Give me Five! 3

ENGLISH

TEACHER'S BOOK

Donna Shaw • Joanne Ramsden

macmillan education

Macmillan Education
4 Crinan Street
London N1 9XW
A division of Macmillan Publishers Limited

Companies and representatives throughout the world

Teacher's Book ISBN 978-1-380-02499-2
Teacher's Book Pack ISBN 978-1-380-02498-5

This edition published 2018
First edition entitled *High Five! English* published 2014 by Macmillan Publishers Limited

Teacher's Edition credits:
Original design by Amanda Easter and Sue Bushell
Page make-up by emc design ltd
Illustrated by Ángeles Peinador
Cover design by Bigtop Design Limited
Cover photographs by Tom, Dick and Debbie Productions

Authors' acknowledgements
The authors would like to thank everyone at Macmillan who has given help and advice throughout this project. Special thanks from Jo to Carlos, Daniel and Alex for their patience and support during this process. Special thanks from Donna to Jose, Elisa, Teresa and Marina for their encouragement and enthusiasm.

The publishers would like to thank the following teachers for their contribution to the project: Ana Postigo, CEIP Vicálvaro, Madrid; Beatriz García Vaquero, CEIP Mariano José Larra, Madrid; Damián Quiralte Fresneda, CEIP Claudio Moyano, Madrid; Eamonn Healy, Colegio SEK Santa Isabel, Madrid; Elvira Robledo Gandarias, Colegio Ayalde, Loiu, Vizcaya; Francisco Javier Navarro Pineda, Colegio Tajamar, Madrid; Guiomar Yagüe Martínez, CEIP Celso Emilio Ferreiro, Móstoles, Madrid; Henar Del Gallo Muñoz, CEIP Cantos Altos, Collado Villalba, Madrid; Ignacio de la Puente Rodríguez, CEIP El Cantizal, Las Rozas, Madrid; Inmaculada Romero Fanego, CEIP Príncipes de Asturias, Pozuelo de Alarcón, Madrid; Laura Tenorio, CEIP Esperanza, Madrid; María del Rosario García Leal, CEIP Rufino Blanco, Madrid; Patricia Sanz, CEIP Félix Rodríguez de la Fuente, Coslada, Madrid; Silvia San José Paul, CEIP El Cantizal, Las Rozas, Madrid; Víctor Molinero Cuartango, CEIP Ciudad de Roma, Madrid; Virginia Escalona Monreal, CEIP La Encina, Las Rozas, Madrid; Laura Zarzuelo, Colegio Virgen de la Almudena, Collado Villalba, Madrid; Eugenio Domínguez, Colegio Virgen de la Almudena, Collado Villalba, Madrid; Silvia Díez de Rivera, Colegio Orvalle, Las Rozas, Madrid; Maite Crespo, Colegio Jesús Nazareno, Madrid; Rocío González, Colegio Jesús Nazareno, Madrid; Silvia Valderrama, CEIP Benito Pérez Galdós, Arganda del Rey, Madrid; Lilian Villafuerte, CEIP Rosa Chacel, Collado Villalba, Madrid; Cristina Baeza, CEIP Rosa Chacel, Collado Villalba, Madrid; Carlota Padovani, CEIP Vicálvaro, Madrid; Leyre Alcalde, CEIP Cortes de Cádiz, Madrid; María Andrés, Colegio Matter Inmaculata, Madrid.

Full acknowledgements for illustrations and photographs in the facsimile pages can be found in the Pupil's Book ISBN 978-1-380-01358-3 and the Activity Book ISBN 978-1-380-01378-1.

Printed and bound in Brazil

2022
25

Give Me Five!

TEACHER'S BOOK 3

Syllabus

Unit	Key Competences and Key Learning Outcomes	Contents
		Lexis
Starter Unit Welcome to the lighthouse!	• Listen, repeat and mime activities (Lesson 2) • Talk about activities you like, love and don't like doing (Lesson 2) • Complete a story summary (Lesson 3) • Learn and practise the numbers 50–100 (Lesson 4) • Review the numbers 1–50 (Lesson 4) • Use the Pupil's App on Navio • Review vocabulary from previous levels (Lesson 1) • Listen for specific information (Lesson 2) • Review and practise saying the alphabet (Lesson 4) • Ask how to spell things (Lesson 4) • Get to know the course characters (Lesson 1) • Ask for and give personal information (Lesson 1) • Work with a Talk Partner to practise and reinforce learning (all lessons) • Sing a song (Lesson 1) • Understand and act out a story (Lesson 3) • Say a rap (Lesson 4)	**Core vocabulary** • *cycling, dancing, flat, grandparents, lighthouse, making models, playing tennis, reading, singing, welcome*; numbers 50–100 **Other vocabulary** • *adventure, blog, bottom, boxes, code, double, explore, help, message, password, scientist, secret, steps, top, travel* **Recycled vocabulary** • The alphabet • Family members • Sports: *cycling, sailing, skateboarding, swimming, volleyball* • Transport: *(sailing) boat, bus, car, helicopter, motorbike* • Animals: *bird / seagull, butterfly, dolphin, fish, rabbit* • Places in a town: *baker's, chemist's, park, post office, restaurant / café, supermarket, swimming pool* • *friend, letter, number, school*
Unit 1 Time for school	• Identify and name places in a school (Lesson 1) • Say the vocabulary chant (Lesson 1) • Understand and act out a dialogue (Lesson 2) • Understand and use *Wh-* question words (Lesson 2) • Review and learn school subjects (Lesson 4) • Use capital letters correctly (Lesson 7) • Watch and understand a video (Video and 21st Century Skills) • Use a code to read a message (Lesson 3) • Use the Pupil's App on Navio • Investigate Ireland (Lesson 8) • Say a tongue twister, learn another spelling for the 'j' sound and practise spelling (Lesson 5) • Practise activity types found in the Cambridge Exams: A1 Movers • Review your own learning (Review) • Understand the importance of helping new pupils at school (Lesson 3) • Ask and answer about new things to try (Video and 21st Century Skills) • Work with a Talk Partner to practise and reinforce learning (all lessons) • Play a communication game and complete a timetable (Lesson 5) • Sing two songs (Lessons 1 and 4) • Understand and act out a story (Lesson 3) • Read and write a poster for a school club (Lessons 6 and 7) • Learn about Ireland (Lesson 8) • Think about your own culture (Lesson 8)	**Core vocabulary** • *basketball court, bike stand, canteen, computer room, corridor, football pitch, gym, library, music room, playground, school hall, vegetable garden* • *Arts and Crafts, Drama, Geography, History, ICT, PE* **Extension vocabulary (optional)** • *changing room, entrance, reception, science lab, staffroom, toilets; Biology, Chemistry, French, Literature* **Other vocabulary** • *balls, club, computer, gloves, helmet, hockey stick, memory stick, pads, rollerblades* • *amazing, bored, comfortable, cool, exciting, fast* **Recycled vocabulary** • Days of the week • Times (o'clock) • Classroom objects • *English, Maths, Music* • *draw pictures, eat lunch, read book, study, throw a ball; classroom, computers, fast, football, games, helmet, hit / kick the ball, hockey, skating, skip, sport, swimming pool*

Competence in linguistic communication | Competence in mathematics, science and technology | Digital competence
Learning to learn | Social and civic competences | Sense of initiative and entrepreneurship | Cultural awareness and expression

Contents					Cross-curricular links
Structures	Phonics	Sociocultural aspects	Culture around the world and Literacy	21st Century Skills	
Core structures • *Who do you live with? I live with my (grandparents).* • *I like (swimming). I love (making models). I don't like (skateboarding).* • *Do you like (singing)? Yes, I do. No, I don't.* **Other structures** • *Can we help you? Who's this? He's our (brother). He's a (scientist).* **Recycled structures** • *What's your name? My name's (Josh). How old are you? I'm (nine). I'm (nine) years old. Where do you live? I live in (the town). How do you spell (letter)?*		**Cooperative learning Skills** • Checking learning (Lesson 1) • Sharing information (Lessons 2 and 4) • Recording answers for a survey (Lesson 2) • Collaborating (Lesson 3)		**Thinking skills** • Categorising (Lesson 1); Sequencing (Lesson 4); Grouping (Lesson 4); Logical thinking (Lesson 4)	
Core structures • *Where do you (play with your friends)? I (play with my friends) (in the playground).* • *When do you (study Maths)? What do you (do in the computer room)?* • *Are you good at (Maths)? Yes, I am. No, I'm not.* • *I'm brilliant / very good / good / not very good at (History). When do we have (Music)? We have (music) on (Monday) at (nine o'clock).* **Other structures** • *The (classes) begin / finish at (five o'clock). We meet on (Tuesday). The classes cost (£2). You need to wear (comfortable clothes). For more information, email (emma@fun.uk).* **Recycled structures** • *This is my school. I go to school. There's a (gym) in our school. There isn't a (music room) in our school. Do you love (hockey)? Do you want to (learn an exciting sport)? My favourite after-school activity is (hockey). I play (a tin whistle).*	• The 'j' sound (**g**iraffes **j**umping **j**udo **g**ym)	**Cooperative learning Skills** • Listening to each other (Lesson 1) • Collaborating (Lessons 2, 4 and 5) • Checking learning (Lesson 5) • Peer evaluation and feedback (Lessons 5 and 7) • Working together (Review) **Values** • Understanding the importance of helping new pupils at school	**Culture around the world** • After-school activities in Ireland **Literacy** **Text type** • A poster (text to persuade) **Reading skills** • Asking yourself a question before you read **Writing skills** • Using capital letters	**21st Century Skills** • Open mindedness and trying new things **Thinking skills** • Predicting (Lessons 3 and 8); Discussing values (Lesson 3); Expressing opinions (Lesson 3); Applying rules (Lesson 4); Making inferences (Lesson 6); Thinking about your culture (Lesson 8); Making connections (Review)	**Link to Science** **Living things** • Listing living and non-living things at school **Arts and Crafts** • Observing proportion in art and the human body and creating a self-portrait

Syllabus

Unit	Key Competences and Key Learning Outcomes	Contents
		Lexis
Unit 2 Helping hands	• Identify and name household chores (Lesson 1) • Say the vocabulary chant (Lesson 1) • Listen, repeat and act out a conversation (Lesson 2) • Talk about routines (Lesson 2) • Identify and name free-time activities (Lesson 4) • Ask and answer about frequency (Lesson 4) • Order adjectives and nouns (Lesson 7) • Watch and understand a video (Video and 21st Century Skills) • Use a code to read a message (Lesson 3) • Use the Pupil's App on Navio • Investigate Scotland (Lesson 8) • Say a tongue twister, learn another spelling for the 'ch' sound and practise spelling (Lesson 5) • Practise activity types found in the Cambridge Exams: A1 Movers • Review your own learning (Review) • Understand the importance of helping at home (Lesson 3) • Work with a Talk Partner to practise and reinforce learning (all lessons) • Do a communication activity (Lesson 5) • Sing two songs (Lessons 1 and 4) • Understand and act out a story (Lesson 3) • Read and understand a fable (Lesson 6) • Plan and write the end of the fable (Lesson 7) • Learn about Scotland (Lesson 8) • Think about your own culture (Lesson 8)	**Core vocabulary** • *clear the table, cook dinner, dust, feed my pet, hoover the floor, lay the table, make my bed, tidy up, walk the dog, wash the car, wash up, water the plants* • *do puzzles, draw pictures, play board games, play computer games, read comics, watch DVDs* **Extension vocabulary (optional)** • *brush the floor, clean the bathroom, fold the clothes, take out the rubbish, wash the clothes, wash the floor; go for a walk, go ice-skating, go shopping, listen to the radio* **Other vocabulary** • *action, chore, fable, ferry, free time, island, look after, north, routine, smell, web, west* • *clever, dirty, greedy, lazy* • *dolphin, seal, turtle* **Recycled vocabulary** • Days of the week • Family members • Household objects • Places in a school • Rooms in a house • *coat, delicious, dirty, drums, farm, hands, help, hot, hungry, legs, long, lunch(time); monkey, rabbit, river, sheep, spider, swim, thin, town, vegetables, walk, wash*
Unit 3 Fit and healthy	• Identify and name health problems (Lesson 1) • Say the vocabulary chant (Lesson 1) • Understand and act out a conversation (Lesson 2) • Identify healthy and unhealthy habits (Lesson 4) • Use 'must' and 'mustn't' (Lesson 4) • Use question marks correctly (Lesson 7) • Watch and understand a video (Video and 21st Century Skills) • Use a code to read a message (Lesson 3) • Do a health quiz (Lesson 6) • Write a quiz about healthy eating (Lesson 7) • Identify how keeping healthy benefits the body (Video and 21st Century Skills) • Use the Pupil's App on Navio • Investigate Malta (Lesson 8) • Say a tongue twister, learn another spelling for the 'k' sound and practise spelling (Lesson 5) • Practise activity types found in the Cambridge Exams: A1 Movers • Review your own learning (Review) • Understand the importance of talking to someone when you've got a problem (Lesson 3) • Work with a Talk Partner to practise and reinforce learning (all lessons) • Play a communication game (Lesson 5) • Sing two songs (Lessons 1 and 4) • Understand and act out a story (Lesson 3) • Learn about Malta (Lesson 8) • Think about your own culture (Lesson 8)	**Core vocabulary** • *broken leg, cold, cough, cut, earache, feel dizzy, feel sick, flu, headache, sore throat, stomach ache, temperature* • *be active, be lazy, eat healthy snacks, eat lots of sweets, go to bed early, go to bed late* **Extension vocabulary (optional)** • *bandage, cast, cream, medicine, plaster, tablets; do exercise, drink water, eat junk food, have fizzy drinks* **Other vocabulary** • *divers, fit, healthy, healthy eating, hurt, ill, points, quiz, rescue centre, sea animal rescue, scientists, skin, vets* **Recycled vocabulary** • *always, every day, five times a week, never, once or twice a week, sometimes; be quiet, beach, breakfast, chores, cold, do sport, dog, drink some water, eat fruit, fingers, run, school, shout, swim, tired, vegetables, watch TV, wear a hat, windy*

Competence in linguistic communication | Competence in mathematics, science and technology | Digital competence | Learning to learn | Social and civic competences | Sense of initiative and entrepreneurship | Cultural awareness and expression

<table>
<tr><th colspan="5">Contents</th><th rowspan="2">Cross-curricular links</th></tr>
<tr><th>Structures</th><th>Phonics</th><th>Sociocultural aspects</th><th>Culture around the world and Literacy</th><th>21st Century Skills</th></tr>
<tr>
<td>Core structures
• My (dad) always / often / sometimes / never (washes up).
• My (sister) doesn't (cook).
• Does she (wash up)? Yes, she does. No, she doesn't.
• How often does (your mum) (watch DVDs)? She (watches DVDs) once a week / five times a week.
• How often do you (make your bed)? I never (make my bed).
Other structures
• How does (Sarah) (travel to school)? There isn't (a school here). What does he do (in his free time)? The (island) is famous for (its sheep). You can (sometimes) see (seals). I (help) (my parents).
Recycled structures
• Do you (dust)? Yes, I do. No, I don't. When do you (dust)? I (dust) (at the weekend). I travel to (school) by (ferry). I love (playing with the baby animals).</td>
<td>• The 'ch' sound (witch chops chicken kitchen)</td>
<td>Cooperative learning Skills
• Sharing information (Lessons 1 and 5)
• Team building (Lesson 4)
• Checking learning (Lesson 5)
• Peer evaluation and feedback (Lesson 7)
• Working together (Review)
Values
• Understanding the importance of helping at home</td>
<td>Culture around the world
• Life on a Scottish island
Literacy
Text type
• A fable (text to entertain)
Reading skills
• Identifying the message of the text
Writing skills
• Placing adjectives in the correct position</td>
<td>21st Century Skills
• Helping others
Thinking skills
• Categorising (Lesson 1); Expressing opinions (Lesson 3); Predicting (Lessons 3 and 6); Discussing values (Lesson 3); Applying rules (Lesson 4); Making inferences (Lesson 6); Visualisation and prediction (Lesson 8); Thinking about your culture (Lesson 8); Making connections (Review)</td>
<td>Link to Science
The senses
• Reviewing how our senses give us information about our environment
Arts and Crafts
• Exploring primary, secondary and tertiary colours and creating a still life</td>
</tr>
<tr>
<td>Core structures
• What's the matter?
• Have they got (a cold)? Yes, they have.
• Has she got (a sore throat)? Yes, she has. No, she hasn't.
• Do they (feel dizzy)? Yes, they do. No, they don't.
Does (your sister) (feel sick)? Yes, she does.
You must (go to bed early). You mustn't (eat lots of sweets).
Other structures
(Marine animals) (sometimes) need (our help). Some (turtles) have got (broken bones). When the (turtles) are (better), (they put them into the sea). Everyone (feels happy) when (the turtles are in the wild).
Recycled structures
How are you today? I'm (fine). Have you got (a headache)? Yes, I have. No, I haven't. Do you (feel dizzy)? Yes, I do. No, I don't. Go (to bed). Are you (fit and healthy)? Yes, I am. Do you (walk to school)? I (never) (walk to school). How often do you (eat fruit)? I (eat fruit) (every day). What time do you (go to bed)? I (go to bed) at about (nine o'clock). How do (you spell) (shoulder)?</td>
<td>• The 'k' sound (pink chameleon headache king stomach ache)</td>
<td>Cooperative learning Skills
• Sharing information (Lessons 1 and 5)
• Collaborating (Lessons 3 and 4)
• Checking learning (Lesson 5)
• Peer evaluation and feedback (Lesson 7)
• Working together (Review)
Values
• Understanding the importance of dealing with problems</td>
<td>Culture around the world
• Sea animal rescue in Malta
Literacy
Text type
• A quiz (information text)
Reading skills
• Activating existing knowledge
Writing skills
• Using question marks</td>
<td>21st Century Skills
• Being fit and healthy
Thinking skills
• Applying rules (Lessons 2 and 4); Remembering (Lesson 2); Predicting (Lessons 3 and 7); Discussing values (Lesson 3); Expressing opinions (Lesson 3); Visual intelligence (Lesson 4); Visualisation and prediction (Lesson 8); Thinking about your culture (Lesson 8); Making connections (Review)</td>
<td>Link to Science
We can move
• Reviewing how we move and what our body needs
Arts and Crafts
• Identifying positive and negative shapes and making a collage</td>
</tr>
</table>

Syllabus

Unit	Key Competences and Key Learning Outcomes	Contents: Lexis
My project 1: The zoo challenge	• Identify animals, services for visitors and animals' living areas in a zoo (Lesson 1) • Present your project (Lesson 2) • Review different types of animals (optional) (Lesson 1) • Find out about three zoo animals (Lesson 2) • Reflect on what you've learnt and how well you've worked together (Lesson 2) • Work together to design a zoo (Lesson 2) • Share information with your group (Lesson 1)	**Key vocabulary** • *crocodile, eagle, elephant, giraffe, lizard, monkey, ostrich, parrot, penguin, snake, tiger, tortoise* • *fish, fruit, grass, insects, leaves, meat, seeds* • *first aid post, picnic area, playground, restaurant, shop, visitors, zoo* • *alone, bird, cage, cave, cold / hot / warm climate, in a group, land, mammal, pool, reptile, rocks, tree, water* **Recycled vocabulary** • Zoo animals • Food zoo animals eat • Services for visitors • Animals' living areas
Unit 4 Creative cooking	• Identify and name different food (Lesson 1) • Say the vocabulary chant (Lesson 1) • Understand and act out a conversation (Lesson 2) • Make requests with 'would like' (Lesson 2) • Follow, complete and correct the grammar tables (Lessons 2 and 4) • Learn adjectives to describe food (Lesson 4) • Talk about what food you prefer (Lesson 4) • Understand that adjectives are the same with singular and plural objects (Lesson 7) • Watch and understand a video (Video and 21st Century Skills) • Use a code to read a message (Lesson 3) • Use the Pupil's App on Navio • Investigate India (Lesson 8) • Say a tongue twister, learn another spelling for the 'z' sound and practise spelling (Lesson 5) • Practise activity types found in the Cambridge Exams: A1 Movers • Review your own learning (Review) • Understand the importance of trying new food (Lesson 3) • Work with a Talk Partner to practise and reinforce learning (all lessons) • Play a communication game (Lesson 5) • Use imagination to create food pictures (Video and 21st Century Skills) • Sing a song (Lesson 1) • Understand and act out a story (Lesson 3) • Say a rap (Lesson 4) • Read and understand a shape poem (Lesson 6) • Plan, write and evaluate a shape poem (Lesson 7) • Learn about India (Lesson 8) • Think about your own culture (Lesson 8)	**Core vocabulary** • *cheese, chillies, mushrooms, olives, onions, peppers, pineapple, prawns, spinach, sweetcorn, tomato sauce, tuna* • *crunchy, plain, savoury, soft, spicy, sweet* **Extension vocabulary (optional)** • *garlic, herbs, mayonnaise, mustard, pepper, vinegar; chewy, delicious, horrible, juicy* **Other vocabulary** • *circle, oval, rectangle, round, shape poem, square, triangle* • *adjectives, descriptions, stories* **Recycled vocabulary** • *apple, banana, big, biscuits, bread, breakfast, brown, cake, chips, chocolate, cold, competition, computer games, cook, crisps, delicious, easy, eat, enormous, grow, hot, ice cream, inside, kiwi, lazy, long, milk, orange, outside, quiz, red, restaurant, rice, small, strawberry, sugar, thin, throw, vegetables, white, yellow, zoo*

- Competence in linguistic communication
- Competence in mathematics, science and technology
- Digital competence
- Learning to learn
- Social and civic competences
- Sense of initiative and entrepreneurship
- Cultural awareness and expression

Contents					Cross-curricular links
Structures	**Phonics**	**Sociocultural aspects**	**Culture around the world and Literacy**	**21st Century Skills**	
Key structures • *What's your (mammal)?* • *It's (an elephant).* • *It lives (in a group).* • *It eats (grass).* • *The zoo is called (Animal Land).* • *There's (a playground) in the zoo.* • *There are (elephants).* • *It's got (a restaurant).* • *They've got (a playground).* • *Children can (play here).* • *That's a (good idea).* • *I'm not sure.*		**Cooperative learning Skills** • Listen to and respect everyone's opinion (Lesson 2)			**Link to Science** **Animals** • Reviewing different types of animals
Core structures • *What would you like (on your pizza)? I'd like some (cheese).* • *Would you like a lot of / lots of (olives)? Yes, please. No, thank you.* • *Which do you prefer? (Apples) or (pears)?* • *Do you prefer (plain) food or (spicy) food? They prefer (sweet) food. She prefers (savoury) food.* **Other structures** • *What do people (have for breakfast)? Which (food) can you buy? Breakfast is (an important meal). People use (milk) to make (cakes). (India) is famous for (its spicy food).* **Recycled structures** • *Do you like (onions)? Yes, I do. No, I don't.* • *There are (lots of toppings). What about you? It's (long and thin). It's got (a stone in the middle).*	• The 'z' sound (zebra sneezes cheese cherries)	**Cooperative learning Skills** • Team building (Lesson 1) • Collaborating (Lesson 4) • Checking learning (Lesson 5) • Sharing information (Lesson 5) • Peer evaluation and feedback (Lesson 7) • Working together (Review) **Values** • Understanding the importance of trying new food	**Culture around the world** • Food in India **Literacy** **Text type** • Shape poems **Reading skills** • Guessing meaning from context (inferring) **Writing skills** • Using adjectives	**21st Century Skills** • Being creative **Thinking skills** • Sequencing (Lesson 1); Applying rules (Lessons 2 and 4); Remembering (Lesson 2); Predicting (Lessons 3 and 8); Discussing values (Lesson 3); Expressing opinions (Lesson 3); Classifying (Lesson 6); Thinking about your culture (Lesson 8); Making connections (Review)	**Link to Science** **Plants** • Reviewing why we need plants **Arts and Crafts** • Identifying patterns using lines, shapes and colours and creating a mosaic

Syllabus

Unit	Key Competences and Key Learning Outcomes	Contents
		Lexis
Unit 5 Under the sea	• Identify and name sea animals (Lesson 1) • Say the vocabulary chant (Lesson 1) • Understand and act out a conversation (Lesson 2) • Use comparative adjectives (Lessons 2 and 4) • Follow, complete and correct the grammar tables (Lessons 2 and 4) • Learn descriptive adjectives (Lesson 4) • Use 'and' to add similar information (Lesson 7) • Watch and understand a video (Video and 21st Century Skills) • Use a code to read a message (Lesson 3) • Read an article about sea animals (Lesson 6) • Plan and write an article about a sea animal (Lesson 7) • Learn interesting facts about sea animals (Video and 21st Century Skills) • Use the Pupil's App on Navio • Investigate Hawaii (Lesson 8) • Say a tongue twister, learn another spelling for the 'w' sound and practise spelling (Lesson 5) • Practise activity types found in the Cambridge Exams: A1 Movers • Review your own learning (Review) • Work with a Talk Partner to practise and reinforce learning (all lessons) • Do a quiz with a partner (Lesson 5) • Understand the importance of protecting sea animals (Lesson 3) • Sing a song (Lesson 1) • Understand and act out a story (Lesson 3) • Say a rap (Lesson 4) • Learn about Hawaii (Lesson 8) • Think about your own culture (Lesson 8)	**Core vocabulary** • *crab, dolphin, fish, jellyfish, octopus, seahorse, seal, shark, squid, starfish, turtle, whale* • *colourful, dangerous, heavy, intelligent, pretty, ugly* **Extension vocabulary (optional)** • *clam, eel, lobster, ray, sea urchin, walrus; boring, friendly, funny, interesting* **Other vocabulary** • *blowhole, blue whale, brain, curled tail, hard / soft skin, krill, long head, round body, spider crab, stomach, super, tongue; light, long, slow, thin* **Recycled vocabulary** • *arms, big, body, car, cat, claw, cow, crocodile, December, dog, elephant, eye, giraffe, hamster, hard skin, head, hippo, legs, May, mouse, old, shell, snail, snake, teeth*
Unit 6 Sports mad	• Identify and name water sports equipment (Lesson 1) • Say the vocabulary chant (Lesson 1) • Understand and act out a conversation (Lesson 2) • Talk and write about future plans (Lesson 2) • Follow, complete and correct the grammar tables (Lessons 2 and 4) • Learn adverbs of manner (Lesson 4) • Learn simple time sequencers for ordering information (Lesson 7) • Watch and understand a video (Video and 21st Century Skills) • Use a code to read a message (Lesson 3) • Use the Pupil's App on Navio • Investigate New Zealand (Lesson 8) • Say a tongue twister, learn another spelling for the 'k' sound and practise spelling (Lesson 5) • Practise activity types found in the Cambridge Exams: A1 Movers • Review your own learning (Review) • Understand the importance of listening to other people's ideas (Lesson 3) • Work with a Talk Partner to practise and reinforce learning (all lessons) • Do a questionnaire in pairs and report on it (Lesson 5) • Reflect on personal safety in sports (Video and 21st Century Skills) • Sing two songs (Lessons 1 and 4) • Understand and act out a story (Lesson 3) • Read and evaluate a letter (Lesson 6) • Write a letter (Lesson 7) • Learn about New Zealand (Lesson 8) • Think about your own culture (Lesson 8)	**Core vocabulary** • *flippers, gloves, helmet, kayak, life jacket, mask, paddle, snorkel, surfboard, swimsuit, water-skis, wetsuit* • *badly, fast, loudly, quickly, quietly, slowly, well* **Extension vocabulary (optional)** • *fishing rod, goggles, jet ski, oars, rope, sailing boat; carefully, dangerously, happily, sadly* **Other vocabulary** • *adventure / sports camp, archery, bungee jumping, extreme sport, forest, horse riding, kayaking, lake, leaflet, letter, mountain biking, rafting, rock climbing, sand surfing, windsurfing, zorbing* **Recycled vocabulary** • *baseball, cycle, dance, go swimming, gymnastics, hockey, play football, ride a horse, rollerblade, sailing, sing, skate, snorkelling, swim, tennis, volleyball, walk, watch TV; adventure, air, beach, camp, faster, hill, lie down, mountains, river, rock, sea animals*

Competence in linguistic communication · Competence in mathematics, science and technology · Digital competence · Learning to learn · Social and civic competences · Sense of initiative and entrepreneurship · Cultural awareness and expression

Contents					Cross-curricular links
Structures	**Phonics**	**Sociocultural aspects**	**Culture around the world and Literacy**	**21st Century Skills**	
Core structures • *A (shark) is (bigger) than a (seahorse).* • *A (shark) is more (dangerous) than a (seahorse).* • *Is a (shark) more (intelligent) than a (dolphin)? Yes, it is. No, it isn't.* **Other structures** • *(Blue whales) are (about 30 metres long). Do you know that (they haven't got any teeth)? How (big) is the animal? What does it (look like)? Where does it (live)? How does it (move)? Why is it (amazing)? What does it (eat)? They're (different sizes) and (colours).* **Recycled structures** • *This (sea animal) has got (sharp teeth). This (sea animal) is (big). There's a (whale). There are (three jellyfish). Which (sea animal) do you like? I like (dolphins). He likes (jellyfish). They've got (soft skin). They eat (fish and plants). Has it got a (shell)? No, it hasn't. Is it a (turtle)? Yes, it is.*	• The 'w' sound (**w**hy **wh**ite **wh**ale **w**earing **w**atch)	**Cooperative learning Skills** • Teamwork (Lesson 1) • Helping each other (Lesson 1) • Collaborating (Lesson 4) • Checking learning (Lesson 5) • Peer evaluation and feedback (Lesson 7) • Working together (Review) **Values** • Understanding the importance of protecting sea animals	**Culture around the world** • Activities in Hawaii **Literacy** **Text type** • A magazine article (information text) **Reading skills** • Activating existing knowledge of content • Reading for information and entertainment **Writing skills** • Using 'and' to add similar information	**21st Century Skills** • Using keywords to find information online **Thinking skills** • Applying rules (Lessons 2 and 4); Spatial thinking (Lesson 2); Predicting (Lessons 3 and 8); Discussing values (Lesson 3); Expressing opinions (Lesson 3); Thinking about your culture (Lesson 8); Making connections (Review)	**Link to Science Habitats** • Reviewing water habitats, the food chain and how to protect ecosystems **Arts and Crafts** • Exploring space in art and creating a three-dimensional landscape with a background, middle ground and foreground to create the illusion of depth
Core structures • *I am / I'm not going to (play football tomorrow).* • *He is / isn't going to (go swimming).* • *They are / aren't going to (watch TV).* • *Are you going to (play football)? Yes, I am. No, I'm not.* • *What are you going to do (on Saturday)?* • *I (play chess) (well). He (dances) (badly).* **Other structures** • *Dear (Grandma), First / Next / Finally, (I'm going to) (go horse riding). See you (soon). Love, (Laura). Which (sport) can you do (in the air)? If you like (travelling fast), (sand surfing) is (the sport for you).* **Recycled structures** • *I'm wearing (a wetsuit). I'm ready to (snorkel). What about you? Are you (ready to snorkel)? He's wearing (gloves). She's got (water-skis). She's ready to (water-ski). You must (run fast). Good idea. Why don't you (play football)? Do you like (adventure)?*	• The 'k' sound (bla**ck** mon**k**ey **k**aya**k**s qui**ck**ly la**k**e)	**Cooperative learning Skills** • Working together (Lesson 1) • Team building (Lesson 2) • Collaborating (Lesson 4) • Checking learning (Lesson 5) • Sharing information (Lesson 5) • Peer evaluation and feedback (Lesson 7) • Working together (Review) **Values** • Understanding the importance of listening to other people's ideas	**Culture around the world** • Extreme sports in New Zealand **Literacy** **Text type** • A letter **Reading skills** • Sequencing parts of a text **Writing skills** • Using time sequencers 'First', 'Next', 'Finally'	**21st Century Skills** • Staying safe when doing sports **Thinking skills** • Applying rules (Lessons 2 and 4); Predicting (Lessons 3 and 8); Discussing values (Lesson 3); Expressing opinions (Lesson 3); Sequencing (Lesson 6); Thinking about your culture (Lesson 8); Making connections (Review)	**Link to Science Water and air on Earth** • Identifying where we find water **Arts and Crafts** • Exploring three-dimensional geometric shapes and constructing a cylindrical Japanese carp kite

Syllabus

Unit	Key Competences and Key Learning Outcomes	Contents Lexis
My project 2: Treasure islands	• Review and learn the names of natural things and man-made things on an island (Lesson 1) • Present your treasure map to other pupils and play a game (Lesson 2) • Talk about the local landscape (optional) (Lesson 1) • Find out about an island (Lesson 1) • Reflect on what you've learnt and how you've worked together (Lesson 2) • Share information with your group (Lesson 1) • Work together to design an island (Lesson 2) • Identify islands in your country (Lesson 1)	**Key vocabulary** • *bay, beach, bridge, cave, cliffs, coast, island, jungle, lake, lighthouse, man-made, natural, port, pyramid, river, rocks, treasure, village, volcano, waterfall* **Recycled vocabulary** • Man-made features on an island • Natural features on an island • *behind, between, in, in front of, on, under*
Unit 7 Detectives	• Identify and name household objects (Lesson 1) • Say the vocabulary chant (Lesson 1) • Understand and act out a conversation (Lesson 2) • Use the past tense with 'was / were' (Lessons 2 and 4) • Follow, complete and correct the grammar tables (Lessons 2 and 4) • Learn names of personal belongings (Lesson 4) • Use exclamation marks (Lesson 7) • Watch and understand a video (Video and 21st Century Skills) • Practise memory skills in a game (Video and 21st Century Skills) • Use a code to read a message (Lesson 3) • Use the Pupil's App on Navio • Investigate Australia (Lesson 8) • Say a tongue twister, learn another spelling for the 'r' sound and practise spelling (Lesson 5) • Practise activity types found in the Cambridge Exams: A1 Movers • Review your own learning (Review) • Understand the importance of looking after personal belongings (Lesson 3) • Work with a Talk Partner to practise and reinforce learning (all lessons) • Play a communication game (Lesson 5) • Sing a song (Lesson 1) • Understand and act out a story (Lesson 3) • Say a chant (Lesson 4) • Read and evaluate a script (Lesson 6) • Plan and write a script (Lesson 7) • Learn about Australia (Lesson 8) • Think about your own culture (Lesson 8) • Learn about unusual houses around the world (Video and 21st Century Skills)	**Core vocabulary** • *armchair, bath, bookcase, cooker, cupboard, fridge, mat, mirror, painting, sink, sofa, wardrobe* • *bracelet, earrings, keys, sunglasses, umbrella, watch* **Extension vocabulary (optional)** • *bedside table, carpet, coffee table, DVD player, microwave, wash basin; brush, comb, diary, toothbrush* **Other vocabulary** • *characters, investigate, necklace, play, police officer, robber, scene, script* • *angry, excited, laughing, nervously, shouting, surprised, whispering* **Recycled vocabulary** • *behind, between, in, in front of, near, on, under; bathroom, bedroom, dining room, hall, kitchen, living room; angrily, happily, quietly, sleepily, slowly; boat, book, build, cinema, comic, DVD, garden, golf, home, library, restaurant, school, shiny, shops, shouting, stone, supermarket, swimming pool, town, walls, window, work, wrist, wrong*

Competence in linguistic communication | Competence in mathematics, science and technology | Digital competence
Learning to learn | Social and civic competences | Sense of initiative and entrepreneurship | Cultural awareness and expression

Contents					Cross-curricular links
Structures	Phonics	Sociocultural aspects	Culture around the world and Literacy	21st Century Skills	
Key structures • *Where's (Hawaii)?* • *It's in (the Pacific Ocean).* • *What's it like?* • *There are (lots of beaches).* • *There's (a jungle).* • *It's (beautiful).* • *Let's (hide the treasure).* • *I think we should (have a lighthouse).* • *I agree.* • *You're right.* • *That's a good idea, but how about (having a waterfall)?* • *Which do you prefer? I prefer (this treasure map).* • *Is the treasure (behind the waterfall)? Yes, it is. No, it isn't.*		**Cooperative learning Skills** • Listen to and respect everyone's opinion (Lesson 2)			**Link to Science** **Landscapes** • Talking about the local landscape
Core structures • *He was / wasn't (at school) (yesterday).* • *They were / weren't (at the cinema) yesterday.* • *Was the (watch) (on the table)? Yes, it was. No, it wasn't.* • *Were the (earrings) (in the cupboard)? Yes, they were. No, they weren't.* **Other structures** • *What's that (noise)? Is it a (fox)? Hands (up)! (Living underground) is (cooler) than (living above ground). I can't (play in the day) because (it's too hot).* **Recycled structures** • *There's a (mystery). Where's the (mirror)? It's in the (living room). It's (between the door and the book case). They're (on the armchair). It's got (three bedrooms). It hasn't got (a window). There's a (sofa) and an (armchair).*	• The 'r' sound (**R**on **r**obber w**r**ites **r**ed w**r**apper)	**Cooperative learning Skills** • Team building (Lesson 2) • Collaborating (Lesson 4) • Checking learning (Lesson 5) • Sharing information (Lesson 5) • Peer evaluation and feedback (Lesson 7) • Working together (Review) **Values** • Understanding the importance of looking after personal belongings	**Culture around the world** • An underground town in Australia **Literacy** **Text type** • A script (text to entertain) **Reading skills** • Predicting content from an image **Writing skills** • Using exclamation marks	**21st Century Skills** • Paying attention **Thinking skills** • Classification (Lesson 1); Applying rules (Lesson 2); Predicting (Lessons 3 and 8); Discussing values (Lesson 3); Expressing opinions (Lesson 3); Remembering (Lesson 4); Sequencing (Lesson 6); Thinking about your culture (Lesson 8); Making connections (Review)	**Link to Science** **The top layer of Earth** • Identifying rocks and minerals **Arts and Crafts** • Exploring organic (natural) forms and finding organic shapes and forms to make a land art collage

Syllabus

Unit	Key Competences and Key Learning Outcomes	Contents Lexis
Unit 8 What's on TV?	• Identify and name TV programmes (Lesson 1) • Say the vocabulary chant (Lesson 1) • Understand and act out a conversation (Lesson 2) • Ask and answer questions with 'did' (Lesson 2) • Follow, complete and correct the grammar tables (Lessons 2 and 4) • Identify and name free-time activities (Lesson 4) • Use regular verbs in the past simple (Lesson 4) • Give reasons with 'because' (Lesson 7) • Watch and understand a video (Video and 21st Century Skills) • Use a code to read a message (Lesson 3) • Use the Pupil's App on Navio • Investigate The USA (Lesson 8) • Say a tongue twister, learn another spelling for the 'f' sound and practise spelling (Lesson 5) • Practise activity types found in the Cambridge Exams: A1 Movers • Review your own learning (Review) • Understand the importance of working together (Lesson 3) • Work collaboratively to plan a video (Video and 21st Century Skills) • Work with a Talk Partner to practise and reinforce learning (all lessons) • Play a communication game (Lesson 5) • Sing two songs (Lessons 1 and 4) • Understand and act out a story (Lesson 3) • Read and evaluate a review (Lesson 6) • Plan and write a review (Lesson 7) • Learn about the USA (Lesson 8) • Think about your own culture (Lesson 8)	**Core vocabulary** • *advert, cartoon, comedy programme, documentary, film, game show, music programme, quiz show, sports programme, talk show, the news, the weather* • *climb a tree, paint a picture, phone a friend, plant seeds, play cards, skip* **Extension vocabulary (optional)** • *actor, camera operator, director, musician, presenter, reporter; bake-baked, skate-skated, study-studied, travel-travelled* **Other vocabulary** • *car chase, channel, editor, judges, prizes, review, reviewer, singers, special effects, star, studio* **Recycled vocabulary** • *adventure, carry, city, clever, climb, dangerous, detective, dog, exciting, famous, farm, fish, flag, frog, funny, fur, hills, information, jump, last night / week, newspaper, pet, photo, scary, scientists, slide, submarine, surprise, team*
Unit 9 Let's celebrate!	• Identify and name attractions at festivals (Lesson 1) • Say the vocabulary chant (Lesson 1) • Understand and act out a conversation (Lesson 2) • Talk about festivals in the past tense (Lesson 2) • Follow, complete and correct the grammar tables (Lessons 2 and 4) • Tell the time (Lesson 4) • Understand how to use 'but' (Lesson 7) • Watch and understand a video (Video and 21st Century Skills) • Use a code to read a message (Lesson 3) • Use the Pupil's App on Navio • Investigate Canada (Lesson 8) • Say a tongue twister, learn another spelling for the 's' sound and practise spelling (Lesson 5) • Practise activity types found in the Cambridge Exams: A1 Movers • Review your own learning (Review) • Understand the importance of doing nice things for others (Lesson 3) • Work collaboratively to plan a fete (Video and 21st Century Skills) • Work with a Talk Partner to practise and reinforce learning (all lessons) • Play a communication game (Lesson 5) • Sing two songs (Lessons 1 and 4) • Understand and act out a story (Lesson 3) • Read an email (Lesson 6) • Plan and write an email (Lesson 7) • Learn about Canada (Lesson 8) • Think about your own culture (Lesson 8)	**Core vocabulary** • *band, big wheel, bumper cars, candyfloss, clown, costume, fireworks, ghost train, merry-go-round, parade, roller coaster, toffee apple* • *ten past (three), twenty past (one), twenty-five past (eleven), twenty-five to (four), ten to (eight), five to (twelve)* **Extension vocabulary (optional)** • *barbecue, bonfire, bouncy castle, display, helter-skelter, stall; five past two, ten past seven, twenty to three, ten to nine* **Other vocabulary** • *concert, email, face painting, haggis, log rolling, lumberjack, maypole, Morris dancers, Mounties, photo, poet, ribbon, school fete, show, snacks, sweets* **Recycled vocabulary** • Months of the year • Ordinal numbers (1st–31st) • *beach, bike, birthday, burger, cake, chocolate, festival, fish, half past, ice cream, last week / night, played, quarter past / to, sunglasses, surprise party, TV programmes, watched TV, water, yesterday (evening)*

Competence in linguistic communication | Competence in mathematics, science and technology | Digital competence
Learning to learn | Social and civic competences | Sense of initiative and entrepreneurship | Cultural awareness and expression

Contents					Cross-curricular links
Structures	**Phonics**	**Sociocultural aspects**	**Culture around the world and Literacy**	**21st Century Skills**	
Core structures • *Did (you) watch (a cartoon) yesterday? Yes, (I) did. No, (I) didn't. I (painted a picture) yesterday. We didn't (watch TV) (last night).* • *What did (Daisy) do (yesterday morning)? She (planted seeds).* **Other structures** • *What type of (TV programme) is it? This (documentary) is about (sea animals). I (love) (this programme) because (it's exciting). What's on (Channel 2) at (five o'clock)? Which of (these programmes) do you (want to watch)? I (don't) think it's (a very good programme).* **Recycled structures** • *I like / love / don't like watching (cartoons). Do you like watching (the news)? Yes, I do. No, I don't. Do you prefer watching (cartoons) or (films)? What do you like watching (in the afternoon)?*	• The 'f' sound (dol**ph**in **f**ished ele**ph**ant **ph**oned **f**riend)	**Cooperative learning Skills** • Working together (Lesson 1) • Discussing survey results (Lesson 2) • Team building (Lesson 3) • Collaborating (Lesson 4) • Checking learning (Lesson 5) • Sharing information (Lesson 5) • Peer evaluation and feedback (Lesson 7) • Working together (Review) **Values** • Understanding the importance of working together	**Culture around the world** • Activities in Hollywood **Literacy** **Text type** • A review (information text) **Reading skills** • Scanning texts for specific information **Writing skills** • Using 'because' to give a reason	**21st Century Skills** • Making a video **Thinking skills** • Ranking (Lesson 1); Applying rules (Lessons 2 and 4); Problem solving (Lesson 2); Predicting (Lessons 3 and 8); Discussing values (Lesson 3); Expressing opinions (Lesson 3); Thinking about your culture (Lesson 8); Making connections (Review)	**Link to Science** **Transport and communication** • Naming TV programmes that provide information **Arts and Crafts** • Identifying the use of balance (symmetry) in art and designing a flying machine
Core structures • *What did (you) wear / eat / drink / do / see (yesterday)? I wore / ate / drank / did / saw; I had / went / rode* • *What time did (you) (go to bed) yesterday? (I) (went to bed) at (twenty past nine).* **Other structures** • *In the (evening), I had (a big dinner). Then I (sang songs), but I didn't (dance). When's (Canada Day)?* **Recycled structures** • *Let's (watch the parade). Do you (eat candyfloss)? Yes, I do. No, I don't. What (a mess)! What did (Peter) watch / ride on / see? What was (Joey's) favourite activity?*	• The 's' sound (**C**ecil **s**nake **s**ang dan**c**ed **c**ity **c**elebration)	**Cooperative learning Skills** • Team building (Lesson 2) • Collaborating (Lesson 3) • Checking learning (Lesson 5) • Sharing information (Lesson 5) • Peer evaluation and feedback (Lesson 7) • Working together (Review) **Values** • Understanding the importance of doing nice things for others	**Culture around the world** • Canada Day celebrations **Literacy** • An email (email form) **Reading skills** • Guessing meaning from context (inferring) **Writing skills** • Using 'but' to give opposite information	**21st Century Skills** • Working in a group: accepting ideas and suggestions **Thinking skills** • Thinking about your culture (Lesson 1); Applying rules (Lessons 2 and 4); Predicting (Lessons 3 and 8); Discussing values (Lesson 3); Expressing opinions (Lesson 3); Making connections (Review)	**Link to Science** **Work** • Reviewing the three job sectors (primary, secondary, tertiary) **Arts and Crafts** • Identifying the use of lines to show movement in illustrations and drawing a comic strip

Syllabus

Unit	Key Competences and Key Learning Outcomes	Contents
		Lexis
My project 3: A London adventure	• Review and learn the names of places and attractions in London (Lesson 1) • Present your project (Lesson 2) • Discuss the advantages and disadvantages of city life (optional) (Lesson 1) • Use the Internet to investigate two London attractions (Lesson 1) • Reflect on what you've learnt and how you've worked together (Lesson 2) • Work together to design a digital presentation of your trip (Lesson 2) • Share information with your group (Lesson 1)	**Key vocabulary** • *bike, boat, bus, taxi, Underground* • *aquarium, attraction, building, cathedral, museum, park, Queen, river cruise, tower, trip, zoo* • *Saturday, Sunday* • *do experiments, ride a bike, take a photo*
Festivals: Chinese New Year	• Learn about Chinese New Year • Write a riddle for a mystery word • Read and solve some riddles • Make a Chinese lantern	**Key vocabulary** • *chopsticks, dragons, envelopes, festival, fish, lanterns, lions, lucky, money, noodles, riddles, soup, tradition*
Festivals: World Book Day	• Ask and answer questions about books and reading • Make a poster about a favourite book • Learn about World Book Day • Read and enjoy a poem	**Key vocabulary** • *adventure, black hole, books, buy, chest, desert, detective, dragon, faraway land, follow, gold, grow, ice, land, magic beans, magic carpet, pirate, poems, read, sand, snow, stories, treasure, tree, white rabbit, witch, write*

Competence in linguistic communication | Competence in mathematics, science and technology | Digital competence
Learning to learn | Social and civic competences | Sense of initiative and entrepreneurship | Cultural awareness and expression

Contents					Cross-curricular links
Structures	Phonics	Sociocultural aspects	Culture around the world and Literacy	21st Century Skills	
Key structures • *What's your (first / second) attraction?* • *What can you (do) there? You can (visit some rooms).* • *You can (do experiments) there.* • *Why don't we (go on the London Eye)?* • *Shall we (go to Regent's Park)?* • *On Saturday we're going to (take the Underground).* • *We're going to visit (Buckingham Palace).*		**Cooperative learning Skills** • Listen to and respect everyone's opinion (Lesson 2)			**Link to Science** **Where we live** • Discussing the advantages and disadvantages of city life
Key structures • *People) eat / use / decorate …* • *(Children) have / receive / read …* • *The (envelopes) have got (money inside them).* • *They often have (drawings of lucky animals).* • *What letter is it?*					
Key structures • *Do you like (writing stories and poems)?* • *How often do (you read a book)? I (read a book) three times a week.* • *What's your (favourite book)? My favourite book is (Geronimo Stilton).* • *What's it (about)? It's (about a mouse).*					

Introduction to *Give Me Five!*

Give Me Five! is a six-level course for pupils who have an extended English timetable and are being taught at a faster pace. It is designed to develop pupils' communicative competences in a systematic and comprehensive manner.

With *Give Me Five! 3*, pupils ...

- **identify language patterns** and use them to personalise and be creative with new language.
- **use new technologies and multimedia** as tools for learning.
- **develop their social and civic competences** through a hands-on cooperative project each term and the integration of collaborative tasks and strategies.
- **link their learning to other areas in the curriculum** such as Science and Arts and Crafts.
- **develop literacy skills** through a range of enjoyable and motivating real-world texts and a focus on the key reading and writing skills.
- **develop a clear and natural pronunciation** through the systematic practice of tricky sounds.
- **communicate confidently and fluently** through well-supported speaking tasks.
- **learn about life in English-speaking countries around the world** and think about their own culture.
- **participate fully** in fun and engaging activities such as songs, stories, games and chants.
- **develop reading, writing, listening and speaking** in a balanced and integrative manner.
- **prepare for Cambridge Exams** through the systematic integration of exam practice material and a dedicated Exams Practice lesson in each unit.
- **become independent and reflective learners** through the integration of learning-to-learn strategies and activities.
- **develop their thinking skills and multiple intelligences** through a variety of stimulating and challenging activities.
- **develop their 21st century skills** through real life videos and interesting tasks to practise and perfect the skills needed in the 21st century.

Meet the characters in *Give Me Five! 3*

Josh and his sister **Lily** are nine and eight years old respectively and have just moved into their new home, a lighthouse.

Together with their friend **Ravi**, they discover that living next to the sea is full of surprises and adventure.

Luke is Josh and Lily's big brother. He's a scientist and a fan of codes and secret messages. The children love reading about the amazing things he sees and does on his trip around the world.

Cooperative learning

Give Me Five! 3 incorporates a variety of **cooperative learning tasks and strategies** which require the pupils to work together in a structured way. Working in pairs and small groups has many benefits. The pupils are prepared to spend more time on the tasks, are motivated to produce more language and are more likely to use creative and logical thinking. Cooperative learning also helps develop a positive classroom environment as the pupils have a greater sense of belonging and learn to understand and value all the members of the group. Finally, cooperative tasks require the pupils to be active and more independent learners, building their self-confidence and their ability to cope with uncertainty and unpredictability.

Give Me Five! 3 makes use of common and well-researched cooperative learning strategies. One of these is **Think-Pair-Share**, where learners listen to a question, think about it individually, discuss the answer with a partner and then share their ideas with the rest of the class. Others include **Talk Partners**, where the pupils test and prompt each other in pairs, and **Writing Partners**, where the pupils work together to plan, write and evaluate a piece of written work. There is also a simple, clearly staged **cooperative project** at the end of each term which provides the pupils with the opportunity to learn and develop **interpersonal skills** such as turn taking, listening to others and dealing with conflict.

In order to support and reinforce these different ways of working, the teacher is provided with a set of **Talk cards**. The cards can be displayed in the classroom and include a **Talk Partners card**, where the pupils work with the person sitting next to them to complete a task, a **Talk in small groups card**, where the pupils work in groups of three or four, and an **Own work, but can help a partner card** where the pupils are encouraged to support and help each other with a reading or writing task.

Cooperative learning activities and strategies bank

1 Three-step interview

The pupils work with a partner to ask and answer questions, e.g. about their preferences or their routines. Once they have completed the task, they turn to a new partner and report what their first partner has told them, e.g. *Peter loves skating.* This strategy can be used for personal questions, for example in some *Talk Partner* activities.

2 Think – write – pair – compare

Ask the pupils a question, e.g. *What water sports do you know?* Each pupil should think and write down their ideas. The pupils then share and compare their ideas with a partner or in a small group. Asking pupils to write down their ideas helps them to organise their thoughts and ensures full participation. This strategy can be used for brainstorming, for example in Lesson 1, Activity 1.

3 Numbered heads

When the class is working in small groups, give each pupil a number (1–3). At the end of the task ask a question and say one of the numbers. The pupil with that number in each group should answer the question. Repeat the process with other questions, choosing a different number to answer each time. This strategy can be used when the pupils are planning and creating projects in small groups or when they are doing the review quiz in pairs at the end of the unit.

4 Round robin

Organise the class into small groups. Then ask an open-ended question. Each pupil should take turns to share their answer with their group. To prevent interruptions, give pupils a *talk token,* e.g. a rubber, to place on the table when they speak. Once they have done this, they cannot speak again until all their group's tokens are on the table. This strategy can be used, for example, when talking about values in Lesson 3 or the children's culture in Lesson 8.

5 Board sharing

When pupils have discussed a question in small groups, ask them to choose their best answer. One pupil from each group should then write the information on the board. The class can then compare and discuss the different answers. This strategy can be used for brainstorming ideas or for making predictions, for example before reading the story in Lesson 3.

6 Reading partners

Organise the class into pairs to read a text. The two pupils should take it in turns to read a section of the text, e.g. a paragraph, to each other. At the end of each section they should check each other's understanding. This strategy can be used, for example, after a class reading of the literacy texts in Lessons 6 and 7.

21st Century learning

Give Me Five! 3 and 21st Century learning

Today's learners are growing up in a complex, changing world where an enormous amount of information is available at the touch of a button and where social media allows them to communicate with people all around the world. Technology is transforming the way we live and the way we learn. A key objective of *Give Me Five! 3* is to support learners in developing the necessary skills for the digital age. Apart from using digital technology, skills such as communicating and collaborating with others, thinking creatively and critically, and working to become a caring global citizen are an essential part of this course.

Give Me Five! 3 takes an integrated approach to the use of digital technology and the teaching of **digital skills**. In each unit there is a comprehensive set of digital practice material for the learner, helping them to become autonomous and digitally confident. Pupils are also supported in developing specific ICT skills. There are tips on how to use the Internet to find, select and present information, and there is a selection of projects with digital outcomes. Guided web quests also support pupils in using the Internet to explore new places around the world.

There are multiple opportunities for **communication** and **collaboration** in *Give Me Five! 3*. Learners are encouraged to work together to discover and build knowledge through quizzes and questionnaires, whole-class discussions and a wide range of *Talk Partner* activities. Pupils also work with *Writing Partners* to plan, write and evaluate pieces of written work, and are encouraged to work cooperatively to review learning and reflect on progress at the end of each unit. Finally, there are structured cooperative projects which by providing opportunities for authentic communication, they encourage the development of interpersonal skills and enable learners to celebrate achievement.

Each unit of *Give Me Five! 3* provides a range of tasks to build the pupil's **critical and creative thinking skills**. These include problem-solving, evaluating information, and using imaginative thinking. The Video and 21st Century Skills lessons also focus on a selection of discrete thinking skills. They provide practical tips and thinking strategies.

The interconnectivity of the 21st Century and the increasing diversity of our communities mean that pupils need to learn how to respect and value other cultures. *Give Me Five! 3* provides learners with historical, geographical and cultural information about nine different places in the world. This rich content provides opportunities for **intercultural learning**, where learners identify cultural differences and similarities and build a positive attitude toward their own and other cultures.

Finally, a dedicated *Values* section in each unit supports learners in developing their **social and civic competencies** and helps them to make a positive difference in the world.

Video and 21st Century Skills lessons

Video generates interest and supports learners' listening skills by providing a clear visual context and model to practise speaking. It is also a flexible tool, allowing teachers to pause the recording or turn off the sound, and can be used as a stimulus for thinking, language practice and communication. Each unit in *Give Me Five! 3* concludes with a Video and 21st Century Skills lesson. These video lessons help to build key 21st Century Skills, develop visual literacy and provide a springboard for authentic communication.

The stars of the videos are Chloe and Mark, the two children presenters of *Channel 21*. The children begin each programme by introducing a new topic and then share a selection of related video clips that they have gathered. These are visually rich videos, bring images of the world into the classroom and offer insights into British culture. The children then discuss the clips and highlight a 21st Century Skill in the material. This serves to contextualise the 21st Century Skill and show the learner how it is relevant in their learning and in their lives.

The 21st Century Skills selected for this level are the following:

Ways of thinking: these skills focus on critical and creative thinking and include open mindedness (Unit 1), using your imagination (Unit 4) and paying attention (Unit 7).

Ways of working: these skills focus on collaboration and communication and include accepting ideas and suggestion when working in groups (Unit 9).

Digital skills: these skills focus on researching, evaluating information and using digital technology and include using keywords to find information online (Unit 5) and making a video (Unit 8).

Living in the world: these skills focus on values, responsibility and cultural awareness and include helping others (Unit 2) being fit and healthy (Unit 3) and staying safe when doing sport (Unit 6).

Multiple Intelligences

According to the theory of **multiple intelligences**, each human being possesses a set of intelligences. As a consequence, learners have different needs, strengths and abilities in the classroom. In *Give Me Five!*, seven key intelligences are highlighted:

Linguistic intelligence

The pupils are supported on their journey to becoming **confident and accurate speakers**, listeners, readers and writers of the English language through a wide variety of activities. The pupils are given opportunities to use this language in a **range of social and cultural contexts**.

Bodily-kinaesthetic intelligence

Physical expression is an important part of communication and the pupils are encouraged to use **mime and gesture to support meaning**. The pupils are also given the opportunity to develop their fine motor skills.

Logical-mathematical intelligence

Integrated activities that require the pupils to use mathematical and logical **thinking skills**. These include **code breaking**, **problem solving**, **hypothesising** and **recording and presenting data**.

Visual-spatial intelligence

The engaging artwork in *Give Me Five!* is used to support meaning and help the pupils to **visualise contexts for language**. **Graphic organisers** help the pupils form their own conceptual links and order new information.

Musical intelligence

The pupils are exposed to **songs**, **chants**, **tongue twisters**, **rhymes**, **riddles** and **poems**. These help them to produce natural-sounding rhythm, stress and intonation.

Interpersonal intelligence

A **values** section in each unit provides an opportunity for the pupils to develop the ability to empathise and respond appropriately to other people and draws their attention to key **social and civic values** and **codes of conduct**.

Intrapersonal intelligence

The pupils are encouraged to think about their **inner feelings**, **values** and **beliefs** through questionnaires and discussion questions. They also carry out several self-evaluation tasks.

Tips for teaching pupils with Special Educational Needs

Setting up the class and Working together

- Change the groupings regularly to make sure the SEN pupils have an opportunity to work with all their classmates.
- Keeping routines is highly important for SEN pupils. Use visuals to reinforce rules and routines.
- Make instructions clear and on a step-by-step basis. Check understanding by giving an example and getting an example from the pupils.
- Use positive classroom language. Say what you want pupils to do, not what you don't want them to do. For example, say ***Look at the board*** not ***Don't keep turning round***.
- Develop a peer mentoring system to encourage pupils to help each other and share skills.

Hearing Impaired (HI) learners

- Write instructions on the board or highlight them on the IWB. Make sure you have your pupil's attention before you read out the instructions or speak.
- Seat your hearing impaired (HI) pupil facing and close to you to make lip reading and following instruction gestures easier.
- Assign or ask for a volunteer helper or note-taker depending on the level. The helper can point out the instructions in the Pupil's Book and a note-taker can take note of the key ideas of a listening to support the hearing impaired pupil.

Visually Impaired (VI) learners

- Say every word you write on the board and use realia to teach vocabulary. Realia allows the visually impaired pupils to use all their senses.
- *Give Me Five! 3* offers plenty of songs, stories and dialogues with lesson tips on how to include total physical response (TPR) activities.
- Encourage other pupils to describe experiences to give plenty of exposure to personal and shared interests.

Dyslexic learners

- For brainstorming activities, do the first few examples with the class. Ask the pupils to do the first part of an activity and check their answers before moving on to the next part. For writing activities at sentence level, provide the pupils with a model which can be done as a whole class first.
- If pupils can't write in their books, provide photocopies to allow pupils with dyslexia to mark the text or cut it and move it around. This allows for information to be processed in manageable chunks.

Key Competences and Key Learning Outcomes

The **Key Competences and Key Learning Outcomes** outline the **knowledge**, **skills** and **behaviour** that the pupils need to develop in order to achieve their full personal potential, participate in an effective and constructive way in society and become responsible and autonomous life-long learners.

Competence in linguistic communication: the ability to use language as an instrument to express and interpret concepts, facts, feelings and ideas in an appropriate and creative way.

Cultural awareness and expression: the ability to understand and appreciate different art and cultural forms.

Competence in mathematics, science and technology: the ability to develop and apply mathematical thinking to solve everyday problems and to use scientific knowledge to explain the natural world and understand the consequences of human action.

Sense of initiative and entrepreneurship: the ability to apply qualities and skills such as creativity, critical thinking and perseverance, and to plan and manage projects.

Digital competence: the ability to use digital technology confidently, critically and responsibly.

Social and civic competences: the ability to understand and appreciate diversity in society and to develop personal and interpersonal competences.

Learning to learn: the ability to organise one's own learning and work efficiently and autonomously as an individual or in a group.

How *Give Me Five! 3* develops the Key Competences and Key Learning Outcomes

Competence in linguistic communication

Give Me Five! 3 develops the pupils' linguistic skills in a systematic and integrative manner. The pupils learn to identify the meaning, sounds and rhythms of words and phrases through **songs**, **chants** and **stories**. The use of short **listening texts** helps them develop the ability to understand simple communicative messages in everyday contexts.

There is systematic practice of **tricky sounds** which helps the pupils develop clear and natural pronunciation. In addition, the structured use of **games**, **personalisation activities** and simple **conversations** provide the pupils with the opportunity to practise real-world exchanges in the classroom and express their feelings and opinions in English. A **cooperative project** each term also helps the pupils develop social competences and introduces language and strategies for working successfully in small groups.

Each unit of *Give Me Five! 3* has a **double-page literacy spread** which introduces the pupils to a variety of engaging real-world texts. **Reading strategies** are systematically introduced to support readers in understanding, responding to and reflecting on these texts, whilst an analysis of features such as the writer's purpose, audience and the informational content of a text help prepare the pupils for writing. Discrete **writing skills** such as the use of capital letters or punctuation are also highlighted in the literacy lessons and the pupils learn and practise **alternative spellings** of consonant sounds in the Lesson 5 **phonics** section.

Competence in mathematics, science and technology

In *Give Me Five! 3*, mathematical competence is developed in a number of ways. The pupils' understanding of **numbers, space, measures and time** is reinforced and **language patterns** are highlighted. The pupils also have the opportunity to work with **number codes, charts and diagrams**, and to do activities which require them to recognise and **solve problems**. Each unit of *Give Me Five! 3* is also **linked to an area of learning in the Science curriculum**, reinforcing key concepts and language across the curriculum.

Digital competence

Give Me Five! 3 uses **digital resources** as tools to support learning, familiarising the pupils with computer technology and showing them how technology can be used for learning purposes. The **Pupil's App on Navio** serves to consolidate class work and allows the pupils to work independently outside the classroom.

Learning to learn

Give Me Five! 3 introduces a variety of **learning strategies** to help the pupils become more independent and reflective learners. Learning outcomes are set at the beginning and reviewed at the end of each lesson to check that the objectives have been met. The pupils are also encouraged to reflect on their learning and progress at the end of each unit through the use of a **self-evaluation task**. A dedicated learning-to-learn section in each unit encourages the pupils to think about how they like to learn and introduces simple strategies which can be used independently, outside the classroom.

Finally, throughout *Give Me Five!* there is an emphasis on good learning habits and the importance of making an effort and being responsible for your work. Personal qualities such as self-confidence, initiative, curiosity, interest and creativity are also explicitly promoted, preparing the pupils for life-long learning.

Social and civic competences

Developing the ability to understand how somebody else is feeling and knowing how to respond appropriately is an important objective of *Give Me Five!*, and emphasis is placed on **positive classroom behaviour**. **Cooperative projects** provide the pupils with the language needed to engage effectively with others and solve problems, whilst the integration of **collaborative activities and strategies** reinforces the importance of active participation, cooperation and respect and support for others.

A **values** section in each unit encourages the pupils to reflect on their natural, social and cultural environment, integrating real-world topics such as protecting natural environments, listening to other people's opinions and making people feel welcome.

Sense of initiative and entrepreneurship

Give Me Five! 3 develops a sense of initiative and entrepreneurship through the inclusion of a **cooperative project** in each term. These require the pupils to work in groups to successfully plan and complete a task, such as designing a zoo or organising a class trip to London. Working together to complete a task helps the pupils to take responsibility for their work and gain confidence in their abilities. Initiative is also encouraged through personalisation activities, problem-solving tasks, creative activities and the opportunity to work independently in pairs and small groups.

Cultural awareness and expression

In *Give Me Five! 3* the pupils are introduced to the real-world culture of different **English-speaking countries around the world**. The content of these lessons has been selected to be of **intrinsic interest** to the pupils and to help them understand and respect different customs. A **Think about your culture** section encourages the pupils to reflect on their own culture and have a clearer idea of their own **cultural identity**.

Give Me Five! 3 also provides the opportunity to experience and appreciate a **range of art forms** such as poems, songs, literature, drawing, mime and performance, and encourages the pupils to express their ideas, experiences and emotions through these mediums.

Give Me Five! 3 Pupil's components

Pupil's Book

This is a 128-page, full-colour, write-in book that contains a Starter Unit and nine thematic units. It also comprises three fun and easy-to-use projects and two festivals sections. Each unit is divided into eight lessons and provides vocabulary input and practice, a short conversation to contextualise and practise chunks of language and a double-page story for language input and consolidation. It also contains a humorous tongue twister to practise a tricky consonant sound, a photographic world culture lesson, an engaging real-world literacy text and a unit review. At the end of each unit there is a Video and 21st Century Skills lesson, and at the back of the book there is practice material for Cambridge English Young Learners exams and a vocabulary and grammar review section.

Activity Book

This 120-page, write-in book works in tandem with the Pupil's Book to reinforce and extend language learning, support and develop reading and writing and provide further practice of the listening and speaking skills. Each unit comprises a variety of activities which are devised to engage and challenge the pupils, activate different intelligences, encourage creativity and allow the pupils to use language in a personal and meaningful way. At the end of each unit there is a full page unit review and a Video and 21st Century Skills lesson. At the back of the book there is practice material for the Cambridge English Young Learners exams and a vocabulary and grammar practice section.

Pupil's App on Navio

Powered By NAVIO

The Pupil's App on Navio is designed to accompany the course and provide extra practice in class or at home. Pupils can create avatars and then explore Navio's immersive worlds. Pupils complete game-based activities designed to practise and review the language and content learnt in class. As they do so, they earn rewards, points and badges. The App tracks pupils' progress so the teacher can see how they are doing and provide extra support where it is needed. The App also includes all the songs, stories and animations from the course so that pupils can review them at home and share them with their family. The access code for the Pupil's App can be found on the inside front cover of the Pupil's Book.

PERFECT PARTNERS WITH

BY ME

Social Science Primary 3 **Natural Science Primary 3**

Arts and Crafts Primary 3

Grammar Goals 3

Give Me Five! 3 Teacher's components

Teacher's Book

This user-friendly, spiral-bound book provides teachers with as much or as little support as they need. The At a Glance Lesson Plans, illustrated with images of the Pupil's Book and Activity Book, clearly highlight the learning aims, key language, materials required, learning routines, key activities and a range of optional extra activities, including Links to Science and cooperative learning activities. These are accompanied by Detailed Lesson Plans which provide complete and concise teaching notes for each activity and answer keys. Full audioscripts can be found at the back of the book. In addition, there is a Reflective Teacher page at the end of each unit for documenting learning, noting ideas and planning actions.

Teacher's App on Navio

Powered By NAVIO

The Teacher's App on Navio offers one-stop access to all the many resources which accompany the course. **Tap and Teach Lessons** with **integrated audio and video** ensure that everything you need to teach each lesson is in one place. You can use the **Classroom Management tool** to award points for good behaviour or success in class, and track your pupils' marks and progress using the **Progress Tracker**. You'll find additional photocopiable resources in the **Teacher's Resource Bank** (see opposite) and **Test Generator**.

Class CDs

Four class CDs provide all the recorded material for the Pupil's Book and Activity Book: songs, chants, dialogues, listening tasks, stories, games, tongue twisters, culture lessons, literacy texts, review material, 21st Century Skills lessons and Cambridge English Young Learners Exams practice material. They also include recordings of the cooperative learning songs and a karaoke version of the Lesson 1 song in each unit.

Flashcards

A set of 118 full-colour flashcards with photographic images of the key vocabulary from Lesson 1 of each unit. Suggestions for using the flashcards are given in the Detailed Lesson Plans and in the Flashcards games bank on page 27.

Teacher's Resource Bank: course resources

The **Teacher's Resource Bank** located within the teacher's app on Navio, contains a wealth of resources that complement *Give Me Five!* In addition to providing downloads for all class audio and video, the resource bank contains:

- **Letters to parents:** an introductory letter, followed by a letter to present each unit.
- **Talk cards:** a set of six cards to support the pupils' understanding of the interaction required at different stages of the lesson.

- **Vocabulary and Grammar worksheets:** to reinforce and extend the vocabulary and grammar syllabus.
- **Evaluation Rubrics:** one grid per unit to evaluate pupils' level of achievement of the Key Learning Outcomes and Key Competences as well as their cooperative learning skills.
- **Tests:** a Diagnostic Test, Unit Tests, Term Tests and an End-of-Year Test with audio and Teacher's Notes. Each test has a standard and a higher level version.

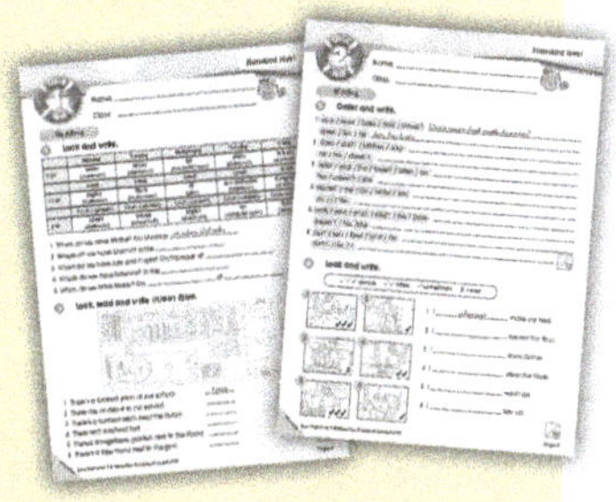

- **Word cards:** A set of 118 word cards. Suggestions for using the word cards can be found in the Detailed Lesson Plans and in the Word cards games bank on page 27.

Teacher's Resource Bank: External Exams Resources

This section in the Teacher's Resource Bank supports teachers who are preparing their pupils for either one of the ***Trinity Graded Exams in Spoken English*** (Elementary Stage, Grades 4 and 5) or the ***Cambridge English Young Learners Movers Test***. The external exams resources contain the following:

- **Videos** of children doing speaking practice.
- **Teacher's Notes** on how to exploit these videos in the classroom.
- Extra **Cambridge Exam Practice material** and **practice tests** and **tips for teachers**.
- **Trinity Exam Practice Worksheets**
- A set of **Trinity Exam Practice cards** for optional Trinity-type speaking practice at the start of each lesson.

Teacher's and Pupil's Apps on Navio

The Navio app which accompanies this course offers one-stop access to the huge range of resources that come with *Give Me Five! 3*. **Tap and Teach Lessons** enable you to move seamlessly between the book and digital components, and you can track your pupils' marks and review their progress using the **Progress Tracker**, and find additional resources in the **Resource Bank** and **Test Generator**.

Accessing the app

To access Navio:

1. Go to www.MacmillanNavio.com/givemefive
2. Follow the onscreen instructions

If you haven't got a Macmillan Education account, you need to create a profile. Then you can enter your access code and download the app for your device (see System Requirements: www.macmillannavio.com/system-requirements).

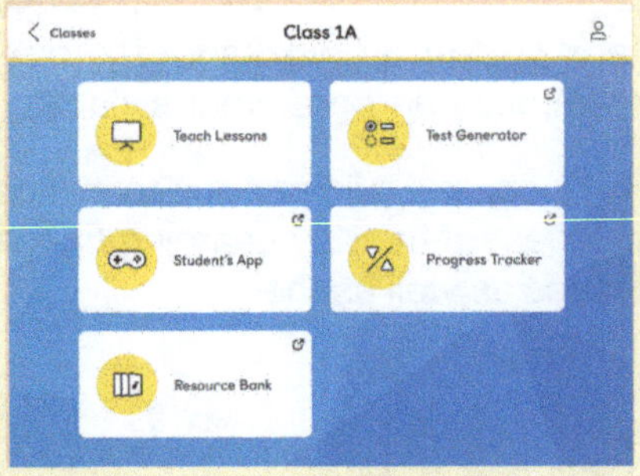

Setting up a class

You, or your school administrator, will need to set up a class and register pupils with their names and the email address of their parents or guardians. Once the class is created, login details can be given to parents. Parents can then log in to the Pupil's App and enter the access code from the inside cover of the Teacher's Book to access the 3D worlds and practice content.

Managing your downloads

Navio makes it easy to manage the storage space on your device, as you can control how much material you download at one time. Navio makes it clear how much storage space your chosen content will need. You can download the complete Teacher's and Pupil's Apps at once, or, if your device has limited storage capacity, you can choose to download only one or two units. And after you finish a unit, you can safely delete the content from your device. You won't lose your pupils' data, as this information is stored online.

Using the Progress Tracker

All the work your pupils complete in the app is recorded in the **Progress Tracker**. You can monitor the progress of a whole class or any individual pupil. Every activity in the App is mapped against the course Learning Outcomes and Skills, so you can easily identify where your pupils need extra support.

Teaching a lesson

Navio makes it easy to plan and teach your lessons with fully interactive **Tap and Teach Lessons** for every lesson in *Give Me Five! 3*. Go to your Class Dashboard and choose Teach Lessons. Find the lesson you want to teach and click to open it. Click on the Toolbar along the bottom of the screen to expand it to Thumbnail view. The Toolbar also contains the Tap and Teach tools you need to teach heads-up, whole-class activities, including a Timer, Pen tool, and Mask tool.

Lessons follow the lesson plans in the Teacher's Book, and provide everything you need to teach from your device in one place. They include digital versions of all the activities in the Pupil's Book, Activity Book and Essential Activity Book, with their answer keys. They also include all the audio and video you need for the lesson, as well as some extra tools such as digital Flashcards. All relevant pages from all three books are also provided so that you can project them in class, to help your pupils and to encourage heads-up participation.

When you teach, move through the lesson slide by slide using the arrows, or double click on a thumbnail to jump straight to a particular activity. If you prefer, you can Filter activities to customise the lesson so it includes only the content you want to teach.

Using the Rewards tool

Navio's new **Rewards tool** is a great way to keep your pupils engaged in class. Much more than just a record of attendance, you can also use it to award points for good behaviour or success in activities. You can even organise your class into teams, and you can award points to individuals, groups or the whole class at any time. When pupils earn points, they appear in the Pupil's App next time they log in, so parents can see their performance.

Pupil's App

As a teacher you can also access a version of the Pupil's App from the Class Dashboard. This has all the same content that your pupils can access at home, but your version is set in **Teacher Mode**. This means that all the activities and worlds are already unlocked, and the App does not record any marks to the Progress Tracker.

We recommend using Teacher Mode when pupils share devices to avoid mixing up pupils' grades and progress. However, if pupils have individual devices or are using the app at home, they should always log in with their own username and password. In this way they can earn points and badges, set up and customise their avatar and build a record of their progress in the Progress Tracker.

Flashcards and Word cards games bank

Flashcard games

1 *What is it?*
Hold up a flashcard so that the pupils can't see the picture and describe what you can see, the colour, shape and texture. You can also state where it's found and what it's used for. Ask **What is it?** The pupils try to guess, for example *Is it a (canoe)?* When the class successfully guesses the picture, show it to them and ask them to repeat the word. Repeat the procedure with all the flashcards in the lexical set.

2 *What's missing?*
Stick eight flashcards in a row on the board and quickly review the vocabulary items. Then say the items in order, deliberately missing one of them out. The pupils should identify the missing word. Repeat the procedure several times, missing out a different item each time. When the pupils are confident, remove the cards and repeat the activity. The pupils should try to identify the missing item, but this time from memory. The pupils can repeat the activity with their Talk Partners.

3 *Disappearing flashcards*
Stick a set of flashcards in a row or in a grid on the board. Point to each card and elicit the word. Repeat until the pupils are saying the words in a fluent and rhythmical manner. Then remove one of the cards. Point to the remaining cards and the empty space in order and prompt the class to say all the words in order once again. Continue removing the cards until there are no cards on the board and the class is chanting the words in order from memory.

4 *Flashcard duel*
Invite two pupils to come to the front of the class and ask them to take a flashcard. They can look at the card, but they mustn't show it to anyone else. The pupils then take three steps away from each other, turn and quickly show their cards. Each pupil should name the activity or item that they can see on the other pupil's card as quickly as possible. Repeat the procedure with different cards and different pairs of pupils.

5 *Flashcard elimination*
Stick a set of flashcards on the board, prompting the class to say each word. Explain to the class that you are thinking of one of the words and challenge them to discover it in five questions. However, you will only answer **yes** or **no**. If necessary, provide a set of closed question prompts, i.e. **Is it …? Has it got …? Do you need …?** Invite a pupil to ask you a question, i.e. *Is the food sweet?* If your answer is **No, it isn't**, the pupil should remove all the flashcards that have sweet foods on them. Repeat the procedure until the pupils have either guessed the word or run out of questions.

6 *Keep talking*
Organise the class into two or more teams. Show the class your first flashcard and elicit the vocabulary item. Then give the card to the first team and ask them to make a sentence about what is on the card, for example *It's yellow* (a banana). If the sentence is acceptable the team wins a point and the card is passed on to the next team who must think up another sentence, e.g. *It's delicious. It's sweet. It comes from the Canary Islands. I eat one every week.* Continue the activity until the groups run out of things to say. Then repeat the procedure with another card.

Word card games

1 *Word dictation*
Choose a word card from the lexical set you want to practise and spell out the word on it. The pupils raise their hands when they recognise the word. Ask a pupil to say it. Repeat with different words, saying the letters faster as the pupils become more confident. You can also invite different pupils to take your role.

2 *Board pelmanism*
Stick a set of flashcards and the corresponding word cards face down on the board in a random order. Number all the cards. Then divide the class into two teams. Each team takes turns to choose two numbers. Turn over the corresponding cards each time. If the cards match, remove them from the board and award the team a point. If they do not match, return them face down to their original positions. Encourage the class to try to remember where the different cards are located. The team with the most points when all the cards have been removed is the winner.

3 *Careful copying*
Organise the class into small groups and place a selection of word cards face down on the table in front of each group. A pupil in each group should turn over one of the cards and show it to the rest of the group for a few seconds. The card is then replaced and everyone in the group writes the word in their notebooks from memory. Afterwards, the pupils should look at the card again to check their spelling.
If everyone has spelt the word correctly, the card stays face up on the table and another card is chosen. However, if anyone in the group has spelt the word incorrectly, the card should be replaced and the group has another go. The group can help each other at this stage. The activity continues until all the cards are face up on the table.

4 *Word detectives*
Stick a set of word cards on the board, prompting the class to read and say each word as you do so. Then organise the class into pairs and explain that they are going to be word detectives. Give the first clue and ask the pairs to discuss which of the words on the board it could be. Repeat the procedure with the other clues. After the class has listened to all five clues, ask different pairs to guess the word. Possible clues include: 1 It's got … letters. 2 It's got … vowels. 3 It rhymes with the word … 4 It finishes with the letter … 5 It begins with the letter …

5 *Word card classification*
Use the word cards to organise and classify vocabulary items. You can use the cards to create a mind map, writing the name of the topic in the centre of the board and then asking the class to organise the word cards into sub-topics around the topic. You can also create Venn diagrams, for example classifying food into groups according to whether it is eaten hot or cold, or organising activities on a line according to how boring or exciting they are.

Using the Pupil's Book and Activity Book

Lessons 1 and 2

The pupils **activate their existing knowledge** by working in small groups to brainstorm words they already know.

Twelve items of vocabulary are introduced and practised using **photographic and picture flashcards**.

Real-world photographic images provide the pupils with a record of new vocabulary. The pupils point to each image and say a **vocabulary chant**.

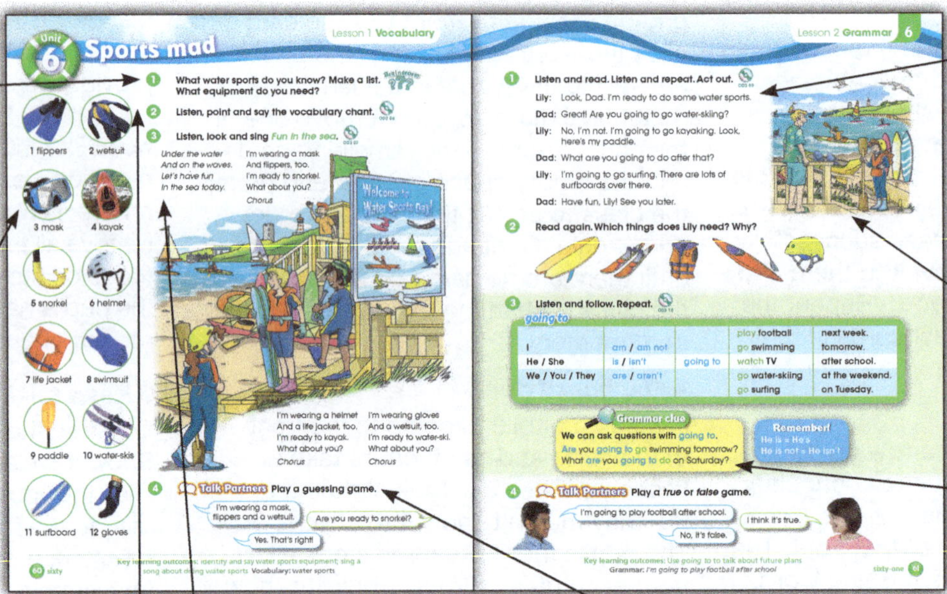

A short conversation places **grammar in a fun and familiar context**.

Attractive artwork engages the pupils and helps contextualise language.

The **grammar table** highlights and practises language patterns. The pupils listen to an audio and point to the different parts of the sentence in the table. They then work with a partner to create their own sentences.

A **fun and easy-to-sing song** builds fluency and makes language more memorable.

The pupils work in pairs to play a **game** using the new vocabulary items.

Fun, game-like activities motivate the pupils to write the new vocabulary items.

The pupils **practise writing** the new vocabulary in a sentence using a recycled structure.

The pupils use a code-breaking activity to **review and recycle** vocabulary from the previous unit at the bottom of each Activity Book page.

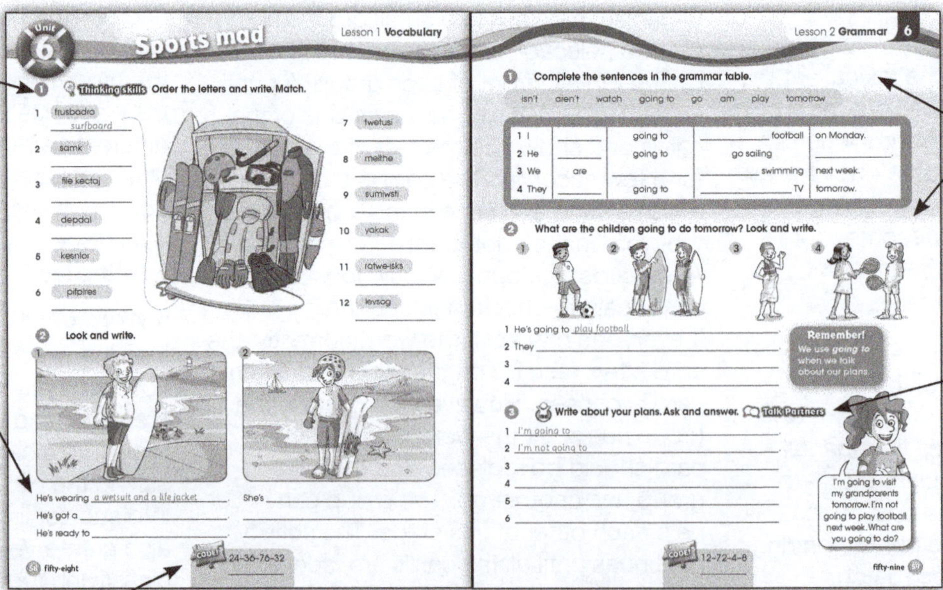

A range of activities give the pupils practice in manipulating the form of the new grammar.

A selection of **thinking skills** such as problem solving and spatial thinking are developed in each unit.

Digital resources

Teacher's Digital: Don't forget you can teach these lessons using the Teacher's App on Navio.

Pupil's Digital: Encourage your pupils to use the Pupil's App on Navio to practise the vocabulary from these lessons.

Powered By NAVIO

Lesson 3

A pre-reading task helps prepare the pupils to read and listen to the story. These include a code-breaking task and predictions about the story content.

In each unit, the pupils enjoy an **exciting adventure** with Lily, Josh and Ravi. A list of frame-by-frame comprehension questions for each story is provided in the Detailed Lesson Plan in the Teacher's Book.

Attractive and humorous pictures and an **exciting audio recording** support the pupils' understanding of the narrative.

The **Values** section encourages the pupils to reflect on the story and relate a personal, social or civic value to their own lives.

The story reinforces language introduced in Lessons 1 and 2 and previews language from Lesson 4.

A range of activities check the pupils' understanding of the story.

Comprehension is reinforced through a **listening activity**.

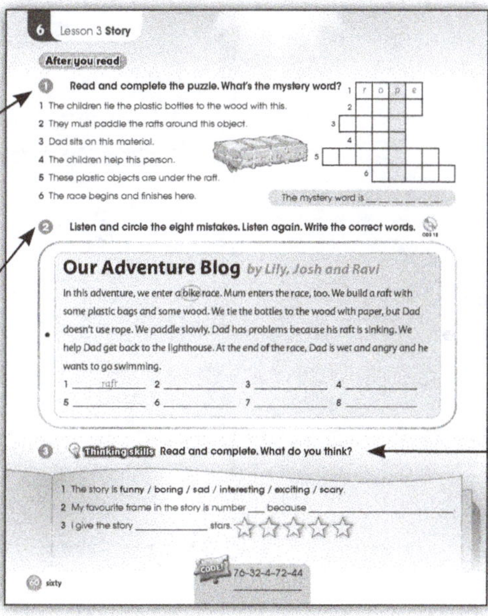

The pupils are encouraged to give a **personal response** to the story as well as an opportunity to practise thinking skills.

Digital resources

Teacher's Digital: Don't forget you can teach this lesson using the Teacher's App on Navio.

Pupil's Digital: Encourage your pupils to use the Pupil's App on Navio to practise the vocabulary from these lessons.

Powered By NAVIO

Using the Pupil's Book and Activity Book

Lessons 4 and 5

Six new items of vocabulary are introduced and practised, using **pictures** and **photos**.

The **Speak and spell** section uses a humorous tongue twister to give the pupils practice in producing **tricky sounds**. It also introduces pupils to **alternative spelling** patterns for these sounds.

A **lively song, chant or rap** gives further practice of the vocabulary and introduces additional grammar.

Grammar clues encourage the pupils to think analytically about new language.

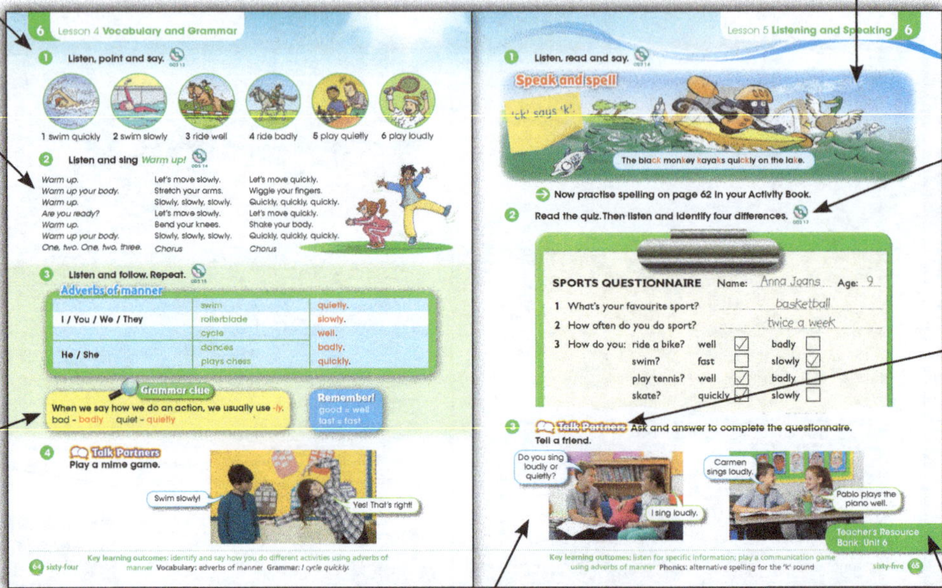

A listening task prepares the pupils for a communicative game. The pupils listen to children using the unit language to play the game.

Talk Partners icons indicate when the pupils have the opportunity to practise speaking in pairs. These activities build confidence and ensure full participation.

The pupils play a **communicative game** in pairs. Each pupil has different information, providing the pupils with a genuine reason for speaking. The Teacher's Notes give clear, precise instructions on how to set up and scaffold the communication game.

In the Teacher's Resource Bank you can find further activities to practise and consolidate learning.

Activities encourage the pupils to recognise and practise the Lesson 4 vocabulary.

Reading and writing activities are carefully staged **to build the pupils' confidence and ensure success**.

The pupils enjoy a full page of activities to practise reading, writing and saying the key letter sounds in each unit.

The activities use recycled words to build the pupils' confidence and link new information to existing knowledge.

The pupils work with their **Talk Partners** to test and prompt each other on the spelling of words that contain the key letter sound.

Digital resources

Teacher's Digital: Don't forget you can teach these lessons using the Teacher's App on Navio.

Pupil's Digital: Encourage your pupils to use the Pupil's App on Navio to practise the vocabulary from these lessons.

Powered By NAVIO

Lessons 6 and 7

The pupils are introduced to a **wide range of reading text types**. These are selected to reflect the interests and experiences of the age group and have an **authentic appearance** that will appeal to learners.

A variety of tasks help the pupils to understand the purpose of a text, the intended audience or what is appropriate content. This helps to develop **literacy** and reading skills.

The **Before you read activities** help prepare the pupils to read. These include activating the pupils' existing knowledge, exploiting visuals, asking questions to raise interest and making predictions.

All texts are supported by an audio recording and attractive visuals.

The pupils are directed to the **After you read activities** in the Activity Book.

A shorter text provides a **writing model** for the pupils to follow.

Guided questions help the pupils identify key text features such as titles, captions and layout.

The **Writing tip** section highlights a discrete writing skill such as using capital letters or connectors.

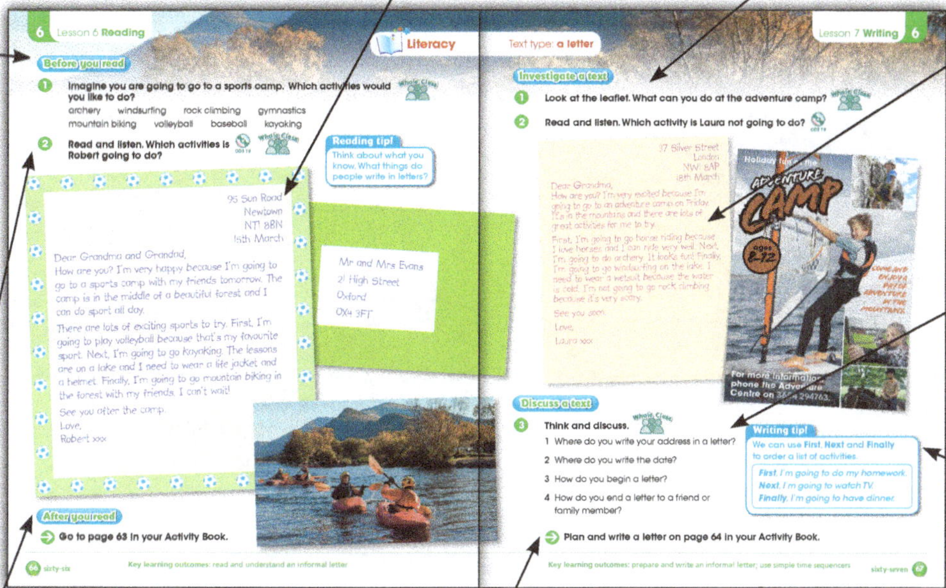

The pupils are directed to the Activity Book to prepare their piece of writing.

A range of **After you read activities** reinforce and check the pupils' understanding of the literacy text.

Reading skills such as skimming and scanning are actively developed.

The pupils work with **charts, graphs** and **graphic organisers** to categorise and order information.

A variety of **enjoyable activities** allow the pupils to respond to the text in a personal and creative way.

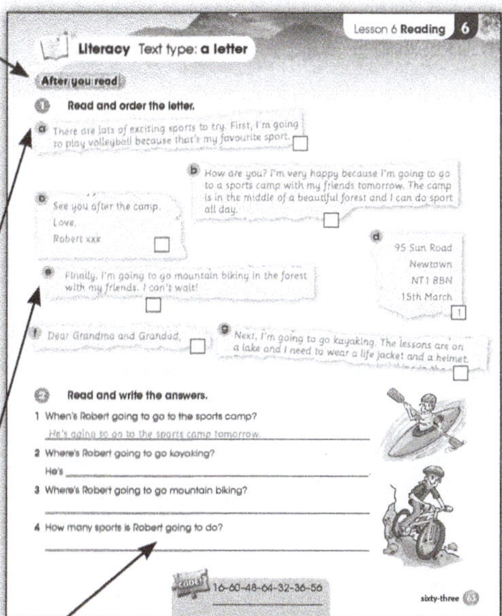

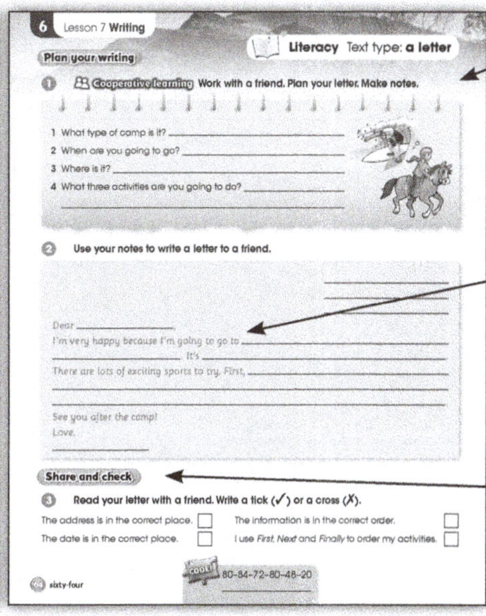

The pupils work with a partner to plan, draft and revise their writing.

Step-by-step instructions and a writing framework provide the pupils with plenty of support in the planning stage and scaffold learning as they write their text.

The pupils **share their work** with another student and use **self-assessment criteria** to check their work.

Digital resources

Teacher's Digital: Don't forget you can teach these lessons using the Teacher's App on Navio.

Pupil's Digital: Encourage your pupils to use the Pupil's App on Navio to practise the vocabulary from these lessons.

Powered By NAVIO

Using the Pupil's Book and Activity Book

Lesson 8, Review and 21st Century Skills

The pupils are introduced to **age-appropriate cultural content** from English-speaking countries around the world.

Josh and Lily's brother Luke introduces the new destination and sets an investigation task.

A webpage showing children in different countries brings the culture to life. This helps foster a positive attitude towards English-speaking countries and English language learning.

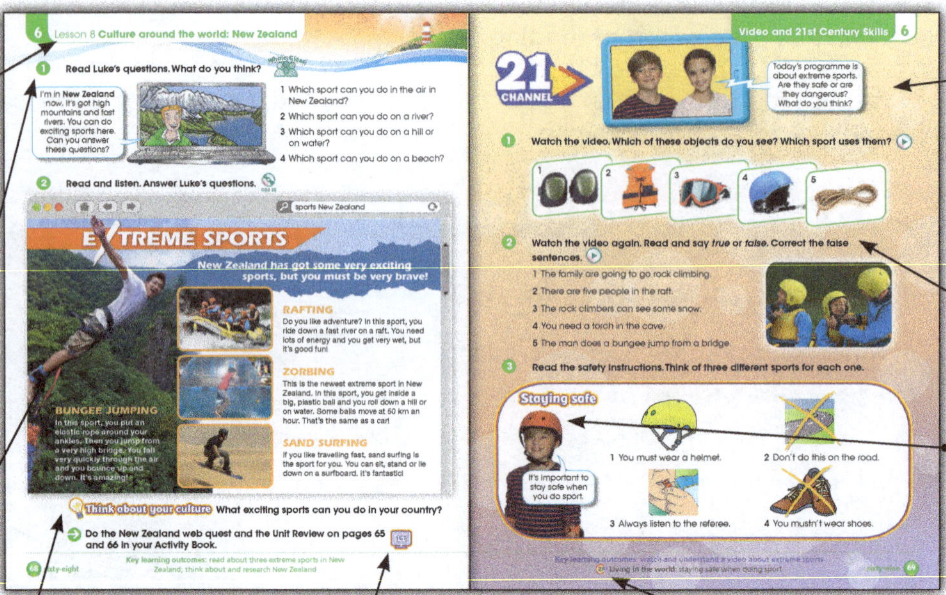

The presenters introduce the video lesson and spark the pupils' interest in a wide range of topics.

The pupils watch an engaging **video** related to the topic of the unit and 21st Century Skills.

In the final activity, pupils have the opportunity to personalise their learning from the lesson. They are encouraged to adopt and put into practise the **21st Century Skill** focus of the lesson by thinking about how it is relevant in their own lives.

The pupils are directed to the Activity Book to do a **web quest** and the **Unit Review**.

The **21st Century Skill** is highlighted at the bottom of the page.

Think about your culture encourages the pupils to identify similarities and differences between the two cultures and to begin to form their own cultural identity.

Understanding of the **cultural content** is consolidated through a listening activity.

An additional task is provided for **independent Internet research**.

The pupils do a simple class **web quest**.

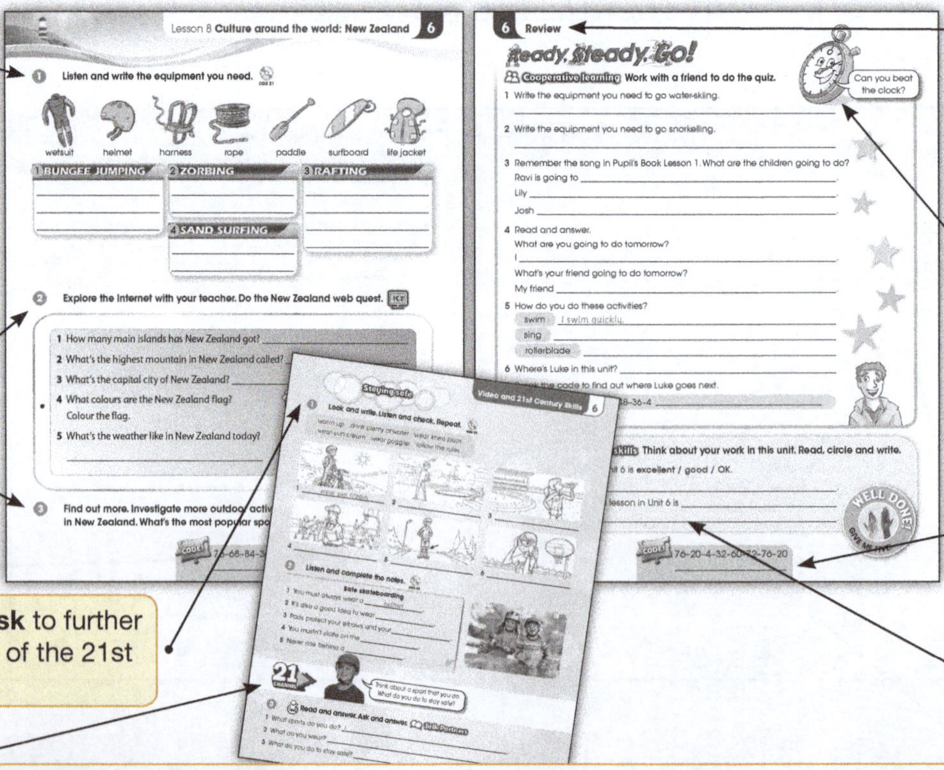

A full-page **Review** checks and reinforces all of the unit vocabulary and grammar.

The pupils **work cooperatively** to check their learning, complete the review and beat the clock.

The pupils do a **code-breaking activity** to find out where Luke travels to in the next unit.

The pupils **reflect on and assess their learning** in the unit.

The pupils do a **listening task** to further develop their understanding of the 21st Century Skill.

The pupils do a **21st Century Skills** task.

Digital resources

Teacher's Digital: Don't forget you can teach these lessons using the Teacher's App on Navio.

Pupil's Digital: Encourage your pupils to use the Pupil's App on Navio to practise the vocabulary from these lessons.

Powered By NAVIO

Using the projects

Give Me Five! 3 provides three fun and highly doable **projects**: The zoo challenge (Term 1), Treasure islands (Term 2) and A London adventure (Term 3). These provide an opportunity for the pupils to **work cooperatively** in a structured way, building autonomy and promoting creativity.

The pupils have the opportunity to **share existing knowledge** about the topic.

Vocabulary is presented in an attractive context. Each project **recycles language** that the pupils have seen, while providing **new input**.

Tasks create **positive interdependence**. Each member's contribution is essential in order to complete the group's task.

The **digital tip** helps pupils practise and expand on a variety of digital skills.

The listening activity gives the pupils the opportunity to check their word lists and to practise saying them correctly.

The pupils go to the Activity Book to record their findings in the individual **investigation task**.

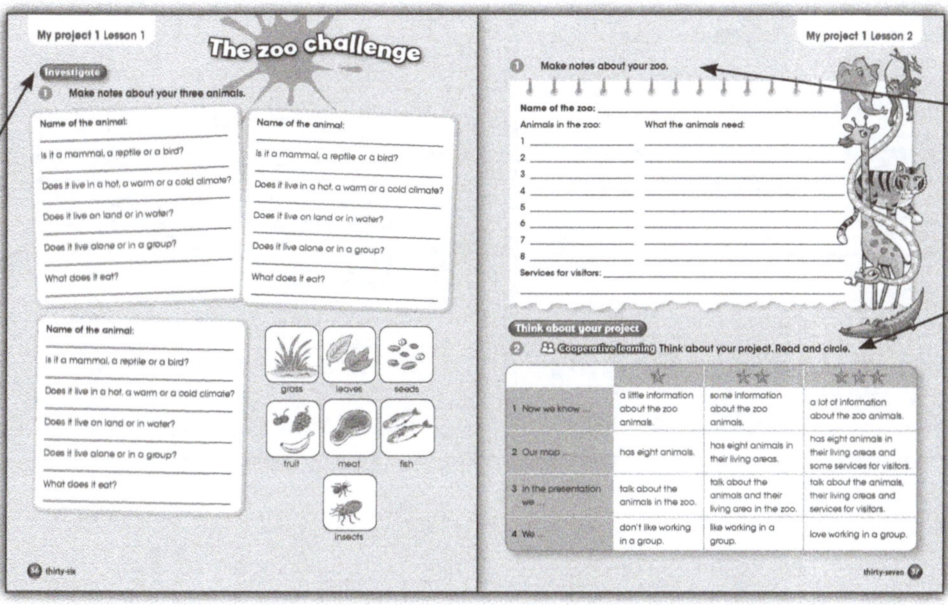

The pupils record their decisions for the group task.

The pupils **reflect on their cooperative skills and how they have worked as a group**.

Digital resources

Teacher's Digital: Don't forget you can teach these lessons using the Teacher's App on Navio.

Pupil's Digital: Encourage your pupils to use the Pupil's App on Navio to practise the vocabulary from these lessons.

Powered By NAVIO

Using the Exams Practice

The **Cambridge Exams Practice** section at the end of both the Pupil's Book and Activity Book introduces the pupils to the activity types found in the different parts of the three papers of the Cambridge English Young Leaners Movers Tests: Listening, Reading and Writing and Speaking.

The twelve Cambridge Exams Practice pages at the back of the Pupil's Book will help the pupils to **develop the necessary skills** to do the Reading and Writing and Speaking papers.

Listening activities provide a realistic model for the pupils to follow before doing Speaking tasks.

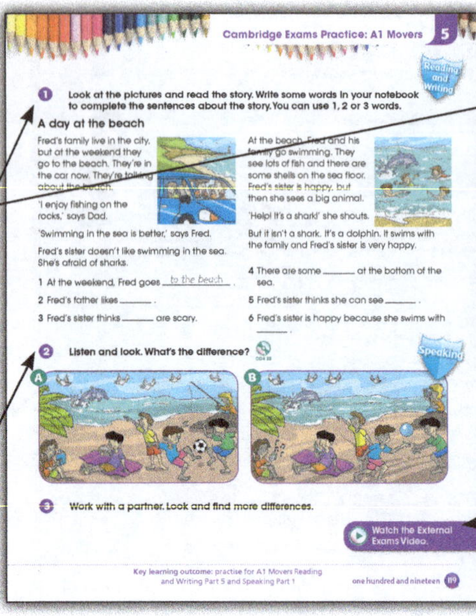
Cambridge Exams Practice: A1 Movers 5

Reading and Writing

1 Look at the pictures and read the story. Write some words in your notebook to complete the sentences about the story. You can use 1, 2 or 3 words.

A day at the beach

Fred's family live in the city, but at the weekend they go to the beach. They're in the car now. They're talking about the beach.

'I enjoy fishing on the rocks,' says Dad.

'Swimming in the sea is better,' says Fred.

Fred's sister doesn't like swimming in the sea. She's afraid of sharks.

At the beach, Fred and his family go swimming. They see lots of fish and there are some shells on the sea floor. Fred's sister is happy, but then she sees a big animal.

'Help! It's a shark!' she shouts.

But it isn't a shark. It's a dolphin. It swims with the family and Fred's sister is very happy.

1 At the weekend, Fred goes to the beach .
2 Fred's father likes ______ .
3 Fred's sister thinks ______ are scary.
4 There are some ______ at the bottom of the sea.
5 Fred's sister thinks she can see ______ .
6 Fred's sister is happy because she swims with ______ .

Speaking

2 Listen and look. What's the difference?

A B

3 Work with a partner. Look and find more differences.

Watch the External Exams Video.

Key learning outcome: practise for A1 Movers Reading and Writing Part 5 and Speaking Part 1

one hundred and nineteen 119

Cambridge Exams Practice: A1 Movers 6

Reading and Writing

1 Read the text and choose the best answer.

1 Vicky: Do you want to go to the sports centre tomorrow, Jack?
Jack: A Yes, I do
B Yes, I can.
C Yes, I am.

2 Vicky: Great! Which sport do you want to do?
Jack: A Yes, that's right.
B What about skateboarding?
C I play basketball.

3 Vicky: Good idea! I love skateboarding.
Jack: A Do we?
B It's fine.
C Me too.

4 Vicky: How often do you go skateboarding?
Jack: A About once a week.
B I skateboard well.
C I skateboard fast.

5 Vicky: What about asking Alice to come too?
Jack: A That's a good idea.
B I'm very well, thank you.
C It's nice.

6 Vicky: I can phone her this afternoon.
Jack: A OK. I'm fine.
B Sorry.
C OK. Thank you.

Watch the External Exams Video.

120 one hundred and twenty

Key learning outcome: practise for A1 Movers Reading and Writing Part 2

For further practice, watch the **External Exams Video** which you can find in the Teacher's Resource Bank.

The nine Cambridge Exams Practice pages at the back of the Activity Book will help the pupils to **develop the necessary skills** to do the Listening and Reading and Writing papers.

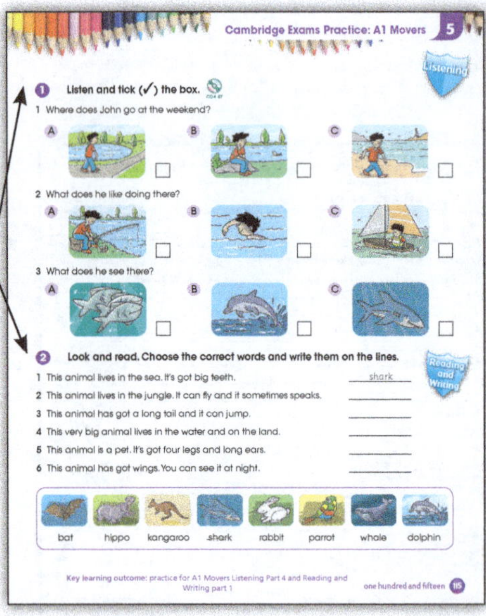
Cambridge Exams Practice: A1 Movers 5

Listening

1 Listen and tick (✓) the box.

1 Where does John go at the weekend?
A B C
2 What does he like doing there?
A B C
3 What does he see there?
A B C

Reading and Writing

2 Look and read. Choose the correct words and write them on the lines.

1 This animal lives in the sea. It's got big teeth. shark
2 This animal lives in the jungle. It can fly and it sometimes speaks. ______
3 This animal has got a long tail and it can jump. ______
4 This very big animal lives in the water and on the land. ______
5 This animal is a pet. It's got four legs and long ears. ______
6 This animal has got wings. You can see it at night. ______

bat hippo kangaroo shark rabbit parrot whale dolphin

Key learning outcome: practice for A1 Movers Listening Part 4 and Reading and Writing part 1

one hundred and fifteen 115

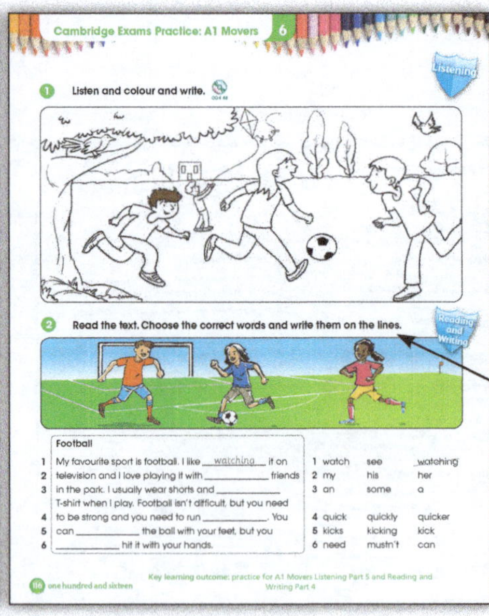
Cambridge Exams Practice: A1 Movers 6

Listening

1 Listen and colour and write.

Reading and Writing

2 Read the text. Choose the correct words and write them on the lines.

Football

1 My favourite sport is football. I like watching it on
2 television and I love playing it with ______ friends
3 in the park. I usually wear shorts and ______ T-shirt when I play. Football isn't difficult, but you need
4 to be strong and you need to run ______ . You
5 can ______ the ball with your feet, but you
6 ______ hit it with your hands.

1	watch	see	watching
2	my	his	her
3	an	some	a
4	quick	quickly	quicker
5	kicks	kicking	kick
6	need	mustn't	can

116 one hundred and sixteen

Key learning outcome: practice for A1 Movers Listening Part 5 and Reading and Writing Part 4

Pupils are encourage to develop their reading and writing skills by practising activities found in the Reading and Writing papers.

Digital resources

Teacher's Digital: Don't forget you can teach this lesson using the Teacher's App on Navio.

Pupil's Digital: Encourage your pupils to use the Pupil's App on Navio to practise the vocabulary from these lessons.

Powered By NAVIO

Exams Practice

Give Me Five! 3 and the external exams

Give Me Five! 3 and *4* provide a wide range of materials to support teachers who are preparing their pupils for the ***Cambridge English Young Learners Movers and Flyers Test***. Reading, writing and listening activity types found in the ***Cambridge English Young Learners Movers and Flyers Tests*** are integrated into the material and each book ends with **Cambridge Exams Practice lessons** in the Pupil's Book and Activity Book. This material is adapted to match the linguistic and cognitive level of the pupils, and language is systematically extended as the course progresses.

There are also **External Exams Resources** which contain videos of children doing the speaking exams, and provide Teacher's Notes on how to exploit these videos in the classroom. These resources, which are part of the **Teacher's Resource Bank**, also include additional External Exams material and practice tests, for both the ***Cambridge English Young Learners Movers and Flyers*** and the ***Trinity Graded Exam in Spoken English*** (Elementary Stage, Grades 4 and 5), material focused on developing specific exam-related skills and a set of Trinity Exam Practice cards.

Trinity Exam Practice cards

The **Trinity Exam Practice cards** are a set of downloadable and photocopiable cards. They can be used to build the pupils' confidence in asking and answering questions. On each card is a question based on the ***Trinity Graded Exam in Spoken English*** syllabus. These recycle questions from the Initial Stage (Grades 2 and 3) and introduce questions from the Elementary Stage (Grades 4 and 5). These cards should be printed out, laminated if possible and filed by unit. They can then be used during the Starting the lesson stage, which systematically recycles language, transferring it to the pupils' long-term memory. For the Trinity Exam Practice cards routine, the teacher selects several cards from previous units. The teacher should choose a different set of cards for each lesson, and tricky questions and recent topics should be revisited more frequently. The teacher then uses the cards to practise asking and answering questions by doing one of the following suggested activities:

Trinity Exam Practice cards activity bank

1 *Ask and answer in Talk Partners*
Point to the Talk Partners Talk card and ask the class to get into pairs. Then hold up one of the selected Trinity Exam Practice cards and ask the class the question. Invite a pupil to answer and repeat their answer for the class. The pupils then ask and answer the same question with their Talk Partner. Repeat the procedure with other cards.

2 *Three-step interview*
Follow the procedure for Activity 1. When the pupils have asked and answered all the questions on the Trinity Exam Practice cards, ask them to get into different pairs. They should then share information about their first partner's responses.

3 *Question bounce*
Select a Trinity Exam Practice card, read out the question and ask the class to think of an answer. Then point around the room, finally choosing one pupil. This pupil should answer the question. If the pupil answers correctly, they should take another card and ask the question to the class. Once again, the class should think of the answer and then the pupil with the card selects another pupil to answer. Repeat the procedure as many times as you wish, ensuring that the questions are 'bounced' to a range of pupils in the class.

4 *Walking questions*
Select six to eight Trinity Exam Practice cards. Drill each question as a class and invite a different pupil to answer each time. Hand out the cards to different pupils. These pupils must move around the class and ask their question to five other pupils. They should then return to their seats. Hand out the cards to six different pupils and repeat the procedure.

5 *Moving questions*
Select eight Trinity Exam Practice cards and stick them on the board, writing a number (one to eight) above each one. Organise the class into small groups of three or four. One pupil from each group should come to the board and read and memorise the first question. They should then return to the group and ask the question. Once everyone in the group has answered, a second pupil should repeat the procedure, reading and memorising the second question. Continue until all eight questions have been asked and answered.

6 *Mix Pair Share*
The pupils should move silently around the room. When you call out the word **pair**, they should form a pair with the person closest to them. Students who haven't found a partner should raise their hands to find each other. Read out a question on one of the Trinity Exam Practice cards. The pupils then tell each other their answers. Encourage the pupils to keep talking as long as possible. When all the pupils have finished, repeat the procedure with other cards.

7 *Snakes and ladders*
Draw a simple snakes and ladders board on the board and draw a question mark in eight to ten of the squares. Divide the class into two teams and ask each team to throw the dice. The team with the highest number should begin. The teams take turns to throw the dice and move along the board. When a team lands on a question mark, read out one of the Trinity Exam Practice cards. The team has to answer correctly to stay on the square. If they don't answer correctly, they move back to their last square. The game continues until a team reaches the 'finish' square.

8 *Class question box*
Make extra copies of the Trinity Exam Practice cards that you have practised in class. Laminate these, if possible, and store them in a class question box. Fast finishers can use these cards to review and practise language, working individually to write the answers in their notebooks or asking and answering the questions with a Talk Partner.

Using the Teacher's Book

The Teacher's Notes have a clear, user-friendly design, offering both an **At a Glance Lesson Plan** and a **Detailed Lesson Plan**. These mirror each other, enabling teachers to move between the two lesson plans with ease.

This box clearly shows the learning outcomes, key active language and materials required for the lesson. The lesson objectives are mapped to the **Key Competences and Key Learning Outcomes**.

The **At a Glance Lesson Plan** provides a brief overview of all the activities in the lesson, including **Starting** and **Ending the lesson activities**, and **Extra activities**. Class audio references are also provided.

Fast Forward icons indicate the **fast route** through the lesson for teachers who have shorter lessons or fewer hours of English.

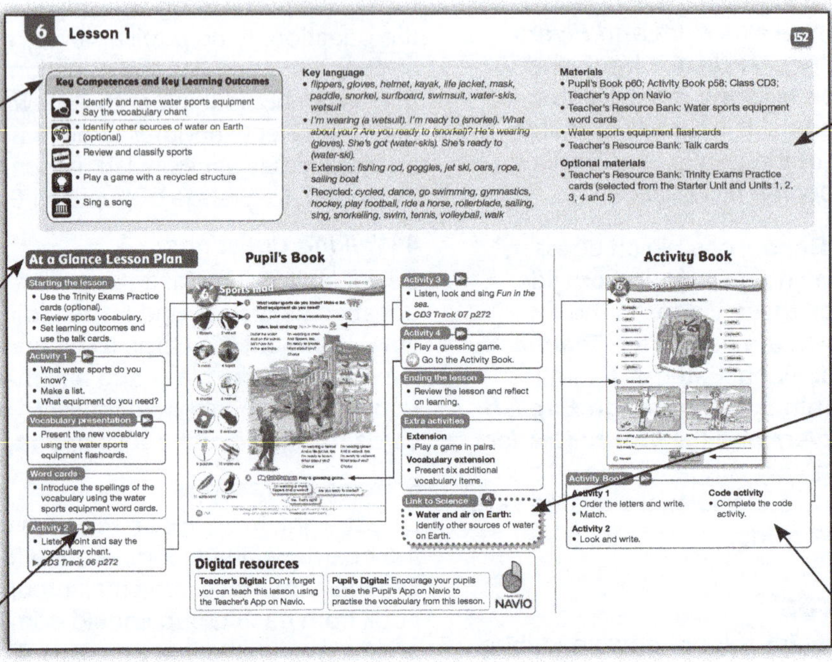

The required and optional materials for each lesson are included in the panel.

Optional **Link to Science** activities in each unit review and reinforce learning from the Science curriculum.

There is also a brief overview of the Activity Book activities.

The **Detailed Lesson Plan** provides more detailed **step-by-step instructions** for each activity.

The activities for **Starting the lesson** include optional use of the **Trinity Exams Practice cards** and the **Talk cards** to give the pupils a clear idea of what they are going to do in the lesson.

A clear layout and clear stages make the plan very easy to follow.

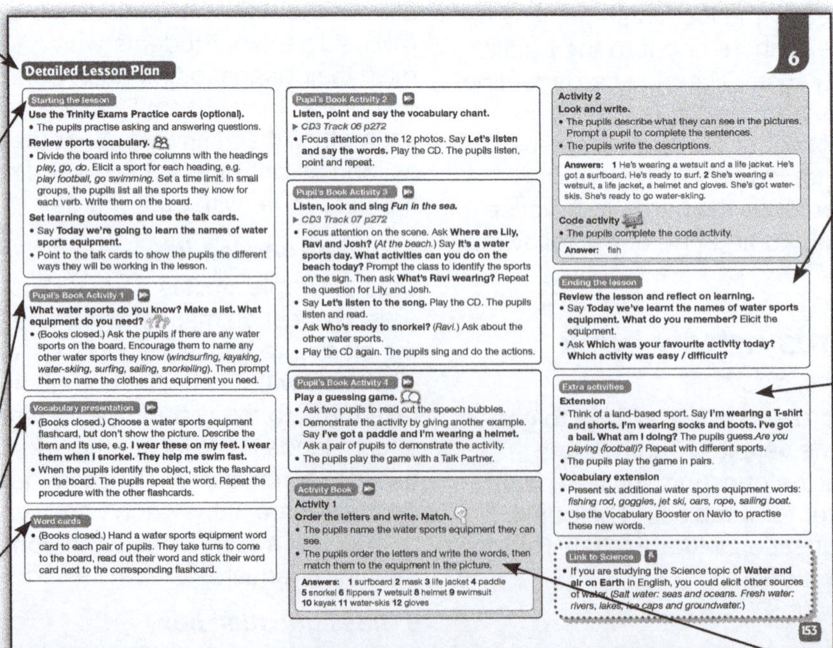

The activities for **Ending the lesson** include reviewing the lesson and reflecting on learning.

Each lesson includes optional **Extra activities** to reinforce and extend learning.

Activity Book teaching notes always appear in a shaded box so they can be easily identified. The answers are also provided.

Unit overview

Key Competences and Key Learning Outcomes

- Listen, repeat and mime activities (Lesson 2)
- Talk about activities you like, love and don't like doing (Lesson 2)
- Complete a story summary (Lesson 3)
- Learn and practise the numbers 50–100 (Lesson 4)
- Listen, follow the grammar table and identify parts of a question (Lesson 4)

- Review the numbers 1–50 (Lesson 4)

- Use the Pupil's App on Navio

- Review vocabulary from previous levels (Lesson 1)
- Listen for specific information (Lesson 2)
- Review and practise saying the alphabet (Lesson 4)
- Ask how to spell things and give the correct spelling (Lesson 4)

- Get to know the course characters (Lesson 1)
- Ask for and give personal information (Lesson 1)

- Work with a Talk Partner to practise and reinforce learning (all lessons)

- Sing a song (Lesson 1)
- Understand and act out a story (Lesson 3)
- Say a rap (Lesson 4)

Vocabulary

Core vocabulary
cycling, dancing, flat, grandparents, lighthouse, making models, playing tennis, reading, singing, welcome; numbers 50–100

Other vocabulary
adventure, blog, bottom, boxes, code, double, explore, help, message, password, scientist, secret, steps, top, travel

Recycled vocabulary
the alphabet; family members; numbers 1–50; sports: *cycling, sailing, skateboarding, swimming, volleyball;* transport: *(sailing) boat, bus, car, helicopter, motorbike;* animals: *bird / seagull, butterfly, dolphin, fish, rabbit;* places in a town: *baker's, chemist's, park, post office, restaurant / café, supermarket, swimming pool; friend, letter, number, school*

Structures

Core structures
Who do you live with? I live with my (grandparents). I like (swimming). I love (making models). I don't like (skateboarding). Do you like (singing)? Yes, I do. No, I don't.

Other structures
Can we help you? Who's this? He's our (brother). He's a (scientist).

Recycled structures
What's your name? My name's (Josh). How old are you? I'm (nine). I'm (nine) years old. Where do you live? I live in (the town). How do you spell (letter)?

Thinking skills

Categorising (Lesson 1); Sequencing (Lesson 4); Grouping (Lesson 4); Logical thinking (Lesson 4)

Cooperative learning

Checking learning (Lesson 1); Sharing information (Lessons 2 and 4); Recording answers for a survey (Lesson 2); Collaborating (Lesson 3)

Key Competences and Key Learning Outcomes

- Review vocabulary from previous levels
- Get to know the course characters
- Ask for and give personal information
- Sing a song

Key language

- *Josh, Lily, Ravi; bottom, explore, flat, grandparents, lighthouse, top, welcome*
- *Who do you live with? I live with my (grandparents).*
- Recycled: the alphabet; family members; numbers (1–50), free-time activities: *cycling, reading, sailing, skateboarding, swimming, volleyball;* transport: *(sailing) boat, bus, car, helicopter, motorbike;* animals: *bird / seagull, butterfly, dolphin, fish, rabbit;* places in a town: *baker's, chemist's, park, post office, restaurant / café, school, supermarket, swimming pool*
- Recycled: *What's your name? My name's (Josh). I'm (nine). How old are you? I'm (nine) years old. Where do you live? I live in (the town).*

Materials

- Pupil's Book pp4–5; Activity Book p2; Class CD1; Teacher's App on Navio; *Josh*, *Lily*, *Ravi* and *lighthouse* flashcards
- Teacher's Resource Bank: *Josh, Lily, Ravi* and *lighthouse* word cards
- Teacher's Resource Bank: Talk cards

At a Glance Lesson Plan

Pupil's Book

Starting the lesson
- Greet the class.
- Set learning outcomes and use the talk cards.

Activity 1
- Find and say.

Activity 2
- Listen and read.
- ▶ *CD1 Track 01 p260*
- Act out.

Activity 3
- Ask and answer.

Activity 4
- Listen and sing *Welcome to the lighthouse!*
- ▶ *CD1 Track 02 p260*
- Go to the Activity Book.

Ending the lesson
- Review the lesson and reflect on learning.

Extra activities

Reinforcement
- Check each other's learning.
- Play *I spy*.

Extension
- Make a class birthday calendar.

Activity Book

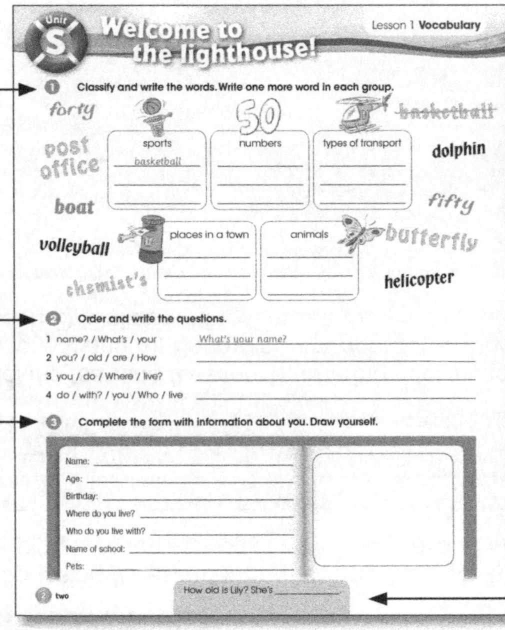

Activity Book

Activity 1
- Classify and write the words.
- Write one more word in each group.

Activity 2
- Order and write the questions.

Activity 3
- Complete the form with information about you.
- Draw yourself.

Footer
- Complete the activity.

Digital resources

Teacher's Digital: You can also teach this lesson using the Teacher's App on Navio.

Pupil's Digital: Encourage your pupils to use the Pupil's App on Navio to practise the activities from this lesson.

Powered By NAVIO

Starting the lesson

Greet the class.

- Introduce yourself and ask the pupils to tell you their names.

Set learning outcomes and use the talk cards.

- Say **Today we're going to remember words we know in English. We're also going to practise asking for personal information and sing a song.**
- Point to the talk cards to show the pupils the different ways they will be working in the lesson.

Pupil's Book Activity 1

Find and say.

- Ask **What can you see in the scene?** Prompt the class to tell you that the family is moving into the lighthouse.
- Organise the class into Talk Partners. The pupils work in pairs to find and name the different things from the five categories listed.
- Check the answers and identify more items.

Answers: **numbers:** 8, 9 in speech bubbles, 10 on car, 20 on van, 30 on road sign, 40 on boat, 50 on sail; **free-time activities:** cycling, reading, sailing, skateboarding, swimming, volleyball; **animals:** butterfly, dolphin, fish, rabbit, seagull; **transport:** boat, bus, car, helicopter, motorbike, sailing boat, van; **places in a town:** baker's, café, chemist's, library, park, post office, restaurant, school, supermarket, swimming pool

Pupil's Book Activity 2

Listen and read. Act out.

▶ *CD1 Track 01 p260*

- Focus the class on the children in the scene. Prompt the class to describe Josh, Lily and Ravi.
- Play the CD. The pupils listen and read the conversation.
- Point to a character and ask **What's his / her name? How old is he / she? Where does he / she live? Who does he / she live with?** Repeat the procedure with the other two characters.
- Play the CD again, pausing after each sentence for the pupils to repeat.
- The pupils act out the conversation in groups of three.

Pupil's Book Activity 3

Ask and answer.

- Focus the class on the activity. Read out the questions and ask different pupils to answer.
- The pupils practise the questions and answers with a Talk Partner.

Pupil's Book Activity 4

Listen and sing *Welcome to the lighthouse!*

▶ *CD1 Track 02 p260*

- Say **Let's listen to a song about the lighthouse.** Play the CD. The pupils listen and read the song lyrics on page 5.
- Play the CD again. The pupils join in, singing the song and doing the actions.
- Ask the pupils what they think it would be like inside a lighthouse.

Activity Book

Activity 1

Classify and write the words. Write one more word in each group.

- Read out the five categories of words. Then invite different pupils to read out and classify a word.
- The pupils work on their own or in pairs to write the words in the correct category. They then add an extra word to each box.
- Check the activity and write the pupils' extra words on the board.

Answers: sports: basketball, volleyball numbers: forty, fifty types of transport: helicopter, boat places in a town: chemist's, post office animals: dolphin, butterfly

Activity 2

Order and write the questions.

- Ask a pupil to point to the jumbled words and show how to order them to make the first question.
- The pupils work on their own or in pairs to order and write the questions.

Answers: **1** What's your name? **2** How old are you? **3** Where do you live? **4** Who do you live with?

Activity 3

Complete the form with information about you. Draw yourself.

- The pupils work on their own to complete the form.
- The pupils draw themselves in the box.
- Ask questions, e.g. **Have you got any pets? When's your birthday?**

Footer

- The pupils complete the activity.

Answer: eight

Ending the lesson

Review the lesson and reflect on learning.

- Say **Today we've remembered words in English. We also met the children in the book. What are their names?**
- Ask **Which was your favourite activity today? Which activity was easy / difficult?**

Extra activities

Reinforcement

- (Books open.) The pupils check each other's learning. Pupil A asks *What are the five (numbers) in the picture?* Pupil B answers. (Pupil A can help Pupil B, if necessary.)
- The pupils swap roles, taking turns to identify all the words in each category.
- Choose an object that appears in the scene. Say **I spy with my little eye something beginning with the letter (b).** The pupil who guesses correctly chooses the next word and says the rhyme. If necessary, write the rhyme on the board as support.
- The pupils play the game in pairs.

Extension

- Make a birthday calendar with the pupils in order to review the phrase *When's your birthday?* and to practise using ordinal numbers.

Key Competences and Key Learning Outcomes

- Listen, repeat and mime activities
- Talk about activities you like, love and don't like doing
- Listen for specific information

Key language

- *cycling, dancing, making models, playing tennis, reading, singing, skateboarding, swimming*
- *I like (swimming). I love (dancing). I don't like (skateboarding). Do you like (dancing)? Yes, I do. No, I don't.*

Materials

- Pupil's Book pp4–5; Activity Book p3; Class CD1; Teacher's App on Navio
- Teacher's Resource Bank: Talk cards

At a Glance Lesson Plan

Pupil's Book

Starting the lesson

- Review vocabulary from Lesson 1.
- Review the *Welcome to the lighthouse!* song.
- ▶ ***CD1 Track 02 p260***
- ▶ ***CD1 Track 03 p260***
- Set learning outcomes and use the talk cards.

Activity 1

- Listen and complete.
- ▶ ***CD1 Track 04 p260***

Activity 2

- Listen and repeat.
- ▶ ***CD1 Track 05 p260***
- Mime.

Activity 3

- Ask and answer.

Ending the lesson

- Review the lesson and reflect on learning.

Extra activity

Reinforcement

- Do a group survey to find the most popular activity.

Activity Book

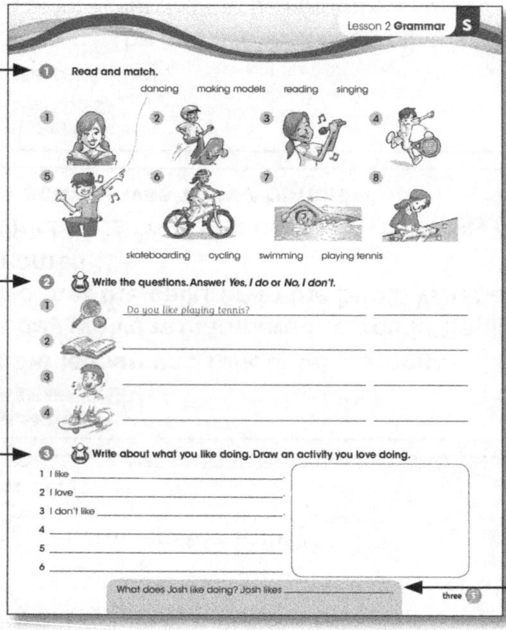

Activity Book

Activity 1

- Read and match.

Activity 2

- Write the questions.
- Answer *Yes, I do* or *No, I don't.*

Activity 3

- Write about what you like doing.
- Draw an activity you love doing.

Footer

- Complete the activity.

Digital resources

Teacher's Digital: You can also teach this lesson using the Teacher's App on Navio.

Pupil's Digital: Encourage your pupils to use the Pupil's App on Navio to practise the activities from this lesson.

Powered By NAVIO

Starting the lesson

Review vocabulary from Lesson 1.

- (Books closed.) Ask **Can you remember ten objects from the last lesson?** The pupils think on their own for a minute. Organise the class into pairs to share their information. Then ask the whole class to list the objects they remember. (Books open.) The pupils look at the scene on pages 4 and 5.

Review the *Welcome to the lighthouse!* song.

▶ *CD1 Track 02 p260*

▶ *CD1 Track 03 p260 (optional karaoke version)*

- Play the CD (or use the karaoke version). The pupils sing and do the actions.

Set learning outcomes and use the talk cards.

- Say **Today we're going to talk about things we like, love and don't like doing.**
- Point to the talk cards to show the pupils the different ways they will be working in the lesson.

Pupil's Book Activity 1

Listen and complete.

▶ *CD1 Track 04 p260*

- Read out the three sentence stems. Say **Let's listen to Josh, Lily and Ravi.** Play the CD, pausing for the pupils to report the correct information.
- Write the complete sentences on the board and highlight that we use the '–ing' form of the verb (gerund) after the verbs 'like', 'love' and 'don't like'.

Answers: Josh likes swimming. Lily loves singing. Ravi doesn't like singing.

Pupil's Book Activity 2

Listen and repeat. Mime.

▶ *CD1 Track 05 p260*

- Read out the activities and check understanding by asking the class to do the mime for each one.
- Play the CD. The pupils repeat the activities and do the corresponding actions.
- Explain that some verbs double their last letter when we use the '–ing' form. The pupils find an example.
- Explain that some verbs lose a letter when we use the '–ing' form. The pupils find an example.

Pupil's Book Activity 3

Ask and answer.

- Ask two pupils to read out the exchange.
- Practise the activity as a class. Ask different pupils the questions and prompt them to answer.
- The pupils practise the questions and answers with a Talk Partner.

Activity Book

Activity 1

Read and match.

- Read out the activities as a class.
- The pupils work on their own to draw the matching lines.

Answers: **1** reading **2** skateboarding **3** singing **4** playing tennis **5** dancing **6** cycling **7** swimming **8** making models

Activity 2

Write the questions. Answer *Yes, I do* or *No, I don't*.

- Read out the example as a class.
- The pupils work on their own to write the questions and their answers.

Answers: **1** Do you like playing tennis? **2** Do you like reading? **3** Do you like singing? **4** Do you like skateboarding?

Activity 3

Write about what you like doing. Draw an activity you love doing.

- Invite different pupils to complete the sentences. Write any new activities the pupils mention on the board.
- The pupils work on their own to write their sentences and draw a picture of an activity they love doing.
- The pupils read out their sentences with a Talk Partner.

Footer

- The pupils complete the activity.

Answer: swimming

Ending the lesson

Review the lesson and reflect on learning.

- Say **Today we've talked about activities you like, love and don't like. What activities do you like / love? What activities don't you like?** Elicit sentences from the pupils.
- Ask **Which was your favourite activity today? Which activity was easy / difficult?**

Extra activity

Reinforcement

- Organise the class into groups of four or five. Then draw a simple chart on the board (see below) and ask one person in each group to copy it into their notebook.
- Explain that the aim is to find out which activity is the most popular. Demonstrate by writing a question in the left-hand column of the chart on the board: **Do you love (swimming)?** The pupils who love this activity should raise their hands. Count the raised hands and write the number in the right-hand column of the chart; for example 卌 卌 卌 III (18).
- The groups work on their own to choose and write five similar questions in their own charts. Then one person from each group should visit the other groups in turn, ask the questions and record the answers. At the same time, the remaining members of the group answer the other groups' questions. When the pupil asking the questions has visited each group, he / she should return and report the findings.
- When the groups have completed their tables, ask each group in turn which activity is the most popular according to their chart.

Activity	How many pupils?
1 Do you love swimming?	卌 卌 卌 III
2	
3	
4	
5	

Key Competences and Key Learning Outcomes

- Complete a story summary
- Understand and act out a story

Key language

- *adventure, blog, boxes, code, help, message, number, password, scientist, secret, steps, travel*
- *Can we (help you)? Who's (this)? He's our (brother). He's a (scientist).*
- Recycled: numbers, the alphabet

Materials

- Pupil's Book p6; Activity Book p4; Class CD1; Teacher's App on Navio
- Teacher's Resource Bank: Talk cards

At a Glance Lesson Plan

Pupil's Book

Starting the lesson

- Review activities that children love, like and don't like doing.
- Review the *Welcome to the lighthouse!* song.
- ▶ *CD1 Track 02 p260*
- ▶ *CD1 Track 03 p260*
- Set learning outcomes and use the talk cards.

Before you read

- Read the title and predict the content of the story.

Activity 1

- Listen and read.
- ▶ *CD1 Track 06 p260*
- Act out.
- Go to the Activity Book.

Ending the lesson

- Review the lesson and reflect on learning.

Extra activity

Reinforcement

- Retell the story as a class.

Activity Book

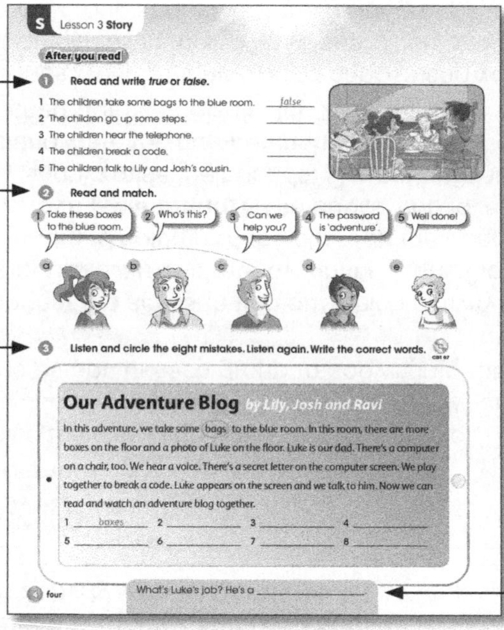

After you read: Activity Book

Activity 1

- Read and write *true* or *false*.

Activity 2

- Read and match.

Activity 3

- Listen and circle the eight mistakes.
- ▶ *CD1 Track 07 p260*
- Listen again.
- Write the correct words.

Footer

- Complete the activity.

Digital resources

Teacher's Digital: You can also teach this lesson using the Teacher's App on Navio.

Pupil's Digital: Encourage your pupils to use the Pupil's App on Navio to practise the activities from this lesson.

Powered By NAVIO

Starting the lesson

Review activities that children love, like and don't like doing.

- Play *Who is it?* Ask five pupils to give you their Activity Books. Look at one of the books, without the pupils seeing who it belongs to, and read out the information from Activity 3, page 3. The class listens and guesses who the pupil is. Repeat the procedure with the other Activity Books.

Review the *Welcome to the lighthouse!* song.

▶ ***CD1 Track 02 p260***

▶ ***CD1 Track 03 p260 (optional karaoke version)***

- Play the CD (or use the karaoke version). The pupils sing and do the actions.

Set learning outcomes and use the talk cards.

- Say **Today we're going to read and listen to a story in English.**
- Point to the talk cards to show the pupils the different ways they will be working in the lesson.

Before you read

- (Books closed.) Read the title of the story. Explain that in the story Ravi, Josh and Lily find a secret message. Ask **Where do they find the message?** Encourage the class to make predictions. Then ask **Who's the message from?**

Pupil's Book Activity 1

Listen and read. Act out.

▶ ***CD1 Track 06 p260***

- Say **Now listen to the story and find out.**
- Play the CD. The pupils follow in their books.
- Confirm that the message is on the computer and it's from Lily and Josh's brother, Luke.
- Ask questions to check understanding.

Suggested comprehension questions

- Frame 1: **Where do the children take the boxes?** (*To the blue room.*)
- Frame 2: **What's on the noticeboard in the blue room?** (*A photo of Lily and Josh's brother, Luke.*)
- Frame 3: **What's on the computer?** (*A message.*) **Who's the message from?** (*Luke.*)
- Frame 4: **Who breaks the alphabet code?** (*Lily, Ravi and Josh.*) **What's the password?** (*A-D-V-E-N-T-U-R-E.*)
- Frame 5: **Who do the children see?** (*Luke.*) **What can the children do with the code?** (*Read Luke's secret messages and his travel blog.*)

- Organise the class into five groups (Lily, Dad, Ravi, Josh and Luke) and play the CD again. Each group joins in when their character speaks. If the pupils need extra support, pause the CD after each utterance and ask them to repeat it instead.
- Repeat, with groups swapping roles.

After you read: Activity Book

Activity 1

Read and write *true* or *false*.

- Ask different pupils to read out the sentences. The pupils answer and write *true* or *false* each time.

Answers: **1** false **2** true **3** false **4** true **5** false

Activity 2

Read and match.

- The pupils work on their own or in pairs to match a speech bubble with a character. They can check their answers in the Pupil's Book.

Answers: **1** c **2** d **3** a **4** e **5** b

Activity 3

Listen and circle the eight mistakes. Listen again. Write the correct words.

▶ ***CD1 Track 07 p260***

- Explain that the children have a blog where they write about their adventures for Luke to read.
- Play the CD. The pupils listen and circle the eight mistakes.
- Play the CD again. The pupils listen and write the correct words.

Answers: **1** ~~bags~~ boxes **2** ~~floor~~ wall **3** ~~dad~~ brother **4** ~~chair~~ table **5** ~~voice~~ noise **6** ~~letter~~ message **7** ~~play~~ work **8** ~~watch~~ write

Footer

- The pupils complete the activity.

Answer: scientist

Ending the lesson

Review the lesson and reflect on learning.

- Say **Today we've listened to a story about a secret message.** Ask **Did you like the story?**
- Ask **Which was your favourite activity today? Which activity was easy / difficult?**

Extra activity

Reinforcement

- Retell the story as a class. Say **Let's tell the story together.** Prompt the class by saying **The children help Dad. They take some …** (*boxes*) **to the …** (*blue room*). **They go …** (*up the steps*). Use mime, gesture and drawings to support the class.

Key Competences and Key Learning Outcomes

- Learn and practise the numbers 50–100
- Listen, follow the grammar table and identify parts of a question
- Review the numbers 1–50
- Review and practise saying the alphabet
- Ask how to spell things and give the correct spelling
- Listen and say a rap about a secret code

Key language

- numbers 50–100; *double (m)*
- Recycled: the alphabet; numbers 1–50; *code, friend, letter, message, number, password, school, secret; How do you spell (letter)?*

Materials

- Pupil's Book p7; Activity Book p5; Class CD1; Teacher's App on Navio
- Teacher's Resource Bank: Talk cards

At a Glance Lesson Plan

Pupil's Book

Starting the lesson

- Review the numbers 1–50.
- Set learning outcomes and use the talk cards.

Activity 1

- Listen and say *The secret code rap.*

▶ ***CD1 Track 08 p260***

Activity 2

- Ask and answer.

Activity 3

- Listen and follow.

▶ ***CD1 Track 09 p260***

- Ask and answer.
- Go to the Activity Book.

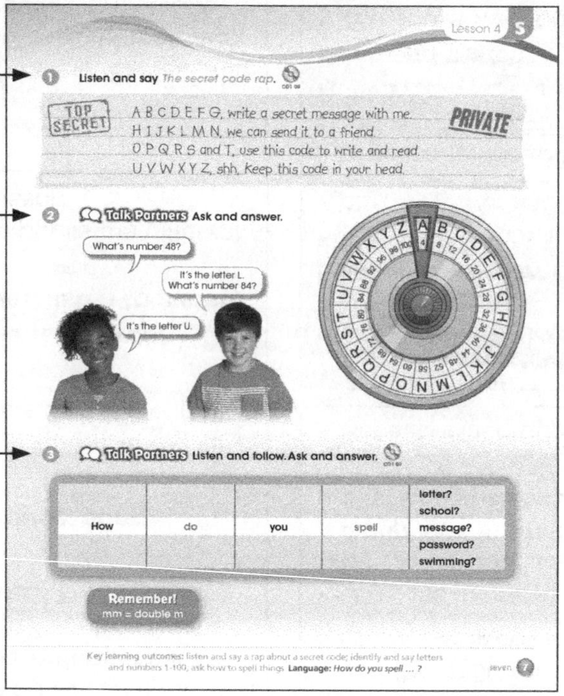

Ending the lesson

- Review the lesson and reflect on learning.

Extra activity

Reinforcement

- Use the code to write a secret message to a friend.
- Invent names and ask and answer how to spell them.

Activity Book

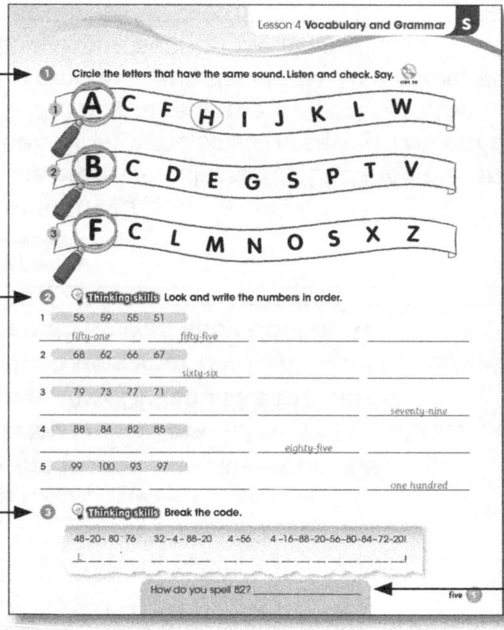

Activity Book

Activity 1

- Circle the letters that have the same sound.
- Listen and check.

▶ ***CD1 Track 10 p260***

- Say.

Activity 2

- Look and write the numbers in order.

Activity 3

- Break the code.

Footer

- Complete the activity.

Digital resources

Teacher's Digital: You can also teach this lesson using the Teacher's App on Navio.

Pupil's Digital: Encourage your pupils to use the Pupil's App on Navio to practise the activities from this lesson.

Powered By NAVIO

Starting the lesson

Review the numbers 1–50.

- Review the numbers 1–50 by counting around the class. Repeat, increasing the speed.
- Explain to the pupils that you are thinking of a number (e.g. 36) and they have ten attempts to guess it. Ask a pupil to make the first guess. Then say **My number is higher / lower than (twenty).** The pupils continue guessing, choosing their number based on the previous guesses.

Set learning outcomes and use the talk cards.

- Say **Today we're going to learn to read a secret code, learn more numbers and practise saying the alphabet.**
- Point to the talk cards to show the pupils the different ways they will be working in the lesson.

Pupil's Book Activity 1

Listen and say *The secret code rap.*

▶ *CD1 Track 08 p260*

- Say **Look at this message. It's top secret.**
- Play the CD. The pupils listen and read.
- Play the CD again. The pupils join in saying the rap.

Pupil's Book Activity 2

Ask and answer.

- Write the number 50 on the board and ask **What number is this? What number is next?** Prompt the pupils to count up to 59 and then teach them the word 'sixty'. Repeat until you reach 100.
- Write random numbers on the board (50–100) and ask the class to say the numbers.
- Ask individual pupils to come to the board and write the numbers you say (50–100).
- Focus the class on the secret code. Invite two pupils to read out the speech bubbles. Then ask **What's number (16)?** The pupils say the corresponding letter. Repeat several times.
- The pupils do the activity in pairs with a Talk Partner.

Pupil's Book Activity 3

Listen and follow. Ask and answer.

▶ *CD1 Track 09 p260*

- Explain that the grammar table shows the parts of a sentence.
- Play the CD. The pupils listen and point to the parts of the sentence. Then ask a pupil to repeat a complete sentence and give the answer by spelling the word. Read the *Remember!* tip to highlight how we use the word 'double' when two of the same letters are next to each other in a word.
- Organise the class into Talk Partners. The pupils ask for and give the spelling of words in the grammar table.

Activity Book

Activity 1

Circle the letters that have the same sound. Listen and check. Say.

▶ *CD1 Track 10 p260*

- Ask the class to name the first letter in row 1 (*A*) and say the vowel sound 'ai'. Read out the next letter (*C*) and ask **Does this have the same sound?**
- Repeat the procedure with the remaining letters. The pupils circle the letters with the same sound.
- Ask the class to say the first letter in rows 2 and 3 (*B and F*). The pupils work in pairs to identify the similar sounds.
- Play the CD. The pupils listen and check their answers.
- Play the CD again. The pupils point to and say the sounds.

Answers: **1** A H J K **2** B C D E G P T V **3** F L M N S X

Activity 2

Look and write the numbers in order.

- Read out the numbers on the first lozenge as a class.
- Ask the class to say the numbers again, but in order. The pupils then write the numbers.
- Repeat with the following set of numbers.
- The pupils complete the activity on their own or in pairs.

Answers: **1** fifty-one, fifty-five, fifty-six, fifty-nine **2** sixty-two, sixty-six, sixty-seven, sixty-eight **3** seventy-one, seventy-three, seventy-seven, seventy-nine **4** eighty-two, eighty-four, eighty-five, eighty-eight **5** ninety-three, ninety-seven, ninety-nine, one hundred

Activity 3

Break the code.

- The pupils use the secret code on Pupil's Book page 7 to discover the secret sentence.

Answer: Let's have an adventure!

Footer

- The pupils complete the activity.

Answer: eighty-two

Ending the lesson

Review the lesson and reflect on learning.

- Say **Today we've practised the alphabet. How many letters are in the English alphabet / your alphabet? We've also learnt some numbers. Can you count from 50 to 100?**
- Ask **Which was your favourite activity today? Which activity was easy / difficult?**

Extra activity

Reinforcement

- The pupils use the code to write a secret message to a friend in English. They swap messages and use the code to read them.
- The pupils invent funny new names for themselves, then write their new names using the code. They swap their coded names for their friend to work out what it is.

Date: ____________________ Unit: __________

1 What did my pupils learn in this unit?

2 How did my pupils work? (✓)

individually ☐ in pairs ☐ in small groups ☐

in large groups ☐ as a class ☐

3 Which key competences did my pupils develop?

- Competence in linguistic communication ☐
- Competence in mathematics, science and technology ☐
- Digital competence ☐
- Learning to learn ☐
- Social and civic competences ☐
- Sense of initiative and entrepreneurship ☐
- Cultural awareness and expression ☐

4 Which lessons / activities were the most successful and why?

5 Which lessons / activities did my pupils find the most difficult and why?

6 What did I try in the classroom for the first time? How did it go?

7 Which resources did I find most useful? (including webpages)

8 What could I do differently next time I teach this unit?

1 Time for school

Unit overview

Key Competences and Key Learning Outcomes

- Identify and say places in a school (Lesson 1)
- Say the vocabulary chant (Lesson 1)
- Listen, read, follow and act out a conversation (Lesson 2)
- Understand and use *Wh-* question words (Lesson 2)
- Follow, complete and correct the grammar tables (Lessons 2 and 4)
- Review and learn school subjects (Lesson 4)
- Use capital letters correctly (Lesson 7)
- Watch and understand a video (Video and 21st Century Skills)

- Use a code to read a message (Lesson 3)

- Use the Pupil's App on Navio
- Investigate Ireland (Lesson 8)

- Review school objects and equipment (Lesson 1)
- Say a tongue twister, learn another spelling for the 'j' sound and practise spelling (Lesson 5)
- Practise activity types found in the Cambridge Exams: A1 Movers
- Review your own learning (Review)

- Understand the importance of helping new pupils at school (Lesson 3)
- Ask and answer about new things to try (Video and 21st Century Skills)

- Work with a Talk Partner to practise and reinforce learning (all lessons)
- Play a communication game (Lesson 5)

- Sing two songs (Lessons 1 and 4)
- Understand, act out and give an opinion on a story (Lesson 3)
- Read and write a poster for a school club (Lessons 6 and 7)
- Learn about Ireland (Lesson 8)
- Think about your own culture (Lesson 8)

Vocabulary

Core vocabulary
basketball court, bike stand, canteen, computer room, corridor, football pitch, gym, library, music room, playground, school hall, vegetable garden; Arts and Crafts, Drama, Geography, History, ICT, PE

Extension vocabulary (optional)
changing room, entrance, reception, science lab, staffroom, toilets; Biology, Chemistry, French, Literature

Other vocabulary
balls, club, computer, gloves, helmet, hockey stick, memory stick, pads, rollerblades; amazing, bored, comfortable, cool, exciting, fast

Recycled vocabulary
days of the week; times (o'clock); classroom objects; *English, Maths, Music, draw pictures, eat lunch, read books, study, throw a ball; classroom, computers, fast, football, games, helmet, hit / kick the ball, hockey, skating, skip, sport, swimming pool*

Structures

Core structures
Where do you (play with your friends)? I (play with my friends) (in the playground). When do you (study Maths)? What do you (do in the computer room)? Are you good at (Maths)? Yes, I am. No, I'm not. I'm brilliant / very good / good / not very good at (History). When do we have (Music)? We have (music) on (Monday) at (nine o'clock).

Other structures
The (classes) begin / finish at (five o'clock). We meet on (Tuesday). The classes cost (£2). You need to wear (comfortable clothes). For more information, email (emma@fun.uk).

Recycled structures
This is my school. I go to school. There's a (gym) in our school. There isn't a (music room) in our school. Do you love (hockey)? Do you want to (learn an exciting sport)? My favourite after-school activity is (hockey). I play (a tin whistle).

Phonics

The 'j' sound (***g****iraffes* ***j****umping* ***j****udo* ***g****ym*)

Literacy

Text type: a poster (text to persuade; writing preparation)
Reading skills: asking yourself a question before you read
Writing skills: using capital letters

Culture ... around the world

After-school activities in Ireland

21st Century Skills

Open mindedness and trying new things

Thinking skills

Predicting (Lessons 3 and 8); Discussing values (Lesson 3); Expressing opinions (Lesson 3); Applying rules (Lesson 4); Making inferences (Lesson 6); Thinking about your culture (Lesson 8); Making connections (Review)

Cooperative learning

Listening to each other (Lesson 1); Collaborating (Lessons 2, 4 and 5); Checking learning (Lesson 5); Peer evaluation and feedback (Lessons 5 and 7); Working together (Review)

Values

The importance of helping new pupils at school

Cross-curricular links

Link to Science
Living things: Listing living and non-living things at school
Suggested Arts and Crafts concepts
Observing proportion in art and the human body and creating a self-portrait

Key Competences and Key Learning Outcomes

- Identify and say places in a school
- Say the vocabulary chant
- List living and non-living things at school (optional)
- Review school objects and equipment
- Talk about your school using a recycled structure
- Sing a song about a school

Key language

- Places in a school: *basketball court, bike stand, canteen, computer room, corridor, football pitch, gym, library, music room, playground, school hall, vegetable garden; go online, hang my coat, play the drums, throw a ball*
- *Where do you (hang your coat)? I (hang my coat) in the (corridor).*
- Extension: *changing room, entrance, reception, science lab, staffroom, toilets*
- Recycled: days of the week; *This is (my school). I go (to school). There's a (gym) in our school. There isn't a (music room) in our school.*

Materials

- Pupil's Book p8; Activity Book p6; Class CD1; Teacher's App on Navio
- Places in a school flashcards
- Teacher's Resource Bank: Talk cards
- Teacher's Resource Bank: Places in a school word cards

Optional materials

- Teacher's Resource Bank: Trinity Exams Practice cards (selected from the Starter Unit)

At a Glance Lesson Plan

Pupil's Book

Starting the lesson

- Use the Trinity Exams Practice cards (optional).
- Review classroom objects and equipment.
- Set learning outcomes and use the talk cards.

Activity 1

- Think of places in your school.
- Make a list.

Vocabulary presentation

- Present the new vocabulary using the places in a school flashcards.

Word cards

- Introduce the spellings of the vocabulary using the places in a school word cards.

Activity 2

- Listen, point and say the vocabulary chant.

▶ ***CD1 Track 11 p260***

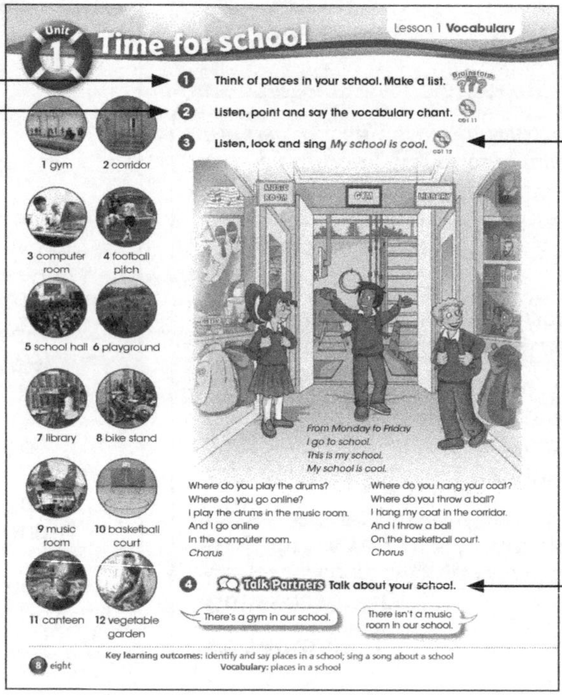

Activity 3

- Listen, look and sing *My school is cool.*

▶ ***CD1 Track 12 p261***

Activity 4

- Talk about your school.
- Go to the Activity Book.

Ending the lesson

- Review the lesson.

Extra activities

Reinforcement

- Make a vocabulary chain.
- Draw and label a plan of the school.

Vocabulary extension

- Present six additional vocabulary items.

Link to Science

- **Living things:** List living and non-living things at school.

Activity Book

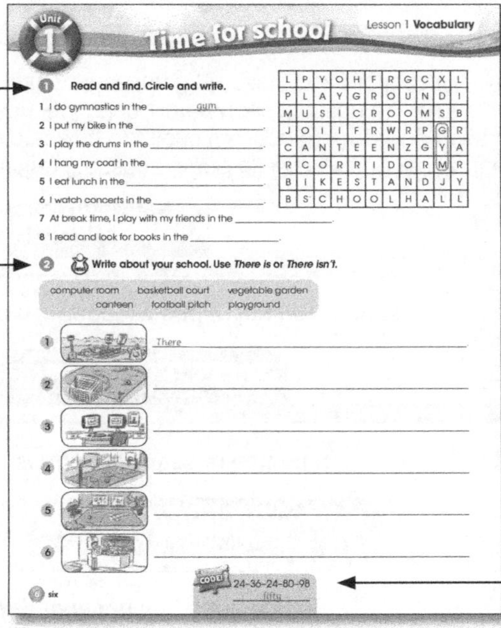

Activity Book

Activity 1

- Read and find.
- Circle and write.

Activity 2

- Write about your school.
- Use *There is* or *There isn't.*

Code activity

- Complete the code activity.

Digital resources

Teacher's Digital: You can also teach this lesson using the Teacher's App on Navio.

Pupil's Digital: Encourage your pupils to use the Pupil's App on Navio to practise the activities from this lesson.

Powered By NAVIO

Starting the lesson

Use the Trinity Exams Practice cards (optional).

- The pupils practise asking and answering questions.

Review classroom objects and equipment.

- Ask **What can you see in the classroom?** Describe the location of one of the objects, e.g. **This object is on the wall next to the board. What is it?** The pupils identify the object. Repeat with different objects.
- The pupils repeat the activity in pairs.

Set learning outcomes and use the talk cards.

- Say **Today we're going to learn the names of places in a school.**
- Point to the talk cards to show the pupils the different ways they will be working in the lesson.

Pupil's Book Activity 1

Think of places in your school. Make a list.

- (Books closed.) Organise the pupils into groups of three or four and ask them to choose a scribe.
- Set a time limit. Each group names places in their school in English. The scribe writes them down.
- At the end of the time, ask the pupils to count their words. The groups then read out their lists.

Vocabulary presentation

- (Books closed.) Hold up the places in a school flashcards in turn and elicit or say the place. Ask **What do you do in the (library)?** (*Read, use the computer, …*).
- Stick the flashcards on the board. The pupils repeat the words.

Word cards

- (Books closed.) Hand a places in a school word card to each pair of pupils.
- The pairs take turns to come to the board, read out their place and stick their word card next to the corresponding flashcard.

Pupil's Book Activity 2

Listen, point and say the vocabulary chant.

▶ ***CD1 Track 11 p260***

- Focus the pupils' attention on the 12 photos. Say **Let's listen and say the chant.** Play the CD. The pupils listen, point and repeat.

Pupil's Book Activity 3

Listen, look and sing *My school is cool*.

▶ ***CD1 Track 12 p261***

- Focus the pupils' attention on the scene. Ask **Where are Lily, Ravi and Josh?** (*At school.*) **What places can you see?** (*corridor, music room, gym, library*) Explain that Ravi is showing Lily and Josh the school because it is their first day.
- Say **Let's listen to the song.** Play the CD. The pupils listen and read. Ask **What places are in the song?**
- Play the CD again. The pupils sing the song and do the actions.

Pupil's Book Activity 4

Talk about your school.

- Ask two pupils to read out the speech bubbles. Remind the pupils that we use 'There is / isn't' when we talk about one object. Elicit more sentences about your school from the class.
- Organise the class into Talk Partners. The pupils point to the photo of each place in a school and say the corresponding sentence about your school.

Activity Book

Activity 1

Read and find. Circle and write.

- Ask different pupils to read out and complete the sentences. The pupils find and circle the places in the wordsearch and write the words in the sentences.

Answers: **1** gym **2** bike stand **3** music room **4** corridor **5** canteen **6** school hall **7** playground **8** library

Activity 2

Write about your school. Use *There is* or *There isn't*.

- Point to the pictures and ask **What's this? Is there a (vegetable garden) in our school?**
- The pupils then write the sentences.

Answers: **1** There is / isn't a vegetable garden in our school. **2** There is / isn't a football pitch. **3** There is / isn't a computer room. **4** There is / isn't a basketball court. **5** There is / isn't a playground. **6** There is / isn't a canteen.

Code activity

- The pupils look at the activity, referring to the code on Pupil's Book page 7.

Answer: fifty

Ending the lesson

Review the lesson and reflect on learning.

- Say **Today we've learnt the names of places in a school.** Elicit the places.
- Ask **Which was your favourite activity today? Which activity was easy / difficult?**

Extra activities

Reinforcement

- In pairs, the pupils take turns to say different places in a school from memory. Can they remember all 12 places between them? Ask confident pairs to say them in front of the class.
- The pupils work together to draw a plan of the school and label the different places.

Vocabulary extension

- Present six additional places in a school: *changing room, entrance, reception, science lab, staffroom, toilets.*
- Use the Vocabulary Booster on Navio to practise these new words.

Link to Science

- If you are studying the Science topic of **Living things** in English, ask the pupils to list different living and non-living things at school. Make two lists on the board.

Key Competences and Key Learning Outcomes

- Listen, read, follow and act out a conversation
- Listen, follow the grammar table and identify the parts of a question
- Understand and use *Wh-* question words

Key language

- *eat lunch, read books, study Maths*
- *Wh-* questions: *Where do you (play with your friends)? When do you (study Maths)? What do you (do in the computer room)? I play with my friends (in the playground).*
- Recycled: days of the week; *basketball court, bike stand, canteen, computer room, corridor, football pitch, gym, library, music room, playground, school hall, vegetable garden*

Materials

- Pupil's Book p9; Activity Book p7; Class CD1; Teacher's App on Navio
- Places in a school flashcards
- Teacher's Resource Bank: Talk cards

Optional materials

- Teacher's Resource Bank: Trinity Exams Practice cards (selected from the Starter Unit)

At a Glance Lesson Plan

Pupil's Book

Starting the lesson

- Use the Trinity Exams Practice cards (optional).
- **Think-Pair-Share.** Review places in a school.
- Review the *My school is cool* song.
- ▶ *CD1 Track 12 p261*
- ▶ *CD1 Track 13 p261*
- Set learning outcomes and use the talk cards.

Activity 1

- Listen and read.
- Listen and repeat.
- ▶ *CD1 Track 14 p261*
- Act out.

Activity 2

- Read again.
- Which places does Ravi talk about?
- What does he do there?

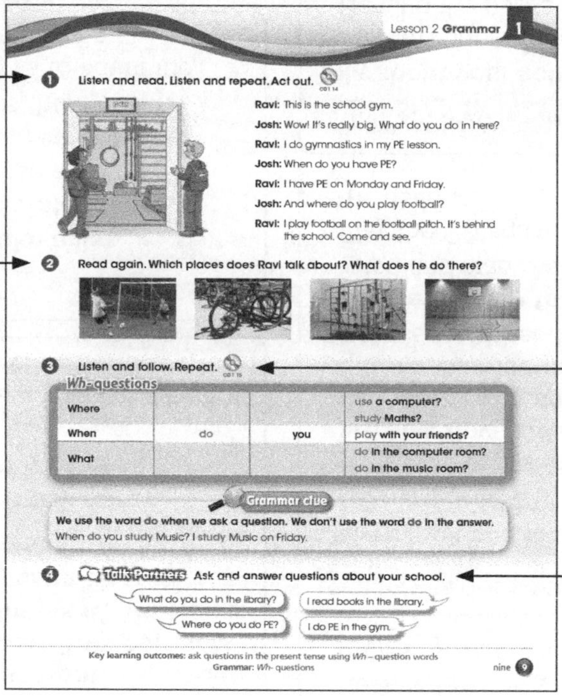

Activity 3

- Listen and follow.
- ▶ *CD1 Track 15 p261*
- Repeat.
- **Grammar clue:** Read about when we use 'do'.

Activity 4

- Ask and answer questions about your school.
- Go to the Activity Book.

Ending the lesson

- Review the lesson and reflect on learning.

Extra activities

Reinforcement

- Use the question words to talk about other daily routines.
- Play *What's missing?*

Activity Book

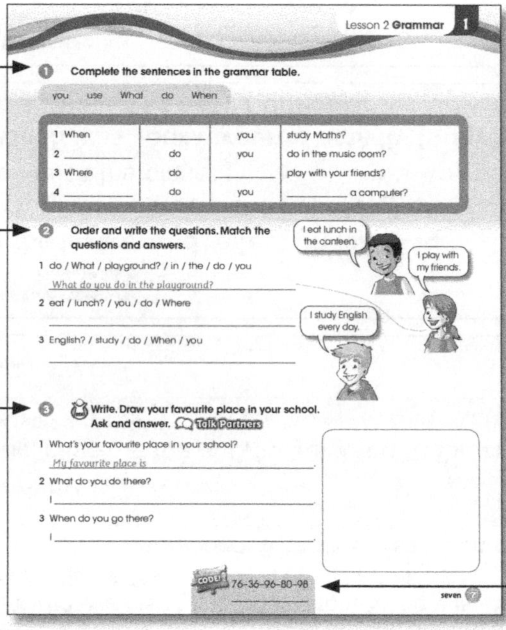

Activity Book

Activity 1

- Complete the sentences in the grammar table.

Activity 2

- Order and write the questions.
- Match the questions and answers.

Activity 3

- Write.
- Draw your favourite place in your school.
- Ask and answer.

Code activity

- Complete the code activity.

Digital resources

Teacher's Digital: You can also teach this lesson using the Teacher's App on Navio.

Pupil's Digital: Encourage your pupils to use the Pupil's App on Navio to practise the activities from this lesson.

Powered By NAVIO

Starting the lesson

Use the Trinity Exams Practice cards (optional).

- The pupils practise asking and answering questions.

Think-Pair-Share. Review places in a school.

- Ask **Can you remember the places in a school?** The class thinks silently for a minute.
- Then the pupils work with a Talk Partner to name the places.
- Invite different Talk Partners to say a different place. Hold up the corresponding flashcard and prompt the class to repeat the word.
- Finally, repeat the procedure, asking different pairs of Talk Partners each time, until all the places in a school have been named.

Review the *My school is cool* song.

▶ *CD1 Track 12 p261*

▶ *CD1 Track 13 p261 (optional karaoke version)*

- Play the CD (or use the karaoke version). The pupils sing and do the actions.

Set learning outcomes and use the talk cards.

- Say **Today we're going to act out a conversation, then ask and answer questions about school.**
- Point to the talk cards to show the pupils the different ways they will be working in the lesson.

Pupil's Book Activity 1

Listen and read. Listen and repeat. Act out.

▶ *CD1 Track 14 p261*

- The pupils look at the picture. Ask **Where are Josh and Ravi?** (*The school gym.*)
- Play the CD. The pupils listen and read the conversation.
- Ask **Do you think Josh likes sport?** (*Yes.*)
- Play the CD again, pausing after each sentence for the pupils to repeat.
- The pupils act out the conversation in pairs.

Pupil's Book Activity 2

Read again. Which places does Ravi talk about? What does he do there?

- The pupils read the conversation again and say what places Ravi talks about and what he does there.

Pupil's Book Activity 3

Listen and follow. Repeat.

▶ *CD1 Track 15 p261*

- Play the CD. The pupils listen to the first question and point to the words they hear.
- The pupils repeat the question and give an answer.
- Repeat the procedure with the other sentences.
- Check that the pupils understand that we use the question word 'Where' when we ask about a place, 'When' when we ask about time and 'What' when we ask about an object or an action.

Grammar clue

- Read the grammar clue as a class. Highlight that the word 'do' (the auxiliary verb) helps the main verb to make a question.

Pupil's Book Activity 4

Ask and answer questions about your school.

- The pupils work in pairs to practise asking and answering questions.

Activity Book

Activity 1

Complete the sentences in the grammar table.

- Invite a pupil to read out the words in the word box.
- The pupils work on their own or with a partner to write the words in the grammar table.

Answers: **1** do **2** What **3** you **4** When, use

Activity 2

Order and write the questions. Match the questions and answers.

- Invite a pupil to order and read out the first question. If necessary, show the class how to refer to the grammar table in Activity 1 to check the order of words. Then ask the pupil to identify the correct speech bubble.
- The pupils work on their own or in pairs to write the sentences and to draw the matching lines to the answers.

Answers: **1** What do you do in the playground? I play with my friends. **2** Where do you eat lunch? I eat lunch in the canteen. **3** When do you study English? I study English every day.

Activity 3

Write. Draw your favourite place in your school. Ask and answer.

- Ask a pupil to read out the first question and invite different responses. Repeat for the remaining questions and write any new vocabulary on the board.
- The pupils work on their own to write their answers and then draw their favourite place in the school.
- Organise the class into small groups. The pupils take turns to show their drawing to their group and talk about their favourite place.

Code activity

- The pupils complete the code activity.

Answer: sixty

Ending the lesson

Review the lesson and reflect on learning.

- Say **Today we've learnt how to ask and answer questions about school.** Invite the class to ask you some of the questions they've learnt.
- Ask **Which was your favourite activity today? Which activity was easy / difficult?**

Extra activities

Reinforcement

- Write the question words 'When', 'Where' and 'What' on the left side of the board. Then brainstorm different daily routines as a class and write these on the right side of the board, e.g. *get up at 7.00am, eat lunch at school, play football after school*.
- Organise the class into small groups and give them five minutes to make as many questions as possible using the information on the board. At the end of that time, the groups ask you their questions.
- Play *What's missing?* (see p27) with the places in a school flashcards.

Key Competences and Key Learning Outcomes

- Read, listen and understand a story about a new school
- Use a code to read a message
- Do a pre-reading task
- Understand the importance of helping new pupils at school
- Understand, enjoy and act out a story
- Give an opinion on the story

Key language

- *Arts and Crafts, basketball, bracelet, break time, brilliant, classroom, Music, swimming lesson, swimming pool*
- *When do we have (PE)? We have (PE) (after the break). I'm not very good at (Music). What's the matter? I can't (play the drums). You can (see the lighthouse). Kick your legs. This is difficult. Where's my (new bracelet)? It's (at the bottom of the pool).*
- Recycled: *playground; boring, exciting, funny, interesting, sad, scary; I love (sport).*

Materials

- Pupil's Book pp10–11; Activity Book p8; Class CD1; Teacher's App on Navio
- Teacher's Resource Bank: Talk cards
- A soft ball

Optional materials

- Teacher's Resource Bank: Trinity Exams Practice cards (selected from the Starter Unit)
- Teacher's Resource Bank: Places in a school word cards

At a Glance Lesson Plan

Pupil's Book

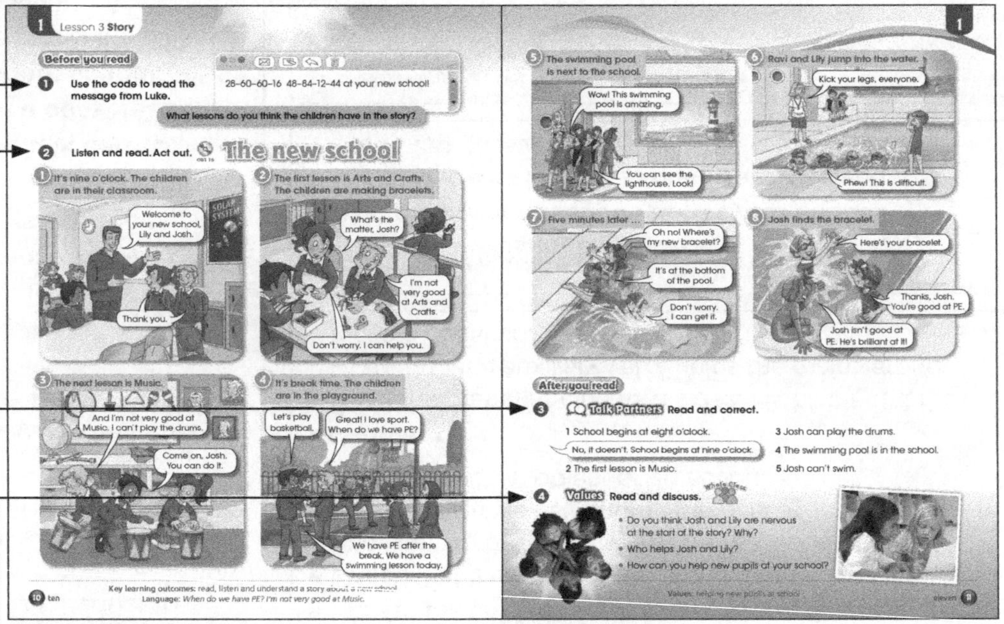

Starting the lesson

- Use the Trinity Exams Practice cards (optional).
- Review places in a school.
- Set learning outcomes and use the talk cards.

Before you read: Activity 1

- Use the code to read the message from Luke.

Activity 2

- Listen and read.
- ▶ *CD1 Track 16 p261*
- Act out.

After you read: Activity 3

- Read and correct.

Activity 4: Values

- Read and discuss.
- Go to the Activity Book.

Ending the lesson

- Review the lesson and reflect on learning.

Extra activity

Reinforcement

- Retell the story as a class.

Activity Book

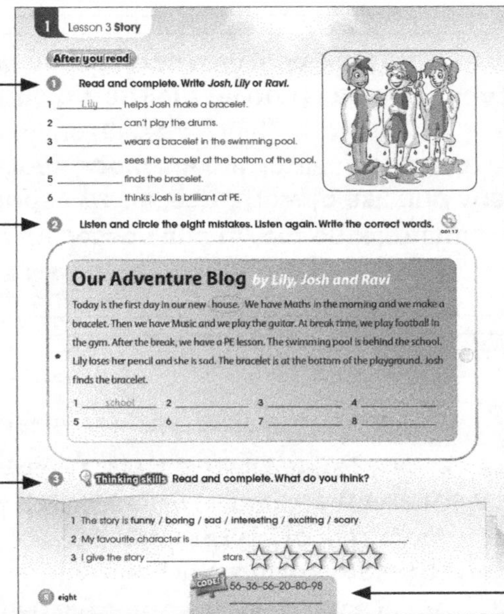

After you read: Activity Book

Activity 1

- Read and complete.
- Write *Josh, Lily* or *Ravi*.

Activity 2

- Listen and circle the eight mistakes.
- ▶ *CD1 Track 17 p261*
- Listen again.
- Write the correct words.

Activity 3

- Read and complete.
- What do you think?

Code activity

- Complete the code activity.

Digital resources

Teacher's Digital: You can also teach this lesson using the Teacher's App on Navio.

Pupil's Digital: Encourage your pupils to use the Pupil's App on Navio to practise the activities from this lesson.

Powered By NAVIO

Starting the lesson

Use the Trinity Exams Practice cards (optional).

- The pupils practise asking and answering questions.

Review places in a school.

- Ask **Where do you (do PE)?** Throw a soft ball to a pupil and prompt him / her to answer. The pupil asks another question about school using the same question form, e.g. **Where do you (hang your coat)?** The pupil then throws the ball to another pupil who should answer. Repeat several times.

Set learning outcomes and use the talk cards.

- Say **Today we're going to listen to and read a story.**
- Point to the talk cards to show the pupils the different ways they will be working in the lesson.

Before you read: Pupil's Book Activity 1

Use the code to read the message from Luke.

- Say **Josh and Lily have received a message from Luke.** Ask the pupils to use the code (Pupil's Book page 7) to discover the mystery words in the message (*good luck*). Prompt the class to think about how Lily and Josh will feel on their first day at their new school.
- Ask **What lessons do you think the children have in the story?** The pupils predict the lessons.

Pupil's Book Activity 2

Listen and read. Act out.

▶ *CD1 Track 16 p261*

- Play the CD. The pupils follow in their books.
- Ask the pupils to look at Frame 1 of the story. Ask **What can you see?** The pupils describe the picture. Highlight the poster of the solar system and ask the pupils to name all the planets that they can.
- Ask additional questions to check understanding.

Suggested comprehension questions

- Frame 1: **When does school begin?** (*At nine o'clock.*)
- Frame 2: **What do the children do in the first lesson?** (*Make bracelets.*) **Is Josh happy?** (*No.*) **Why not?** (*He's not very good at Arts and Crafts.*)
- Frame 3: **What's the next lesson?** (*Music.*) **Why isn't Josh happy?** (*He's not very good at Music.*)
- Frame 4: **What do the children play in the playground?** (*Basketball.*)
- Frame 5: **What do the children do after the break?** (*They have a swimming lesson.*)
- Frame 6: **Is it easy?** (*No, it's difficult.*)
- Frame 7: **What's at the bottom of the pool?** (*Lily's new bracelet.*)
- Frame 8: **Who finds the bracelet for Lily?** (*Josh.*) **Can Josh swim very well?** (*Yes, he can.*)

- Organise the class into five groups (Teacher, Lily, Ravi, Josh, swimming instructor) and play the CD. Each group joins in when their character speaks. If pupils need extra support, pause the CD after each utterance and ask them to repeat it instead.
- Repeat, with groups swapping roles.

After you read: Pupil's Book Activity 3

Read and correct.

- Ask a pupil to read out the first sentence and its correction. Ask the class to identify the story frame which has this information (*Frame 1*).
- The pupils work in pairs to find the information in the story and correct each sentence. They can do this orally or in their notebooks.

Answers: **1** No, it doesn't. School begins at nine o'clock. **2** No, it isn't. The first lesson is Arts and Crafts. **3** No, he can't. Josh can't play the drums. **4** No, it isn't. The swimming pool is next to the school. **5** Yes, he can. Josh can swim very well.

Pupil's Book Activity 4: Values

Read and discuss.

- Read out the questions and discuss them as a class.
- Prompt the class to think of ways they can help new pupils, e.g. play with them in the playground, show them where things are.

After you read: Activity Book

Activity 1

Read and complete. Write *Josh, Lily* or *Ravi*.

- The pupils work on their own to read and complete the sentences.

Answers: **1** Lily **2** Josh **3** Lily **4** Ravi **5** Josh **6** Ravi

Activity 2

Listen and circle the eight mistakes. Listen again. Write the correct words.

▶ *CD1 Track 17 p261*

- Play the CD. The pupils circle the eight mistakes.
- Play the CD again. The pupils write the correct words.

Answers: **1** ~~house~~ school **2** ~~Maths~~ Arts and Crafts **3** ~~guitar~~ drums **4** ~~football~~ basketball **5** ~~gym~~ playground **6** ~~behind~~ next to **7** ~~pencil~~ bracelet **8** ~~playground~~ swimming pool

Activity 3

Read and complete. What do you think?

- Ask a pupil to read out the first statement. The pupils circle the adjective that best describes the story.
- The pupils complete the second sentence and give a reason. They then rate the story from one to five stars.
- The pupils share opinions with a Talk Partner.

Code activity CODE!

- The pupils complete the code activity.

Answer: ninety

Ending the lesson

Review the lesson and reflect on learning.

- Say **Today we've listened to a story about Lily and Josh's new school.** Elicit the story.
- Ask **Which was your favourite activity today? Which activity was easy / difficult?**

Extra activity

Reinforcement

- Retell the story as a class. Say **Let's tell the story together.** Prompt the class by saying **The first lesson is ...** (*Arts and Crafts*). Use mime for support.

Key Competences and Key Learning Outcomes

- Review and learn additional school subjects
- Follow and correct the grammar tables
- Sing a song

Key language

- School subjects: *Arts and Crafts, Drama, Geography, History, ICT, PE*
- *I'm brilliant / very good / good / not very good at (History). Are you good at (Maths)? Yes, I am. No, I'm not.*
- Extension: *Biology, Chemistry, French, Literature*
- Recycled: *English, Maths*

Materials

- Pupil's Book p12; Activity Book p9; Class CD1; Teacher's App on Navio
- Teacher's Resource Bank: Talk cards

Optional materials

- Teacher's Resource Bank: Trinity Exams Practice cards (selected from the Starter Unit)

At a Glance Lesson Plan

Pupil's Book

Starting the lesson

- Use the Trinity Exams Practice cards (optional).
- Review school subjects.
- Set learning outcomes and use the talk cards.

Activity 1

- Listen, point and say.
- ▶ *CD1 Track 18 p261*

Activity 2

- Listen and sing *I'm brilliant at PE.*
- ▶ *CD1 Track 19 p261*

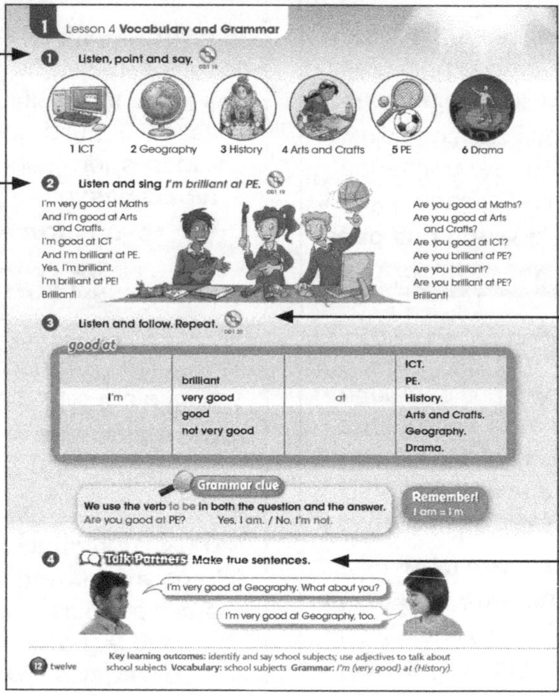
1 Lesson 4 Vocabulary and Grammar

1 Listen, point and say.

1 ICT 2 Geography 3 History 4 Arts and Crafts 5 PE 6 Drama

2 Listen and sing *I'm brilliant at PE.*

I'm very good at Maths
And I'm good at Arts
and Crafts.
I'm good at ICT
And I'm brilliant at PE.
Yes, I'm brilliant.
I'm brilliant at PE!
Brilliant!

Are you good at Maths?
Are you good at Arts
and Crafts?
Are you good at ICT?
Are you brilliant at PE?
Are you brilliant?
Are you brilliant at PE?
Brilliant!

3 Listen and follow. Repeat.

good at

I'm	brilliant very good good not very good	at	ICT. PE. History. Arts and Crafts. Geography. Drama.

Grammar clue

We use the verb *to be* in both the question and the answer.
Are you good at PE? Yes, I am. / No, I'm not.

Remember! I am = I'm

4 Talk Partners Make true sentences.

12 twelve Key learning outcomes: identify and say school subjects; use adjectives to talk about school subjects Vocabulary: school subjects Grammar: *I'm (very good) at (History).*

Activity 3

- Listen and follow.
- ▶ *CD1 Track 20 p261*
- Repeat.
- **Grammar clue:** Read about using the verb 'to be' in questions and answers.

Activity 4

- Make true sentences.
- Go to the Activity Book.

Ending the lesson

- Review the lesson and reflect on learning.

Extra activities

Reinforcement

- Ask and answer questions about what you're good at.

Vocabulary extension

- Present four additional vocabulary items.

Activity Book

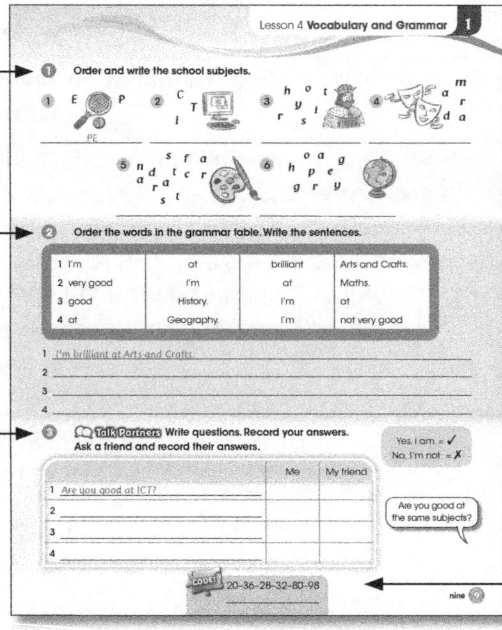
Lesson 4 Vocabulary and Grammar 1

1 Order and write the school subjects.

2 Order the words in the grammar table. Write the sentences.

1 I'm	at	brilliant	Arts and Crafts.
2 very good	I'm	at	Maths.
3 good	History.	I'm	at
4 at	Geography.	I'm	not very good

1 I'm brilliant at Arts and Crafts.
2
3
4

3 Talk Partners Write questions. Record your answers. Ask a friend and record their answers.

Yes, I am. = ✓ No, I'm not. = ✗

	Me	My friend
1 Are you good at ICT?		
2		
3		
4		

CODE! 20-36-28-32-80-98

nine 9

Activity Book

Activity 1

- Order and write the school subjects.

Activity 2

- Order the words in the grammar table.
- Write the sentences.

Activity 3

- Write questions.
- Record your answers.
- Ask a friend and record their answers.

Code activity

- Complete the code activity.

Digital resources

Teacher's Digital: You can also teach this lesson using the Teacher's App on Navio.

Pupil's Digital: Encourage your pupils to use the Pupil's App on Navio to practise the activities from this lesson.

Powered By NAVIO

Starting the lesson

Use the Trinity Exams Practice cards (optional).

- The pupils practise asking and answering questions.

Review school subjects.

- Play *Lifeboat*. Draw a figure on a raft at sea. Then draw a line for each letter of a school subject, e.g. _ _ _ _ _ (Maths), and ask the class to guess the letters. Write the letters the pupils guess correctly on the lines. For incorrect letters, erase part of the raft. Can the pupils guess the school subject before the figure falls into the water?
- Repeat with other school subjects the pupils know.

Set learning outcomes and use the talk cards.

- Say **Today we're going to learn the names of some more school subjects and talk about them.**
- Point to the talk cards to show the pupils the different ways they will be working in the lesson.

Pupil's Book Activity 1

Listen, point and say.

▶ ***CD1 Track 18 p261***

- Point to the first picture and say **Look. This school subject is ICT.** The class repeats the name of the subject. Ask **Do you study ICT at school?**
- Play the CD. The pupils listen, point to each picture and repeat the subject.

Pupil's Book Activity 2

Listen and sing *I'm brilliant at PE.*

▶ ***CD1 Track 19 p261***

- Say **Look at Ravi. What subject is he good at?** Repeat for Lily and Josh.
- Play the CD. The pupils listen and read. Confirm that Ravi is very good at Maths, Lily is good at Arts and Crafts, and Josh is good at ICT and brilliant at PE.
- Play the CD again. The pupils join in singing the song and doing the actions.

Pupil's Book Activity 3

Listen and follow. Repeat.

▶ ***CD1 Track 20 p261***

- Focus the pupils on the grammar table.
- Play the CD. The pupils listen to the first sentence, pointing to the corresponding parts of the sentence.
- The pupils repeat the complete sentence and say if it is true or false for them.
- Repeat the procedure with the other sentences.

Grammar clue

- Read the grammar clue as a class. Encourage the pupils to make questions and to answer. Read the *Remember!* tip.

Pupil's Book Activity 4

Make true sentences.

- Organise the class into Talk Partners. The pupils take turns to ask and answer questions.

Activity Book

Activity 1

Order and write the school subjects.

- Ask the pupils to name the school subjects.
- The pupils work on their own to write the words.

Answers: **1** PE **2** ICT **3** History **4** Drama **5** Arts and Crafts **6** Geography

Activity 2

Order the words in the grammar table. Write the sentences.

- Explain that the grammar table is mixed up and that the pupils need to reorder the words. Invite a pupil to read out the first sentence.
- The pupils order and write the remaining sentences. If they need more support, remind them that a sentence begins with a capital letter and ends with a full stop.

Answers: **1** I'm brilliant at Arts and Crafts. **2** I'm very good at Maths. **3** I'm good at History. **4** I'm not very good at Geography.

Activity 3

Write questions. Record your answers. Ask a friend and record their answers.

- Invite a pupil to read out the first question. Quickly review school subjects. The pupils then write their own questions.
- Working with a Talk Partner, the pupils take turns to ask and answer the questions. They record answers for themselves and for their partners.
- Ask **Are you good at the same subjects?** Prompt the pairs to say which subjects they are both good at, e.g. *We're good at* (*Maths*) *and* (*PE*).

Code activity

- The pupils complete the code activity.

Answer: eighty

Ending the lesson

Review the lesson and reflect on learning.

- Say **Today we've learnt some new school subjects. What are they?** Elicit the school subjects.
- Ask **Which was your favourite activity today? Which activity was easy / difficult?**

Extra activities

Reinforcement

- Review the activities from the unit so far and ask the pupils to think of a question, e.g. *Are you good at* (*skateboarding*)? The class moves around the room. When you say **Freeze**, the pupils stop where they are. When you say **Pair**, they get into a pair with a pupil standing nearby. Finally, when you say **Share**, they ask and answer their questions. Repeat several times.

Vocabulary extension

- Use the Vocabulary Booster on Navio and present and practise four additional school subjects: *Biology*, *Chemistry*, *French*, *Literature*.

Key Competences and Key Learning Outcomes

- Say a tongue twister with the 'j' sound
- Practise spelling and learn an alternative spelling for the 'j' sound
- Listen for specific information

- Play a communication game using *Wh-* questions and complete a timetable

Key language

- *giraffe, jeans, jelly, judo, juice, jump, orange, page, timetable*
- *When do we have (Music)? We have (Music) on (Monday) at (nine o'clock). Where do we have (Music)? We have it in (the music room).*
- Recycled: *Arts and Crafts, Drama, English, Geography, History, ICT, Maths, Music, PE, Science; classroom, computer room, gym, music room, school hall, swimming pool;* days of the week

Materials

- Pupil's Book p13; Activity Book p10; Class CD1; Teacher's App on Navio
- Teacher's Resource Bank: Talk cards
- Teacher's Resource Bank: Unit 1 Lesson 5 Communication Activity

Optional materials

- Teacher's Resource Bank: Trinity Exams Practice cards (selected from the Starter Unit)
- Teacher's Resource Bank: Places in a school word cards
- Places in a school flashcards

At a Glance Lesson Plan

Pupil's Book

Starting the lesson

- Use the Trinity Exams Practice cards (optional).
- **Think-Pair-Share.** Review school subjects.
- Review the *I'm brilliant at PE* song.

▶ ***CD1 Track 19 p261***

- Set learning outcomes and use the talk cards.

Activity 1: Speak and spell

- Listen, read and say.

▶ ***CD1 Track 21 p262***

Go to the Activity Book.

Activity 2

- Read the timetable.

▶ ***CD1 Track 22 p262***

- Listen and identify four differences.

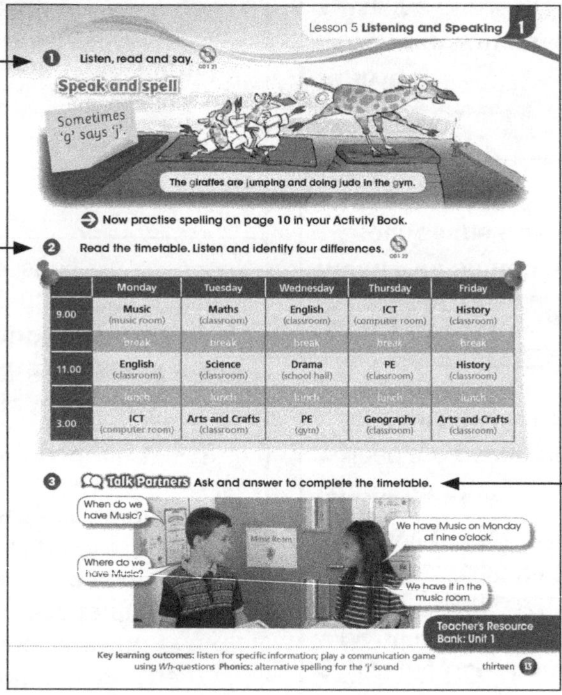

Activity 3

- Ask and answer to complete the timetable (Teacher's Resource Bank: Unit 1).

Ending the lesson

- Review the lesson and reflect on learning.

Extra activities

Reinforcement

- Talk about your own school timetable.
- Play *Board pelmanism.*

Activity Book

Activity Book

Activity 1: Speak and spell

- Complete and say.

Activity 2

- Find and circle the words.
- Classify and write.

Activity 3

- Test your friend.
- Ask and answer.

Code activity

- Complete the code activity.

Digital resources

Teacher's Digital: You can also teach this lesson using the Teacher's App on Navio.

Pupil's Digital: Encourage your pupils to use the Pupil's App on Navio to practise the activities from this lesson.

Powered By NAVIO

Starting the lesson

Use the Trinity Exams Practice cards (optional).

- The pupils practise asking and answering questions.

Think-Pair-Share. Review school subjects.

- Ask **Can you remember eight school subjects?** The class thinks silently for a minute.
- Then the pupils work with a Talk Partner to name the subjects.
- Invite different pairs of Talk Partners to come to the board and write a school subject.
- Finally, repeat the procedure, asking different pairs of Talk Partners each time, until all the school subjects have been named.
- Point to each school subject in turn and ask **Are you good at (Maths)?** The class responds.

Review the *I'm brilliant at PE* song.

▶ *CD1 Track 19 p261*

- Play the CD. The pupils sing and do the actions.

Set learning outcomes and use the talk cards.

- Say **Today we're going to say a tongue twister, practise spelling and complete a timetable.**
- Point to the talk cards to show the pupils the different ways they will be working in the lesson.

Pupil's Book Activity 1: Speak and spell

Listen, read and say.

▶ *CD1 Track 21 p262*

- (Books closed.) Write the letter 'g' on the board and ask **What sound does this letter make?** (*'g'*) List the words that the pupils know with this sound, e.g. *girl, go, goat*. Explain that sometimes this letter makes another sound.
- (Books open.) Focus the class on the picture and ask **What can you see here? What's this giraffe doing? What are these giraffes doing?**
- Say **Let's listen to a tongue twister.** Play the CD. The pupils follow the text in their books.
- Play the CD again. The pupils join in with the tongue twister.
- Ask **How do you spell judo? How do you spell gym?** Highlight the two ways of spelling the 'j' sound and focus the class on the yellow note.
- Highlight that the letter 'g' is usually a hard sound, e.g. 'go', but when it is followed by the letters 'e', 'i' or 'y' it can have a soft sound.

Activity Book

Activity 1: Speak and spell

Complete and say.

- The pupils complete and say the words in the tongue twister.

Answer: The giraffes are jumping and doing judo in the gym.

Activity 2

Find and circle the words. Classify and write.

- The pupils find and circle the words in the border which contain the 'j' sound.
- The pupils classify and write the words according to whether they are written with 'j' or 'g'.

Answers: j: juice, jelly, jump, jeans, judo g: giraffe, gym, geography, orange, page

Activity 3

Talk Partners. Test your friend. Ask and answer.

- Invite two pupils to read out the speech bubbles.
- Organise the pupils into Talk Partners. The pupils take it in turns to test their partner on the spelling of the words in Activity 2. Stress the importance of prompting, encouraging and helping each other.

Code activity

- The pupils complete the code activity.

Answer: seventy

Pupil's Book Activity 2

Read the timetable. Listen and identify four differences.

▶ *CD1 Track 22 p262*

- Focus the class on the timetable and ask questions to familiarise the pupils with the content, e.g. **When do the children have (Maths)? What do the children have on (Thursday) at (nine o'clock)?**
- Say **Let's listen to two children talking about the timetable. Listen for the four differences.** Play the CD, pausing after each difference for the pupils to say what it is.

Answers: **1** Music in the ~~music room~~ classroom **2** Science on ~~Tuesday~~ Thursday **3** 11.00 Friday ~~History~~ Maths **4** Drama in ~~school hall~~ gym

Pupil's Book Activity 3

Ask and answer to complete the timetable (Teacher's Resource Bank: Unit 1).

- Invite two volunteers to read out the speech bubbles.
- Explain that the pupils are going to work in pairs to complete a timetable.
- Organise the class into Talk Partners. Pupil A uses Timetable 1. Pupil B uses Timetable 2. The partners ask questions about the different subjects to complete the timetable.
- At the end, the pupils compare and check their completed timetables.

Ending the lesson

Review the lesson and reflect on learning.

- Say **Today we've practised a tongue twister.** Elicit the tongue twister from the pupils.
- Ask **Which was your favourite activity today? Which activity was easy / difficult?**

Extra activities

Reinforcement

- Ask the pupils to look at their own school timetable and to say which lessons they have and the times they have them.
- Make a statement about the class timetable, e.g. **You have Maths on Monday morning.** The pupils listen and decide whether the statement is true or false.
- Play *Board pelmanism* (see p27) with the places in a school flashcards and word cards.

Key Competences and Key Learning Outcomes

- Read and understand a poster
- Write and talk about your favourite after-school activity

- Do a pre-reading task
- Read the text for general understanding
- Scan the text to find specific information
- Use context clues

Key language

- *balls, gloves, helmet, hockey stick, pads, rollerblades; comfortable, fast, text message*
- *Are you bored? Do you want to learn (an exciting sport?) The classes begin / finish at (five o'clock). We meet on (Tuesday). The classes cost (£2). You need to wear (comfortable clothes). For more information, email (emma@fun.uk).*
- Recycled: *bored, exciting, playground, sport*

Materials

- Pupil's Book p14; Activity Book p11; Class CD1; Teacher's App on Navio
- Teacher's Resource Bank: Talk cards

Optional materials

- Teacher's Resource Bank: Trinity Exams Practice cards (selected from the Starter Unit)

At a Glance Lesson Plan

Pupil's Book

Starting the lesson

- Use the Trinity Exams Practice cards (optional).
- Review the tongue twister.
- ▶ *CD1 Track 21 p262*
- Set learning outcomes and use the talk cards.

Before you read: Activity 1

- Look at the photo on the poster.
- What can you do at this club?

Before you read: Activity 2

- Think of a question to ask about the club.

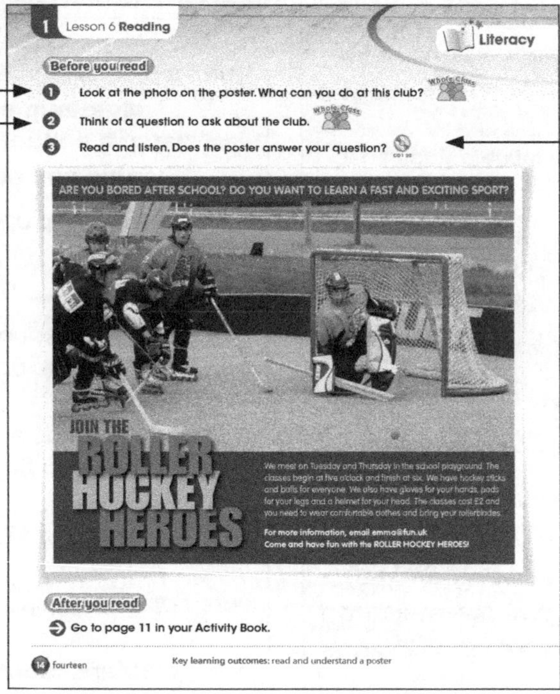

Activity 3

- Read and listen.
- ▶ *CD1 Track 23 p262*
- Does the poster answer your question?
- Go to the Activity Book.

Ending the lesson

- Review the lesson and reflect on learning.

Extra activity

Extension

- Plan an English club for the school.

Activity Book

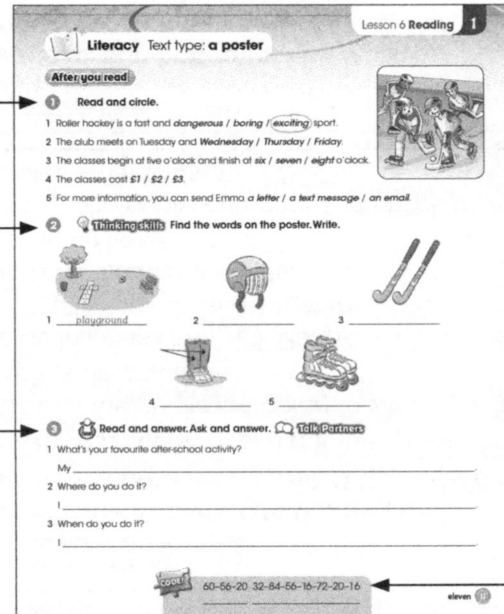

After you read: Activity Book

Activity 1

- Read and circle.

Activity 2

- Find the words on the poster.
- Write.

Activity 3

- Read and answer.
- Ask and answer.

Code activity

- Complete the code activity.

Digital resources

Teacher's Digital: You can also teach this lesson using the Teacher's App on Navio.

Pupil's Digital: Encourage your pupils to use the Pupil's App on Navio to practise the activities from this lesson.

Powered By NAVIO

Starting the lesson

Use the Trinity Exams Practice cards (optional).

- The pupils practise asking and answering questions.

Review the tongue twister.

▶ *CD1 Track 21 p262*

- Ask **What sound did you practise in the tongue twister?** (*'j'*)
- Ask **Can you remember the tongue twister?** (*The giraffes are jumping and doing judo in the gym.*)
- Play the CD. Practise the tongue twister as a class.
- Remind the pupils that they know two spellings for this sound ('j' and 'g'). The pupils list the words they know which have these letters.

Set learning outcomes and use the talk cards.

- Say **Today we're going to read a poster.**
- Point to the talk cards to show the pupils the different ways they will be working in the lesson.

Before you read: Pupil's Book Activity 1

Look at the photo on the poster. What can you do at this club?

- Invite a pupil to read the question in the rubric.
- Prompt the pupils to look at the poster and describe what they can see.

Answer: You can play roller hockey.

Before you read: Pupil's Book Activity 2

Think of a question to ask about the club.

- Encourage the pupils to think of questions about the club. If necessary, prompt them by providing the question words 'When?' 'How much?' and 'What?'. Write the questions on the board.

Pupil's Book Activity 3

Read and listen. Does the poster answer your question?

▶ *CD1 Track 23 p262*

- Invite a pupil to read the rubric. Explain to the pupils that the first time they read, they should try to understand the most important information.
- If you want the pupils to read the text without the support of the CD, set a time limit for this task. Otherwise, play the CD.
- The pupils report which of the questions on the board have been answered.

After you read: Activity Book

Activity 1

Read and circle.

- The pupils work on their own or in pairs to read each sentence and identify the correct option. The pupils should refer back to the text in the Pupil's Book when necessary.

Answers: **1** exciting **2** Thursday **3** six **4** £2 **5** an email

Activity 2

Find the words on the poster. Write.

- The pupils work on their own or in pairs to label the pictures. They should refer back to the text in the Pupil's Book to find the word each time. Highlight clues such as *pads* ***for your legs,*** *a helmet* ***for your head***.

Answers: **1** playground **2** helmet **3** hockey sticks **4** pads **5** rollerblades

Activity 3

Read and answer. Ask and answer.

- Read the questions as a class and encourage different pupils to answer. If necessary, write keywords and new vocabulary on the board.
- The pupils work on their own to write their answers.
- The pupils ask and answer the questions with a Talk Partner.

Code activity

- The pupils complete the code activity.

Answer: one hundred

Ending the lesson

Review the lesson and reflect on learning.

- Say **Today we've read a poster. Do you think it's a good poster? Would you like to join the Roller Hockey Heroes?** Elicit the pupils' opinions.
- Ask **Which was your favourite activity today? Which activity was easy / difficult?**

Extra activity

Extension

- Explain to the pupils that you want them to plan an English club for the school.
- As a class, decide when and where the club is to meet.
- Organise the pupils into Talk Partners or small groups and ask them to think of activities children can do to practise their English and have fun at the club. The pupils should list the activities they think of.
- After a few minutes, ask the groups or Talk Partners to share their ideas with the rest of the class.

Key Competences and Key Learning Outcomes

- Use capital letters correctly

- Identify the audience of a poster
- Identify informational content
- Identify the text features of a poster
- Use criteria to check your writing

- Share your writing with a partner

- Plan, prepare and write a poster about an after-school club

Key language

- *capital letter, computers, computer programmers, draw pictures, free, games, join, memory stick, painting, skating, teachers*
- *Do you love (computers)? Do you want to (play games)? The classes begin / finish at (five o'clock). We meet on (Wednesday). You need to bring (a memory stick). For more information, contact (Mr Smith).*
- Recycled: *exciting*

Materials

- Pupil's Book p15; Activity Book p12; Class CD1; Teacher's App on Navio
- Teacher's Resource Bank: Talk cards

Optional materials

- Teacher's Resource Bank: Trinity Exams Practice cards (selected from the Starter Unit)
- Large pieces of paper; computers; word-processing program; magazine pictures; glue
- Crayons or coloured pencils

At a Glance Lesson Plan

Pupil's Book

Starting the lesson

- Use the Trinity Exams Practice cards (optional).
- Review after-school activities.
- Set learning outcomes and use the talk cards.

Investigate a text: Activity 1

- Read and listen.
- ▶ *CD1 Track 24 p262*
- Which questions does the poster answer?

Discuss a text: Activity 2

- Think and discuss.
- **Writing tip:** Read about using capital letters.
- Go to the Activity Book.

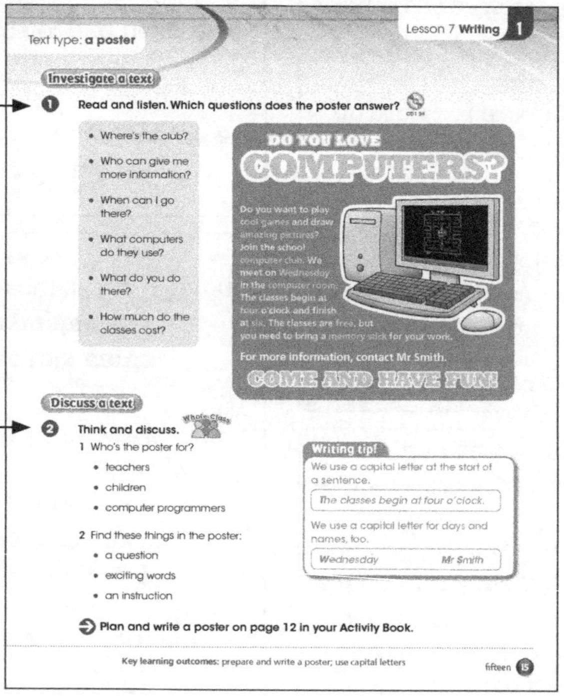

Text type: a poster Lesson 7 Writing 1

Investigate a text

1 Read and listen. Which questions does the poster answer?

- Where's the club?
- Who can give me more information?
- When can I go there?
- What computers do they use?
- What do you do there?
- How much do the classes cost?

DO YOU LOVE COMPUTERS?

For more information, contact Mr Smith.

COME AND HAVE FUN!

Discuss a text

2 Think and discuss.

1 Who's the poster for?
- teachers
- children
- computer programmers

2 Find these things in the poster:
- a question
- exciting words
- an instruction

Writing tip!

We use a capital letter at the start of a sentence.

The classes begin at four o'clock.

We use a capital letter for days and names, too.

Wednesday *Mr Smith*

Plan and write a poster on page 12 in your Activity Book.

Key learning outcomes: prepare and write a poster; use capital letters fifteen 15

Ending the lesson

- Review the lesson and reflect on learning.

Extra activity

Extension

- Create posters and make a wall display.

Activity Book

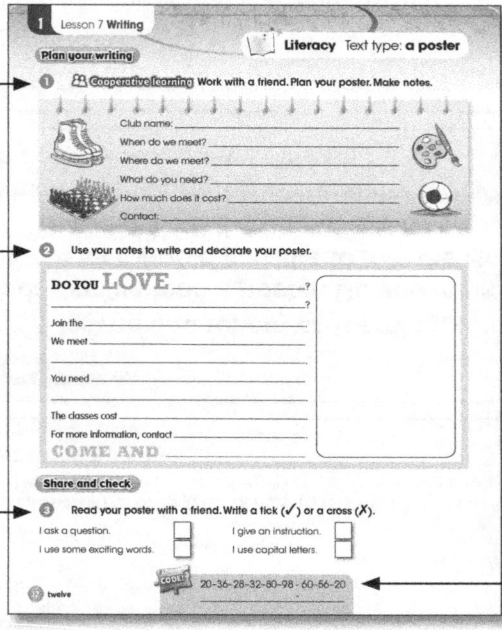

1 Lesson 7 Writing

Literacy Text type: a poster

Plan your writing

1 Cooperative learning Work with a friend. Plan your poster. Make notes.

Club name:
When do we meet?
Where do we meet?
What do you need?
How much does it cost?
Contact:

2 Use your notes to write and decorate your poster.

DO YOU LOVE ___?
___?
Join the ___
We meet ___
You need ___
The classes cost ___
For more information, contact ___
COME AND ___

Share and check

3 Read your poster with a friend. Write a tick (✓) or a cross (✗).

I ask a question.		I give an instruction.	
I use some exciting words.		I use capital letters.	

CODE! 20-36-28-32-80-98-60-56-20

twelve

Activity Book

Plan your writing:
Activity 1

- Work with a friend.
- Plan your poster.
- Make notes.

Activity 2

- Use your notes to write and decorate your poster.

Share and check:
Activity 3

- Read your poster with a friend.
- Write a tick (✓) or a cross (✗).

Code activity

- Complete the code activity

Digital resources

Teacher's Digital: You can also teach this lesson using the Teacher's App on Navio.

Pupil's Digital: Encourage your pupils to use the Pupil's App on Navio to practise the activities from this lesson.

Powered By NAVIO

Starting the lesson

Use the Trinity Exams Practice cards (optional).

- The pupils practise asking and answering questions.

Review after-school activities.

- Ask **What activities do you do after school?** Invite a pupil to come to the front of the class and to make a statement, e.g. *I (play football).*
- Invite a second pupil to come to the front of the class. This pupil should say *(Mario) plays football and I (go swimming).* If necessary, highlight the third-person form.
- Continue in this way to make a memory chain. Challenge the class to make a chain of ten pupils or more.

Set learning outcomes and use the talk cards.

- Ask **What did we read in the last lesson?** (*A poster.*) Say **Today we're going to investigate another poster. Then we're going to plan and write our own posters.**
- Point to the talk cards to show the pupils the different ways they will be working in the lesson.

Investigate a text: Pupil's Book Activity 1

Read and listen. Which questions does the poster answer?

▶ *CD1 Track 24 p262*

- Read the questions as a class. Explain that some of the questions are answered in the text. The pupils should read the text to identify which information is included.
- If you want the pupils to read the text without the support of the CD, set a time limit for this task. Otherwise, play the CD.
- The pupils report which questions are answered. They then read the text again to find the answers to these questions.

Answers: Where's the club? Who can give me more information? When can I go there? What do you do there? How much do the classes cost?

Discuss a text: Pupil's Book Activity 2

Think and discuss.

- Read the first question and identify who the poster is for.
- Discuss why the text is for children. (*The members play games, draw pictures and it's a school club.*)
- Read the next instruction and prompt the pupils to find a question in the text. (*Do you love computers? Do you want to play cool games and draw amazing pictures?*) Explain that questions get the readers' attention and make them want to read more.
- Prompt the class to find examples of exciting (emotive) language. (*cool, amazing, fun*) Explain that these words make the club sound more attractive.
- Prompt the class to find an instruction. (*Join the school computer club. Come and have fun!*) Explain that instructions tell people what to do.

Writing tip

- Read the information and ask the pupils to find examples of capital letters in the text.
- Remind / teach the pupils that we also use capital letters for cities, countries, months and school subjects.

Activity Book

Plan your writing: Activity 1

Writing Partners. Work with a friend. Plan your poster. Make notes.

- Invite a pupil to read out the questions and prompts.
- Organise the class into pairs to plan their posters. The pairs should choose or invent a school club and make notes.

Activity 2

Use your notes to write and decorate your poster.

- Focus the class on the activity. If necessary, model how to complete the framework on the board, with the pupils making suggestions. Show the class how to begin with a question to get the reader's attention, finish with an instruction, and include exciting (emotive) vocabulary.
- The pupils work in pairs to write their text based on their notes and then draw a picture for their poster.

Share and check: Activity 3

Writing Partners. Read your poster with a friend. Write a tick (✓) or a cross (✗).

- Read the statements as a class.
- Organise the class into new pairs. One pupil in each pair should read their text aloud to their partner. The other pupil listens. The pupils work together to decide if the text fulfils all the criteria and tick or cross the corresponding boxes. The pupils can add to, improve, or correct the text at this stage.
- The pupils swap roles.

Code activity

- The pupils complete the code activity.

Answer: eighty-one

Ending the lesson

Review the lesson and reflect on learning.

- Say **Today we've written a poster. Are you happy with your posters?** Elicit the pupils' opinions.
- Ask **Which was your favourite activity today? Which activity was easy / difficult?**

Extra activity

Extension

- If you have access to computers, show the class how to use a word-processing program to create their posters. The pupils can print out their posters and make a wall display.
- Alternatively, the pupils can copy their work onto large pieces of paper. They can then decorate their posters with drawings and pictures from magazines.

Key Competences and Key Learning Outcomes

- Use the Internet to investigate Ireland
- Read and listen for specific information
- Learn about after-school activities in Ireland
- Think about your own culture and identity

Key language

- *beautiful, competitions, concert, dresses, Gaelic football, helmet, hurling, Ireland, Irish dancing, jump, noise, passing the ball, practise, running, skip, small, sport, tin whistle, traditional; carry / hit / kick the ball*
- *My favourite activity is* (Gaelic football). *I play* (a tin whistle). *I practise on* (Tuesday evenings). *I go to* (a dance class).
- Recycled: days of the week

Materials

- Pupil's Book p16; Activity Book p13; Class CD1; Teacher's App on Navio
- Teacher's Resource Bank: Talk cards
- An online world map
- Coloured pencils (green, orange, white)

Optional materials

- Teacher's Resource Bank: Trinity Exams Practice cards (selected from the Starter Unit)

At a Glance Lesson Plan

Pupil's Book

Starting the lesson

- Use the Trinity Exams Practice cards (optional).
- Review the days of the week.
- Set learning outcomes and use the talk cards.

Activity 1

- Read Luke's questions.
- What do you think?

Activity 2

- Read and listen.
- ▶ ***CD1 Track 25 p262***
- Answer Luke's questions.
- **Think about your culture** What activities do children do after school in your country?

Go to the Activity Book.

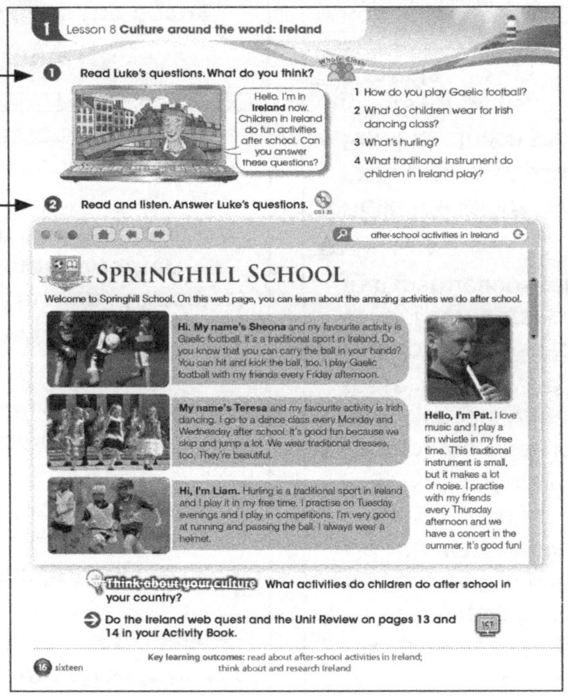

1 Lesson 8 **Culture around the world: Ireland**

1 **Read Luke's questions. What do you think?**

Hello. I'm in **Ireland** now. Children in Ireland do fun activities after school. Can you answer these questions?

1 How do you play Gaelic football?
2 What do children wear for Irish dancing class?
3 What's hurling?
4 What traditional instrument do children in Ireland play?

2 **Read and listen. Answer Luke's questions.**

SPRINGHILL SCHOOL

Welcome to Springhill School. On this web page, you can learn about the amazing activities we do after school.

Hi. My name's Sheona and my favourite activity is Gaelic football. It's a traditional sport in Ireland. Do you know that you can carry the ball in your hands? You can hit and kick the ball, too. I play Gaelic football with my friends every Friday afternoon.

My name's Teresa and my favourite activity is Irish dancing. I go to a dance class every Monday and Wednesday after school. It's good fun because we skip and jump a lot. We wear traditional dresses, too. They're beautiful.

Hi, I'm Liam. Hurling is a traditional sport in Ireland and I play it in my free time. I practise on Tuesday evenings and I play in competitions. I'm very good at running and passing the ball. I always wear a helmet.

Hello, I'm Pat. I love music and I play a tin whistle in my free time. This traditional instrument is small, but it makes a lot of noise. I practise with my friends every Thursday afternoon and we have a concert in the summer. It's good fun!

Think about your culture What activities do children do after school in your country?

Do the Ireland web quest and the Unit Review on pages 13 and 14 in your Activity Book.

16 sixteen

Key learning outcomes: read about after-school activities in Ireland; think about and research Ireland

Ending the lesson

- Review the lesson and reflect on learning.

Activity Book

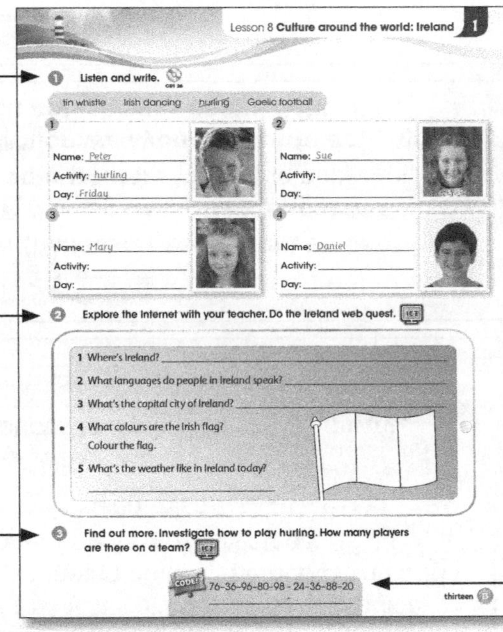

Lesson 8 **Culture around the world: Ireland** 1

1 **Listen and write.**

tin whistle Irish dancing hurling Gaelic football

1 Name: Peter Activity: hurling Day: Friday
2 Name: Sue Activity: Day:
3 Name: Mary Activity: Day:
4 Name: Daniel Activity: Day:

2 **Explore the Internet with your teacher. Do the Ireland web quest.**

1 Where's Ireland?
2 What languages do people in Ireland speak?
3 What's the capital city of Ireland?
4 What colours are the Irish flag? Colour the flag.
5 What's the weather like in Ireland today?

3 **Find out more. Investigate how to play hurling. How many players are there on a team?**

CODE! 76-36-96-80-98-24-36-88-20

thirteen 13

Activity Book

Activity 1

- Listen and write.
- ▶ ***CD1 Track 26 p262***

Activity 2

- Explore the Internet with your teacher. Do the Ireland web quest.

Activity 3

- Find out more. Investigate how to play hurling. How many players are there on a team?

Code activity

- Complete the code activity.

Digital resources

Teacher's Digital: You can also teach this lesson using the Teacher's App on Navio.

Powered By NAVIO

Starting the lesson

Use the Trinity Exams Practice cards (optional).

- The pupils practise asking and answering questions.

Review the days of the week.

- Ask the pupils to say the days of the week in order, around the class. As the pupils become more confident, prompt them to say the days faster.
- Ask the class to spell the days of the week. Choose a pupil to write the days on the board as they are spelt out.

Set learning outcomes and use the talk cards.

- Say **Today we're going to investigate Ireland.**
- Point to the talk cards to show the pupils the different ways they will be working in the lesson.

Pupil's Book Activity 1

Read Luke's questions. What do you think?

- Read the speech bubble as a class. Encourage the pupils to tell you what they know about Ireland. Show them where the country is on an online world map.
- Read the questions as a class. Encourage the pupils to predict the answers.

Pupil's Book Activity 2

Read and listen. Answer Luke's questions.

▶ *CD1 Track 25 p262*

- Focus the class on the photos. Ask **What can you see?**
- Play the CD, pausing after each section to check understanding. The pupils answer Luke's questions.

Answers: **1** You can carry the ball in your hands and hit and kick it. **2** Girls wear traditional dresses. **3** Hurling is a traditional sport in Ireland. **4** They play the tin whistle.

Think about your culture

- Read out the question and prompt different pupils to tell you about the activities children do after school in their country. Ask **Do children (play hurling) after school here?**

Activity Book

Activity 1

Listen and write.

▶ *CD1 Track 26 p262*

- Ask the pupils to read out the after-school activities in the word box. Play the CD, pausing after the first exchange for the pupils to say the activity and the day.
- Repeat the procedure for the other exchanges, with the pupils writing the answers.

Answers: **1** Peter, hurling, Friday **2** Sue, Irish dancing, Wednesday **3** Mary, tin whistle, Monday **4** Daniel, Gaelic football, Thursday

Activity 2

Explore the Internet with your teacher. Do the Ireland web quest.

- Read out the instructions and connect to a children's website that provides geographical information about Ireland. (See suggested websites opposite.) Read out questions 1 to 4. The pupils work as a class to find and write the answers. They should also colour the Irish flag.
- Read out question 5. Connect to a website that shows the weather around the world. (See suggested website opposite.) The pupils complete the information about the day's weather.

Answers: **1** next to the UK / in Europe **2** English and Irish **3** Dublin **4** green, white and orange

Activity 3

Find out more. Investigate how to play hurling. How many players are there on a team?

- Read the rubric and encourage the pupils to predict how many players there are on a hurling team.
- If you are doing the investigation as a class, go to a suitable website and ask the pupils to scan the information to find the answer.
- If you are working in a computer room, organise the class into small groups.

Answer: There are 15 players on the hurling team.

Suggested websites

- Use a range of trusted Internet sites such as:
  http://www.enchantedlearning.com/europe/ireland
  http://www.bbc.co.uk/weather
  http://www.safesearchkids.com

Code activity

- The pupils complete the code activity.

Answer: sixty-five

Ending the lesson

Review the lesson and reflect on learning.

- Say **Today we've learnt about Ireland. What traditional sport do children play?** Elicit the information from the pupils.
- Ask **Which was your favourite activity today? Which activity was easy / difficult?**

Go to the AB Unit Review on page 243.

Key Competences and Key Learning Outcomes

- Watch and understand a video about after-school activities
- Ask and answer about new things to try
- Think about new activities they would like to try
- Learn about other after-school activities

Key language

- *dancing, drums, goalkeeper, pottery, robotics, robots, rugby*
- Recycled: *gloves, helmet, pads, roller hockey; brilliant, fast, slow*
- *Do you want to (play the guitar)? Yes, I do. (Music is fun.) What activities do you do after school?*

Materials

- Pupil's Book p17; Activity Book p15; Class CD1; Teacher's App on Navio
- Teacher's Resource Bank: Talk cards

Optional materials

- Teacher's Resource Bank: Trinity Exams Practice cards (selected from the Starter Unit)

At a Glance Lesson Plan

Pupil's Book

Starting the lesson

- Use the Trinity Exams Practice cards (optional).
- **Think-Pair-Share.** Review after-school activities.
- Set learning outcomes and use the talk cards.

Activity 1

- Before you watch
- Watch the video.
- *Unit 1 video p284*
- Which after-school activities use these objects?

Activity 2

- Watch the video again.
- *Unit 1 video*
- Read and say *true* or *false*.
- Correct the false sentences.

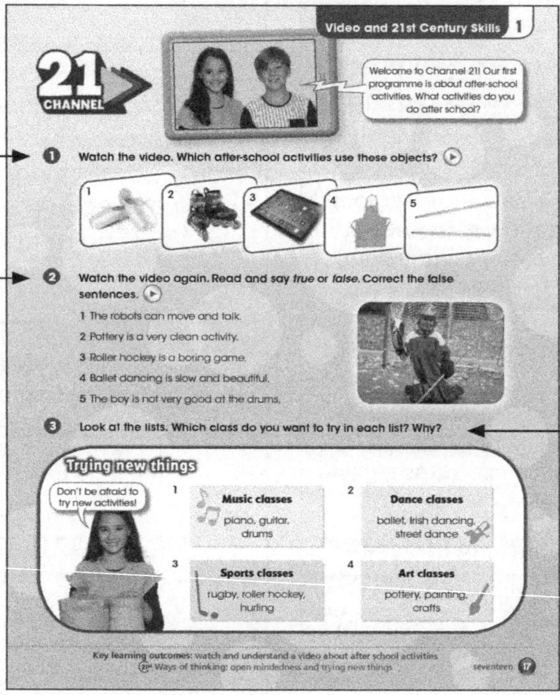

Activity 3

- Look at the lists.
- Which class do you want to try in each list?
- Why?
- Go to the Activity Book.

Ending the lesson

- Review the lesson and reflect on learning.

Extra activity

Reinforcement

- Play a mime game to review new things we want to try.

Activity Book

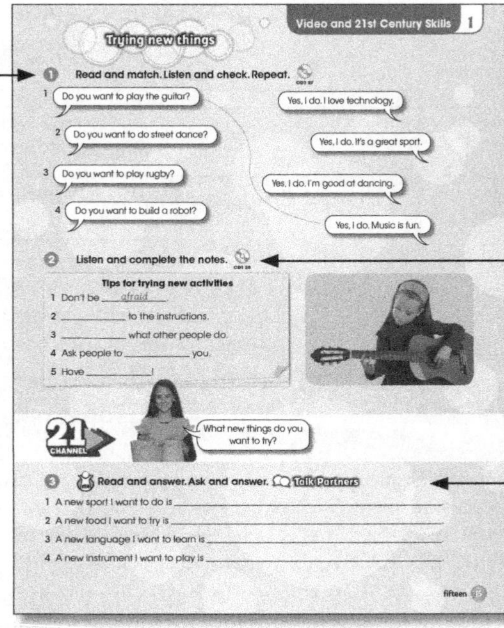

Activity Book

Activity 1

- Read and match.
- Listen and check.
- ▶ *CD1 Track 27 p262*
- Repeat.

Activity 2

- Listen and complete the notes.
- ▶ *CD1 Track 28 p263*

Activity 3

- Read and answer.
- Ask and answer.

Digital resources

Teacher's Digital: You can also teach this lesson using the Teacher's App on Navio.

Pupil's Digital: Encourage your pupils to use the Pupil's App on Navio to practise the activities from this lesson.

Powered By NAVIO

Starting the lesson

Use the Trinity Exams Practice cards (optional).

- The pupils practise asking and answering questions.

Think-Pair-Share. Review after-school activities.

- Ask **How many different after-school clubs can you think of?** The class thinks silently for a minute.
- Then the pupils work with a Talk Partner to name after-school clubs and activities.
- Invite different Talk Partners to say a different after-school club. Write the activity on the board and prompt the class to repeat the club.

Set learning outcomes and use the talk cards.

- Say **Today we're going to watch a video and then ask and answer questions about after-school clubs and activities**.
- Explain to the pupils that in every unit they will watch a TV programme called Channel 21, which is presented by two children called Chloe and Mark.
- Point to the talk cards to show the pupils the different ways they will be working in the lesson.

Pupil's Book Activity 1

Before you watch

- Point to the photo of Chloe and Mark. Ask **Who are these children?** (*The presenters of Channel 21.*)
- Read the speech bubble to pupils. Ask **What activities do you do after school?** Elicit responses from a number of pupils.

Watch the video. Which after-school activities use these objects? *p284*

- Watch Part 1. Ask pupils **What are you going to see next?** Check they understand that they will see short video clips about different after-school activities.
- Play Part 2. Ask general questions to check understanding. Focus the pupils on the photos in Activity 1. Say **Which after-school activities use these objects?** Elicit ideas.
- Play Part 2 for the pupils to answer the questions. Check answers as a class.

Answers: **1** dance class **2** roller hockey **3** robotics club **4** pottery class **5** drum class

Pupil's Book Activity 2

Watch the video again. Read and say *true* or *false*. Correct the false sentences.

- Ask a pupil to read out sentence 1. Ask the class whether they think the sentence is true or false. Repeat with sentences 2–5.
- Play Part 2. Students work in pairs to decide whether the sentences are true or false. They correct the false sentences.

Answers: **1** F The robots can move, but they can't talk. **2** F Pottery is a very dirty activity. **3** F Roller hockey is an exciting game. **4** T **5** F The boy is brilliant at the drums.

Pupil's Book Activity 3

Look at the lists. Which class do you want to try in each list? Why?

- Tell pupils that in the last part of the video Chloe and Mark talk about trying new activities. Ask **What activity does Mark want to do?** (*Play the drums.*) **Why doesn't he go to the class after school?** (*He's not very good at music.*) **What does Chloe say?** (*It's important to try new activities.*)
- Explain that pupils are going to choose some new classes to try. Read the lists with the class and check vocabulary.
- Ask one pupil **Do you want to play the piano?** Elicit both responses, *Yes, I do* and *No, I don't*. For extra challenge you could prompt pupils to give a reason, for example, *Yes, I do. I love music!*
- Pupils work in pairs to ask and answer questions. They choose one class from each list.

Activity Book

Activity 1

Read and match. Listen and check. Repeat.

▶ *CD1 Track 27 p262*

- Ask **Do you want to play rugby?** and prompt a pupil to answer. The pupil then asks you the same (or a similar) question. Say **Yes, I do. I love sport.**
- The pupils work on their own to match the question and answer speech bubbles.
- Play the CD and check answers.

Answers: **1** Do you want to play the guitar? Yes, I do. Music is fun. **2** Do you want to do street dance? Yes, I do. I'm good at dancing. **3** Do you want to play rugby? Yes, I do. It's a great sport. **4** Do you want to build a robot? Yes, I do. I love technology.

Activity 2

Listen and complete the notes.

▶ *CD1 Track 28 p263*

- Read out the first sentence and ask the pupils if they think it is good advice for trying new activities.
- Play the CD, pausing to allow the pupils to write.
- Play the CD again without pausing. Elicit answers.

Answers: **1** afraid **2** Listen **3** Watch **4** help **5** fun

Activity 3

Read and answer. Ask and answer.

- Read out the speech bubble and elicit answers from the class. Once pupils are confident answering, you could make the question more specific and ask about sport, food, language, etc.
- The pupils write sentences about new things they want to try using the prompts.
- Organise the pupils into Talk Partners. The pupils take it in turns to ask and answer questions.

Ending the lesson

Review the lesson and reflect on learning.

- Say **Today we've watched a video about after-school activities. What have we learnt about trying new things?** Elicit the information from the pupils.
- Ask **Which was your favourite activity today? Which activity was easy / difficult?**

Extra activity

Reinforcement

- Ask a pupil to mime an activity that he / she would like to try. Other pupils ask *Do you want to do (ballet)?* The pupil answers, *Yes, I do. (Ballet) is (beautiful).*

Date: ______________________ Unit: __________

1 What did my pupils learn in this unit?

2 How did my pupils work? (✓)

individually ☐ in pairs ☐ in small groups ☐

in large groups ☐ as a class ☐

3 Which key competences did my pupils develop?

- Competence in linguistic communication ☐
- Competence in mathematics, science and technology ☐
- Digital competence ☐
- Learning to learn ☐
- Social and civic competences ☐
- Sense of initiative and entrepreneurship ☐
- Cultural awareness and expression ☐

4 Which lessons / activities were the most successful and why?

5 Which lessons / activities did my pupils find the most difficult and why?

6 What did I try in the classroom for the first time? How did it go?

7 Which resources did I find most useful? (including webpages)

8 What could I do differently next time I teach this unit?

2 Helping hands

Unit overview

Key Competences and Key Learning Outcomes

- Identify and name household chores (Lesson 1)
- Say the vocabulary chant (Lesson 1)
- Listen, repeat and act out a conversation (Lesson 2)
- Talk about chores using adverbs of frequency (Lesson 2)
- Follow, complete and correct the grammar tables (Lessons 2 and 4)
- Identify and name free-time activities (Lesson 4)
- Ask and answer about frequency (Lesson 4)
- Order adjectives and nouns (Lesson 7)
- Watch and understand a video (Video and 21st Century Skills)

- Use a code to read a message (Lesson 3)

- Use the Pupil's App on Navio
- Investigate Scotland (Lesson 8)

- Say a tongue twister, learn another spelling for the 'ch' sound and practise spelling (Lesson 5)
- Practise activity types found in the Cambridge Exams: A1 Movers
- Review your own learning (Review)

- Understand the importance of helping at home (Lesson 3 and Video and 21st Century Skills)

- Work with a Talk Partner to practise and reinforce learning (all lessons)
- Do a communication activity (Lesson 5)

- Sing two songs (Lessons 1 and 4)
- Understand, act out and give an opinion on a story (Lesson 3)
- Read and understand a fable (Lesson 6)
- Plan and write the end of the fable (Lesson 7)
- Learn about Scotland (Lesson 8)
- Think about your own culture (Lesson 8)

Vocabulary

Core vocabulary
clear the table, cook dinner, dust, feed my pet, hoover the floor, lay the table, make my bed, tidy up, walk the dog, wash the car, wash up, water the plants; do puzzles, draw pictures, play board games, play computer games, read comics, watch DVDs

Extension vocabulary (optional)
brush the floor, clean the bathroom, fold the clothes, take out the rubbish, wash the clothes, wash the floor; go for a walk, go ice-skating, go shopping, listen to the radio

Other vocabulary
action, chore, fable, ferry, free time, island, look after, north, routine, smell, web, west; clever, dirty, greedy, lazy; dolphin, seal, turtle

Recycled vocabulary
days of the week; family members; household objects; places in a school; rooms in a house; *coat, delicious, dirty, drums, farm, hands, help, hot, hungry, legs, long, lunch(time); monkey, rabbit, river, sheep, spider, swim, thin, town, vegetables, walk, wash*

Structures

Core structures
My (dad) always / often / sometimes / never (washes up). My (sister) doesn't (cook). Does she (wash up)? Yes, she does. No, she doesn't. How often does (your mum) (watch DVDs)? She (watches DVDs) once a week / five times a week. How often do you (make your bed)? I never (make my bed).

Other structures
How does (Sarah) (travel to school)? There isn't (a school here). What does he do (in his free time)? The (island) is famous for (its sheep). You can (sometimes) see (seals). I (help) (my parents).

Recycled structures
Do you (dust)? Yes, I do. No, I don't. When do you (dust)? I (dust) (at the weekend). I travel to school by (ferry). I love (playing with the baby animals).

Phonics

The 'ch' sound (*wit**ch** **ch**ops **ch**icken kit**ch**en*)

Literacy

Text type: a fable (text to entertain; writing preparation)
Reading skills: identifying the message of the text
Writing skills: placing adjectives in the correct position

Culture ... around the world

Life on a Scottish island

21st Century Skills

Helping others

Thinking skills

Categorising (Lesson 1); Expressing opinions (Lesson 3); Predicting (Lessons 3 and 6); Discussing values (Lesson 3); Applying rules (Lesson 4); Making inferences (Lesson 6); Visualisation and prediction (Lesson 8); Thinking about your culture (Lesson 8); Making connections (Review)

Cooperative learning

Sharing information (Lessons 1 and 5); Team building (Lesson 4); Checking learning (Lesson 5); Peer evaluation and feedback (Lesson 7); Working together (Review)

Values

Understanding the importance of helping at home

Cross-curricular links

Link to Science
The senses: Reviewing how our senses give us information about our environment
Suggested Arts and Crafts concepts
Exploring primary, secondary and tertiary colours and creating a still life

Key Competences and Key Learning Outcomes

- Identify and name household chores
- Say the vocabulary chant
- Write about chores you do and don't do
- Review rooms and objects in a house
- Ask and answer questions using a recycled structure
- Sing a song

Key language

- Household chores: *clear the table, cook dinner, dust, feed my pet, hoover the floor, lay the table, make my bed, tidy up, walk the dog, wash the car, wash up, water the plants*
- *We do (chores) (in the morning). What a (busy day)!*
- Extension: *brush the floor, clean the bathroom, fold the clothes, take out the rubbish, wash the clothes, wash the floor*
- Recycled: rooms in a house; household objects; *Do you (dust)? Yes, I do. No, I don't. When do you (dust)? I (dust) (at the weekend).*

Materials

- Pupil's Book p18; Activity Book p16; Class CD1; Teacher's App on Navio
- Teacher's Resource Bank: Household chores word cards
- Household chores flashcards
- Teacher's Resource Bank: Talk cards

Optional materials

- Teacher's Resource Bank: Trinity Exams Practice cards (selected from the Starter Unit and Unit 1)
- A piece of paper for each group

At a Glance Lesson Plan

Pupil's Book

Starting the lesson

- Use the Trinity Exams Practice cards (optional).
- Review rooms and objects in a house.
- Set learning outcomes and use the talk cards.

Activity 1

- How do you help at home?
- Make a list.

Vocabulary presentation

- Present the new vocabulary using the household chores flashcards.

Word cards

- Introduce the spellings of the vocabulary using the household chores word cards.

Activity 2

- Listen, point and say the vocabulary chant.

▶ *CD1 Track 29 p263*

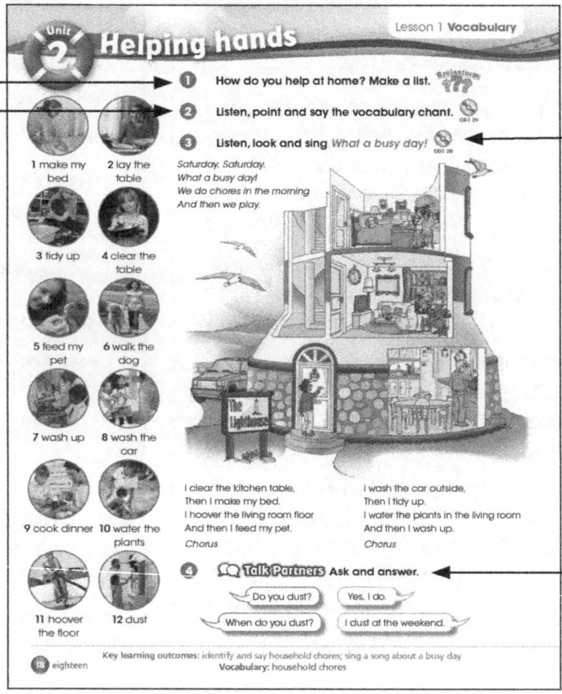

Activity 3

- Listen, look and sing *What a busy day!*

▶ *CD1 Track 30 p263*

Activity 4

- Ask and answer.
- Go to the Activity Book.

Ending the lesson

- Review the lesson and reflect on learning.

Extra activities

Extension

- Use a Venn diagram to categorise the chores.

Vocabulary extension

- Present six additional vocabulary items.

Activity Book

Activity Book

Activity 1

- Read and complete.

Activity 2

- Write about the chores you do and don't do.

Code activity

- Complete the code activity.

Digital resources

Teacher's Digital: You can also teach this lesson using the Teacher's App on Navio.

Pupil's Digital: Encourage your pupils to use the Pupil's App on Navio to practise the activities from this lesson.

Powered By NAVIO

Starting the lesson

Use the Trinity Exams Practice cards (optional).

- The pupils practise asking and answering questions.

Review rooms and objects in a house.

- Draw a house on the board and elicit the rooms, e.g. *living room, bedroom, kitchen, bathroom, dining room, garage.* Ask **Have you got a (kitchen) in your house? What do you do in the (living room)?**
- Organise the class into small groups and give each group a piece of paper with the name of a room at the top. The groups have two minutes to write the names of objects you can find in those rooms.
- Ask the groups to pass their piece of paper to the next group on the left. The pupils have two minutes to read the list of objects and add any other objects they know.
- Repeat two or three more times. Then return the papers to their original groups. Invite one pupil from each group to read out their list of words.

Set learning outcomes and use the talk cards.

- Say **Today we're going to learn the names of household chores.** Explain that household chores are jobs that you do in the house.
- Point to the talk cards to show the pupils the different ways they will be working in the lesson.

Pupil's Book Activity 1

How do you help at home? Make a list.

- (Books closed.) Ask **Do you help at home?** Encourage the pupils to say how they help and praise them for their efforts.
- Make a class list of the chores the pupils do.

Vocabulary presentation

- (Books closed.) Tell the class that you do lots of chores. Hold up the *make my bed* flashcard and say **I make my bed.** Prompt the class to mime the action and repeat the sentence. Stick the flashcard on the board.
- Repeat the procedure with the other flashcards.

Word cards

- (Books closed.) Hand out a household chores word card to each pair of pupils.
- The pairs take turns to come to the board, read out their household chore and stick their word card next to the corresponding flashcard.

Pupil's Book Activity 2

Listen, point and say the vocabulary chant.

▶ ***CD1 Track 29 p263***

- Focus the pupils' attention on the 12 photos. Say **Let's listen and say the words.** Play the CD. The pupils listen, point and repeat.

Pupil's Book Activity 3

Listen, look and sing *What a busy day!*

▶ ***CD1 Track 30 p263***

- Focus the pupils' attention on the scene. Ask **What rooms can you see in the lighthouse?** (*Kitchen, living room, bedroom.*) **Where's Lily?** (*In her bedroom.*) **What's she doing?** (*Feeding her pet goldfish.*) Repeat the questions for Josh and Dad.
- Say **Let's listen to the song.** Play the CD. The pupils listen and read.
- Play the CD again. The pupils join in, singing the song and doing the corresponding actions.

Pupil's Book Activity 4

Ask and answer.

- Ask two pupils to read out the speech bubbles. Prompt the pair to have a similar exchange about another chore.
- Working with a Talk Partner, the pupils point to each of the 12 chores and ask and answer the questions.

Activity Book

Activity 1

Read and complete.

- Ask different pupils to read out and complete the information in the first note. The pupils then work on their own or in pairs to complete the activity.

Answers: **1** make **2** feed **3** hoover **4** lay **5** cook **6** walk **7** tidy **8** wash **9** water **10** dust **11** clear **12** wash

Activity 2

Write about the chores you do and don't do.

- Ask the class to read out the words in the word box. Invite pupils to say which chores they do and don't do.
- The pupils write their sentences. Then they read them out to a Talk Partner.

Code activity

- The pupils complete the code activity.

Answer: canteen

Ending the lesson

Review the lesson and reflect on learning.

- Say **Today we've learnt the names of chores. What household chores do you remember?** Elicit the chores from the pupils.
- Ask **Which was your favourite activity today? Which activity was easy / difficult?**

Extra activities

Extension

- Draw a simple Venn diagram on the board with two circles labelled 'Inside' and 'Outside'. Hold up a household chores flashcard and ask **Do you (wash the car) inside or outside the house?** Stick the flashcard on the diagram. Repeat with the other flashcards.

Vocabulary extension

- Present six additional chores: *brush the floor, clean the bathroom, fold the clothes, take out the rubbish, wash the clothes, wash the floor.*
- Use the Vocabulary Booster on Navio to practise these new words.

Key Competences and Key Learning Outcomes

- Listen, repeat and act out a conversation
- Listen, follow the grammar table and identify the parts of a sentence
- Talk about household chores in the present simple using adverbs of frequency

Key language

- *fair, friend, routines*
- *My (dad) always / often / sometimes / never (washes up). My (sister) doesn't (cook). Does your sister (wash up)? Yes, she does. No, she doesn't.*
- Recycled: *clear the table, cook dinner, dust, feed my pet, hoover the floor, lay the table, make my bed, tidy up, walk the dog, wash the car, wash up, water the plants;* family members

Materials

- Pupil's Book p19; Activity Book p17; Class CD1; Teacher's App on Navio
- Household chores flashcards
- Teacher's Resource Bank: Talk cards

Optional materials

- Teacher's Resource Bank: Trinity Exams Practice cards (selected from the Starter Unit and Unit 1)

At a Glance Lesson Plan

Pupil's Book

Starting the lesson

- Use the Trinity Exams Practice cards (optional).
- **Think-Pair-Share.** Review household chores vocabulary.
- Review the *What a busy day!* song.

▶ *CD1 Track 30 p263*

▶ *CD1 Track 31 p263*

- Set learning outcomes and use the talk cards.

Activity 1

- Listen and read.
- Listen and repeat.

▶ *CD1 Track 32 p263*

- Act out.

Activity 2

- Read again.
- What does Lily do at home?
- And Josh?

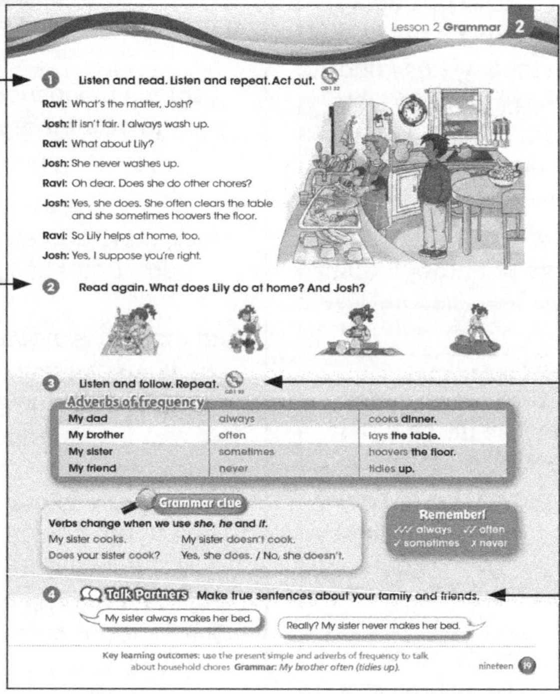

Lesson 2 Grammar 2

1 Listen and read. Listen and repeat. Act out.

Ravi: What's the matter, Josh?
Josh: It isn't fair. I always wash up.
Ravi: What about Lily?
Josh: She never washes up.
Ravi: Oh dear. Does she do other chores?
Josh: Yes, she does. She often clears the table and she sometimes hoovers the floor.
Ravi: So Lily helps at home, too.
Josh: Yes, I suppose you're right.

2 Read again. What does Lily do at home? And Josh?

3 Listen and follow. Repeat.

Adverbs of frequency

My dad	always	cooks dinner.
My brother	often	lays the table.
My sister	sometimes	hoovers the floor.
My friend	never	tidies up.

Grammar clue

Verbs change when we use *she, he* and *it.*
My sister cooks. My sister doesn't cook.
Does your sister cook? Yes, she does. / No, she doesn't.

Remember!
✓✓✓ always ✓✓ often
✓ sometimes ✗ never

4 Talk Partners Make true sentences about your family and friends.

My sister always makes her bed.
Really? My sister never makes her bed.

Key learning outcomes: use the present simple and adverbs of frequency to talk about household chores. Grammar: *My brother often (tidies up).*

nineteen 19

Activity 3

- Listen and follow.

▶ *CD1 Track 33 p263*

- Repeat.
- **Grammar clue:** Read about how verbs change when we use *she, he* and *it*.

Activity 4

- Make true sentences about your family and friends.

Go to the Activity Book.

Ending the lesson

- Review the lesson and reflect on learning.

Extra activity

Reinforcement

- Play a mime game to review chores we do at the weekend.

Activity Book

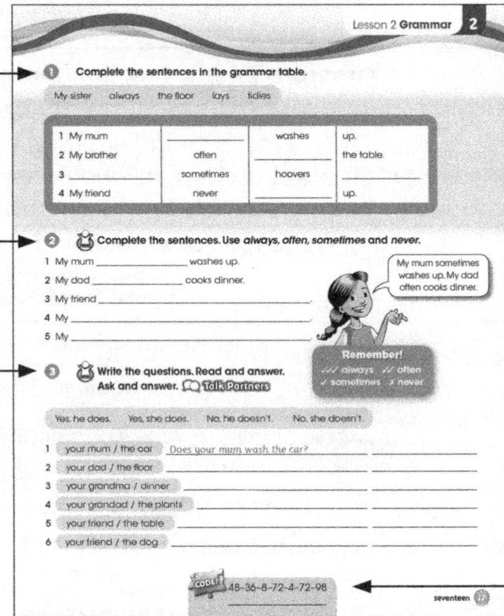

Lesson 2 Grammar 2

1 Complete the sentences in the grammar table.

My sister always the floor lays tidies

1 My mum	______	washes	up.
2 My brother	often	______	the table.
3 ______	sometimes	hoovers	______
4 My friend	never	______	up.

2 Complete the sentences. Use *always, often, sometimes* and *never.*

1 My mum ______ washes up.
2 My dad ______ cooks dinner.
3 My friend ______
4 My ______
5 My ______

My mum sometimes washes up. My dad often cooks dinner.

3 Write the questions. Read and answer. Ask and answer. Talk Partners

Remember!
✓✓✓ always ✓✓ often
✓ sometimes ✗ never

Yes, he does. Yes, she does. No, he doesn't. No, she doesn't.

1 your mum / the car — Does your mum wash the car?
2 your dad / the floor
3 your grandma / dinner
4 your grandad / the plants
5 your friend / the table
6 your friend / the dog

Code! 48-36-8-72-4-72-98

seventeen 17

Activity Book

Activity 1

- Complete the sentences in the grammar table.

Activity 2

- Complete the sentences. Use *always, often, sometimes* and *never.*

Activity 3

- Write the questions.
- Read and answer.
- Ask and answer.

Code activity

- Complete the code activity.

Digital resources

Teacher's Digital: You can also teach this lesson using the Teacher's App on Navio.

Pupil's Digital: Encourage your pupils to use the Pupil's App on Navio to practise the activities from this lesson.

Powered By NAVIO

Starting the lesson

Use the Trinity Exams Practice cards (optional).

- The pupils practise asking and answering questions.

Think-Pair-Share. Review household chores vocabulary.

- Ask **Can you remember the household chores vocabulary?** The class thinks silently for a minute.
- Then the pupils work with a Talk Partner to name the household chores.
- Invite different Talk Partners to say a different household chore. Hold up the corresponding flashcard and prompt the class to repeat the words.

Review the *What a busy day!* song.

▶ ***CD1 Track 30 p263***

▶ ***CD1 Track 31 p263 (optional karaoke version)***

- Play the CD (or use the karaoke version). The pupils sing and do the actions.

Set learning outcomes and use the talk cards.

- Say **Today we're going to talk about who does the chores in your family.**
- Point to the talk cards to show the pupils the different ways they will be working in the lesson.

Pupil's Book Activity 1

Listen and read. Listen and repeat. Act out.

▶ ***CD1 Track 32 p263***

- The pupils look at the picture. Ask **What's Josh doing? Is he happy?**
- Play the CD. The pupils listen and read the conversation.
- Ask **Does Josh do chores? Does Lily do chores? Is it fair?**
- Play the CD again, pausing after each sentence for the pupils to repeat.
- The pupils act out the conversation in pairs.

Pupil's Book Activity 2

Read again. What does Lily do at home? And Josh?

- The pupils read the conversation again and say what Lily and Josh do at home.

Pupil's Book Activity 3

Listen and follow. Repeat.

▶ ***CD1 Track 33 p263***

- Play the CD. The pupils listen to the first sentence and point to the words they hear. They then repeat the complete sentence. Repeat the procedure with the other sentences.
- Read the *Remember!* tip. Then invite different pupils to make true sentences using the grammar table.

Grammar clue

- Read the grammar clue as a class. Highlight that we add 's' to most verbs in the third-person singular, but when a verb finishes in 's', 'ss', 'sh', 'ch', 'x' or 'o', we add 'es', and when a verb finishes in a consonant + 'y', we add 'ies'.

Pupil's Book Activity 4

Make true sentences about your family and friends.

- The pupils work in pairs to make true sentences about their family and friends.

Activity Book

Activity 1

Complete the sentences in the grammar table.

- Invite a pupil to read out the words in the word box.
- The pupils work on their own or with a partner to complete the sentences in the grammar table.

Answers: **1** always **2** lays **3** My sister, the floor **4** tidies

Activity 2

Complete the sentences. Use *always, often, sometimes* and *never.*

- Ask a pupil to read out the speech bubble.
- Invite different pupils to complete the first two sentences using adverbs of frequency.
- The pupils work on their own to complete the sentences in their Activity Books. Point out that the last two sentences should be about family members.

Activity 3

Write the questions. Read and answer. Ask and answer.

- Invite a pupil to read out the model question and to give their answer. If necessary, show the pupils how to refer to the grammar table in Activity 1 to check the order of words.
- The pupils write questions and answers using the prompts and the words in the word box.
- The pupils ask and answer the questions with a Talk Partner.

Answers: **1** Does your mum wash the car? **2** Does your dad hoover the floor? **3** Does your grandma cook dinner? **4** Does your grandad water the plants? **5** Does your friend lay / clear the table? **6** Does your friend walk the dog?

Code activity

- The pupils complete the code activity.

Answer: library

Ending the lesson

Review the lesson and reflect on learning.

- Say **Today we've learnt how to say who does the chores in our family.** Invite different pupils to say a sentence about their family.
- Ask **Which was your favourite activity today? Which activity was easy / difficult?**

Extra activity

Reinforcement

- Invite a pupil to the front of the class. Ask him / her to mime an activity that he / she does at the weekend. Ask **What does (Carmen) do at the weekend?** The rest of the class attempts to identify the activity, e.g. *She goes shopping.* Repeat with different individual pupils.

Key Competences and Key Learning Outcomes
• Read, listen and understand a story about a secret tunnel
• Use a code to read a message • Review how our senses give us information about our environment (optional)
• Do a pre-reading task
• Understand the importance of helping at home
• Understand, enjoy and act out the story • Give an opinion on the story

Key language

- *cave, curtain, dark, explore, ghost, secret tunnel, shadow, surprise, wet*
- *I practise here (once a week). Are you ready to (play)? Not yet. I need to (hoover the floor). Is it (scary)?*
- Recycled: *drums, hoover the floor, living room; Does (Josh) (play the drums)? No, he doesn't. Yes, he does. Grandad (always) (tidies up on Saturday morning).*

Materials

- Pupil's Book pp20–21; Activity Book p18; Class CD1; Teacher's App on Navio
- Teacher's Resource Bank: Talk cards

Optional materials

- Teacher's Resource Bank: Trinity Exams Practice cards (selected from the Starter Unit and Unit 1)

At a Glance Lesson Plan

Starting the lesson

- Use the Trinity Exams Practice cards (optional).
- Review household chores.
- Set learning outcomes and use the talk cards.

Before you read: Activity 1

- Use the code to read the message from Luke.

Activity 2

- Listen and read.
- ▶ *CD1 Track 34 p263*
- Act out.

After you read: Activity 3

- Ask and answer.

Activity 4: Values

- Read and discuss.
- Go to the Activity Book.

Pupil's Book

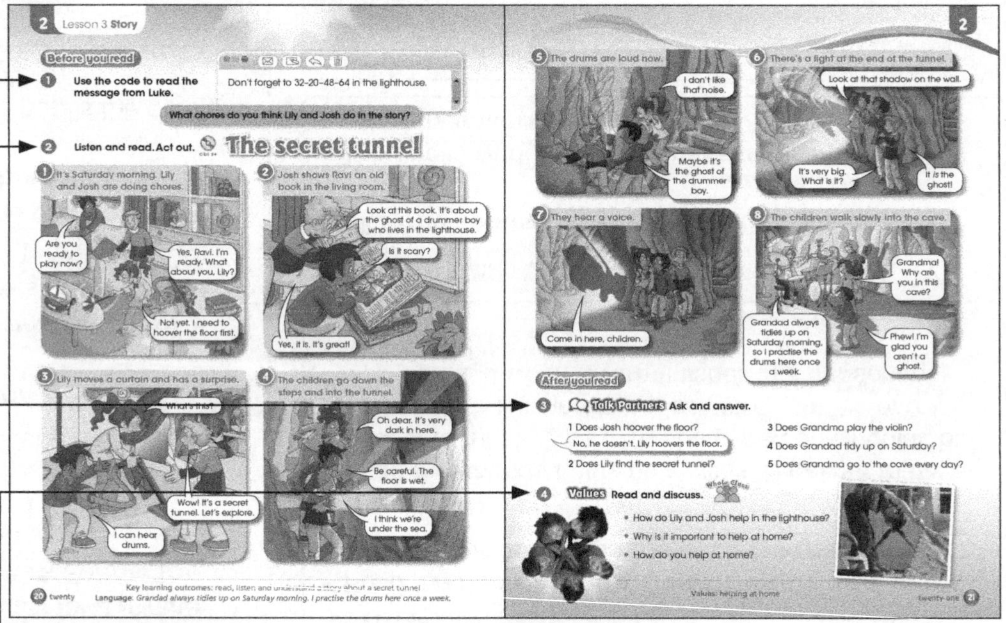

Ending the lesson

- Review the lesson and reflect on learning.

Extra activity

Reinforcement

- Find the character.

Activity Book

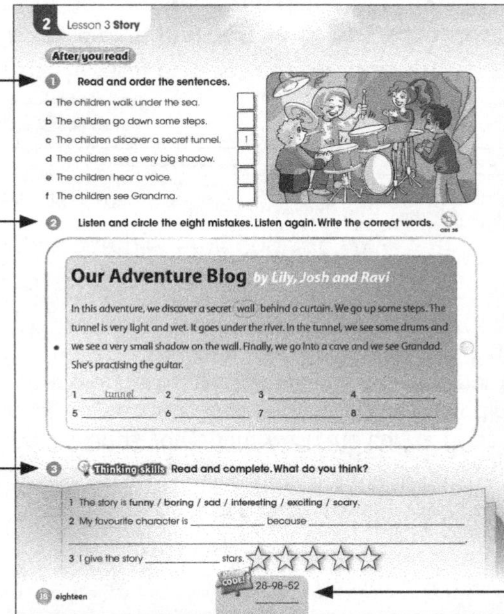

After you read: Activity Book

Activity 1

- Read and order the sentences.

Activity 2

- Listen and circle the eight mistakes.
- ▶ *CD1 Track 35 p263*
- Listen again.
- Write the correct words.

Activity 3

- Read and complete.
- What do you think?

Code activity

- Complete the code activity.

Digital resources

Teacher's Digital: You can also teach this lesson using the Teacher's App on Navio.

Pupil's Digital: Encourage your pupils to use the Pupil's App on Navio to practise the activities from this lesson.

Powered By NAVIO

Link to Science

- **The senses:** Review how our senses give us information about our environment.

Starting the lesson

Use the Trinity Exams Practice cards (optional).

- The pupils practise asking and answering questions.

Review household chores.

- Invite a pupil to the front of the class. Ask **Does (Maria) wash up?** The rest of the class guesses *Yes, she does. / No, she doesn't.* The pupil at the front then answers. Repeat with another pupil.

Set learning outcomes and use the talk cards.

- Say **Today we're going to read and listen to a story.**
- Point to the talk cards to show the pupils the different ways they will be working in the lesson.

Before you read: Pupil's Book Activity 1

Use the code to read the message from Luke.

- Say **Josh and Lily have received a message from Luke.** Ask the pupils to use the code (Pupil's Book page 7) to discover the mystery word (*help*).
- Ask **What chores do you think Lily and Josh do in the story?** The pupils make predictions.

Pupil's Book Activity 2

Listen and read. Act out.

▶ *CD1 Track 34 p263*

- Play the CD. The pupils follow in their books.
- Ask questions to check comprehension.

Suggested comprehension questions

- Frame 1: **What do Ravi and Josh want to do?** (*Play.*) **What does Lily need to do?** (*Hoover the floor.*)
- Frame 2: **What do Josh and Ravi look at?** (*An old book.*)
- Frame 3: **Where's the tunnel?** (*Behind a curtain.*)
- Frame 4: **Where do the children go?** (*Down the steps and into the tunnel.*)
- Frame 5: **What can the children hear?** (*Drums.*)
- Frame 6: **What do the children see?** (*A shadow.*)
- Frame 7: **What do the children hear?** (*A voice.*)
- Frame 8: **Who's in the cave?** (*Grandma.*) **What's she doing?** (*Practising the drums.*)

- Organise the class into four groups (Lily, Ravi, Josh and Grandma) and play the CD. Each group joins in when their character speaks. If pupils need extra support, pause the CD after each utterance and ask them to repeat it.
- Repeat, with groups swapping roles.

After you read: Pupil's Book Activity 3

Ask and answer.

- Invite pupils to ask and answer the questions.
- Organise the class into Talk Partners to practise asking and answering the questions. They can do this orally or in their notebooks.

Answers: **1** No, he doesn't. Lily hoovers the floor. **2** Yes, she does. **3** No, she doesn't. She plays the drums. **4** Yes, he does. **5** No, she doesn't. She goes to the cave once a week.

Pupil's Book Activity 4: Values

Read and discuss.

- Read out the questions and discuss them as a class.
- Prompt the pupils to say which chores they like and don't like. Ask **Is it important to help at home?**

After you read: Activity Book

Activity 1

Read and order the sentences.

- Read out the sentences. The pupils follow in their books.
- Read out the sentence that comes first and ask the class to identify the next sentence.
- The pupils work on their own or in pairs to number the remaining sentences.

Answers: **a** 3 **b** 2 **c** 1 **d** 4 **e** 5 **f** 6

Activity 2

Listen and circle the eight mistakes. Listen again. Write the correct words.

▶ *CD1 Track 35 p263*

- Play the CD. The pupils circle the mistakes.
- Play the CD again. The pupils write the correct words.

Answers: **1** ~~wall~~ tunnel **2** ~~up~~ down **3** ~~light~~ dark **4** ~~river~~ sea **5** ~~see~~ hear **6** ~~small~~ big **7** ~~Grandad~~ Grandma **8** ~~guitar~~ drums

Activity 3

Read and complete. What do you think?

- Invite pupils to read out and complete the sentences.
- The pupils complete the task in their Activity Books and then share opinions with a Talk Partner.

Code activity

- The pupils complete the code activity.

Answer: gym

Ending the lesson

Review the lesson and reflect on learning.

- Say **Today we've listened to a story about a secret tunnel.**
- Retell the story as a class. Say **Let's tell the story together.** Prompt the pupils by saying **Lily needs to …** (*hoover the floor*). **Ravi and Josh read …** (*a book*). Use mime, gesture and drawings to support the class.
- Ask **Which was your favourite activity today? Which activity was easy / difficult?**

Extra activity

Reinforcement

- Read out one of the speech bubbles from the story. The pupils find the text and say the name of the character who said the words.

Link to Science

- If you are studying the Science topic of **The senses** in English, use the story to review how our senses give us information about our environment. Ask **Which senses do the children use?** Ask the class to name the other senses. Then ask the pupils to imagine that they are outside the cave, next to the sea. Elicit what they can see, smell, touch, taste and hear.

Key Competences and Key Learning Outcomes

- Identify and say free-time activities
- Follow and correct the grammar tables
- Ask and answer questions about frequency of free-time activities

- Sing a song

Key language

- Free-time activities: *do puzzles, draw pictures, play board games, play computer games, read comics, watch DVDs; after school, at the weekend, every day, never, once / twice / three times a week; free time*
- *How often does (your sister) (do puzzles)? She (does puzzles) (twice a week).*
- Extension: *go for a walk, go ice-skating, go shopping, listen to the radio*
- Recycled: days of the week

Materials

- Pupil's Book p22; Activity Book p19; Class CD1; Teacher's App on Navio
- Teacher's Resource Bank: Talk cards

Optional materials

- Teacher's Resource Bank: Trinity Exams Practice cards (selected from the Starter Unit and Unit 1)

At a Glance Lesson Plan

Pupil's Book

Starting the lesson

- Use the Trinity Exams Practice cards (optional).
- Review free-time activities.
- Play *Two truths and a lie*.
- Set learning outcomes and use the talk cards.

Activity 1

- Listen, point and say.

▶ *CD1 Track 36 p264*

Activity 2

- Listen and sing *Free time*.

▶ *CD1 Track 37 p264*

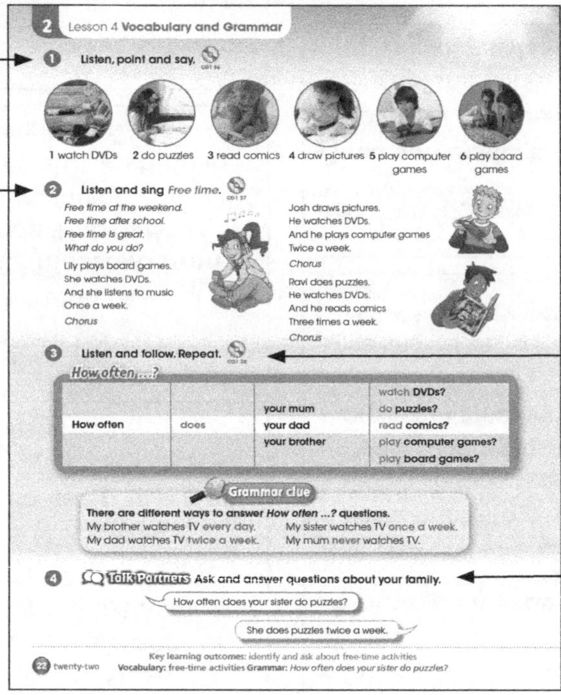
2 Lesson 4 Vocabulary and Grammar

1 Listen, point and say.

1 watch DVDs 2 do puzzles 3 read comics 4 draw pictures 5 play computer games 6 play board games

2 Listen and sing *Free time.*

Free time at the weekend.
Free time after school.
Free time is great.
What do you do?
Lily plays board games.
She watches DVDs.
And she listens to music
Once a week.
Chorus

Josh draws pictures.
He watches DVDs.
And he plays computer games
Twice a week.
Chorus
Ravi does puzzles.
He watches DVDs.
And he reads comics
Three times a week.
Chorus

3 Listen and follow. Repeat.

How often ...?

How often	does	your mum	watch DVDs?
		your dad	do puzzles?
		your brother	read comics?
			play computer games?
			play board games?

Grammar clue

There are different ways to answer *How often ...?* questions.
My brother watches TV every day. My sister watches TV once a week.
My dad watches TV twice a week. My mum never watches TV.

4 Talk Partners Ask and answer questions about your family.

How often does your sister do puzzles?

She does puzzles twice a week.

22 twenty-two

Key learning outcomes: identify and ask about free-time activities
Vocabulary: free-time activities Grammar: *How often does your sister do puzzles?*

Activity 3

- Listen and follow.

▶ *CD1 Track 38 p264*

- Repeat.
- **Grammar clue**: Read about different ways to answer *How often ...?* questions.

Activity 4

- Ask and answer questions about your family.

Go to the Activity Book.

Ending the lesson

- Review the lesson and reflect on learning.

Extra activities

Reinforcement

- Talk about how often you do things at school.

Vocabulary extension

- Present four additional vocabulary items.

Activity Book

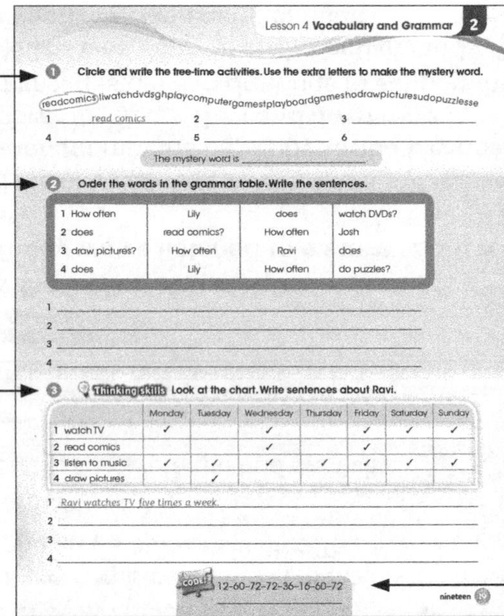
Lesson 4 Vocabulary and Grammar 2

1 Circle and write the free-time activities. Use the extra letters to make the mystery word.

readcomicsliwatchdvdsghplaycomputergamesplayboardgameshodrawpicturesudopuzzlesse

1 read comics 2 ____ 3 ____
4 ____ 5 ____ 6 ____

The mystery word is ____

2 Order the words in the grammar table. Write the sentences.

1 How often	Lily	does	watch DVDs?
2 does	read comics?	How often	Josh
3 draw pictures?	How often	Ravi	does
4 does	Lily	How often	do puzzles?

1 ____
2 ____
3 ____
4 ____

3 Thinking skills Look at the chart. Write sentences about Ravi.

	Monday	Tuesday	Wednesday	Thursday	Friday	Saturday	Sunday
1 watch TV	✓		✓		✓	✓	✓
2 read comics			✓		✓		
3 listen to music	✓	✓	✓	✓	✓	✓	✓
4 draw pictures		✓					

1 Ravi watches TV five times a week.
2 ____
3 ____
4 ____

Code 12-60-72-72-36-16-60-72

nineteen 19

Activity Book

Activity 1

- Circle and write the free-time activities.
- Use the extra letters to make the mystery word.

Activity 2

- Order the words in the grammar table.
- Write the sentences.

Activity 3

- Look at the chart.
- Write sentences about Ravi.

Code activity

- Complete the code activity.

Digital resources

Teacher's Digital: You can also teach this lesson using the Teacher's App on Navio.

Pupil's Digital: Encourage your pupils to use the Pupil's App on Navio to practise the activities from this lesson.

Powered By NAVIO

Starting the lesson

Use the Trinity Exams Practice cards (optional).

- The pupils practise asking and answering questions.

Review free-time activities.

- Ask **What activities do you do in your free time?** Prompt the class to list the free-time activities they do and, if necessary, write the words on the board.
- Play *Two truths and a lie*. Say **Listen to my information. I (play tennis) at the weekend. I (watch TV) at night. I (ride a horse) on Saturdays. One sentence is false. Which sentence is false?** Encourage the class to guess the false information. Then tell them which sentence is untrue.
- Invite different pupils to take your role. The pupils can also do the activity with a Talk Partner.

Set learning outcomes and use the talk cards.

- Say **Today we're going to learn the names of some more free-time activities.**
- Point to the talk cards to show the pupils the different ways they will be working in the lesson.

Pupil's Book Activity 1

Listen, point and say.

▶ ***CD1 Track 36 p264***

- Point to the first picture and say **Look. He's watching DVDs.** Ask **Do you watch DVDs in your free time?** Prompt the class to answer and then repeat the name of the activity. Repeat the procedure with the other free-time activities.
- Play the CD. The pupils listen, point and repeat.

Pupil's Book Activity 2

Listen and sing *Free time.*

▶ ***CD1 Track 37 p264***

- Focus the class on the activity and ask **What's Josh doing?** (*Playing a computer game.*) Repeat the question for Lily and Ravi.
- Play the CD. The pupils listen and read.
- Play the CD again. The pupils join in singing the song and doing the actions.
- Ask **Does Lily listen to music every day?** (*No.*) **How often does she listen to music?** Hold up one finger and say **She listens to music once a week.** Repeat the procedure with the other characters.

Pupil's Book Activity 3

Listen and follow. Repeat.

▶ ***CD1 Track 38 p264***

- Focus the class on the grammar table.
- Play the CD. The pupils listen to the first sentence and point to the corresponding parts of the sentence. The pupils repeat the complete sentence. Repeat the procedure with the other sentences.

Grammar clue

- Read about different ways to answer *How often …?* questions. Encourage the pupils to make and answer questions as a class.

Pupil's Book Activity 4

Ask and answer questions about your family.

- Organise the class into Talk Partners. The pupils take turns to ask and answer questions.

Activity Book

Activity 1

Circle and write the free-time activities. Use the extra letters to make the mystery word.

- The pupils circle the free-time activities in the word snake, then write the words on their own.
- The pupils identify the extra letters to make the mystery word.

Answers: **1** read comics **2** watch DVDs **3** play computer games **4** play board games **5** draw pictures **6** do puzzles The mystery word is lighthouse.

Activity 2

Order the words in the grammar table. Write the sentences.

- Explain that the grammar table is mixed up and that the pupils need to reorder the words. Invite a pupil to read out the first sentence.
- The pupils order and write the remaining sentences. If they need more support, remind them that a sentence begins with a capital letter and ends with a full stop.

Answers: **1** How often does Lily watch DVDs? **2** How often does Josh read comics? **3** How often does Ravi draw pictures? **4** How often does Lily do puzzles?

Activity 3

Look at the chart. Write sentences about Ravi.

- Quickly review the days of the week. Then point to the chart and ask **How often does Ravi watch TV?** Repeat the procedure with the other activities.
- The pupils write the sentences about Ravi.

Answers: **1** Ravi watches TV five times a week. **2** Ravi reads comics twice a week. **3** Ravi listens to music every day. **4** Ravi draws pictures once a week.

Code activity

- The pupils complete the code activity.

Answer: corridor

Ending the lesson

Review the lesson and reflect on learning.

- Say **Today we've learnt some new free-time activities. What activities are they?**
- Ask **Which was your favourite activity today? Which activity was easy / difficult?**

Extra activities

Reinforcement

- Ask the pupils to take out their timetables, then ask **How often do you study (Maths)?** The class counts the lessons and responds. Repeat the procedure with other subjects and activities. Then invite individual pupils to ask their own questions.

Vocabulary extension

- Use the Vocabulary Booster on Navio and present and practise four additional free-time activities: *go for a walk, go ice-skating, go shopping, listen to the radio.*

Key Competences and Key Learning Outcomes

- Say a tongue twister with the 'ch' sound
- Practise spelling and learn an alternative spelling for the 'ch' sound
- Listen for specific information

- Play a communication game using adverbs of frequency

Key language

- *beach, catch, chair, chicken, chop, chore, kitchen, pitch, torch, watch, witch*
- *How often do you (wash the car)? I (never) (wash the car). I (make my bed) (every day). (Marcus) (makes his bed) (every day).*
- Recycled: *hoover the floor, lay the table, make your bed, tidy up, wash the car, water the plants; every day, never, once / twice / three times a week*

Materials

- Pupil's Book p23; Activity Book p20; Class CD1; Teacher's App on Navio
- Teacher's Resource Bank: Talk cards
- Teacher's Resource Bank: Unit 2 Lesson 5 Communication Activity

Optional materials

- Teacher's Resource Bank: Trinity Exams Practice cards (selected from the Starter Unit and Unit 1)
- Household chores flashcards

At a Glance Lesson Plan

Pupil's Book

Starting the lesson

- Use the Trinity Exams Practice cards (optional).
- **Think-Pair-Share.** Review free-time activities.
- Review the *Free time* song.

▶ *CD1 Track 37 p264*

- Set learning outcomes and use the talk cards.

Activity 1: Speak and spell

- Listen, read and say.

▶ *CD1 Track 39 p264*

Go to the Activity Book.

Activity 2

- Read the questionnaire.

▶ *CD1 Track 40 p264*

- Listen and identify four differences.

Lesson 5 Listening and Speaking 2

1 Listen, read and say.

Speak and spell

The witch chops chicken in the kitchen.

Now practise spelling on page 20 in your Activity Book.

2 Read the questionnaire. Listen and identify four differences.

	never	once a week	twice a week	three times a week	every day
clear the table?				✓	
feed your pet?					✓
walk the dog?			✓		
wash up?	✓				
cook dinner?		✓			

3 Talk Partners Ask and answer to complete the questionnaire. Tick (✓). Tell a friend.

Key learning outcomes: listen for specific information; play a communication game using adverbs of frequency. Phonics: alternative spelling for the 'ch' sound

twenty-three 23

Activity 3

- Ask and answer to complete the questionnaire.
- Tick (✓).
- Tell a friend (Teacher's Resource Bank: Unit 2).

Ending the lesson

- Review the lesson and reflect on learning.

Extra activities

Reinforcement

- Create your own tongue twister.
- Play *Disappearing flashcards*.

Activity Book

2 Lesson 5 Speaking and Spelling

1 Complete and say.

2 Find and circle the words. Classify and write.

3 Talk Partners Test your friend. Ask and answer.

20 twenty

Activity Book

Activity 1: Speak and spell

- Complete and say.

Activity 2

- Find and circle the words.
- Classify and write.

Activity 3

- Test your friend.
- Ask and answer.

Code activity

- Complete the code activity.

Digital resources

Teacher's Digital: You can also teach this lesson using the Teacher's App on Navio.

Pupil's Digital: Encourage your pupils to use the Pupil's App on Navio to practise the activities from this lesson.

Powered By NAVIO

Starting the lesson

Use the Trinity Exams Practice cards (optional).

- The pupils practise asking and answering questions.

Think-Pair-Share. Review free-time activities.

- Ask **Can you remember the free-time activities vocabulary?** The class thinks silently for a minute.
- Then the pupils work with a Talk Partner to name the free-time activities.
- Invite different Talk Partners to say a different free-time activity.
- Finally, repeat the procedure, asking different pairs of Talk Partners each time, until all the free-time activities have been named.

Review the *Free time* song.

▶ *CD1 Track 37 p264*

- Play the CD. The pupils join in singing and doing the actions.

Set learning outcomes and use the talk cards.

- Say **Today we're going to say a tongue twister, practise spelling and complete a questionnaire.**
- Point to the talk cards to show the pupils the different ways they will be working in the lesson.

Pupil's Book Activity 1: Speak and spell

Listen, read and say.

▶ *CD1 Track 39 p264*

- (Books closed.) Write the letters 'ch' on the board and ask **What sound do these letters make?** (*'ch'*) List the words the pupils know with this sound, e.g. *chicken, chips, cheese.* Say **Today you're going to learn another way of writing the 'ch' sound.**
- (Books open.) Focus the class on the picture. Ask **What can you see here? What's the witch doing?** Confirm that she's cooking and use mime to explain the verb 'chop'.
- Say **Let's listen to the tongue twister.** Play the CD. The pupils follow the text in their books.
- Play the CD again. The pupils join in with the tongue twister.
- Finally, ask the class to identify the alternative way of writing the 'ch' sound ('tch').

Activity Book

Activity 1: Speak and spell

Complete and say.

- The pupils complete and say the words in the tongue twister.

Answer: The witch chops chicken in the kitchen.

Activity 2

Find and circle the words. Classify and write.

- The pupils find and circle the words in the border that contain the 'ch' sound.
- The pupils classify and write the words according to whether they are written with 'ch' or 'tch'.

Answers: ch: chair, chicken, chore, beach, torch
tch: witch, kitchen, pitch, catch, watch

Activity 3

Talk Partners. Test your friend. Ask and answer.

- Invite two pupils to read out the speech bubbles.
- Organise the pupils into Talk Partners. The pupils take it in turns to spell out and identify the words in Activity 2. Stress the importance of prompting, encouraging and helping each other.

Code activity CODE!

- The pupils complete the code activity.

Answer: playground

Pupil's Book Activity 2

Read the questionnaire. Listen and identify four differences.

▶ *CD1 Track 40 p264*

- Focus the pupils on the questionnaire and ask **How often does Marc clear the table?** Play the CD, pausing after Marc answers the question. The pupils look at the chart again to check if this is correct. Elicit that the chart is incorrect, and that Marc clears the table twice a week.
- Repeat the procedure with the other chores.
- Elicit the four differences between the CD and the chart from the class.

Answers: Marc clears the table twice a week. He never walks the dog. He washes up every day. He helps cook dinner once a week.

Pupil's Book Activity 3

Ask and answer to complete the questionnaire. Tick (✓). Tell a friend (Teacher's Resource Bank: Unit 2).

- Invite two pupils to read out the speech bubbles. Explain to the pupils that they are going to do a questionnaire.
- Organise the class into Talk Partners. Pupil A uses questionnaire 1 and Pupil B uses questionnaire 2. The pupils should take turns to ask and answer the questions.
- When the pupils have completed the questionnaire, invite individual pupils to report what they have learnt about their partner. If necessary, highlight that we use 'his' for boys and 'her' for girls (*tidies up his bedroom, makes her bed*).
- Organise the class into new pairs. The pupils should report on the information in the questionnaire.

Ending the lesson

Review the lesson and reflect on learning.

- Say **Today we've practised a tongue twister.** Elicit the tongue twister from the pupils.
- Ask **Which was your favourite activity today? Which activity was easy / difficult?**

Extra activities

Reinforcement

- Organise the class into pairs and ask them to invent a new tongue twister to practise the 'ch' sound. The pupils should practise the tongue twister in their pairs. If time permits, invite different pairs of pupils to teach the rest of the class their tongue twister.
- Play *Disappearing flashcards* (see p27) with the household chores flashcards.

Key Competences and Key Learning Outcomes

- Identify the message of the fable
- Read the text for general understanding
- Scan the text for specific information

- Read and understand a fable
- Order and act out the story conversation

Key language

- *beans, clever, climbs out, cooking, fall, greedy, honey, hungry, idea, lazy, pull, surprised, web*
- *(Pull this web) when (lunch is ready). They smell (delicious). What are you (cooking)? I'm (cooking vegetables). Do you want (to have lunch) with me?*
- Recycled: *chores, delicious, help, legs, long, lunchtime, monkey, rabbit, river, spider, thin, vegetables*

Materials

- Pupil's Book p24; Activity Book p21; Class CD1; Teacher's App on Navio
- Teacher's Resource Bank: Talk cards

Optional materials

- Teacher's Resource Bank: Trinity Exams Practice cards (selected from the Starter Unit and Unit 1)

At a Glance Lesson Plan

Pupil's Book

Starting the lesson

- Use the Trinity Exams Practice cards (optional).
- Review the tongue twister.
- ▶ *CD1 Track 39 p264*
- Set learning outcomes and use the talk cards.

Before you read: Activity 1

- When and where do you listen to stories?
- Can we learn things from stories?

Activity 2: Before you read

- Read the title of the fable.
- Who do you think Anansi is?

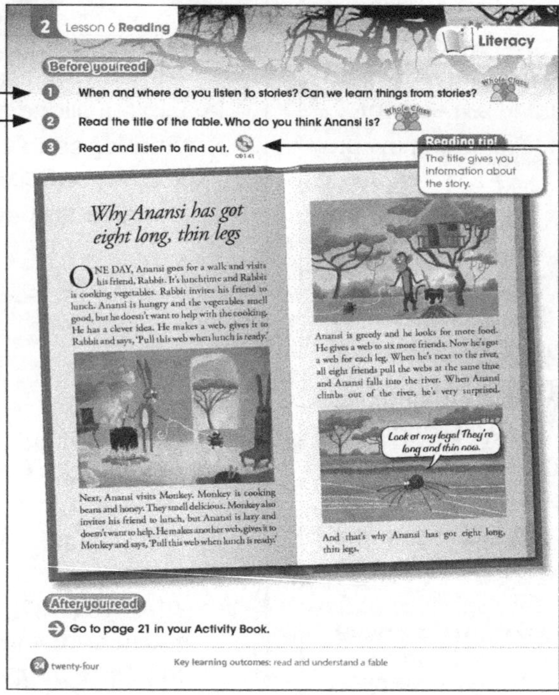

2 Lesson 6 **Reading** Literacy

Before you read

1 When and where do you listen to stories? Can we learn things from stories?

2 Read the title of the fable. Who do you think Anansi is?

3 Read and listen to find out. CD1 41

Reading tip! The title gives you information about the story.

Why Anansi has got eight long, thin legs

ONE DAY, Anansi goes for a walk and visits his friend, Rabbit. It's lunchtime and Rabbit is cooking vegetables. Rabbit invites his friend to lunch. Anansi is hungry and the vegetables smell good, but he doesn't want to help with the cooking. He has a clever idea. He makes a web, gives it to Rabbit and says, 'Pull this web when lunch is ready.'

Next, Anansi visits Monkey. Monkey is cooking beans and honey. They smell delicious. Monkey also invites his friend to lunch, but Anansi is lazy and doesn't want to help. He makes another web, gives it to Monkey and says, 'Pull this web when lunch is ready.'

Anansi is greedy and he looks for more food. He gives a web to six more friends. Now he's got a web for each leg. When he's next to the river, all eight friends pull the webs at the same time and Anansi falls into the river. When Anansi climbs out of the river, he's very surprised.

Look at my legs! They're long and thin now.

And that's why Anansi has got eight long, thin legs.

After you read

Go to page 21 in your Activity Book.

24 twenty-four Key learning outcomes: read and understand a fable

Activity 3

- Read and listen to find out.
- ▶ *CD1 Track 41 p264*
- Go to the Activity Book.

Ending the lesson

- Review the lesson and reflect on learning.

Extra activity

Reinforcement

- Watch an animated version of the fable online.

Activity Book

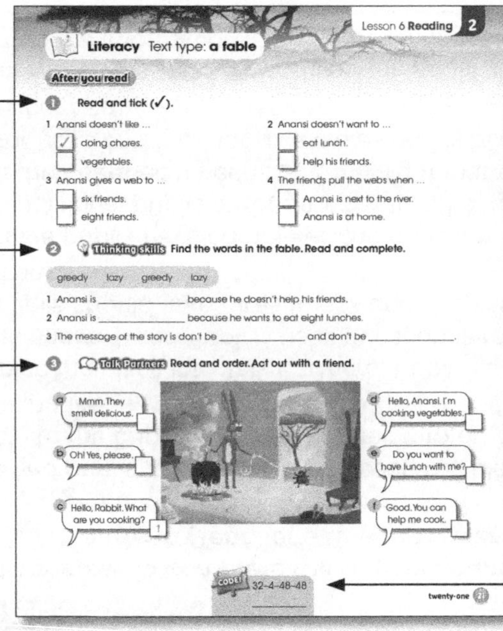

Lesson 6 **Reading** 2

Literacy Text type: **a fable**

After you read

1 Read and tick (✓).

1 Anansi doesn't like ... ✓ doing chores. / vegetables.

2 Anansi doesn't want to ... eat lunch. / help his friends.

3 Anansi gives a web to ... six friends. / eight friends.

4 The friends pull the webs when ... Anansi is next to the river. / Anansi is at home.

2 Thinking skills Find the words in the fable. Read and complete.

greedy lazy greedy lazy

1 Anansi is ________ because he doesn't help his friends.

2 Anansi is ________ because he wants to eat eight lunches.

3 The message of the story is don't be ________ and don't be ________.

3 Talk Partners Read and order. Act out with a friend.

a Mmm. They smell delicious.

b Oh! Yes, please.

c Hello, Rabbit. What are you cooking? 1

d Hello, Anansi. I'm cooking vegetables.

e Do you want to have lunch with me?

f Good. You can help me cook.

CODE! 32-4-48-48

twenty-one 21

After you read: Activity Book

Activity 1

- Read and tick (✓).

Activity 2

- Find the words in the fable.
- Read and complete.

Activity 3

- Read and order.
- Act out with a friend.

Code activity

- Complete the code activity.

Digital resources

Teacher's Digital: You can also teach this lesson using the Teacher's App on Navio.

Pupil's Digital: Encourage your pupils to use the Pupil's App on Navio to practise the activities from this lesson.

Powered By NAVIO

Starting the lesson

Use the Trinity Exams Practice cards (optional).

- The pupils practise asking and answering questions.

Review the tongue twister.

▶ *CD1 Track 39 p264*

- Ask **What sound did you practise in the tongue twister?** *('ch')*
- Play the CD. Practise the tongue twister as a class.
- Remind the pupils that they know two spellings for this sound ('ch' and 'tch').
- The pupils list the words they know which contain these letters.

Set learning outcomes and use the talk cards.

- Say **Today we're going to read a fable from Africa.** Explain that a fable is a traditional story.
- Point to the talk cards to show the pupils the different ways they will be working in the lesson.

Before you read: Pupil's Book Activity 1

When and where do you listen to stories? Can we learn things from stories?

- Invite a pupil to read the first question in the rubric. Prompt the pupils to think about when and where they hear stories (*at home, from grandparents and parents, in the classroom*). Ask **Can we learn things from stories?** Explain that in many countries, stories are used to pass knowledge from one generation to the next.
- Tell the pupils that the fable they are going to read is used to teach us a lesson.

Before you read: Pupil's Book Activity 2

Read the title of the fable. Who do you think Anansi is?

- Invite a pupil to read the title of the fable. Ask who the pupils think Anansi might be.

Pupil's Book Activity 3

Read and listen to find out.

▶ *CD1 Track 41 p264*

- Explain that the first time the pupils read, they should try to understand the most important information.
- If you want the pupils to read the text without the support of the CD, set a time limit for this task. Otherwise, play the CD.
- The pupils confirm / report that Anansi is a spider.

After you read: Activity Book

Activity 1

Read and tick (✓).

- The pupils work on their own or in pairs to read each sentence stem and identify the correct ending, referring to the Pupil's Book when necessary.

Answers: **1** doing chores. **2** help his friends. **3** eight friends. **4** Anansi is next to the river.

Activity 2

Find the words in the fable. Read and complete.

- Read the words in the word box and ask the pupils to find them in the fable. Encourage the class to guess the meaning of each word from the context.
- Read out the first sentence and prompt the pupils to tell you the missing word. Repeat with the remaining sentences.
- The pupils work on their own to complete the sentences.

Answers: **1** lazy **2** greedy **3** greedy, lazy

Activity 3

Read and order. Act out with a friend.

- Read out speech bubble **c**. Explain that this is the first speech bubble in the conversation.
- Ask the pupils to put the speech bubbles in the correct order, writing the numbers.
- Invite two pupils to read out the conversation, one taking the role of Anansi and the other taking the role of Rabbit. Then organise the class into Talk Partners to practise reading the conversation.
- Invite pairs of pupils to act out the conversation for their classmates.

Answers: **a** 3 **b** 5 **c** 1 **d** 2 **e** 4 **f** 6

Code activity

- The pupils complete the code activity.

Answer: hall

Ending the lesson

Review the lesson and reflect on learning.

- Say **Today we've read a fable. Do you think it's a good story? Do you think Anansi is funny?** Elicit the pupils' opinions.
- Ask **Which was your favourite activity today? Which activity was easy / difficult?**

Extra activity

Reinforcement

- If you have access to the Internet, you can find animated versions of this fable on YouTube.

Key Competences and Key Learning Outcomes

- Use adjectives before nouns

- Read the text and choose the best title
- Identify the text features of a fable
- Use criteria to check your writing

- Share your writing with a partner

- Prepare and write an ending for a fable

Key language

- *clever, dirty, greedy, heavy, lunch, share, turtle*
- *You can't (wear a coat) when you (eat lunch).*
- Recycled: *coat, delicious, food, hands, hungry, idea, river, spider, swim, walk, wash*

Materials

- Pupil's Book p25; Activity Book p22; Class CD1; Teacher's App on Navio
- Teacher's Resource Bank: Talk cards

Optional materials

- Teacher's Resource Bank: Trinity Exams Practice cards (selected from the Starter Unit and Unit 1)
- Teacher's Resource Bank: Household chores word cards

At a Glance Lesson Plan

Pupil's Book

Starting the lesson

- Use the Trinity Exams Practice cards (optional).
- Review adjectives to describe feelings and emotions.
- Set learning outcomes and use the talk cards.

Investigate a text: Activity 1

- What do you remember about Anansi?

Activity 2

- Read and listen.
- ▶ *CD1 Track 42 p264*
- Choose the best title for this Anansi fable.

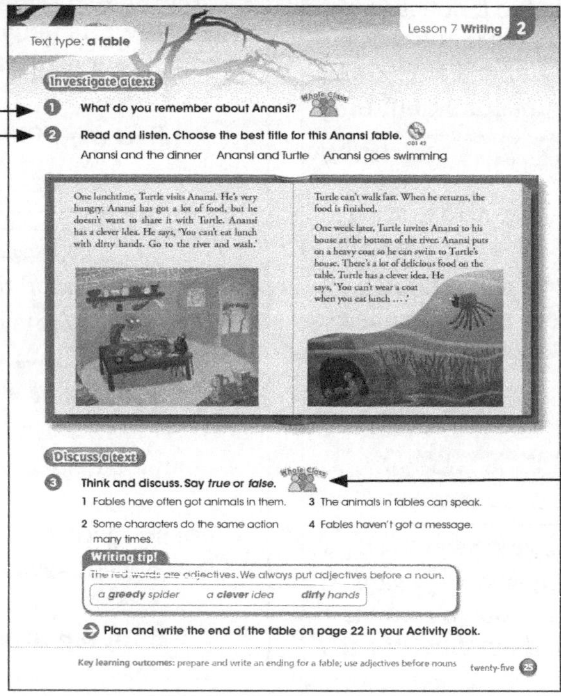

Discuss a text: Activity 3

- Think and discuss.
- Say *true* or *false*.
- **Writing tip:** Read about adjectives and word order.
- Go to the Activity Book.

Ending the lesson

- Review the lesson and reflect on learning.

Extra activities

Reinforcement

- Watch an animated version of the story.
- Play *Careful copying.*

Activity Book

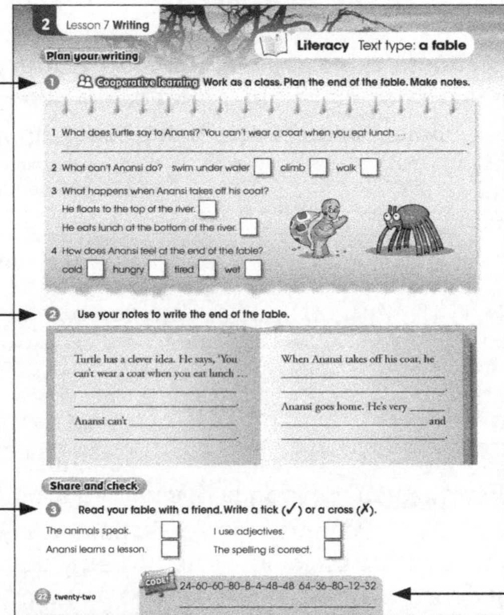

Activity Book

Plan your writing:

Activity 1

- Work as a class. Plan the end of the fable.
- Make notes.

Activity 2

- Use your notes to write the end of the fable.

Share and check:

Activity 3

- Read your fable with a friend.
- Write a tick (✓) or a cross (✗).

Code activity

- Complete the code

Digital resources

Teacher's Digital: You can also teach this lesson using the Teacher's App on Navio.

Pupil's Digital: Encourage your pupils to use the Pupil's App on Navio to practise the activities from this lesson.

Powered By NAVIO

Starting the lesson

Use the Trinity Exams Practice cards (optional).

- The pupils practise asking and answering questions.

Review adjectives to describe feelings and emotions.

- Ask **How are you feeling today?** Encourage the pupils to say how they are feeling and why. If necessary, prompt them by asking **Are you happy? Why are you happy?** Other adjectives include tired, sad, angry, excited, worried. Explain that the words to describe how we feel are called adjectives.

Set learning outcomes and use the talk cards.

- Ask **What kind of story did we read in the last lesson?** (*A fable.*) Say **Today we're going to investigate another fable. Then we're going to plan and write the end of the fable.**
- Point to the talk cards to show the pupils the different ways they will be working in the lesson.

Investigate a text: Pupil's Book Activity 1

What do you remember about Anansi?

- Read the question as a class. Encourage the pupils to tell you what they remember about Anansi from Lesson 6. (*He's a spider. He's greedy, clever and lazy.*)

Pupil's Book Activity 2

Read and listen. Choose the best title for this Anansi fable.

▶ *CD1 Track 42 p264*

- Invite a pupil to read out the three possible titles for the fable. Explain that the class should read the text to decide which title is best. If you want the pupils to read the text without the support of the CD, set a time limit for this task. Otherwise, play the CD.
- Listen to the pupils' ideas and confirm that the best title for the story is *Anansi and Turtle*.

Discuss a text: Pupil's Book Activity 3

Think and discuss. Say *true* or *false*.

- Invite a pupil to read out the first statement and say whether it's true or false. Confirm that it's true and identify the animals that appear in the two fables. (*A spider, a rabbit, a monkey and a turtle.*)
- Repeat the procedure with the other sentences, encouraging the class to find examples in the texts each time.

Answers: **1** true **2** true **3** true **4** false

Writing tip

- Read the information about adjectives and word order.
- Ask the class to give you other examples of adjectives + nouns. Prompt the pupils by giving them different nouns, e.g. dog, house, car, turtle.

Activity Book

Plan your writing: Activity 1

Work as a class. Plan the end of the fable. Make notes.

- Read out each question and encourage the class to answer. The pupils write the answer and tick the boxes as a class.

Activity 2

Use your notes to write the end of the fable.

- Focus the class on the activity. If necessary, model how to complete the framework. The pupils work as a class to give you the information as you write the full text on the board. The pupils then work on their own to write their text in their Activity Books.

Suggested answers: Turtle has a clever idea. He says, 'You can't wear a coat when you eat lunch. **Take your coat off.'** Anansi can't **swim under water**. When Anansi takes off his coat, he **floats to the top of the river.** Anansi goes home. He's very **cold, wet** and **hungry**.

Share and check: Activity 3

Writing Partners. Read your fable with a friend. Write a tick (✓) or a cross (✗).

- Focus the class on the statements.
- Organise the class into pairs. One pupil in each pair should read their fable ending aloud to their partner. The other pupil listens. The pupils work together to decide if the text fulfils all the criteria and tick or cross the corresponding boxes. The pupils can add to, improve, or correct the text at this stage.
- The pupils swap roles.

Code activity

- The pupils complete the code activity.

Answer: football pitch

Ending the lesson

Review the lesson and reflect on learning.

- Say **Today we've written the ending for a fable. Are you happy with it?** Elicit the pupils' opinions.
- Ask **Which was your favourite activity today? Which activity was easy / difficult?**

Extra activities

Reinforcement

- Search for 'Anansi and the turtle' on YouTube to watch an animated version of the fable with your class.
- Play *Careful copying* (see p27) with the household chores word cards.

Key Competences and Key Learning Outcomes

- Use the Internet to investigate Scotland
- Read and listen for specific information
- Read about life on a Scottish island
- Think about your own culture and identity

Key language

- *ferry, island, look after, north, safe, Scotland, seals, west*
- *I travel to (school) by (ferry). I often (feed the sheep). I love (playing with the baby animals).*
- Recycled: *dolphins, farm, free time, sheep, town*

Materials

- Pupil's Book p26; Activity Book p23; Class CD1; Teacher's App on Navio
- Teacher's Resource Bank: Talk cards
- An online world map
- Coloured pencils (blue and white)

Optional materials

- Teacher's Resource Bank: Trinity Exams Practice cards (selected from the Starter Unit and Unit 1)

At a Glance Lesson Plan

Pupil's Book

Starting the lesson

- Use the Trinity Exams Practice cards (optional).
- Review vocabulary for towns and cities.
- Set learning outcomes and use the talk cards.

Activity 1

- Read Luke's questions.
- What do you think?

Activity 2

- Read and listen.

▶ ***CD1 Track 43 p264***

- Answer Luke's questions.
- **Think about your culture** Do you live in a village, a town or a big city? What routines have you got?

Go to the Activity Book.

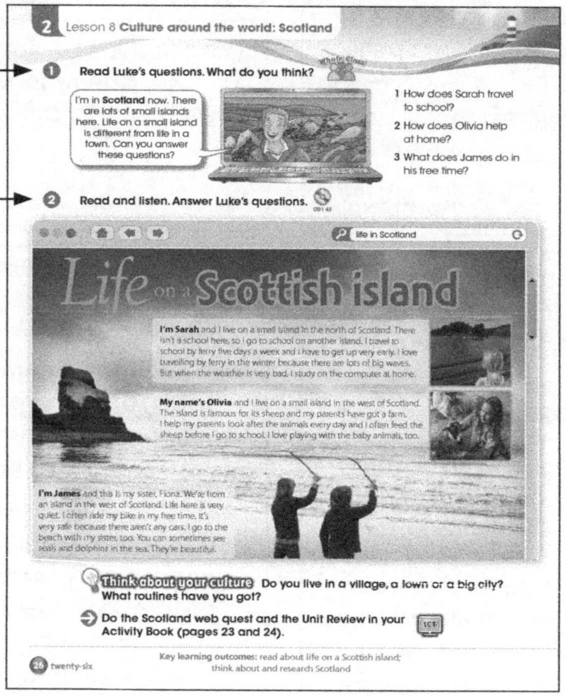

Ending the lesson

- Review the lesson and reflect on learning.

Extra activity

Extension

- Write a description of what you can see and do on Scottish islands.

Activity Book

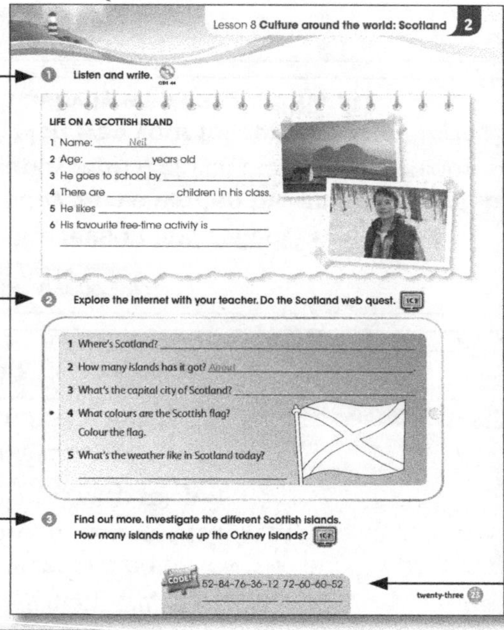

Activity Book

Activity 1

- Listen and write.

▶ ***CD1 Track 44 p265***

Activity 2

- Explore the Internet with your teacher. Do the Scotland web quest.

Activity 3

- Find out more. Investigate the different Scottish islands. How many islands make up the Orkney Islands?

Code activity

- Complete the code activity.

Digital resources

Teacher's Digital: You can also teach this lesson using the Teacher's App on Navio.

Powered By NAVIO

Starting the lesson

Use the Trinity Exams Practice cards (optional).

- The pupils practise asking and answering questions.

Review vocabulary for towns and cities.

- Ask the pupils to close their eyes and imagine they are in the centre of their town. Ask **What can you see? What can you hear?**
- Ask the pupils to open their eyes and report back to the class. Praise the pupils for their ideas and write any key vocabulary on the board.

Set learning outcomes and use the talk cards.

- Say **Today we're going to investigate a new country: Scotland.**
- Point to the talk cards to show the pupils the different ways they will be working in the lesson.

Pupil's Book Activity 1

Read Luke's questions. What do you think?

- Read the speech bubble as a class. Encourage the pupils to tell you what they know about Scotland. Show the pupils where the country is on an online world map.
- Read the questions as a class. Encourage the pupils to predict the answers.

Pupil's Book Activity 2

Read and listen. Answer Luke's questions.

▸ *CD1 Track 43 p264*

- Focus the class on the photos. Ask **What can you see?** (*A child on a ferry, a girl feeding sheep, children on a beach.*)
- Ask the pupils to read the text. If you want the pupils to read the text without the support of the CD, set a time limit for this task. Otherwise, play the CD, pausing after each section to check understanding.
- The pupils answer Luke's questions.
- Ask **Would you like to live on a small island?**

Answers: **1** Sarah travels to school by ferry. **2** Olivia helps her parents look after the animals and she feeds the sheep. **3** In his free time, James rides his bike and he goes to the beach.

Think about your culture

- Discuss the questions. Ask different pupils to tell you about their routines, prompting them if necessary with additional questions, e.g. **How do you travel to school? How do you help at home? What do you do in your free time?**

Activity Book

Activity 1

Listen and write.

▸ *CD1 Track 44 p265*

- Read out the information in the notebook. Then play the CD, pausing to allow the pupils to write the missing information each time.
- Play the CD again without stopping. The pupils listen and check their answers.

Answers: **1** Neil **2** nine **3** bike **4** six **5** playing basketball **6** sailing

Activity 2

Explore the Internet with your teacher. Do the Scotland web quest.

- Read out the instructions for the activity.
- Connect to a children's website that provides geographical information about Scotland. (See suggested websites opposite.) Read out questions 1–4. The pupils work as a class to find and write the answers. They should also colour the Scottish flag.
- Read out question 5. Connect to a website that shows the weather around the world. The pupils complete the information about the day's weather.

Answers: **1** in the UK above / north of England **2** About 790 **3** Edinburgh **4** blue and white

Activity 3

Find out more. Investigate the different Scottish islands. How many islands make up the Orkney Islands?

- Tell the pupils that they are going to investigate the different Scottish islands. Ask them to predict how many islands make up the Orkney Islands. The pupils research how many islands make up the Orkney Islands.

Answer: Approximately 70 islands make up the Orkney Islands.

Suggested websites

- Use a range of trusted Internet sites such as:

www.bbc.co.uk/schools
http://www.visitscotland.com
http://maps.google.es/
http://www.bbc.co.uk/weather

Code activity

- The pupils complete the code activity.

Answer: music room

Ending the lesson

Review the lesson and reflect on learning.

- Say **Today we've learnt about Scotland. What activities do some school children do?**
- Ask **Which was your favourite activity today? Which activity was easy / difficult?**

Extra activity

Extension

- Ask the pupils to connect to a Scottish islands tourism website. They look at the photos and then choose the ones they like the most.
- The pupils work together to write a description of what they can see and do on their favourite Scottish island or group of islands.

Go to the AB Unit Review on page 245.

Key Competences and Key Learning Outcomes

- Watch and understand a video about helping at home
- Understand the importance of helping at home
- Identify when a person may need help

Key language

- *evening, morning; help, read a story, share a snack, take out the rubbish, tidy the bedroom, wash the car*
- Recycled: *cook dinner, lay the table, walk the dog, water the plants*
- *Do you help people?, I (tidy up) my bedroom, Let's tidy up together*

Materials

- Pupil's Book p27; Activity Book p25; Class CD1; Teacher's App on Navio
- Teacher's Resource Bank: Talk cards

Optional materials

- Teacher's Resource Bank: Trinity Exams Practice cards (selected from the Starter Unit and Unit 1)

At a Glance Lesson Plan

Pupil's Book

Starting the lesson

- Use the Trinity Exams Practice cards (optional).
- **Think-Pair-Share.** Review household chores vocabulary.
- Set learning outcomes and use the talk cards.

Activity 1

- Before you watch
- Watch the video.
- *Unit 2 video p284*
- What do the children do with these objects?

Activity 2

- Watch the video again.
- *Unit 2 video*
- Read and answer the questions.

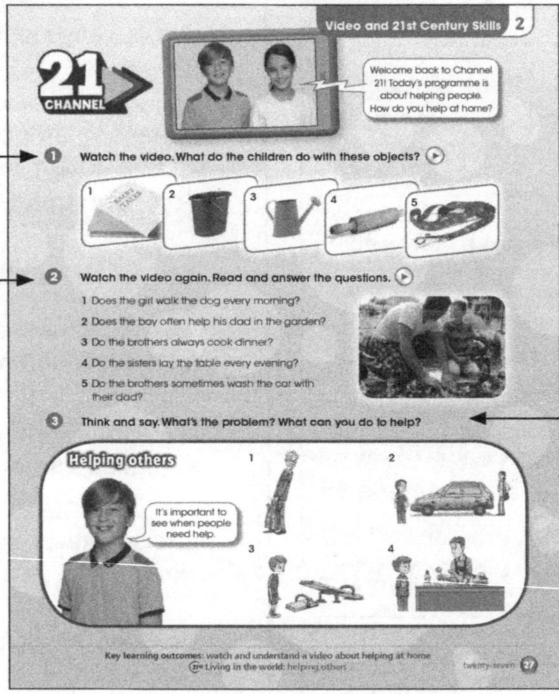

Activity 3

- Think and say.
- What's the problem?
- What can you do to help?
- Go to the Activity Book.

Ending the lesson

- Review the lesson and reflect on learning.

Extra activity

Reinforcement

- Talk about how often you help others.

Activity Book

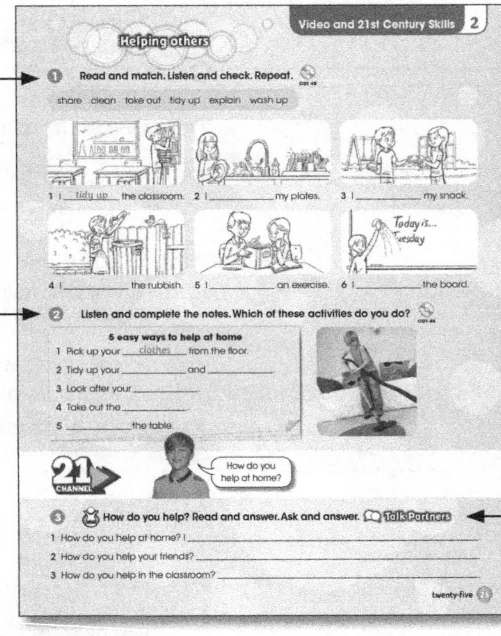

Activity Book

Activity 1

- Read and match.
- Listen and check.
- ▶ *CD1 Track 45 p265*
- Repeat.

Activity 2

- Listen and complete the notes.
- ▶ *CD1 Track 46 p265*
- Which of these activities do you do?

Activity 3

- How do you help?
- Read and answer.
- Ask and answer.

Digital resources

Teacher's Digital: You can also teach this lesson using the Teacher's App on Navio.

Pupil's Digital: Encourage your pupils to use the Pupil's App on Navio to practise the activities from this lesson.

Powered By NAVIO

Starting the lesson

Use the Trinity Exams Practice cards (optional).

- The pupils practise asking and answering questions.

Think-Pair-Share. Review household chores vocabulary.

- Ask **Can you remember the household chores vocabulary?** The class thinks silently for a minute.
- Then the pupils work with a Talk Partner to name household chores.
- Invite different Talk Partners to say a different household chore. Write the chore on the board and prompt the class to repeat the chore.
- Finally, repeat the procedure, asking different pairs of Talk Partners each time, until all the ideas have been recorded.

Set learning outcomes and use the talk cards.

- Say **Today we're going to watch a video and then ask and answer questions about helping at home**.
- Point to the talk cards to show the pupils the different ways they will be working in the lesson.

Pupil's Book Activity 1

Before you watch

- Read the speech bubble to pupils. Ask **How do you help at home?** Elicit responses from a number of pupils.

Watch the video. What do the children do with these objects? *p284*

- Watch Part 1. Ask pupils **What are you going to see next?** Check that they understand that they will see how other children help at home.
- Play Part 2. Ask general questions to check understanding. Focus the pupils on the photos in Activity 1. Say **What do the children do with these objects?** Elicit ideas.
- Play Part 2 again for the pupils to answer the questions. Check answers as a class.

Answers: **1** reads to brother **2** wash the car **3** water the plants **4** cook dinner **5** walks the dog

Pupil's Book Activity 2

Watch the video again. Read and answer the questions.

- Review adverbs of frequency. Ask pupils to put the adverbs *always*, *often*, *sometimes* and *never* into order of frequency.
- Ask a pupil to read out sentence 1. Ask the class what they think the answer is. Repeat with sentences 2–5.
- Play Part 2. Students work in pairs to answer the questions.

Answers: **1** No, she walks the dog after school. **2** Yes, he does. **3** No, they sometimes cook dinner. **4** Yes, they do. **5** No, they usually wash the car with their dad.

Pupil's Book Activity 3

Think and say. What's the problem? What can you do to help?

- Ask **What is the problem at the end of the video?** (*The studio is a mess.*) **What do Chloe and Mark do to help?** (*They tidy up.*)
- Look at the pictures with pupils and explain that they need to identify the problem in each one and suggest what they can do to help. Look at the pictures with the class and check vocabulary.
- Pupils work in pairs to identify the problem and suggest what they can do to help.
- Check answers with the class. Say **What is the problem? What can you do to help?**

Activity Book

Activity 1

Read and match. Listen and check. Repeat.

▸ *CD1 Track 45 p265*

- Look at the words in the box and check vocabulary.
- Pupils work on their own to complete the sentences.
- Play the CD and check answers.

Answers: **1** tidy up **2** wash up **3** share **4** take out **5** explain **6** clean

Activity 2

Listen and complete the notes. Which of these activities do you do?

▸ *CD1 Track 46 p265*

- Explain to the pupils that they are going to listen to two people talking about what children can do to help at home. Ask pupils for ideas of what they can do to help at home. Read out the information. Then play the CD, pausing to allow the pupils to write the missing information.
- Play the CD again without pausing. Elicit answers.

Answers: **1** clothes **2** toys and games **3** pets **4** rubbish **5** Lay

Activity 3

How do you help? Read and answer. Ask and answer.

- Read out the speech bubble and elicit answers from the class. Once pupils are confident answering, you could make the question more specific and ask about helping friends, helping in the classroom, etc.
- The pupils write answers to the questions about how they help other people.
- Organise the pupils into Talk Partners. The pupils take it in turns to ask and answer questions.

Ending the lesson

Review the lesson and reflect on learning.

- Say **Today we've watched a video about helping at home and we've come up with ideas how we can help people.**
- Ask **Which was your favourite activity today? Which activity was easy / difficult?**

Extra activity

Reinforcement

- Ask a pupil **How often do you lay the table?** Encourage the pupil to reply using an adverb of frequency. Repeat the procedure with other household chores or more general helpful activities. Then invite pupils to ask and answer in pairs.

Date: ____________________ Unit: __________

1 What did my pupils learn in this unit?

2 How did my pupils work? (✓)

individually ☐ in pairs ☐ in small groups ☐

in large groups ☐ as a class ☐

3 Which key competences did my pupils develop?

- Competence in linguistic communication ☐
- Competence in mathematics, science and technology ☐
- Digital competence ☐
- Learning to learn ☐
- Social and civic competences ☐
- Sense of initiative and entrepreneurship ☐
- Cultural awareness and expression ☐

4 Which lessons / activities were the most successful and why?

5 Which lessons / activities did my pupils find the most difficult and why?

6 What did I try in the classroom for the first time? How did it go?

7 Which resources did I find most useful? (including webpages)

8 What could I do differently next time I teach this unit?

3 Fit and healthy

Unit overview

Key Competences and Key Learning Outcomes

- Identify and name health problems (Lesson 1)
- Say the vocabulary chant (Lesson 1)
- Understand and act out a conversation (Lesson 2)
- Follow, complete and correct the grammar tables (Lessons 2 and 4)
- Identify healthy and unhealthy habits (Lesson 4)
- Use 'must' and 'mustn't' (Lesson 4)
- Use question marks correctly (Lesson 7)
- Watch and understand a video (Video and 21st Century Skills)

- Use a code to read a message (Lesson 3)
- Do a health quiz (Lesson 6)
- Write a quiz about healthy eating (Lesson 7)
- Identify how keeping healthy benefits the body (Video and 21st Century)

- Use the Pupil's App on Navio
- Investigate Malta (Lesson 8)

- Say a tongue twister, learn another spelling for the 'k' sound and practise spelling (Lesson 5)
- Practise activity types found in the Cambridge Exams: A1 Movers
- Review your own learning (Review)

- Understand the importance of talking to someone when you've got a problem (Lesson 3)

- Work with a Talk Partner to practise and reinforce learning (all lessons)
- Play a communication game (Lesson 5)

- Sing two songs (Lessons 1 and 4)
- Understand, act out and give an opinion on a story (Lesson 3)
- Learn about Malta (Lesson 8)
- Think about your own culture (Lesson 8)

Vocabulary

Core vocabulary
broken leg, cold, cough, cut, earache, feel dizzy, feel sick, flu, headache, sore throat, stomach ache, temperature; be active, be lazy, eat healthy snacks, eat lots of sweets, go to bed early, go to bed late

Extension vocabulary (optional)
bandage, cast, cream, medicine, plaster, tablets; do exercise, drink water, eat junk food, have fizzy drinks

Other vocabulary
divers, fit, healthy, healthy eating, hurt, ill, points, quiz, rescue centre, sea animal rescue, scientists, skin, vets

Recycled vocabulary
always, every day, five times a week, never, once or twice a week, sometimes; be quiet, beach, breakfast, chores, cold, do sport, dog, drink some water, eat fruit, fingers, run, school, shout, swim, tired, vegetables, watch TV, wear a hat, windy

Structures

Core structures
What's the matter? Have they got (a cold)? Yes, they have. Has she got (a sore throat)? Yes, she has. No, she hasn't. Do they (feel dizzy)? Yes, they do. No, they don't. Does (your sister) (feel sick)? Yes, she does. You must (go to bed early). You mustn't (eat lots of sweets).

Other structures
(Marine animals) (sometimes) need (our help). Some (turtles) have got (broken bones). When the (turtles) are (better), (they put them into the sea). Everyone (feels happy) when (the turtles are in the wild.)

Recycled structures
How are you today? I'm (fine). Have you got (a headache)? Yes, I have. No, I haven't. Do you (feel dizzy)? Yes, I do. No, I don't. Go (to bed). Are you (fit and healthy)? Yes, I am. Do you (walk to school)? I (never) walk to school. How often do you (eat fruit)? I (eat fruit) (every day). What time do you (go to bed)? I (go to bed) at about (nine o'clock). How do (you spell) (shoulder)?

Phonics

The 'k' sound (*pin**k** **ch**ameleon heada**che** **k**ing stoma**ch** a**che***)

Literacy

Text type: a quiz (information text; writing preparation)
Reading skills: activating existing knowledge
Writing skills: using question marks

Culture ... around the world

Sea animal rescue in Malta

21st Century Skills

Being fit and healthy

Thinking skills

Applying rules (Lessons 2 and 4); Remembering (Lesson 2); Predicting (Lessons 3 and 7); Discussing values (Lesson 3); Expressing opinions (Lesson 3); Visual intelligence (Lesson 4); Visualisation and prediction (Lesson 8); Thinking about your culture (Lesson 8); Making connections (Review)

Cooperative learning

Sharing information (Lessons 1 and 5); Collaborating (Lessons 3 and 4); Checking learning (Lesson 5); Peer evaluation and feedback (Lesson 7); Working together (Review)

Values

Understanding the importance of dealing with problems

Cross-curricular links

Link to Science
We can move: Reviewing how we move and what our body needs
Suggested Arts and Crafts concepts
Identifying positive and negative shapes and making a collage

Key Competences and Key Learning Outcomes

- Identify and name health problems
- Say the vocabulary chant
- Review joints in the human body (optional)
- Review the question *How are you today?* and brainstorm possible responses
- Play a game using a recycled structure
- Sing a song

Key language

- Health problems: *broken leg, cold, cough, cut, earache, feel dizzy, feel sick, flu, headache, sore throat, stomach ache, temperature*
- *Have I got (flu)? I'm not (very well). I (feel sick). You aren't (very well).*
- Extension: *bandage, cast, cream, medicine, plaster, tablets*
- Recycled: *How are you today? I'm (fine). Have you got a (headache)? Yes, I have. No, I haven't. Do you (feel dizzy)? Yes, I do. No, I don't. Go (to bed).*

Materials

- Pupil's Book p28; Activity Book p26; Class CD1; Teacher's App on Navio
- Teacher's Resource Bank: Health problems word cards
- Health problems flashcards
- Teacher's Resource Bank: Talk cards
- A large piece of paper for each group of 3–4 pupils

Optional materials

- Teacher's Resource Bank: Trinity Exams Practice cards (selected from the Starter Unit and Units 1 and 2)

At a Glance Lesson Plan

Pupil's Book

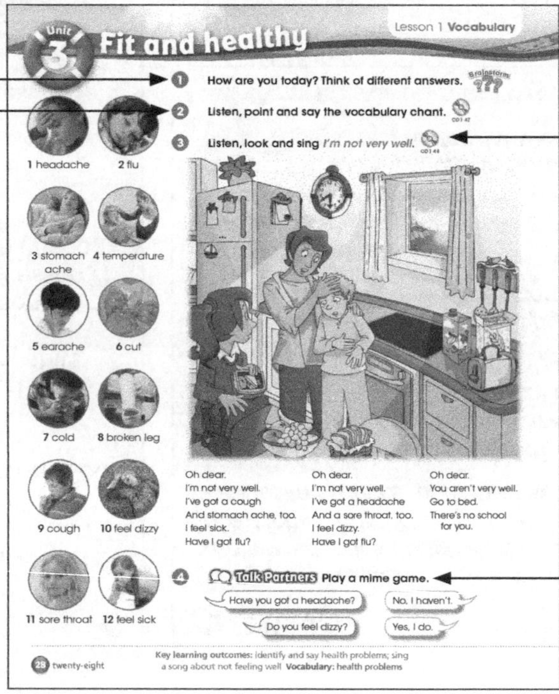

Starting the lesson
- Use the Trinity Exams Practice cards (optional).
- Review parts of the body.
- Set learning outcomes and use the talk cards.

Activity 1
- How are you today?
- Think of different answers.

Vocabulary presentation
- Present the new vocabulary using the health problems flashcards.

Word cards
- Introduce the spellings of the vocabulary using the health problems word cards.

Activity 2
- Listen, point and say the vocabulary chant.

▶ *CD1 Track 47 p265*

Activity 3
- Listen, look and sing *I'm not very well.*

▶ *CD1 Track 48 p265*

Activity 4
- Play a mime game.

Go to the Activity Book.

Ending the lesson
- Review the lesson and reflect on learning.

Extra activities

Extension
- Play a game in pairs.

Vocabulary extension
- Present six additional vocabulary items.

Link to Science
- **We can move:** Review joints in the human body and how we move.

Digital resources

Teacher's Digital: You can also teach this lesson using the Teacher's App on Navio.

Pupil's Digital: Encourage your pupils to use the Pupil's App on Navio to practise the activities from this lesson.

Powered By NAVIO

Activity Book

Activity Book

Activity 1
- Look and complete the puzzle.
- What's the mystery word?

Activity 2
- Look and complete the sentences.

Code activity
- Complete the code activity.

Starting the lesson

Use the Trinity Exams Practice cards (optional).

- The pupils practise asking and answering questions.

Review parts of the body.

- Organise the class into small groups. Ask a pupil in each group to draw the outline of a person on a large piece of paper. The groups have three minutes to label as many parts of the body as possible.
- Ask the groups to pass their paper to the group on the left. The groups have two minutes to read the labels and add any other body words they know. Repeat the procedure. Then ask different groups to read out their words.

Set learning outcomes and use the talk cards.

- Say **Today we're going to learn how to explain when we're not very well.**
- Point to the talk cards to show the pupils the different ways they will be working in the lesson.

Pupil's Book Activity 1

How are you today? Think of different answers.

- (Books closed.) Ask **How are you today?** Encourage the pupils to think of different answers, e.g. *I'm fine. I'm (not) very well. I'm tired / hungry / hot / cold.*

Vocabulary presentation

- (Books closed.) Tell the class that you don't feel well. Mime a health problem and stick the corresponding flashcard on the board. Say **I've got a (headache).** Prompt the class to mime the problem and repeat. Repeat with the other flashcards.

Word cards

- (Books closed.) Hand a health problem word card to each pair of pupils. The pairs take turns to come to the board, read out their health problem and stick their word card next to the corresponding flashcard.

Pupil's Book Activity 2

Listen, point and say the vocabulary chant.

▶ *CD1 Track 47 p265*

- Focus the pupils' attention on the 12 photos. Say **Let's listen and say the words.** Play the CD. The pupils listen, point and repeat.

Pupil's Book Activity 3

Listen, look and sing *I'm not very well.*

▶ *CD1 Track 48 p265*

- Focus the pupils' attention on the scene. Ask **Where are they? What's the matter with Josh?** (*He's not very well.*)
- Say **Let's listen to the song.** Play the CD. The pupils listen and read.
- Play the CD again. The pupils sing the song and mime the health problems.
- Ask the pupils if they think Josh has got flu.

Pupil's Book Activity 4

Play a mime game.

- Ask two pupils to read out the speech bubbles. Then mime one of the health problems for the class to guess, using the same sentence structure. Repeat several times.
- The pupils play the game with a Talk Partner.

Activity Book

Activity 1

Look and complete the puzzle. What's the mystery word?

- Point to each picture and ask the pupils to name the health problems.
- The pupils write the words in the puzzle to discover and write the mystery word.

Answers: **1** broken leg **2** stomach ache **3** sore throat **4** headache **5** cut **6** cough **7** temperature
The mystery word is earache.

Activity 2

Look and complete the sentences.

- Ask the class to read out the words in the word box.
- Invite different pupils to complete the speech bubbles.
- The pupils write the sentences.

Answers: **1** I've got flu. **2** I feel dizzy. **3** I've got earache. **4** I've got a cold. **5** I've got a cough. **6** I feel sick.

Code activity

- The pupils complete the code activity.

Answer: wash up

Ending the lesson

Review the lesson and reflect on learning.

- Say **Today we've learnt the names of health problems. What health problems do you remember?** Elicit the words from the pupils.
- Ask **Which was your favourite activity today? Which activity was easy / difficult?**

Extra activities

Extension

- Organise the class into pairs. Pupil A chooses a health problem and says what he / she can't do because of the problem, e.g. *I can't eat ice cream / sweets.* Pupil B guesses the health problem. (*Feel sick.*) The pupils then change roles.

Vocabulary extension

- Present six additional health problem related words: *bandage, cast, cream, medicine, plaster, tablets.*
- Use the Vocabulary Booster on Navio to practise these new words.

Link to Science

- If you are studying the Science topic of **We can move** in English, review the main joints (*wrist, elbow, shoulder, ankle, knee, hip, neck, back / vertebrae*) and how we move our bodies. The pupils can also identify whether these joints are flexible, semi-flexible or fixed.

Key Competences and Key Learning Outcomes

- Listen, repeat and act out a conversation
- Listen, follow the grammar table and identify the parts of a question
- Use *has / have got* and *do / does* to talk about feeling unwell

Key language

- *What's the matter? Poor (Josh!)*
- *Have they got (a cold)? Yes, they have. Has she got (a sore throat)? Yes, she has. Do they (feel dizzy)? Yes, they do. Does (your sister) (feel sick)? Yes, she does.*
- Recycled: *broken leg, cold, cough, cut, earache, feel dizzy, feel sick, flu, headache, sore throat, stomach ache, temperature; Have you got (a cold)? Yes, I have. No, I haven't.*

Materials

- Pupil's Book p29; Activity Book p27; Class CD1 and 2; Teacher's App on Navio
- Teacher's Resource Bank: Health problems word cards
- Health problems flashcards
- Teacher's Resource Bank: Talk cards

Optional materials

- Teacher's Resource Bank: Trinity Exams Practice cards (selected from the Starter Unit and Units 1 and 2)

At a Glance Lesson Plan

Pupil's Book

Starting the lesson

- Use the Trinity Exams Practice cards (optional).
- **Think-Pair-Share.** Review health problems.
- Review the *I'm not very well* song.
- ▶ *CD1 Track 48 p265*
- ▶ *CD2 Track 01 p265*
- Set learning outcomes and use the talk cards.

Activity 1

- Listen and read.
- Listen and repeat.
- ▶ *CD2 Track 02 p265*
- Act out.

Activity 2

- Read again.
- What's the matter with Josh?
- Which problems has he got?

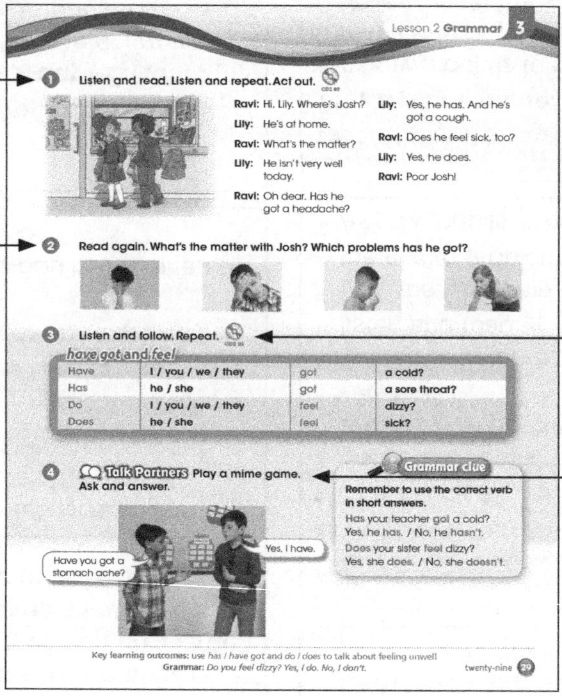

Activity 3

- Listen and follow.
- ▶ *CD2 Track 03 p265*
- Repeat.
- **Grammar clue:** Read about short answers and using the correct verb.

Activity 4

- Play a mime game.
- Ask and answer.
- Go to the Activity Book.

Ending the lesson

- Review the lesson and reflect on learning.

Extra activities

Reinforcement

- Play *What is it?*
- Play a spelling game.

Activity Book

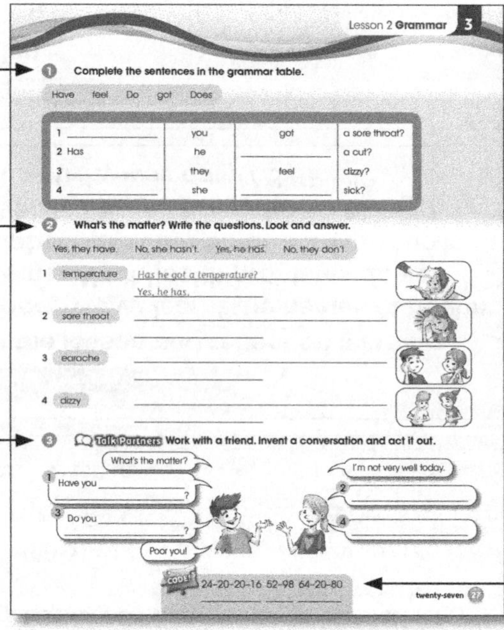

Activity Book

Activity 1

- Complete the sentences in the grammar table.

Activity 2

- What's the matter?
- Write the questions.
- Look and answer.

Activity 3

- Work with a friend.
- Invent a conversation and act it out.

Code activity

- Complete the code activity.

Digital resources

Teacher's Digital: You can also teach this lesson using the Teacher's App on Navio.

Pupil's Digital: Encourage your pupils to use the Pupil's App on Navio to practise the activities from this lesson.

Powered By NAVIO

Starting the lesson

Use the Trinity Exams Practice cards (optional).

- The pupils practise asking and answering questions.

Think-Pair-Share. Review health problems.

- Ask **Can you remember the health problems?** The class thinks silently for a minute.
- Then the pupils work with a Talk Partner to name health problems.
- Invite different Talk Partners to say a different health problem. Hold up the corresponding flashcard and prompt the class to repeat the word.

Review the *I'm not very well* song.

▸ *CD1 Track 48 p265*

▸ *CD2 Track 01 p265 (optional karaoke version)*

- Organise the class into pairs and explain that one pupil is Josh and the other is Mum or Dad. Play the CD. The pupils sing along with their character and do the actions. Mum and Dad should touch their partner's forehead when they sing their part.

Set learning outcomes and use the talk cards.

- Say **Today we're going to act out a conversation and ask and answer questions about health.**
- Point to the talk cards to show the pupils the different ways they will be working in the lesson.

Pupil's Book Activity 1

Listen and read. Listen and repeat. Act out.

▸ *CD2 Track 02 p265*

- Focus on the picture. Ask **Where are Lily and Ravi? What do you think they are talking about?**
- Play the CD. The pupils listen and read the conversation. Confirm they are talking about Josh.
- Play the CD again, pausing after each sentence for the pupils to repeat.
- The pupils act out the conversation in pairs.

Pupil's Book Activity 2

Read again. What's the matter with Josh? Which problems has he got?

- The pupils read the conversation again and say what is the matter with Josh and name the problems he has got.

Pupil's Book Activity 3

Listen and follow. Repeat.

▸ *CD2 Track 03 p265*

- Play the CD. The pupils listen to the first sentence and point to the words they hear. They repeat the complete sentence. Repeat the procedure with the other sentences.
- Say **Have I got a sore throat? Has (Maria) got a cold? Do (Javier and Susana) feel dizzy? Does she feel sick?** Invite different pupils to make similar questions using the grammar table.

Grammar clue

- Read the grammar clue about short answers. If necessary, demonstrate the meaning of the different personal pronouns by pointing to different people (he, she, they, etc.).

Pupil's Book Activity 4

Play a mime game. Ask and answer.

- The pupils work in pairs to perform mimes and ask and answer questions.

Activity Book

Activity 1

Complete the sentences in the grammar table.

- Invite a pupil to read out the words in the word box.
- The pupils work on their own or with a partner to write the words in the grammar table.

Answers: 1 Have **2** got **3** Do **4** Does, feel

Activity 2

What's the matter? Write the questions. Look and answer.

- Invite a pupil to read out the words in the word box. Then point to each picture in turn and elicit a question from the class.
- The pupils write the questions.
- They then look at the pictures and answer the questions.

Answers: **1** Has he got a temperature? Yes, he has. **2** Has she got a sore throat? No, she hasn't. **3** Have they got earache? Yes, they have. **4** Do they feel dizzy? No, they don't.

Activity 3

Work with a friend. Invent a conversation and act it out.

- Explain that the pupils are going to invent a conversation. Read out the first two speech bubbles then elicit possible content for the other speech bubbles. If necessary, write the pupils' suggestions on the board.
- The pupils work with a Talk Partner to write their own conversation.
- The pairs practise the conversation and then act it out for the class.

Suggested conversation: **1** Have you got a headache? **2** No, I haven't. **3** Do you feel dizzy? **4** Yes, I do. **5** Poor you!

Code activity

- The pupils complete the code activity.

Answer: feed my pet

Ending the lesson

Review the lesson and reflect on learning.

- Say **Today we've learnt how to talk about health.** Invite different pupils in the class to say a sentence about themselves.
- Ask **Which was your favourite activity today? Which activity was easy / difficult?**

Extra activities

Reinforcement

- Play *What is it?* (see p27) with the health problems flashcards.
- Play a spelling game with the class. Take one of the health problems word cards and ask the class **How do you spell (temperature)?** Prompt a pupil to give the first letter (*T*). The pupil sitting next to him / her gives the next letter (*E*). If a pupil makes a mistake, the next pupil should begin the word again.

Key Competences and Key Learning Outcomes

- Read, listen and understand a story about a dolphin rescue
- Do a pre-reading task
- Think about the people you can talk to when there's a problem
- Understand, enjoy and act out the story
- Give an opinion on the story

Key language

- *barking, clever, dolphin, hurt, shout, skin, TV station, vet, well done*
- *Are you (better)? Yes, I am. How's (the dolphin)? It's got (some cuts). Put (your coat on). We mustn't shout.*
- Recycled: *beach, cold, dog, tired, windy; What's the matter?*

Materials

- Pupil's Book pp30–31; Activity Book p28; Class CD2; Teacher's App on Navio
- Teacher's Resource Bank: Talk cards

Optional materials

- Teacher's Resource Bank: Trinity Exams Practice cards (selected from the Starter Unit and Units 1 and 2)

At a Glance Lesson Plan

Pupil's Book

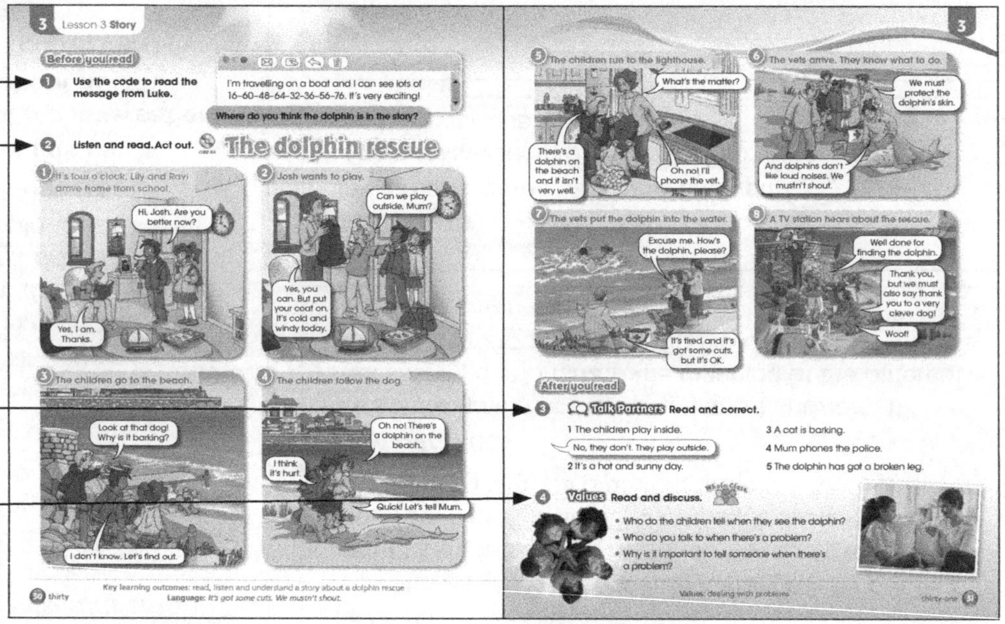

Starting the lesson

- Use the Trinity Exams Practice cards (optional).
- Review the conversation from Lesson 2.
- Set learning outcomes and use the talk cards.

Before you read: Activity 1

- Use the code to read the message from Luke.

Activity 2

- Listen and read.
- ▶ *CD2 Track 04 p265*
- Act out.

After you read: Activity 3

- Read and correct.

Activity 4: Values

- Read and discuss.
- Go to the Activity Book.

Ending the lesson

- Review the lesson and reflect on learning.

Extra activity

Reinforcement

- Retell the story as a class.

Activity Book

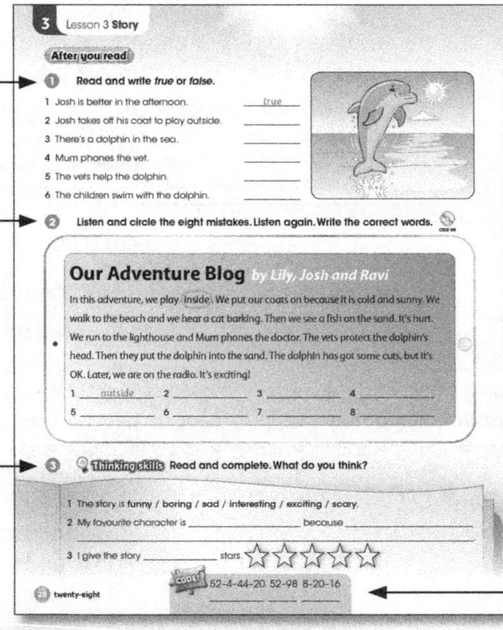

After you read: Activity Book

Activity 1

- Read and write *true* or *false*.

Activity 2

- Listen and circle the eight mistakes.
- ▶ *CD2 Track 05 p266*
- Listen again.
- Write the correct words.

Activity 3

- Read and complete.
- What do you think?

Code activity

- Complete the code activity.

Digital resources

Teacher's Digital: You can also teach this lesson using the Teacher's App on Navio.

Pupil's Digital: Encourage your pupils to use the Pupil's App on Navio to practise the activities from this lesson.

Powered By NAVIO

Starting the lesson

Use the Trinity Exams Practice cards (optional).

- The pupils practise asking and answering questions.

Review the conversation from Lesson 2.

- Ask **Do you remember what Lily and Ravi say in Lesson 2?** Write the first line of the conversation on the board and ask the class to give the next line. Prompt them by providing the first word of the question that follows and write the pupils' ideas on the board. Repeat the procedure with the rest of the conversation. The pupils then open their Pupil's Books at page 29 to compare the conversations.

Set learning outcomes and use the talk cards.

- Say **Today we're going to read and listen to a story.**
- Point to the talk cards to show the pupils the different ways they will be working in the lesson.

Pupil's Book Activity 1: Before you read

Use the code to read the message from Luke.

- Say **Josh and Lily have received a message from Luke.** Ask the pupils to use the code (Pupil's Book page 7) to discover the mystery word (*dolphins*).
- Ask the class to read the title of the story and ask **Where do you think the dolphin is in the story?** The pupils predict where it is.

Pupil's Book Activity 2

Listen and read. Act out.

▶ *CD2 Track 04 p265*

- Play the CD. The pupils follow in their books.
- Ask questions to check comprehension.

Suggested comprehension questions

- Frame 1: **Is Josh well now?** (*Yes, he is.*)
- Frame 2: **Where do the children play?** (*Outside.*)
- Frame 3: **What's the dog doing?** (*Barking.*)
- Frame 4: **What can the children see?** (*A dolphin.*)
- Frame 5: **Who does Mum phone?** (*The vet.*)
- Frame 6: **What do the vets do?** (*They protect the dolphin's skin.*)
- Frame 7: **Is the dolphin hurt?** (*It's got some cuts.*)
- Frame 8: **Who's clever?** (*The dog.*)

- Organise the class into groups (one for each character) and play the CD. Each group joins in when their character speaks. If pupils need extra support, pause the CD after each utterance and ask them to repeat it instead.
- Repeat, with groups swapping roles.

After you read: Pupil's Book Activity 3

Read and correct.

- Ask a pupil to read out the first sentence and its correction. Ask the class to identify the story frame which has this information (*Frame 2*).
- Organise the class into Talk Partners. The pupils find the information and correct each sentence. They can do this orally or in their notebooks.

Answers: **1** No, they don't. They play outside. **2** No, it isn't. It's cold and windy. **3** No, it isn't. A dog is barking. **4** No, she doesn't. She phones the vet. **5** No, it hasn't. It's got some cuts.

Pupil's Book Activity 4: Values

Read and discuss.

- Read out the questions and discuss them as a class. You may want to describe typical situations that the pupils know and ask **Who do you talk to / tell?** Possible situations include: You don't feel very well. You can't find your coat. You're hungry. You don't understand an activity.

After you read: Activity Book

Activity 1

Read and write *true* or *false*.

- The pupils work on their own or in pairs to read the statements and write *true* or *false*.

Answers: **1** true **2** false **3** false **4** true **5** true **6** false

Activity 2

Listen and circle the eight mistakes. Listen again. Write the correct words.

▶ *CD2 Track 05 p266*

- Play the CD. The pupils listen to the blog and circle the eight mistakes.
- Play the CD again. The pupils write the correct words.

Answers: **1** ~~inside~~ outside **2** ~~sunny~~ windy **3** ~~cat~~ dog **4** ~~fish~~ dolphin **5** ~~doctor~~ vet **6** ~~head~~ skin **7** ~~sand~~ water **8** ~~radio~~ TV

Activity 3

Read and complete. What do you think?

- Invite pupils to read out and complete the sentences.
- The pupils complete the task in their Activity Books and then share opinions with a Talk Partner.

Code activity

- The pupils complete the code activity.

Answer: make my bed

Ending the lesson

Review the lesson and reflect on learning.

- Say **Today we've listened to a story about a dolphin.** Elicit the story from the pupils.
- Ask **Which was your favourite activity today? Which activity was easy / difficult?**

Extra activity

Reinforcement

- Retell the story as a class. Say **Let's tell the story together.** Prompt the class by saying **In the afternoon Josh is …** (*better*). **The children play …** (*outside*). Use mime, gesture and drawings to support the class.

Key Competences and Key Learning Outcomes

- Identify and say healthy activities
- Follow and correct the grammar tables
- Use 'must' and 'mustn't' for rules and instructions

- Play a game

- Sing a song

Key language

- Healthy and unhealthy activities: *be active, be lazy, eat healthy snacks, eat lots of sweets, go to bed early, go to bed late; fit, healthy*
- *You must (go to bed early). You mustn't (eat lots of sweets).*
- Extension: *do exercise, drink water, eat junk food, have fizzy drinks*
- Recycled: *every day, lazy, run*

Materials

- Pupil's Book p32; Activity Book p29; Class CD2; Teacher's App on Navio
- Teacher's Resource Bank: Talk cards

Optional materials

- Teacher's Resource Bank: Trinity Exams Practice cards (selected from the Starter Unit and Units 1 and 2)

At a Glance Lesson Plan

Pupil's Book

Starting the lesson

- Use the Trinity Exams Practice cards (optional).
- Review the story.
- Set learning outcomes and use the talk cards.

Activity 1

- Listen, point and say.
- ▶ *CD2 Track 06 p266*

Activity 2

- Listen and sing *Fit and healthy*.
- ▶ *CD2 Track 07 p266*

Activity 3

- Listen and follow.
- ▶ *CD2 Track 08 p266*
- Repeat.
- **Grammar clue:** Read about using *must* and *mustn't* for rules and instructions.

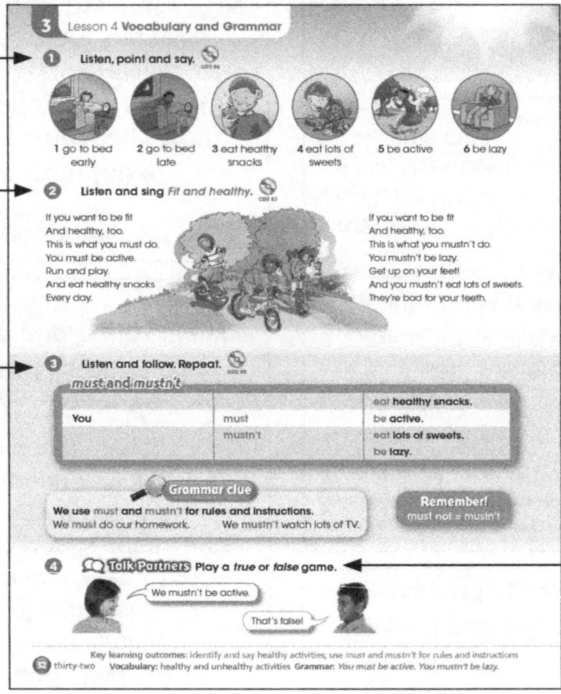
3 Lesson 4 Vocabulary and Grammar

1 Listen, point and say.

1 go to bed early 2 go to bed late 3 eat healthy snacks 4 eat lots of sweets 5 be active 6 be lazy

2 Listen and sing *Fit and healthy*.

If you want to be fit
And healthy, too.
This is what you must do.
You must be active.
Run and play.
And eat healthy snacks
Every day.

If you want to be fit
And healthy, too.
This is what you mustn't do.
You mustn't be lazy.
Get up on your feet!
And you mustn't eat lots of sweets.
They're bad for your teeth.

3 Listen and follow. Repeat.

must and mustn't

You	must	eat healthy snacks.
	mustn't	be active.
		eat lots of sweets.
		be lazy.

Grammar clue
We use must and mustn't for rules and instructions.
We must do our homework. We mustn't watch lots of TV.

Remember! must not = mustn't

4 Talk Partners Play a *true* or *false* game.

Key learning outcomes: identify and say healthy activities; use must and mustn't for rules and instructions
thirty-two Vocabulary: healthy and unhealthy activities Grammar: You must be active. You mustn't be lazy.

Activity 4

- Play a *true* or *false* game.
- Go to the Activity Book.

Ending the lesson

- Review the lesson and reflect on learning.

Extra activities

Reinforcement

- Talk about being happy and safe at school.

Vocabulary extension

- Present four additional vocabulary items.

Link to Science

- **We can move:** Review what our body needs to keep healthy.

Activity Book

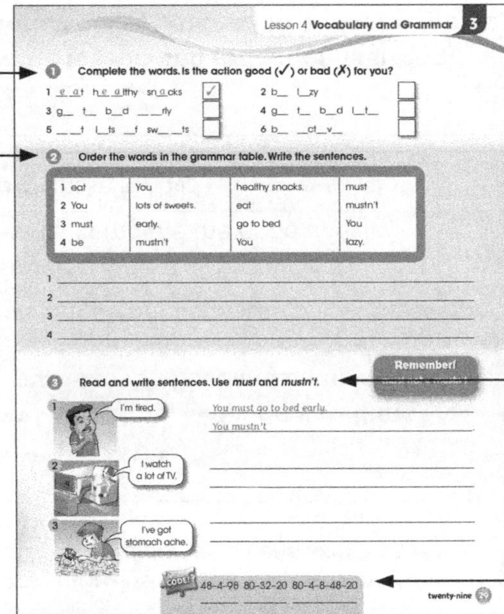
Lesson 4 Vocabulary and Grammar 3

1 Complete the words. Is the action good (✓) or bad (✗) for you?

1 eat healthy snacks ✓ 2 b_ l_zy
3 g_ t_ b_d __rly 4 g_ t_ b_d l_t_
5 __t l_ts _f sw__ts 6 b_ _ct_v_

2 Order the words in the grammar table. Write the sentences.

1 eat	You	healthy snacks.	must
2 You	lots of sweets.	eat	mustn't
3 must	early.	go to bed	You
4 be	mustn't	You	lazy.

3 Read and write sentences. Use *must* and *mustn't*.

You must go to bed early.
You mustn't

CODE! 48-4-98 80-32-20 80-4-8-48-20

twenty-nine

Activity Book

Activity 1

- Complete the words.
- Is the action good (✓) or bad (✗) for you?

Activity 2

- Order the words in the grammar table.
- Write the sentences.

Activity 3

- Read and write sentences.
- Use *must* and *mustn't.*

Code activity

- Complete the code activity.

Digital resources

Teacher's Digital: You can also teach this lesson using the Teacher's App on Navio.

Pupil's Digital: Encourage your pupils to use the Pupil's App on Navio to practise the activities from this lesson.

Powered By NAVIO

Starting the lesson

Use the Trinity Exams Practice cards (optional).

- The pupils practise asking and answering questions.

Review the story.

- Ask the pupils if they remember the story from the last lesson. Organise the class into small groups. Ask each group a question about the story. The pupils should collaborate before they answer.

Set learning outcomes and use the talk cards.

- Say **Today we're going to learn the names of habits that are good for us and habits that are bad for us.**
- Point to the talk cards to show the pupils the different ways they will be working in the lesson.

Pupil's Book Activity 1

Listen, point and say.

▶ *CD2 Track 06 p266*

- (Books closed.) Ask **What activities are / aren't good for us?** Discuss the pupils' ideas as a class.
- (Books open.) Point to the first picture and ask **Is this good for you? Do you go to bed early?** The pupils respond and then repeat *go to bed early*. Repeat the procedure with the other words.
- Play the CD. The pupils listen, point and say.

Pupil's Book Activity 2

Listen and sing *Fit and healthy.*

▶ *CD2 Track 07 p266*

- Focus the class on the picture and ask **What are Lily, Josh and Ravi doing? Are they doing healthy activities?**
- Play the CD. The pupils listen and read.
- Play the CD again. The pupils sing and do the actions.

Pupil's Book Activity 3

Listen and follow. Repeat.

▶ *CD2 Track 08 p266*

- Focus the class on the grammar table, then play the CD. The pupils listen to the first sentence and point to the corresponding parts of the sentence, then repeat the sentence. Repeat the procedure with the other sentences.

Grammar clue

- Read about the use of 'must' and 'mustn't' for rules and instructions. Read the *Remember!* tip.
- Elicit sentences with *must* and *mustn't* from the class. If they need help, they can look at the *Fit and healthy* song for ideas.

Pupil's Book Activity 4

Play a *true* or *false* game.

- (Books closed.) Say **Is this true or false? You (mustn't eat healthy snacks).** Then repeat with a true statement for the class to respond.
- Organise the class into Talk Partners. The pupils play the game.

Activity Book

Activity 1

Complete the words. Is the action good (✓) or bad (✗) for you?

- Say **Some of the letters are missing.** Point to the first missing letter and ask **What's this letter?** Repeat until the pupils can decipher the words. Then ask **Is the action good for you or bad for you?**
- The pupils complete the words and tick / cross the boxes.

Answers: **1** eat healthy snacks (✓) **2** be lazy (✗) **3** go to bed early (✓) **4** go to bed late (✗) **5** eat lots of sweets (✗) **6** be active (✓)

Activity 2

Order the words in the grammar table. Write the sentences.

- Explain that the grammar table is mixed up and that the pupils need to reorder the words. Invite a pupil to read out the first sentence.
- The pupils order and write the remaining sentences. If they need more support, remind them that a sentence begins with a capital letter and ends with a full stop.

Answers: **1** You must eat healthy snacks. **2** You mustn't eat lots of sweets. **3** You must go to bed early. **4** You mustn't be lazy.

Activity 3

Read and write sentences. Use *must* and *mustn't.*

- Invite two pupils to read and complete the first pair of sentences using the lesson's vocabulary.
- The pupils read and write the sentences.

Answers: **1** You must go to bed early. You mustn't go to bed late. **2** You must be active. You mustn't be lazy. **3** You must eat healthy snacks. You mustn't eat lots of sweets.

Code activity

- The pupils complete the code activity.

Answer: lay the table

Ending the lesson

Review the lesson and reflect on learning.

- Say **Today we've learnt the names of habits that are good for us and habits that are bad for us. Tell me what you must / mustn't do to be healthy.**
- Ask **Which was your favourite activity today? Which activity was easy / difficult?**

Extra activities

Reinforcement

- Explain that everybody needs to be safe and happy in school. Ask **What must we do to be safe at school? What mustn't we do? What must we do to be happy in the classroom? What mustn't we do?**

Vocabulary extension

- Use the Vocabulary Booster on Navio and present and practise four additional habits: *do exercise, drink water, eat junk food, have fizzy drinks.*

Link to Science

- If you are studying the Science topic of **We can move** in English, review what we must do to keep our bodies healthy and strong. The pupils work in groups to list healthy and unhealthy habits under the headings *You must* and *You mustn't.*

Key Competences and Key Learning Outcomes

- Say a tongue twister with the 'k' sound
- Practise spelling and learn an alternative spelling for the 'k' sound
- Listen for specific information

- Play a communication game using *must* and *mustn't*

Key language

- *chameleon, chemist's, key, king, kiss, kite; hospital, medicine*
- *You must (take some medicine) and you mustn't (shout). OK. Thank you, (Doctor).*
- Recycled: *broken leg, cold, cough, cut, earache, feel dizzy, feel sick, flu, headache, sore throat, stomach ache, temperature; be quiet, drink some water, wear a hat; run, school, swim; What's the matter? I've got (a sore throat).*

Materials

- Pupil's Book p33; Activity Book p30; Class CD2; Teacher's App on Navio
- Teacher's Resource Bank: Talk cards
- Teacher's Resource Bank: Unit 3 Lesson 5 Communication Activity

Optional materials

- Teacher's Resource Bank: Trinity Exams Practice cards (selected from the Starter Unit and Units 1 and 2)
- Teacher's Resource Bank: Health problems word cards

At a Glance Lesson Plan

Pupil's Book

Starting the lesson

- Use the Trinity Exams Practice cards (optional).
- Review the *Fit and healthy* song.

▶ ***CD2 Track 07 p266***

- Set learning outcomes and use the talk cards.

Activity 1: Speak and spell

- Listen, read and say.

▶ ***CD2 Track 09 p266***

Go to the Activity Book.

Activity 2

- Read the doctor's notes.
- Listen and identify four differences.

▶ ***CD2 Track 10 p266***

Activity 3

- Listen and say what your partner must and mustn't do (Teacher's Resource Bank: Unit 3).

Ending the lesson

- Review the lesson and reflect on learning.

Extra activities

Reinforcement

- Play *Word dictation*.
- Create and act out a doctor / patient conversation in pairs.

Activity Book

Activity Book

Activity 1: Speak and spell

- Complete and say.

Activity 2

- Find and circle the words.
- Classify and write.

Activity 3

- Test your friend.
- Ask and answer.

Code activity

- Complete the code activity.

Digital resources

Teacher's Digital: You can also teach this lesson using the Teacher's App on Navio.

Pupil's Digital: Encourage your pupils to use the Pupil's App on Navio to practise the activities from this lesson.

Powered By NAVIO

Starting the lesson

Use the Trinity Exams Practice cards (optional).

- The pupils practise asking and answering questions.

Review the *Fit and healthy* song.

▶ *CD2 Track 07 p266*

- Play the CD. The pupils sing along and do the actions.

Set learning outcomes and use the talk cards.

- Say **Today we're going to say a tongue twister, practise spelling and play a game.**
- Point to the talk cards to show the pupils the different ways they will be working in the lesson.

Pupil's Book Activity 1: Speak and spell

Listen, read and say.

▶ *CD2 Track 09 p266*

- (Books closed.) Write the letter 'k' on the board and ask **What sound does this letter make?** (*'k'*) List the words the pupils know that contain this letter. Then say **In the last unit, you learnt about another letter that has this sound. What letter is it?** (*'c'*) Once again, elicit words that contain the hard sound of the letter 'c'. Say **Today you're going to learn another way of writing the 'k' sound.**
- (Books open.) Focus the class on the picture and ask **What can you see?** (*A king and a chameleon.*) **Where are they?** (*In a chemist's.*) **What's the problem?**
- Say **Let's listen to the tongue twister.** Play the CD. The pupils follow the text in their books.
- Play the CD again. The pupils join in with the tongue twister.
- Finally, ask the class to identify the alternative way of writing the 'k' sound (*'ch'*).

Activity Book

Activity 1: Speak and spell

Complete and say.

- The pupils complete and say the tongue twister.

Answer: The pink chameleon's got a headache and the king's got stomach ache.

Activity 2

Find and circle the words. Classify and write.

- The pupils find and circle the words in the border that contain the 'k' sound.
- The pupils classify and write the words according to whether they are written with 'ch' or 'k'.

Answers: ch: chameleon, school, stomach, chemist's, earache k: king, key, karate, kite, kiss

Activity 3

Talk Partners. Test your friend. Ask and answer.

- Invite two pupils to read out the speech bubbles.
- Organise the pupils into Talk Partners. The pupils take it in turns to test their partner on the spelling of the words in Activity 2. Stress the importance of prompting, encouraging and helping each other.

Code activity

- The pupils complete the code activity.

Answer: clear the table

Pupil's Book Activity 2

Read the doctor's notes. Listen and identify four differences.

▶ *CD2 Track 10 p266*

- Explain that the pupils are going to listen to two children playing a game. In the game, one child is a doctor and the other isn't very well. The pupils must listen out for four differences between the doctor's notes and what they hear.
- Play the CD, pausing after the first difference. Prompt the pupils to repeat the health problem (*earache*). Then play the rest of the exchange. The pupils repeat the doctor's advice and identify the differences. Repeat the procedure with the other exchanges.

Answers:
1 I've got a headache earache.
2 You mustn't eat sweets go swimming.
3 I've got stomach ache a sore throat.
4 You mustn't run shout.

Pupil's Book Activity 3

Listen and say what your partner must and mustn't do (Teacher's Resource Bank: Unit 3).

- Invite two pupils to read out the speech bubbles.
- Organise the class into Talk Partners. Invite a pair of pupils to demonstrate the game. The Talk Partners then do the role play.
- After a few minutes, ask the partners to swap roles.

Ending the lesson

Review the lesson and reflect on learning.

- Say **Today we've practised a tongue twister.** Elicit the tongue twister from the pupils.
- Ask **Which was your favourite activity today? Which activity was easy / difficult?**

Extra activities

Reinforcement

- Play *Word dictation* (see p27) with the health problems word cards.
- The pupils work in pairs to create a doctor / patient conversation and perform it to the class.

Key Competences and Key Learning Outcomes

- Read and understand a quiz about healthy activities
- Do the quiz with a partner
- Report what you have discovered about a friend's health

- Activate existing knowledge before reading
- Scan the quiz to find specific information

Key language

- *not bad, quiz, well done; does, eats, goes, walks, watches*
- *How much (TV do you watch)? Try to (do more exercise).*
- Recycled: *do sport, eat fruit, go to bed, watch TV; always, every day, five times a week, never, once or twice a week; Are you (fit and healthy)? Do you (walk to school)? I (never) (walk to school). How often do you (eat fruit)? I (eat fruit) (every day). What time do you (go to bed)? I (go to bed) at about (nine o'clock).*

Materials

- Pupil's Book p34; Activity Book p31; Class CD2; Teacher's App on Navio
- Teacher's Resource Bank: Talk cards

Optional materials

- Teacher's Resource Bank: Trinity Exams Practice cards (selected from the Starter Unit and Units 1 and 2)

At a Glance Lesson Plan

Pupil's Book

Starting the lesson

- Use the Trinity Exams Practice cards (optional).
- Review the tongue twister.

▶ *CD2 Track 09 p266*

- Set learning outcomes and use the talk cards.

Before you read: Activity 1

- Look at the quiz title.
- What must you do to be fit and healthy?
- What mustn't you do?

Activity 2

- Read and listen.

▶ *CD2 Track 11 p266*

- Do the quiz with a partner.

Go to the Activity Book.

3 Lesson 6 Reading

Literacy

Before you read

1 Look at the quiz title. What must you do to be fit and healthy? What mustn't you do?

2 Talk Partners Read and listen. Do the quiz with a partner.

Are you fit and healthy?

1 Do you walk to school?
a) always b) sometimes c) never

2 How often do you eat fruit?
a) every day b) five times a week c) once or twice a week

3 What time do you go to bed?
a) about nine o'clock b) about ten o'clock c) about eleven o'clock

4 How much TV do you watch every day?
a) less than one hour b) one to two hours c) more than two hours

5 How often do you do sport?
a) every day b) five times a week c) once or twice a week

After you read

Go to page 31 in your Activity Book.

thirty-four Key learning outcomes: read and understand about healthy activities

Ending the lesson

- Review the lesson and reflect on learning.

Extra activity

Reinforcement

- Use the Internet to investigate other quizzes.

Activity Book

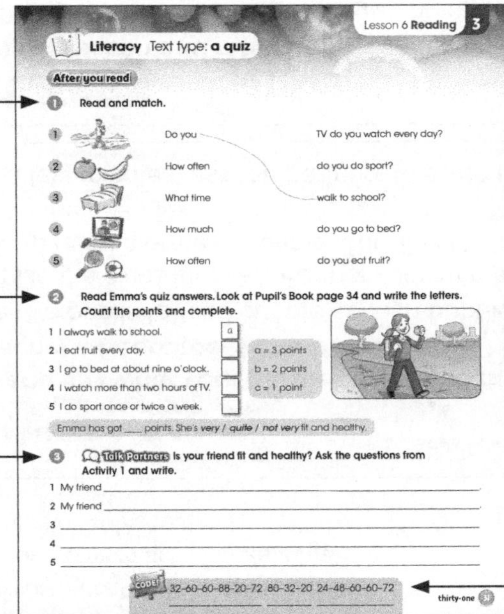

Lesson 6 Reading 3

Literacy Text type: a quiz

After you read

1 Read and match.

1	Do you	TV do you watch every day?
2	How often	do you do sport?
3	What time	walk to school?
4	How much	do you go to bed?
5	How often	do you eat fruit?

2 Read Emma's quiz answers. Look at Pupil's Book page 34 and write the letters. Count the points and complete.

1 I always walk to school. a
2 I eat fruit every day.
3 I go to bed at about nine o'clock.
4 I watch more than two hours of TV.
5 I do sport once or twice a week.

a = 3 points
b = 2 points
c = 1 point

Emma has got ___ points. She's *very / quite / not very* fit and healthy.

3 Talk Partners Is your friend fit and healthy? Ask the questions from Activity 1 and write.

1 My friend ___
2 My friend ___
3 ___
4 ___
5 ___

CODE 32-60-60-88-20-72 80-32-20 24-48-60-60-72

thirty-one

After you read: Activity Book

Activity 1

- Read and match.

Activity 2

- Read Emma's quiz answers.
- Look at Pupil's Book page 34 and write the letters.
- Count the points and

Activity 3

- Is your friend fit and healthy?
- Ask the questions from Activity 1 and write.

Code activity

- Complete the code activity.

Digital resources

Teacher's Digital: You can also teach this lesson using the Teacher's App on Navio.

Pupil's Digital: Encourage your pupils to use the Pupil's App on Navio to practise the activities from this lesson.

Powered By NAVIO

Starting the lesson

Use the Trinity Exams Practice cards (optional).

- The pupils practise asking and answering questions.

Review the tongue twister.

▶ ***CD2 Track 09 p266***

- Ask **What sound did you practise in the tongue twister?** (*'k'*)
- Play the CD. Practise the tongue twister as a class.
- Remind the pupils that they know three spellings for the 'k' sound: 'k', 'c' and 'ch'.

Set learning outcomes and use the talk cards.

- Say **Today we're going to read and do a quiz.** Explain that we can find out information about ourselves from quizzes. Explain that in this quiz there are lots of questions.
- Point to the talk cards to show the pupils the different ways they will be working in the lesson.

Before you read: Pupil's Book Activity 1

Look at the quiz title. What must you do to be fit and healthy? What mustn't you do?

- Invite a pupil to read the title of the quiz. Then use the prompts to elicit all the different things you must / mustn't do to be fit and healthy.

Pupil's Book Activity 2

Read and listen. Do the quiz with a partner.

▶ ***CD2 Track 11 p266***

- Play the CD. The pupils read and listen.
- Read the quiz again as a class, inviting different pupils to read out and respond to each question. Encourage the pupils to give a full response and, if necessary, remind the class of the position of the adverb of frequency and time expression in the sentence.
- Organise the class into Talk Partners. Pupil A asks the questions and records the answers (a, b or c) in their notebook. At the end of the quiz, Pupil A adds up the score for Pupil B. The pupils then swap roles.
- The pupils report back to the class on how fit and healthy their partner is.

After you read: Activity Book

Activity 1

Read and match.

- The pupils work on their own or in pairs to read the beginning of each question and identify the correct ending, using the pictures to help them.
- The pupils check the answers in their Pupil's Books.

Answers: **1** Do you walk to school? **2** How often do you eat fruit? **3** What time do you go to bed? **4** How much TV do you watch every day? **5** How often do you do sport?

Activity 2

Read Emma's quiz answers. Look at Pupil's Book page 34 and write the letters. Count the points and complete.

- The pupils work on their own or in pairs to read Emma's quiz answers. They look at Pupil's Book page 34 and write the corresponding letters from the answer key.
- The pupils add up the score and work out if Emma is very, quite or not very fit and healthy.

Answers: **1** a **2** a **3** a **4** c **5** c Emma has got 11 points. She's very fit and healthy.

Activity 3

Is your friend fit and healthy? Ask the questions from Activity 1 and write.

- Working with a Talk Partner, the pupils ask the questions from Activity 1.
- Highlight the use of the third-person form of the verb and invite different pupils to spell the words. Write the words on the board: *watches, does, walks, goes, eats.*
- The pupils work on their own to write the sentences.

Code activity

- The pupils complete the code activity.

Answer: hoover the floor

Ending the lesson

Review the lesson and reflect on learning.

- Say **Today we've done a quiz. What's the title of the quiz? What questions does it ask? Are you fit and healthy?** Elicit the pupils' responses.
- Ask **Which was your favourite activity today? Which activity was easy / difficult?**

Extra activity

Reinforcement

- If you have an Internet connection, you can show the pupils other quizzes. There are quizzes about animals, music, films and what's on in the news on the CBBC site: http://www.bbc.co.uk/newsround

Key Competences and Key Learning Outcomes

- Use question marks
- Prepare and write a quiz about healthy eating
- Predict the questions that will appear in a quiz
- Identify some of the text features of a quiz
- Use criteria to check your writing
- Share your writing with a partner

Key language

- *answer, dinner, fizzy drinks, healthy diet, question*
- *Do you have (a healthy diet)? Do (the quiz to find out). Do you (eat breakfast)? How often do you (eat vegetables)?*
- Recycled: *always, every day, five times a week, never, once or twice a week, sometimes; breakfast, quiz, vegetables*

Materials

- Pupil's Book p35; Activity Book p32; Class CD2; Teacher's App on Navio
- Teacher's Resource Bank: Talk cards

Optional materials

- Teacher's Resource Bank: Trinity Exams Practice cards (selected from the Starter Unit and Units 1 and 2)
- Paper or card for signs

At a Glance Lesson Plan

Pupil's Book

Starting the lesson

- Use the Trinity Exams Practice cards (optional).
- Review questions that begin with 'What'.
- Set learning outcomes and use the talk cards.

Investigate a text: Activity 1

- Think of questions for a quiz about healthy eating.

Investigate a text: Activity 2

- Read and listen.
- ▶ *CD2 Track 12 p266*
- Can you see your questions?

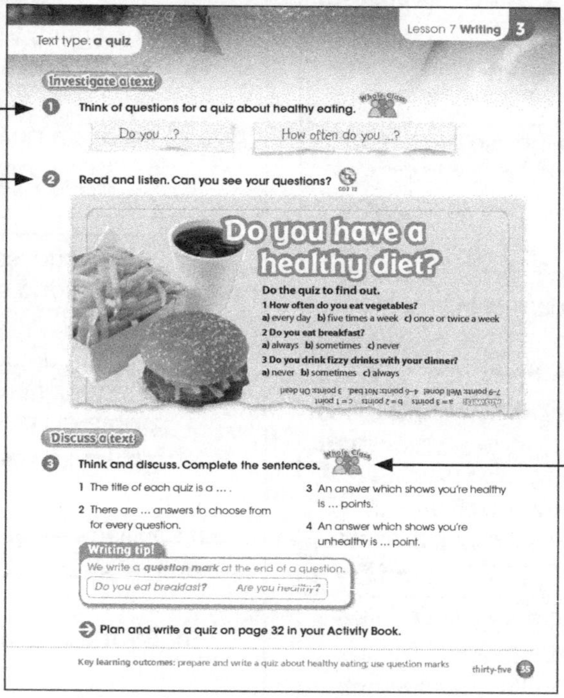

Discuss a text: Activity 3

- Think and discuss.
- Complete the sentences.
- **Writing tip:** Read about question marks.

Go to the Activity Book.

Ending the lesson

- Review the lesson and reflect on learning.

Extra activity

Reinforcement

- Make a sign about being healthy.

Link to Science

- **We can move:** Review what our bodies need to be healthy.

Activity Book

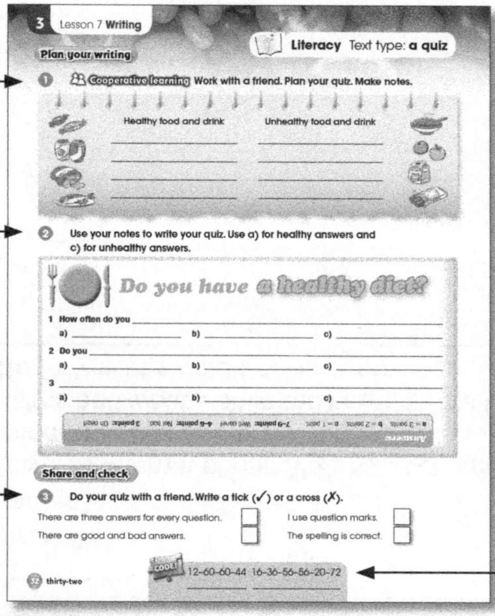

Activity Book

Plan your writing: Activity 1

- Work with a friend.
- Plan your quiz.
- Make notes.

Activity 2

- Use your notes to write your quiz.
- Use a) for healthy answers and c) for unhealthy answers

Share and check: Activity 3

- Do your quiz with a friend.
- Write a tick (✓) or a cross (✗).

Code activity

- Complete the code activity.

Digital resources

Teacher's Digital: You can also teach this lesson using the Teacher's App on Navio.

Pupil's Digital: Encourage your pupils to use the Pupil's App on Navio to practise the activities from this lesson.

Powered By NAVIO

Starting the lesson

Use the Trinity Exams Practice cards (optional).

- The pupils practise asking and answering questions.

Review questions that begin with 'What'.

- Write *What* on the board and elicit different questions which begin with this question word, e.g. *What's your name? What's your favourite (food)?* Then elicit other ways of beginning a question and encourage the class to give you examples. Write the question words in a random order on the board.
- Place a chair in the middle of the room and say **This is the hot seat.** Invite a confident pupil to sit in the seat and then prompt the rest of the class to ask him / her questions. After one minute, stop the activity.
- Repeat with different pupils in the hot seat.

Set learning outcomes and use the talk cards.

- Ask **What did we read in the last lesson?** (*A quiz.*) Say **Today we're going to investigate another quiz. Then we're going to plan and write our own quiz.**
- Point to the talk cards to show the pupils the different ways they will be working in the lesson.

Investigate a text: Pupil's Book Activity 1

Think of questions for a quiz about healthy eating.

- Read the instructions for the activity and prompt the pupils to predict the questions that may appear in a quiz about healthy eating.

Investigate a text: Pupil's Book Activity 2

Read and listen. Can you see your questions?

▶ *CD2 Track 12 p266*

- Play the CD. The pupils listen and read.
- The pupils read the quiz again to check how many questions they guessed correctly.

Discuss a text: Pupil's Book Activity 3

Think and discuss. Complete the sentences.

- Invite a pupil to read out the first statement and to complete the sentence.
- Repeat the procedure with the other statements.

Answers: **1** question **2** three **3** three **4** one

Writing tip

- Read the information. Ask the class to think of questions in their language. Do they finish with a question mark? Do they have one or two question marks?

Activity Book

Plan your writing: Activity 1

Writing Partners. Work with a friend. Plan your quiz. Make notes.

- Point to and name the healthy and unhealthy foods which illustrate the activity.
- Organise the class into Talk Partners. The partners write a list of healthy and unhealthy foods in their Activity Books.

Activity 2

Use your notes to write your quiz. Use a) for healthy answers and c) for unhealthy answers.

- Focus the class on the activity. If necessary, model how to complete the quiz framework. The pupils work as a class to give you the information. Write the questions and three possible answers on the board. Make sure that the healthiest answer is always answer **a** and the least healthy answer is always answer **c**.
- The Talk Partners write their quiz in their Activity Books.

Share and check: Activity 3

Writing Partners. Do your quiz with a friend. Write a tick (✓) or a cross (✗).

- Organise the class into new pairs. The pupils ask their new partner the questions in their quiz. They then calculate the score and give a result.
- Focus the class on the statements. Read through the statements as a class.
- The pupils work in their new pairs to decide if their quiz fulfils all the criteria and tick or cross the corresponding boxes.

Code activity

- The pupils complete the code activity.

Answer: cook dinner

Ending the lesson

Review the lesson and reflect on learning.

- Say **Today we've written a quiz. Are you happy with it?** The pupils give their opinions.
- Ask **Which was your favourite activity today? Which activity was easy / difficult?**

Extra activity

Reinforcement

- Organise the class into pairs. Explain that you want them to design a poster to tell people how to be healthy.
- The pupils work with their partner to design and make the poster.
- Use the finished posters to make an attractive wall display.

Link to Science

- If you are studying the Science topic of **We can move** in English, you could take this opportunity to review what our bodies need. Talk about healthy and unhealthy food and elicit other important things, e.g. sleep, rest and exercise.

Key Competences and Key Learning Outcomes

- Use the Internet to investigate Malta
- Read and listen for specific information
- Read about sea animal rescue in Malta
- Think about your own culture and identity

Key language

- *broken bones, divers, ill, inspect, investigate, marine / sea animals, rescue centre, scientists, turtles, warm, wild, work hard*
- *(Turtles) sometimes need help because (they eat plastic bags). When (the turtles are better), the vets (put them back into the sea).*
- Recycled: *cuts, hurt, medicine, vets*

Materials

- Pupil's Book p36; Activity Book p33; Class CD2; Teacher's App on Navio
- Teacher's Resource Bank: Talk cards
- An online world map
- Coloured pencils (white and red)

Optional materials

- Teacher's Resource Bank: Trinity Exams Practice cards (selected from the Starter Unit and Units 1 and 2)

At a Glance Lesson Plan

Pupil's Book

Starting the lesson

- Use the Trinity Exams Practice cards (optional).
- Review domestic and wild animals.
- Set learning outcomes and use the talk cards.

Activity 1

- Read Luke's questions.
- What do you think?

Activity 2

- Read and listen.
- ▶ *CD2 Track 13 p267*
- Answer Luke's questions.
- **Think about your culture** Do people help wild animals in your country? Which animals do they help?
- Go to the Activity Book.

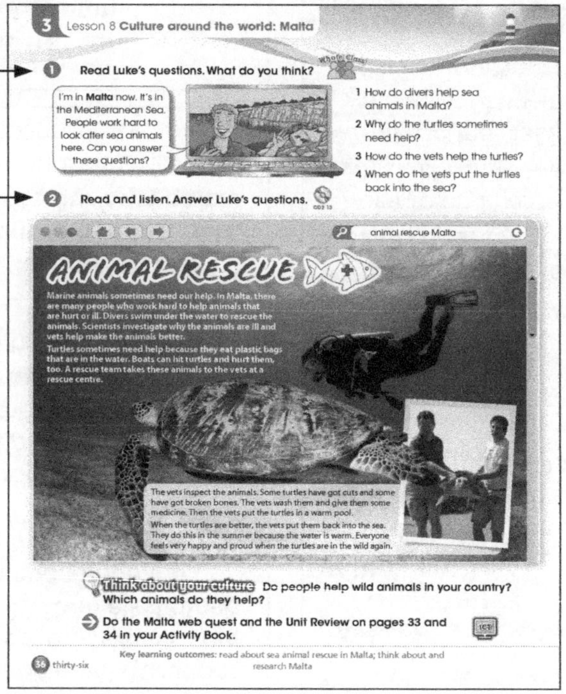

Ending the lesson

- Review the lesson and reflect on learning.

Activity Book

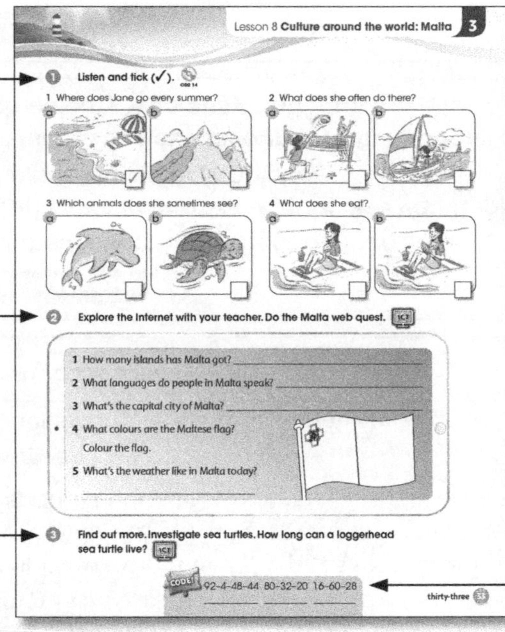

Activity Book

Activity 1

- Listen and tick (✓).
- ▶ *CD2 Track 14 p267*

Activity 2

- Explore the Internet with your teacher. Do the Malta web quest.

Activity 3

- Find out more. Investigate sea turtles. How long can a loggerhead sea turtle live?

Code activity

- Complete the code activity.

Digital resources

Teacher's Digital: You can also teach this lesson using the Teacher's App on Navio.

Starting the lesson

Use the Trinity Exams Practice cards (optional).

- The pupils practise asking and answering questions.

Review domestic and wild animals.

- Divide the board into two halves and write the headings *Domestic animals* and *Wild animals*. Hand the chalk or board pen to the first pupil who writes the name of an animal in the correct section. That pupil then passes the pen to the next pupil, who adds a word. The rest of the class can suggest words or help with spelling, but they cannot repeat an animal. The activity finishes when each pupil has written an animal on the board.

Set learning outcomes and use the talk cards.

- Say **Today we're going to investigate Malta.**
- Point to the talk cards to show the pupils the different ways they will be working in the lesson.

Pupil's Book Activity 1

Read Luke's questions. What do you think?

- Read the speech bubble as a class. Encourage the class to tell you where the Mediterranean Sea is. Then show the pupils where Malta is on a world map.
- Read Luke's questions as a class. Encourage the pupils to predict the answers.

Pupil's Book Activity 2

Read and listen. Answer Luke's questions.

▸ *CD2 Track 13 p267*

- Focus the class on the photos. Ask **What can you see?** (*A diver, a turtle, vets helping a turtle.*)
- Ask the pupils to read the text. If you want them to read the text without the support of the CD, set a time limit for this task. Otherwise, play the CD, pausing after each paragraph to check understanding.
- Ask **What animals do they rescue?** (*Turtles.*) **Are they wild animals or pets?** (*Wild animals.*) **Who helps them?** (*Divers, vets and scientists.*)
- The pupils answer Luke's questions.

Answers: **1** They swim under water to rescue the animals. **2** They sometimes eat plastic bags and boats can also hurt them. **3** They inspect the animals, wash them, give them medicine and put them in a warm pool. **4** They put them back into the sea when they are better, during the summer.

Think about your culture

- Read out the questions and prompt different pupils to tell you about the wild animals that are protected in their country.

Activity Book

Activity 1

Listen and tick (✓).

▸ *CD2 Track 14 p267*

- Ask the pupils to read out the first question and name the two places (*beach and mountains*). Then play the CD, pausing to allow the pupils to tick.
- Repeat the procedure with the other questions.

Answers: **1** a **2** b **3** a **4** b

Activity 2

Explore the Internet with your teacher. Do the Malta web quest.

- Read out the instructions for the activity.
- Connect to a children's website that provides geographical information about Malta. (See suggested websites opposite.) Read out questions 1–4. The pupils work as a class to find and write the answers. They should also colour the Maltese flag.
- Read out question 5. Connect to a website which shows the weather around the world. (See suggested link opposite.) The pupils complete the information about the day's weather.

Answers: **1** three **2** Maltese and English **3** Valletta **4** white and red

Activity 3

Find out more. Investigate sea turtles. How long can a loggerhead sea turtle live?

- Encourage the pupils to predict how long a loggerhead sea turtle can live for.
- If you are doing the investigation as a class, go to a suitable website, e.g. National Geographic Kids. The pupils should read the information to find and note interesting facts about sea turtles. They should also scan the information to find out how long a loggerhead sea turtle can live for.
- Alternatively, organise the class into small groups. The groups should connect to a suitable website and do the investigation.
- The pupils share their information with the rest of the class.

Answer: A loggerhead sea turtle can live for more than 50 years.

Suggested websites

http://maps.google.es/
http://www.ducksters.com and search for 'Malta'
http://www.bbc.co.uk/weather

Code activity

- The pupils complete the code activity.

Answer: walk the dog

Ending the lesson

Review the lesson and reflect on learning.

- Say **Today we've learnt about Malta. Which animals do people help there?** Elicit the information from the pupils.
- Ask **Which was your favourite activity today? Which activity was easy / difficult?**

Go to the AB Unit Review on page 247.

Key Competences and Key Learning Outcomes
• Watch and understand a video about being healthy
• Review ways to be fit and healthy • Identify how keeping healthy benefits the body

Key language

- *burgers, fruit, lunch, salad, sandwich, snack, sugar, thirsty, water*
- Recycled: *exercise, fit, fizzy drink, healthy, unhealthy*
- *What do you do to stay fit and healthy? Fruit is a fantastic snack. Why don't you eat a(n) (orange)? How often do you (do exercise)? I (do exercise) (once a week).*

Materials

- Pupil's Book p37; Activity Book p35; Class CD2; Teacher's App on Navio
- Teacher's Resource Bank: Talk cards

Optional materials

- Teacher's Resource Bank: Trinity Exams Practice cards (selected from the Starter Unit and Units 1 and 2)

At a Glance Lesson Plan

Pupil's Book

Starting the lesson

- Use the Trinity Exams Practice cards (optional).
- **Think-Pair-Share.** Review habits that are good for us and habits that are bad for us.
- Set learning outcomes and use the talk cards.

Activity 1

- Before you watch
- Watch the video.
- *Unit 3 video p285*
- Which healthy activities do the children do?

Activity 2

- Watch the video again.
- *Unit 3 video*
- Read and say *true* or *false*.
- Correct the false sentences.

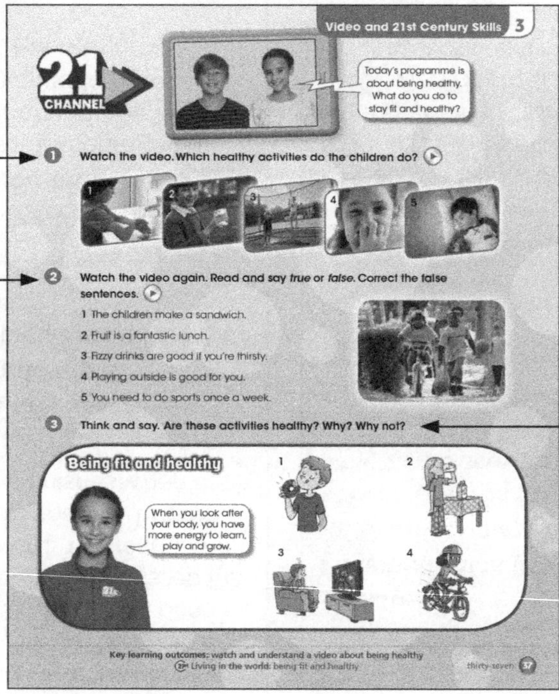

Activity 3

- Think and say.
- Are these activities healthy?
- Why? Why not?
- Go to the Activity Book.

Ending the lesson

- Review the lesson and reflect on learning.

Extra activity

Reinforcement

- Give advice using *must* or *mustn't*.

Activity Book

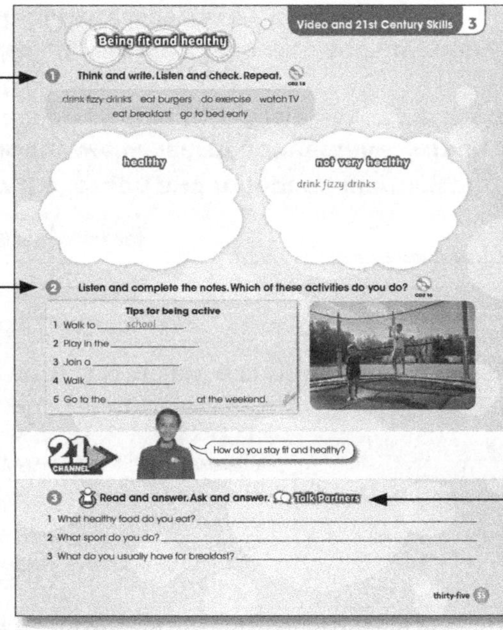

Activity Book

Activity 1

- Think and write.
- Listen and check.
- ▶ *CD2 Track 15 p267*
- Repeat.

Activity 2

- Listen and complete the notes.
- ▶ *CD2 Track 16 p267*
- Which of these activities do you do?

Activity 3

- Read and answer.
- Ask and answer.

Digital resources

Teacher's Digital: You can also teach this lesson using the Teacher's App on Navio.

Pupil's Digital: Encourage your pupils to use the Pupil's App on Navio to practise the activities from this lesson.

Powered By NAVIO

Starting the lesson

Use the Trinity Exams Practice cards (optional).

- The pupils practise asking and answering questions.

Think-Pair-Share. Review habits that are good for us and habits that are bad for us.

- Ask **Can you remember which habits are good for us and which are bad for us?** The class thinks silently for a minute.
- Then the pupils work with a Talk Partner to name good and bad habits.
- Invite different Talk Partners to say a different habit. The rest of the class decide whether it is a good habit or a bad habit. Write the habit on the board (under *Good* or *Bad*) and prompt the class to repeat it.
- Finally, repeat the procedure, asking different pairs of Talk Partners, until all the ideas have been recorded.

Set learning outcomes and use the talk cards.

- Say **Today we're going to watch a video and then ask and answer questions about being healthy**.
- Point to the talk cards to show the pupils the different ways they will be working in the lesson.

Pupil's Book Activity 1

Before you watch

- Read the speech bubble to pupils. Ask **What do you do to stay fit and healthy?** Elicit responses from a number of pupils.

Watch the video. Which healthy activities do the children do? *p285*

- Watch Part 1. Ask pupils **What do you think you are going to see next?** Elicit ideas and explain that they will see how other children stay fit and healthy.
- Play Part 2. Ask general questions to check understanding. Focus the pupils on the photos in Activity 1. Check vocabulary. Say **Which healthy activities do the children do?** Elicit ideas.
- Play Part 2 again for the pupils to answer the questions. Check answers as a class.

Answers: **2** drink water **3** do exercise **4** eat fruit

Pupil's Book Activity 2

Watch the video again. Read and say *true* or *false*. Correct the false sentences.

- Ask a pupil to read out sentence 1. Ask the class whether they think the sentence is true or false. Repeat with sentences 2–5.
- Play Part 2. Students work in pairs to decide whether the sentences are true or false. They correct the false sentences.

Answers: **1** F The children make a salad. **2** F Fruit is a fantastic snack. **3** F Don't drink fizzy drinks when you're thirsty. Drink water. **4** T **5** F You need to do sports two or three times a week.

Pupil's Book Activity 3

Think and say. Are these activities healthy? Why? Why not?

- Ask **What do Chloe and Mark do at the end of the video?** (*They go for a run.*) **Is this healthy?** (*Yes.*) **Why?** (*You must be active.*)
- Review the use of *must* and *mustn't* if necessary.
- Look at the pictures with pupils and explain that they need to decide whether the activity in each one is healthy or unhealthy. They should also say why or why not. Look at the pictures with the class and check vocabulary.
- Pupils work in pairs to decide whether the activity is healthy or unhealthy and give a reason using *must* or *mustn't*.
- Check answers with the class. Say **Is this healthy or unhealthy? Why?**

Activity Book

Activity 1

Think and write. Listen and check. Repeat.

CD2 Track 15 p267

- Look at the words in the box and check vocabulary.
- Pupils work on their own to put the activities in the correct spaces.
- Play the CD and check answers.

Answers: healthy: do exercise, eat breakfast, go to bed early; not very healthy: drink fizzy drinks, eat burgers, watch TV

Activity 2

Listen and complete the notes. Which of these activities do you do?

CD2 Track 16 p267

- Ask pupils for ideas of how to be more active. Read out the information. Then play the CD, pausing to allow the pupils to write the missing information.
- Play the CD again without pausing.

Answers: **1** school **2** playground **3** sports club **4** the dog **5** park

Activity 3

Read and answer. Ask and answer.

- Read out the speech bubble and elicit answers from the class. Once pupils are confident answering, you could make the question more specific and ask about healthy food, what sports they do, etc.
- The pupils write answers to the questions about how they stay fit and healthy.
- Organise the pupils into Talk Partners. The pupils take it in turns to ask and answer questions.

Ending the lesson

Review the lesson and reflect on learning.

- Say **Today we've watched a video about staying fit and healthy.** Ask **What must we do to stay fit and healthy? What mustn't we do?**
- Ask **Which was your favourite activity today? Which activity was easy / difficult?**

Extra activity

Reinforcement

- Say **I often drink fizzy drinks. I must drink water.** Say another unhealthy activity and encourage a pupil to tell you what you *must* or *mustn't* do.
- The pupils work in pairs to say unhealthy activities and what they *must* or *mustn't* do.

My project 1: The zoo challenge

Key Competences and Key Learning Outcomes

- Remember and learn the names of things you can see at a zoo
- Review different types of animals (optional)
- Investigate a zoo
- Share information with your group

Key language

- *crocodile, eagle, elephant, giraffe, lizard, monkey, ostrich, parrot, penguin, snake, tiger, tortoise; fish, fruit, grass, insects, leaves, meat, seeds; first aid post, picnic area, playground, restaurant, shop, visitors, zoo; alone, bird, cage, cave, cold / hot / warm climate, in a group, land, mammal, pool, reptile, rocks, tree, water*
- *What's your (mammal)? It's (an elephant). It lives (in a group). It eats (grass).*

Materials

- Pupil's Book p38; Activity Book p36; CD2
- Teacher's Resource Bank: Talk cards

Optional materials

- Teacher's Resource Bank: Trinity Exams Practice cards (selected from the Starter Unit and Units 1, 2 and 3)

At a Glance Lesson Plan

Pupil's Book

Starting the lesson

- Use the Trinity Exams Practice cards (optional).
- Set learning outcomes and use the talk cards.

Investigate: Activity 1

- Is there a zoo in your town?
- What can you see and do at a zoo?

Investigate: Activity 2

- Work in groups.
- Look at the map of a zoo and make lists.

Activity 3

- Listen and check your lists.
- ▶ *CD2 Track 17 p267*
- Listen again and repeat the words.

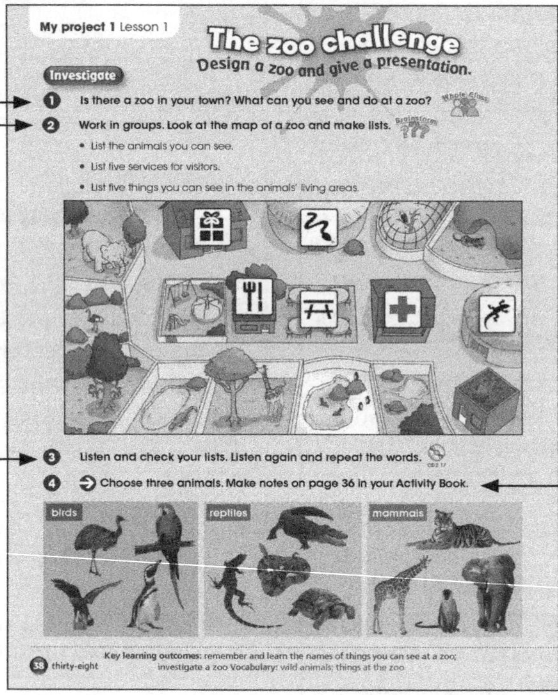

Activity 4

- Choose three animals.
- Make notes on page 36 in your Activity Book.

Ending the lesson

- Review the lesson and reflect on learning.

Extra activity

Reinforcement

- Practise describing animals.

Link to Science

- **Animals:** Review different types of animals.

Activity Book

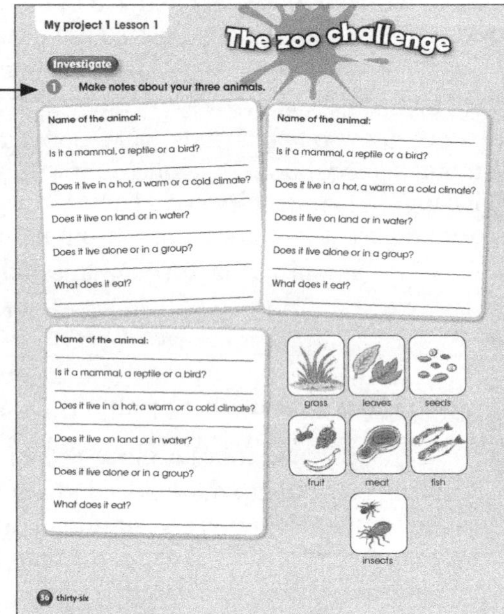

Activity Book

Activity 1

- Make notes about your three animals.

Digital resources

Teacher's Digital: You can also teach this lesson using the Teacher's App on Navio.

Pupil's Digital: Encourage your pupils to use the Pupil's App on Navio to practise the activities from this lesson.

Starting the lesson

Use the Trinity Exams Practice cards (optional).

- The pupils practise asking and answering questions.

Set learning outcomes and use the talk cards.

- Say **Today we're going to begin a project.**
- Point to the talk cards to show the pupils the different ways they will be working in the lesson.

Investigate: Pupil's Book Activity 1

Is there a zoo in your town? What can you see and do at a zoo?

- (Books closed.) Encourage the pupils to tell you if there is a zoo in or near your town and what you can see and do there. Ask **Do you like going to the zoo? Which is your favourite animal? Where do the animals live?**
- (Books open.) Focus the pupils' attention on the task at the top of the page. Read the challenge.

Investigate: Pupil's Book Activity 2

Work in groups. Look at the map of a zoo and make lists.

- Focus the class on the map and ask **What can you see?** Read the three tasks, check understanding and prompt the class to find examples.
- Organise the class into groups of four and ask each group to choose a scribe who will write the lists in his / her notebook. Set a time limit. The pupils should work together to identify and list items that appear on the map. Remind the pupils that everyone should contribute when they are working in a group.
- At the end of the time, prompt different groups to read out their lists. Write the words on the board and then elicit / give the names of any unknown items.

Suggested answers: Animals: elephant, ostrich, snake, monkey, parrot, lizard, crocodile, tiger, penguin, giraffe, tortoise, eagle
Services for visitors: restaurant, playground, picnic area, shop, first aid post
Living areas: cave, tree, cage, rock, pool

Pupil's Book Activity 3

Listen and check your lists. Listen again and repeat the words.

▶ *CD2 Track 17 p267*

- Pupils listen and check their lists. Then they listen again and repeat the words.

Pupil's Book Activity 4

Choose three animals. Make notes on page 36 in your Activity Book.

- Explain that there are three groups of animals shown in the photos: mammals, reptiles and birds.
- Ask the class to name the animals in the pictures.
- Pupils choose three animals and make notes on page 36 of their Activity Book.

Activity Book

Activity 1

Make notes about your three animals.

- Focus the pupils' attention on the activity and check understanding. If they need support, complete the notes for one of the animals on the board with the class. Point out the pictures and labels on the page.
- The pupils work on their own to complete the notes about their three animals. If there is a pupil who needs extra support, pair him / her up with another pupil who is making notes about the same group of animals.

Ending the lesson

Review the lesson and reflect on learning.

- Say **Today we've learnt about zoos. What can you tell me about animals in a zoo?** Elicit the pupils' responses.
- Ask **Which was your favourite activity today? Which activity was easy / difficult?**

Extra activity

Reinforcement

- Say **I'm thinking of an animal. Which animal am I thinking of?** Prompt the class to ask you closed questions, e.g. *Can it (fly)? Is it (a lion)? Has it got (wings)? Does it (climb)?* When a pupil guesses correctly, invite him / her to think of a different animal and continue with the game.

Link to Science

- If you are studying the Science topic of **Animals** in English, you could take this opportunity to review different types of animals and classify them as vertebrates or invertebrates. You could also review the classification of vertebrates as mammals, reptiles, birds, fish or amphibians. Make a list of zoo animals as a class. (There should be three different species from each animal class in the list.)

My project 1: The zoo challenge

Key Competences and Key Learning Outcomes

- Present your zoo to the class
- Reflect on what you've learnt and how well you've worked together
- Work together to design a zoo
- Use the Internet to find animal photos

Key language

- Recycled: zoo animals; food that zoo animals eat; services for visitors; animals' living areas
- *Let's call the zoo … We can have (some elephants). The (crocodile) needs (a pool). The zoo is called (Animal Land). There's (a playground) in the zoo. There are (elephants). It's got (a restaurant). They've got (a playground). Children can (play here). That's a (good idea). I'm not sure.*

Materials

- Pupil's Book p39; Activity Book p37
- Teacher's Resource Bank: Talk cards
- A large piece of paper or card for each group of four pupils; coloured pens and pencils

Optional materials

- Teacher's Resource Bank: Trinity Exams Practice cards (selected from the Starter Unit and Units 1, 2 and 3)

At a Glance Lesson Plan

Pupil's Book

Starting the lesson

- Use the Trinity Exams Practice cards (optional).
- Set learning outcomes and use the talk cards.

Plan and create your project: Activity 1

- Discuss the questions.
- Write the information on page 37 in your Activity Book.

Go to the Activity Book.

Cooperative learning

- Take turns to speak when you work in a group.

Activity 2

- Design and draw your zoo.

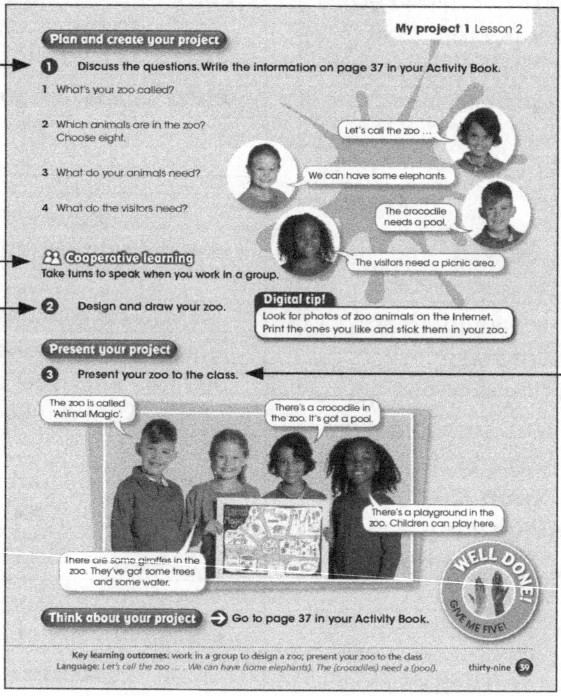

My project 1 Lesson 2

Plan and create your project

1 Discuss the questions. Write the information on page 37 in your Activity Book.

1 What's your zoo called?

2 Which animals are in the zoo? Choose eight.

3 What do your animals need?

4 What do the visitors need?

Cooperative learning: Take turns to speak when you work in a group.

2 Design and draw your zoo.

Digital tip! Look for photos of zoo animals on the Internet. Print the ones you like and stick them in your zoo.

Present your project

3 Present your zoo to the class.

Think about your project → Go to page 37 in your Activity Book.

Key learning outcomes: work in a group to design a zoo; present your zoo to the class
Language: Let's call the zoo … We can have (some elephants). The (crocodiles) need a (pool).

thirty-nine 39

Present your project: Activity 3

- Present your zoo to the class.
- Think about your project

Go to the Activity Book.

Ending the lesson

- Review the lesson and reflect on learning.

Extra activity

Reinforcement

- Create a radio advert.

Activity Book

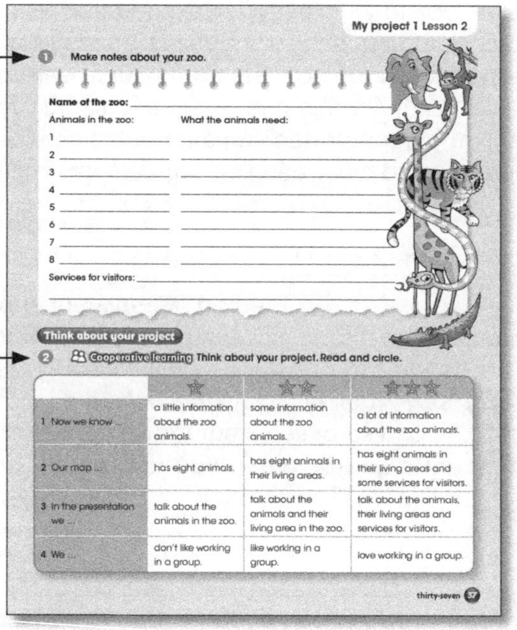

My project 1 Lesson 2

1 Make notes about your zoo.

Name of the zoo:

Animals in the zoo:	What the animals need:
1	
2	
3	
4	
5	
6	
7	
8	

Services for visitors:

Think about your project

2 Cooperative learning: Think about your project. Read and circle.

	★	★★	★★★
1 Now we know …	a little information about the zoo animals.	some information about the zoo animals.	a lot of information about the zoo animals.
2 Our map …	has eight animals.	has eight animals in their living areas.	has eight animals in their living areas and some services for visitors.
3 In the presentation we …	talk about the animals in the zoo.	talk about the animals and their living area in the zoo.	talk about the animals, their living areas and services for visitors.
4 We …	don't like working in a group.	like working in a group.	love working in a group.

thirty-seven 37

Activity Book

Activity 1

- Make notes about your zoo.

Think about your project: Activity 2

- Think about your project
- Read and circle.

Digital resources

Teacher's Digital: You can also teach this lesson using the Teacher's App on Navio.

Pupil's Digital: Encourage your pupils to use the Pupil's App on Navio to practise the activities from this lesson.

Powered By NAVIO

Starting the lesson

Use the Trinity Exams Practice cards (optional).
- The pupils practise asking and answering questions.

Set learning outcomes and use the talk cards.
- Say **Today we're going to continue the project.** Prompt the class to tell you what they did in the last lesson.
- Point to the talk cards to show the pupils the different ways they will be working in the lesson.
- Highlight that the pupils will be working in small groups and prompt the class to tell you what they must do when they work in groups (*listen, take turns, respect different opinions*, etc.).

Plan and create your project: Pupil's Book Activity 1

Discuss the questions. Write the information on page 37 in your Activity Book.
- Focus the class on the activity and invite a pupil to read out the questions. Explain that the pupils should work in their groups to decide on: a name for the zoo, eight animals for the zoo, the things the eight animals need, and services for the visitors. This information is recorded on page 37 of the Activity Book.
- If pupils need more support with this activity, ask the groups to do one task at a time. First, ask the groups to choose the zoo's name and record it in their Activity Books. Then repeat for the remaining tasks.

Activity Book

Activity 1

Make notes about your zoo.
- The pupils record their decisions about the zoo, the animals, what the animals need, and services for visitors.

Take turns to speak when you work in a group.
- Read out the rubric. Discuss with the class how we should show respect for each other and allow each other to speak.
- Emphasise the importance of listening to others.

Plan and create your project: Pupil's Book Activity 2

Design and draw your zoo.
- Once the pupils have completed their plan, they design and draw their zoo.
- Hand out a large piece of card or paper to each group and ask them to take out their coloured pens and pencils. The pupils work as a group to draw their zoo. If possible, students can use the Internet to find pictures of animals for their zoo as per the Digital tip.

Present your project: Pupil's Book Activity 3

Present your zoo to the class.
- Focus the class on the photo and encourage the pupils to talk about what they can see. Ask **What are the children talking about? What can you see on their poster?** Then ask a pupil to read out the speech bubbles.
- Invite different groups in turn to present their design to the rest of the class. Ensure that each pupil in the group participates in the presentation, but accept that some pupils may contribute more than others. At the end of each presentation, ask the group a question and encourage the rest of the class to do the same.
- If you wish, ask the class to vote on which zoo is the best. Write the names of the different zoos on the board and explain that the pupils can only vote for one zoo and they can't vote for their own zoo. Say the name of each zoo in turn and ask the pupils to raise their hands if they think that zoo is the best. Write the number of votes next to the zoo's name.

Think about your project
- Tell the pupils that they are now going to think about what they have achieved and evaluate how their project went. Ask the pupils to turn to page 37 in their Activity Book.

Activity Book

Activity 2

Think about your project. Read and circle.
- Ask the pupils to think about their project. Read out each statement and ask the pupils to circle one, two or three stars depending on their project.

Ending the lesson

Review the lesson and reflect on learning.
- Say **We've completed a project about zoos. What was your job? Are you pleased with what you achieved?** Elicit the pupils' answers.
- Ask **Which was your favourite activity? Which activity was easy / difficult?**

Extra activity

Reinforcement
- Ask the class how they can advertise their zoo (*newspapers, radio, TV, posters*). Tell the pupils they are going to write a short radio advertisement. Write examples of language on the board: *Come to (Animal Land)! You can see (amazing animals). You can play (in the playground). You can feed (the penguins). There are (so many attractions). It's (fantastic)!*
- The pupils work in groups to write their adverts. When they have finished, the groups read them out to the rest of the class or make a recording of them on a computer.

Date: ______________ Unit: ________

1 What did my pupils learn in this unit?

2 How did my pupils work? (✓)

individually ☐ in pairs ☐ in small groups ☐

in large groups ☐ as a class ☐

3 Which key competences did my pupils develop?

- Competence in linguistic communication ☐
- Competence in mathematics, science and technology ☐
- Digital competence ☐
- Learning to learn ☐
- Social and civic competences ☐
- Sense of initiative and entrepreneurship ☐
- Cultural awareness and expression ☐

4 Which lessons / activities were the most successful and why?

5 Which lessons / activities did my pupils find the most difficult and why?

6 What did I try in the classroom for the first time? How did it go?

7 Which resources did I find most useful? (including webpages)

8 What could I do differently next time I teach this unit?

4 Creative cooking

Unit overview

Key Competences and Key Learning Outcomes

- Identify and name different food (Lesson 1)
- Say the vocabulary chant (Lesson 1)
- Understand and act out a conversation (Lesson 2)
- Make requests with 'would like' (Lesson 2)
- Follow, complete and correct the grammar tables (Lessons 2 and 4)
- Learn adjectives to describe food (Lesson 4)
- Talk about what food you prefer (Lesson 4)
- Understand that adjectives are the same with singular and plural objects (Lesson 7)
- Watch and understand a video (Video and 21st Century Skills)

- Use a code to read a message (Lesson 3)

- Use the Pupil's App on Navio
- Investigate India (Lesson 8)

- Say a tongue twister, learn another spelling for the 'z' sound and practise spelling (Lesson 5)
- Practise activity types found in the Cambridge Exams: A1 Movers
- Review your own learning (Review)

- Understand the importance of trying new food (Lesson 3)

- Work with a Talk Partner to practise and reinforce learning (all lessons)
- Play a communication game (Lesson 5)
- Use imagination to create food pictures (Video and 21st Century Skills)

- Sing a song (Lesson 1)
- Understand, act out and give an opinion on a story (Lesson 3)
- Say a rap (Lesson 4)
- Read and understand a shape poem (Lesson 6)
- Plan, write and evaluate a shape poem (Lesson 7)
- Learn about India (Lesson 8)
- Think about your own culture (Lesson 8)

Vocabulary

Core vocabulary
cheese, chillies, mushrooms, olives, onions, peppers, pineapple, prawns, spinach, sweetcorn, tomato sauce, tuna; crunchy, plain, savoury, soft, spicy, sweet

Extension vocabulary (optional)
garlic, herbs, mayonnaise, mustard, pepper, vinegar; chewy, delicious, horrible, juicy

Other vocabulary
circle, oval, rectangle, round, shape poem, square, triangle; adjectives, descriptions, stories

Recycled vocabulary
apple, banana, big, biscuits, bread, breakfast, brown, cake, chips, chocolate, cold, competition, computer games, cook, crisps, delicious, easy, eat, enormous, grow, hot, ice cream, inside, kiwi, lazy, long, meat, milk, orange, outside, quiz, red, restaurant, rice, small, strawberry, sugar, thin, throw, vegetables, white, yellow, zoo

Structures

Core structures
What would you like (on your pizza)? I'd like some (cheese). Would you like a lot of / lots of (olives)? Yes, please. No, thank you. Which do you prefer? (Apples) or (pears)? Do you prefer (plain) food or (spicy) food? They prefer (sweet food). She prefers (savoury) food.

Other structures
What do people (have for breakfast)? Which (food) can you buy? Breakfast is (an important meal). People use (milk) to make (cakes). (India) is famous for (its spicy food).

Recycled structures
Do you like (onions)? Yes, I do. No, I don't. There are (lots of toppings). What about you? It's (long and thin). It's got (a stone in the middle). How many flowers are on the plant?

Phonics

The 'z' sound (*zebra sneezes cheese cherries*)

Literacy

Text type: shape poems (poem; writing preparation)
Reading skills: guessing meaning from context (inferring)
Writing skills: using adjectives

Culture ... around the world

Food in India

21st Century Skills

Being creative

Thinking skills

Sequencing (Lesson 1); Applying rules (Lessons 2 and 4); Remembering (Lesson 2); Predicting (Lessons 3 and 8); Discussing values (Lesson 3); Expressing opinions (Lesson 3); Classifying (Lesson 6); Thinking about your culture (Lesson 8); Making connections (Review)

Cooperative learning

Team building (Lesson 1); Collaborating (Lesson 4); Checking learning (Lesson 5); Sharing information (Lesson 5); Peer evaluation and feedback (Lesson 7); Working together (Review)

Values

Understanding the importance of trying new food

Cross-curricular links

Link to Science
Plants: Reviewing why we need plants
Suggested Arts and Crafts concepts
Identifying patterns using lines, shapes and colours and creating a mosaic

Key Competences and Key Learning Outcomes

- Identify and say food
- Say the vocabulary chant
- Draw and write about a pizza
- Review why we need plants (optional)
- Review pizza toppings
- Ask and answer questions using a recycled structure
- Sing a song about making pizza

Key language
- Food: *cheese, chillies, mushrooms, olives, onions, peppers, pineapple, prawns, spinach, sweetcorn, tomato sauce, tuna; pizza topping; add, choose, mix, push, roll*
- *They're delicious. There are (lots of toppings). You can add (tuna).*
- Extension: *garlic, herbs, mayonnaise, mustard, pepper, vinegar*
- Recycled: *throw; Do you like (onions on your pizza)? Yes, I do. No, I don't.*

Materials
- Pupil's Book p40; Activity Book p38; Class CD2; Teacher's App on Navio
- Teacher's Resource Bank: Food word cards
- Food flashcards
- Teacher's Resource Bank: Talk cards

Optional materials
- Teacher's Resource Bank: Trinity Exams Practice cards (selected from the Starter Unit and Units 1, 2 and 3)

At a Glance Lesson Plan

Starting the lesson
- Use the Trinity Exams Practice cards (optional).
- Review food vocabulary.
- Set learning outcomes and use the talk cards.

Activity 1
- Make a list of toppings you can put on a pizza.
- Which are your favourites?

Vocabulary presentation
- Present the new vocabulary using the food flashcards.

Word cards
- Introduce the spellings of the vocabulary using the food word cards.

Activity 2
- Listen, point and say the vocabulary chant.

▶ *CD2 Track 18 p267*

Pupil's Book

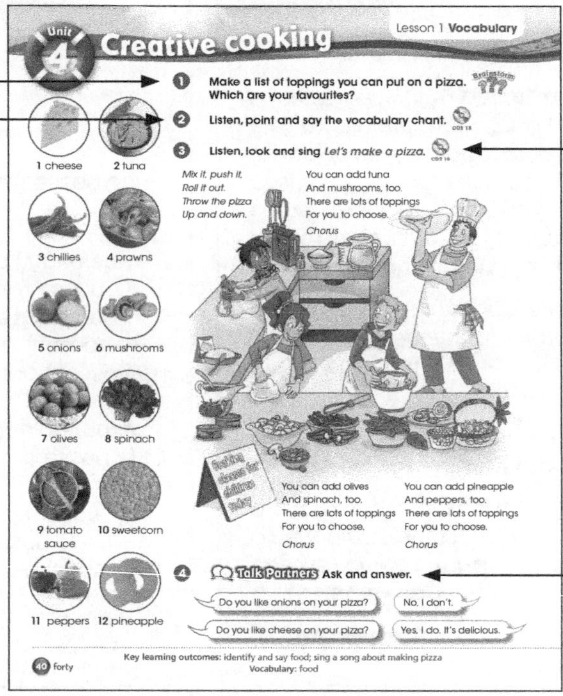

Activity 3
- Listen, look and sing *Let's make a pizza.*

▶ *CD2 Track 19 p267*

Activity 4
- Ask and answer.

Go to the Activity Book.

Ending the lesson
- Review the lesson and reflect on learning.

Extra activities

Reinforcement
- Order the ingredients in alphabetical order.

Vocabulary extension
- Present six additional vocabulary items.

Link to Science
- **Plants:** Review why we need plants.

Activity Book

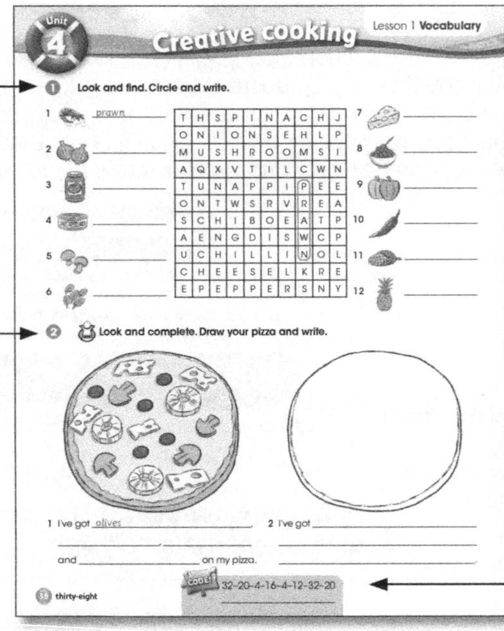

Activity Book

Activity 1
- Look and find.
- Circle and write.

Activity 2
- Look and complete.
- Draw your pizza and write.

Code activity
- Complete the code activity.

Digital resources

Teacher's Digital: You can also teach this lesson using the Teacher's App on Navio.

Pupil's Digital: Encourage your pupils to use the Pupil's App on Navio to practise the activities from this lesson.

Powered By NAVIO

Starting the lesson

Use the Trinity Exams Practice cards (optional).

- The pupils practise asking and answering questions.

Review food vocabulary.

- Elicit the alphabet and write the letters on the board. Elicit a food beginning with 'A' and write it next to the letter: *A apple*. The pupils think of a food that begins with each letter. Choose a pupil to write the words or invite different individual pupils to write the word each time.

Set learning outcomes and use the talk cards.

- Say **Today we're going to talk about food.**
- Point to the talk cards to show the pupils the different ways they will be working in the lesson.

Pupil's Book Activity 1

Make a list of toppings you can put on a pizza. Which are your favourites?

- (Books closed.) Ask **Who likes pizza? Do you make pizza at home? What's your favourite topping?** Encourage the pupils to answer in as much detail as possible and brainstorm a list.

Vocabulary presentation

- (Books closed.) Explain that you have pictures of pizza toppings, but don't let the pupils see the food flashcards. Describe a food item on a flashcard, e.g. **This topping can be red, green or yellow. It grows on a plant.** The pupils raise their hands when they have identified the food (*peppers*). Show the class the flashcard and say the word. The pupils repeat the word.
- Stick the flashcard on the board and repeat the procedure with the other flashcards.

Word cards

- (Books closed.) Hand a food word card to each pair of pupils. The pairs of pupils take turns to come to the board, read out their word and stick their word card next to the corresponding flashcard.

Pupil's Book Activity 2

Listen, point and say the vocabulary chant.

▶ *CD2 Track 18 p267*

- Focus the pupils' attention on the 12 photos. Say **Let's listen and say the words.** Play the CD. The pupils listen, point and repeat.

Pupil's Book Activity 3

Listen, look and sing *Let's make a pizza.*

▶ *CD2 Track 19 p267*

- Focus the pupils' attention on the scene. Ask **What are the children doing?** Then say **Josh is mixing.** Mime mixing ingredients in a bowl and prompt the class to do the same. Repeat the procedure with Lily (*pushing*) and Ravi (*rolling*). Ask **What's the teacher doing?** (*Throwing the pizza dough up and down.*)
- Say **Let's listen to the song.** Play the CD. The pupils listen and read.
- Play the CD again. The pupils sing the song and mime the different actions.

Pupil's Book Activity 4

Ask and answer.

- Ask two pupils to read out the speech bubbles.
- Working with a Talk Partner, the pupils take turns to ask and answer questions about the 12 food items.

Activity Book

Activity 1

Look and find. Circle and write.

- Point to each picture in turn and ask the pupils to name the different food items. The pupils work on their own to find and circle the words in the wordsearch and to write the words next to the corresponding pictures.

Answers: **1** prawn **2** onions **3** tomato sauce **4** tuna **5** mushrooms **6** spinach **7** cheese **8** olives **9** peppers **10** chilli **11** sweetcorn **12** pineapple

Activity 2

Look and complete. Draw your pizza and write.

- Focus the pupils on the drawing of the first pizza and ask them to name the different toppings. The pupils then complete the sentence below the picture.
- The pupils draw four toppings on the second pizza and write a short description below it.

Answers: **1** I've got olives, pineapple, mushrooms and cheese on my pizza. **2** Pupils' own answers

Code activity

- The pupils complete the code activity.

Answer: headache

Ending the lesson

Review the lesson and reflect on learning.

- Say **Today we've learnt the names of foods. Which foods do you remember?** Elicit the food from the pupils.
- Ask **Which was your favourite activity today? Which activity was easy / difficult?**

Extra activities

Reinforcement

- Organise the class into pairs. Challenge them to write the food words in alphabetical order. Set a time limit.

Vocabulary extension

- Present six additional food words: *garlic, herbs, mayonnaise, mustard, pepper, vinegar.*
- Use the Vocabulary Booster on Navio to practise these new words.

Link to Science

- If you are studying the Science topic of **Plants**, remind the pupils that plants are a source of food and that we need plants in order to have a healthy diet. Ask the class to classify the food flashcards into food from animals or from plants.

Key Competences and Key Learning Outcomes

- Listen, repeat and act out a conversation
- Listen, follow the grammar table and identify the parts of a sentence
- Use *would like* to make requests

Key language

- *good evening, here you are, Madam, salad*
- *What would you like (on your pizza)? I'd like some (tuna), please. Would you like a lot of (mushrooms)? Yes, please. No, thank you. We would like some / a lot of / lots of (cheese). Would you like (anything else)?*
- Recycled: *cheese, chillies, mushrooms, olives, onions, peppers, pineapple, prawns, spinach, sweetcorn, tomato sauce, topping, tuna*

Materials

- Pupil's Book p41; Activity Book p39; Class CD2; Teacher's App on Navio
- Food flashcards
- Teacher's Resource Bank: Talk cards

Optional materials

- Teacher's Resource Bank: Trinity Exams Practice cards (selected from the Starter Unit and Units 1, 2 and 3)
- Play food

At a Glance Lesson Plan

Starting the lesson

- Use the Trinity Exams Practice cards (optional).
- **Think-Pair-Share.** Review food vocabulary.
- Review the *Let's make a pizza* song.

▶ *CD2 Track 19 p267*

▶ *CD2 Track 20 p268*

- Set learning outcomes and use the talk cards.

Activity 1

- Listen and read.
- Listen and repeat.

▶ *CD2 Track 21 p268*

- Act out.

Activity 2

- Read again.
- What would Grandma like in her salad?

Activity 3

- Listen and follow.

▶ *CD2 Track 22 p268*

- Repeat.
- **Grammar clue:** Read about word order in questions.

Pupil's Book

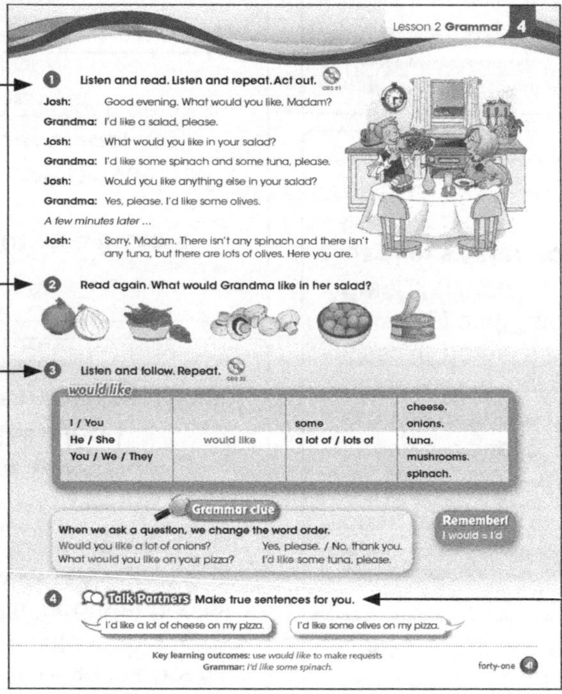

Lesson 2 Grammar 4

1 Listen and read. Listen and repeat. Act out.

Josh: Good evening. What would you like, Madam?
Grandma: I'd like a salad, please.
Josh: What would you like in your salad?
Grandma: I'd like some spinach and some tuna, please.
Josh: Would you like anything else in your salad?
Grandma: Yes, please. I'd like some olives.
A few minutes later ...
Josh: Sorry, Madam. There isn't any spinach and there isn't any tuna, but there are lots of olives. Here you are.

2 Read again. What would Grandma like in her salad?

3 Listen and follow. Repeat.

would like

I / You		some	cheese.
He / She	would like	a lot of / lots of	onions. tuna.
You / We / They			mushrooms. spinach.

Grammar clue

When we ask a question, we change the word order.
Would you like a lot of onions? Yes, please. / No, thank you.
What would you like on your pizza? I'd like some tuna, please.

Remember! I would = I'd

4 Talk Partners Make true sentences for you.

I'd like a lot of cheese on my pizza.
I'd like some olives on my pizza.

Key learning outcomes: use *would like* to make requests
Grammar: *I'd like some spinach.*

forty-one 41

Activity 4

- Make true sentences for you.
- Go to the Activity Book.

Ending the lesson

- Review the lesson and reflect on learning.

Extra activity

Reinforcement

- Do a guided role play using play food.

Activity Book

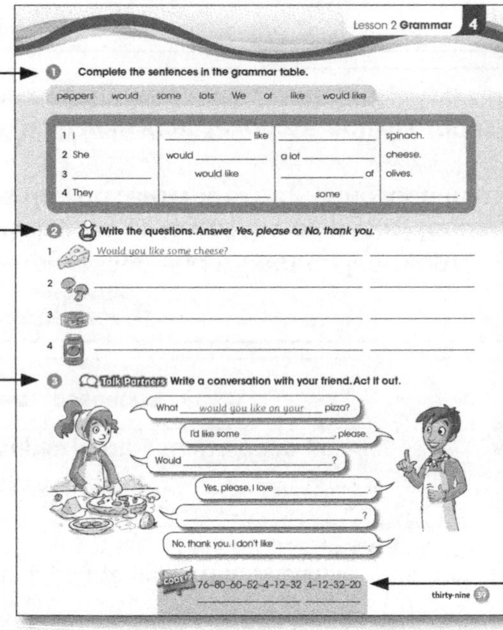

Lesson 2 Grammar 4

1 Complete the sentences in the grammar table.

peppers would some lots We of like would like

1 I	______ like	______	spinach.
2 She	would ______	a lot ______	cheese.
3 ______	would like	______ of	olives.
4 They	______	some	______

2 Write the questions. Answer *Yes, please* or *No, thank you.*

1 Would you like some cheese?
2
3
4

3 Talk Partners Write a conversation with your friend. Act it out.

What would you like on your pizza?
I'd like some ______, please.
Would ______?
Yes, please. I love ______
______?
No, thank you. I don't like ______

Code 76-80-60-62-4-12-32 4-12-32-20

thirty-nine 39

Activity Book

Activity 1

- Complete the sentences in the grammar table.

Activity 2

- Write the questions.
- Answer *Yes, please* or *No, thank you.*

Activity 3

- Write a conversation with your friend.
- Act it out.

Code activity

- Complete the code activity.

Digital resources

Teacher's Digital: You can also teach this lesson using the Teacher's App on Navio.

Pupil's Digital: Encourage your pupils to use the Pupil's App on Navio to practise the activities from this lesson.

Powered By NAVIO

Starting the lesson

Use the Trinity Exams Practice cards (optional).

- The pupils practise asking and answering questions.

Think-Pair-Share. Review food vocabulary.

- Ask **Can you remember the food vocabulary?** The class thinks silently for a minute.
- Then the pupils work with a Talk Partner to name the food vocabulary.
- Invite different Talk Partners to say a different food word. Hold up the corresponding flashcard and prompt the class to repeat the word.
- Repeat the procedure, asking different Talk Partners each time, until all the food words have been named.

Review the *Let's make a pizza* song.

▶ *CD2 Track 19 p267*

▶ *CD2 Track 20 p268 (optional karaoke version)*

- Play the CD (or use the karaoke version). The pupils sing and do the actions.

Set learning outcomes and use the talk cards.

- Say **Today we're going to learn a polite way of asking for food.**
- Point to the talk cards to show the pupils the different ways they will be working in the lesson.

Pupil's Book Activity 1

Listen and read. Listen and repeat. Act out.

▶ *CD2 Track 21 p268*

- The pupils look at the picture. Ask **Who can you see? Where are they? What's Josh doing?**
- Play the CD. The pupils listen and read the conversation. Confirm that Josh is pretending to be a waiter, taking his grandma's food order.
- Play the CD again, pausing after each sentence for the pupils to repeat.
- The pupils act out the conversation in pairs.

Pupil's Book Activity 2

Read again. What would Grandma like in her salad?

- The pupils read the conversation again and say what Grandma would like in her salad.

Answers: spinach, tuna and olives

Pupil's Book Activity 3

Listen and follow. Repeat.

▶ *CD2 Track 22 p268*

- Play the CD. The pupils listen to the first sentence and point to the words they hear. The pupils repeat the complete sentence. Repeat the procedure with the other sentences.
- Explain that 'would like' is a polite way of asking for things in English. If necessary, drill the pronunciation of these words until the pupils feel confident.

Grammar clue

- Read the grammar clue as a class. Read the *Remember!* tip and focus on the contracted form of 'I would': 'I'd'.
- Ask a pupil **Would you like some cheese?** Mime offering the food item to the pupil and prompt him / her to say *Yes, please* or *No, thank you.* Repeat.

Pupil's Book Activity 4

Make true sentences for you.

- Organise the class into Talk Partners. The pupils practise offering and accepting or refusing the different food items, making true sentences.

Activity Book

Activity 1

Complete the sentences in the grammar table.

- Invite a pupil to read out the words in the word box.
- The pupils work on their own or with a partner to write the words in the grammar table.

Answers: **1** would, some **2** like, of **3** We, lots **4** would like, peppers

Activity 2

Write the questions. Answer *Yes, please* or *No, thank you.*

- A pupil reads out and answers the first question.
- The pupils work on their own to write and respond to the questions.

Suggested answers: **1** Would you like some cheese? **2** Would you like some mushrooms? **3** Would you like lots of tuna? **4** Would you like a lot of tomato sauce?

Activity 3

Write a conversation with your friend. Act it out.

- Explain to the pupils that they are going to invent a conversation. Read out the first speech bubble as an example, then prompt the class to complete the remaining speech bubbles.
- The pupils work with a Talk Partner to write and practise their own conversation.
- Invite different pairs of pupils to read out their completed conversation.

Suggested answers: What would you like on your pizza? I'd like some peppers, please. Would you like anything else? Yes, please. I love olives. Would you like some mushrooms? No, thank you. I don't like mushrooms.

Code activity

- The pupils complete the code activity.

Answer: stomach ache

Ending the lesson

Review the lesson and reflect on learning.

- Say **Today we've learnt how to ask for food politely.** Ask **What food would you like now?** Prompt the class to tell you the food they'd like to eat.
- Ask **Which was your favourite activity today? Which activity was easy / difficult?**

Extra activity

Reinforcement

- Set up a guided role play. Place a desk and two chairs at the front of the class and invite two pupils to be the customers. Then place play food on another desk and invite a pupil to stand behind it to be the chef. Finally, invite a pupil to be the waiter. The waiter takes the customers' orders and reports them to the chef. The chef passes the food to the waiter, who then serves it to the customers.

Key Competences and Key Learning Outcomes

- Read, listen and understand a story about an amazing pizza
- Use a code to read a message
- Do a pre-reading task
- Understand the importance of trying new food
- Understand, enjoy and act out the story
- Give an opinion on the story

Key language

- *bake, enormous, forget, ingredients, judges, oven, prize, savoury, spicy, sweet*
- *What (toppings) would you like (on your slice of pizza)? I'd like some (olives), please. I prefer (sweet food).*
- Recycled: *cheese, chillies, mushrooms, olives, onions, peppers, pineapple, prawns, spinach, sweetcorn, tomato sauce, tuna; banana, competition, computer games, grow, lunch, mix, pizza, restaurant, roll, toppings; What about you?*

Materials

- Pupil's Book pp42–43; Activity Book p40; Class CD2; Teacher's App on Navio
- Food flashcards
- Teacher's Resource Bank: Talk cards

Optional materials

- Teacher's Resource Bank: Trinity Exams Practice cards (selected from the Starter Unit and Units 1, 2 and 3)

At a Glance Lesson Plan

Pupil's Book

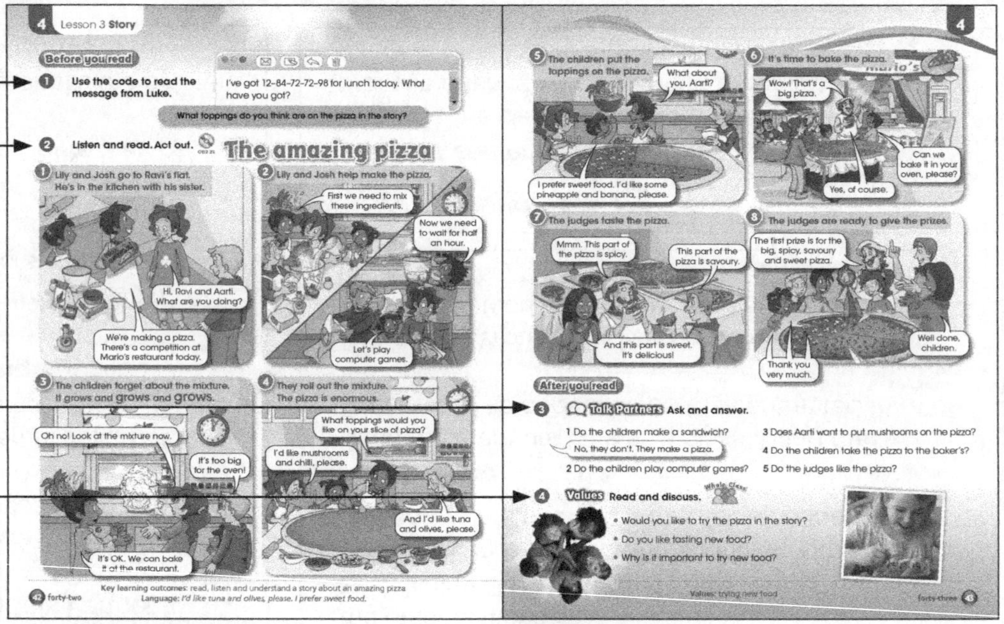

Starting the lesson

- Use the Trinity Exams Practice cards (optional).
- Review food vocabulary.
- Set learning outcomes and use the talk cards.

Before you read: Activity 1

- Use the code to read the message from Luke.

Activity 2

- Listen and read.
- ▶ *CD2 Track 23 p268*
- Act out.

After you read: Activity 3

- Ask and answer.

Activity 4: Values

- Read and discuss.
- Go to the Activity Book.

Ending the lesson

- Review the lesson and reflect on learning.

Extra activity

Reinforcement

- Retell the story as a class.

Digital resources

Teacher's Digital: You can also teach this lesson using the Teacher's App on Navio.

Pupil's Digital: Encourage your pupils to use the Pupil's App on Navio to practise the activities from this lesson.

Powered By NAVIO

Activity Book

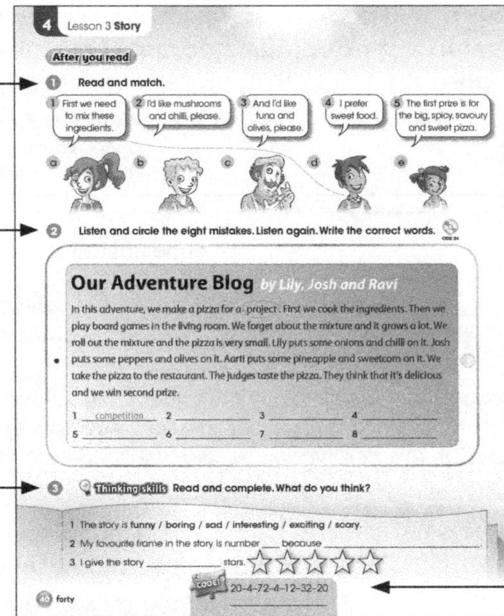

After you read: Activity Book

Activity 1

- Read and match.

Activity 2

- Listen and circle the eight mistakes.
- ▶ *CD2 Track 24 p268*
- Listen again.
- Write the correct words.

Activity 3

- Read and complete.
- What do you think?

Code activity

- Complete the code activity.

Starting the lesson

Use the Trinity Exams Practice cards (optional).

- The pupils practise asking and answering questions.

Review food vocabulary.

- Take a food flashcard and ask a pupil **Would you like some (spinach)?** Prompt the pupil to respond by saying *Yes, please* or *No, thank you.* If the pupil wants the food item, give him / her the flashcard. If the pupil doesn't want it, ask other pupils.
- Invite four pupils to the front of the class and give them three food flashcards each. These pupils move around the class asking the question. The aim is to give away all their flashcards, but they can only give the flashcard to somebody who doesn't already have one.
- Repeat with four more pupils.

Set learning outcomes and use the talk cards.

- Say **Today we're going to read and listen to a story.**
- Point to the talk cards to show the pupils the different ways they will be working in the lesson.

Before you read: Pupil's Book Activity 1

Use the code to read the message from Luke.

- Say **Josh and Lily have received a message from Luke.** Ask the pupils to use the code (Pupil's Book page 7) to discover the mystery word (*curry*). Check that the pupils know what this food is.
- Read the title of the story. Ask **What toppings do you think are on the pizza in the story?** The pupils predict the toppings.

Pupil's Book Activity 2

Listen and read. Act out.

▶ *CD2 Track 23 p268*

- Play the CD. The pupils follow in their books.
- Ask questions to check comprehension.

Suggested comprehension questions

- Frame 1: **Where are the children?** (*At Ravi's flat.*) **Why are Ravi and his sister making a pizza?** (*There's a competition.*)
- Frame 2: **Why do the children play computer games?** (*They have to wait for half an hour.*)
- Frame 3: **What happens to the mixture?** (*It grows very big.*)
- Frames 4 and 5: **What toppings do the children put on the pizza?** (*Mushrooms, chilli, tuna, olives, pineapple and banana.*)
- Frame 6: **Where do they take the pizza?** (*To the restaurant.*)
- Frame 7: **Do the judges like the pizza?** (*Yes.*)
- Frame 8: **Do the children win?** (*Yes, first prize.*)
- Organise the class into groups (one for each character) and play the CD. Each group joins in when their character speaks. If the pupils need extra support, pause the CD after each utterance and ask them to repeat it instead.
- Repeat with groups swapping roles.

After you read: Pupil's Book Activity 3

Ask and answer.

- Ask a pupil to read out the first question and answer. Then invite other pupils to ask and answer the other questions. If necessary, ask the whole class to repeat the answer each time.
- The pupils practise asking and answering the questions with a Talk Partner. They can do this orally or in their notebooks.

Answers: **1** No, they don't. They make a pizza. **2** Yes, they do. **3** No, she doesn't. She wants to put pineapple and banana on the pizza. **4** No, they don't. They take the pizza to the restaurant. **5** Yes, they do. They give it first prize.

Pupil's Book Activity 4: Values

Read and discuss.

- Ask the pupils to read the first question and elicit answers.
- Read out the second question. The pupils respond.
- Read out and discuss the third question as a class.

After you read: Activity Book

Activity 1

Read and match.

- Ask a pupil to match a speech bubble with a character. The pupils then draw matching lines and check their answers in the Pupil's Book.

Answers: **1** d **2** a **3** b **4** e **5** c

Activity 2

Listen and circle the eight mistakes. Listen again. Write the correct words.

▶ *CD2 Track 24 p268*

- Play the CD. The pupils circle the eight mistakes.
- Play the CD again. The pupils write the correct words.

Answers: **1** ~~project~~ competition **2** ~~cook~~ mix **3** ~~board~~ computer **4** ~~small~~ big **5** ~~onions~~ mushrooms **6** ~~peppers~~ tuna **7** ~~sweetcorn~~ banana **8** ~~second~~ first

Activity 3

Read and complete. What do you think?

- Invite pupils to read out and complete the sentences.
- The pupils complete the task in their Activity Books and then share opinions with a Talk Partner.

Code activity

- The pupils complete the code activity.

Answer: earache

Ending the lesson

Review the lesson and reflect on learning.

- Say **Today we've listened to a story about an amazing pizza.** Elicit the story.
- Ask **Which was your favourite activity today? Which activity was easy / difficult?**

Extra activity

Reinforcement

- Say **Let's tell the story together.** Prompt the class by saying **Ravi and his sister are in the ...** (*kitchen*). Use mime, gesture and drawings to support the class.

Lesson 4

Key Competences and Key Learning Outcomes

- Identify and say adjectives to describe food
- Follow and correct the grammar tables
- Use *prefer* to talk about preferences

- Say a rap

Key language

- Adjectives: *crunchy, plain, savoury, soft, spicy, sweet*
- *Which do you prefer? (Apples) or (pears)? She prefers (savoury food). They prefer (sweet food).*
- Extension: *chewy, delicious, horrible, juicy*
- Recycled: *apples, chilli, chocolate, crisps, ice cream, rice*

Materials

- Pupil's Book p44; Activity Book p41; Class CD2; Teacher's App on Navio
- Teacher's Resource Bank: Talk cards

Optional materials

- Teacher's Resource Bank: Trinity Exams Practice cards (selected from the Starter Unit and Units 1, 2 and 3)

At a Glance Lesson Plan

Pupil's Book

Starting the lesson

- Use the Trinity Exams Practice cards (optional).
- Review the story.
- Set learning outcomes and use the talk cards.

Activity 1

- Listen, point and say.
- ▶ *CD2 Track 25 p268*

Activity 2

- Listen and sing *The delicious food rap.*
- ▶ *CD2 Track 26 p268*

Activity 3

- Listen and follow.
- ▶ *CD2 Track 27 p268*
- Repeat.
- **Grammar clue:** Read about asking questions with 'prefer'.

Activity 4

- Ask and answer.
- Go to the Activity Book.

4 Lesson 4 Vocabulary and Grammar

1 Listen, point and say.

1 sweet 2 savoury 3 plain 4 spicy 5 soft 6 crunchy

2 Listen and sing *The delicious food rap.*

Food, food.
Delicious food.
Which do you prefer?
Sweet or Savoury?
Plain or Spicy?

Soft or crunchy?
Food, food.
Delicious food.
Which do you prefer?

3 Listen and follow. Repeat.

prefer		
		plain food.
I / You / We / They	prefer	spicy food.
He / She	prefers	soft food.
		crunchy food.

Grammar clue

We can ask questions with prefer, too.
Which do you prefer? Apples or pears? Does she prefer chocolate or sweets?

4 Talk Partners Ask and answer.

Which do you prefer? Sweet or savoury food? — I prefer sweet food.
Which do you prefer? Pasta or rice? — I prefer pasta.

44 forty-four

Key learning outcomes: identify and say adjectives to describe food; use *prefer* to talk about preferences Vocabulary: adjectives Grammar: *I prefer (crunchy) food.*

Ending the lesson

- Review the lesson and reflect on learning.

Extra activities

Reinforcement

- Describe your mid-morning snack.

Vocabulary extension

- Present four additional vocabulary items.

Digital resources

Teacher's Digital: You can also teach this lesson using the Teacher's App on Navio.

Pupil's Digital: Encourage your pupils to use the Pupil's App on Navio to practise the activities from this lesson.

Powered By NAVIO

Activity Book

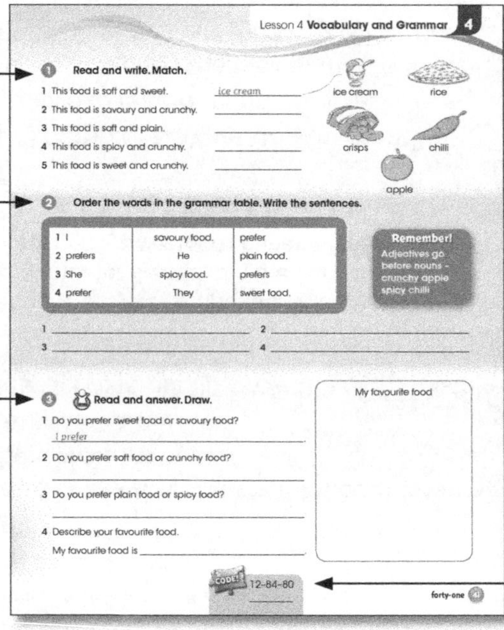

Lesson 4 Vocabulary and Grammar 4

1 Read and write. Match.

1 This food is soft and sweet. ice cream
2 This food is savoury and crunchy.
3 This food is soft and plain.
4 This food is spicy and crunchy.
5 This food is sweet and crunchy.

2 Order the words in the grammar table. Write the sentences.

1 I	savoury food.	prefer
2 prefers	He	plain food.
3 She	spicy food.	prefers
4 prefer	They	sweet food.

Remember! Adjectives go before nouns - crunchy apple spicy chilli

1 ___ 2 ___
3 ___ 4 ___

3 Read and answer. Draw.

1 Do you prefer sweet food or savoury food? I prefer
2 Do you prefer soft food or crunchy food?
3 Do you prefer plain food or spicy food?
4 Describe your favourite food.
My favourite food is ___

My favourite food

CODE 12-84-80

forty-one 41

Activity Book

Activity 1

- Read and write.
- Match.

Activity 2

- Order the words in the grammar table.
- Write the sentences.

Activity 3

- Read and answer.
- Draw.

Code activity

- Complete the code activity.

Starting the lesson

Use the Trinity Exams Practice cards (optional).

- The pupils practise asking and answering questions.

Review the story.

- Ask the pupils if they remember the story that they read in the last lesson.
- Organise the class into small groups. Ask each group in turn a question about the story. The pupils should collaborate before they give their answer.

Set learning outcomes and use the talk cards.

- Say **Today we're going to learn how to describe food.**
- Point to the talk cards to show the pupils the different ways they will be working in the lesson.

Pupil's Book Activity 1

Listen, point and say.

▶ ***CD2 Track 25 p268***

- Point to the first photo and say **This food is sweet. What other food is sweet? Do you like sweet food?** Encourage different pupils to respond to the questions. Then say the adjective once more and prompt the class to repeat. Repeat the procedure with the other adjectives.
- Play the CD. The pupils listen, point to each photo and repeat the word.

Pupil's Book Activity 2

Listen and sing *The delicious food rap.*

▶ ***CD2 Track 26 p268***

- Focus the class on the picture. Ask the class to name the food items (*sweets, popcorn, sandwiches, curry, apple, ice cream*) and to use adjectives to describe each one.
- Play the CD. The pupils listen and read.
- Play the CD again. The pupils join in saying the rap.

Pupil's Book Activity 3

Listen and follow. Repeat.

▶ ***CD2 Track 27 p268***

- Focus the class on the grammar table.
- Play the CD. The pupils listen to the first sentence and point to the corresponding parts of the sentence. The pupils repeat the complete sentence. Repeat the procedure with the other sentences.

Grammar clue

- Read the grammar clue as a class. Explain that when we ask questions with 'prefer', we ask someone to choose between two or more things.
- Ask **Do you prefer chocolate or sweets?** Invite different pupils to answer. Ask more questions about different food items, e.g. **Which do you prefer? Pasta or rice?** Ask the class to say the questions with you several times. Then invite other pupils to make similar questions.

Pupil's Book Activity 4

Ask and answer.

- Organise the class into Talk Partners. The pupils take turns to make true sentences about preferences.

Activity Book

Activity 1

Read and write. Match.

- Read out the names of the food items with the class.
- Invite a pupil to read out the first description and to identify the food.
- The pupils work on their own or in pairs to read the descriptions and write the food words. Then they draw matching lines from the sentences to the pictures.

Answers: 1 ice cream **2** crisps **3** rice **4** chilli **5** apple

Activity 2

Order the words in the grammar table. Write the sentences.

- Explain that the grammar table is mixed up and that the pupils need to reorder the words. Invite a pupil to read out the first sentence.
- The pupils order and write the remaining sentences. If they need more support, remind them that a sentence begins with a capital letter and ends with a full stop.

Answers: 1 I prefer savoury food. **2** He prefers plain food. **3** She prefers spicy food. **4** They prefer sweet food.

Activity 3

Read and answer. Draw.

- Invite a pupil to read out and answer the first question. Repeat the procedure with the other questions.
- The pupils answer the questions in their Activity Books. They then draw their favourite food.
- Invite different pupils to read out their descriptions of their favourite food to the rest of the class. Their classmates try to guess the food.

Code activity

- The pupils complete the code activity.

Answer: cut

Ending the lesson

Review the lesson and reflect on learning.

- Say **Today we've learnt some words to describe food. Which words are they?** The pupils list the six adjectives.
- Ask **Which was your favourite activity today? Which activity was easy / difficult?**

Extra activities

Reinforcement

- If the lesson is in the morning, ask a pupil to take out his / her mid-morning snack and show it to the class. Prompt the pupil to describe the food they have. Then ask **Do you like your snack? Would you prefer a different snack?** Repeat the procedure with different individual pupils. If the lesson is in the afternoon, ask the pupils to describe a mid-morning snack they often have.

Vocabulary extension

- Use the Vocabulary Booster on Navio and present and practise four additional adjectives to describe food: *chewy, delicious, horrible, juicy.*

Key Competences and Key Learning Outcomes

- Say a tongue twister with the 'z' sound
- Practise spelling and learn an alternative spelling for the 'z' sound
- Listen for specific information
- Play a communication game using adjectives to describe food

Key language

- *curry, nose, pancakes, popcorn, sneeze, zebra*
- *Do you prefer (crunchy) food or (soft) food? I prefer (crunchy) food. Your favourite food is (rice).*
- Recycled: *apple, cake, cheese, cherries, chips, crisps, easy, ice cream, lazy, olives, please, prize, quiz, rice, salad, zoo; crunchy, plain, savoury, soft, spicy, sweet; hot, cold*

Materials

- Pupil's Book p45; Activity Book p42; Class CD2; Teacher's App on Navio
- Teacher's Resource Bank: Talk cards
- Food flashcards
- Teacher's Resource Bank: Unit 4 Lesson 5 Communication Activity

Optional materials

- Teacher's Resource Bank: Trinity Exams Practice cards (selected from the Starter Unit and Units 1, 2 and 3)

At a Glance Lesson Plan

Pupil's Book

Starting the lesson

- Use the Trinity Exams Practice cards (optional).
- **Think-Pair-Share.** Review adjectives to describe food.
- Review *The delicious food rap.*
- ▶ *CD2 Track 26 p268*
- Set learning outcomes and use the talk cards.

Activity 1: Speak and spell

- Listen, read and say.
- ▶ *CD2 Track 28 p268*
- Go to the Activity Book.

Activity 2

- Listen to children playing a game.
- ▶ *CD2 Track 29 p269*
- Are their answers *right* or *wrong*?

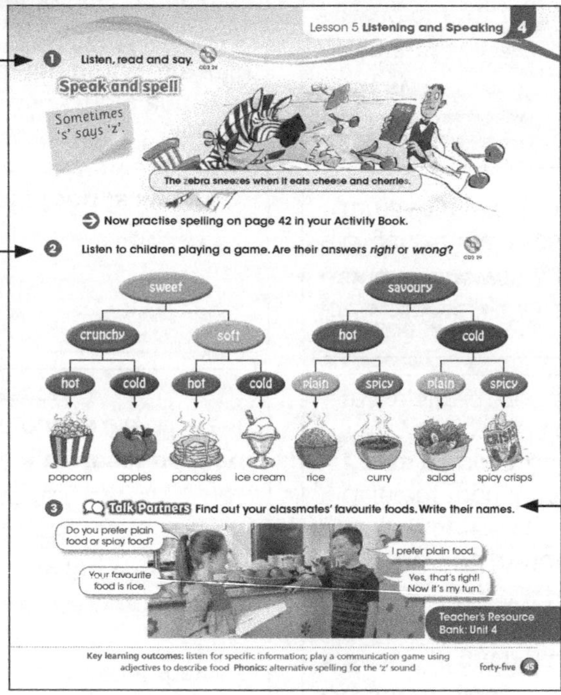

Activity 3

- Find out your classmates' favourite foods.
- Write their names (Teacher's Resource Bank: Unit 4).

Ending the lesson

- Review the lesson and reflect on learning.

Extra activity

Reinforcement

- Write a description of one of the foods in the lesson.

Activity Book

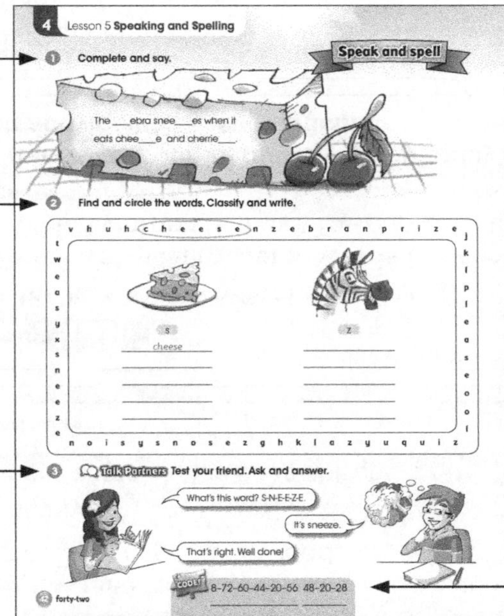

Activity Book

Activity 1: Speak and spell
- Complete and say.

Activity 2
- Find and circle the words.
- Classify and write.

Activity 3
- Test your friend.
- Ask and answer.

Code activity
- Complete the code activity.

Digital resources

Teacher's Digital: You can also teach this lesson using the Teacher's App on Navio.

Pupil's Digital: Encourage your pupils to use the Pupil's App on Navio to practise the activities from this lesson.

Powered By NAVIO

Starting the lesson

Use the Trinity Exams Practice cards (optional).

- The pupils practise asking and answering questions.

Think-Pair-Share. Review adjectives to describe food.

- Ask **Can you remember the adjectives to describe food?** The class thinks silently for a minute.
- Then the pupils work with a Talk Partner to name the adjectives to describe food.
- Invite different Talk Partners to say a different adjective. Hold up the food flashcards one by one and prompt the pupils to describe them in as much detail as possible (size, shape, colour, smell, etc.).
- Finally, repeat the procedure, asking different pairs of Talk Partners each time.

Review *The delicious food* rap.

▶ *CD2 Track 26 p268*

- Play the CD. The pupils listen and say the rap.

Set learning outcomes and use the talk cards.

- Say **Today we're going to say a tongue twister, practise spelling and play a game.**
- Point to the talk cards to show the pupils the different ways they will be working in the lesson.

Pupil's Book Activity 1: Speak and spell

Listen, read and say.

▶ *CD2 Track 28 p268*

- (Books closed.) Write the letter 'z' on the board and ask **What sound does this letter make?** ('z') List the words the pupils know that contain this letter. Say **Today you're going to learn another way of writing the 'z' sound.**
- (Books open.) Focus the class on the picture and ask **What can you see?** (*A zebra.*) **What's he eating?** (*Cheese and cherries.*) **What's he doing?** (*Sneezing.*)
- Say **Let's listen to the tongue twister.** Play the CD. The pupils follow the text in their books.
- Play the CD again. The pupils join in.
- Finally, ask the class to identify the alternative way of writing the 'z' sound *('s')*.

Activity Book

Activity 1: Speak and spell

Complete and say.

- The pupils write the letters, then say the tongue twister.

Answer: The zebra sneezes when it eats cheese and cherries.

Activity 2

Find and circle the words. Classify and write.

- The pupils find and circle the words in the border which contain the 'z' sound.
- The pupils classify and write the words according to whether they are written with 'z' or 's'.

Answers: s: cheese, please, easy, noisy, nose
z: zebra, sneeze, prize, lazy, quiz

Activity 3

Talk Partners. Test your friend. Ask and answer.

- Invite two pupils to read out the speech bubbles.
- Organise the pupils into Talk Partners. The pupils take it in turns to identify the words in Activity 2. Stress the importance of prompting, encouraging and helping each other.

Code activity

- The pupils complete the code activity.

Answer: broken leg

Pupil's Book Activity 2

Listen to children playing a game. Are their answers *right* or *wrong*?

▶ *CD2 Track 29 p269*

- Explain that a girl and a boy are playing a game to find out each other's favourite food.
- Point to the pictures and make sure that pupils understand the diagram.
- Play the first part of the conversation on the CD, pausing after each question to allow the pupils to point to the relevant part of the diagram. The pupils identify and name the boy's favourite food.
- Repeat the procedure with the other parts of the conversation.

Answers: **1** curry **2** ice cream **3** spicy crisps **4** pancakes

Pupil's Book Activity 3

Find out your classmates' favourite foods. Write their names. (Teacher's Resource Bank: Unit 4).

- Invite two pupils to read out the speech bubbles. Explain that the pupils are going to find out their classmates' favourite food.
- Give the class the worksheet from Teacher's Resource Bank: Unit 4. Elicit the food items at the bottom of the diagram.
- Invite a confident pupil to choose a favourite food from the diagram. He / She can show the rest of the class which item it is, but you mustn't see it. Explain to the pupil that you are going to ask questions to find out their favourite food. Ask **Do you prefer sweet or savoury food?** The pupil answers. Depending on their answer, ask **Do you prefer crunchy or soft food?** or **Do you prefer hot or cold food?** Finally, move down the diagram and ask either **Do you prefer hot or cold food?** or **Do you prefer plain or spicy food?** to discover the pupil's favourite food.
- Invite a pair of pupils to repeat the procedure.
- Ask the pupils to go around the classroom, asking a few classmates the questions to find out their favourite foods. Explain that they should write their classmates' names under the relevant food item.

Ending the lesson

Review the lesson and reflect on learning.

- Say **Today we've practised a tongue twister.** Elicit the tongue twister from the pupils.
- Ask **Which was your favourite activity today? Which activity was easy / difficult?**

Extra activity

Reinforcement

- Ask the pupils to choose one of the foods in the lesson and write a description of it in their notebooks.

Key Competences and Key Learning Outcomes

- Classify information in a chart

- Scan the poems to find words
- Guess the meaning of words from context (inferring)

- Read and understand three shape poems

Key language

- *jam, juicy, round, shape, shiny, slice, square, sticky, stone*
- *I sometimes (toast) it. I eat it (in the summer). I peel / cook / eat it.*
- Recycled: *banana, bread, brown, cheese, cherry, delicious, inside, long, meat, outside, red, savoury, small, soft, sweet, thin, white, yellow; It's (long and thin). It's got (a stone in the middle).*

Materials

- Pupil's Book p46; Activity Book p43; Class CD2; Teacher's App on Navio
- Teacher's Resource Bank: Talk cards

Optional materials

- Teacher's Resource Bank: Trinity Exams Practice cards (selected from the Starter Unit and Units 1, 2 and 3)
- Bilingual dictionaries

At a Glance Lesson Plan

Pupil's Book

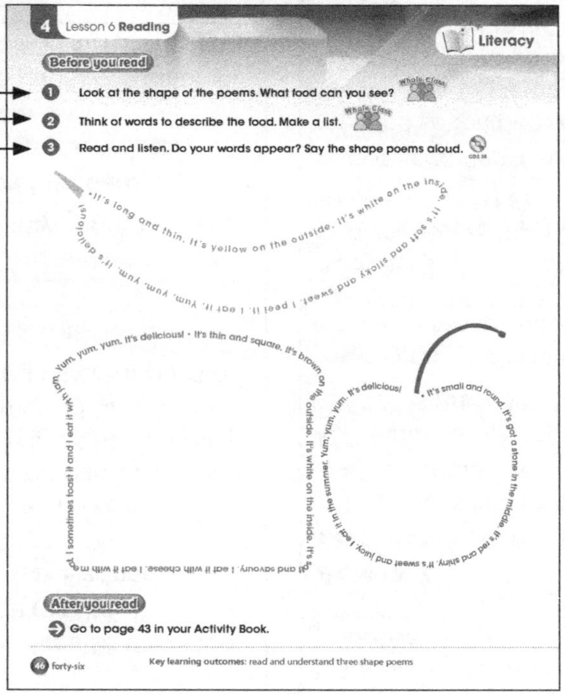
4 Lesson 6 Reading | Literacy

Before you read

1 Look at the shape of the poems. What food can you see?

2 Think of words to describe the food. Make a list.

3 Read and listen. Do your words appear? Say the shape poems aloud.

It's long and thin. It's yellow on the outside. It's white on the inside. It's soft and sticky and sweet. I peel it. I eat it. Yum, yum, yum, it's delicious!

Yum, yum, yum, it's delicious! It's thin and square. It's brown on the outside. It's white on the inside. It's soft and savoury. I eat it with cheese. I eat it with meat. I sometimes toast it and I eat it with jam.

It's small and round. It's got a stone in the middle. It's red and shiny. It's sweet and juicy. I eat it in the summer. Yum, yum, it's delicious!

After you read

Go to page 43 in your Activity Book.

46 forty-six Key learning outcomes: read and understand three shape poems

Starting the lesson

- Use the Trinity Exams Practice cards (optional).
- Review the tongue twister.

▶ *CD2 Track 28 p268*

- Set learning outcomes and use the talk cards.

Before you read: Activity 1

- Look at the shape of the poems.
- What food can you see?

Before you read: Activity 2

- Think of words to describe the food.
- Make a list.

Activity 3

- Read and listen.

▶ *CD2 Track 30 p269*

- Do your words appear?
- Say the shape poems aloud.

Go to the Activity Book.

Ending the lesson

- Review the lesson and reflect on learning.

Extra activity

Reinforcement

- List two-syllable words that end with the letter 'y'.

Activity Book

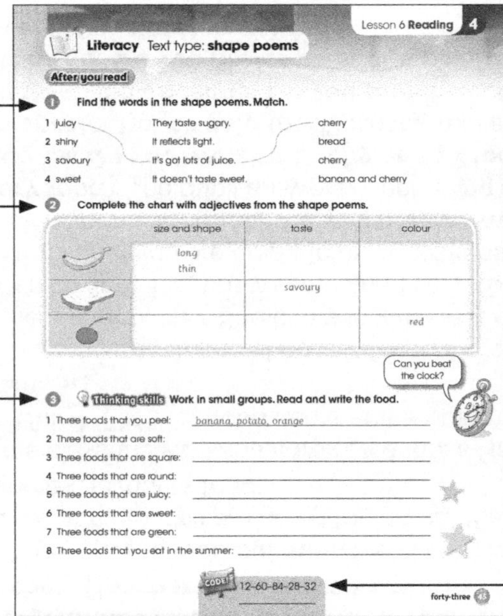
Lesson 6 Reading 4

Literacy Text type: shape poems

After you read

1 Find the words in the shape poems. Match.

1 juicy	They taste sugary.	cherry
2 shiny	It reflects light.	bread
3 savoury	It's got lots of juice.	cherry
4 sweet	It doesn't taste sweet.	banana and cherry

2 Complete the chart with adjectives from the shape poems.

	size and shape	taste	colour
	long thin		
		savoury	
			red

Can you beat the clock?

3 Thinking skills Work in small groups. Read and write the food.

1 Three foods that you peel: banana, potato, orange
2 Three foods that are soft:
3 Three foods that are square:
4 Three foods that are round:
5 Three foods that are juicy:
6 Three foods that are sweet:
7 Three foods that are green:
8 Three foods that you eat in the summer:

CODE 12-60-84-28-32

forty-three 43

After you read: Activity Book

Activity 1

- Find the words in the shape poems.
- Match.

Activity 2

- Complete the chart with adjectives from the shape poems.

Activity 3

- Work in small groups.
- Read and write the food.

Code activity

- Complete the code activity.

Digital resources

Teacher's Digital: You can also teach this lesson using the Teacher's App on Navio.

Pupil's Digital: Encourage your pupils to use the Pupil's App on Navio to practise the activities from this lesson.

Powered By NAVIO

Starting the lesson

Use the Trinity Exams Practice cards (optional).

- The pupils practise asking and answering questions.

Review the tongue twister.

▶ *CD 2 Track 28 p268*

- Ask **What sound did you practise in the tongue twister?** ('z')
- Play the CD. Practise the tongue twister as a class.
- Remind the pupils that they know two spellings for the 'z' sound: 's' and 'z'. The pupils list the words they know which contain these letters.

Set learning outcomes and use the talk cards.

- Say **Today we're going to read some poems.** Ask **Do you like poems? Are poems usually short or long? Do poems have a shape? What shape can they be?** Explain that in this lesson the pupils are going to look at shape poems.
- Point to the talk cards to show the pupils the different ways they will be working in the lesson.

Before you read: Pupil's Book Activity 1

Look at the shape of the poems. What food can you see?

- Invite a pupil to read the instructions. The pupils identify the food from the shapes.

Answers: a banana, a slice of bread, a cherry

Pupil's Book Activity 2

Think of words to describe the food. Make a list.

- Ask the pupils to think of words to describe a banana, a slice of bread and a cherry, e.g. *soft, savoury, sweet.*
- Invite different pupils to tell you their words. List their words on the board.

Pupil's Book Activity 3

Read and listen. Do your words appear? Say the shape poems aloud.

▶ *CD2 Track 30 p269*

- Play the CD. The pupils listen to and read the poems.
- Ask the class if any of the words they listed appear. Then identify new words and check understanding.
- Explain that a lot of poetry (but not all) is written to be spoken. Read out the first poem, sentence by sentence, and ask the class to repeat it as fluently as possible. Then play the CD. The pupils listen and read the poem aloud. Repeat with the other shape poems.
- If the CD is too fast for your pupils, read the poem as a class, with you directing the speed and rhythm.

After you read: Activity Book

Activity 1

Find the words in the shape poems. Match.

- Read the example word 'juicy' in the first column. The pupils scan the poems in the Pupil's Book to find the word. Match it with its meaning in the second column and with the food in the third column.
- The pupils work on their own or in pairs to find the other words in the poems, work out their meaning and draw the matching lines.

Answers: **1** juicy – It's got lots of juice. – cherry **2** shiny – It reflects light. – cherry **3** savoury – It doesn't taste sweet. – bread **4** sweet – They taste sugary. – banana and cherry

Activity 2

Complete the chart with adjectives from the shape poems.

- The pupils work on their own or in pairs to read each poem and find the words to complete the chart.

Answers:

	size and shape	taste	colour
	long, thin	sweet	yellow, white
	thin, square	savoury	brown, white
	small, round	sweet	red

Activity 3

Work in small groups. Read and write the food.

- Invite a pupil to read out the instructions. Organise the class into small groups. Set a time limit for the challenge, e.g. ten minutes.
- The pupils read and write the food.
- If you wish to make the activity more challenging, you can say that pupils aren't allowed to repeat a food. This activity is also a good opportunity for pupils to work with a bilingual dictionary.

Suggested answers: **1** banana, potato, orange **2** banana, rice, bread **3** bread, cheese, crackers **4** apple, orange, tomato **5** pineapple, mango, cherry **6** popcorn, ice cream, jam **7** apple, cabbage, green pepper **8** ice cream, salad, strawberries

Code activity

- The pupils complete the code activity.

Answer: cough

Ending the lesson

Review the lesson and reflect on learning.

- Say **Today we've read some poems. What type of poems were they? Did you like them? Which was your favourite poem?** Elicit the pupils' responses.
- Ask **Which was your favourite activity today? Which activity was easy / difficult?**

Extra activity

Reinforcement

- Ask the class to find examples in the poems of two-syllable words that end with the letter 'y' (*sticky, juicy, shiny, cherry*).
- Organise the class into pairs. The pupils make a list of other words they know that end in 'y' (*baby, city, happy*, etc.).

Key Competences and Key Learning Outcomes

- Use adjectives with singular and plural nouns
- Identify different shapes in food
- Identify the features of a shape poem
- Use criteria to check your writing
- Share your writing with a partner
- Prepare and write a shape poem

Key language

- *circle, oval, rectangle, round, triangle; favourite, flavour, lick, lollipop, stick, strawberry*
- *It's (big). I (lick) it. I (hold) the stick. My favourite flavour is (strawberry). A (lollipop) is (sweet). (Cherries) are (sweet).*
- Recycled: *big, green, shape, sticky, sweet, yellow*

Materials

- Pupil's Book p47; Activity Book p44; Class CD2; Teacher's App on Navio
- Teacher's Resource Bank: Talk cards

Optional materials

- Teacher's Resource Bank: Trinity Exams Practice cards (selected from the Starter Unit and Units 1, 2 and 3)
- Coloured pencils
- A piece of paper for each pupil
- Food word cards

At a Glance Lesson Plan

Pupil's Book

Starting the lesson

- Use the Trinity Exams Practice cards (optional).
- Review basic shapes.
- Set learning outcomes and use the talk cards.

Investigate a text: Activity 1

- Think of foods which are these shapes.

Investigate a text: Activity 2

- Look at the poem. What shape is it?
- Read and listen.
- ▶ *CD2 Track 31 p269*
- Name the food.

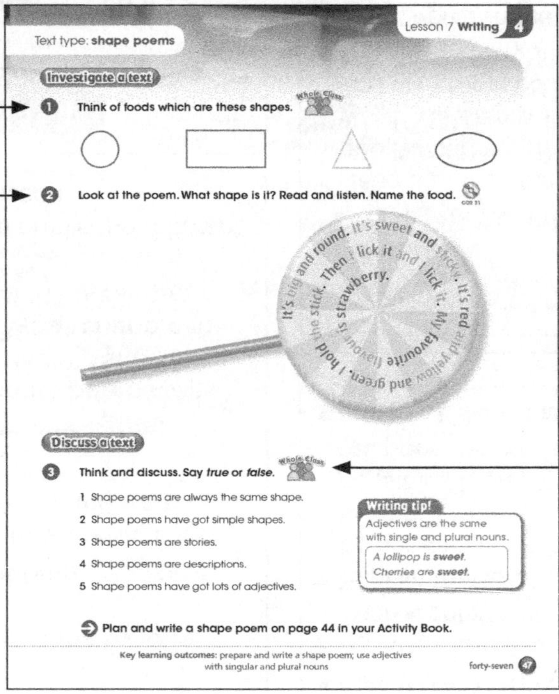

Discuss a text: Activity 3

- Think and discuss.
- Say *true* or *false*.
- **Writing tip:** Read about adjectives with singular and plural nouns.

Go to the Activity Book.

Ending the lesson

- Review the lesson and reflect on learning.

Extra activities

Reinforcement

- Make a class display of shape poems.
- Play *Word detectives*.

Activity Book

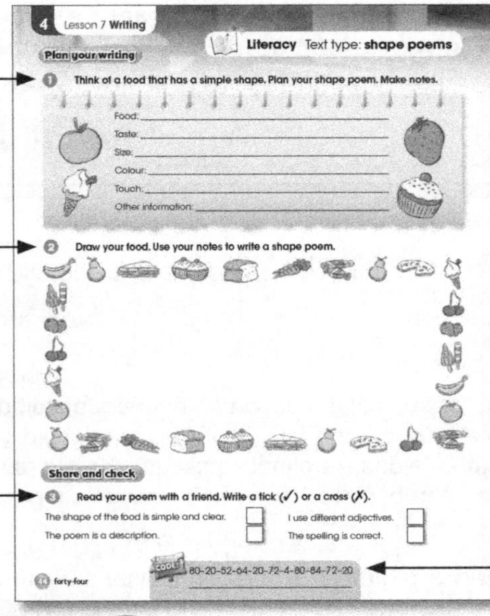

Activity Book

Plan your writing: Activity 1

- Think of a food that has a simple shape.
- Plan your shape poem.
- Make notes.

Activity 2

- Draw your food.
- Use your notes to write a shape poem.

Share and check: Activity 3

- Read your poem with a friend.
- Write a tick (✓) or a cross (✗).

Code activity

- Complete the code activity.

Digital resources

Teacher's Digital: You can also teach this lesson using the Teacher's App on Navio.

Pupil's Digital: Encourage your pupils to use the Pupil's App on Navio to practise the activities from this lesson.

Powered By NAVIO

Starting the lesson

Use the Trinity Exams Practice cards (optional).

- The pupils practise asking and answering questions.

Review basic shapes.

- Draw a square on the board and ask **What shape is this?** Then ask **Can you see a square shape in the classroom?** Repeat the procedure with a triangle, a rectangle and an oval. Point to each shape in turn and say the word. The pupils repeat two or three times.

Set learning outcomes and use the talk cards.

- Ask **What did we read in the last lesson?** (*Shape poems.*) Say **Today we're going to investigate another shape poem. Then we're going to plan and write our own shape poem.**
- Point to the talk cards to show the pupils the different ways they will be working in the lesson.

Investigate a text: Pupil's Book Activity 1

Think of foods which are these shapes.

- Read the instructions for the activity and prompt the pupils to name the shapes (*circle, rectangle, triangle, oval*). Ask the class to think of different foods that are these shapes.

Investigate a text: Pupil's Book Activity 2

Look at the poem. What shape is it? Read and listen. Name the food.

▶ *CD2 Track 31 p269*

- Focus the pupils on the poem and ask them to name the shape and guess what food it is.
- The pupils read and listen to the poem and identify the food.
- The pupils read the poem again on their own. Check comprehension and explain any unknown vocabulary.

Answer: It's round. It's a lollipop.

Discuss a text: Pupil's Book Activity 3

Think and discuss. Say *true* or *false*.

- Invite a pupil to read out the first statement and to say whether it's true or false. Repeat the procedure with the other statements.
- Confirm that shape poems have got simple shapes. Shape poems are usually descriptions and they have got lots of adjectives.

Answers: **1** false **2** true **3** false **4** true **5** true

Writing tip

- Read the information as a class. Ask the pupils to think of how adjectives are used in their language. Is the adjective the same when there's a singular noun and when there's a plural noun?

Activity Book

Plan your writing: Activity 1

Think of a food that has a simple shape. Plan your shape poem. Make notes.

- Read out the headings and give examples for each section. If necessary, write ideas on the board.
- The pupils work on their own to think of a food and then complete their notes.

Activity 2

Draw your food. Use your notes to write a shape poem.

- Ask the pupils to use their notes to write a draft of their shape poem in their notebooks. The pupils should use the poems that they saw in Lessons 6 and 7 as models. Move around the class, monitoring and supporting pupils as they write.
- Organise the class into pairs and ask the pupils to check each other's work for mistakes. They can also suggest other ideas or improvements.
- The pupils work on their own to draw the outline shape of their food in pencil in their Activity Books. They should then copy their corrected poems onto the outline or inside the shape. The pupils can also colour and decorate their drawing.

Share and check: Activity 3

Writing Partners. Read your poem with a friend. Write a tick (✓) or a cross (✗).

- Focus the pupils on the statements. Read through the statements as a class.
- Organise the class into new pairs. Pupil A reads their poem aloud to their partner. Pupil B listens. The pupils work together to decide if the poem fulfils all the criteria and tick or cross the corresponding boxes.
- The pupils swap roles.

Code activity

- The pupils complete the code activity.

Answer: temperature

Ending the lesson

Review the lesson and reflect on learning.

- Say **Today you've written a shape poem. Are you happy with it?** Elicit the pupils' responses.
- Ask **Which was your favourite activity today? Which activity was easy / difficult?**

Extra activities

Reinforcement

- The pupils copy their shape poems onto a piece of paper and decorate their work.
- Use the poems to make a class display.
- Play *Word detectives* (see p27) with food word cards.

Key Competences and Key Learning Outcomes

- Use the Internet to investigate India
- Read and listen for specific information
- Read about food in India
- Think about your own culture and identity

Key language

- *festival days, fingers, meal, nuts, sauces, snacks, soup*
- *(India) is famous for (its spicy food). Do you know that (you can only eat with your right hand in India)?*
- Recycled: *bread, breakfast, cakes, cheese, curry, milk, rice, savoury, small, spicy, sticky, sugar, sweet, vegetables*

Materials

- Pupil's Book p48; Activity Book p45; Class CD2; Teacher's App on Navio
- Teacher's Resource Bank: Talk cards
- Coloured pencils (orange, white and green)
- An online world map

Optional materials

- Teacher's Resource Bank: Trinity Exams Practice cards (selected from the Starter Unit and Units 1, 2 and 3)
- Food flashcards

At a Glance Lesson Plan

Pupil's Book

Starting the lesson

- Use the Trinity Exams Practice cards (optional).
- Review the code message in Lesson 3.
- Set learning outcomes and use the talk cards.

Activity 1

- Read Luke's questions.
- What do you think?

Activity 2

- Read and listen.
- ▶ *CD2 Track 32 p269*
- Answer Luke's questions.
- **Think about your culture** What food is typical in your country?
- Go to the Activity Book.

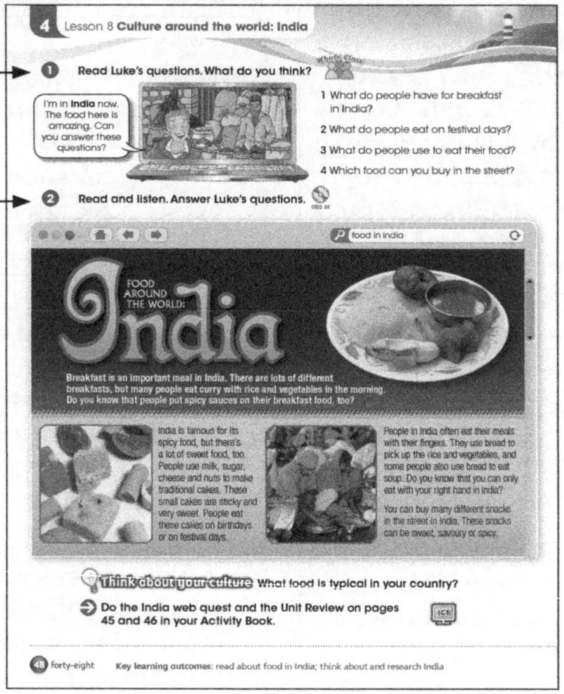

4 Lesson 8 Culture around the world: India

1 Read Luke's questions. What do you think?

I'm in India now. The food here is amazing. Can you answer these questions?

1 What do people have for breakfast in India?
2 What do people eat on festival days?
3 What do people use to eat their food?
4 Which food can you buy in the street?

2 Read and listen. Answer Luke's questions.

Breakfast is an important meal in India. There are lots of different breakfasts, but many people eat curry with rice and vegetables in the morning. Do you know that people put spicy sauces on their breakfast food, too?

India is famous for its spicy food, but there's a lot of sweet food, too. People use milk, sugar, cheese and nuts to make traditional cakes. These small cakes are sticky and very sweet. People eat these cakes on birthdays or on festival days.

People in India often eat their meals with their fingers. They use bread to pick up the rice and vegetables, and some people also use bread to eat soup. Do you know that you can only eat with your right hand in India?

You can buy many different snacks in the street in India. These snacks can be sweet, savoury or spicy.

Think about your culture What food is typical in your country?

Do the India web quest and the Unit Review on pages 45 and 46 in your Activity Book.

48 forty-eight Key learning outcomes: read about food in India; think about and research India

Ending the lesson

- Review the lesson and reflect on learning.

Extra activity

Reinforcement

- Play *Keep talking*.

Activity Book

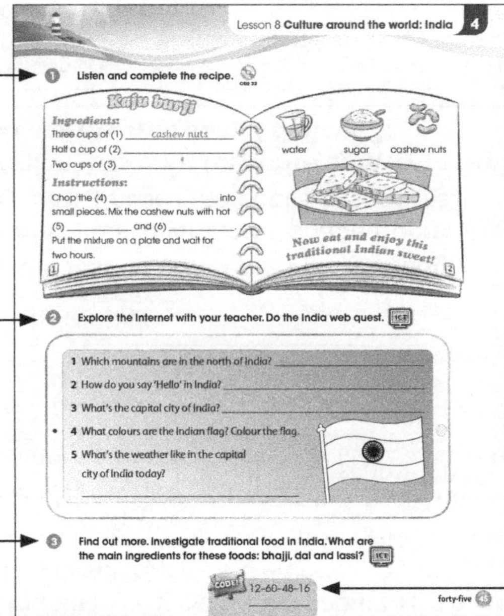

Lesson 8 Culture around the world: India 4

1 Listen and complete the recipe.

2 Explore the Internet with your teacher. Do the India web quest.

1 Which mountains are in the north of India?
2 How do you say 'Hello' in India?
3 What's the capital city of India?
4 What colours are the Indian flag? Colour the flag.
5 What's the weather like in the capital city of India today?

3 Find out more. Investigate traditional food in India. What are the main ingredients for these foods: bhajji, dal and lassi?

CODE 12-60-48-16

forty-five 45

Activity Book

Activity 1

- Listen and complete the recipe.
- ▶ *CD2 Track 33 p269*

Activity 2

- Explore the Internet with your teacher. Do the India web quest.

Activity 3

- Find out more. Investigate traditional food in India. What are the main ingredients for these foods: bhajji, dal and lassi?

Code activity

- Complete the code activity.

Digital resources

Teacher's Digital: You can also teach this lesson using the Teacher's App on Navio.

Powered By NAVIO

Starting the lesson

Use the Trinity Exams Practice cards (optional).

- The pupils practise asking and answering questions.

Review the code message in Lesson 3.

- Ask **Do you remember Luke's secret message? What food does he have for lunch?** (*Curry.*) **Do you like curry? Where do people eat curry?**

Set learning outcomes and use the talk cards.

- Say **Today we're going to investigate food in India.**
- Point to the talk cards to show the pupils the different ways they will be working in the lesson.

Pupil's Book Activity 1

Read Luke's questions. What do you think?

- Read the speech bubble as a class. Ask what the pupils know about India. Show them where the country is on an online world map.
- Read the questions as a class. Encourage the pupils to predict the answers.

Pupil's Book Activity 2

Read and listen. Answer Luke's questions.

▶ *CD2 Track 32 p269*

- Focus the class on the photos. Ask **What can you see?**
- Ask the pupils to read the text. If you want the pupils to read the text without the support of the CD, set a time limit. Otherwise, play the CD, pausing after each section to check understanding.
- The pupils answer Luke's questions.
- Ask **Would you like to eat curry for breakfast? Would you like to try Indian sweets? What food do you eat with your fingers? What snacks do you buy in the street?**

Answers: **1** Many people eat curry with rice and vegetables and spicy sauces. **2** People eat traditional cakes. **3** People often eat with their fingers, using their right hand only. They also use bread. **4** You can buy sweet, savoury or spicy snacks.

Think about your culture

- Read out the question and prompt different pupils to tell you about typical food in their country.

Activity Book

Activity 1

Listen and complete the recipe.

▶ *CD2 Track 33 p269*

- Read out the information. Use mime to explain the meaning of 'chop'. Then play the CD, pausing to allow the pupils to write the words.
- Play the CD again without pausing.
- Ask the pupils if they think the recipe sounds delicious.

Answers: **1** cashew nuts **2** water **3** sugar **4** cashew nuts **5** water **6** sugar

Activity 2

Explore the Internet with your teacher. Do the India web quest.

- Read out the instructions for the activity.
- Connect to a children's website that provides geographical information about India. (See suggested websites opposite.) Read out questions 1–4. The pupils work as a class to find and write the answers, then they colour the flag.
- Read out question 5. Connect to a website that shows the weather around the world. (See suggested websites opposite.) The pupils complete the information about the day's weather.

Answers: **1** the Himalayas **2** Namaste **3** New Delhi **4** orange, white and green

Activity 3

Find out more. Investigate traditional food in India. What are the main ingredients for these foods: bhajji, dal and lassi?

- Tell the pupils that they are going to investigate traditional food in India. Ask them to predict the main ingredients in bhajji, dal and lassi.
- If you are doing the investigation as a class, go to a suitable website and ask the pupils to scan the information to find the answer.
- If you are working in a computer room, organise the class into small groups. The groups should go to the website and find the answers.

Answers: Bhajjis are made with vegetables and spices. Dal is made with pulses like lentils and chickpeas. Lassi is made with yoghurt.

Suggested websites

http://maps.google.es/

https://www.natgeokids.com/uk/

http://www.bbc.co.uk/weather

Code activity

- The pupils complete the code activity.

Answer: cold

Ending the lesson

Review the lesson and reflect on learning.

- Say **Today we've learnt about India. What food do people eat there?** Elicit the information.
- Ask **Which was your favourite activity today? Which activity was easy / difficult?**

Extra activity

Reinforcement

- Play *Keep talking* (see p27) with the food flashcards.

Go to the AB Unit Review on page 249.

Key Competences and Key Learning Outcomes

- Watch and understand a video about being creative with fruit
- Use imagination to create food pictures
- Work together to decorate pictures

Key language

- *apple, banana, grapes, lemon, melon, orange, pear, pineapple, strawberries, watermelon; bird, crab, dessert, dolphins, flowers, imagination, leaves, palm tree, plant; amazing, creative, fantastic, happy*
- *Which shape do you prefer? How many flowers are on the plant?*
- Recycled: *crunchy, soft*

Materials

- Pupil's Book p49; Activity Book p47; Class CD2; Teacher's App on Navio
- Teacher's Resource Bank: Talk cards

Optional materials

- Teacher's Resource Bank: Trinity Exams Practice cards (selected from the Starter Unit and Units 1, 2 and 3)

At a Glance Lesson Plan

Pupil's Book

Starting the lesson

- Use the Trinity Exams Practice cards (optional).
- **Think-Pair-Share.** Review fruit vocabulary.
- Set learning outcomes and use the talk cards.

Activity 1

- Before you watch
- Watch the video.

Unit 4 video p285

- Which fruits do you see in the video?
- What pictures do the fruits make?

Activity 2

- Watch the video again.

Unit 4 video

- Read and answer the questions.

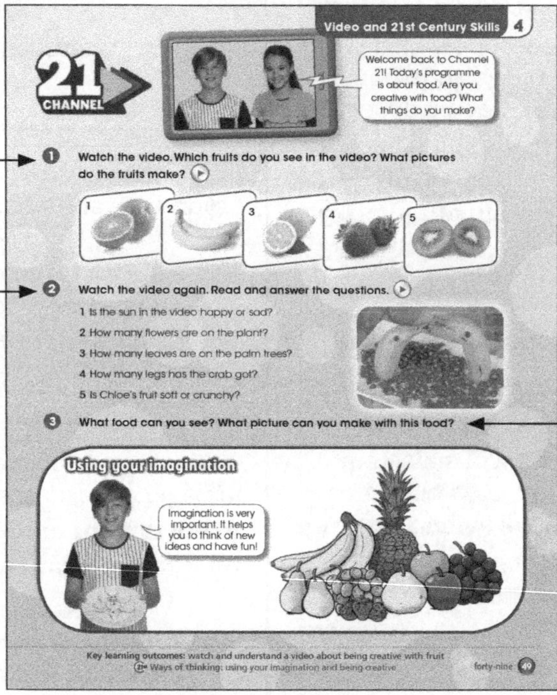
Video and 21st Century Skills 4
Welcome back to Channel 21! Today's programme is about food. Are you creative with food? What things do you make?
1 Watch the video. Which fruits do you see in the video? What pictures do the fruits make?
2 Watch the video again. Read and answer the questions.
1 Is the sun in the video happy or sad?
2 How many flowers are on the plant?
3 How many leaves are on the palm trees?
4 How many legs has the crab got?
5 Is Chloe's fruit soft or crunchy?
3 What food can you see? What picture can you make with this food?
Using your imagination
Imagination is very important. It helps you to think of new ideas and have fun!
forty-nine

Activity 3

- What food can you see?
- What picture can you make with this food?

Go to the Activity Book.

Ending the lesson

- Review the lesson and reflect on learning.

Extra activity

Reinforcement

- Use your imagination to be creative with vegetables.

Activity Book

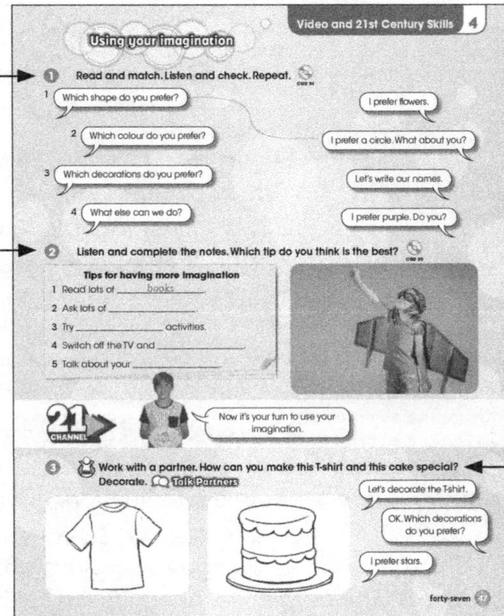
Video and 21st Century Skills 4
Using your imagination
1 Read and match. Listen and check. Repeat.
1 Which shape do you prefer? — I prefer flowers.
2 Which colour do you prefer? — I prefer a circle. What about you?
3 Which decorations do you prefer? — Let's write our names.
4 What else can we do? — I prefer purple. Do you?
2 Listen and complete the notes. Which tip do you think is the best?
Tips for having more imagination
1 Read lots of books
2 Ask lots of
3 Try activities.
4 Switch off the TV and
5 Talk about your
Now it's your turn to use your imagination.
3 Work with a partner. How can you make this T-shirt and this cake special? Decorate.
Let's decorate the T-shirt.
OK. Which decorations do you prefer?
I prefer stars.
forty-seven

Activity Book

Activity 1

- Read and match.
- Listen and check.

▶ *CD2 Track 34 p269*

- Repeat.

Activity 2

- Listen and complete the notes.

▶ *CD2 Track 35 p269*

- Which tip do you think is the best?

Activity 3

- Work with a partner.
- How can you make this T-shirt and this cake special?
- Decorate

Digital resources

Teacher's Digital: You can also teach this lesson using the Teacher's App on Navio.

Pupil's Digital: Encourage your pupils to use the Pupil's App on Navio to practise the activities from this lesson.

Powered By NAVIO

Starting the lesson

Use the Trinity Exams Practice cards (optional).

- The pupils practise asking and answering questions.

Think-Pair-Share. Review fruit vocabulary.

- Ask **Can you remember the names of fruits?** The class thinks silently for a minute.
- Then the pupils work with a Talk Partner to name different types of fruit.
- Invite different Talk Partners to say a different fruit. Write the fruit on the board and prompt the class to repeat the fruit.
- Finally, repeat the procedure, asking different pairs of Talk Partners each time, until all the ideas have been recorded.

Set learning outcomes and use the talk cards.

- Say **Today we're going to watch a video and then ask and answer questions about being creative**.
- Point to the talk cards to show the pupils the different ways they will be working in the lesson.

Pupil's Book Activity 1

Before you watch

- Read the speech bubble to pupils. Ask **Are you creative with food? What things do you make?** Elicit responses from a number of pupils.

Watch the video. Which fruits do you see in the video? What pictures do the fruits make? *p285*

- Watch Part 1. Ask pupils **What do you think you are going to see next?** Elicit ideas and explain that they will see a video about being creative with fruit.
- Play Part 2. Ask general questions to check understanding. Focus the pupils on the photos in Activity 1 and check vocabulary. Say **Which fruits do you see in the video? What pictures do the fruits make?** Elicit ideas.
- Play Part 2 again for the pupils to answer the questions. Check answers as a class.

Answers: **1** (flowers), **2** (palm trees, dolphins), **4** (sun), **5** (palm trees)

Pupil's Book Activity 2

Watch the video again. Read and answer the questions.

- Ask a pupil to read out sentence 1. Ask the class what they think the answer is. Repeat with sentences 2–5.
- Play Part 2. Students work in pairs to answer the questions.

Answers: **1** happy **2** four **3** ten **4** eight **5** crunchy

Pupil's Book Activity 3

What food can you see? What picture can you make with this food?

- Ask **What does Chloe say about eating fruit at the start of the video?** (*It's boring.*) **How does Chloe describe the fruit at the end?** (*Delicious.*) **How does Mark change her opinion?** (*He is creative with the fruit.*)
- Explain that this activity is all about using your imagination to change boring food into delicious creations. Look at the pictures with the class and check vocabulary.
- Pupils work in pairs to use the food to create a picture.
- Invite pairs to show their pictures to the class. Ask **Which picture do you prefer?** Say **I prefer …**

Activity Book

Activity 1

Read and match. Listen and check. Repeat.

▶ *CD2 Track 34 p269*

- Ask the pupils to read out the speech bubbles. Check vocabulary. The pupils work on their own to match the speech bubbles.
- Play the CD and check answers.

Answers: **1** I prefer a circle. What about you? **2** I prefer purple. Do you? **3** I prefer flowers. **4** Let's write our names.

Activity 2

Listen and complete the notes. Which tip do you think is the best?

▶ *CD2 Track 35 p269*

- Explain to the pupils that they are going to listen to a girl and her mum talking about how she can have more imagination. Ask pupils for ideas of how to improve their imagination. Read out the information. Then play the CD, pausing to allow the pupils to write the missing information.
- Play the CD again without pausing.

Answers: **1** books **2** questions **3** new **4** play **5** ideas

- Ask the pupils **Which tip do you think is the best? How good is your imagination?**

Activity 3

Work with a partner. How can you make this T-shirt and this cake special? Decorate.

- Read out the speech bubbles. Explain that pupils will work in pairs to decorate a T-shirt and a cake. Remind them that they need to use their imagination.
- Organise the pupils into Talk Partners. The pupils decorate their T-shirt and cake.
- Invite pairs to show their designs to the class.

Ending the lesson

Review the lesson and reflect on learning.

- Say **Today we've watched a video about being creative with fruit.** Ask **What fruit picture would you prefer to eat?**
- Ask **Which was your favourite activity today? Which activity was easy / difficult?**

Extra activity

Reinforcement

- Ask the pupils to create something from a vegetable, for example a book character, a musical instrument, or a vehicle. They could draw their design in their notebooks or actually make the creation for homework.

Date: ____________ Unit: ____________

1 What did my pupils learn in this unit?

2 How did my pupils work? (✓)

individually ☐ in pairs ☐ in small groups ☐

in large groups ☐ as a class ☐

3 Which key competences did my pupils develop?

- Competence in linguistic communication ☐
- Competence in mathematics, science and technology ☐
- Digital competence ☐
- Learning to learn ☐
- Social and civic competences ☐
- Sense of initiative and entrepreneurship ☐
- Cultural awareness and expression ☐

4 Which lessons / activities were the most successful and why?

5 Which lessons / activities did my pupils find the most difficult and why?

6 What did I try in the classroom for the first time? How did it go?

7 Which resources did I find most useful? (including webpages)

8 What could I do differently next time I teach this unit?

Unit 5 Under the sea

Unit overview

Key Competences and Key Learning Outcomes

- Identify and name sea animals (Lesson 1)
- Say the vocabulary chant (Lesson 1)
- Understand and act out a conversation (Lesson 2)
- Use comparative adjectives (Lessons 2 and 4)
- Follow, complete and correct the grammar tables (Lessons 2 and 4)
- Learn descriptive adjectives (Lesson 4)
- Use 'and' to add similar information (Lesson 7)
- Watch and understand a video (Video and 21st Century Skills)

- Use a code to read a message (Lesson 3)
- Read about sea animals (Lesson 6)
- Plan and write an article about sea animals (Lesson 7)
- Learn interesting facts about sea animals (Video and 21st Century Skills)

- Use the Pupil's App on Navio
- Investigate Hawaii (Lesson 8)

- Say a tongue twister, learn another spelling for the 'w' sound and practise spelling (Lesson 5)
- Practise activity types found in the Cambridge Exams: A1 Movers
- Review your own learning (Review)

- Work with a Talk Partner to practise and reinforce learning (all lessons)
- Do a quiz with a partner (Lesson 5)

- Understand the importance of protecting sea animals (Lesson 3)

- Sing a song (Lesson 1)
- Understand, act out and give an opinion on a story (Lesson 3)
- Say a rap (Lesson 4)
- Learn about Hawaii (Lesson 8)
- Think about your own culture (Lesson 8)

Vocabulary

Core vocabulary
crab, dolphin, fish, jellyfish, octopus, seahorse, seal, shark, squid, starfish, turtle, whale; colourful, dangerous, heavy, intelligent, pretty, ugly

Extension vocabulary (optional)
clam, eel, lobster, ray, sea urchin, walrus; boring, friendly, funny, interesting

Other vocabulary
blowhole, blue whale, brain, curled tail, hard / soft skin, krill, long head, round body, spider crab, stomach, super, tongue; light, long, slow, thin

Recycled vocabulary
arms, big, body, car, cat, cow, claw, crocodile, December, dog, elephant, eye, giraffe, hamster, hard skin, head, hippo, legs, May, mouse, old, shell, snail, snake, teeth

Structures

Core structures
A (shark) is (bigger) than a (seahorse). A (shark) is more (dangerous) than a (seahorse). Is a (shark) more (intelligent) than a (dolphin)? Yes, it is. No, it isn't.

Other structures
(Blue whales) are (about 30 metres long). Do you know that (they haven't got any teeth)? How (big) is the animal? What does it (look like)? Where does it (live)? How does it (move)? Why is it (amazing)? What does it (eat)? They're (different sizes) and (colours). How many (eyes) has a (starfish) got? How fast does a (great white shark) (swim)?

Recycled structures
This (sea animal) has got (sharp teeth). This (sea animal) is (big). There's a (whale). There are (three jellyfish). Which (sea animals) do you like? I like (dolphins). He likes (jellyfish). They've got (soft skin). They eat (fish and plants). Has it got a (shell)? No, it hasn't. Is it a (turtle)? Yes, it is.

Phonics

The 'w' sound (***wh**y **wh**ite **wh**ale **w**earing **w**atch*)

Literacy

Text type: a magazine article (information text; writing preparation)
Reading skills: activating existing knowledge of content; reading for information and entertainment
Writing skills: using 'and' to add similar information

Culture ... around the world

Activities in Hawaii

21st Century Skills

Using keywords to find information online

Thinking skills

Applying rules (Lessons 2 and 4); Spatial thinking (Lesson 2); Predicting (Lessons 3 and 8); Discussing values (Lesson 3); Expressing opinions (Lesson 3); Thinking about your culture (Lesson 8); Making connections (Review)

Cooperative learning

Teamwork (Lesson 1); Helping each other (Lesson 1); Collaborating (Lesson 4); Checking learning (Lesson 5); Peer evaluation and feedback (Lesson 7); Working together (Review)

Values

Understanding the importance of protecting sea animals

Cross-curricular links

Link to Science
Habitats: Reviewing water habitats, the food chain and how to protect ecosystems
Suggested Arts and Crafts concepts
Exploring space in art and creating a three-dimensional landscape with a background, middle ground and foreground to create the illusion of depth

Key Competences and Key Learning Outcomes

- Identify and say sea animals
- Say the vocabulary chant
- Create a water habitat drawing (optional)
- Review animal vocabulary
- Play a game with a recycled structure
- Sing a song about sea animals

Key language

- Sea animals: *crab, dolphin, fish, jellyfish, octopus, seahorse, seal, shark, squid, starfish, turtle, whale; claws, fur, sea floor, seaweed, sharp, sting, tentacles, under the sea*
- Extension: *clam, eel, lobster, ray, sea urchin, walrus*
- Recycled: *big, legs, teeth; There are (three jellyfish). There's a (whale). This sea animal is (very big). This sea animal has got (sharp teeth).*

Materials

- Pupil's Book p50; Activity Book p48; Class CD2; Teacher's App on Navio
- Teacher's Resource Bank: Sea animals word cards
- Sea animals flashcards
- Teacher's Resource Bank: Talk cards

Optional materials

- Teacher's Resource Bank: Trinity Exams Practice cards (selected from the Starter Unit and Units 1, 2, 3 and 4)

At a Glance Lesson Plan

Starting the lesson

- Use the Trinity Exams Practice cards (optional).
- Review animal vocabulary.
- Set learning outcomes and use the talk cards.

Activity 1

- What animals live under the sea?
- Make a list.

Vocabulary presentation

- Present the new vocabulary using the sea animals flashcards.

Word cards

- Introduce the spellings of the vocabulary using the sea animals word cards.

Activity 2

- Listen, point and say the vocabulary chant.

▶ *CD2 Track 36 p270*

Pupil's Book

Activity 3

- Listen, look and sing *Under the sea.*

▶ *CD2 Track 37 p270*

Activity 4

- Play a memory game.
- Go to the Activity Book.

Ending the lesson

- Review the lesson and reflect on learning.

Extra activities

Reinforcement

- Memorise the keywords.

Vocabulary extension

- Present six additional vocabulary items.

Link to Science

- **Habitats:** Create a water habitat drawing.

Activity Book

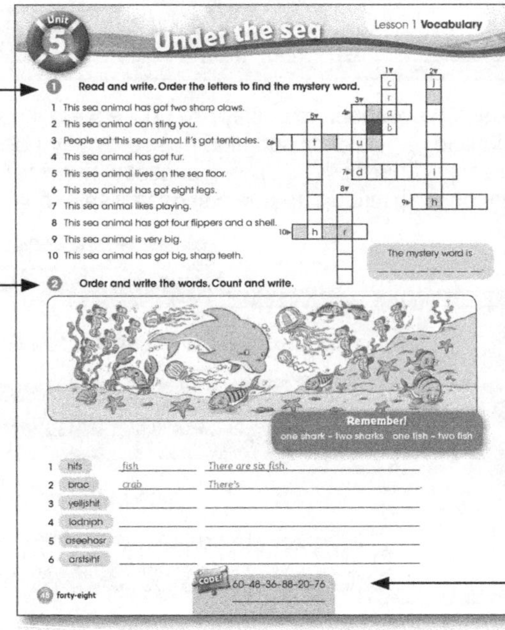

Activity Book

Activity 1

- Read and write.
- Order the letters to find the mystery word.

Activity 2

- Order and write the words.
- Count and write.

Code activity

- Complete the code activity.

Digital resources

Teacher's Digital: You can also teach this lesson using the Teacher's App on Navio.

Pupil's Digital: Encourage your pupils to use the Pupil's App on Navio to practise the activities from this lesson.

Powered By NAVIO

Starting the lesson

Use the Trinity Exams Practice cards (optional).

- The pupils practise asking and answering questions.

Review animal vocabulary.

- Organise the class into small groups and ask them to choose a scribe. Say **Write the names of four animals that have got fur.** When they have finished, the whole group puts their hands up. Check answers and repeat with another category (animals that can fly / have got wings / are nocturnal / eat meat / eat plants).

Set learning outcomes and use the talk cards.

- Say **Today we're going to learn the names of animals that live in the sea.**
- Point to the talk cards to show the pupils the different ways they will be working in the lesson.

Pupil's Book Activity 1

What animals live under the sea? Make a list.

- (Books closed.) Work as a class to brainstorm the names of sea animals that pupils know. Make a list.

Vocabulary presentation

- (Books closed.) Explain that you have some pictures of sea animals, but don't let the pupils see the flashcards. Describe the animal on the first sea animals flashcard, e.g. **This sea animal has got eight legs. It's got big eyes.** The pupils raise their hands when they know the animal. Show the class the flashcard and say the word. The pupils repeat.
- Stick the flashcard on the board and repeat the procedure with the other flashcards.

Word cards

- (Books closed.) Hand a sea animals word card to each pair of pupils.
- The pairs take turns to come to the board, read out their word and stick their word card next to the corresponding flashcard.

Pupil's Book Activity 2

Listen, point and say the vocabulary chant.

▶ *CD2 Track 36 p270*

- Focus the pupils' attention on the 12 photos. Say **Let's listen and say the words.** Play the CD. The pupils listen, point and repeat.

Pupil's Book Activity 3

Listen, look and sing *Under the sea.*

▶ *CD2 Track 37 p270*

- Ask **Where are Lily, Ravi, Josh and Josh's grandad?** (*At an aquarium.*) **What sea animals can they see?**
- Play the CD. The pupils listen and read.
- Ask **What sea animals are in the song?**
- Play the CD again. The pupils sing and point to the sea animals.

Pupil's Book Activity 4

Play a memory game.

- Ask two pupils to read out the speech bubbles. Remind the class that we use 'There is' for one object and 'There are' for more than one object.
- Give the pupils one minute to study the scene and count the sea animals.
- (Books closed.) Say sentences about the scene. The pupils say if the sentences are right or wrong.
- The pupils play the game with a Talk Partner.

Activity Book

Activity 1

Read and write. Order the letters to find the mystery word.

- The pupils complete the crossword, then order the shaded letters to discover the mystery word.

Answers: **1** crab **2** jellyfish **3** squid **4** seal **5** starfish **6** octopus **7** dolphin **8** turtle **9** whale **10** shark
Mystery word: seahorse

Activity 2

Order and write the words. Count and write.

- Ask the pupils to describe the picture. Then focus their attention on the jumbled words and ask them to identify the sea animals.
- Focus the pupils on the *Remember!* tip and remind them when to use 'There is' or 'There are'.
- The pupils count the animals and write the sentences.

Answers: **1** fish – There are six fish. **2** crab – There's one crab. **3** jellyfish – There are four jellyfish. **4** dolphin – There's one dolphin. **5** seahorse – There are nine seahorses. **6** starfish – There are seven starfish.

Code activity

- The pupils complete the code activity.

Answer: olives

Ending the lesson

Review the lesson and reflect on learning.

- Say **Today we've learnt the names of sea animals. What animals do you remember?**
- Ask **Which was your favourite activity today? Which activity was easy / difficult?**

Extra activities

Reinforcement

- The pupils look at the 12 keywords on Pupil's Book page 50 for one minute. Then try to remember them in pairs.

Vocabulary extension

- Present six additional sea animals: *clam, eel, lobster, ray, sea urchin, walrus.*
- Use the Vocabulary Booster on Navio to practise these new words.

Link to Science

- Review the plants and animals that live in water **habitats**. Create a class drawing of a water scene. Invite pupils to draw and label an animal or a plant.

Key Competences and Key Learning Outcomes

- Listen, repeat and act out a conversation
- Listen, follow the grammar table and identify the parts of a sentence
- Use comparative adjectives with '-er'

Key language
- *bigger, faster, lighter, longer, slower, smaller, thinner*
- *A (shark) is bigger than a (seahorse).*
- Recycled: *crab, dolphin, fish, jellyfish, octopus, seahorse, seal, shark, squid, starfish, turtle, whale; car*

Materials
- Pupil's Book p51; Activity Book p49; Class CD2; Teacher's App on Navio
- Sea animals flashcards
- Teacher's Resource Bank: Talk cards

Optional materials
- Teacher's Resource Bank: Trinity Exams Practice cards (selected from the Starter Unit and Units 1, 2, 3 and 4)

At a Glance Lesson Plan

Pupil's Book

Starting the lesson
- Use the Trinity Exams Practice cards (optional).
- **Think-Pair-Share.** Review sea animals vocabulary.
- Review the *Under the sea* song.
- ▶ *CD2 Track 37 p270*
- ▶ *CD2 Track 38 p270*
- Set learning outcomes and use the talk cards.

Activity 1
- Listen and read.
- Listen and repeat.
- ▶ *CD2 Track 39 p270*
- Act out.

Activity 2
- Read again.
- Which picture is correct?

Activity 3
- Listen and follow.
- ▶ *CD2 Track 40 p270*
- Repeat.
- **Grammar clue:** Read about making comparative adjectives with '–er'.

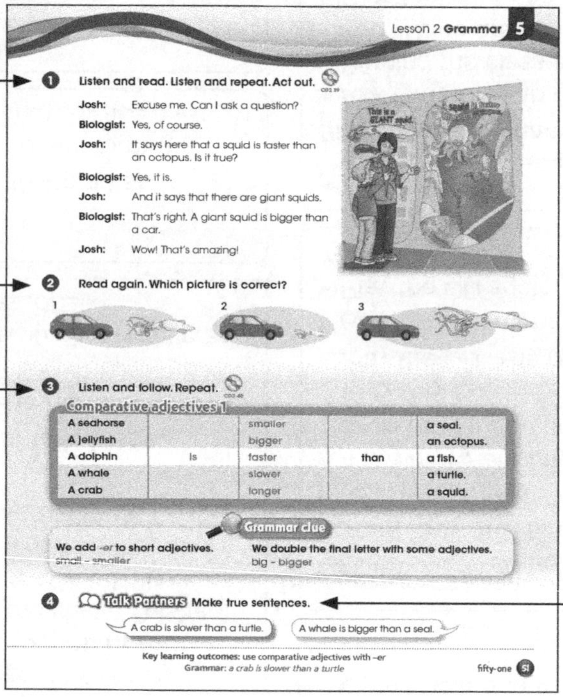

Lesson 2 Grammar 5

1 Listen and read. Listen and repeat. Act out.

Josh: Excuse me. Can I ask a question?
Biologist: Yes, of course.
Josh: It says here that a squid is faster than an octopus. Is it true?
Biologist: Yes, it is.
Josh: And it says that there are giant squids.
Biologist: That's right. A giant squid is bigger than a car.
Josh: Wow! That's amazing!

2 Read again. Which picture is correct?

3 Listen and follow. Repeat.

Comparative adjectives 1

A seahorse		smaller		a seal.
A jellyfish		bigger		an octopus.
A dolphin	is	faster	than	a fish.
A whale		slower		a turtle.
A crab		longer		a squid.

Grammar clue
We add -er to short adjectives. small – smaller
We double the final letter with some adjectives. big – bigger

4 Talk Partners Make true sentences.
A crab is slower than a turtle. A whale is bigger than a seal.

Key learning outcomes: use comparative adjectives with -er
Grammar: a crab is slower than a turtle

fifty-one 51

Activity 4
- Make true sentences.
- Go to the Activity Book.

Ending the lesson
- Review the lesson and reflect on learning.

Extra activity

Reinforcement
- Make a line and compare ages.

Activity Book

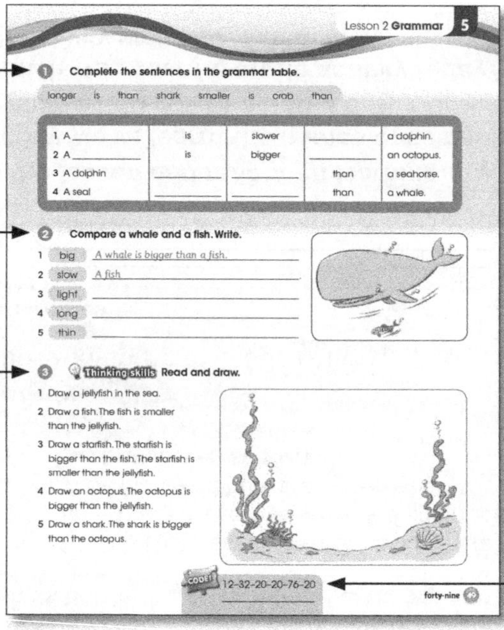

Lesson 2 Grammar 5

1 Complete the sentences in the grammar table.
longer is than shark smaller is crab than

1 A ____	is	slower	____	a dolphin.
2 A ____	is	bigger	____	an octopus.
3 A dolphin	____	____	than	a seahorse.
4 A seal	____	____	than	a whale.

2 Compare a whale and a fish. Write.
1 big A whale is bigger than a fish.
2 slow A fish
3 light
4 long
5 thin

3 Thinking skills Read and draw.
1 Draw a jellyfish in the sea.
2 Draw a fish. The fish is smaller than the jellyfish.
3 Draw a starfish. The starfish is bigger than the fish. The starfish is smaller than the jellyfish.
4 Draw an octopus. The octopus is bigger than the jellyfish.
5 Draw a shark. The shark is bigger than the octopus.

CODE! 12-32-20-20-76-20

forty-nine 49

Activity Book

Activity 1
- Complete the sentences in the grammar table.

Activity 2
- Compare a whale and a fish.
- Write.

Activity 3
- Read and draw.

Code activity
- Complete the code activity.

Digital resources

Teacher's Digital: You can also teach this lesson using the Teacher's App on Navio.

Pupil's Digital: Encourage your pupils to use the Pupil's App on Navio to practise the activities from this lesson.

Powered By NAVIO

Starting the lesson

Use the Trinity Exams Practice cards (optional).

- The pupils practise asking and answering questions.

Think-Pair-Share. Review sea animals vocabulary.

- Ask **Can you remember the sea animals vocabulary?** The class thinks silently for a minute.
- Then the pupils work with a Talk Partner to name the sea animals.
- Invite different Talk Partners to say a different animal. Hold up the corresponding flashcard and prompt the class to repeat the word.
- Finally, repeat the procedure, asking different pairs of Talk Partners each time, until all the sea animals have been named.

Review the *Under the sea* song.

▶ *CD2 Track 37 p270*

▶ *CD2 Track 38 p270 (optional karaoke version)*

- Play the CD (or use the karaoke version). The pupils sing and mime the different animals.

Set learning outcomes and use the talk cards.

- Say **Today we're going to learn how to compare two animals in English.**
- Point to the talk cards to show the pupils the different ways they will be working in the lesson.

Pupil's Book Activity 1

Listen and read. Listen and repeat. Act out.

▶ *CD2 Track 39 p270*

- The pupils look at the picture. Ask **Where's Josh? What's he doing?**
- Play the CD. The pupils listen and read the conversation.
- Ask **Are squids interesting?**
- Play the CD again, pausing after each sentence for the pupils to repeat.
- The pupils act out the conversation in pairs.

Pupil's Book Activity 2

Read again. Which picture is correct?

- The pupils read the conversation again and say which picture is correct.

Answer: the third picture

Pupil's Book Activity 3

Listen and follow. Repeat.

▶ *CD2 Track 40 p270*

- Play the CD. The pupils listen to the first sentence and point to the words they hear. The pupils repeat the complete sentence. Repeat the procedure with the other sentences.
- Highlight that the verb 'to be' (*is* / *are*) is always before the adjective and the word 'than' always follows the adjective.

Grammar clue

- Read the first grammar clue as a class. Invite a pupil to give another example.
- Read the second grammar clue as a class. Ask the pupils to think of another adjective where we double the last letter when we add –er (*thin*). Explain that this only happens in short adjectives that finish in a vowel and a consonant sound. The adjective 'slow' does not have a double letter because the final sound is a diphthong.

Pupil's Book Activity 4

Make true sentences.

- Organise the class into Talk Partners. The Talk Partners use the grammar table to make more true sentences. They can do this orally or in their notebooks.

Activity Book

Activity 1

Complete the sentences in the grammar table.

- Invite a pupil to read out the words in the word box.
- The pupils work on their own or with a partner to write the words in the grammar table.

Answers: **1** crab, than **2** shark, than **3** is longer **4** is smaller

Activity 2

Compare a whale and a fish. Write.

- Ask a pupil to name the two animals in the picture and to read out the first sentence. If necessary, ask different individual pupils to say the other comparative sentences.
- The pupils work on their own or with a partner to write the sentences.

Answers: **1** A whale is bigger than a fish. **2** A fish is slower than a whale. **3** A fish is lighter than a whale. **4** A whale is longer than a fish. **5** A fish is thinner than a whale.

Activity 3

Read and draw.

- Ask a pupil to read out the first instruction. The pupils draw a jellyfish in the frame. Tell them not to draw it too big, as they need to leave space for other animals.
- Repeat the procedure with the other instructions, inviting different pupils to read out the comparative sentences.

Code activity

- The pupils complete the code activity.

Answer: cheese

Ending the lesson

Review the lesson and reflect on learning.

- Say **Today we've learnt how to compare sea animals.** Hold up two of the sea animals flashcards and ask the class to compare them. Repeat the procedure with another pair of flashcards.
- Ask **Which was your favourite activity today? Which activity was easy / difficult?**

Extra activity

Reinforcement

- Ask ten pupils to line up according to their ages. Then ask each pupil to make two sentences, e.g. *I'm older than* (the pupil on their left). *I'm younger than* (the pupil on their right).

Key Competences and Key Learning Outcomes

- Read the story with some fluency
- Use a code to read a message
- Make a sign or poster about protecting ecosystems (optional)
- Do a pre-reading task
- Understand the importance of protecting sea animals
- Read, listen and understand a story about an underwater adventure
- Give an opinion on the story

Key language

- *aquarium, captain, gold coins, rich, robot, sand, submarine*
- *Let's (see some sea animals in the wild). We're going (to the bottom of the sea).*
- Recycled: *bin, cans, fish, shark, shiny, whale; It's (bigger) than (a fish). It's (heavier) than a (shark).*

Materials

- Pupil's Book pp52–53; Activity Book p50; Class CD2; Teacher's App on Navio
- Sea animals flashcards
- Teacher's Resource Bank: Talk cards

Optional materials

- Teacher's Resource Bank: Trinity Exams Practice cards (selected from the Starter Unit and Units 1, 2, 3 and 4)

At a Glance Lesson Plan

Pupil's Book

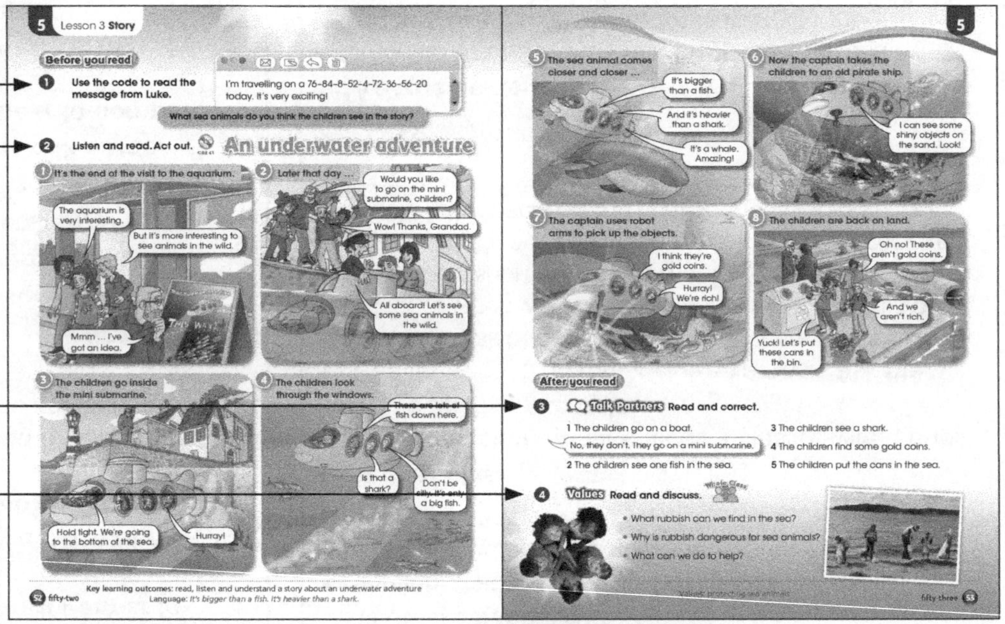

Activity Book

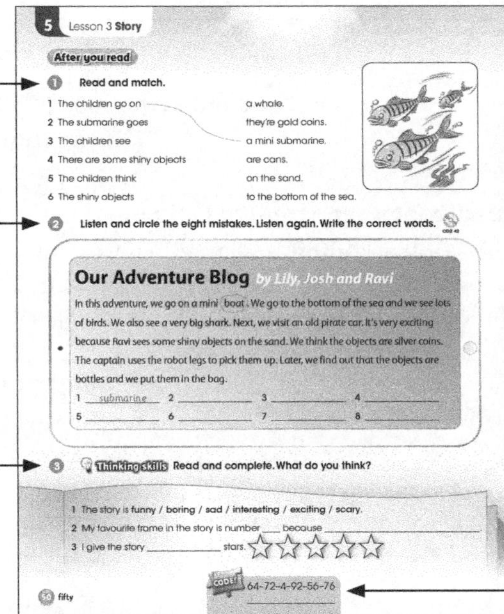

Starting the lesson

- Use the Trinity Exams Practice cards (optional).
- Review adjectives to compare two sea animals.
- Set learning outcomes and use the talk cards.

Before you read: Activity 1

- Use the code to read the message from Luke.

Activity 2

- Listen and read.
- ▶ *CD2 Track 41 p270*
- Act out.

After you read: Activity 3

- Read and correct.

Activity 4: Values

- Read and discuss.
- Go to the Activity Book.

Ending the lesson

- Review the lesson and reflect on learning.

Extra activity

Reinforcement

- Play *Broken CD player*.

Link to Science

- **Habitats:** Make a sign or poster about the importance of protecting ecosystems.

Digital resources

Teacher's Digital: You can also teach this lesson using the Teacher's App on Navio.

Pupil's Digital: Encourage your pupils to use the Pupil's App on Navio to practise the activities from this lesson.

Powered By NAVIO

After you read: Activity Book

Activity 1

- Read and match.

Activity 2

- Listen and circle the eight mistakes.
- ▶ *CD2 Track 42 p270*
- Listen again.
- Write the correct words.

Activity 3

- Read and complete.
- What do you think?

Code activity

- Complete the code activity.

Starting the lesson

Use the Trinity Exams Practice cards (optional).

- The pupils practise asking and answering questions.

Review adjectives to compare two sea animals.

- Stick six sea animals flashcards on the left of the board and six on the right. Write in the middle: *small, big, fast, slow, long.* Invite a pupil to come to the board and compare two of the animals, pointing to the words, e.g. *A whale is bigger than a dolphin.* Repeat with other pupils.

Set learning outcomes and use the talk cards.

- Say **Today we're going to read and listen to a story.**
- Point to the talk cards to show the pupils the different ways they will be working in the lesson.

Before you read: Pupil's Book Activity 1

Use the code to read the message from Luke.

- Say **Josh and Lily have received another message from Luke.** The pupils use the code (Pupil's Book page 7) to discover the mystery word (*submarine*). Ask **What do you know about submarines?** (*They travel under water.*) Explain that some submarines have windows. You can see under the sea in them.
- Read the title of the story. Ask **What sea animals do you think the children see in the story?** The pupils make predictions.

Pupil's Book Activity 2

Listen and read. Act out.

▶ *CD2 Track 41 p270*

- Play the CD. The pupils follow in their books.
- Ask questions to check comprehension.

Suggested comprehension questions

- Frame 1: **Do the children like the aquarium?** (*Yes.*)
- Frame 2: **What transport do they use?** (*A mini submarine.*)
- Frame 3: **Where does the mini submarine go?** (*To the bottom of the sea.*)
- Frame 4: **What does Lily think the big sea animal is?** (*A shark.*)
- Frame 5: **Is the big sea animal heavier than a shark?** (*Yes.*) **What is it?** (*A whale.*)
- Frame 6: **What type of ship is at the bottom of the sea?** (*An old pirate ship.*)
- Frame 7: **What do the children think the shiny objects are?** (*Gold coins.*)
- Frame 8: **What are the shiny objects?** (*Cans.*)
- Organise the class into five groups (Lily, Ravi, Josh, Grandad and the captain) and play the CD. Each group joins in when their character speaks.

After you read: Pupil's Book Activity 3

Read and correct.

- Ask a pupil to read out the first sentence and its correction. Ask the class to identify the story frame which has this information. (*Frame 2.*)
- Organise the class into Talk Partners to find the information and correct each sentence.

Answers: **1** No, they don't. They go on a mini submarine. **2** No, they don't. They see lots of fish. **3** No, they don't. They see a whale. **4** No, they don't. They find some cans. **5** No, they don't. They put them in the recycling bin.

Pupil's Book Activity 4: Values

Read and discuss.

- Read out the questions and discuss them as a class. Prompt the class to name the types of rubbish that you can find in the sea (*bottles, plastic bags, cans*) and why these are dangerous for sea animals.
- Ask **What can we do to help keep the sea clean?**

After you read: Activity Book

Activity 1

Read and match.

- The pupils read and match the sentence halves.

Answers: **1** The children go on a mini submarine. **2** The submarine goes to the bottom of the sea. **3** The children see a whale. **4** There are some shiny objects on the sand. **5** The children think they're gold coins. **6** The shiny objects are cans.

Activity 2

Listen and circle the eight mistakes. Listen again. Write the correct words.

▶ *CD2 Track 42 p270*

- Play the CD. The pupils circle the eight mistakes.
- Play the CD again. The pupils write the correct words.

Answers: **1** ~~boat~~ submarine **2** ~~birds~~ fish **3** ~~shark~~ whale **4** ~~car~~ ship **5** ~~silver~~ gold **6** ~~legs~~ arms **7** ~~bottles~~ cans **8** ~~bag~~ bin

Activity 3

Read and complete. What do you think?

- Invite pupils to read out and complete the sentences.
- The pupils complete the task in their Activity Books and then share opinions with a Talk Partner.

Code activity

- The pupils complete the code activity.

Answer: prawns

Ending the lesson

Review the lesson and reflect on learning.

- Say **Today we've listened to a story about an underwater adventure.** Retell the story as a class. Prompt the class by saying **The children have a ride in a …** (*submarine*). **They travel to …** (*the bottom of the sea*). Use mime, gesture and drawings to support the pupils.
- Ask **Which was your favourite activity today? Which activity was easy / difficult?**

Extra activity

Reinforcement

- Play *Broken CD player.* Read the story or play the CD again. The pupils follow in their books. Pause at different stages of the story. The class say the next word or phrase.

Link to Science

- If you are studying the Science topic of **Habitats** in English, reinforce the importance of protecting oceans and other natural spaces. Ask the class to design signs or posters.

Key Competences and Key Learning Outcomes

- Identify and say adjectives to describe animals and people
- Follow and correct the grammar tables
- Use comparative adjectives with '-ier' and 'more'
- Play a game
- Say a rap

Key language

- Adjectives: *colourful, dangerous, heavy, intelligent, pretty, ugly*
- *A (dolphin) is heavier than a (seahorse). A (shark) is (more dangerous) than a (turtle). Which (sea animal) do you like? I like (dolphins). She likes (jellyfish).*
- Extension: *boring, friendly, funny, interesting*
- Recycled: *dog, elephant, hamster, hippo, lion, mouse, parrot, penguin, snake, spider, tiger, turtle*

Materials

- Pupil's Book p54; Activity Book p51; Class CD2; Teacher's App on Navio
- Teacher's Resource Bank: Talk cards

Optional materials

- Teacher's Resource Bank: Trinity Exams Practice cards (selected from the Starter Unit and Units 1, 2, 3 and 4)

At a Glance Lesson Plan

Pupil's Book

Starting the lesson

- Use the Trinity Exams Practice cards (optional).
- Review the story.
- Set learning outcomes and use the talk cards.

Activity 1

- Listen, point and say.

▶ *CD2 Track 43 p270*

Activity 2

- Listen and say *The sea animal rap.*

▶ *CD2 Track 44 p271*

Activity 3

- Listen and follow.

▶ *CD2 Track 45 p271*

- Repeat.
- **Grammar clue:** Read about comparative adjectives with '-ier' and 'more'.

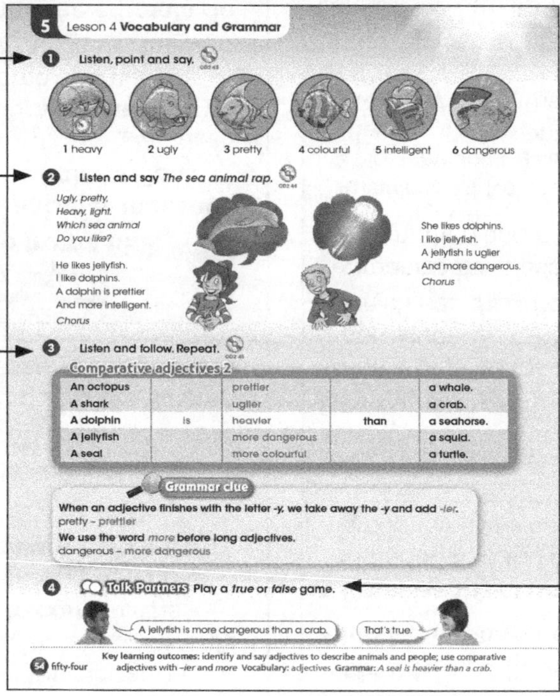

5 Lesson 4 **Vocabulary and Grammar**

1 Listen, point and say.

1 heavy 2 ugly 3 pretty 4 colourful 5 intelligent 6 dangerous

2 Listen and say *The sea animal rap.*

Ugly, pretty,
Heavy, light,
Which sea animal
Do you like?

He likes jellyfish.
I like dolphins.
A dolphin is prettier
And more intelligent.
Chorus

She likes dolphins.
I like jellyfish.
A jellyfish is uglier
And more dangerous.
Chorus

3 Listen and follow. Repeat.

Comparative adjectives 2

An octopus		prettier		a whale.
A shark		uglier		a crab.
A dolphin	is	heavier	than	a seahorse.
A jellyfish		more dangerous		a squid.
A seal		more colourful		a turtle.

Grammar clue

When an adjective finishes with the letter -y, we take away the -y and add -ier.
pretty – prettier
We use the word *more* before long adjectives.
dangerous – more dangerous

4 Talk Partners Play a *true* or *false* game.

A jellyfish is more dangerous than a crab.
That's true.

54 fifty-four

Key learning outcomes: identify and say adjectives to describe animals and people; use comparative adjectives with -ier and more Vocabulary: adjectives Grammar: *A seal is heavier than a crab.*

Activity 4

- Play a *true* or *false* game.
- Go to the Activity Book.

Ending the lesson

- Review the lesson and reflect on learning.

Extra activities

Reinforcement

- List and compare ten animals.

Vocabulary extension

- Present four additional vocabulary items.

Activity Book

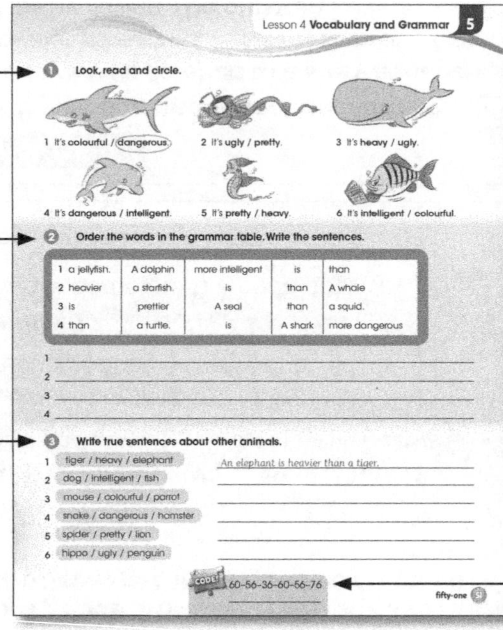

Lesson 4 **Vocabulary and Grammar** 5

1 Look, read and circle.

1 It's colourful / dangerous. 2 It's ugly / pretty. 3 It's heavy / ugly.
4 It's dangerous / intelligent. 5 It's pretty / heavy. 6 It's intelligent / colourful.

2 Order the words in the grammar table. Write the sentences.

1 a jellyfish.	A dolphin	more intelligent	is	than
2 heavier	a starfish.	is	than	A whale
3 is	prettier	A seal	than	a squid.
4 than	a turtle.	is	A shark	more dangerous

1
2
3
4

3 Write true sentences about other animals.

1 tiger / heavy / elephant — An elephant is heavier than a tiger.
2 dog / intelligent / fish
3 mouse / colourful / parrot
4 snake / dangerous / hamster
5 spider / pretty / lion
6 hippo / ugly / penguin

CODE 60-56-36-60-56-76

fifty-one 51

Activity Book

Activity 1

- Look, read and circle.

Activity 2

- Order the words in the grammar table.
- Write the sentences.

Activity 3

- Write true sentences about other animals.

Code activity

- Complete the code activity.

Digital resources

Teacher's Digital: You can also teach this lesson using the Teacher's App on Navio.

Pupil's Digital: Encourage your pupils to use the Pupil's App on Navio to practise the activities from this lesson.

Powered By NAVIO

Starting the lesson

Use the Trinity Exams Practice cards (optional).

- The pupils practise asking and answering questions.

Review the story.

- Ask the pupils if they remember the story from the last lesson.
- Organise the class into small groups. Ask each group in turn a question about the story. The pupils should collaborate before they give the answer.

Set learning outcomes and use the talk cards.

- Say **Today we're going to learn some new adjectives and we're going to use these adjectives to compare animals.**
- Point to the talk cards to show the pupils the different ways they will be working in the lesson.

Pupil's Book Activity 1

Listen, point and say.

▶ *CD2 Track 43 p270*

- Point to the first picture and say **Look at this fish.** Mime holding something heavy and say **It's heavy.** Ask the class to think of an animal that is heavy (*an elephant, a hippo*). Repeat the procedure with the other adjectives.
- Play the CD. The pupils listen, point to each picture and repeat the words.

Pupil's Book Activity 2

Listen and say *The sea animal rap.*

▶ *CD2 Track 44 p271*

- Explain that the rap is about sea animals that Lily and Josh like. Ask **Which animal does Lily like? Which adjectives describe a dolphin?** Repeat with Josh.
- Play the CD. The pupils listen and read.
- Play the CD again. The pupils join in saying the rap.

Pupil's Book Activity 3

Listen and follow. Repeat.

▶ *CD2 Track 45 p271*

- Focus the class on the grammar table.
- Play the CD. The pupils listen to the first sentence and point to the corresponding parts in the table. The pupils then repeat the complete sentence. Repeat the procedure with the other sentences.

Grammar clue

- Read the first grammar clue as a class. Encourage the pupils to think of other adjectives they know which finish with the letter 'y' (*happy, scary*).
- Read the second grammar clue as a class. Encourage the pupils to think of other adjectives they know which have two or more syllables.

Pupil's Book Activity 4

Play a *true* or *false* game.

- (Books closed.) Explain that the pupils are going to play a *true* or *false* game. Say **An octopus is heavier than a whale. True or false?** Repeat, making different sentences.
- The pupils play the game with a Talk Partner.

Activity Book

Activity 1

Look, read and circle.

- Ask the pupils to name the first sea animal and to read out the corresponding adjective. Repeat with the second animal.
- The pupils work on their own to circle the correct words.

Answers: 1 dangerous 2 ugly 3 heavy 4 intelligent 5 pretty 6 intelligent

Activity 2

Order the words in the grammar table. Write the sentences.

- Explain that the grammar table is mixed up and that the pupils need to reorder the words. Invite a pupil to read out the first sentence.
- The pupils order and write the remaining sentences. If they need more support, remind them that a sentence begins with a capital letter and ends with a full stop.

Answers: 1 A dolphin is more intelligent than a jellyfish. 2 A whale is heavier than a starfish. 3 A seal is prettier than a squid. 4 A shark is more dangerous than a turtle.

Activity 3

Write true sentences about other animals.

- Invite a pupil to read out the model sentence. Then read out the other prompts.
- The pupils work on their own to write the sentences.

Answers: 1 An elephant is heavier than a tiger. 2 A dog is more intelligent than a fish. 3 A parrot is more colourful than a mouse. 4 A snake is more dangerous than a hamster. 5 A lion is prettier than a spider. 6 A hippo is uglier than a penguin.

Code activity

- The pupils complete the code activity.

Answer: onions

Ending the lesson

Review the lesson and reflect on learning.

- Say **Today we've learnt some new adjectives. What are they?** Elicit the adjectives from the pupils.
- Ask **Which was your favourite activity today? Which activity was easy / difficult?**

Extra activities

Reinforcement

- Ask the pupils to name ten different animals and write them on the board. Then ask them to make a sentence comparing two of these animals. Cross out the two animals they use.
- The pupils continue the activity in pairs.

Vocabulary extension

- Use the Vocabulary Booster on Navio and present and practise four additional adjectives: *boring, friendly, funny, interesting.*

Key Competences and Key Learning Outcomes

- Say a tongue twister with the 'w' sound
- Practise spelling and learn an alternative spelling for the 'w' sound
- Read and listen for specific information
- Play a communication game using comparative adjectives

Key language

- *walk, watch, wearing, weather, what, when, white, why, window*
- *Is an (elephant) taller than a (giraffe)? Yes, it is. No, it isn't.*
- Recycled: *dog, elephant, giraffe, hippo, snail, water, whale*

Materials

- Pupil's Book p55; Activity Book pp52; Class CD2; Teacher's App on Navio
- Teacher's Resource Bank: Sea animals word cards
- Sea animals flashcards
- Teacher's Resource Bank: Talk cards
- Teacher's Resource Bank: Unit 5 Lesson 5 Communication Activity

Optional materials

- Teacher's Resource Bank: Trinity Exams Practice cards (selected from the Starter Unit and Units 1, 2, 3 and 4)

At a Glance Lesson Plan

Pupil's Book

Starting the lesson

- Use the Trinity Exams Practice cards (optional).
- Review sea animals vocabulary.
- Review *The sea animal rap.*
- ▶ ***CD2 Track 44 p271***
- Set learning outcomes and use the talk cards.

Activity 1: Speak and spell

- Listen, read and say.
- ▶ ***CD2 Track 46 p271***
- Go to the Activity Book.

Activity 2

- Read the animal quiz.
- Listen and find out the correct answers.
- ▶ ***CD2 Track 47 p271***

Activity 3

- Do a quiz with your partner (Teacher's Resource Bank: Unit 5).

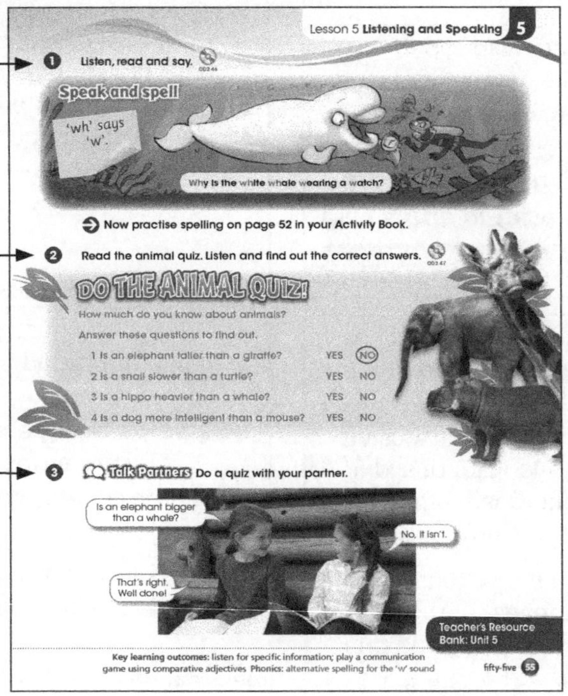

Ending the lesson

- Review the lesson and reflect on learning.

Extra activities

Reinforcement

- Play *Word card classification*.

Extension

- Investigate more animals and write your own quiz questions.

Digital resources

Teacher's Digital: You can also teach this lesson using the Teacher's App on Navio.

Pupil's Digital: Encourage your pupils to use the Pupil's App on Navio to practise the activities from this lesson.

Powered By NAVIO

Activity Book

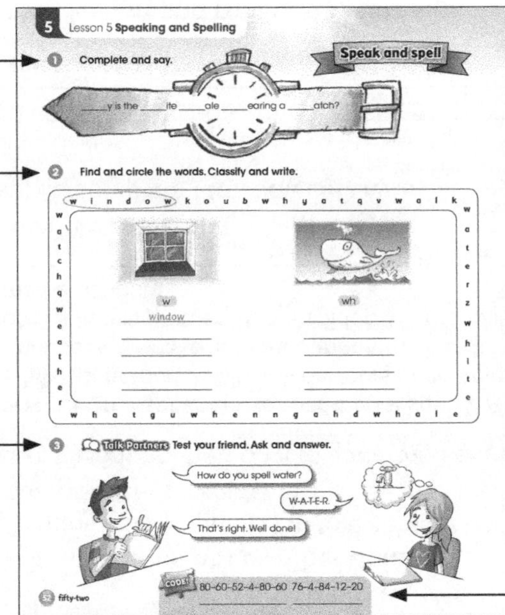

Activity Book

Activity 1: Speak and spell

- Complete and say.

Activity 2

- Find and circle the words.
- Classify and write.

Activity 3

- Test your friend.
- Ask and answer.

Code activity

- Complete the code activity.

Starting the lesson

Use the Trinity Exams Practice cards (optional).
- The pupils practise asking and answering questions.

Review sea animals vocabulary.
- Hold up one of the sea animals flashcards so that the pupils can't see it and say **This sea animal is (smaller) than (a whale). Which animal is it?** Invite a pupil to make a guess. Then, if they guess incorrectly, give another clue. **This sea animal is (more dangerous) than (a jellyfish). Which animal is it?** When the class guesses the animal correctly (*shark*), choose another flashcard and repeat the procedure.
- If the class is confident with the language, invite a pupil to take your role.

Review *The sea animal rap.*

▶ *CD2 Track 44 p271*
- Play the CD. The pupils join in saying the rap.

Set learning outcomes and use the talk cards.
- Say **Today we're going to say a tongue twister, practise spelling and do an animal quiz.**
- Point to the talk cards to show the pupils the different ways they will be working in the lesson.

Pupil's Book Activity 1: Speak and spell

Listen, read and say.

▶ *CD2 Track 46 p271*
- (Books closed.) Write the letter 'w' on the board and ask **What sound does this letter make?** *('w')* List the words the pupils know that contain this letter. Say **Today you're going to learn another way of writing the 'w' sound.**
- (Books open.) Focus on the picture and ask **What can you see here? What colour is the whale? What's the whale wearing?**
- Say **Let's listen to the tongue twister.** Play the CD. The pupils follow the text in their books.
- Play the CD again. The pupils join in with the tongue twister.
- Finally, ask the class to identify the alternative way of writing the 'w' sound (*'wh'*).

Activity Book

Activity 1: Speak and spell

Complete and say.
- The pupils write the letters and say the tongue twister.

Answer: Why is the white whale wearing a watch?

Activity 2

Find and circle the words. Classify and write.
- The pupils find and circle the words in the border that begin with the 'w' sound.
- The pupils classify and write the words according to whether they begin with 'w' or 'wh'.

Answers: w: window, walk, water, watch, weather
wh: whale, white, what, when, why

Activity 3

Talk Partners. Test your friend. Ask and answer.
- Invite two pupils to read out the speech bubbles.
- Organise the pupils into Talk Partners. The pupils take it in turns to test their partner on the spelling of the words in Activity 2. Stress the importance of prompting, encouraging and helping each other.

Code activity
- The pupils complete the code activity.

Answer: tomato sauce

Pupil's Book Activity 2

Read the animal quiz. Listen and find out the correct answers.

▶ *CD2 Track 47 p271*
- Read out the introduction to the animal quiz.
- Invite a pupil to read out the first question and prompt the whole class to respond.
- Repeat the procedure with the remaining questions.
- Say **Let's listen to two children doing the quiz.** Play the CD, pausing after each answer.
- Ask **How many of your answers were correct?**

Answers: **1** No. **2** Yes. **3** No. **4** Yes.

Pupil's Book Activity 3

Do a quiz with your partner (Teacher's Resource Bank: Unit 5).
- Invite two pupils to read out the speech bubbles. Explain that the pupils are going to write their own quiz.
- Organise the class into Talk Partners. Pupil A uses quiz 1 and Pupil B uses quiz 2. The pupils should complete the questions in the quiz.
- The pupils ask and answer the questions. At the end of the quiz, they give and receive a final score.

Ending the lesson

Review the lesson and reflect on learning.
- Say **Today we've practised a tongue twister.** Elicit the tongue twister from the pupils.
- Ask **Which was your favourite activity today? Which activity was easy / difficult?**

Extra activities

Reinforcement
- Play *Word card classification* (see p27) with the sea animals word cards. Ask the pupils to find the names of more sea animals to add to their classification before doing the Extension activity.

Extension
- The pupils investigate more animals and write their own quiz questions. They can do this individually or in pairs.
- When they have finished writing their quiz, the pupils swap their quizzes and answer the questions.

Key Competences and Key Learning Outcomes

- Read and understand a magazine article
- Review what marine animals consume and link them together in a food chain (optional)

- Do a pre-reading task to activate existing knowledge
- Read the text for general understanding
- Scan the text to find specific information

- Play a game

Key language

- *blowhole, blue whale, curled tail, hard / soft skin, krill, long head, round body, seahorse, spider crab, stomach, tongue*
- *(Blue whales) are (about 30 metres long). Do you know that (they haven't got any teeth)?*
- Recycled: *claw, legs, shell; They've got (soft skin). They eat (fish and plants). Has it got (a shell)? No, it hasn't. Is it a (turtle)? Yes, it is.*

Materials

- Pupil's Book p56; Activity Book p53; Class CD2; Teacher's App on Navio
- Teacher's Resource Bank: Talk cards

Optional materials

- Teacher's Resource Bank: Trinity Exams Practice cards (selected from the Starter Unit and Units 1, 2, 3 and 4)

At a Glance Lesson Plan

Pupil's Book

Starting the lesson

- Use the Trinity Exams Practice cards (optional).
- Review the tongue twister.
- ▶ ***CD2 Track 46 p271***
- Set learning outcomes and use the talk cards.

Before you read: Activity 1

- Look at the title of the article.
- Do you know any amazing animals?

Before you read: Activity 2

- Look at the photos.
- What do you know about these animals?

Activity 3

- Read and listen.
- ▶ ***CD2 Track 48 p271***
- Find an amazing fact for each animal.

Go to the Activity Book.

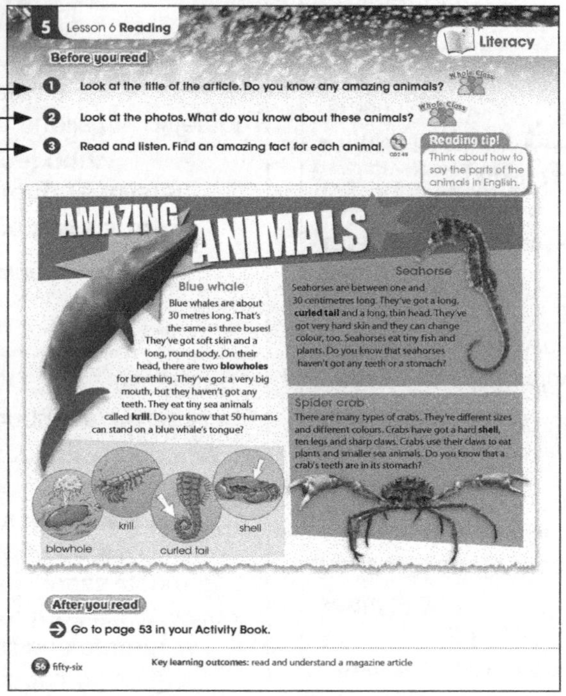
5 Lesson 6 Reading

Literacy

Before you read

1 Look at the title of the article. Do you know any amazing animals?

2 Look at the photos. What do you know about these animals?

3 Read and listen. Find an amazing fact for each animal.

Reading tip! Think about how to say the parts of the animals in English.

AMAZING ANIMALS

Blue whale

Blue whales are about 30 metres long. That's the same as three buses! They've got soft skin and a long, round body. On their head, there are two **blowholes** for breathing. They've got a very big mouth, but they haven't got any teeth. They eat tiny sea animals called **krill**. Do you know that 50 humans can stand on a blue whale's tongue?

Seahorse

Seahorses are between one and 30 centimetres long. They've got a long, **curled tail** and a long, thin head. They've got very hard skin and they can change colour, too. Seahorses eat tiny fish and plants. Do you know that seahorses haven't got any teeth or a stomach?

Spider crab

There are many types of crabs. They're different sizes and different colours. Crabs have got a hard **shell**, ten legs and sharp claws. Crabs use their claws to eat plants and smaller sea animals. Do you know that a crab's teeth are in its stomach?

After you read

Go to page 53 in your Activity Book.

56 fifty-six

Key learning outcomes: read and understand a magazine article

Ending the lesson

- Review the lesson and reflect on learning.

Extra activity

Extension

- Investigate blue whales, seahorses and crabs further and find out one more fact for each animal.

Link to Science

- **Habitats:** Review what marine animals consume and link them together in a food chain.

Activity Book

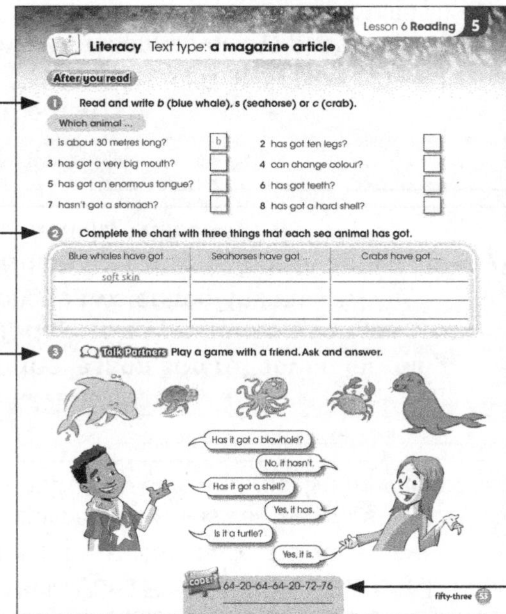
Lesson 6 Reading 5

Literacy Text type: **a magazine article**

After you read

1 Read and write *b* (blue whale), *s* (seahorse) or *c* (crab).

Which animal ...

1 is about 30 metres long? b
2 has got ten legs?
3 has got a very big mouth?
4 can change colour?
5 has got an enormous tongue?
6 has got teeth?
7 hasn't got a stomach?
8 has got a hard shell?

2 Complete the chart with three things that each sea animal has got.

Blue whales have got ...	Seahorses have got ...	Crabs have got ...
soft skin		

3 Talk Partners Play a game with a friend. Ask and answer.

CODE! 64-20-64-64-20-72-76

fifty-three 53

After you read: Activity Book

Activity 1

- Read and write *b* (blue whale), *s* (seahorse) or *c* (crab).

Activity 2

- Complete the chart with three things that each sea animal has got.

Activity 3

- Play a game with a friend.
- Ask and answer.

Code activity

- Complete the code activity.

Digital resources

Teacher's Digital: You can also teach this lesson using the Teacher's App on Navio.

Pupil's Digital: Encourage your pupils to use the Pupil's App on Navio to practise the activities from this lesson.

Powered By NAVIO

Starting the lesson

Use the Trinity Exams Practice cards (optional).

- The pupils practise asking and answering questions.

Review the tongue twister.

▶ *CD2 Track 46 p271*

- Ask **What sound did you practise in the tongue twister?** *('w')*
- Play the CD. Practise the tongue twister as a class.
- Remind the pupils that they know two spellings for this sound ('w' and 'wh'). The pupils list the words they know which begin with these letters.

Set learning outcomes and use the talk cards.

- Say **Today we're going to read a magazine article.** Check that the pupils know what a magazine is. Give the titles of children's magazines that they may be familiar with as examples.
- Point to the talk cards to show the pupils the different ways they will be working in the lesson.

Before you read: Pupil's Book Activity 1

Look at the title of the article. Do you know any amazing animals?

- Invite a pupil to read the rubric. Prompt the class to name any amazing animals they know and to say why they are amazing.

Before you read: Pupil's Book Activity 2

Look at the photos. What do you know about these animals?

- Invite a pupil to read the rubric. Encourage the class to look at each photo in turn and to share what they know about the animal. If necessary, use prompts: **What does a (blue whale) look like? What does (a seahorse) eat? Where does (a spider crab) live? What can (a blue whale) do?** Write keywords on the board.

Pupil's Book Activity 3

Read and listen. Find an amazing fact for each animal.

▶ *CD2 Track 48 p271*

- Invite a pupil to read the instructions. Explain to the pupils that the first time they read, they should try to understand the most important information. If you want the pupils to read the text without the support of the CD, set a time limit for this task. Otherwise, play the CD, pausing after each animal report.
- The pupils report an amazing fact for each animal.

After you read: Activity Book

Activity 1

Read and write *b* (blue whale), *s* (seahorse) or *c* (crab).

- The pupils work on their own or in pairs to read each question and identify the animal. The pupils should refer back to the text in the Pupil's Book when necessary.

Answers: **1** b **2** c **3** b **4** s **5** b **6** c **7** s **8** c

Activity 2

Complete the chart with three things that each sea animal has got.

- The pupils work on their own or in pairs to complete the chart. They should refer back to the text in the Pupil's Book when necessary.

Possible answers:

Blue whales have got …	Seahorses have got …	Crabs have got …
soft skin	a curled tail	a hard shell
two blowholes	hard skin	ten legs
a big mouth	a thin head	sharp claws

Activity 3

Play a game with a friend. Ask and answer.

- Ask the class to name the five animals in the activity.
- Invite two pupils to read out the speech bubbles.
- Play the game as a class. Choose one of the animals and prompt the pupils to ask you questions until they identify the animal.
- The pupils play the same game with a Talk Partner.

Code activity

- The pupils complete the code activity.

Answer: peppers

Ending the lesson

Review the lesson and reflect on learning.

- Say **Today we've read a magazine article. What do we know about blue whales?** Repeat the question for seahorses and spider crabs.
- Ask **Which was your favourite activity today? Which activity was easy / difficult?**

Extra activity

Extension

- The pupils investigate blue whales, seahorses and crabs further and write one more fact for each animal. The pupils can do this individually or in pairs.

Link to Science

- If you are studying the Science topic of **Habitats** in English, elicit and review the plants and animals that live in water habitats. Review the foods that different marine animals consume.
- Write the names of different sea animals on the board and ask the class to link them together in a food chain, e.g. *plants – krill – fish – seal – shark.*

Key Competences and Key Learning Outcomes

- Use 'and' to add similar information
- Prepare and write a magazine article about a sea animal
- Investigate a sea animal
- Identify the audience of magazine articles
- Identify the informational content and text features of magazine articles
- Share your writing with a partner

Key language
- *brain, super*
- *How (big) is (the animal)? What does it (look like)? Where does it (live)? How does it (move)? Why is it (amazing)? What does it (eat)? They're (different sizes) and (colours).*
- Recycled: *arms, eye, hard skin, starfish*

Materials
- Pupil's Book p57; Activity Book p54; Class CD3; Teacher's App on Navio
- Sea animals flashcards
- Teacher's Resource Bank: Talk cards

Optional materials
- Teacher's Resource Bank: Trinity Exams Practice cards (selected from the Starter Unit and Units 1, 2, 3 and 4)
- A piece of paper for each pupil, a stapler, string, drawing pins

At a Glance Lesson Plan

Pupil's Book

Starting the lesson
- Use the Trinity Exams Practice cards (optional).
- Review vocabulary for describing animals.
- Set learning outcomes and use the talk cards.

Investigate a text: Activity 1
- Read and listen.
- ▶ *CD3 Track 01 p271*
- Which questions does the article answer?

Discuss a text: Activity 2
- Think and discuss.
- **Writing tip:** Read about using 'and'.
- Go to the Activity Book.

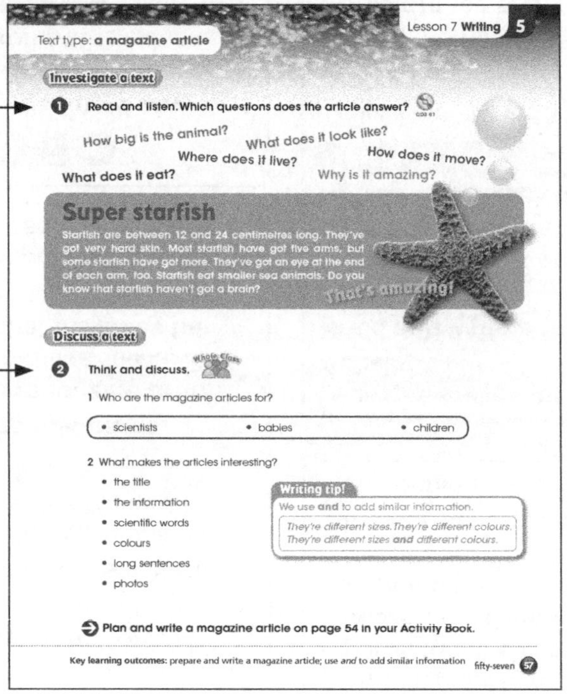
Lesson 7 Writing 5

Text type: **a magazine article**

Investigate a text

1 Read and listen. Which questions does the article answer?

How big is the animal? What does it look like? Where does it live? How does it move? What does it eat? Why is it amazing?

Super starfish

Starfish are between 12 and 24 centimetres long. They've got very hard skin. Most starfish have got five arms, but some starfish have got more. They've got an eye at the end of each arm, too. Starfish eat smaller sea animals. Do you know that starfish haven't got a brain?

That's amazing!

Discuss a text

2 Think and discuss.

1 Who are the magazine articles for?
- scientists
- babies
- children

2 What makes the articles interesting?
- the title
- the information
- scientific words
- colours
- long sentences
- photos

Writing tip!
We use **and** to add similar information.
They're different sizes. They're different colours.
They're different sizes **and** *different colours.*

Plan and write a magazine article on page 54 in your Activity Book.

Key learning outcomes: prepare and write a magazine article; use *and* to add similar information

fifty-seven 57

Ending the lesson
- Review the lesson and reflect on learning.

Extra activity

Reinforcement
- Make an animal magazine.

Activity Book

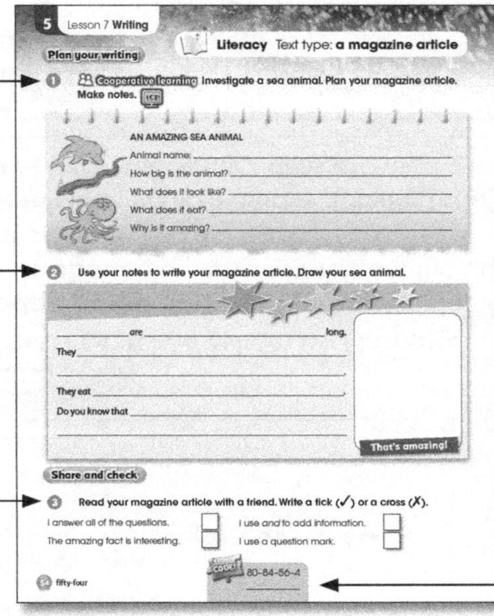
5 Lesson 7 Writing

Plan your writing

Literacy Text type: **a magazine article**

1 Cooperative learning Investigate a sea animal. Plan your magazine article. Make notes.

AN AMAZING SEA ANIMAL
Animal name: ______
How big is the animal? ______
What does it look like? ______
What does it eat? ______
Why is it amazing? ______

2 Use your notes to write your magazine article. Draw your sea animal.

______ are ______ long.
They ______
They eat ______
Do you know that ______

That's amazing!

Share and check

3 Read your magazine article with a friend. Write a tick (✓) or a cross (✗).

I answer all of the questions. ☐ I use and to add information. ☐
The amazing fact is interesting. ☐ I use a question mark. ☐

Code! 80-84-56-4

fifty-four

Activity Book

Plan your writing:

Activity 1
- Investigate a sea animal.
- Plan your magazine article.
- Make notes.

Activity 2
- Use your notes to write your magazine article.
- Draw your sea animal.

Share and check:

Activity 3
- Read your magazine article with a friend.
- Write a tick (✓) or a cross (✗).

Code activity
- Complete the code activity.

Digital resources

Teacher's Digital: You can also teach this lesson using the Teacher's App on Navio.

Pupil's Digital: Encourage your pupils to use the Pupil's App on Navio to practise the activities from this lesson.

Powered By NAVIO

Starting the lesson

Use the Trinity Exams Practice cards (optional).

- The pupils practise asking and answering questions.

Review vocabulary for describing animals.

- Explain to the class that when we want to know about the appearance of something we use the question **What does it look like?** Hold up a selection of sea animals flashcards and ask the question. The pupils describe each one. Prompt the pupils to use the language they saw in the *Amazing Animals* magazine article in Lesson 6 (*hard / soft skin, blowhole, claws, shell, curled tail, long / round body*).

Set learning outcomes and use the talk cards.

- Ask the class **What did we read in the last lesson?** (*A magazine article.*) Say **Today we're going to investigate another magazine article. Then we're going to plan and write a magazine article.**
- Point to the talk cards to show the pupils the different ways they will be working in the lesson.

Investigate a text: Pupil's Book Activity 1

Read and listen. Which questions does the article answer?

▶ *CD3 Track 01 p271*

- Read the six questions as a class. Explain that some of the questions are answered in the text and others are not. The pupils should read the text to identify which information is included.
- If you want the pupils to read the text without the support of the CD, set a time limit for this task. Otherwise, play the CD, pausing after each sentence.
- The pupils report which questions are answered.
- The pupils read the text again to find the answers to these questions.

Answers: How big is the animal? What does it look like? What does it eat? Why is it amazing?

Discuss a text: Pupil's Book Activity 2

Think and discuss.

- Read the first question and identify who the magazine articles in Lessons 6 and 7 are written for. Discuss why the texts are not for babies or scientists. Explain that the purpose of these magazine articles is to give information and to entertain.
- Read the second question and discuss which of the features make the articles interesting. (*The titles are exciting and the repetition of sounds makes them memorable. The information that's included is interesting. The use of bright colours catches your attention. The photos are exciting.*)

Writing tip

- Read the information and ask the pupils to find other examples in the magazine articles.
- Prompt the pupils to create their own sentences using 'and'.

Activity Book

Plan your writing: Activity 1

Writing Partners. Investigate a sea animal. Plan your magazine article. Make notes.

- Read out the headings and give examples of how pupils can complete each section. If necessary, write these ideas on the board.
- Arrange for the pupils to have access to a computer or the library to research their animals. The pupils work in pairs to choose a sea animal and complete the notes in their Activity Books. Alternatively, use an interactive whiteboard to research a sea animal and make notes as a class.

Suggested websites

http://kids.nationalgeographic.com/ and search for 'animals'.

http://easyscienceforkids.com/

Activity 2

Use your notes to write your magazine article. Draw your sea animal.

- Focus the class on the activity. If necessary, model how to complete the framework. The pupils work as a class to give you the information. Write the text on the board.
- The pupils work in their pairs to write their text in their Activity Books and draw their sea animal.

Share and check: Activity 3

Writing Partners. Read your magazine article with a friend. Write a tick (✓) or a cross (✗).

- Read through the statements as a class.
- Organise the class into new pairs. One pupil in each pair should read their text aloud to their partner. The other pupil listens. The pupils work together to decide if the text fulfils all the criteria and tick or cross the corresponding boxes. The pupils can add to, improve, or correct the text at this stage.
- The pupils swap roles.

Code activity

- The pupils complete the code activity.

Answer: tuna

Ending the lesson

Review the lesson and reflect on learning.

- Say **Today we've written a magazine article. Are you happy with your article? Elicit responses.**
- Ask **Which was your favourite activity today? Which activity was easy / difficult?**

Extra activity

Reinforcement

- Ask the pupils to copy their text and drawing onto a piece of paper. Staple about eight of the pieces of paper together down the left side of the page. Then tie a piece of string around the stapled edge and pin the end of the string to a class noticeboard. Repeat with the other pages. The pupils can read these simple magazines whenever they like.

Key Competences and Key Learning Outcomes

- Use the Internet to investigate Hawaii
- Read and listen for specific information
- Read about Hawaii
- Think about your own culture and identity

Key language

- *boat trip, coral reefs, humpback whale, islands, make a sandcastle, manta ray, snorkel, surf, tropical fish*
- *The trip begins / finishes at (11 o'clock).*
- Recycled: *beaches, December, May, sand; There are (eight big islands).*

Materials

- Pupil's Book p58; Activity Book p55; Class CD3; Teacher's App on Navio
- Teacher's Resource Bank: Talk cards
- An online world map
- Coloured pencils (red, white and blue)

Optional materials

- Teacher's Resource Bank: Trinity Exams Practice cards (selected from the Starter Unit and Units 1, 2, 3 and 4)

At a Glance Lesson Plan

Pupil's Book

Starting the lesson

- Use the Trinity Exams Practice cards (optional).
- Review language for expressing preferences.
- Set learning outcomes and use the talk cards.

Activity 1

- Read Luke's questions.
- What do you think?

Activity 2

- Read and listen.
- ▶ *CD3 Track 02 p271*
- Answer Luke's questions.
- **Think about your culture** What water activities can you do in your country?

Go to the Activity Book.

5 Lesson 8 **Culture around the world: Hawaii**

1 Read Luke's questions. What do you think?

I'm in Hawaii now. It's in the Pacific Ocean and there are eight big islands. It's an exciting place to visit. Can you answer these questions?

1 Where can you learn to surf in Hawaii?
2 When can you see whales?
3 Which animals live in the reefs?
4 What colour is the sand?

2 Read and listen. Answer Luke's questions.

Welcome to the islands of Hawaii

There are lots of exciting activities for all the family.

Watch the whales More than 6,000 humpback whales visit Hawaii every year. They arrive in December and stay until May. Take a boat trip and get close to these amazing animals. If you're lucky, you can see them jump out of the water. It's amazing!

Learn to surf Do you like water sports? In Hawaii, there are lots of beaches where you can learn to surf. It isn't easy, but it's exciting and fun. Give it a try!

Snorkel There are beautiful coral reefs around the islands of Hawaii. You can swim with colourful tropical fish and see enormous manta rays. Manta rays look quite scary, but they aren't dangerous.

Make a sandcastle Hawaii is famous for its beautiful beaches, but the sand isn't always yellow. You can find red, black, green and white sand here. It's the perfect place to make a fantastic sandcastle!

Think about your culture What water activities can you do in your country?

Do the Hawaii web quest and the Unit Review on pages 55 and 56 in your Activity Book.

58 fifty-eight Key learning outcomes: read about Hawaii; think about and research Hawaii

Ending the lesson

- Review the lesson and reflect on learning.

Extra activity

Extension

- Investigate other activities you can do in Hawaii.

Activity Book

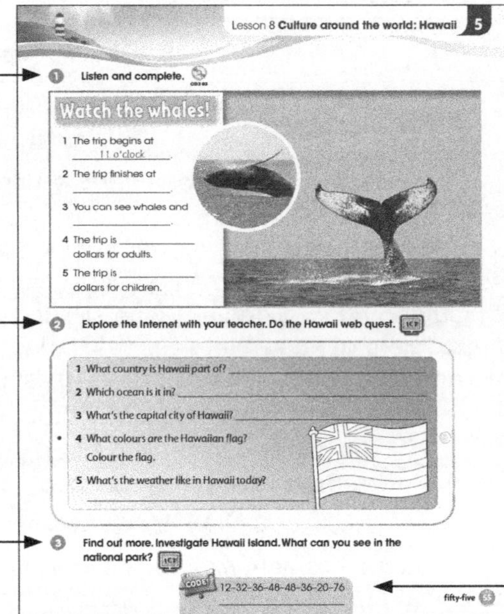

Lesson 8 **Culture around the world: Hawaii** 5

1 Listen and complete.

Watch the whales!

1 The trip begins at 11 o'clock.
2 The trip finishes at ______
3 You can see whales and ______
4 The trip is ______ dollars for adults.
5 The trip is ______ dollars for children.

2 Explore the Internet with your teacher. Do the Hawaii web quest.

1 What country is Hawaii part of? ______
2 Which ocean is it in? ______
3 What's the capital city of Hawaii? ______
4 What colours are the Hawaiian flag? Colour the flag.
5 What's the weather like in Hawaii today? ______

3 Find out more. Investigate Hawaii Island. What can you see in the national park?

12-32-36-48-48-36-20-76

fifty-five 55

Activity Book

Activity 1

- Listen and complete.
- ▶ *CD3 Track 03 p271*

Activity 2

- Explore the Internet with your teacher. Do the Hawaii web quest.

Activity 3

- Find out more. Investigate Hawaii Island. What can you see in the national park?

Code activity

- Complete the code activity.

Digital resources

Teacher's Digital: You can also teach this lesson using the Teacher's App on Navio.

Powered By NAVIO

Starting the lesson

Use the Trinity Exams Practice cards (optional).

- The pupils practise asking and answering questions.

Review language for expressing preferences.

- Ask **Which do you prefer? The beach or the mountains?** Encourage the pupils to tell you which place they prefer. Ask **Why do you prefer the (beach)?** Prompt the class to compare the two places. (*The beach is warmer than the mountains. The mountains are cleaner than the beach.)*

Set learning outcomes and use the talk cards.

- Say **Today we're going to investigate Hawaii.**
- Point to the talk cards to show the pupils the different ways they will be working in the lesson.

Pupil's Book Activity 1

Read Luke's questions. What do you think?

- Read the speech bubble as a class. Encourage the pupils to tell you what they know about Hawaii. Show the pupils where the islands are on an online world map.
- Read the questions as a class. Encourage the pupils to predict the answers.

Pupil's Book Activity 2

Read and listen. Answer Luke's questions.

▶ *CD3 Track 02 p271*

- Focus the class on the photos. Ask **What can you see?** Then focus the class on the subheadings and ask **What activities can you do in Hawaii?**
- Ask the pupils to read the text. If you want the pupils to read the text without the support of the CD, set a time limit for this task. Otherwise, play the CD, pausing after each section to check understanding.
- The pupils answer Luke's questions.

Answers: **1** You can learn to surf on the beaches. **2** You can see whales from December to May. **3** Tropical fish and manta rays. **4** It's red, black, green, white and yellow.

Think about your culture

- Read out the question and prompt different pupils to tell you about water activities in their country.

Activity Book

Activity 1

Listen and complete.

▶ *CD3 Track 03 p271*

- Read out the text. Then play the CD, pausing to allow the pupils to write the missing information.
- Play the CD again without pausing.
- Ask the pupils if they think the boat trip sounds fun.

Answers: **1** 11 o'clock **2** 12 o'clock **3** dolphins **4** ten **5** five

Activity 2

Explore the Internet with your teacher. Do the Hawaii web quest.

- Read out the instructions for the activity.
- Connect to a children's website (see suggested websites opposite) that provides geographical information about Hawaii. Read out questions 1–4. The pupils work as a class to find and write the answers. They should also colour the Hawaiian flag.
- Read out question 5. Connect to a website that shows the weather around the world. The pupils complete the information about the day's weather.

Answers: **1** the USA **2** Pacific Ocean **3** Honolulu **4** red, white and blue

Activity 3

Find out more. Investigate Hawaii Island. What can you see in the national park?

- Read the rubric as a class. Encourage the pupils to predict what you can see in the national park.
- If you are doing the investigation as a class, go to a suitable website, e.g. gohawaii.com, and ask the pupils to scan the information to find the answer.
- If you are working in a computer room, organise the class into small groups. The groups should go to the website and find the answer.

Answer: You can see active volcanoes.

Suggested websites

http://maps.google.es/
http://www.bbc.co.uk/weather
http://www.gohawaii.com

Code activity

- The pupils complete the code activity.

Answer: chillies

Ending the lesson

Review the lesson and reflect on learning.

- Say **Today we've learnt about Hawaii. Is it an interesting place? What can you see and do there?** Elicit the information from the pupils.
- Ask **Which was your favourite activity today? Which activity was easy / difficult?**

Extra activity

Extension

- Use a tourism website to investigate other activities you can do on the islands.
- If you are working as a class, ask the pupils to choose an island to visit from the home page. Click on the name of the island and use the interactive map to discover the different activities. The pupils should choose one of these activities, scan the information and take notes.
- If you are working in a computer room, organise the class into small groups and allocate an island to each group. The groups should investigate the activities on their island. Ask each group to share their information with the rest of the class.

Go to the AB Unit Review on page 251.

Key Competences and Key Learning Outcomes

- Watch and understand a video about sea animals
- Review sea animals
- Learn interesting facts about sea animals
- Learn to use keywords to search for information online
- Investigate a sea animal

Key language

- *crab, jellyfish, octopus, seahorse, sea turtle, shark; keywords, search engine, webpage, website*
- *How many eyes has a (starfish) got? How do whales communicate?*

Materials

- Pupil's Book p59; Activity Book p57; Class CD3; Teacher's App on Navio
- Sea animals flashcards
- Teacher's Resource Bank: Talk cards

Optional materials

- Teacher's Resource Bank: Trinity Exams Practice cards (selected from the Starter Unit and Units 1, 2, 3 and 4)

At a Glance Lesson Plan

Pupil's Book

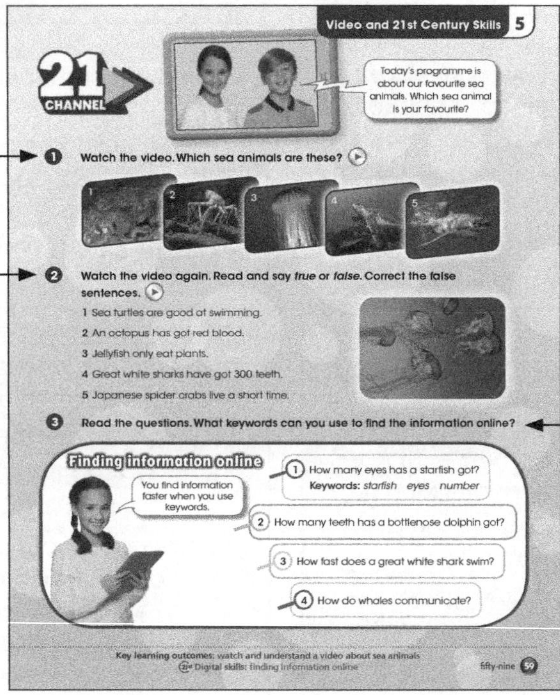

Starting the lesson

- Use the Trinity Exams Practice cards (optional).
- **Think-Pair-Share.** Review sea animals vocabulary.
- Set learning outcomes and use the talk cards.

Activity 1

- Before you watch
- Watch the video.
- *Unit 5 video p285*
- Which sea animals are these?

Activity 2

- Watch the video again.
- *Unit 5 video*
- Read and say *true* or *false*.
- Correct the false sentences.

Activity 3

- Read the questions.
- What keywords can you use to find the information online?
- Go to the Activity Book.

Ending the lesson

- Review the lesson and reflect on learning.

Extra activity

Reinforcement

- Find the best keywords to find information online.

Activity Book

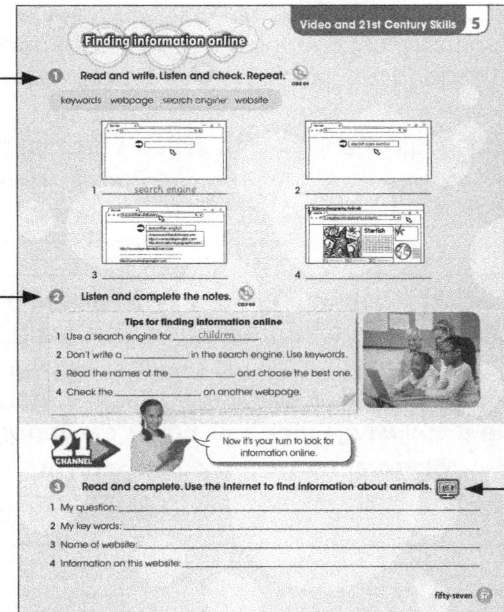

Activity Book

Activity 1

- Read and write.
- Listen and check.
- ▶ *CD3 Track 04 p272*
- Repeat.

Activity 2

- Listen and complete the notes.
- ▶ *CD3 Track 05 p272*

Activity 3

- Read and complete.
- Use the Internet to find information about animals.

Digital resources

Teacher's Digital: You can also teach this lesson using the Teacher's App on Navio.

Pupil's Digital: Encourage your pupils to use the Pupil's App on Navio to practise the activities from this lesson.

Powered By NAVIO

Starting the lesson

Use the Trinity Exams Practice cards (optional).

- The pupils practise asking and answering questions.

Think-Pair-Share. Review sea animals vocabulary.

- Ask **Can you remember the sea animals vocabulary?** The class thinks silently for a minute.
- Then the pupils work with a Talk Partner to name the sea animals.
- Invite different Talk Partners to say a different animal. Hold up the corresponding flashcard and prompt the class to repeat the word.
- Finally, repeat the procedure, asking different pairs of Talk Partners each time, until all the sea animals have been named.

Set learning outcomes and use the talk cards.

- Say **Today we're going to watch a video and then ask and answer questions about sea animals.**
- Point to the talk cards to show the pupils the different ways they will be working in the lesson.

Pupil's Book Activity 1

Before you watch

- Read the speech bubble to pupils. Ask **Which sea animal is your favourite?** Elicit responses from a number of pupils.

Watch the video. Which sea animals are these? *p285*

- Watch Part 1. Ask pupils **What are you going to see next?** Check that they understand that they will see lots of short video clips about different sea animals.
- Play Part 2. Ask general questions to check understanding. Focus the pupils on the photos in Activity 1. Say **Which sea animals are these?** Elicit ideas.
- Play Part 2 again for the pupils to answer the questions. Check answers as a class.

Answers: **1** octopus **2** Japanese spider crab **3** jellyfish **4** sea turtle **5** great white shark

Pupil's Book Activity 2

Watch the video again. Read and say *true* or *false*. Correct the false sentences.

- Explain that you are going to do a true or false activity.
- Ask a pupil to read out sentence 1. Ask the class whether they think the sentence is true or false. Repeat with sentences 2–5.
- Play Part 2. Students work in pairs to decide whether the sentences are true or false. They correct the false sentences.

Answers: **1** T **2** F An octopus has got blue blood. **3** F Jellyfish eat small fish and crabs. **4** T **5** F Japanese spider crabs live 100 years.

Pupil's Book Activity 3

Read the questions. What keywords can you use to find the information online?

- Tell pupils that in the last part of the video Chloe and Mark talk about finding information online. Ask **What animal does Chloe want to find out about?** (*Seahorse.*) **What detail does she want to know about?** (*What they eat/Food.*) **What keywords does Chloe use?** (*seahorse; food*)
- Explain that in this activity, pupils want to find information online and they need to choose what keywords to use. Read the questions with the class and check vocabulary.
- Write question 1 on the board. Ask **What animal do I want to find out about?** (*Starfish.*) **What detail do I want to know about?** (*eyes, how many*)
- Pupils work in pairs to read the questions and choose the best keywords to use.

Activity Book

Activity 1

Read and write. Listen and check. Repeat.

▶ *CD3 Track 04 p272*

- Pupils work on their own to match the words to the pictures.
- Play the CD and check answers.

Answers: **1** search engine **2** keywords **3** website **4** webpage

Activity 2

Listen and complete the notes.

▶ *CD3 Track 05 p272*

- Explain to the pupils that they are going to listen to a girl and her dad talking about finding information online. Ask pupils if they can suggest any tips. Read out the information. Then play the CD, pausing to allow the pupils to write the missing information.
- Play the CD again without pausing.

Answers: **1** children **2** question **3** websites **4** information

- Ask the pupils if they think the tips sound helpful.

Activity 3

Read and complete. Use the Internet to find information about animals. ICT

- Read out the speech bubble and tell pupils that they are going to use the Internet to find out information about animals. Remind pupils how to break down their question to identify the best keywords to use.
- The pupils complete the information in class or for homework.
- Invite pupils to share their information with the class.

Ending the lesson

Review the lesson and reflect on learning.

- Say **Today we've watched a video about sea animals. What have we learnt about finding information online?** Elicit the information from the pupils.
- Ask **Which was your favourite activity today? Which activity was easy / difficult?**

Extra activity

Reinforcement

- Tell the class something that you would like to find out about. It could be on the topic of sea animals or another topic. Pupils suggest suitable keywords for you to use to find the information online. You could try this on the whiteboard using a suitable children's search engine and see which keywords give the best results.

Date: ______________ Unit: ______________

1 **What did my pupils learn in this unit?**

2 **How did my pupils work? (✓)**

individually ☐ in pairs ☐ in small groups ☐

in large groups ☐ as a class ☐

3 **Which key competences did my pupils develop?**

- Competence in linguistic communication ☐
- Competence in mathematics, science and technology ☐
- Digital competence ☐
- Learning to learn ☐
- Social and civic competences ☐
- Sense of initiative and entrepreneurship ☐
- Cultural awareness and expression ☐

4 **Which lessons / activities were the most successful and why?**

5 **Which lessons / activities did my pupils find the most difficult and why?**

6 **What did I try in the classroom for the first time? How did it go?**

7 **Which resources did I find most useful? (including webpages)**

8 **What could I do differently next time I teach this unit?**

Unit 6 Sports mad

Unit overview

Key Competences and Key Learning Outcomes

- Identify and name water sports equipment (Lesson 1)
- Say the vocabulary chant (Lesson 1)
- Understand and act out a conversation (Lesson 2)
- Talk and write about future plans (Lesson 2)
- Follow, complete and correct the grammar tables (Lessons 2 and 4)
- Learn adverbs of manner (Lesson 4)
- Learn simple time sequencers for ordering information (Lesson 7)
- Watch and understand a video (Video and 21st Century Skills)

- Use a code to read a message (Lesson 3)

- Use the Pupil's App on Navio
- Investigate New Zealand (Lesson 8)

- Say a tongue twister, learn another spelling for the 'k' sound and practise spelling (Lesson 5)
- Practise activity types found in the Cambridge Exams: A1 Movers
- Review your own learning (Review)

- Understand the importance of listening to other people's ideas (Lesson 3)

- Work with a Talk Partner to practise and reinforce learning (all lessons)
- Do a questionnaire in pairs and report on it (Lesson 5)
- Reflect on personal safety in sports (Video and 21st Century Skills)

- Sing two songs (Lessons 1 and 4)
- Understand, act out and give an opinion on a story (Lesson 3)
- Read and evaluate a letter (Lesson 6)
- Write a letter (Lesson 7)
- Learn about New Zealand (Lesson 8)
- Think about your own culture (Lesson 8)

Vocabulary

Core vocabulary
flippers, gloves, helmet, kayak, life jacket, mask, paddle, snorkel, surfboard, swimsuit, water-skis, wetsuit; badly, fast, loudly, quickly, quietly, slowly, well

Extension vocabulary (optional)
fishing rod, goggles, jet ski, oars, rope, sailing boat; carefully, dangerously, happily, sadly

Other vocabulary
adventure / sports camp, archery, bungee jumping, extreme sport, forest, horse riding, kayaking, lake, leaflet, letter, mountain biking, rafting, rock climbing, sand surfing, windsurfing, zorbing

Recycled vocabulary
baseball, cycle, dance, go swimming, gymnastics, hockey, play football, ride a horse, rollerblade, sailing, sing, skate, snorkelling, swim, tennis, volleyball, walk, watch TV; adventure, air, beach, camp, faster, hill, lie down, mountains, river, rock, sea animals

Structures

Core structures
I am / I'm not going to (play football (tomorrow). He is / isn't going to (go swimming). They are / aren't going to (watch TV). Are you going to (play football)? Yes, I am. No, I'm not. What are you going to do (on Saturday)? I (play chess) (well). He (dances) (badly).

Other structures
Dear (Grandma), First / Next / Finally, (I'm going to) (go horse riding). See you (soon). Love, (Laura). Which (sport) can you do (in the air)? If you like (travelling fast), (sand surfing) is (the sport for you).

Recycled structures
I'm wearing (a wetsuit). I'm ready to (snorkel). What about you? Are you (ready to snorkel)? He's wearing (gloves). She's got (water-skis). She's ready to (water-ski). You must (run fast). Good idea. Why don't you (play football)? Do you like (adventure)?

Phonics

The 'k' sound (*bla**ck** mon**k**ey **k**aya**k**s qui**ck**ly la**k**e*)

Literacy

Text type: a letter (writing preparation)
Reading skills: sequencing parts of a text
Writing skills: using time sequencers 'First', 'Next', 'Finally'

Culture ... around the world

Extreme sports in New Zealand

21st Century Skills

Staying safe when doing sports.

Thinking skills

Applying rules (Lessons 2 and 4); Predicting (Lessons 3 and 8); Discussing values (Lesson 3); Expressing opinions (Lesson 3); Sequencing (Lesson 6); Thinking about your culture (Lesson 8); Making connections (Review)

Cooperative learning

Working together (Lesson 1); Team building (Lesson 2); Collaborating (Lesson 4); Checking learning (Lesson 5); Sharing information (Lesson 5); Peer evaluation and feedback (Lesson 7); Working together (Review)

Values

Understanding the importance of listening to other people's ideas

Cross-curricular links

Link to Science
Water and air on Earth: Identifying where we find water
Suggested Arts and Crafts concepts
Exploring three-dimensional geometric shapes and constructing a cylindrical Japanese carp kite

Key Competences and Key Learning Outcomes

- Identify and name water sports equipment
- Say the vocabulary chant
- Identify other sources of water on Earth (optional)
- Review and classify sports
- Play a game with a recycled structure
- Sing a song

Key language

- *flippers, gloves, helmet, kayak, life jacket, mask, paddle, snorkel, surfboard, swimsuit, water-skis, wetsuit*
- *I'm wearing (a wetsuit). I'm ready to (snorkel). What about you? Are you ready to (snorkel)? He's wearing (gloves). She's got (water-skis). She's ready to (water-ski).*
- Extension: *fishing rod, goggles, jet ski, oars, rope, sailing boat*
- Recycled: *cycled, dance, go swimming, gymnastics, hockey, play football, ride a horse, rollerblade, sailing, sing, snorkelling, swim, tennis, volleyball, walk*

Materials

- Pupil's Book p60; Activity Book p58; Class CD3; Teacher's App on Navio
- Teacher's Resource Bank: Water sports equipment word cards
- Water sports equipment flashcards
- Teacher's Resource Bank: Talk cards

Optional materials

- Teacher's Resource Bank: Trinity Exams Practice cards (selected from the Starter Unit and Units 1, 2, 3, 4 and 5)

At a Glance Lesson Plan

Pupil's Book

Starting the lesson
- Use the Trinity Exams Practice cards (optional).
- Review sports vocabulary.
- Set learning outcomes and use the talk cards.

Activity 1
- What water sports do you know?
- Make a list.
- What equipment do you need?

Vocabulary presentation
- Present the new vocabulary using the water sports equipment flashcards.

Word cards
- Introduce the spellings of the vocabulary using the water sports equipment word cards.

Activity 2
- Listen, point and say the vocabulary chant.
- ▶ *CD3 Track 06 p272*

Activity 3
- Listen, look and sing *Fun in the sea.*
- ▶ *CD3 Track 07 p272*

Activity 4
- Play a guessing game.
- Go to the Activity Book.

Ending the lesson
- Review the lesson and reflect on learning.

Extra activities

Extension
- Play a game in pairs.

Vocabulary extension
- Present six additional vocabulary items.

Link to Science
- **Water and air on Earth:** Identify other sources of water on Earth.

Digital resources

Teacher's Digital: Don't forget you can teach this lesson using the Teacher's App on Navio.

Pupil's Digital: Encourage your pupils to use the Pupil's App on Navio to practise the vocabulary from this lesson.

Powered By NAVIO

Activity Book

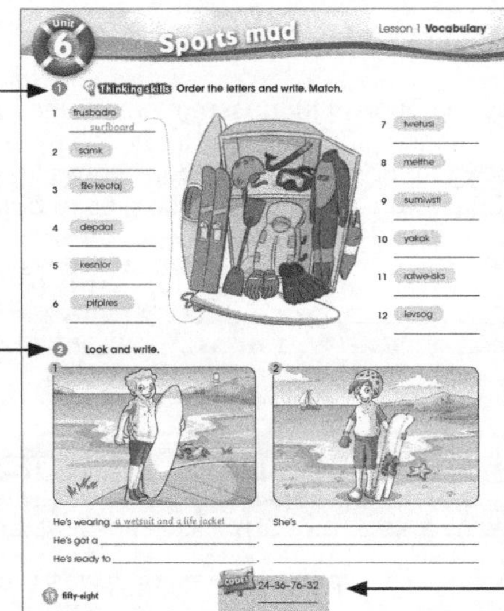

Activity Book

Activity 1
- Order the letters and write.
- Match.

Activity 2
- Look and write.

Code activity
- Complete the code activity.

Starting the lesson

Use the Trinity Exams Practice cards (optional).

- The pupils practise asking and answering questions.

Review sports vocabulary.

- Divide the board into three columns with the headings *play, go, do*. Elicit a sport for each heading, e.g. *play football, go swimming*. Set a time limit. In small groups, the pupils list all the sports they know for each verb. Write them on the board.

Set learning outcomes and use the talk cards.

- Say **Today we're going to learn the names of water sports equipment.**
- Point to the talk cards to show the pupils the different ways they will be working in the lesson.

Pupil's Book Activity 1

What water sports do you know? Make a list. What equipment do you need?

- (Books closed.) Ask the pupils if there are any water sports on the board. Encourage them to name any other water sports they know (*windsurfing, kayaking, water-skiing, surfing, sailing, snorkelling*). Then prompt them to name the clothes and equipment you need.

Vocabulary presentation

- (Books closed.) Choose a water sports equipment flashcard, but don't show the picture. Describe the item and its use, e.g. **I wear these on my feet. I wear them when I snorkel. They help me swim fast.**
- When the pupils identify the object, stick the flashcard on the board. The pupils repeat the word. Repeat the procedure with the other flashcards.

Word cards

- (Books closed.) Hand a water sports equipment word card to each pair of pupils. They take turns to come to the board, read out their word and stick their word card next to the corresponding flashcard.

Pupil's Book Activity 2

Listen, point and say the vocabulary chant.

▶ ***CD3 Track 06 p272***

- Focus attention on the 12 photos. Say **Let's listen and say the words.** Play the CD. The pupils listen, point and repeat.

Pupil's Book Activity 3

Listen, look and sing *Fun in the sea.*

▶ ***CD3 Track 07 p272***

- Focus attention on the scene. Ask **Where are Lily, Ravi and Josh?** (*At the beach.*) Say **It's a water sports day. What activities can you do on the beach today?** Prompt the class to identify the sports on the sign. Then ask **What's Ravi wearing?** Repeat the question for Lily and Josh.
- Say **Let's listen to the song.** Play the CD. The pupils listen and read.
- Ask **Who's ready to snorkel?** (*Ravi.*) Ask about the other water sports.
- Play the CD again. The pupils sing and do the actions.

Pupil's Book Activity 4

Play a guessing game.

- Ask two pupils to read out the speech bubbles.
- Demonstrate the activity by giving another example. Say **I've got a paddle and I'm wearing a helmet.** Ask a pair of pupils to demonstrate the activity.
- The pupils play the game with a Talk Partner.

Activity Book

Activity 1

Order the letters and write. Match.

- The pupils name the water sports equipment they can see.
- The pupils order the letters and write the words, then match them to the equipment in the picture.

Answers: **1** surfboard **2** mask **3** life jacket **4** paddle **5** snorkel **6** flippers **7** wetsuit **8** helmet **9** swimsuit **10** kayak **11** water-skis **12** gloves

Activity 2

Look and write.

- The pupils describe what they can see in the pictures. Prompt a pupil to complete the sentences.
- The pupils write the descriptions.

Answers: **1** He's wearing a wetsuit and a life jacket. He's got a surfboard. He's ready to surf. **2** She's wearing a wetsuit, a life jacket, a helmet and gloves. She's got water-skis. She's ready to go water-skiing.

Code activity

- The pupils complete the code activity.

Answer: fish

Ending the lesson

Review the lesson and reflect on learning.

- Say **Today we've learnt the names of water sports equipment. What do you remember?** Elicit the equipment.
- Ask **Which was your favourite activity today? Which activity was easy / difficult?**

Extra activities

Extension

- Think of a land-based sport. Say **I'm wearing a T-shirt and shorts. I'm wearing socks and boots. I've got a ball. What am I doing?** The pupils guess.*Are you playing (football)?* Repeat with different sports.
- The pupils play the game in pairs.

Vocabulary extension

- Present six additional water sports equipment words: *fishing rod, goggles, jet ski, oars, rope, sailing boat.*
- Use the Vocabulary Booster on Navio to practise these new words.

Link to Science

- If you are studying the Science topic of **Water and air on Earth** in English, you could elicit other sources of water. (*Salt water: seas and oceans. Fresh water: rivers, lakes, ice caps and groundwater.*)

Key Competences and Key Learning Outcomes

- Listen, read, repeat and act out a conversation
- Read and identify water sports equipment.
- Listen, follow the grammar table and identify the parts of a sentence
- Talk and write about future plans using 'going to'

Key language

- *go kayaking, go sailing, go surfing, go swimming, go water-skiing, play football / tennis, watch TV; after school, at the weekend, next week, tomorrow*
- *I am / I'm not going to (play football). He is / isn't going to (go swimming). They are / aren't going to (watch TV). Are you going to (play football)? Yes, I am. No, I'm not. What are you going to do (on Saturday)?*
- Recycled: *flippers, gloves, helmet, kayak, life jacket, mask, paddle, snorkel, surfboard, swimsuit, water-skis, wetsuit; water sports*

Materials

- Pupil's Book p61; Activity Book p59; Class CD3; Teacher's App on Navio
- Water sports equipment flashcards
- Teacher's Resource Bank: Talk cards

Optional materials

- Teacher's Resource Bank: Trinity Exams Practice cards (selected from the Starter Unit and Units 1, 2, 3, 4 and 5)

At a Glance Lesson Plan

Pupil's Book

Starting the lesson

- Use the Trinity Exams Practice cards (optional).
- **Think-Pair-Share.** Review water sports equipment vocabulary.
- Review the *Fun in the sea* song.
- ▶ *CD3 Track 07 p272*
- ▶ *CD3 Track 08 p272*
- Set learning outcomes and use the talk cards.

Activity 1

- Listen and read. Listen and repeat.
- ▶ *CD3 Track 09 p272*
- Act out.

Activity 2

- Read again. Which things does Lily need? Why?

Activity 3

- Listen and follow.
- ▶ *CD3 Track 10 p272*
- Repeat.
- **Grammar clue:** Read about asking questions with *'going to'*.

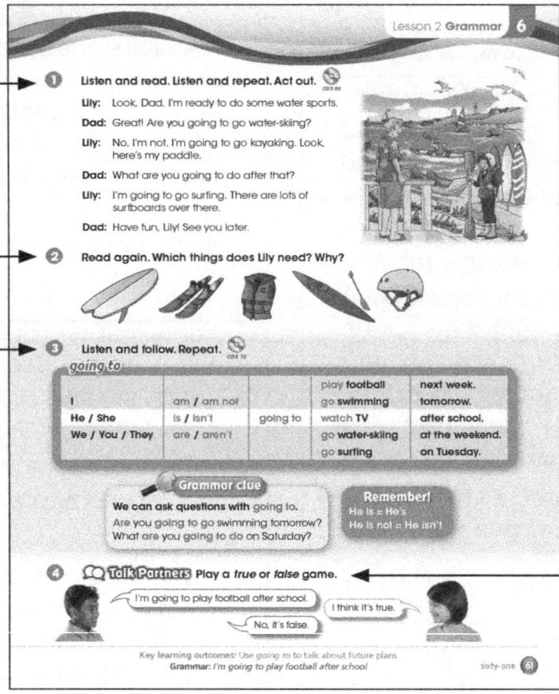

Lesson 2 Grammar 6

1 Listen and read. Listen and repeat. Act out.

Lily: Look, Dad. I'm ready to do some water sports.
Dad: Great! Are you going to go water-skiing?
Lily: No, I'm not. I'm going to go kayaking. Look, here's my paddle.
Dad: What are you going to do after that?
Lily: I'm going to go surfing. There are lots of surfboards over there.
Dad: Have fun, Lily! See you later.

2 Read again. Which things does Lily need? Why?

3 Listen and follow. Repeat.

going to

I	am / am not	going to	play football	next week.
He / She	is / isn't		go swimming	tomorrow.
We / You / They	are / aren't		watch TV	after school.
			go water-skiing	at the weekend.
			go surfing	on Tuesday.

Grammar clue: We can ask questions with going to. Are you going to go swimming tomorrow? What are you going to do on Saturday?

Remember! He is = He's. He is not = He isn't

4 Talk Partners Play a *true* or *false* game.

Key learning outcome: Use going to to talk about future plans
Grammar: I'm going to play football after school

sixty-one 61

Activity 4

- Play a *true* or *false* game.
- Go to the Activity Book.

Ending the lesson

- Review the lesson and reflect on learning.

Extra activities

Reinforcement

- Play *Two truths and a lie*.
- Play *Flashcard duel*.

Digital resources

Teacher's Digital: Don't forget you can teach this lesson using the Teacher's App on Navio.

Pupil's Digital: Encourage your pupils to use the Pupil's App on Navio to practise the grammar from this lesson.

Powered By NAVIO

Activity Book

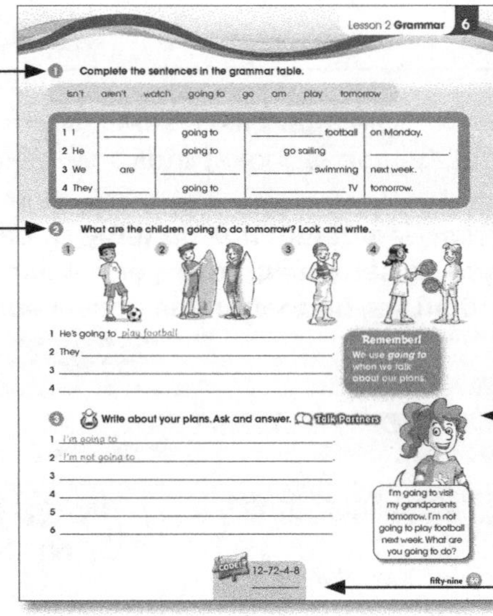

Lesson 2 Grammar 6

1 Complete the sentences in the grammar table.

isn't aren't watch going to go am play tomorrow

1 I	___	going to	___ football	on Monday.
2 He	___	going to	go sailing	___
3 We	are	___	___ swimming	next week.
4 They	___	going to	___ TV	tomorrow.

2 What are the children going to do tomorrow? Look and write.

1 He's going to play football
2 They
3
4

Remember! We use going to when we talk about our plans.

3 Write about your plans. Ask and answer. Talk Partners

1 I'm going to
2 I'm not going to
3
4
5
6

Code 12-72-4-8

fifty-nine 59

Activity Book

Activity 1

- Complete the sentences in the grammar table.

Activity 2

- What are the children going to do tomorrow?
- Look and write.

Activity 3

- Write about your plans.
- Ask and answer.

Code activity

- Complete the code activity.

Starting the lesson

Use the Trinity Exams Practice cards (optional).

- The pupils practise asking and answering questions.

Think-Pair-Share. Review water sports equipment vocabulary.

- Ask **Can you remember the water sports equipment vocabulary?** The class thinks silently for a minute.
- Then the pupils work with a Talk Partner to name the water sports equipment.
- Invite different Talk Partners to say a different item. Hold up the corresponding flashcard and prompt the class to repeat the word.

Review the *Fun in the sea* song.

▶ *CD3 Track 07 p272*

▶ *CD3 Track 08 p272 (optional karaoke version)*

- Organise the class into three groups. Play the CD (or use the karaoke version). The pupils sing along with their verse and do the actions.

Set learning outcomes and use the talk cards.

- Say **Today we're going to talk about plans.**
- Point to the talk cards to show the pupils the different ways they will be working in the lesson.

Pupil's Book Activity 1

Listen and read. Listen and repeat. Act out.

▶ *CD3 Track 09 p272*

- The pupils look at the picture and describe what they can see. Ask **What's Lily ready to do?**
- Play the CD. The pupils listen and read the conversation.
- Confirm that Lily is ready to do some water sports. Ask **Is she going to go water-skiing?** (*No, she's going to go kayaking*.)
- Play the CD again, pausing after each sentence for the pupils to repeat.
- The pupils act out the conversation with a Talk Partner.

Pupil's Book Activity 2

Read again. Which things does Lily need? Why?

- The pupils read the conversation again and say which things Lily needs and why.

Pupil's Book Activity 3

Listen and follow. Repeat.

▶ *CD3 Track 10 p272*

- Play the CD. The pupils listen to the first sentence and point to the words they hear. The pupils then repeat the complete sentence. Repeat the procedure with the other sentences.

Grammar clue

- Read the grammar clue and the *Remember!* tip as a class. Ask individual pupils a question about their plans and prompt them to respond. Then invite different individual pupils to ask you similar questions.
- Organise the class into Talk Partners. The pupils take turns to ask and answer questions.
- Use the grammar table to make sentences about future plans: **I am not going to (go water-skiing) (tomorrow).**
- With a Talk Partner, the pupils take turns to make similar sentences.

Pupil's Book Activity 4

Play a *true* or *false* game.

- The pupils work in pairs to make similar sentences and say if they are true or false.

Activity Book

Activity 1

Complete the sentences in the grammar table.

- Invite a pupil to read out the words in the word box.
- The pupils work on their own or with a partner to write the words in the grammar table.

Answers: 1 am, play **2** isn't, tomorrow **3** going to, go **4** aren't, watch

Activity 2

What are the children going to do tomorrow? Look and write.

- Focus the class on the first picture and elicit that the boy is going to play football. Repeat with the other pictures.
- The pupils write the sentences.

Answers: **1** He's going to play football. **2** They are going to go surfing. **3** She's going to go swimming. **4** They are going to play tennis.

Activity 3

Write about your plans. Ask and answer.

- Read the speech bubble and the *Remember!* tip.
- Invite the pupils to complete the first sentence in as many ways as possible. Write any new vocabulary on the board.
- The pupils write their own six sentences.
- Working with a Talk Partner, the pupils ask and answer questions about what they are going to do in the future. They can record the answers in their notebooks.

Code activity

- The pupils complete the code activity.

Answer: crab

Ending the lesson

Review the lesson and reflect on learning.

- Say **Today we've learnt how to talk about our plans.** Ask **What are you going to do after this lesson?** Prompt the pupils to answer.
- Ask **Which was your favourite activity today? Which activity was easy / difficult?**

Extra activities

Reinforcement

- Play *Two truths and a lie*. Say three things that you are going to do tomorrow (two true things and one lie). The pupils must identify the lie.
- The pupils write their own sentences about tomorrow. Invite pupils to read out their three sentences in order for the rest of the class to identify the lie.
- Play *Flashcard duel* (see p27) with the water sports equipment flashcards.

Key Competences and Key Learning Outcomes

- Read the story with some fluency
- Use a code to read a message
- Do a pre-reading task
- Understand the importance of listening to other people's ideas
- Understand, enjoy and act out the story
- Give an opinion on the story

Key language

- *build, faster, flag, plastic bottles, race, raft, rope, sinking, wood*
- *Are you (going to enter the race)?*
- Recycled: *There's a (raft race). You must (build your raft with these things). Why don't you (use this rope)? Good idea.*

Materials

- Pupil's Book pp62–63; Activity Book p60; Class CD3; Teacher's App on Navio
- Teacher's Resource Bank: Talk cards

Optional materials

- Teacher's Resource Bank: Trinity Exams Practice cards (selected from the Starter Unit and Units 1, 2, 3, 4 and 5)

At a Glance Lesson Plan

Pupil's Book

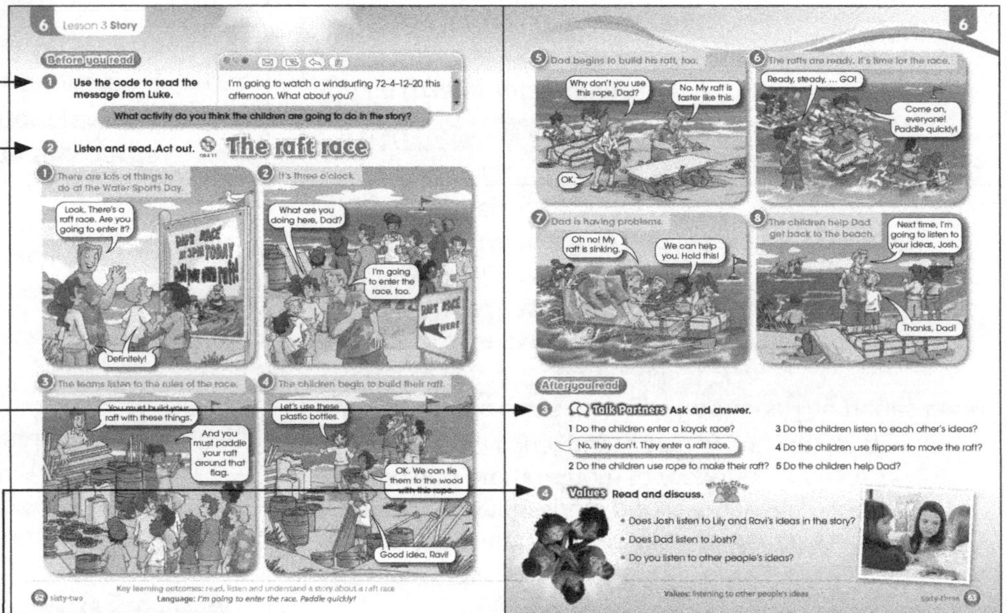

Activity Book

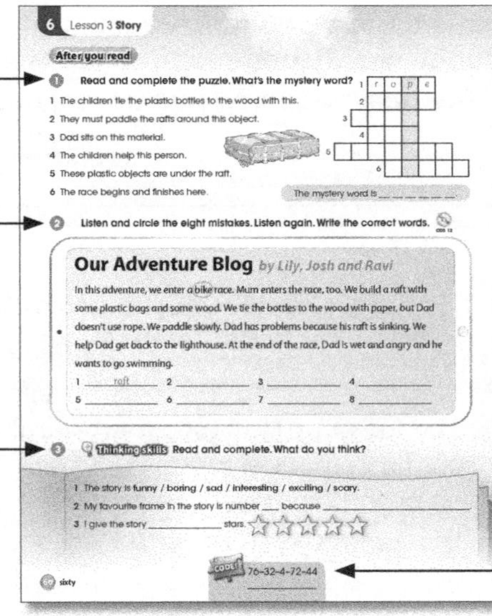

Starting the lesson

- Use the Trinity Exams Practice cards (optional).
- Review the grammar from Lesson 2.
- Set learning outcomes and use the talk cards.

Before you read: Activity 1

- Use the code to read the message from Luke.

Activity 2

- Listen and read.
- ▶ *CD3 Track 11 p272*
- Act out.

After you read: Activity 3

- Ask and answer.

Values: Activity 4

- Read and discuss.
- Go to the Activity Book.

Ending the lesson

- Review the lesson and reflect on learning.

Extra activity

Reinforcement

- Retell the story as a class.

Activity Book: After you read

Activity 1

- Read and complete the puzzle.
- What's the mystery word?

Activity 2

- Listen and circle the eight mistakes.
- ▶ *CD3 Track 12 p273*
- Listen again.
- Write the correct words.

Activity 3

- Read and complete.
- What do you think?

Code activity

- Complete the code activity.

Digital resources

Teacher's Digital: Don't forget you can teach this lesson using the Teacher's App on Navio.

Pupil's Digital: Encourage your pupils to use the Pupil's App on Navio to practise the reading the story again at home.

Powered By NAVIO

Starting the lesson

Use the Trinity Exams Practice cards (optional).

- The pupils practise asking and answering questions.

Review the grammar from Lesson 2.

- Think of a place and say **I'm going to eat an ice cream tomorrow. Where am I going?** Prompt a pupil to guess. (*Are you going to (a restaurant)?*) If the guess is incorrect, say another thing you are going to do. **I'm going to make a sandcastle, too.**
- Repeat the procedure with a different place.

Set learning outcomes and use the talk cards.

- Say **Today we're going to read and listen to a story.**
- Point to the talk cards to show the pupils the different ways they will be working in the lesson.

Before you read: Pupil's Book Activity 1

Use the code to read the message from Luke.

- Say **Josh and Lily have received another message from Luke.** The pupils use the code (Pupil's Book page 7) to discover the mystery word (*race*). Ask **Do you think a windsurfing race is exciting?**
- Ask **What activity do you think the children are going to do in the story?** The pupils make predictions.
- Read the title of the story and explain that a raft is a flat boat with no sides. Confirm that the children do a raft race in the story.

Pupil's Book Activity 2

Listen and read. Act out.

▶ *CD3 Track 11 p272*

- Play the CD. The pupils follow in their books.
- Ask questions to check comprehension.

Suggested comprehension questions

- Frame 1: **Are the children going to enter the raft race?** (*Yes.*)
- Frame 2: **What time is it?** (*Three o'clock.*) **Who is also going to enter the race?** (*Dad.*)
- Frame 3: **What do the teams listen to?** (*The rules.*)
- Frame 4: **What do the children use to build their raft?** (*Plastic bottles, wood and rope.*)
- Frame 5: **Does Dad use the rope?** (*No.*)
- Frame 6: **What words start the race?** (*Ready, steady, go!*)
- Frame 7: **Why does Dad's raft sink?** (*The raft isn't tied together.*) **Who helps him?** (*Lily, Josh and Ravi.*)
- Frame 8: **What is Dad going to do next time?** (*Listen to Josh's ideas.*)
- Organise the class into six groups (Lily, Ravi, Josh, Dad and race monitors) and play the CD. Each group joins in when their character speaks.
- Repeat, with groups swapping roles.

After you read: Pupil's Book Activity 3

Ask and answer.

- Invite pupils to ask and answer the questions. If necessary, ask the whole class to repeat the answer each time.
- Organise the class into Talk Partners. The pupils practise asking and answering the questions. They can do this orally or in their notebooks.

Answers: **1** No, they don't. They enter a raft race. **2** Yes, they do. They use rope, wood and plastic bottles. **3** Yes, they do. They work together. **4** No, they don't. They use paddles. **5** Yes, they do. They help him get back to the beach.

Values: Pupil's Book Activity 4

Read and discuss.

- Read out the questions and discuss them as a class.
- Encourage the class to think about the importance of listening to other pupils' opinions and ideas in class.

Activity Book: After you read

Activity 1

Read and complete the puzzle. What's the mystery word?

- The pupils read the clues and complete the puzzle and mystery word, referring to the story.

Answers: **1** rope **2** flag **3** wood **4** Dad **5** bottles **6** beach
The mystery word is paddle.

Activity 2

Listen and circle the eight mistakes. Listen again. Write the correct words.

▶ *CD3 Track 12 p273*

- Play the CD. The pupils circle the eight mistakes.
- Play the CD again. The pupils write the correct words.

Answers: **1** ~~bike~~ raft **2** ~~Mum~~ Dad **3** ~~bags~~ bottles **4** ~~paper~~ rope **5** ~~slowly~~ quickly **6** ~~lighthouse~~ beach **7** ~~angry~~ tired **8** ~~swimming~~ home

Activity 3

Read and complete. What do you think?

- Invite pupils to read out and complete the sentences.
- The pupils complete the task in their Activity Books and then share opinions with a Talk Partner.

Code activity

- The pupils complete the code activity.

Answer: shark

Ending the lesson

Review the lesson and reflect on learning.

- Say **Today we've listened to a story about a raft race.** Elicit the story.
- Ask **Which was your favourite activity today? Which activity was easy / difficult?**

Extra activity

Reinforcement

- Retell the story as a class. Say **Let's tell the story together.** Prompt the class by saying **The children and Dad enter a …** (*raft race*). **The teams listen to the …** (*rules*). Use mime, gesture and drawings to support the class.

Key Competences and Key Learning Outcomes
• Learn adverbs of manner • Follow and correct the grammar tables
• Play a mime game
• Sing a song

Key language

- *(play) loudly, (play) quietly, (ride) badly, (ride) well, (swim) quickly, (swim) slowly; play chess, warm up*
- *Bend (your knees). Shake (your body). Stretch (your arms). Wiggle (your fingers). You (play chess) well. She (dances) badly. What do you do (well)? I (swim) (very) well.*
- Extension: *carefully, dangerously, happily, sadly*
- Recycled: *cycle, dance, play football, play tennis, rollerblade, sing, swim, (walk)*

Materials

- Pupil's Book p64; Activity Book p61; Class CD3; Teacher's App on Navio
- Teacher's Resource Bank: Talk cards

Optional materials

- Teacher's Resource Bank: Trinity Exams Practice cards (selected from the Starter Unit and Units 1, 2, 3, 4 and 5)
- A dice for each pair of pupils

At a Glance Lesson Plan

Pupil's Book

Starting the lesson

- Use the Trinity Exams Practice cards (optional).
- Review the story.
- Set learning outcomes and use the talk cards.

Activity 1

- Listen, point and say.
- ▶ ***CD3 Track 13 p273***

Activity 2

- Listen and sing *Warm up!*
- ▶ ***CD3 Track 14 p273***

Activity 3

- Listen and follow.
- ▶ ***CD3 Track 15 p273***
- Repeat.
- **Grammar clue:** Read about using '-ly'.

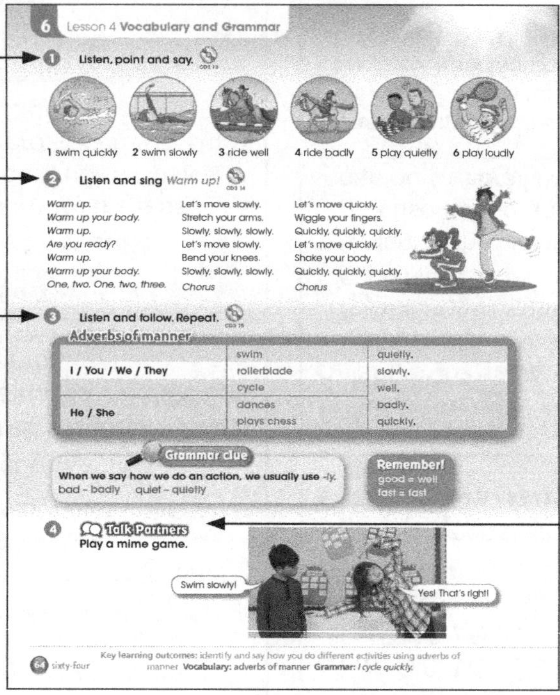

Activity 4

- Play a mime game.
- Go to the Activity Book.

Ending the lesson

- Review the lesson and reflect on learning.

Extra activities

Reinforcement

- Play a dice game to practise adverbs of manner.

Vocabulary extension

- Present four additional vocabulary items.

Activity Book

Activity Book

Activity 1

- Look, read and circle.

Activity 2

- Order the words in the grammar table.
- Write the sentences.

Activity 3

- Read and answer.
- Ask and answer.

Code activity

- Complete the code activity.

Digital resources

Teacher's Digital: Don't forget you can teach this lesson using the Teacher's App on Navio.

Pupil's Digital: Encourage your pupils to use the Pupil's App on Navio to practise the grammar from this lesson.

Powered By NAVIO

Starting the lesson

Use the Trinity Exams Practice cards (optional).

- The pupils practise asking and answering questions.

Review the story.

- Ask the class if they remember the story from the previous lesson. Organise the class into small groups. Ask each group a question about the story. The pupils collaborate before they answer.

Set learning outcomes and use the talk cards.

- Say **Today we're going to talk about the way that we do different actions.**
- Point to the talk cards to show the pupils the different ways they will be working in the lesson.

Pupil's Book Activity 1

Listen, point and say.

▶ *CD3 Track 13 p273*

- Point to the first picture and ask **What's he doing? Is he swimming quickly or slowly?** Mime swimming quickly and then slowly. Repeat the procedure, comparing 'well' and 'badly', and 'quietly' and 'loudly'.
- Play the CD. The pupils listen, point to each picture and say the phrases.

Pupil's Book Activity 2

Listen and sing *Warm up!*

▶ *CD3 Track 14 p273*

- Explain that it's important to warm up your body before you do exercise.
- Say **Lily's stretching her arms and bending her knees.** Encourage the pupils to do the action. Then say **Ravi's wiggling his fingers and shaking his body.** The class does the actions.
- Play the CD. The pupils listen and read.
- Play the CD again. The pupils join in singing the song and doing the actions slowly and quickly.

Pupil's Book Activity 3

Listen and follow. Repeat.

▶ *CD3 Track 15 p273*

- Focus the class on the grammar table.
- Play the CD. The pupils listen to the first sentence and point to the corresponding parts of the sentence in the table. They should then repeat the complete sentence. Repeat the procedure with the other sentences.
- Say **Everybody swim slowly.** The class does the mime. Repeat, choosing a different sport and adverb.
- Introduce other actions and adverbs, e.g. **Brush your teeth sleepily. Eat an ice cream happily.**

Grammar clue

- Read the grammar clue as a class. Highlight that most adverbs of manner are formed by an adjective + '–ly'. Say some adjectives (*angry, sad*) and prompt the class to make the adverbs. Read the *Remember!* tip. Point out that 'good' and 'fast' are exceptions.

Pupil's Book Activity 4

Play a mime game.

- The pupils work in pairs to mime an action and guess the sport and the adverb.

Activity Book

Activity 1

Look, read and circle.

- Focus on the first picture. Then invite a pupil to read out the first sentence, choosing the correct adverb.
- The pupils work on their own to read the remaining sentences and circle the correct adverbs.

Answers: **1** well **2** badly **3** loudly **4** quickly

Activity 2

Order the words in the grammar table. Write the sentences.

- Explain that the grammar table is mixed up and that the pupils need to order the words.
- Invite a pupil to read out the first sentence.
- The pupils write the sentences.

Answers: **1** I sing loudly. **2** You walk slowly. **3** He cycles quickly. **4** They dance well.

Activity 3

Read and answer. Ask and answer.

- Invite different pupils to read out and answer the first question. Repeat with the other questions.
- The pupils write their answers.
- The pupils take turns to ask and answer with a Talk Partner.

Code activity

- The pupils complete the code activity.

Answer: whale

Ending the lesson

Review the lesson and reflect on learning.

- Say **Today we've learnt to say how a person does an activity.** Ask **How can you talk?** (*Quietly / loudly.*) **How can you run?** (*Fast / slowly.*) **What do you do well or badly?**
- Ask **Which was your favourite activity today? Which activity was easy / difficult?**

Extra activities

Reinforcement

- Write the numbers 1–6 in a column on the left of the board and invite the class to name six sports. Write a sport next to each number. Then write another column of numbers (1–6) on the right side and invite the pupils to name six adverbs of manner, e.g. *sleepily, well, badly.* Write them next to the numbers.
- Roll a dice twice without revealing the numbers. The first number is a sport and the second number is an adverb. Do a mime and invite pupils to guess, e.g. *You're playing football slowly.*
- Invite different pupils to take your role.
- Give each pair of pupils a dice and ask them to play the game.

Vocabulary extension

- Use the Vocabulary Booster on Navio and present and practise four additional adverbs: *carefully, dangerously, happily, sadly.*

Key Competences and Key Learning Outcomes

- Say a tongue twister with the 'k' sound
- Practise spelling and learn an alternative spelling for the 'k' sound
- Predict answers then listen for specific information

- Play a communication game using adverbs of manner

Key language
- *lake*
- *Do you (rollerblade) fast or slowly? I (rollerblade) (slowly). Pablo (sings) (well).*
- Recycled: *badly, loudly, quickly, quietly, slowly, well; black, hockey, kayak, kite, monkey, rock, shark, snake*

Materials
- Pupil's Book p65; Activity Book p62; Class CD3; Teacher's App on Navio
- Teacher's Resource Bank: Talk cards
- Teacher's Resource Bank: Unit 6 Lesson 5 Communication Activity

Optional materials
- Teacher's Resource Bank: Trinity Exams Practice cards (selected from the Starter Unit and Units 1, 2, 3, 4 and 5)

At a Glance Lesson Plan

Pupil's Book

Starting the lesson
- Use the Trinity Exams Practice cards (optional).
- Review adverbs of manner.
- Review the *Warm up!* song.
- ▶ ***CD3 Track 14 p273***
- Set learning outcomes and use the talk cards.

Activity 1: Speak and spell
- Listen, read and say.
- ▶ ***CD3 Track 16 p273***
- Go to the Activity Book.

Activity 2
- Read the quiz.
- Then listen and identify four differences.
- ▶ ***CD3 Track 17 p273***

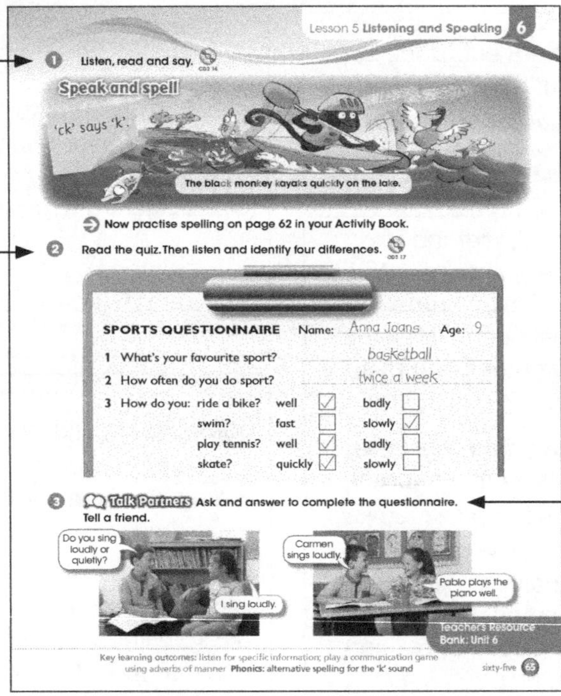

Activity 3
- Ask and answer to complete the questionnaire.
- Tell a friend (Teacher's Resource Bank: Unit 6).

Ending the lesson
- Review the lesson and reflect on learning.

Extra activity

Reinforcement
- Make similar questionnaires in pairs.

Activity Book

Activity Book

Activity 1: Speak and spell
- Complete and say.

Activity 2
- Find and circle the words.
- Classify and write.

Activity 3
- Test your friend.
- Ask and answer.

Code activity
- Complete the code activity.

Digital resources

Teacher's Digital: You can also teach this lesson using the Teacher's App on Navio.

Pupil's Digital: Encourage your pupils to use the Pupil's App on Navio to practise the activities from this lesson.

Powered By NAVIO

Starting the lesson

Use the Trinity Exams Practice cards (optional).
- The pupils practise asking and answering questions.

Review adverbs of manner.
- Ask the pupils to stand up. Then ask them to do an action, e.g. **Swim slowly**. Ask them to do the same action **quickly, quietly, happily, angrily**. Repeat the procedure with different actions. Then, if you wish, invite different pupils to take your role and give the class similar instructions.

Review the *Warm up!* song.
▶ *CD3 Track 14 p273*
- Play the CD. The pupils sing and do the actions.

Set learning outcomes and use the talk cards.
- Say **Today we're going to say a tongue twister, practise spelling and do a questionnaire together.**
- Point to the talk cards to show the pupils the different ways they will be working in the lesson.

Pupil's Book Activity 1: Speak and spell

Listen, read and say.
▶ *CD3 Track 16 p273*
- (Books closed.) Write the letter 'k' on the board and ask **What sound does this letter make?** (*'k'*) List the words the pupils know that begin with this letter. Say **Today you're going to learn another way of writing the 'k' sound.**
- (Books open.) Focus the class on the monkey in the picture and say **What colour is the monkey?** (*Black.*) **What's he doing?** (*Kayaking.*) **Where is he kayaking?** (*On a lake.*)
- Say **Let's listen to the tongue twister.** Play the CD. The pupils follow the text in their books.
- Play the CD again. The pupils join in with the tongue twister.
- Finally, ask the class to identify the alternative way of writing the 'k' sound ('ck').

Activity Book

Activity 1: Speak and spell
Complete and say.
- The pupils write and say the words in the tongue twister.

Answer: The black monkey kayaks quickly on the lake.

Activity 2
Find and circle the words. Classify and write.
- The pupils find and circle the words in the border which contain 'k' and 'ck'.
- The pupils classify and write the words according to whether they are spelt with 'k' or 'ck'.

Answers: ck: hockey, rock, black, back, neck, k: snake, kite, shark, kayak, mask

Activity 3
Talk Partners. Test your friend. Ask and answer.
- Invite two pupils to read out the speech bubbles.
- Organise the pupils into Talk Partners. The pupils take it in turns to spell the words in Activity 2. Stress the importance of prompting, encouraging and helping each other.

Code activity
- The pupils complete the code activity.

Answer: seal

Pupil's Book Activity 2

Read the quiz. Then listen and identify four differences.
▶ *CD3 Track 17 p273*
- Focus the pupils on the questionnaire. Explain that they are going to listen to Anna answering the questions, and they will need to identify four differences. Ask the pupils to look at Anna's answers.
- Play the CD, pausing after the first question and answer. Elicit the difference between the questionnaire and what they heard on the audio. Repeat the procedure with the remaining questions and answers.

Answers: Her surname is spelt J-O-N-E-S; her favourite sport is volleyball; she does sport three times a week; she swims fast

Pupil's Book Activity 3

Ask and answer to complete the questionnaire. Tell a friend (Teacher's Resource Bank: Unit 6).
- Invite three pupils to read out the speech bubbles.
- Explain to the class that they are going to do a similar questionnaire with a Talk Partner.
- Organise the class into Talk Partners. Pupil A uses questionnaire 1 and Pupil B uses questionnaire 2. Check that the pupils know all the activities that appear in their questionnaire.
- The pupils take turns to ask and answer the questions.
- When the pupils have completed the questionnaires, invite individual pupils to report what they have learnt about their Talk Partner.
- Organise the class into new pairs. The pupils should report the information in the questionnaire.

Ending the lesson

Review the lesson and reflect on learning.
- Say **Today we've practised a tongue twister.** Elicit the tongue twister from the pupils.
- Ask **Which was your favourite activity today? Which activity was easy / difficult?**

Extra activity

Reinforcement
- The pupils work in pairs to create a similar questionnaire.
- Organise the class into new pairs to ask and answer the questions.

Key Competences and Key Learning Outcomes

LEARN
- Do a pre-reading task to set the context
- Read the text for general understanding
- Sequence the parts of a letter

- Read and understand an informal letter

Key language
- *archery, mountain biking, rock climbing; forest, lessons, letter; first, next, finally; fish (v)*
- *Which activities is (Robert) going to do?*
- Recycled: *baseball, camp, gymnastics, helmet, kayaking, lake, life jacket, volleyball, windsurfing; I'm going to (go kayaking).*

Materials
- Pupil's Book p66; Activity Book p63; Class CD3; Teacher's App on Navio
- Teacher's Resource Bank: Talk cards

Optional materials
- Teacher's Resource Bank: Trinity Exams Practice cards (selected from the Starter Unit and Units 1, 2, 3, 4 and 5)

At a Glance Lesson Plan

Pupil's Book

Starting the lesson
- Use the Trinity Exams Practice cards (optional).
- Review the tongue twister.
- ▶ *CD3 Track 16 p273*
- Set learning outcomes and use the talk cards.

Before you read: Activity 1
- Imagine you are going to go to a sports camp.
- Which activities would you like to do?

Activity 2
- Read and listen.
- ▶ *CD3 Track 18 p273*
- Which activities is Robert going to do?

Go to the Activity Book.

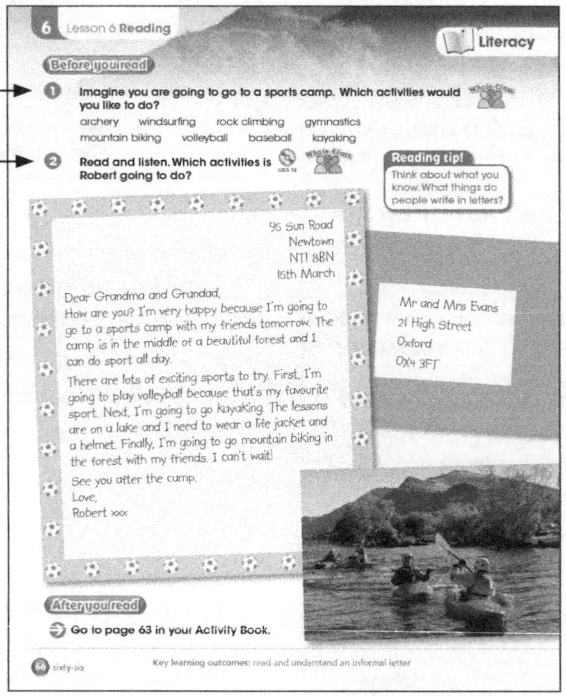
6 Lesson 6 Reading

Literacy

Before you read

1 Imagine you are going to go to a sports camp. Which activities would you like to do?

archery windsurfing rock climbing gymnastics mountain biking volleyball baseball kayaking

2 Read and listen. Which activities is Robert going to do?

Reading tip! Think about what you know. What things do people write in letters?

95 Sun Road
Newtown
NT1 8BN
15th March

Dear Grandma and Grandad,
How are you? I'm very happy because I'm going to go to a sports camp with my friends tomorrow. The camp is in the middle of a beautiful forest and I can do sport all day.
There are lots of exciting sports to try. First, I'm going to play volleyball because that's my favourite sport. Next, I'm going to go kayaking. The lessons are on a lake and I need to wear a life jacket and a helmet. Finally, I'm going to go mountain biking in the forest with my friends. I can't wait!
See you after the camp.
Love,
Robert xxx

Mr and Mrs Evans
21 High Street
Oxford
OX4 3FT

After you read

Go to page 63 in your Activity Book.

66 sixty-six Key learning outcomes: read and understand an informal letter

Ending the lesson
- Review the lesson and reflect on learning.

Extra activity

Reinforcement
- Listen and identify the mistakes in the letter.

Activity Book

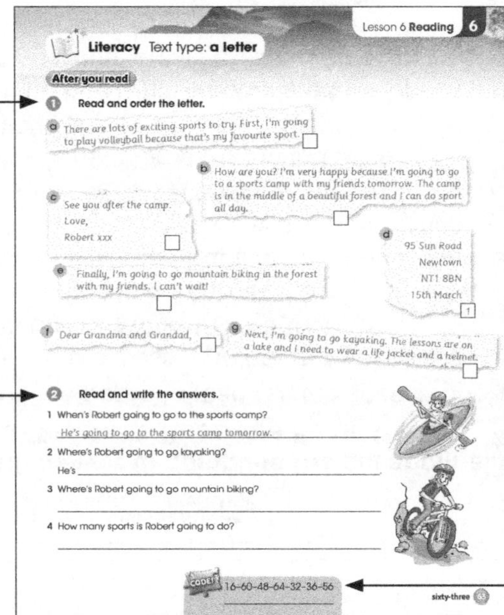
Lesson 6 Reading 6

Literacy Text type: a letter

After you read

1 Read and order the letter.

a There are lots of exciting sports to try. First, I'm going to play volleyball because that's my favourite sport.

b How are you? I'm very happy because I'm going to go to a sports camp with my friends tomorrow. The camp is in the middle of a beautiful forest and I can do sport all day.

c See you after the camp. Love, Robert xxx

d 95 Sun Road Newtown NT1 8BN 15th March 1

e Finally, I'm going to go mountain biking in the forest with my friends. I can't wait!

f Dear Grandma and Grandad,

g Next, I'm going to go kayaking. The lessons are on a lake and I need to wear a life jacket and a helmet.

2 Read and write the answers.

1 When's Robert going to go to the sports camp?
He's going to go to the sports camp tomorrow.
2 Where's Robert going to go kayaking?
He's
3 Where's Robert going to go mountain biking?
4 How many sports is Robert going to do?

CODE 16-60-48-64-32-36-56

sixty-three 63

After you read: Activity Book

Activity 1
- Read and order the letter.

Activity 2
- Read and write the answers.

Code activity
- Complete the code activity.

Digital resources

Teacher's Digital: You can also teach this lesson using the Teacher's App on Navio.

Pupil's Digital: Encourage your pupils to use the Pupil's App on Navio to practise the activities from this lesson.

Powered By NAVIO

Starting the lesson

Use the Trinity Exams Practice cards (optional).

- The pupils practise asking and answering questions.

Review the tongue twister.

▶ *CD3 Track 16 p273*

- Ask **What sound did you practise in the tongue twister?** (*'k'*)
- Play the CD. Practise the tongue twister as a class.
- Remind the pupils that they know four spellings for this sound ('c', 'ch', 'k' and 'ck'). The pupils list the words they know that begin with these letters.

Set learning outcomes and use the talk cards.

- Say **Today we're going to read a letter.** Check understanding by asking **Who brings letters to your house? Do you write letters? Do people write letters to you?** Encourage the pupils to talk about any letters they have sent or received.
- Point to the talk cards to show the pupils the different ways they will be working in the lesson.

Before you read: Pupil's Book Activity 1

Imagine you are going to go to a sports camp. Which activities would you like to do?

- Invite a pupil to read the rubric. Explain any unknown sports in the list and encourage the pupils to tell you which activities they would like to do and why. Give your opinion, too, e.g. **I would like to (go windsurfing) because it's (fun / exciting / fast).**

Pupil's Book Activity 2

Read and listen. Which activities is Robert going to do?

▶ *CD3 Track 18 p273*

- Focus the class on the letter and ask **Who is the letter to?** (*Grandma and Grandad.*) **Who is the letter from?** (*Robert.*) **What's the date on the letter?** (*15th March.*) **Where does Robert live?** (*In Newtown.*) **Where do his grandparents live?** (*In Oxford.*)
- Explain to the class that Robert is writing to his grandparents about the sports camp. Then ask the pupils to read the letter quickly to find out which activities Robert is going to do there. If you want the pupils to read the text without the support of the CD, set a time limit for this task. Otherwise play the CD, pausing at the end of each section of the text.

Answer: Robert is going to play volleyball, go kayaking and go mountain biking.

After you read: Activity Book

Activity 1

Read and order the letter.

- Focus the class on the activity and ask a pupil to read out the first part of the letter.
- Ask the class to scan the other pieces of the letter to find the next part. The pupils should compare their answer with a Talk Partner. Then invite a pupil to read out the second part.
- Highlight 'clues' in the text, such as the question 'How are you?' to begin a letter in the first paragraph.
- Repeat the procedure with the remaining parts of the text.

Answers: **1** d **2** f **3** b **4** a **5** g **6** e **7** c

Activity 2

Read and write the answers.

- Invite a pupil to read out the first question and the example answer. Ask different pupils to read out the other questions.
- The pupils work on their own or in pairs to write the answers.

Answers: **1** He's going to go to the sports camp tomorrow. **2** He's going to go kayaking on a lake. **3** He's going to go mountain biking in the forest. **4** He's going to do three sports.

Code activity

- The pupils complete the code activity.

Answer: dolphin

Ending the lesson

Review the lesson and reflect on learning.

- Say **Today we've read a letter. Will Robert's grandparents like the letter? What do you think?** Elicit the pupils' ideas.
- Ask **Which was your favourite activity today? Which activity was easy / difficult?**

Extra activity

Reinforcement

- (Books closed.) Explain that you are going to read Robert's letter, but you're going to make some mistakes. The pupils should raise their hands or 'fish' the mistakes (mime reeling in a fish) when they hear something that is wrong.
- Read the letter slowly, changing the information at regular intervals, e.g. **Dear Mum and Dad.** Prompt the class to give you the correct information each time.

Key Competences and Key Learning Outcomes

- Learn simple time sequencers and how we begin and end an informal letter
- Learn about the layout of a letter
- Plan an informal letter with a partner
- Use criteria to check your writing
- Share your writing with a partner
- Prepare and write an informal letter

Key language

- *adventure, scary*
- *I'm going to (go horse riding). I'm not going to (go rock climbing). I can (ride) (very well).*
- Recycled: *archery, camp, horse riding, lake, rock climbing, wetsuit, windsurfing; first, next, finally; Which activity is (Laura) not going to do?*

Materials

- Pupil's Book p67; Activity Book p64; Class CD3; Teacher's App on Navio
- Teacher's Resource Bank: Talk cards

Optional materials

- Teacher's Resource Bank: Trinity Exams Practice cards (selected from the Starter Unit and Units 1, 2, 3, 4 and 5)
- A piece of paper for each pupil

At a Glance Lesson Plan

Pupil's Book

Starting the lesson

- Use the Trinity Exams Practice cards (optional).
- Review vocabulary for sports activities.
- Set learning outcomes and use the talk cards.

Investigate a text: Activity 1

- Look at the leaflet.
- What can you do at the adventure camp?

Investigate a text: Activity 2

- Read and listen.
- ▶ *CD3 Track 19 p273*
- Which activity is Laura not going to do?

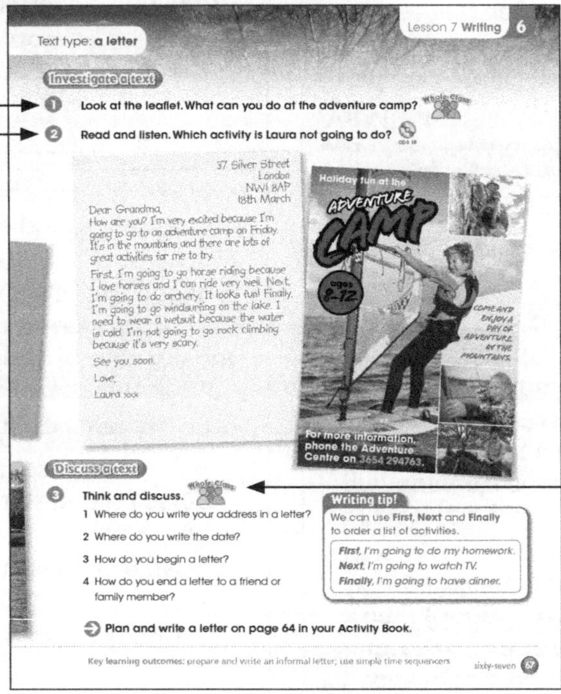

Text type: a letter

Lesson 7 Writing 6

Investigate a text

1 Look at the leaflet. What can you do at the adventure camp?

2 Read and listen. Which activity is Laura not going to do?

Discuss a text

3 Think and discuss.

1 Where do you write your address in a letter?
2 Where do you write the date?
3 How do you begin a letter?
4 How do you end a letter to a friend or family member?

Writing tip! We can use First, Next and Finally to order a list of activities. First, I'm going to do my homework. Next, I'm going to watch TV. Finally, I'm going to have dinner.

Plan and write a letter on page 64 in your Activity Book.

Key learning outcomes: prepare and write an informal letter; use simple time sequencers sixty-seven

Discuss a text: Activity 3

- Think and discuss.
- **Writing tip:** Read about time sequencers.

Go to the Activity Book.

Ending the lesson

- Review the lesson and reflect on learning.

Extra activity

Reinforcement

- Write a letter to a classmate.

Activity Book

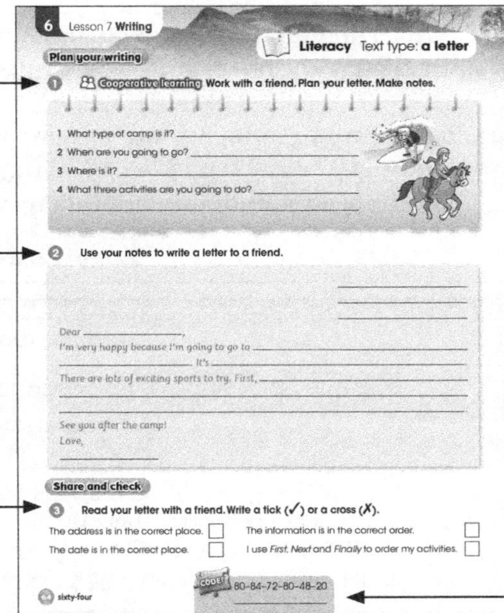

6 Lesson 7 Writing

Literacy Text type: a letter

Plan your writing

1 Cooperative learning Work with a friend. Plan your letter. Make notes.

1 What type of camp is it?
2 When are you going to go?
3 Where is it?
4 What three activities are you going to do?

2 Use your notes to write a letter to a friend.

Share and check

3 Read your letter with a friend. Write a tick (✓) or a cross (✗).

The address is in the correct place. The information is in the correct order.
The date is in the correct place. I use First, Next and Finally to order my activities.

CODE 80-84-72-80-48-20

sixty-four

Activity Book

Plan your writing: Activity 1

- Work with a friend.
- Plan your letter.
- Make notes.

Activity 2

- Use your notes to write a letter to a friend.

Share and check: Activity 3

- Read your letter with a friend.
- Write a tick (✓) or a cross (✗).

Code activity

- Complete the code activity.

Digital resources

Teacher's Digital: You can also teach this lesson using the Teacher's App on Navio.

Pupil's Digital: Encourage your pupils to use the Pupil's App on Navio to practise the activities from this lesson.

Powered By NAVIO

Starting the lesson

Use the Trinity Exams Practice cards (optional).

- The pupils practise asking and answering questions.

Review vocabulary for sports activities.

- Write the following prompts on the board: *I love … I like … I don't like …* Then tell the pupils about the sports you love doing and why. Encourage individual pupils to make similar sentences. Repeat the procedure with the other two prompts.
- Organise the class into Talk Partners and ask them to tell each other about the sports they love, like and don't like.

Set learning outcomes and use the talk cards.

- Ask **What did we read in the last lesson?** (*A letter.*) Say **Today we're going to investigate another letter. Then we're going to plan and write a letter.**
- Point to the talk cards to show the pupils the different ways they will be working in the lesson.

Investigate a text: Pupil's Book Activity 1

Look at the leaflet. What can you do at the adventure camp?

- Focus the class on the photos on the leaflet. The pupils identify the activities you can do at the adventure camp. (*Windsurfing, horse riding, archery, rock climbing.*) Ask the pupils if they think the adventure camp looks fun / exciting.

Investigate a text: Pupil's Book Activity 2

Read and listen. Which activity is Laura not going to do?

▶ *CD3 Track 19 p273*

- Explain that Laura is writing to her grandmother about the adventure camp. Then ask the pupils to read the letter quickly to find out which activity Laura is not going to do there. If you want the pupils to read the text without the support of the CD, set a time limit for this task. Otherwise, play the CD, pausing at the end of each section of the text.

Answer: Laura isn't going to go rock climbing.

Discuss a text: Pupil's Book Activity 3

Think and discuss.

- Read the first question and ask the class to look at the letter. Confirm that you write your address at the top of the letter, on the right. Repeat the procedure with the remaining questions. (*You write the date below the address. You begin a letter with 'Dear' and you end an informal letter with 'Love'.*)

Writing tip

- Read the information about time sequencers as a class.
- Prompt the pupils to find examples of 'First', 'Next' and 'Finally' in the letter.

Activity Book

Plan your writing: Activity 1

Writing Partners. Work with a friend. Plan your letter. Make notes.

- Read out the questions as a class. Organise the pupils into pairs and ask them to invent an exciting day at an activity camp and make notes about it. The pupils do not have to write complete sentences at this stage.
- Alternatively, if the pupils need more support, do this activity as a class.

Activity 2

Use your notes to write a letter to a friend.

- Focus the class on the activity. If necessary, model how to write a letter. The pupils work as a class to give you the information. Write the text on the board.
- The pupils work on their own or with their partner to write their letter in their Activity Books.

Share and check: Activity 3

Writing Partners. Read your letter with a friend. Write a tick (✓) or a cross (✗).

- Read through the statements as a class.
- Organise the class into new pairs. One pupil in each pair reads their text aloud to their partner. The other pupil listens. The pupils work together to decide if the text fulfils all the criteria and tick or cross the corresponding boxes. The pupils can add to, improve, or correct the text at this stage.
- The pupils swap roles.

Code activity

- The pupils complete the code activity.

Answer: turtle

Ending the lesson

Review the lesson and reflect on learning.

- Say **Today we've written a letter. Are you happy with your letter?** Elicit the pupils' responses.
- Ask **Which was your favourite activity today? Which activity was easy / difficult?**

Extra activity

Reinforcement

- Give each pupil the name of a classmate to write a letter to.
- The pupils write a short letter to their classmate saying what they are going to do at the weekend.
- The pupils copy their letter onto a piece of paper, fold it and write their friend's name on the reverse side.
- Collect the letters. Then ask a pupil to be the postman or postwoman and to deliver the letters to the classmates.

Key Competences and Key Learning Outcomes

- Use the Internet to investigate New Zealand
- Read and listen for specific information
- Read about three extreme sports in New Zealand
- Think about your own culture and identity

Key language

- *ankles, bridge, bungee jumping, elastic rope, energy, exciting, extreme sports, harness, rafting, sand surfing, zorbing*
- *If you like (travelling fast), (sand surfing) is the sport for you.*
- Recycled: *adventure, air, beach, helmet, hill, jump, lie down, life jacket, mountains, paddle, plastic ball, raft, ride, river, roll, rope, sit, stand, surfboard, surfing, wet, wetsuit; You must (be very brave). Do you like (adventure)?*

Materials

- Pupil's Book p68; Activity Book p65; Class CD3; Teacher's App on Navio
- Teacher's Resource Bank: Talk cards
- An online world map
- Coloured pencils (red, white and blue)

Optional materials

- Teacher's Resource Bank: Trinity Exams Practice cards (selected from the Starter Unit and Units 1, 2, 3, 4 and 5)

At a Glance Lesson Plan

Pupil's Book

Starting the lesson
- Use the Trinity Exams Practice cards (optional).
- Review preferences for different sports and make comparisons.
- Set learning outcomes and use the talk cards.

Activity 1
- Read Luke's questions.
- What do you think?

Activity 2
- Read and listen.

▶ *CD3 Track 20 p274*
- Answer Luke's questions.
- **Think about your culture** What exciting sports can you do in your country?

Go to the Activity Book.

Ending the lesson
- Review the lesson and reflect on learning.

Activity Book

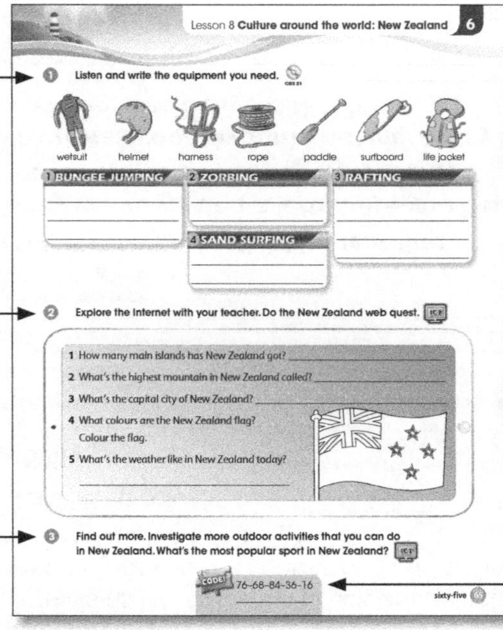

Activity Book

Activity 1
- Listen and write the equipment you need.

▶ *CD3 Track 21 p274*

Activity 2
- Explore the Internet with your teacher. Do the New Zealand web quest.

Activity 3
- Find out more. Investigate more outdoor activities that you can do in New Zealand. What's the most popular sport in New Zealand?

Code activity
- Complete the code activity.

Digital resources

Teacher's Digital: You can also teach this lesson using the Teacher's App on Navio.

Powered By NAVIO

Starting the lesson

Use the Trinity Exams Practice cards (optional).

- The pupils practise asking and answering questions.

Review preferences for different sports and make comparisons.

- Ask a pupil **Do you prefer (rugby) or (football)?** Prompt the pupil to give the full answer and ask **Why?** Prompt the pupil to make a comparison, e.g. (*Football*) *is more exciting than* (*rugby*). Repeat the procedure with different pupils.

Set learning outcomes and use the talk cards.

- Say **Today we're going to investigate New Zealand.**
- Point to the talk cards to show the pupils the different ways they will be working in the lesson.

Pupil's Book Activity 1

Read Luke's questions. What do you think?

- Read the speech bubble as a class.
- Encourage the class to tell you what they know about New Zealand. Show the pupils where New Zealand is on an online world map.
- Read the questions. The pupils predict the answers.

Pupil's Book Activity 2

Read and listen. Answer Luke's questions.

▶ *CD3 Track 20 p274*

- Focus the class on the photos. Ask **What can you see in the photos?**
- The pupils read the text. If you want them to read the text without the support of the CD, set a time limit. Otherwise, play the CD, pausing after each paragraph to check understanding.
- The pupils answer Luke's questions.

Answers: **1** You can do bungee jumping. **2** You can do rafting. **3** You can do zorbing. **4** You can do sand surfing.

Think about your culture

- Read out the question and prompt different pupils to answer. Suggestions might include skiing, kayaking, snowboarding, rafting or rock climbing.

Activity Book

Activity 1

Listen and write the equipment you need.

▶ *CD3 Track 21 p274*

- Say the sports equipment as a class.
- Play the CD, pausing after the first exchange to check pupils' understanding and to allow them to write the equipment needed.
- Repeat the procedure with the other exchanges.

Answers: **1** helmet, harness, rope **2** helmet, harness **3** wetsuit, helmet, paddle, life jacket **4** surfboard, helmet

Activity 2

Explore the Internet with your teacher. Do the New Zealand web quest.

- Read out the instructions for the activity.
- Connect to a children's website (see suggested websites opposite) that provides geographical information about New Zealand. Read out questions 1–4. The pupils work as a class to find and write the answers. They should also colour the flag.
- Read out question 5. Connect to a website that shows the weather around the world. The pupils complete the information about the day's weather.

Answers: **1** two **2** Aoraki / Mount Cook **3** Wellington **4** red, white and blue

Activity 3

Find out more. Investigate more outdoor activities that you can do in New Zealand. What's the most popular sport in New Zealand?

- Tell the pupils that they are going to investigate more outdoor activities in New Zealand and find out the most popular sport.
- If you are doing the investigation as a class, go to a suitable website, e.g. Kids National Geographic, and ask the pupils to scan the information to find the answers.
- If you are working in a computer room, organise the class into small groups. The groups should go to the site and find the answer.

Answer: Rugby is the most popular sport in New Zealand.

Suggested websites

http://maps.google.es/
http://kids.nationalgeographic.com
http://www.bbc.co.uk/weather

Code activity

- The pupils complete the code activity.

Answer: squid

Ending the lesson

Review the lesson and reflect on learning.

- Say **Today we've learnt about New Zealand. Is it an interesting place? What can you see and do there?** Elicit the information from the pupils.
- Ask **Which was your favourite activity today? Which activity was easy / difficult?**

Go to the AB Unit Review on page 253.

Key Competences and Key Learning Outcomes

- Watch and understand a video about doing extreme sports
- Identify ways to stay safe when doing sport
- Reflect on personal safety in sports

Key language

- *bungee jump, caving, gloves, goggles, harness, helmet, knee pads, life jacket, mountain biking, rafting, rock climbing, rope, skateboarding, torch, zorbing*
- *You must (wear a helmet). You need a (torch in the cave). What do you do to stay safe?*

Materials

- Pupil's Book p69; Activity Book p67; Class CD3; Teacher's App on Navio
- Sports equipment flashcards
- Teacher's Resource Bank: Talk cards

Optional materials

- Teacher's Resource Bank: Trinity Exams Practice cards (selected from the Starter Unit and Units 1, 2, 3, 4 and 5)

At a Glance Lesson Plan

Pupil's Book

Starting the lesson

- Use the Trinity Exams Practice cards (optional).
- **Think-Pair-Share.** Review sports equipment vocabulary.
- Set learning outcomes and use the talk cards.

Activity 1

- Before you watch
- Watch the video.
  Unit 6 video p285
- Which of these objects do you see? Which sport uses them?

Activity 2

- Watch the video again.
  Unit 6 video
- Read and say *true* or *false*.
- Correct the false sentences.

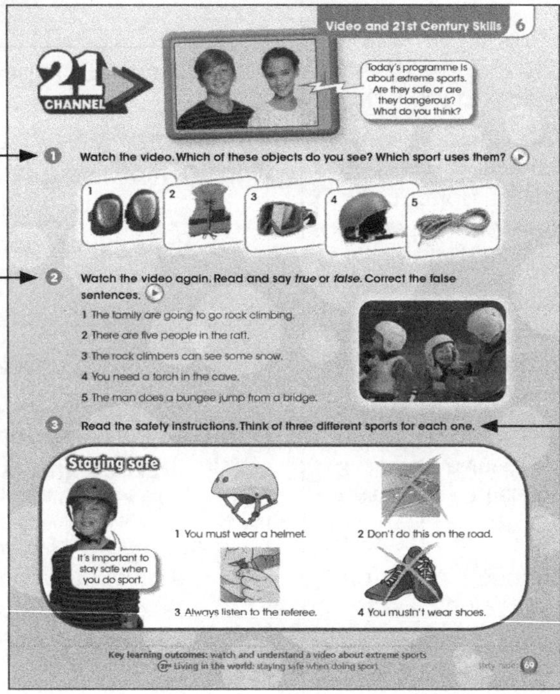

Activity 3

- Read the safety instructions.
- Think of three different sports for each one.
  Go to the Activity Book.

Ending the lesson

- Review the lesson and reflect on learning.

Extra activity

Reinforcement

- Play a guessing game.

Activity Book

Activity Book

Activity 1

- Look and write.
- Listen and check.
- ▶ *CD3 Track 22 p274*
- Repeat.

Activity 2

- Listen and complete the notes.
- ▶ *CD3 Track 23 p274*

Activity 3

- Read and answer.
- Ask and answer.

Digital resources

Teacher's Digital: You can also teach this lesson using the Teacher's App on Navio.

Pupil's Digital: Encourage your pupils to use the Pupil's App on Navio to practise the activities from this lesson.

Powered By NAVIO

Starting the lesson

Use the Trinity Exams Practice cards (optional).

- The pupils practise asking and answering questions.

Think-Pair-Share. Review sports equipment vocabulary.

- Ask **Can you remember the sports equipment vocabulary?** The class thinks silently for a minute.
- Then the pupils work with a Talk Partner to name the sports equipment.
- Invite different Talk Partners to say a different item. Hold up the corresponding flashcard and prompt the class to repeat the word.
- Finally, repeat the procedure, asking different pairs of Talk Partners each time, until all the sports equipment has been named.
- Introduce the extension vocabulary *knee pads* and *goggles* which will be used in the video pages.

Set learning outcomes and use the talk cards.

- Say **Today we're going to watch a video and then ask and answer questions about extreme sports.**
- Point to the talk cards to show the pupils the different ways they will be working in the lesson.

Pupil's Book Activity 1

Before you watch

- Read the speech bubble to pupils. Ask **Which extreme sports can you name?** Elicit responses from a number of pupils. Talk about whether pupils think that these sports are safe or dangerous.

Watch the video. Which of these objects do you see? Which sport uses them? *p285*

- Watch Part 1. Ask pupils **What are you going to see next?** Check that they understand that they will see lots of short video clips about different extreme sports.
- Play Part 2. Ask general questions to check understanding. Focus the pupils' attention on the photos in Activity 1. Say **Which of these objects do you see in the video?** Elicit ideas.
- Play Part 2 again for the pupils to answer the questions. Check answers as a class.

Answers: **1** skateboarding **2** rafting **3** not in video **4** rafting, rock climbing, caving, skateboarding **5** rock climbing, bungee jumping

Pupil's Book Activity 2

Watch the video again. Read and say *true* or *false*. Correct the false sentences.

- Explain that you are going to do a true or false activity.
- Ask a pupil to read out sentence 1. Ask the class whether they think the sentence is true or false. Repeat with sentences 2–5.
- Play Part 2. Students work in pairs to decide whether the sentences are true or false. They correct the false sentences.

Answers: **1** F The family are going to go rafting. **2** F There are seven people in the raft. **3** T **4** T **5** T

Pupil's Book Activity 3

Read the safety instructions. Think of three different sports for each one.

- Tell pupils that in the last part of the video Chloe and Mark talk about having the correct equipment to stay safe when doing sport. Ask **What activity is Chloe going to do?** (*Skateboarding.*) **What safety equipment does she use?** (*Helmet, gloves, knee pads.*) Ask pupils if they can think of any other safety equipment (*goggles*, *elbow pads*) or safety instructions (*don't skateboard on the road*) that could be used when skateboarding.
- Explain that pupils are going to read some safety instructions and have to think of three different sports for each instruction. Read the instructions with the class and check vocabulary.
- Pupils work in pairs to think of different sports. Collate ideas on the board and see how many sports you can come up with for each safety instruction.

Activity Book

Activity 1

Look and write. Listen and check. Repeat.

▶ *CD3 Track 22 p274*

- Look at the words in the box and check vocabulary.
- Pupils work on their own to match the safety instructions to the pictures.
- Play the CD and check answers.

Answers: **1** wear sun cream **2** warm up **3** drink plenty of water **4** follow the rules **5** wear knee pads **6** wear goggles

Activity 2

Listen and complete the notes.

▶ *CD3 Track 23 p274*

- Explain to the pupils that they are going to listen to the safety rules at a skateboarding class. Ask pupils for ideas of possible rules. Read out the information. Then play the CD, pausing to allow the pupils to write the missing information.
- Play the CD again without pausing.

Answers: **1** helmet **2** gloves **3** knees **4** road **5** bike

- Ask pupils what they think the most important rule is. Can they give a reason why?

Activity 3

Read and answer. Ask and answer.

- Read out the speech bubble. Ask the three questions to one pupil (or three different pupils). Establish a model for the answers required.
- The pupils write answers to the questions about how they stay safe when doing sport.
- Organise the pupils into Talk Partners. The pupils take it in turns to ask and answer questions.

Ending the lesson

Review the lesson and reflect on learning.

- Say **Today we've watched a video about extreme sports. What equipment can we use to stay safe when doing sport?** Elicit the information from the pupils.
- Ask **Which was your favourite activity today? Which activity was easy / difficult?**

Extra activity

Reinforcement

- Think of an extreme sport. Say **I'm wearing a helmet and a life jacket. I'm wearing a wetsuit. I must hold the paddle tight. What am I doing?** The pupils guess *Are you rafting?* Repeat with different sports.
- The pupils play the game in pairs.

My project 2: Treasure islands

Key Competences and Key Learning Outcomes

- Remember and learn the names of natural and man-made things on an island
- Talk about the local landscape (optional)
- Use the Internet to find out about an island
- Share information with your group
- Identify islands in your country

Key language

- Natural and man-made things on an island: *bay, beach, bridge, cave, cliffs, coast, island, jungle, lake, lighthouse, man-made, natural, port, pyramid, river, rocks, treasure, village, volcano, waterfall*
- *Where's (Hawaii)? It's in (the Pacific Ocean). What's it like? There are (lots of beaches). There's (a jungle). It's (beautiful).*

Materials

- Pupil's Book p70; Activity Book p68; Class CD3
- Teacher's Resource Bank: Talk cards

Optional materials

- Teacher's Resource Bank: Trinity Exams Practice cards (selected from the Starter Unit and Units 1, 2, 3, 4, 5 and 6)
- An online world map
- Computers

At a Glance Lesson Plan

Pupil's Book

Starting the lesson

- Use the Trinity Exams Practice cards (optional).
- Set learning outcomes and use the talk cards.

Investigate: Activity 1

- Are there any islands in your country?
- Where are they?
- How can you travel there?

Investigate: Activity 2

- Work in groups of three.
- Look at the map and make lists.
- Where's the treasure?

Activity 3

- Listen and check your lists.
- ▶ *CD3 Track 24 p274*
- Listen again and repeat the words.

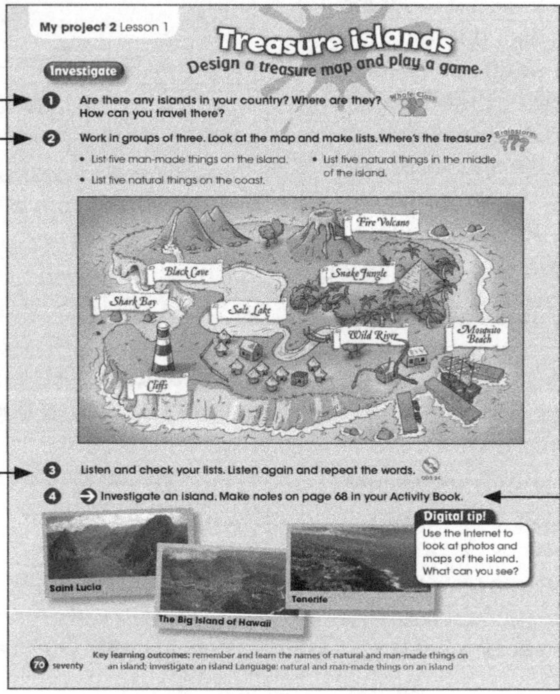

Activity 4

- Investigate an island.
- Make notes on page 68 in your Activity Book.

Go to the Activity Book.

Ending the lesson

- Review the lesson and reflect on learning.

Extra activity

Extension

- Use the Internet to investigate the islands further.

Link to Science

- **Landscapes:** Talk about the local landscape.

Activity Book

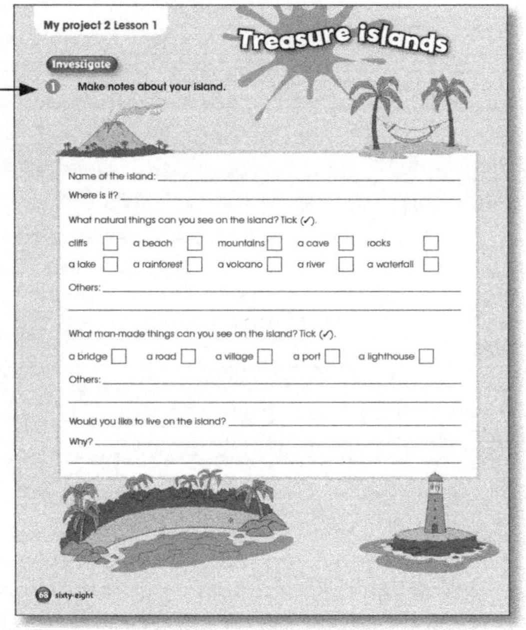

Activity Book

Activity 1

- Make notes about your island.

Digital resources

Teacher's Digital: You can also teach this lesson using the Teacher's App on Navio.

Pupil's Digital: Encourage your pupils to use the Pupil's App on Navio to practise the activities from this lesson.

Powered By NAVIO

Starting the lesson

Use the Trinity Exams Practice cards (optional).

- The pupils practise asking and answering questions.

Set learning outcomes and use the talk cards.

- Say **Today we're going to begin another project.**
- Point to the talk cards to show the pupils the different ways they will be working in the lesson.
- Focus the pupils' attention on the challenge at the top of Pupil's Book page 70. Read the text.

Investigate: Pupil's Book Activity 1

Are there any islands in your country? Where are they? How can you travel there?

- Read out the questions to be discussed as a class. Encourage the pupils to name the islands in their country. Prompt the class to give more information by asking **Have you been to one of the islands? How did you travel there? What did you see?**

Investigate: Pupil's Book Activity 2

Work in groups of three. Look at the map and make lists. Where's the treasure?

- Focus the class on the map of the island and ask **What can you see?**
- Read out the three tasks, check understanding and prompt the class to find examples.
- Organise the class into groups of three and ask each group to choose a scribe to write the lists in his / her notebook. Set a time limit for the groups to list items that appear on the map.
- At the end of the time, prompt different groups to read out their lists. Write the words on the board and give the pupils the names of any unknown items.

Suggested answers: Man-made things on the island: a bridge, a pyramid, a village, a port, a lighthouse
Natural things in the middle of the island: a lake, a jungle, a volcano, a river, a waterfall
Natural things on the coast: a bay, a beach, cliffs, a cave, rocks

Pupil's Book Activity 3

Listen and check your lists. Listen again and repeat the words.

▶ *CD3 Track 24 p274*

- Pupils listen and check their lists. Then they listen again and repeat the words.

Pupil's Book Activity 4

Investigate an island. Make notes on page 68 in your Activity Book.

- The pupils can do this as a whole-class activity or in groups.
- Ask the pupils to describe what they can see in the photos. Point out that these islands are in different parts of the world. If possible, students can use the Internet to find pictures of islands as per the Digital tip.
- Organise the class back into their groups of three and ask them to decide which island each group member is going to investigate.

Activity Book

Activity 1

Make notes about your island.

- Ask a pupil to read the information. Check understanding.
- If you do the investigation as a whole-class activity, use an online map to explore each island in turn. You can look at satellite photos to explore the natural and man-made features of the island's landscape. The whole class can talk about what you can see, but only the pupils who have been allocated this island should make notes.
- If you have access to several computers, organise the class so that the pupils who are investigating the same island are working together. Give each group the link to the online map and ask them to make notes. http://maps.google.es/

Ending the lesson

Review the lesson and reflect on learning.

- Say **We've learnt about islands. Which island did you investigate? What can you remember?** Elicit the pupils' answers.
- Ask **Which was your favourite activity? Which activity was easy / difficult?**

Extra activity

Extension

- Ask the pupils to use the Internet to investigate their islands further. The pupils should find the names of the biggest town, rivers, lakes, mountains and forests.

Link to Science

- If you are studying the Science topic of **Landscapes** in English, talk about the landscape where you live. Encourage the class to identify the different natural and man-made features in their environment.

My project 2: Treasure islands

Key Competences and Key Learning Outcomes

- Remember and learn the names of natural and man-made things on an island
- Present your treasure map to other pupils and play a game
- Reflect on what you've learnt and how you've worked together
- Work together to design an island

Key language

- Recycled: man-made features on an island; natural features on an island; *behind, between, in, in front of, on, under*
- *Let's (hide the treasure). I think we should (have a lighthouse). I agree. You're right. That's a good idea, but how about (having a waterfall)? Which do you prefer? I prefer (this treasure map). Is the treasure (behind the waterfall)? Yes, it is. No, it isn't.*

Materials

- Pupil's Book p71; Activity Book p69
- Teacher's Resource Bank: Talk cards
- A large piece of paper or card for each group of three pupils; coloured pens and pencils

Optional materials

- Teacher's Resource Bank: Trinity Exams Practice cards (selected from the Starter Unit and Units 1, 2, 3, 4, 5 and 6)

At a Glance Lesson Plan

Pupil's Book

Starting the lesson

- Use the Trinity Exams Practice cards (optional).
- Set learning outcomes and use the talk cards.

Plan and create your project: Activity 1

- Discuss the questions.
- Write the information on page 69 in your Activity Book.

Go to the Activity Book.

Cooperative learning

- Listen to and respect everyone's opinion.

Activity 2

- Draw your treasure map and hide your treasure.

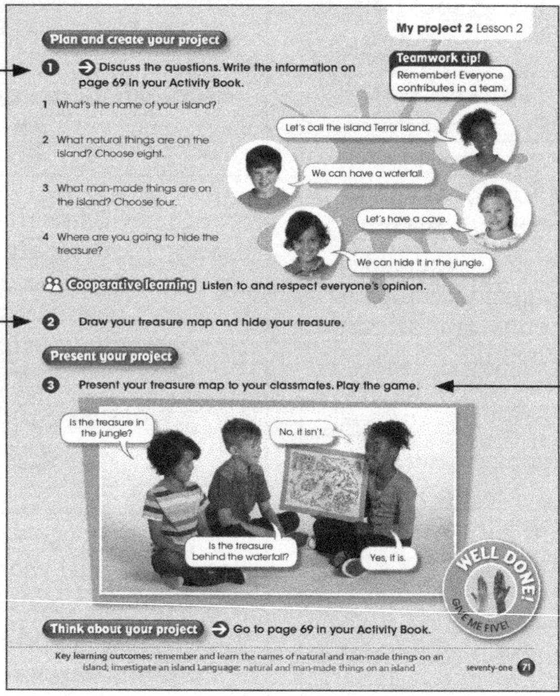

My project 2 Lesson 2

Plan and create your project

1 Discuss the questions. Write the information on page 69 in your Activity Book.

1 What's the name of your island?

2 What natural things are on the island? Choose eight.

3 What man-made things are on the island? Choose four.

4 Where are you going to hide the treasure?

Teamwork tip! Remember! Everyone contributes in a team.

Cooperative learning Listen to and respect everyone's opinion.

2 Draw your treasure map and hide your treasure.

Present your project

3 Present your treasure map to your classmates. Play the game.

Think about your project Go to page 69 in your Activity Book.

Key learning outcomes: remember and learn the names of natural and man-made things on an island; investigate an island Language: natural and man-made things on an island

seventy-one 71

Present your project: Activity 3

- Present your treasure map to your classmates.
- Play the game.
- Think about your project

Go to the Activity Book.

Ending the lesson

- Review the lesson and reflect on learning.

Extra activity

Reinforcement

- Write a description of your island.

Activity Book

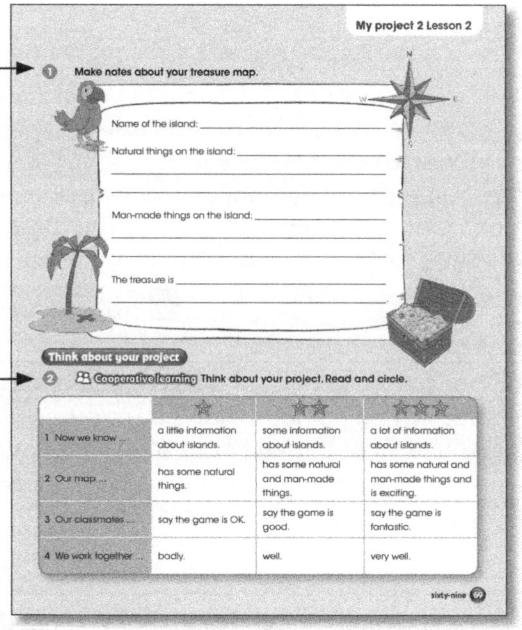

My project 2 Lesson 2

1 Make notes about your treasure map.

Name of the island: ______

Natural things on the island: ______

Man-made things on the island: ______

The treasure is ______

Think about your project

2 Cooperative learning Think about your project. Read and circle.

	☆	☆☆	☆☆☆
1 Now we know ...	a little information about islands.	some information about islands.	a lot of information about islands.
2 Our map ...	has some natural things.	has some natural and man-made things.	has some natural and man-made things and is exciting.
3 Our classmates ...	say the game is OK.	say the game is good.	say the game is fantastic.
4 We work together ...	badly.	well.	very well.

sixty-nine 69

Activity Book

Activity 1

- Make notes about your treasure map.

Think about your project: Activity 2

- Think about your project.
- Read and circle.

Digital resources

Teacher's Digital: You can also teach this lesson using the Teacher's App on Navio.

Pupil's Digital: Encourage your pupils to use the Pupil's App on Navio to practise the activities from this lesson.

Powered By NAVIO

Starting the lesson

Use the Trinity Exams Practice cards (optional).

- The pupils practise asking and answering questions.

Set learning outcomes and use the talk cards.

- Say **Today we're going to continue the project.** Prompt the class to tell you what they did in the last lesson.
- Point to the talk cards to show the pupils the different ways they will be working in the lesson.
- Highlight that the pupils will be working in small groups and prompt the class to tell you what they must do when they work in groups: *listen, take turns, respect different opinions,* etc.

Plan and create your project: Pupil's Book Activity 1

Discuss the questions. Write the information on page 69 in your Activity Book.

- Invite a pupil to read out the text. Highlight the two structures for making suggestions: *Let's … We can …* Encourage the pupils to use these structures to make suggestions as a class.
- Organise the class into their groups of three from the previous lesson. Explain that the pupils should work in their groups to decide on a name for their island, eight natural things on their island, four man-made things on their island, and a place to hide the treasure. They should record this information in their Activity Books.
- If pupils need more support with this activity, ask the groups to do one task at a time. Offer suggestions to help with the first task. Then move on to the second task and third task. Before the pupils do the fourth task, review the prepositions of place that the pupils know and write them on the board: *in, on, under, between, in front of, behind.*

Activity Book

Activity 1

Make notes about your treasure map.

- The pupils record their decisions about their island.

Cooperative learning

Listen to and respect everyone's opinion.

- Read out the rubric. Discuss with the class ways in which we can show respect for each others' opinions.
- Emphasise the importance of being polite and listening carefully to others.

Pupil's Book Activity 2

Draw your treasure map and hide your treasure.

- Hand out a large piece of card or paper to each group. The pupils work as a group to design their island and draw their treasure map. Tell the pupils that they mustn't draw the treasure on their map.

Present your project: Pupil's Book Activity 3

Present your treasure map to your classmates. Play the game.

- Reorganise the groups by asking two pupils in each group to stand up. Each pair should move to the next group and sit down. The treasure map should stay with the pupil who hasn't moved. Remind the pupil with the map that the location of the treasure is a secret and is written in their Activity Book.
- Focus the class on the photo and ask **What are the children doing? What can you see on the island?** Then ask three pupils to read out the speech bubbles.
- The pupil with the map shows it to the new pair and explains the different features. The pair then have ten attempts to guess where the treasure is. Invite a group to demonstrate.
- Regroup the pupils and play again. Find out how many pairs managed to find the treasure.
- If you wish, ask the class to vote on which treasure map is the best. Explain that the pupils can only vote for one treasure map and they can't vote for their own. Say the name of each map in turn and ask the pupils to raise their hands if they think that map is the best.

Think about your project

- Tell the pupils that they are now going to think about what they have achieved and evaluate how their project went. Ask the pupils to turn to page 69 in their Activity Book.

Activity Book

Activity 2: Think about your project

Read and circle.

- Explain that the pupils are now going to think about how they've worked as a group. Read out each statement and ask the pupils to circle one, two or three stars depending on their project.

Ending the lesson

Review the lesson and reflect on learning.

- Say **We've completed a project about treasure islands.** Ask **Would you like to live on an island?**
- Ask **Which was your favourite activity? Which activity was easy / difficult?**

Extra activity

Reinforcement

- Ask the pupils to write a short description of their island. They can do this in groups or on their own.

Date: ______________ Unit: ______________

1 What did my pupils learn in this unit?

2 How did my pupils work? (✓)

individually ☐ in pairs ☐ in small groups ☐

in large groups ☐ as a class ☐

3 Which key competences did my pupils develop?

- Competence in linguistic communication ☐
- Competence in mathematics, science and technology ☐
- Digital competence ☐
- Learning to learn ☐
- Social and civic competences ☐
- Sense of initiative and entrepreneurship ☐
- Cultural awareness and expression ☐

4 Which lessons / activities were the most successful and why?

5 Which lessons / activities did my pupils find the most difficult and why?

6 What did I try in the classroom for the first time? How did it go?

7 Which resources did I find most useful? (including webpages)

8 What could I do differently next time I teach this unit?

7 Detectives

Unit overview

Key Competences and Key Learning Outcomes

- Identify and name household objects (Lesson 1)
- Say the vocabulary chant (Lesson 1)
- Understand and act out a conversation (Lesson 2)
- Use the past tense with 'was' / 'were' (Lessons 2 and 4)
- Follow, complete and correct the grammar tables (Lessons 2 and 4)
- Learn names of personal belongings (Lesson 4)
- Use exclamation marks (Lesson 7)
- Watch and understand a video (Video and 21st Century Skills)
- Practise memory skills in a game (Video and 21st Century Skills)

- Use a code to read a message (Lesson 3)

- Use the Pupil's App on Navio
- Investigate Australia (Lesson 8)

- Say a tongue twister, learn another spelling for the 'r' sound and practise spelling (Lesson 5)
- Practise activity types found in the Cambridge Exams: A1 Movers
- Review your own learning (Review)

- Understand the importance of looking after personal belongings (Lesson 3)

- Work with a Talk Partner (all lessons)
- Play a communication game (Lesson 5)

- Sing a song (Lesson 1)
- Understand, act out and give an opinion on a story (Lesson 3)
- Say a chant (Lesson 4)
- Read and evaluate a script (Lesson 6)
- Plan and write a script (Lesson 7)
- Learn about Australia (Lesson 8)
- Think about your own culture (Lesson 8)
- Learn about unusual houses around the world (Video and 21st Century Skills)

Vocabulary

Core vocabulary
armchair, bath, bookcase, cooker, cupboard, fridge, mat, mirror, painting, sink, sofa, wardrobe; bracelet, earrings, keys, sunglasses, umbrella, watch

Extension vocabulary (optional)
bedside table, carpet, coffee table, DVD player, microwave, wash basin; brush, comb, diary, toothbrush

Other vocabulary
characters, investigate, necklace, play, police officer, robber, scene, script; angry, excited, laughing, nervously, shouting, surprised, whispering

Recycled vocabulary
behind, between, in, in front of, near, on, under; bathroom, bedroom, dining room, hall, kitchen, living room; angrily, happily, quietly, sleepily, slowly; boat, book, build, cinema, comic, DVD, garden, golf, home, library, restaurant, school, shiny, shops, shouting, stone, supermarket, swimming pool, town, walls, window, work, wrist, wrong

Structures

Core structures
He was / wasn't (at school) (yesterday). They were / weren't (at the cinema) yesterday. Was the (watch) (on the table)? Yes, it was. No, it wasn't. Were the (earrings) (in the cupboard)? Yes, they were. No, they weren't.

Other structures
What's that (noise)? Is it a (fox)? Hands (up)! (Living underground) is (cooler) than (living above ground). I can't (play in the day) because (it's too hot).

Recycled structures
There's a (mystery). Where's the (mirror)? It's in the (living room). It's (between the door and the book case). They're (on the armchair). It's got (three bedrooms). It hasn't got (a window). There's a (sofa) and an (armchair).

Phonics

The 'r' sound (***R**on **r**obber **wr**ites **r**ed **wr**apper*)

Literacy

Text type: a script (text to entertain; writing preparation)
Reading skills: predicting content from an image
Writing skills: using exclamation marks

Culture ... around the world

An underground town in Australia

21st Century Skills

Paying attention

Thinking skills

Classification (Lesson 1); Applying rules (Lesson 2); Predicting (Lessons 3 and 8); Discussing values (Lesson 3); Expressing opinions (Lesson 3); Remembering (Lesson 4); Sequencing (Lesson 6); Thinking about your culture (Lesson 8); Making connections (Review)

Cooperative learning

Team building (Lesson 2); Collaborating (Lesson 4); Checking learning (Lesson 5); Sharing information (Lesson 5); Peer evaluation and feedback (Lesson 7); Working together (Review)

Values

Understanding the importance of looking after personal belongings

Cross-curricular links

Link to Science
The top layer of Earth: Identifying rocks and minerals.

Suggested Arts and Crafts concepts
Exploring organic (natural) forms and finding organic shapes and forms to make a land art collage

Key Competences and Key Learning Outcomes

- Identify and say household objects
- Say the vocabulary chant
- Review the rooms in a house and objects in each room
- Play a game with a recycled structure
- Sing a song about a mystery

Key language

- Household objects: *armchair, bath, bookcase, cooker, cupboard, fridge, mat, mirror, painting, sink, sofa, wardrobe; detectives, mystery, tracks*
- Extension: *bedside table, carpet, coffee table, DVD player, microwave, wash basin*
- Recycled: *bathroom, bedroom, dining room, hall, kitchen, living room; behind, between, in, in front of, near, on, under; There's a (mystery). Where's the (mirror)? It's in the (living room). It's (between the door and the bookcase). They're (on the armchair).*

Materials

- Pupil's Book p72; Activity Book p70; Class CD3; Teacher's App on Navio
- Teacher's Resource Bank: Household objects word cards
- Household objects flashcards
- Teacher's Resource Bank: Talk cards
- 6 pieces of A4 paper

Optional materials

- Teacher's Resource Bank: Trinity Exams Practice cards (selected from the Starter Unit and Units 1, 2, 3, 4, 5 and 6)

At a Glance Lesson Plan

Starting the lesson

- Use the Trinity Exams Practice cards (optional).
- Review household vocabulary.
- Set learning outcomes and use the talk cards.

Activity 1

- Can you name the rooms in a house?
- List three objects in each room.

Vocabulary presentation

- Present the new vocabulary using the household objects flashcards.

Word cards

- Introduce the spellings of the vocabulary using the household objects word cards.

Activity 2

- Listen, point and say the vocabulary chant.

▶ *CD3 Track 25 p274*

Pupil's Book

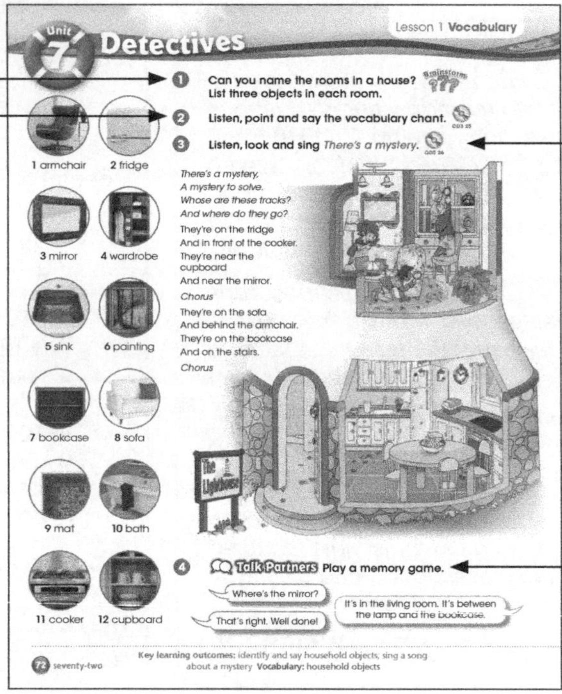

Activity 3

- Listen, look and sing *There's a mystery.*

▶ *CD3 Track 26 p274*

Activity 4

- Play a memory game.
- Go to the Activity Book.

Ending the lesson

- Review the lesson and reflect on learning.

Extra activities

Reinforcement

- Write the new vocabulary in alphabetical order.

Vocabulary extension

- Present six additional vocabulary items.

Digital resources

Teacher's Digital: You can also teach this lesson using the Teacher's App on Navio.

Pupil's Digital: Encourage your pupils to use the Pupil's App on Navio to practise the activities from this lesson.

Powered By NAVIO

Activity Book

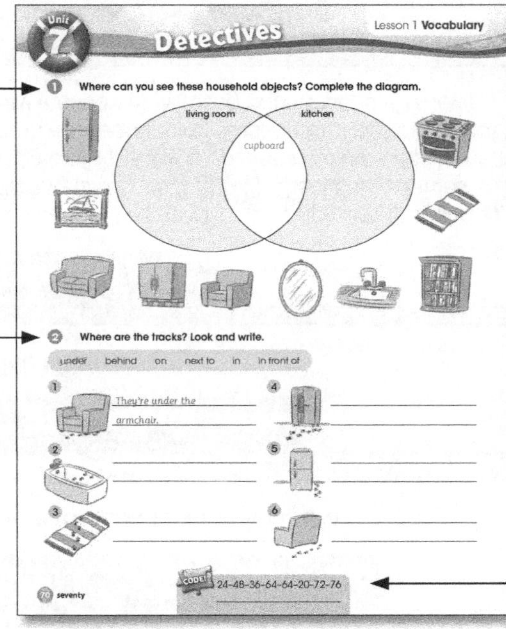

Activity Book

Activity 1

- Where can you see these household objects?
- Complete the diagram.

Activity 2

- Where are the tracks?
- Look and write.

Code activity

- Complete the code activity.

Starting the lesson

Use the Trinity Exams Practice cards (optional).

- The pupils practise asking and answering questions.

Review household vocabulary.

- Draw one line of a house on the board and ask **What am I drawing?** Then draw a bit more of the house, e.g. part of the staircase, part of the chimney, or the doorknob. Encourage the pupils to guess what it is. Finish the drawing and ask the class to name the parts of the house (*walls, chimney*, etc.).

Set learning outcomes and use the talk cards.

- Say **Today we're going to learn the names of household objects.**
- Point to the talk cards to show the pupils the different ways they will be working in the lesson.

Pupil's Book Activity 1

Can you name the rooms in a house? List three objects in each room.

- (Books closed.) Ask the pupils to remember the rooms in a house. Write the words on the board.
- Organise the class into six groups and give each group a piece of paper. Give each group a different room to write at the top of the page. Then give the groups 30 seconds to write three objects you find in that room.
- The groups pass their paper to the next group. The groups should add any other objects they know to the new list. Repeat until this has been done for all six rooms.
- Return the papers to the original groups and ask them to read out their words.

Vocabulary presentation

- (Books closed.) Choose a household objects flashcard without showing the picture. Describe the location and use of the object, e.g. **This is in the living room. Two or three people can sit on it.** (*Sofa.*)
- When the pupils identify the object, tell them the name in English. Stick the flashcard on the board. The pupils repeat the word.

Word cards

- (Books closed.) Hand a household objects word card to each pair of pupils.
- The pairs take turns to come to the board, read out their word and stick their word card next to the corresponding flashcard.

Pupil's Book Activity 2

Listen, point and say the vocabulary chant.

▶ ***CD3 Track 25 p274***

- Focus the pupils' attention on the 12 photos. Say **Let's listen and say the words.** Play the CD. The pupils listen, point and repeat.

Pupil's Book Activity 3

Listen, look and sing *There's a mystery.*

▶ ***CD3 Track 26 p274***

- Focus the pupils' attention on the scene. Ask **Where are Lily, Ravi and Josh?** (*In the living room.*) Say **What's the problem with the room?** (*It's dirty.*) Explain that the children are looking at tracks (marks / footprints left by a human or animal). Ask **Where are the tracks?** Encourage the class to use prepositions of place.
- Say **Let's listen to the song.** Play the CD. The pupils listen and read.
- Ask **What do the children want to know?** (*Whose are the tracks? Where do they go?*)
- Play the CD again. The pupils sing the song.
- Ask the pupils to guess whose tracks they are.

Pupil's Book Activity 4

Play a memory game.

- Ask two pupils to read out the speech bubbles.
- Close your book and prompt a pupil to ask you a question, e.g. *Where's the cooker?* Say **It's next to the cupboard.** Then prompt other pupils to ask similar questions.
- The pupils play the game with a Talk Partner.

Activity Book

Activity 1

Where can you see these household objects? Complete the diagram.

- The pupils name the household objects. Draw the Venn diagram on the board. Invite pupils to stick a flashcard or word card onto the diagram.
- The pupils complete the activity in their books.

Answers: living room: sofa, armchair, bookcase kitchen: fridge, sink, cooker both: cupboard, painting, mirror, mat

Activity 2

Where are the tracks? Look and write.

- A pupil reads the example sentence.
- The pupils write the other sentences.

Answers: **1** They're under the armchair. **2** They're in the bath. **3** They're on the mat. **4** They're in front of the wardrobe. **5** They're next to the fridge. **6** They're behind the sofa.

Code activity

- The pupils complete the code activity.

Answer: flippers

Ending the lesson

Review the lesson and reflect on learning.

- Say **Today we've learnt the names of household objects.** Elicit the objects.
- Ask **Which was your favourite activity today? Which activity was easy / difficult?**

Extra activities

Reinforcement

- The pupils work in pairs to write the new vocabulary in alphabetical order in their notebooks.

Vocabulary extension

- Introduce six additional household items: *bedside table, carpet, coffee table, DVD player, microwave, wash basin.*
- Use the Vocabulary Booster on Navio to practise these new words.

Key Competences and Key Learning Outcomes

- Listen, repeat and act out a conversation
- Listen, follow the grammar table and identify the parts of a sentence
- Use *was* / *wasn't* and *were* / *weren't* in past simple sentences

Key language

- *last night / week, yesterday afternoon / evening / morning*
- *She was / wasn't (at school) yesterday. You weren't (at the cinema) yesterday. Whose are these (tracks)?*
- Recycled: *cinema, home, library, school, supermarket, swimming pool, work*

Materials

- Pupil's Book p73; Activity Book p71; Class CD3; Teacher's App on Navio
- Household objects flashcards
- Teacher's Resource Bank: Talk cards

Optional materials

- Teacher's Resource Bank: Trinity Exams Practice cards (selected from the Starter Unit and Units 1, 2, 3, 4, 5 and 6)

At a Glance Lesson Plan

Pupil's Book

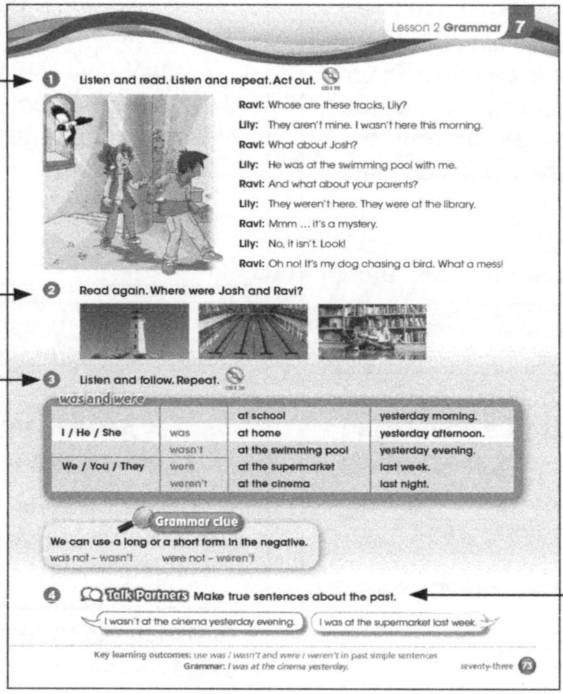
Lesson 2 Grammar 7

1 Listen and read. Listen and repeat. Act out.

Ravi: Whose are these tracks, Lily?
Lily: They aren't mine. I wasn't here this morning.
Ravi: What about Josh?
Lily: He was at the swimming pool with me.
Ravi: And what about your parents?
Lily: They weren't here. They were at the library.
Ravi: Mmm … it's a mystery.
Lily: No, it isn't. Look!
Ravi: Oh no! It's my dog chasing a bird. What a mess!

2 Read again. Where were Josh and Ravi?

3 Listen and follow. Repeat.

was and were

		at school	yesterday morning.
I / He / She	was	at home	yesterday afternoon.
	wasn't	at the swimming pool	yesterday evening.
We / You / They	were	at the supermarket	last week.
	weren't	at the cinema	last night.

Grammar clue
We can use a long or a short form in the negative.
was not – wasn't were not – weren't

4 Talk Partners Make true sentences about the past.

I wasn't at the cinema yesterday evening. I was at the supermarket last week.

Key learning outcomes: use was / wasn't and were / weren't in past simple sentences
Grammar: I was at the cinema yesterday.

seventy-three 73

Starting the lesson

- Use the Trinity Exams Practice cards (optional).
- **Think-Pair-Share.** Review vocabulary for household objects.
- Review the *There's a mystery* song.
- ▶ ***CD3 Track 26 p274***
- ▶ ***CD3 Track 27 p275***
- Set learning outcomes and use the talk cards.

Activity 1

- Listen and read.
- Listen and repeat.
- ▶ ***CD3 Track 28 p275***
- Act out.

Activity 2

- Read again.
- Where were Josh and Ravi?

Activity 3

- Listen and follow.
- ▶ ***CD3 Track 29 p275***
- Repeat.
- **Grammar clue:** Read about using a long and a short form in the negative.

Activity 4

- Make true sentences about the past.
- Go to the Activity Book.

Ending the lesson

- Review the lesson and reflect on learning.

Extra activity

Reinforcement

- Play *Two truths and a lie.*

Digital resources

Teacher's Digital: You can also teach this lesson using the Teacher's App on Navio.

Pupil's Digital: Encourage your pupils to use the Pupil's App on Navio to practise the activities from this lesson.

Powered By NAVIO

Activity Book

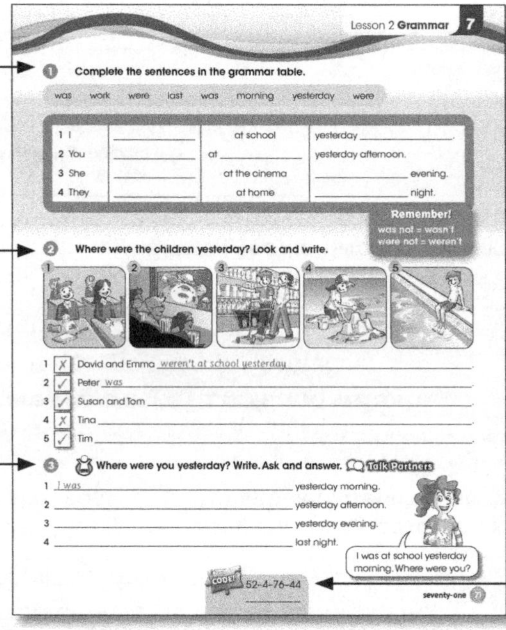
Lesson 2 Grammar 7

1 Complete the sentences in the grammar table.

was work were last was morning yesterday were

1 I		at school	yesterday ___
2 You		at ___	yesterday afternoon.
3 She		at the cinema	___ evening.
4 They		at home	___ night.

Remember!
was not = wasn't
were not = weren't

2 Where were the children yesterday? Look and write.

1 ✗ David and Emma weren't at school yesterday
2 ✓ Peter was
3 ✓ Susan and Tom
4 ✗ Tina
5 ✓ Tim

3 Where were you yesterday? Write. Ask and answer. Talk Partners

1 I was ___ yesterday morning.
2 ___ yesterday afternoon.
3 ___ yesterday evening.
4 ___ last night.

I was at school yesterday morning. Where were you?

CODE 52-4-76-44

seventy-one 71

Activity Book

Activity 1

- Complete the sentences in the grammar table.

Activity 2

- Where were the children yesterday?
- Look and write.

Activity 3

- Where were you yesterday?
- Write.
- Ask and answer.

Code activity

- Complete the code activity.

Starting the lesson

Use the Trinity Exams Practice cards (optional).

- The pupils practise asking and answering questions.

Think-Pair-Share. Review vocabulary for household objects.

- Ask **Can you remember the vocabulary for household objects?** The class thinks silently for a minute.
- Then the pupils work with a Talk Partner to name the household objects.
- Invite Talk Partners to say a different household object. Hold up the corresponding flashcard and prompt the class to repeat the word.
- Repeat the procedure, asking different Talk Partners each time, until all the household objects have been named.

Review the *There's a mystery* song.

▶ *CD3 Track 26 p274*

▶ *CD3 Track 27 p275 (optional karaoke version)*

- Ask the pupils to open their Pupil's Books at page 72 again. Remind them about the tracks, then play the CD. The pupils sing along and point to the objects.

Set learning outcomes and use the talk cards.

- Say **Today we're going to remember / learn how to talk about the past.** Quickly check the concept by asking **What day is it today? What day was it yesterday?**
- Point to the talk cards to show the pupils the different ways they will be working in the lesson.

Pupil's Book Activity 1

Listen and read. Listen and repeat. Act out.

▶ *CD3 Track 28 p275*

- The pupils look at the picture. Ask **Where are Lily and Ravi? What do you think they are talking about?**
- Play the CD. The pupils listen and read the conversation.
- Confirm that they are talking about the tracks. Ask **Whose are the tracks?** (*They are Ravi's dog's tracks, chasing a bird.*)
- Play the CD again, pausing after each sentence for the pupils to repeat.
- The pupils act out the conversation in pairs.

Pupil's Book Activity 2

Read again. Where were Josh and Ravi?

- The pupils read the conversation again and say which picture is correct.

Answer: the second picture

Pupil's Book Activity 3

Listen and follow. Repeat.

▶ *CD3 Track 29 p275*

- Play the CD. The pupils listen to the first sentence and point to the words they hear. They then repeat the complete sentence. Repeat the procedure with the other sentences.
- Model true sentences with the table. Highlight that we can substitute 'he' with 'my brother, dad, friend, teacher' and 'she' with 'my sister, mum, friend, teacher'.

Grammar clue

- Read the grammar clue as a class. The pupils then practise saying 'wasn't' and 'weren't'.

Pupil's Book Activity 4

Make true sentences about the past.

- Organise the class into Talk Partners. They use the grammar table to make more true sentences. They can do this orally or in their notebooks.

Activity Book

Activity 1

Complete the sentences in the grammar table.

- Invite a pupil to read out the words in the word box.
- Remind the pupils of the *Remember!* tip.
- The pupils write the words in the grammar table.

Answers: **1** was, morning **2** were, work **3** was, yesterday **4** were, last

Activity 2

Where were the children yesterday? Look and write.

- Focus the class on the first picture and the cross and elicit that David and Emma weren't at school yesterday. Stress that here we need to use the plural form 'weren't'.
- Repeat the procedure with the second picture.
- The pupils complete the sentences.

Answers: **1** David and Emma weren't at school yesterday. **2** Peter was at the cinema yesterday. **3** Susan and Tom were at the supermarket yesterday. **4** Tina wasn't at the beach yesterday. **5** Tim was at the swimming pool yesterday.

Activity 3

Where were you yesterday? Write. Ask and answer.

- Prompt individual pupils to say where they were yesterday.
- The pupils work on their own to write the sentences.
- The pupils read out their sentences to a Talk Partner.
- Ask the pupils to report to the class if they were in the same place as their Talk Partner yesterday.

Code activity

- The pupils complete the code activity.

Answer: mask

Ending the lesson

Review the lesson and reflect on learning.

- Say **Today we've learnt how to talk about the past. Where were you yesterday?** Elicit the pupils' answers.
- Ask **Which was your favourite activity today? Which activity was easy / difficult?**

Extra activity

Reinforcement

- Play *Two truths and a lie.* Say three sentences about where you were yesterday (two true and one a lie), e.g. **I was at school in the morning. I was at a fair in the afternoon. I was at the sports centre in the evening.** The pupils guess which sentence is a lie.
- The pupils write three sentences about where they were (two true and one a lie). Ask different pupils to read out their sentences for the class to identify the lie.

Key Competences and Key Learning Outcomes
• Read the story with some fluency
• Use a code to read a message
• Do a pre-reading task
• Understand the importance of looking after personal belongings
• Read, listen and understand a story about a mystery • Give an opinion on the story

Key language

- *bracelet, castle, clues, feather, look for, magpie, marbles, missing, mystery, nest, sweet wrapper, watch*
- *Where was it? It was in the (living room). It was (in a magpie's nest in the castle).*
- Recycled: *boat, island, shiny, wardrobe*

Materials

- Pupil's Book pp74–75; Activity Book p72; Class CD3; Teacher's App on Navio
- Teacher's Resource Bank: Talk cards

Optional materials

- Teacher's Resource Bank: Trinity Exams Practice cards (selected from the Starter Unit and Units 1, 2, 3, 4, 5 and 6)

At a Glance Lesson Plan

Pupil's Book

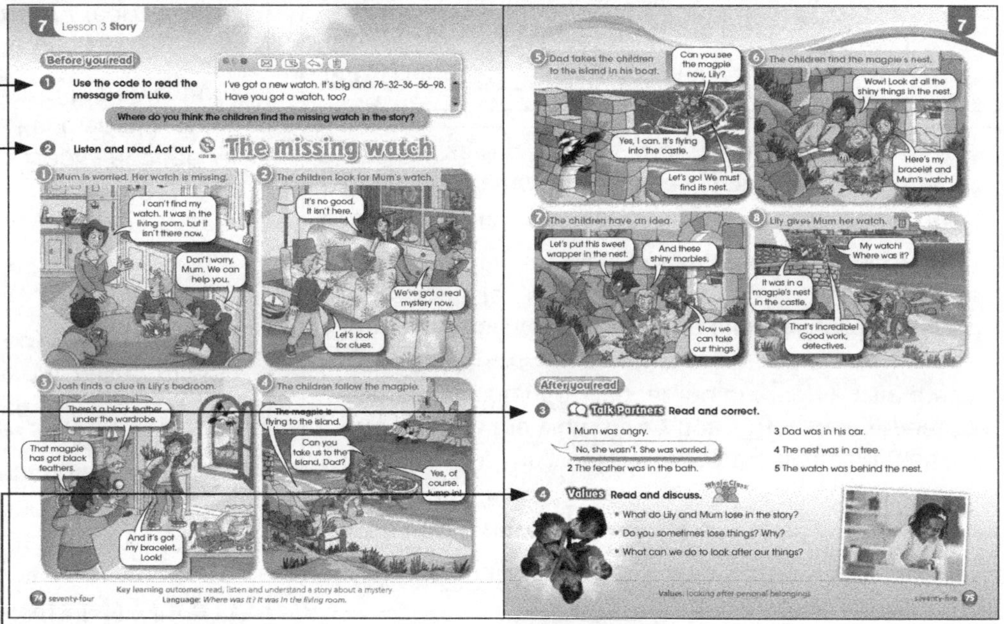

Starting the lesson

- Use the Trinity Exams Practice cards (optional).
- Review the past simple.
- Set learning outcomes and use the talk cards.

Before you read: Activity 1

- Use the code to read the message from Luke.

Activity 2

- Listen and read.
- ▶ *CD3 Track 30 p275*
- Act out.

After you read: Activity 3

- Read and correct.

Activity 4: Values

- Read and discuss.
- Go to the Activity Book.

Ending the lesson

- Review the lesson and reflect on learning.

Extra activity

Reinforcement

- Find the frame.

Activity Book

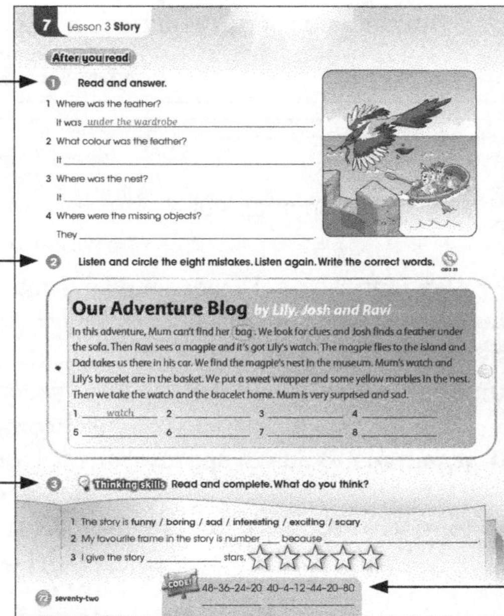

After you read: Activity Book

Activity 1

- Read and answer.

Activity 2

- Listen and circle the eight mistakes.
- ▶ *CD3 Track 31 p275*
- Listen again.
- Write the correct words.

Activity 3

- Read and complete.
- What do you think?

Code activity

- Complete the code activity.

Digital resources

Teacher's Digital: You can also teach this lesson using the Teacher's App on Navio.

Pupil's Digital: Encourage your pupils to use the Pupil's App on Navio to practise the activities from this lesson.

Powered By NAVIO

Starting the lesson

Use the Trinity Exams Practice cards (optional).

- The pupils practise asking and answering questions.

Review the past simple.

- Ask different pupils **Where were you yesterday morning?**
- In pairs, the pupils say where they were yesterday morning / afternoon / evening and last night.

Set learning outcomes and use the talk cards.

- Say **Today we're going to read and listen to a story in English.**
- Point to the talk cards to show the pupils the different ways they will be working in the lesson.

Before you read: Pupil's Book Activity 1

Use the code to read the message from Luke.

- Say **Josh and Lily have received another message from Luke.** Ask the pupils to use the code (Pupil's Book page 7) to discover the mystery word (*shiny*). Then ask the pupils if they have got a watch. Ask different pupils to show and describe their watch.
- Read the title of the story and ask **Where do you think the children find the missing watch in the story?** The pupils make their predictions.

Pupil's Book Activity 2

Listen and read. Act out.

▶ *CD3 Track 30 p275*

- Play the CD. The pupils follow in their books.
- Confirm that the watch was in a magpie's nest in the castle. Then ask questions to check comprehension.

Suggested comprehension questions

- Frame 1: **Where was the watch?** (*In the living room.*)
- Frame 2: **Where do the children look for the watch?** (*In the living room.*) **Do they find it?** (*No.*)
- Frame 3: **What does Josh find in the bedroom?** (*A black feather.*) **Whose is the feather?** (*A magpie's.*) **What has the magpie got?** (*Lily's bracelet.*)
- Frame 4: **Where does the magpie go?** (*To the island.*)
- Frame 5: **Where is the magpie's nest?** (*In the castle.*)
- Frame 6: **What do the children find in the nest?** (*Shiny things.*)
- Frame 7: **What do the children put in the nest?** (*A sweet wrapper and marbles.*) **What do they take out of the nest?** (*Lily's bracelet and Mum's watch.*)
- Frame 8: **How does Mum feel?** (*Happy.*)
- Organise the class into five groups (Lily, Ravi, Josh, Mum and Dad) and play the CD. Each group joins in when their character speaks. If pupils need extra support, pause the CD after each utterance and ask them to repeat it instead.
- Repeat, with groups swapping roles.

After you read: Pupil's Book Activity 3

Read and correct.

- Ask a pupil to read out the first sentence and its correction. The class then identifies the story frame which has this information. (*Frame 1.*)
- In pairs, the pupils correct each sentence. They can do this orally or in their notebooks.

Answers: **1** No, she wasn't. She was worried. **2** No, it wasn't. It was under the wardrobe. **3** No, he wasn't. He was in his boat. **4** No, it wasn't. It was in the castle. **5** No, it wasn't. It was in the nest.

Pupil's Book Activity 4: Values

Read and discuss.

- Read out the questions and discuss them as a class.
- Encourage the class to think about the things they sometimes lose (pencils, coats, toys) and how they feel when they lose something. Then talk about the importance of looking after personal belongings.

After you read: Activity Book

Activity 1

Read and answer.

- Ask different pupils to read out the questions.
- The pupils work on their own or in pairs to write their answers.

Answers: **1** It was under the wardrobe. **2** It was black. **3** It was in the castle. **4** They were in the nest.

Activity 2

Listen and circle the eight mistakes. Listen again. Write the correct words.

▶ *CD3 Track 31 p275*

- Play the CD. The pupils circle the eight mistakes.
- Play the CD again. The pupils write the correct words.

Answers: **1** ~~bag~~ watch **2** ~~sofa~~ wardrobe **3** ~~watch~~ bracelet **4** ~~car~~ boat **5** ~~museum~~ castle **6** ~~basket~~ nest **7** ~~yellow~~ shiny **8** ~~sad~~ happy

Activity 3

Read and complete. What do you think?

- Invite pupils to read out and complete the sentences.
- The pupils complete the task in their Activity Books and then share opinions with a Talk Partner.

Code activity

- The pupils complete the code activity.

Answer: life jacket

Ending the lesson

Review the lesson and reflect on learning.

- Say **Today we've listened to a story about a missing watch. Retell the story as a class.** Say **Let's tell the story together.** Prompt the class by saying **Mum can't find her …** (*watch*). Use mime, gesture and drawings to support the class.
- Ask **Which was your favourite activity today? Which activity was easy / difficult?**

Extra activity

Reinforcement

- Describe what you can see in one of the frames. Say **There are three children. They are looking at a nest. There is a watch in the nest.** The pupils listen and identify the frame (frame 6).

Key Competences and Key Learning Outcomes

- Identify and say personal belongings
- Say a chant
- Follow and correct the grammar tables

- Play a memory game using 'was' / 'were'

Key language
- Personal belongings: *bracelet, earrings, keys, sunglasses, umbrella, watch*
- *Was the (watch on the table)? Yes, it was. No, it wasn't. It was under the desk. Were the (earrings in the cupboard)? Yes, they were. No, they weren't.*
- Extension: *brush, comb, diary, toothbrush*
- Recycled: *box, floor; behind, in, in front of, on, under; armchair, cupboard, fridge, mat, sofa, table; wrist*

Materials
- Pupil's Book p76; Activity Book p73; Class CD3; Teacher's App on Navio
- Teacher's Resource Bank: Talk cards

Optional materials
- Teacher's Resource Bank: Trinity Exams Practice cards (selected from the Starter Unit and Units 1, 2, 3, 4, 5 and 6)

At a Glance Lesson Plan

Pupil's Book

Starting the lesson
- Use the Trinity Exams Practice cards (optional).
- Review the story.
- Set learning outcomes and use the talk cards.

Activity 1
- Listen, point and say.

▶ *CD3 Track 32 p275*

Activity 2
- Listen and say *The memory chant.*

▶ *CD3 Track 33 p275*

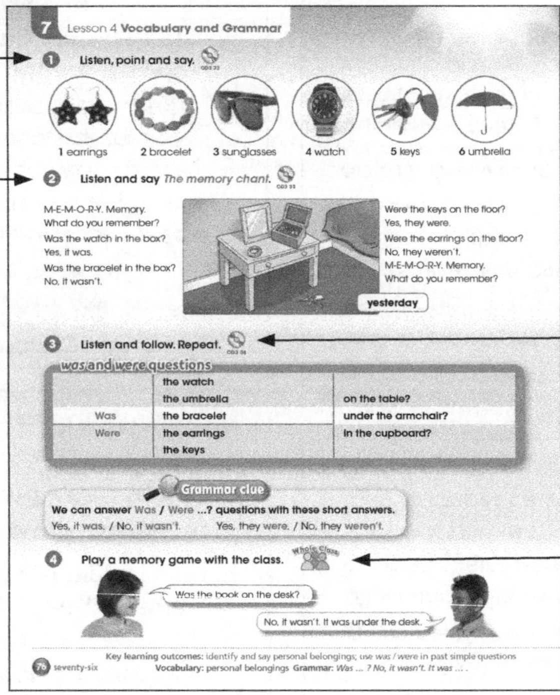
7 Lesson 4 Vocabulary and Grammar

1 Listen, point and say.

1 earrings 2 bracelet 3 sunglasses 4 watch 5 keys 6 umbrella

2 Listen and say *The memory chant.*

M-E-M-O-R-Y. Memory.
What do you remember?
Was the watch in the box?
Yes, it was.
Was the bracelet in the box?
No, it wasn't.

Were the keys on the floor?
Yes, they were.
Were the earrings on the floor?
No, they weren't.
M-E-M-O-R-Y. Memory.
What do you remember?

yesterday

3 Listen and follow. Repeat.

was and *were* questions

	the watch	
	the umbrella	on the table?
Was	the bracelet	under the armchair?
Were	the earrings	in the cupboard?
	the keys	

Grammar clue

We can answer Was / Were ...? questions with these short answers.
Yes, it was. / No, it wasn't. Yes, they were. / No, they weren't.

4 Play a memory game with the class.

Was the book on the desk?

No, it wasn't. It was under the desk.

76 seventy-six

Activity 3
- Listen and follow.

▶ *CD3 Track 34 p275*
- Repeat.
- **Grammar clue:** Read about answering 'Was' / 'Were' questions with short answers.

Activity 4
- Play a memory game with the class.

Go to the Activity Book.

Ending the lesson
- Review the lesson and reflect on learning.

Extra activities

Reinforcement
- Play another memory game.

Vocabulary extension
- Present four additional vocabulary items.

Activity Book

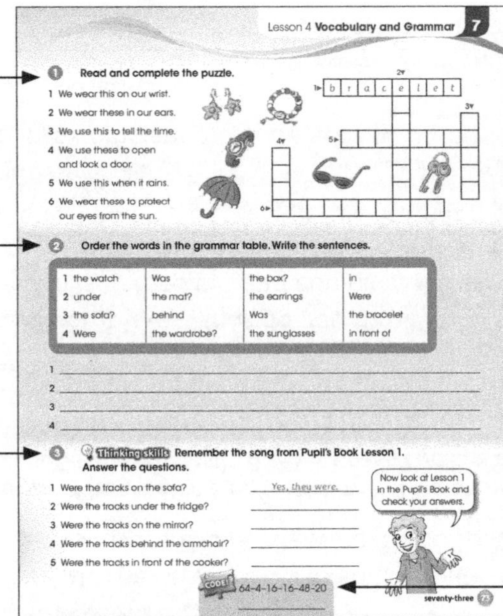
Lesson 4 Vocabulary and Grammar 7

1 Read and complete the puzzle.

1 We wear this on our wrist.
2 We wear these in our ears.
3 We use this to tell the time.
4 We use these to open and lock a door.
5 We use this when it rains.
6 We wear these to protect our eyes from the sun.

b r a c e l e t

2 Order the words in the grammar table. Write the sentences.

1 the watch	Was	the box?	in
2 under	the mat?	the earrings	Were
3 the sofa?	behind	Was	the bracelet
4 Were	the wardrobe?	the sunglasses	in front of

1 ___
2 ___
3 ___
4 ___

3 Thinking skills Remember the song from Pupil's Book Lesson 1. Answer the questions.

1 Were the tracks on the sofa? Yes, they were.
2 Were the tracks under the fridge? ___
3 Were the tracks on the mirror? ___
4 Were the tracks behind the armchair? ___
5 Were the tracks in front of the cooker? ___

Now look at Lesson 1 in the Pupil's Book and check your answers.

Code 64-4-16-16-48-20

seventy-three 73

Activity Book

Activity 1
- Read and complete the puzzle.

Activity 2
- Order the words in the grammar table.
- Write the sentences.

Activity 3
- Remember the song from Pupil's Book Lesson 1.
- Answer the questions.

Code activity
- Complete the code activity.

Digital resources

Teacher's Digital: You can also teach this lesson using the Teacher's App on Navio.

Pupil's Digital: Encourage your pupils to use the Pupil's App on Navio to practise the activities from this lesson.

Powered By NAVIO

Starting the lesson

Use the Trinity Exams Practice cards (optional).

- The pupils practise asking and answering questions.

Review the story.

- Ask the pupils to remember the story from the last lesson. Organise the class into small groups. Ask each group a question about the story. The pupils collaborate before they give the answer.

Set learning outcomes and use the talk cards.

- Say **Today we're going to learn the names of some personal belongings and we're going to practise asking questions about the past.**
- Point to the talk cards to show the pupils the different ways they will be working in the lesson.

Pupil's Book Activity 1

Listen, point and say.

▶ *CD3 Track 32 p275*

- Say **Look at the earrings. What colours are they? Who's wearing earrings today?**
- Repeat the procedure with the other photos, each time encouraging the class to describe the objects and to say whether they are wearing / have got them.
- Play the CD. The pupils listen, point and say.

Pupil's Book Activity 2

Listen and say *The memory chant.*

▶ *CD3 Track 33 p275*

- Ask **Have you got a good memory?** Focus on the picture showing the scene yesterday. Give the pupils one minute to study the picture.
- (Books closed.) Ask questions, e.g. **Was the watch in the box yesterday?** (*Yes.*) **Were the earrings on the floor yesterday?** (*No.*)
- Play the CD. The pupils listen and read the chant.
- Play the CD again. The pupils join in saying the chant.

Pupil's Book Activity 3

Listen and follow. Repeat.

▶ *CD3 Track 34 p275*

- Focus the class on the grammar table. Play the CD. The pupils listen to the first sentence and point to the parts of the sentence in the table. They repeat the complete sentence. Repeat the procedure with the other sentences.

Grammar clue

- Read the grammar clue as a class. Say the four short answers and ask the class to repeat them.

Pupil's Book Activity 4

Play a memory game with the class.

- Invite a pupil to the front of the class and ask him / her to face the wall. Place an object, e.g. a pupil's bag, on your desk. The pupil turns around and asks the class three questions about the object, e.g. *Was the bag under a desk?* The class answers.
- The pupils play the game with a Talk Partner, using objects placed on the desk in front of them.

Activity Book

Activity 1

Read and complete the puzzle.

- Ask pupils to read out the clues and name the objects. They write the words in the puzzle.

Answers: **1** bracelet **2** earrings **3** watch **4** keys **5** umbrella **6** sunglasses

Activity 2

Order the words in the grammar table. Write the sentences.

- Explain that the grammar table is mixed up and that the pupils need to reorder the words. Invite a pupil to read out the first sentence.
- The pupils order and write the remaining sentences. If they need more support, remind them that a sentence begins with a capital letter and ends with a full stop.

Answers: **1** Was the watch in the box? **2** Were the earrings under the mat? **3** Was the bracelet behind the sofa? **4** Were the sunglasses in front of the wardrobe?

Activity 3

Remember the song from Pupil's Book Lesson 1. Answer the questions.

- Tell the pupils to think about the song from Lesson 1. Then ask pupils to read out and answer the questions. If necessary, write the short answers on the board.
- The pupils write the answers.
- The pupils turn to page 72 in the Pupil's Book to check their answers.

Answers: **1** Yes, they were. **2** No, they weren't. **3** No, they weren't. **4** Yes, they were. **5** Yes, they were.

Code activity

- The pupils complete the code activity.

Answer: paddle

Ending the lesson

Review the lesson and reflect on learning.

- Say **Today we've learnt the names of some personal belongings and we've practised asking questions about yesterday.** Elicit the objects and some example questions.
- Ask **Which was your favourite activity today? Which activity was easy / difficult?**

Extra activities

Reinforcement

- Choose a scene in the Pupil's Book, e.g. the opening scene (pp4–5). Ask the class to study it for a minute.
- (Books closed.) Ask questions about the scene, e.g. **Was the motorbike behind the car?** The pupils answer.
- In pairs, the pupils continue asking and answering questions about a scene in the Pupil's Book.

Vocabulary extension

- Use the Vocabulary Booster on Navio and present and practise four additional personal belongings: *brush, comb, diary, toothbrush.*

Key Competences and Key Learning Outcomes

- Say a tongue twister with the 'r' sound
- Practise spelling and learn an alternative spelling for the 'r' sound
- Listen for specific information
- Play a communication game using *was* / *were*

Key language

- *ring, robber, rubbish*
- *Where was the (book) yesterday? It was (on the table). Where were the (sunglasses) yesterday? They were (on the bookcase).*
- Recycled: *armchair, book, bookcase, cupboard, mat, mirror, painting, sofa; bracelet, comic, DVD, earrings, keys, mobile phone, rabbit, radio, red, restaurant, rope, sunglasses, table, umbrella, watch, wrapper, wrist, write, wrong*

Materials

- Pupil's Book p77; Activity Book p74; Class CD3; Teacher's App on Navio
- Teacher's Resource Bank: Talk cards
- Teacher's Resource Bank: Unit 7 Lesson 5 Communication Activity

Optional materials

- Teacher's Resource Bank: Trinity Exams Practice cards (selected from the Starter Unit and Units 1, 2, 3, 4, 5 and 6)
- Approximately ten different objects or the household objects flashcards
- A piece of cloth

At a Glance Lesson Plan

Pupil's Book

Starting the lesson

- Use the Trinity Exams Practice cards (optional).
- Review the spelling of vocabulary from Lesson 4.
- Review *The memory chant*.
- ▶ ***CD3 Track 33 p275***
- Set learning outcomes and use the talk cards.

Activity 1: Speak and spell

- Listen, read and say.
- ▶ ***CD3 Track 35 p275***
- Go to the Activity Book.

Activity 2

- Look at the picture.
- Listen to children playing a memory game.
- ▶ ***CD3 Track 36 p275***
- How many answers are correct?

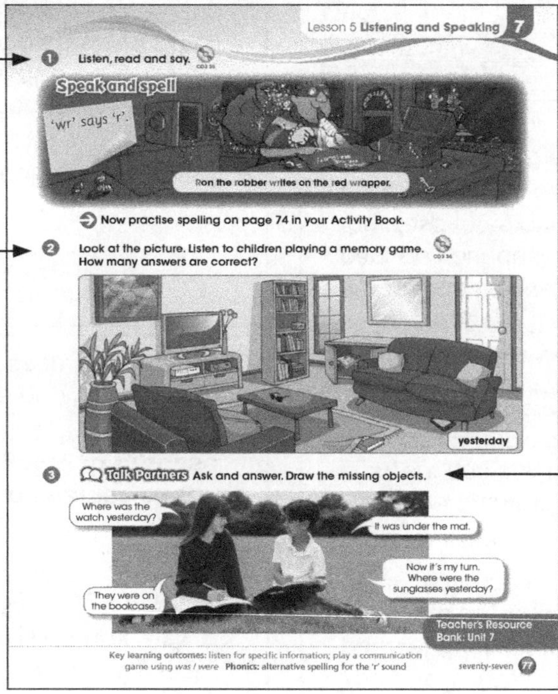

Activity 3

- Ask and answer.
- Draw the missing objects (Teacher's Resource Bank: Unit 7).

Ending the lesson

- Review the lesson and reflect on learning.

Extra activity

Reinforcement

- Play a memory game with different objects or flashcards.

Activity Book

Activity Book

Activity 1: Speak and spell

- Complete and say.

Activity 2

- Find and circle the words.
- Classify and write.

Activity 3

- Test your friend.
- Ask and answer.

Code activity

- Complete the code activity.

Digital resources

Teacher's Digital: You can also teach this lesson using the Teacher's App on Navio.

Pupil's Digital: Encourage your pupils to use the Pupil's App on Navio to practise the activities from this lesson.

Powered By NAVIO

Starting the lesson

Use the Trinity Exams Practice cards (optional).

- The pupils practise asking and answering questions.

Review the spelling of vocabulary from Lesson 4.

- Ask **Which word is this? W-A-T-C-H** (Use the letter names rather than the sounds.) The pupils say the word. Repeat the procedure with the other vocabulary items.
- Ask **How do you spell 'watch'?** Prompt the class to visualise the word and then slowly spell the word back to you. Support the class by writing the letters on the board as the pupils say them. Repeat the procedure with the other items from Lesson 4.

Review *The memory chant*.

▶ *CD3 Track 33 p275*

- Ask the class **How do you spell 'memory'?** Elicit the spelling. Then play the CD. The pupils join in saying the chant.

Set learning outcomes and use the talk cards.

- Say **Today we're going to say a tongue twister, practise spelling and complete a drawing together.**
- Point to the talk cards to show the pupils the different ways they will be working in the lesson.

Pupil's Book Activity 1: Speak and spell

Listen, read and say.

▶ *CD3 Track 35 p275*

- (Books closed.) Write the letter 'r' on the board and ask **What sound does this letter make?** *('r')* List the words the pupils know that begin with this letter. Say **Today you're going to learn another way of writing the 'r' sound.**
- (Books open.) Focus on the picture and ask **Who can you see?** Explain that he is a robber and then ask **What's he doing?** (*Writing.*)
- Say **Let's listen to the tongue twister.** Play the CD. The pupils follow the text in their books.
- Play the CD again. The pupils join in with the tongue twister.
- Finally, ask the class to identify the alternative way of writing the 'r' sound (*'wr'*).

Activity Book

Activity 1: Speak and spell

Complete and say.

- The pupils write the letters and say the tongue twister.

Answer: Ron the robber writes on the red wrapper.

Activity 2

Find and circle the words. Classify and write.

- The pupils find and circle the words in the border which begin with the 'r' sound.
- The pupils classify and write the words according to whether they are spelt with 'r' or 'wr'.

Answers: r: ring, rabbit, restaurant, rope, rubbish
wr: wrist, wrapper, write, wrong

Activity 3

Talk Partners. Test your friend. Ask and answer.

- Invite two pupils to read out the speech bubbles.
- Organise the pupils into Talk Partners. The pupils take it in turns to test their partner on the spelling of the words in Activity 2. Stress the importance of prompting, encouraging and helping each other.

Code activity

- The pupils complete the code activity.

Answer: snorkel

Pupil's Book Activity 2

Look at the picture. Listen to children playing a memory game. How many answers are correct?

▶ *CD3 Track 36 p275*

- Focus the class on the picture and ask the pupils to describe what they can see.
- Explain to the pupils that they are going to listen to two children playing a memory game. The pupils should listen and point to where the children on the CD draw the objects.
- Play the CD, pausing after the first exchange to confirm where the object was yesterday. Repeat the procedure with the other exchanges.

Answer: two (**1** sunglasses: on the table **2** mobile phone: behind the sofa **3** magazine: under the cupboard **4** book: under the mat **5** earrings: in front of the TV)

Pupil's Book Activity 3

Ask and answer. Draw the missing objects (Teacher's Resource Bank: Unit 7).

- Explain to the pupils that they are going to play the same drawing game with a Talk Partner. Invite two pupils to read out the speech bubbles.
- Organise the class into pairs. Check that the pupils know all the objects that appear above the main picture.
- The pupils take turns to ask and answer the questions and draw the objects in the picture.

Ending the lesson

Review the lesson and reflect on learning.

- Say **Today we've practised a tongue twister.** Elicit the tongue twister from the pupils.
- Ask **Which was your favourite activity today? Which activity was easy / difficult?**

Extra activity

Reinforcement

- Place approximately ten objects on your desk. Alternatively, use the household objects flashcards. Give groups of pupils one minute to come and look at the objects before covering them with a piece of cloth. The groups try to remember all the items that are on the desk and write sentences: *There was a (clock) / an (orange). There were some (pens).*

Key Competences and Key Learning Outcomes

- Do a pre-reading task to predict content
- Read the text for general understanding
- Apply learning: read, complete and act out another script

- Read and understand a script

Key language
- *characters, diamond, investigate, nervously, police officer*
- *What's (the problem)? Where (was it?) It (was) (on the table).*
- Recycled: *missing, necklace, robber, shouting, sofa; angrily, happily, quietly, sleepily, slowly*

Materials
- Pupil's Book p78; Activity Book p75; Class CD3; Teacher's App on Navio
- Teacher's Resource Bank: Talk cards

Optional materials
- Teacher's Resource Bank: Trinity Exams Practice cards (selected from the Starter Unit and Units 1, 2, 3, 4, 5 and 6)
- Teacher's Resource Bank: Household objects word cards

At a Glance Lesson Plan

Pupil's Book

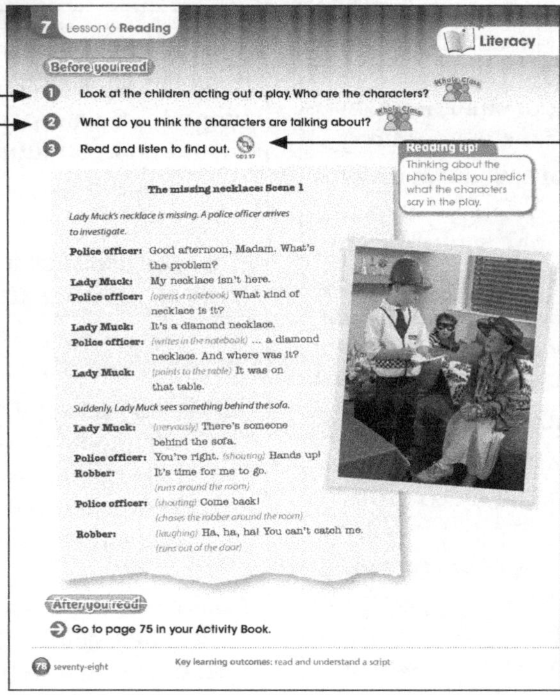
7 Lesson 6 Reading

Literacy

Before you read

1 Look at the children acting out a play. Who are the characters?

2 What do you think the characters are talking about?

3 Read and listen to find out.

Reading tip!
Thinking about the photo helps you predict what the characters say in the play.

The missing necklace: Scene 1

Lady Muck's necklace is missing. A police officer arrives to investigate.

Police officer: Good afternoon, Madam. What's the problem?
Lady Muck: My necklace isn't here.
Police officer: *(opens a notebook)* What kind of necklace is it?
Lady Muck: It's a diamond necklace.
Police officer: *(writes in the notebook)* ... a diamond necklace. And where was it?
Lady Muck: *(points to the table)* It was on that table.

Suddenly, Lady Muck sees something behind the sofa.

Lady Muck: *(nervously)* There's someone behind the sofa.
Police officer: You're right. *(shouting)* Hands up!
Robber: It's time for me to go. *(runs around the room)*
Police officer: *(shouting)* Come back! *(chases the robber around the room)*
Robber: *(laughing)* Ha, ha, ha! You can't catch me. *(runs out of the door)*

After you read

Go to page 75 in your Activity Book.

78 seventy-eight Key learning outcomes: read and understand a script

Starting the lesson
- Use the Trinity Exams Practice cards (optional).
- Review the tongue twister.

▶ *CD3 Track 35 p275*
- Set learning outcomes and use the talk cards.

Before you read: Activity 1
- Look at the children acting out a play.
- Who are the characters?

Before you read: Activity 2
- What do you think the characters are talking about?

Activity 3
- Read and listen to find out.

▶ *CD3 Track 37 p276*

Go to the Activity Book.

Ending the lesson
- Review the lesson and reflect on learning.

Extra activities
Reinforcement
- Continue the playscript from the Activity Book.
- Play *Word dictation.*

Activity Book

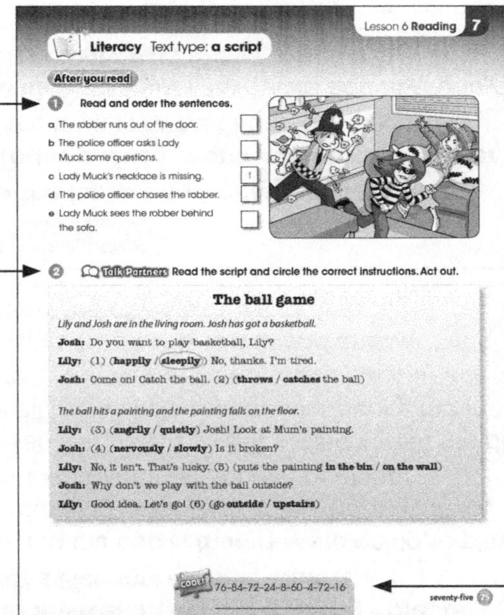
Lesson 6 Reading 7

Literacy Text type: **a script**

After you read

1 Read and order the sentences.

a The robber runs out of the door.
b The police officer asks Lady Muck some questions.
c Lady Muck's necklace is missing. 1
d The police officer chases the robber.
e Lady Muck sees the robber behind the sofa.

2 Talk Partners Read the script and circle the correct instructions. Act out.

The ball game

Lily and Josh are in the living room. Josh has got a basketball.

Josh: Do you want to play basketball, Lily?
Lily: (1) (**happily** / **sleepily**) No, thanks. I'm tired.
Josh: Come on! Catch the ball. (2) (**throws** / **catches** the ball)

The ball hits a painting and the painting falls on the floor.

Lily: (3) (**angrily** / **quietly**) Josh! Look at Mum's painting.
Josh: (4) (**nervously** / **slowly**) Is it broken?
Lily: No, it isn't. That's lucky. (5) (puts the painting **in the bin** / **on the wall**)
Josh: Why don't we play with the ball outside?
Lily: Good idea. Let's go! (6) (go **outside** / **upstairs**)

Code! 76-84-72-24-8-60-4-72-16

seventy-five 75

After you read: Activity Book

Activity 1
- Read and order the sentences.

Activity 2
- Read the script and circle the correct instructions.
- Act out.

Code activity
- Complete the code activity.

Digital resources

Teacher's Digital: You can also teach this lesson using the Teacher's App on Navio.

Pupil's Digital: Encourage your pupils to use the Pupil's App on Navio to practise the activities from this lesson.

Powered By NAVIO

Starting the lesson

Use the Trinity Exams Practice cards (optional).

- The pupils practise asking and answering questions.

Review the tongue twister.

▶ *CD3 Track 35 p275*

- Ask **What sound did you practise in the tongue twister?** (*'r'*)
- Play the CD. Practise the tongue twister as a class.
- Remind the pupils that they know two spellings for this sound ('r' and 'wr'). The pupils list the words they know which begin with these letters.

Set learning outcomes and use the talk cards.

- Say **Today we're going to read a script.** Explain that a script tells actors what they have to say and do. Actors use scripts in films, television programmes and the theatre.
- Point to the talk cards to show the pupils the different ways they will be working in the lesson.

Before you read: Pupil's Book Activity 1

Look at the children acting out a play. Who are the characters?

- Invite a pupil to read out the rubric. The pupils then look at the photo and discuss who the characters might be.

Answers: a police officer, a robber and a woman

Before you read: Pupil's Book Activity 2

What do you think the characters are talking about?

- Ask the pupils to say what they think the three characters are doing and to make predictions about what they are saying.

Pupil's Book Activity 3

Read and listen to find out.

▶ *CD3 Track 37 p276*

- Explain to the pupils that the first time they read they should try to understand the most important information. Then play the CD. The pupils listen and follow in their books.
- The pupils report back about what the characters say.
- Ask the pupils to read the text again without the support of the CD. Set a time limit for this task.

After you read: Activity Book

Activity 1

Read and order the sentences.

- Read out the sentences and ask the pupils to follow in their books. Check understanding if necessary.
- Read out sentence number 1 (c) and then ask the class to identify sentence number 2.
- The pupils work on their own or in pairs to number the remaining sentences.

Answers: **a** 5 **b** 2 **c** 1 **d** 4 **e** 3

Activity 2

Read the script and circle the correct instructions. Act out.

- Explain to the pupils that they are going to read another script. Read out the script without pausing. The pupils should just listen at this stage.
- If necessary, read the script again, pausing at each number to elicit the correct action or the adverb of manner from the class. The pupils then work on their own or in pairs to circle the correct instructions.
- Organise the class into Talk Partners. The pupils practise reading out the script in their pairs, paying attention to the stage directions as they read.
- Invite different pairs of pupils to the front of the class to act out the scene for their classmates.

Answers: **1** sleepily **2** throws **3** angrily **4** nervously **5** on the wall **6** outside

Code activity

- The pupils complete the code activity.

Answer: surfboard

Ending the lesson

Review the lesson and reflect on learning.

- Say **Today we've read a script about a necklace.** Then ask **Who are the characters? Where are they? What happens?**
- Ask **Which was your favourite activity today? Which activity was easy / difficult?**

Extra activities

Reinforcement

- Tell the pupils that they are going to continue the script from the Activity Book. Explain that Josh and Lily are now outside and are playing with the ball.
- Elicit ideas from the pupils about what the characters could say and do.
- Organise the pupils into pairs and ask them to write three or four lines of script in their notebooks.
- Invite pairs to act out their new script for the class.
- Play *Word dictation* (see p27) with the household objects word cards.

Key Competences and Key Learning Outcomes

- Use exclamation marks
- Identify the text features of a script and explain what happens
- Use criteria to check your writing
- Share your writing with a partner
- Prepare and write a script

Key language

- *fox, laughing, queen, whispering, witch, wolf*
- *What's that noise? Is it a (fox)? No, it isn't.*
- Recycled: *angrily, happily, quietly, shouting, sleepily, slowly; characters, detective, diamond, missing necklace, police officer, pop star, restaurant, robber, school*

Materials

- Pupil's Book p79; Activity Book p76; Class CD3; Teacher's App on Navio
- Teacher's Resource Bank: Talk cards

Optional materials

- Teacher's Resource Bank: Trinity Exams Practice cards (selected from the Starter Unit and Units 1, 2, 3, 4, 5 and 6)

At a Glance Lesson Plan

Pupil's Book

Starting the lesson

- Use the Trinity Exams Practice cards (optional).
- Review *The missing necklace: Scene 1.*
- Set learning outcomes and use the talk cards.

Investigate a text: Activity 1

- Read and listen.
- ▶ *CD3 Track 38 p276*
- Imagine what happens next.

Investigate a text: Activity 2

- Read and listen.
- ▶ *CD3 Track 39 p276*
- What happens?

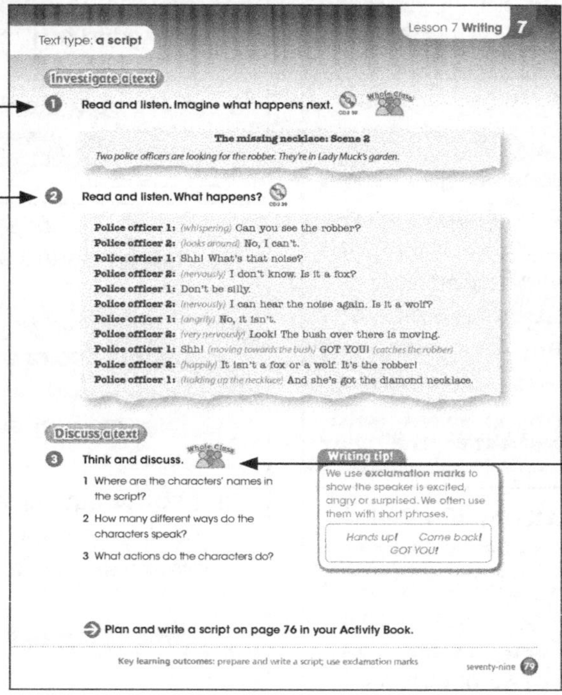

Lesson 7 Writing 7

Text type: **a script**

Investigate a text

1 Read and listen. Imagine what happens next.

The missing necklace: Scene 2

Two police officers are looking for the robber. They're in Lady Muck's garden.

2 Read and listen. What happens?

Police officer 1: *(whispering)* Can you see the robber?
Police officer 2: *(looks around)* No, I can't.
Police officer 1: Shh! What's that noise?
Police officer 2: *(nervously)* I don't know. Is it a fox?
Police officer 1: Don't be silly.
Police officer 2: *(nervously)* I can hear the noise again. Is it a wolf?
Police officer 1: *(angrily)* No, it isn't.
Police officer 2: *(very nervously)* Look! The bush over there is moving.
Police officer 1: Shh! *(moving towards the bush)* GOT YOU! *(catches the robber)*
Police officer 2: *(happily)* It isn't a fox or a wolf. It's the robber!
Police officer 1: *(holding up the necklace)* And she's got the diamond necklace.

Discuss a text

3 Think and discuss.

1 Where are the characters' names in the script?
2 How many different ways do the characters speak?
3 What actions do the characters do?

Writing tip!
We use **exclamation marks** to show the speaker is excited, angry or surprised. We often use them with short phrases.
Hands up! Come back! GOT YOU!

Plan and write a script on page 76 in your Activity Book.

Key learning outcomes: prepare and write a script; use exclamation marks

seventy-nine 79

Discuss a text: Activity 3

- Think and discuss.
- **Writing tip:** Read about exclamation marks.
- Go to the Activity Book.

Ending the lesson

- Review the lesson and reflect on learning.

Extra activity

Reinforcement

- Act out your script for the rest of the class.

Activity Book

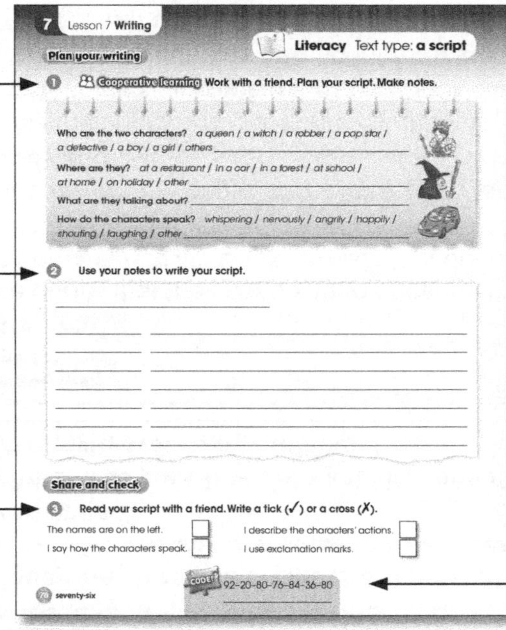

7 Lesson 7 Writing

Literacy Text type: **a script**

Plan your writing

1 Cooperative learning Work with a friend. Plan your script. Make notes.

Who are the two characters? *a queen / a witch / a robber / a pop star / a detective / a boy / a girl / others*

Where are they? *at a restaurant / in a car / in a forest / at school / at home / on holiday / other*

What are they talking about?

How do the characters speak? *whispering / nervously / angrily / happily / shouting / laughing / other*

2 Use your notes to write your script.

Share and check

3 Read your script with a friend. Write a tick (✓) or a cross (✗).

The names are on the left. ☐ I describe the characters' actions. ☐
I say how the characters speak. ☐ I use exclamation marks. ☐

CODE! 92-20-80-76-84-36-80

76 seventy-six

Activity Book

Plan your writing: Activity 1

- Work with a friend.
- Plan your script.
- Make notes.

Activity 2

- Use your notes to write your script.

Share and check: Activity 3

- Read your script with a friend.
- Write a tick (✓) or a cross (✗).

Code activity

- Complete the code activity.

Digital resources

Teacher's Digital: You can also teach this lesson using the Teacher's App on Navio.

Pupil's Digital: Encourage your pupils to use the Pupil's App on Navio to practise the activities from this lesson.

Powered By NAVIO

Starting the lesson

Use the Trinity Exams Practice cards (optional).

- The pupils practise asking and answering questions.

Review *The missing necklace: Scene 1.*

- Ask **What was the title of the script we read in the last lesson?** (*The missing necklace*.)
- Ask three pupils to read out *The missing necklace: Scene 1* (Pupil's Book page 78).

Set learning outcomes and use the talk cards.

- Say **Today we're going to read the end of the script. Then we're going to plan and write another script.**
- Point to the talk cards to show the pupils the different ways they will be working in the lesson.

Investigate a text: Pupil's Book Activity 1

Read and listen. Imagine what happens next.

▶ *CD3 Track 38 p276*

- Play the CD. The pupils listen and read the introduction to Scene 2.
- Encourage the class to predict what will happen in the scene.

Investigate a text: Pupil's Book Activity 2

Read and listen. What happens?

▶ *CD3 Track 39 p276*

- The pupils read the rest of Scene 2 to find out if their predictions were right. If you want the pupils to read the text without the support of the CD, set a time limit for this task. Otherwise, play the CD.
- The pupils report what happens.

Discuss a text: Pupil's Book Activity 3

Think and discuss.

- Read the first question. Confirm that the characters' names are on the left of the script and that they are followed by a colon.
- Read the second question and prompt the pupils to find all the ways of speaking that appear in Scenes 1 and 2. (*Shouting, laughing, whispering, nervously, angrily, happily.*) Highlight that these directions are inside brackets and they come before what the person says.
- Read the third question and elicit some of the actions the characters do. Once again, highlight that these directions appear in brackets and are written in the present tense.

Writing tip

- Read the information about exclamation marks.
- Prompt the pupils to find other examples in the text and to practise saying the exclamations with emotion.

Activity Book

Plan your writing: Activity 1

Writing Partners. Work with a friend. Plan your script. Make notes.

- Organise the class into Talk Partners and explain that they are going to write a short script.
- The pupils work together to decide on the characters and the place. They should also decide on the subject of the exchange and on what will happen at the beginning, middle and end. Finally, they decide on how the characters will speak.

Activity 2

Use your notes to write your script.

- Focus the class on the activity. If necessary, model how to write a script. Choose two characters and a setting and prompt the class to create a script with you. Correct or fine-tune their suggestions and write the text on the board.
- The Talk Partners write their own text in their Activity Books. This text may be as short or as long as the pupils like.

Share and check: Activity 3

Writing Partners. Read your script with a friend. Write a tick (✓) or a cross (✗).

- Read through the statements as a class.
- Organise the class into new pairs. One pupil in each pair should read their text aloud to their partner. The other pupil listens. The pupils work together to decide if the text fulfils all the criteria and tick or cross the corresponding boxes. The pupils can add to, improve, or correct the text at this stage.
- The pupils swap roles.

Code activity CODE

- The pupils complete the code activity.

Answer: wetsuit

Ending the lesson

Review the lesson and reflect on learning.

- Say **Today we've written a script. Are you happy with your script?** Elicit the pupils' opinions.
- Ask **Which was your favourite activity today? Which activity was easy / difficult?**

Extra activity

Reinforcement

- Ask the pupils to practise reading their scripts in pairs. Then invite different pupils to the front of the class to act out the scene for their classmates.

Key Competences and Key Learning Outcomes

- Identify rocks and minerals (optional)
- Think about and research Australia
- Read and listen for specific information
- Read about living in an underground town in Australia
- Think about your own culture and identity

Key language

- *blanket, build, cool, dark, desert, golf, sand, underground*
- Recycled: *bathroom, bedroom, kitchen, library, living room, museum, pictures, shops, stone, town, walls, window; There isn't (a lot of rain). (Living underground) is (cooler) than (living above ground). It's got (three bedrooms). It hasn't got (a window).*

Materials

- Pupil's Book p80; Activity Book p77; Class CD3; Teacher's App on Navio
- Teacher's Resource Bank: Talk cards
- An online world map
- Coloured pencils (red, white and blue)

Optional materials

- Teacher's Resource Bank: Trinity Exams Practice cards (selected from the Starter Unit and Units 1, 2, 3, 4, 5 and 6)

At a Glance Lesson Plan

Pupil's Book

Starting the lesson

- Use the Trinity Exams Practice cards (optional).
- Review household objects vocabulary.
- Set learning outcomes and use the talk cards.

Activity 1

- Read Luke's questions.
- What do you think?

Activity 2

- Read and listen.
- ▶ *CD3 Track 40 p276*
- Answer Luke's questions.
- **Think about your culture** What different kinds of homes have people got in your country?

Go to the Activity Book.

Ending the lesson

- Review the lesson and reflect on learning.

Extra activity

Reinforcement

- Compare living in a house / flat to living underground.

Link to Science

- **The top layer of Earth:** Identify rocks and minerals.

Activity Book

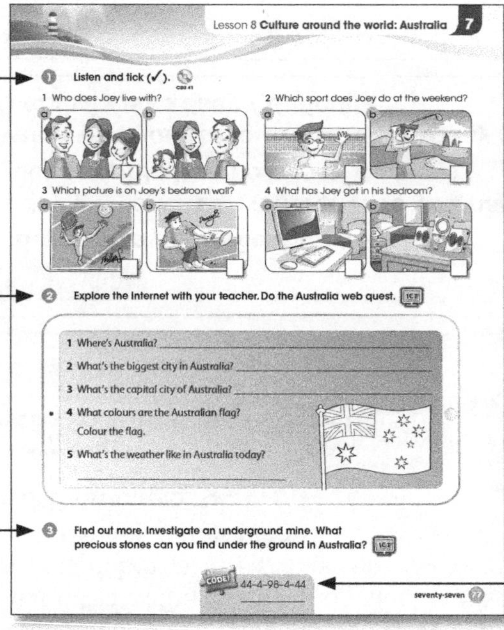

Activity Book

Activity 1

- Listen and tick (✓).
- ▶ *CD3 Track 41 p276*

Activity 2

- Explore the Internet with your teacher. Do the Australia web quest.

Activity 3

- Find out more. Investigate an underground mine. What precious stones can you find under the ground in Australia?

Code activity

- Complete the code activity.

Digital resources

Teacher's Digital: You can also teach this lesson using the Teacher's App on Navio.

Powered By NAVIO

Starting the lesson

Use the Trinity Exams Practice cards (optional).

- The pupils practise asking and answering questions.

Review household objects vocabulary.

- Challenge the pupils to remember ten items. Say **In my house, there's a (cooker).** The pupil next to you continues the chain: *In my house, there's a (cooker) and a (fridge).* Continue around the class.
- Alternatively, organise the class into pairs to play.

Set learning outcomes and use the talk cards.

- Say **Today we're going to investigate Australia.**
- Point to the talk cards to show the pupils the different ways they will be working in the lesson.

Pupil's Book Activity 1

Read Luke's questions. What do you think?

- Read the speech bubble as a class.
- Encourage the pupils to tell you what they know about Australia. Show the pupils where Australia is on an online world map. Then show them where the town of Coober Pedy is in the state of South Australia.
- Read the questions as a class. Encourage the pupils to predict the answers.

Pupil's Book Activity 2

Read and listen. Answer Luke's questions.

▸ *CD3 Track 40 p276*

- Focus on the photos. Ask **What can you see?**
- The pupils read the text. If you want them to do this without the support of the CD, set a time limit for this task. Otherwise, play the CD, pausing after each paragraph to check understanding.
- The pupils answer Luke's questions.

Answers: **1** It's very hot. **2** It's underground. **3** It's got stone walls, a colourful blanket on the bed, and pictures of sports stars on the walls. **4** You can visit an underground museum, go shopping and play golf at night.

Think about your culture

- Read out the question and prompt the pupils to tell you about the different types of homes people have got in their country.

Activity Book

Activity 1

Listen and tick (✓).

▸ *CD3 Track 41 p276*

- Invite a pupil to read out the first question. Play the CD, pausing at the end of the first exchange to identify Joey's family.
- Repeat the procedure with the remaining questions. The pupils listen and tick the corresponding pictures.

Answers: **1** a **2** b **3** b **4** b

Activity 2

Explore the Internet with your teacher. Do the Australia web quest. ICT

- Read out the instructions for the activity.
- Connect to a children's website (see suggested websites opposite) that provides geographical information about Australia. Read out questions 1–4. The pupils work as a class to find and write the answers. They should also colour the flag.
- Read out question 5. Connect to a website that shows the weather around the world. The pupils complete the information about the day's weather.

Answers: **1** between the Pacific and Indian Oceans, near New Zealand **2** Sydney **3** Canberra **4** red, white and blue

Activity 3

Find out more. Investigate an underground mine. What precious stones can you find under the ground in Australia? ICT

- If you are doing the investigation as a class, go to a suitable website and ask the pupils to scan the information to find the answer.
- If you are working in a computer room, organise the class into small groups. The groups should go to a suitable website and find the answer.

Answer: opals

Suggested websites

http://maps.google.es/
http://www.enchantedlearning.com
http://www.bbc.co.uk/weather

Code activity CODE!

- The pupils complete the code activity.

Answer: kayak

Ending the lesson

Review the lesson and reflect on learning.

- Say **Today we've learnt about Coober Pedy in Australia. Is it an interesting place? What can you see and do there?** Elicit the information.
- Ask **Which was your favourite activity today? Which activity was easy / difficult?**

Extra activity

Reinforcement

- The pupils compare their houses with an underground house in Australia. Ask **Which do you prefer? A house / flat or an underground house? Why?**

Link to Science

- If you are studying the Science topic of **The top layer of Earth** in English, find out more about a mine in Coober Pedy.
- Play the video of the mine (available online) and ask the class to identify and describe the rocks and minerals.
- Ask **What can you see / do at the mine?**

Go to the AB Unit Review on page 255.

Key Competences and Key Learning Outcomes

- Watch and understand a video about houses
- Practise memory skills in a game
- Practise asking and answering questions using *was* and *were*

- Learn about unusual houses around the world

Key language

- *chimney, grass, lighthouse, shell, train, turtle, wheels*
- *How many (legs) has the (lighthouse) got? Where's the (house in Portugal)? Where were (the flowers)? Was the (painting next to the door)?*

Materials

- Pupil's Book p81; Activity Book p79; Class CD3; Teacher's App on Navio
- Household objects flashcards
- Teacher's Resource Bank: Talk cards

Optional materials

- Teacher's Resource Bank: Trinity Exams Practice cards (selected from the Starter Unit and Units 1, 2, 3, 4, 5 and 6)

At a Glance Lesson Plan

Pupil's Book

Starting the lesson

- Use the Trinity Exams Practice cards (optional).
- **Think-Pair-Share.** Review vocabulary related to houses.
- Set learning outcomes and use the talk cards.

Activity 1

- Before you watch
- Watch the video.

Unit 7 video p286

- Which of these don't you see in the video?

Activity 2

- Watch the video again.

Unit 7 video

- Read and answer the questions.

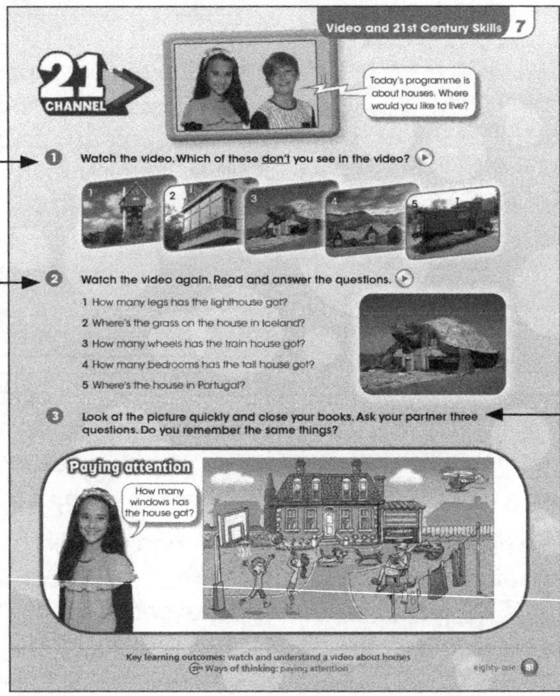

Video and 21st Century Skills 7

1 Watch the video. Which of these don't you see in the video?

2 Watch the video again. Read and answer the questions.

1 How many legs has the lighthouse got?
2 Where's the grass on the house in Iceland?
3 How many wheels has the train house got?
4 How many bedrooms has the tall house got?
5 Where's the house in Portugal?

3 Look at the picture quickly and close your books. Ask your partner three questions. Do you remember the same things?

Activity 3

- Look at the picture quickly and close your books.
- Ask your partner three questions.
- Do you remember the same things?

Go to the Activity Book.

Ending the lesson

- Review the lesson and reflect on learning.

Extra activity

Reinforcement

- Play a memory game.

Activity Book

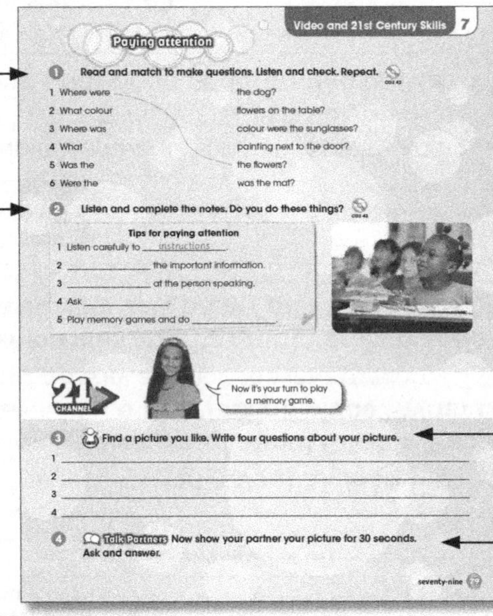

Video and 21st Century Skills 7

Paying attention

1 Read and match to make questions. Listen and check. Repeat.

1 Where were ... the dog?
2 What colour ... flowers on the table?
3 Where was ... colour were the sunglasses?
4 What ... painting next to the door?
5 Was the ... the flowers?
6 Were the ... was the mat?

2 Listen and complete the notes. Do you do these things?

Tips for paying attention
1 Listen carefully to instructions.
2 ______ the important information.
3 ______ at the person speaking.
4 Ask ______
5 Play memory games and do ______

3 Find a picture you like. Write four questions about your picture.

4 Talk Partners Now show your partner your picture for 30 seconds. Ask and answer.

Activity Book

Activity 1

- Read and match to make questions.
- Listen and check.

▶ *CD3 Track 42 p276*

- Repeat.

Activity 2

- Listen and complete the notes.

▶ *CD3 Track 43 p276*

- Do you do these things?

Activity 3

- Find a picture you like.
- Write four questions about your picture.

Activity 4

- Now show your partner your picture for 30 seconds.
- Ask and answer.

Digital resources

Teacher's Digital: You can also teach this lesson using the Teacher's App on Navio.

Pupil's Digital: Encourage your pupils to use the Pupil's App on Navio to practise the activities from this lesson.

Powered By NAVIO

Starting the lesson

Use the Trinity Exams Practice cards (optional).

- The pupils practise asking and answering questions.

Think-Pair-Share. Review vocabulary related to houses.

- Ask **What rooms or parts of a house can you remember?** The class thinks silently for a minute.
- Then the pupils work with a Talk Partner to name rooms or parts of a house.
- Invite different Talk Partners to say a different room or part of a house. Write the word on the board and prompt the class to repeat.

Set learning outcomes and use the talk cards.

- Say **Today we're going to watch a video and then ask and answer questions about houses and paying attention**.
- Point to the talk cards to show the pupils the different ways they will be working in the lesson.

Pupil's Book Activity 1

Before you watch

- Read the speech bubble to pupils. Ask **Where would you like to live?** Elicit responses.

Watch the video. Which of these don't you see in the video? *p286*

- Watch Part 1. Ask pupils **What are you going to see next?** Check that they understand that they will see lots of interesting houses.
- Play Part 2. Ask general questions to check understanding. Focus the pupils' attention on the photos in Activity 1. Say **Which of these don't you see in the video?** Elicit ideas.
- Play Part 2 again for the pupils to answer the questions. Check answers as a class.

Answer: You don't see number 2.

Pupil's Book Activity 2

Watch the video again. Read and answer the questions.

- Read out sentence 1. Ask the class what they think the answer is. Repeat with sentences 2–5.
- Play Part 2. Students work in pairs to answer the questions.

Answers: **1** nine **2** on the roof **3** none **4** five **5** under a big rock

Pupil's Book Activity 3

Look at the picture quickly and close your books. Ask your partner three questions. Do you remember the same things?

- (Books closed.) Ask **What question does Mark ask at the end of the video?** (*What colour was (the lighthouse)?*) **What does Chloe say?** (*Was it blue and white? Or was it green and white?*)
- Review asking *was* and *were* questions and *was / were* short answers.
- Organise the class into Talk Partners.
- (Books open.) Pupils look at the picture for 30 seconds.
- (Books closed.) Pupils work in pairs to ask and answer questions about the picture.
- At the end of the activity, ask **How well did you pay attention to what you saw in the picture?**

Activity Book

Activity 1

Read and match to make questions. Listen and check. Repeat.

▸ *CD3 Track 42 p276*

- Pupils work on their own to make *was / were* questions.
- Play the CD and check answers.

Answers: **1** Where were the flowers? **2** What colour was the mat? **3** Where was the dog? **4** What colour were the sunglasses? **5** Was the painting next to the door? **6** Were the flowers on the table?

Activity 2

Listen and complete the notes. Do you do these things?

▸ *CD3 Track 43 p276*

- Explain to the pupils that they are going to listen to a dad giving his daughter tips for paying attention in class. Ask pupils for their own ideas. Read out the information. Then play the CD, pausing to allow the pupils to write the missing information.
- Play the CD again without pausing.

Answers: **1** instructions **2** Repeat **3** Look **4** questions **5** puzzles

- Ask the pupils **Do you do these things?**

Activity 3

Find a picture you like. Write four questions about your picture.

- Read out the speech bubble.
- Ask pupils to find a fairly detailed picture that they like. They could do this in class or at home.
- Pupils write four questions about the details in their picture. Encourage them to use *was / were* questions.

Activity 4

Now show your partner your picture for 30 seconds. Ask and answer.

- Organise the pupils into Talk Partners. The pupils take it in turns to ask and answer questions.
- At the end of the activity, ask **How well did you pay attention to what you saw in the picture?**

Ending the lesson

Review the lesson and reflect on learning.

- Say **Today we've watched a video about houses and we've tested how well we pay attention.**
- Ask **Which was your favourite activity today? Which activity was easy / difficult?**

Extra activity

Reinforcement

- Use the household objects flashcards to play a memory game. Lay out a selection and ask pupils to study them for a minute. Then hide the flashcards and ask pupils to recall the items they saw.
- Repeat the game. Does playing memory games help pupils to pay attention?

Date: ______________________ **Unit:** __________

1 What did my pupils learn in this unit?

____

____

____

____

2 How did my pupils work? (✓)

individually ☐ in pairs ☐ in small groups ☐

in large groups ☐ as a class ☐

3 Which key competences did my pupils develop?

- Competence in linguistic communication ☐
- Competence in mathematics, science and technology ☐
- Digital competence ☐
- LEARN Learning to learn ☐
- Social and civic competences ☐
- Sense of initiative and entrepreneurship ☐
- Cultural awareness and expression ☐

4 Which lessons / activities were the most successful and why?

____

____

____

____

5 Which lessons / activities did my pupils find the most difficult and why?

____

____

____

____

6 What did I try in the classroom for the first time? How did it go?

____

____

____

____

7 Which resources did I find most useful? (including webpages)

____

____

____

____

____

____

8 What could I do differently next time I teach this unit?

____

____

____

____

8 What's on TV?

Unit overview

Key Competences and Key Learning Outcomes

- Identify and name TV programmes (Lesson 1)
- Say the vocabulary chant (Lesson 1)
- Understand and act out a conversation (Lesson 2)
- Ask and answer questions with 'did' (Lesson 2)
- Follow, complete and correct the grammar tables (Lessons 2 and 4)
- Identify and name free-time activities (Lesson 4)
- Use regular verbs in the past (Lesson 4)
- Give reasons with 'because' (Lesson 7)
- Watch and understand a video (Video and 21st Century Skills)

- Use a code to read a message (Lesson 3)

- Use the Pupil's App on Navio
- Investigate the USA (Lesson 8)

- Say a tongue twister, learn another spelling for the 'f' sound and practise spelling (Lesson 5)
- Practise activity types found in the Cambridge Exams: A1 Movers
- Review your own learning (Review)

- Understand the importance of working together (Lesson 3)
- Work collaboratively to plan a video (Video and 21st Century Skills)

- Work with a Talk Partner to practise and reinforce learning (all lessons)
- Play a communication game (Lesson 5)

- Sing two songs (Lessons 1 and 4)
- Understand, act out and give an opinion on a story (Lesson 3)
- Read and evaluate a review (Lesson 6)
- Plan and write a review (Lesson 7)
- Learn about the USA (Lesson 8)
- Think about your own culture (Lesson 8)

Vocabulary

Core vocabulary
advert, cartoon, comedy programme, documentary, film, game show, music programme, quiz show, sports programme, talk show, the news, the weather; climb a tree, paint a picture, phone a friend, plant seeds, play cards, skip

Extension vocabulary (optional)
actor, camera operator, director, musician, presenter, reporter; bake – baked, skate – skated, study – studied, travel – travelled

Other vocabulary
car chase, channel, editor, judges, prizes, review, reviewer, singers, special effects, star, studio

Recycled vocabulary
adventure, carry, city, clever, climb, dangerous, detective, dog, exciting, famous, farm, fish, flag, frog, funny, fur, hills, information, jump, last night / week, newspaper, pet, photo, scary, scientists, slide, submarine, surprise, team

Structures

Core structures
Did (you) watch (a cartoon) yesterday? Yes, (I) did. No, (I) didn't. I (painted a picture) yesterday. We didn't (watch TV) (last night). What did (Daisy) do (yesterday morning)? She (planted seeds).

Other structures
What type of (TV programme) is it? This (documentary) is about (sea animals). I (love) (this programme) because (it's exciting). What's on (Channel 2) at (five o'clock)? Which of (these programmes) do you (want to watch)? I (don't) think it's (a very good programme).

Recycled structures
I like / love / don't like watching (cartoons). Do you like watching (the news)? Yes, I do. No, I don't. Do you prefer watching (cartoons) or (films)? What do you like watching (in the afternoon)?

Phonics

The 'f' sound (*dol**ph**in **f**ished ele**ph**ant **ph**oned **f**riend*)

Literacy

Text type: a review (information text; writing preparation)
Reading skills: scanning texts for specific information
Writing skills: using 'because' to give a reason

Culture ... around the world

Activities in Hollywood

21st Century Skills

Making a video

Thinking skills

Ranking (Lesson 1); Applying rules (Lessons 2 and 4); Problem solving (Lesson 2); Predicting (Lessons 3 and 8); Discussing values (Lesson 3); Expressing opinions (Lesson 3); Thinking about your culture (Lesson 8); Making connections (Review)

Cooperative learning

Working together (Lesson 1); Discussing survey results (Lesson 2); Team building (Lesson 3); Collaborating (Lesson 4); Checking learning (Lesson 5); Sharing information (Lesson 5); Peer evaluation and feedback (Lesson 7); Working together (Review)

Values

Understanding the importance of working together

Cross-curricular links

Link to Science
Transport and communication: Naming TV programmes that provide information
Suggested Arts and Crafts concepts
Identifying the use of balance (symmetry) in art and designing a flying machine

Key Competences and Key Learning Outcomes

- Identify and say types of TV programmes
- Say the vocabulary chant
- Name the TV programmes that provide information (optional)
- Review free-time activities
- Ask and answer questions using a recycled structure
- Sing a song about TV

Key language

- TV programmes: *advert, cartoon, comedy programme, documentary, film, game show, music programme, quiz show, sports programme, talk show, the news, the weather*
- *What's on (Channel 2) at (five o'clock)? A (talk show).*
- Extension: *actor, camera operator, director, musician, presenter, reporter*
- Recycled: *I like / love / don't like watching (cartoons). Do you like watching (the news)? Yes, I do. No, I don't. Do you prefer watching (cartoons) or (films)? I prefer watching (cartoons). What do you like watching (in the afternoon)?*

Materials

- Pupil's Book p82; Activity Book p80; Class CD3; Teacher's App on Navio
- Teacher's Resource Bank: TV programmes word cards
- TV programmes flashcards
- Teacher's Resource Bank: Talk cards

Optional materials

- Teacher's Resource Bank: Trinity Exams Practice cards (selected from the Starter Unit and Units 1, 2, 3, 4, 5, 6 and 7)

At a Glance Lesson Plan

Pupil's Book

Starting the lesson
- Use the Trinity Exams Practice cards (optional).
- Review vocabulary for free-time activities.
- Set learning outcomes and use the talk cards.

Activity 1
- When do you watch TV?
- Which programmes do you watch?
- Make a list.

Vocabulary presentation
- Present the new vocabulary using the TV programmes flashcards.

Word cards
- Introduce the spellings of the vocabulary using the TV programmes word cards.

Activity 2
- Listen, point and say the vocabulary chant.
▶ *CD3 Track 44 p277*

Activity 3
- Listen, look and sing *The TV song.*
▶ *CD3 Track 45 p277*

Activity 4
- Ask and answer.
- Go to the Activity Book.

Ending the lesson
- Review the lesson and reflect on learning.

Extra activities

Reinforcement
- Rank the TV programmes.

Vocabulary extension
- Present six additional vocabulary items.

Link to Science
- **Transport and communication:** Name the TV programmes that provide information.

Activity Book

Activity Book

Activity 1
- Read and complete.
- Ask and answer.

Activity 2
- What do you like watching on TV?
- Read and write.

Code activity
- Complete the code activity.

Digital resources

Teacher's Digital: You can also teach this lesson using the Teacher's App on Navio

Pupil's Digital: Encourage your pupils to use the Pupil's App on Navio to practise the activities from this lesson

Starting the lesson

Use the Trinity Exams Practice cards (optional).

- The pupils practise asking and answering questions.

Review vocabulary for free-time activities.

- Ask **What do you do in your free time?** The pupils answer using adverbs of frequency (*always, often, sometimes, never*).
- The pupils ask and answer the question in pairs.

Set learning outcomes and use the talk cards.

- Ask **Do you watch TV in your free time?** Then say **Today we're going to learn the names of different types of TV programmes.**
- Point to the talk cards to show the pupils the different ways they will be working in the lesson.

Pupil's Book Activity 1

When do you watch TV? Which programmes do you watch? Make a list.

- (Books closed.) Ask **When do you watch TV? Which programmes do you watch?** Prompt the pupils to answer using frequency expressions: *once/twice/ three times a week, every day.*

Vocabulary presentation

- (Books closed.) Choose a TV programmes flashcard without showing the picture. Describe the TV programme, e.g. **I like watching this programme. It's very interesting. I learn a lot about animals and different places.** (*Documentary.*)
- When the pupils identify the programmes, give them the names in English. Stick the flashcards on the board. The pupils repeat the words.

Word cards

- (Books closed.) Hand a TV programmes word card to each pair of pupils.
- The pairs take turns to come to the board, read out their TV programme and stick their word card next to the corresponding flashcard.

Pupil's Book Activity 2

Listen, point and say the vocabulary chant.

▶ ***CD3 Track 44 p277***

- Focus the pupils' attention on the 12 illustrations. Say **Let's listen and say the words.** Play the CD. The pupils listen, point and repeat.

Pupil's Book Activity 3

Listen, look and sing *The TV song.*

▶ ***CD3 Track 45 p277***

- Ask **Where are Lily, Ravi and Josh?** (*Outside a TV studio.*)
- Play the CD. The pupils listen and read.
- Ask **What does Lily / Josh like watching?**
- Play the CD again. The pupils sing and point to the posters.

Pupil's Book Activity 4

Ask and answer.

- Ask two pupils to read out the speech bubbles.
- Prompt a pupil to ask you a similar question. Give your answer. Then prompt other pupils to ask questions.
- The pupils ask and answer questions with a Talk Partner.

Activity Book

Activity 1

Read and complete. Ask and answer.

- Highlight that all the missing letters are vowels. The pupils read and complete the TV guide.
- Ask two pupils to read out the speech bubbles. Then ask the class similar questions.
- (Books closed.) Working with a Talk Partner, the pupils ask and answer questions from memory.

Answers: **Channel 1** 5:00 cartoon 5:30 game show 6:00 documentary 7:00 film 9:00 the news 9:30 the weather **Channel 2** 5:00 talk show 6:00 comedy programme 7:00 quiz show 7:30 sports programme 8:00 music programme 8:30 advert

Activity 2

What do you like watching on TV? Read and write.

- Invite a pupil to read out and complete the first sentence. Repeat the procedure with the next two sentences.
- The pupils write the sentences.

Code activity

- The pupils complete the code activity.

Answer: armchair

Ending the lesson

Review the lesson and reflect on learning.

- Say **Today we've learnt the names of types of TV programme. What do you remember?** Elicit the programmes from the pupils.
- Ask **Which was your favourite activity today? Which activity was easy / difficult?**

Extra activities

Reinforcement

- Say **I like watching (documentaries) the most.** Write *(1) documentaries* on the board. Then write the number 2 and say **Next, I like watching (films).** Repeat for numbers 3–5.
- The pupils rank their favourite programmes from 1 to 5.

Vocabulary extension

- Present six additional TV professions: *actor, camera operator, director, musician, presenter, reporter.*
- Use the Vocabulary Booster on Navio to practise these new words.

Link to Science

- If you are studying the Science topic of **Transport and communication** in English, remind the pupils that TV entertains and communicates information. Elicit the types of programme that give us information (*the news, the weather, documentaries, adverts, talk shows, sports programmes*).

Key Competences and Key Learning Outcomes

- Listen, repeat and act out a conversation
- Listen, follow the grammar table and identify the parts of a question
- Ask and answer questions with *did*

- Calculate how much TV people watched

Key language

- *TV programmes*
- *Did you watch (a cartoon) yesterday? Yes, I did. No, I didn't. What did you (watch)? Can you (guess)? It's my (favourite programme). How much (TV did he watch) yesterday?*
- Recycled: *advert, cartoon, comedy programme, documentary, film, game show, music programme, quiz show, sports programme, talk show, the news, the weather*

Materials

- Pupil's Book p83; Activity Book p81; Class CD3; Teacher's App on Navio
- TV programmes flashcards
- Teacher's Resource Bank: Talk cards

Optional materials

- Teacher's Resource Bank: Trinity Exams Practice cards (selected from the Starter Unit and Units 1, 2, 3, 4, 5, 6 and 7)

At a Glance Lesson Plan

Pupil's Book

Starting the lesson

- Use the Trinity Exams Practice cards (optional).
- **Think-Pair-Share.** Review TV programmes.
- Review *The TV song.*
- ▶ *CD3 Track 45 p277*
- ▶ *CD3 Track 46 p277*
- Set learning outcomes and use the talk cards.

Activity 1

- Listen and read.
- Listen and repeat.
- ▶ *CD3 Track 47 p277*
- Act out.

Activity 2

- Read again.
- What type of programme did Josh watch yesterday?

Activity 3

- Listen and follow.
- ▶ *CD3 Track 48 p277*
- Repeat.
- **Grammar clue:** Read about using short answers to answer *Did …?* questions.

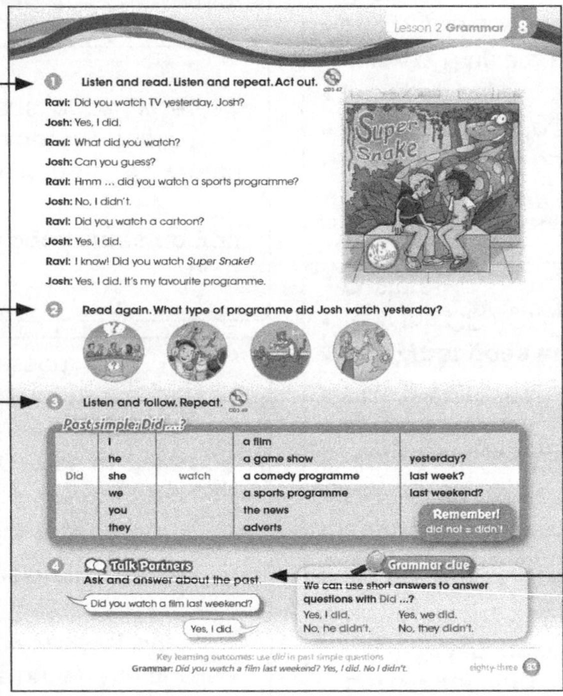

Lesson 2 Grammar 8

1 Listen and read. Listen and repeat. Act out.

Ravi: Did you watch TV yesterday, Josh?
Josh: Yes, I did.
Ravi: What did you watch?
Josh: Can you guess?
Ravi: Hmm … did you watch a sports programme?
Josh: No, I didn't.
Ravi: Did you watch a cartoon?
Josh: Yes, I did.
Ravi: I know! Did you watch *Super Snake?*
Josh: Yes, I did. It's my favourite programme.

2 Read again. What type of programme did Josh watch yesterday?

3 Listen and follow. Repeat.

Past simple: Did …?

	I		a film	
	he		a game show	yesterday?
Did	she	watch	a comedy programme	last week?
	we		a sports programme	last weekend?
	you		the news	
	they		adverts	

Remember! did not = didn't

4 Talk Partners Ask and answer about the past.

Did you watch a film last weekend?
Yes, I did.

Grammar clue
We can use short answers to answer questions with Did …?
Yes, I did. Yes, we did.
No, he didn't. No, they didn't.

Key learning outcomes: use did in past simple questions
Grammar: Did you watch a film last weekend? Yes, I did. No I didn't.

eighty-three 83

Activity 4

- Ask and answer about the past.
- Go to the Activity Book.

Ending the lesson

- Review the lesson and reflect on learning.

Extra activity

Reinforcement

- Class survey: how much TV did you watch last night?

Digital resources

Teacher's Digital: You can also teach this lesson using the Teacher's App on Navio.

Pupil's Digital: Encourage your pupils to use the Pupil's App on Navio to practise the activities from this lesson.

Powered By NAVIO

Activity Book

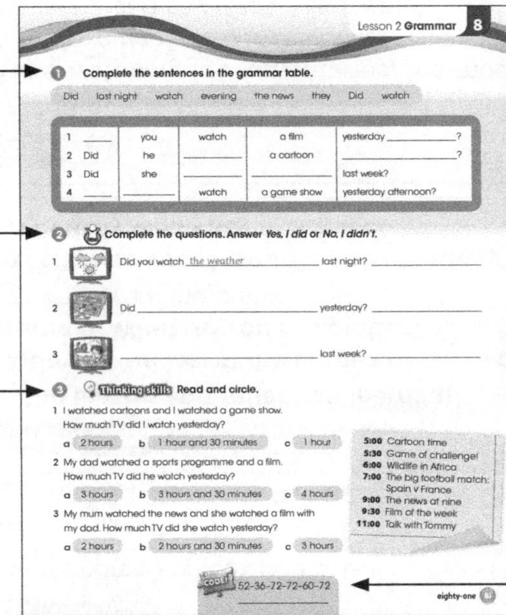

Lesson 2 Grammar 8

1 Complete the sentences in the grammar table.

Did last night watch evening the news they Did watch

1 ___	you	watch	a film	yesterday ___?
2 Did	he	___	a cartoon	___?
3 Did	she	___	___	last week?
4 ___	___	watch	a game show	yesterday afternoon?

2 Complete the questions. Answer *Yes, I did* or *No, I didn't*.

1 Did you watch the weather ___ last night? ___
2 Did ___ yesterday? ___
3 ___ last week? ___

3 Thinking skills Read and circle.

1 I watched cartoons and I watched a game show. How much TV did I watch yesterday?
a 2 hours b 1 hour and 30 minutes c 1 hour
2 My dad watched a sports programme and a film. How much TV did he watch yesterday?
a 3 hours b 3 hours and 30 minutes c 4 hours
3 My mum watched the news and she watched a film with my dad. How much TV did she watch yesterday?
a 2 hours b 2 hours and 30 minutes c 3 hours

5:00 Cartoon time
5:30 Game of challenge!
6:00 Wildlife in Africa
7:00 The big football match: Spain v France
9:00 The news at nine
9:30 Film of the week
11:00 Talk with Tommy

Code 52-36-72-72-60-72

eighty-one 81

Activity Book

Activity 1

- Complete the sentences in the grammar table.

Activity 2

- Complete the questions.
- Answer *Yes, I did* or *No, I didn't.*

Activity 3

- Read and circle.

Code activity

- Complete the code activity.

Starting the lesson

Use the Trinity Exams Practice cards (optional).

- The pupils practise asking and answering questions.

Think-Pair-Share. Review TV programmes.

- Ask **Can you remember the vocabulary for TV programmes?** The class thinks silently for a minute.
- Take a TV programmes flashcard and ask the pupil on your right **Do you like watching (the news)?** The pupil answers, takes the flashcard from you and asks the same question to the pupil on his / her right. Continue the question chain until all the pupils have asked and answered the question.
- Repeat, but this time add more flashcards.

Review *The TV song*.

▶ *CD3 Track 45 p277*

▶ *CD3 Track 46 p277 (optional karaoke version)*

- Give flashcards of the TV programmes that appear in *The TV song* to a few pupils. Play the CD (or use the karaoke version). The pupils with flashcards stand up when they hear their programme. The rest of the class sings along.

Set learning outcomes and use the talk cards.

- Say **Today we're going to ask questions about what we watched on TV yesterday.** Quickly check the concept by asking **What day is it today? What day was it yesterday?**
- Point to the talk cards to show the pupils the different ways they will be working in the lesson.

Pupil's Book Activity 1

Listen and read. Listen and repeat. Act out.

▶ *CD3 Track 47 p277*

- The pupils look at the picture. Ask **Where are Ravi and Josh? What do you think they are talking about?**
- Play the CD. The pupils listen and read the conversation.
- Confirm that they are talking about TV programmes. Ask **What did Josh watch on TV yesterday?**
- Play the CD again, pausing after each sentence for the pupils to repeat.
- The pupils act out the conversation in pairs.

Pupil's Book Activity 2

Read again. What type of programme did Josh watch yesterday?

- The pupils read the conversation again and say which picture is correct.

Answer: the third picture (a cartoon)

Pupil's Book Activity 3

Listen and follow. Repeat.

▶ *CD3 Track 48 p277*

- Play the CD. The pupils listen to the first sentence and point to the words. They repeat the complete sentence. Repeat the procedure with the other sentences.

Grammar clue

- Read the grammar clue as a class. Practise saying the short answers. Read the *Remember!* tip.
- Highlight that 'did' is the past of the verb 'do'. Write *Do you watch a film on Saturday?* ➜ *Did you watch a film on Saturday?*

Pupil's Book Activity 4

Ask and answer about the past.

- Ask **Can you guess what I watched yesterday?** The pupils use the grammar questions, e.g. *Did you watch (a game show yesterday)?*
- The pupils use the grammar table to ask a Talk Partner what they watched on TV.

Activity Book

Activity 1

Complete the sentences in the grammar table.

- Invite a pupil to read out the words in the word box.
- The pupils write the words in the grammar table.

Answers: **1** Did, evening **2** watch, last night **3** watch, the news **4** Did, they

Activity 2

Complete the questions. Answer *Yes, I did* or *No, I didn't*.

- Invite a pupil to read out and answer the first question. If necessary, the pupils can refer to the grammar table.
- The pupils write the questions and answers.

Answers: **1** the weather **2** you watch a sports programme **3** Did you watch a documentary

Activity 3

Read and circle.

- Read out the names of the programmes in the TV guide and elicit what types of programme they are. Then ask **What time does *Wildlife in Africa* begin? What time does *Wildlife in Africa* finish? How long is the programme?** Repeat with other programmes.
- Read out the first question and work out with the class the total amount of TV watched. (*1 hour.*)
- Organise the class into pairs or small groups to calculate how much TV Dad and Mum watched.
- Check the answers as a class.

Answers: **1** c **2** b **3** a

Code activity

- The pupils complete the code activity.

Answer: mirror

Ending the lesson

Review the lesson and reflect on learning.

- Say **Today we've learnt how to talk about the past.** Ask **What did Josh watch yesterday?** (*A cartoon.*) **What did you watch yesterday?** Elicit responses.
- Ask **Which was your favourite activity today? Which activity was easy / difficult?**

Extra activity

Reinforcement

- Draw the chart (see below) on the board.
- Ask the class to work out how much TV they watched yesterday. Invite pupils to say how much TV they watched and tick the corresponding part of the chart. Discuss the results.

0–1 hour	1–2 hours	2–3 hours	3–4 hours	4–5 hours

Key Competences and Key Learning Outcomes

- Read the story with some fluency
- Use a code to read a message
- Do a pre-reading task
- Understand the importance of working together
- Read, listen and understand a story about teamwork
- Give an opinion on the story

Key language
- *pole, rings, slippery, teamwork, work together*
- *It was fantastic! How did you (win)? First, (we carried some water), Then (we all jumped together).*
- Recycled: *carry, climb, documentary, flag, jump, slide, team, TV programme*

Materials
- Pupil's Book pp84–85; Activity Book p82; Class CD3 and 4; Teacher's App on Navio
- Teacher's Resource Bank: Talk cards

Optional materials
- Teacher's Resource Bank: Trinity Exams Practice cards (selected from the Starter Unit and Units 1, 2, 3, 4, 5, 6 and 7)

At a Glance Lesson Plan

Pupil's Book

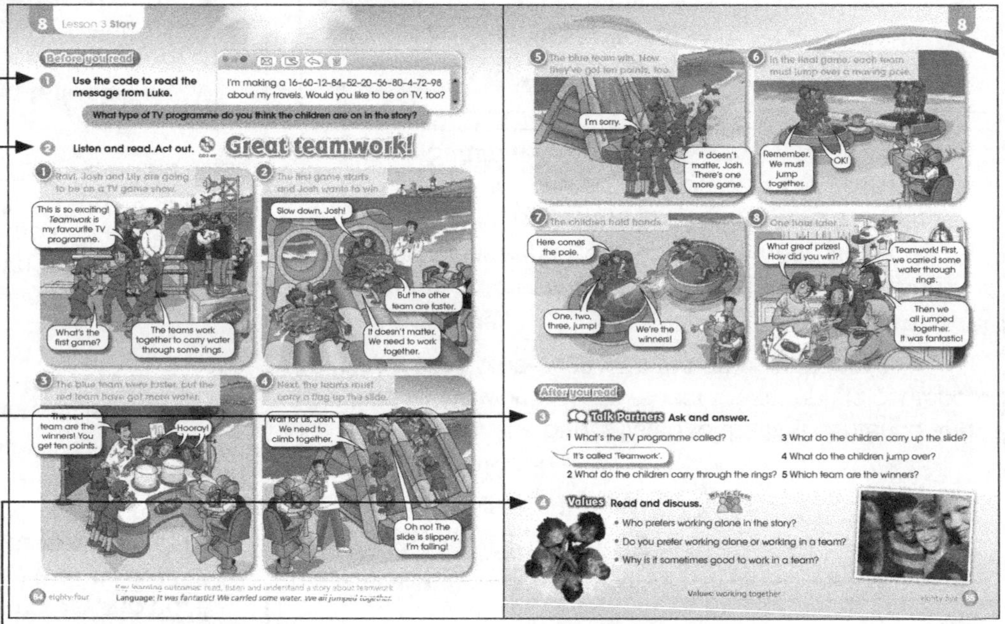

Starting the lesson
- Use the Trinity Exams Practice cards (optional).
- Review TV vocabulary and the past tense.
- Set learning outcomes and use the talk cards.

Before you read: Activity 1
- Use the code to read the message from Luke.

Activity 2
- Listen and read.
- ▶ *CD3 Track 49 p277*
- Act out.

After you read: Activity 3
- Ask and answer.

Activity 4: Values
- Read and discuss.
- Go to the Activity Book.

Ending the lesson
- Review the lesson and reflect on learning.

Extra activity

Reinforcement
- Retell the story as a class.

Activity Book

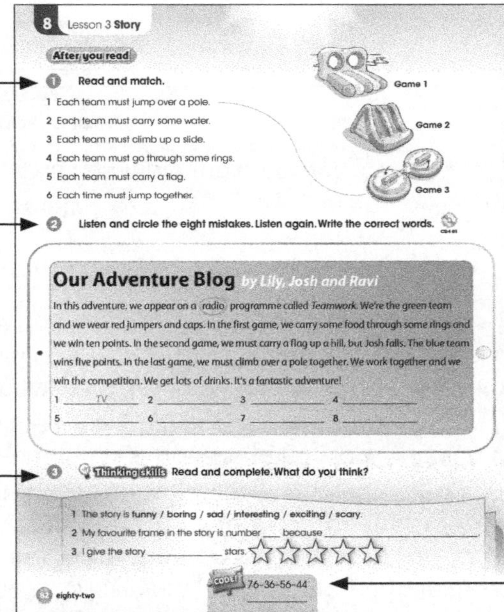

After you read: Activity Book

Activity 1
- Read and match.

Activity 2
- Listen and circle the eight mistakes.
- ▶ *CD4 Track 01 p277*
- Listen again.
- Write the correct words.

Activity 3
- Read and complete.
- What do you think?

Code activity
- Complete the code activity.

Digital resources

Teacher's Digital: You can also teach this lesson using the Teacher's App on Navio.

Pupil's Digital: Encourage your pupils to use the Pupil's App on Navio to practise the activities from this lesson.

Powered By NAVIO

Starting the lesson

Use the Trinity Exams Practice cards (optional).

- The pupils practise asking and answering questions.

Review TV vocabulary and the past tense.

- Drill the question **What did you watch on TV yesterday?** Then prompt a pupil to ask you the question and give an answer, e.g. **I watched the news.** Prompt pairs of pupils to ask and answer the question.
- Ask the class to move around the room. When you clap your hands, the pupils ask and answer the question with someone nearby. When you clap your hands again, they continue moving. Repeat five or six times.

Set learning outcomes and use the talk cards.

- Say **Today we're going to read and listen to a story.**
- Point to the talk cards to show the pupils the different ways they will be working in the lesson.

Before you read: Pupil's Book Activity 1

Use the code to read the message from Luke.

- Say **Josh and Lily have received another message from Luke.** Ask the pupils to use the code (Pupil's Book page 7) to discover the mystery word (*documentary*). Then ask the pupils if they would like to appear on TV.
- Read the title of the story and ask **What type of TV programme do you think the children are on in the story?** The pupils make their predictions.

Pupil's Book Activity 2

Listen and read. Act out.

▶ *CD3 Track 49 p277*

- Play the CD. The pupils follow in their books.
- Confirm that the children work together on a TV game show. They jump, climb, and carry water and a flag.
- Ask additional questions to check understanding.

Suggested comprehension questions

- Frame 1: **What's the TV programme called?** ('*Teamwork*'.) **What do the teams do in the first game?** (*Carry water through some rings.*)
- Frame 2: **How many teams are there?** (*Two.*)
- Frame 3: **Which team wins the first game?** (*The red team.*)
- Frame 4: **What do the children do in the second game?** (*Carry a flag up a slide.*)
- Frame 5: **Which team wins the second game?** (*The blue team.*)
- Frame 6: **What do the children do in the last game?** (*Jump over a moving pole.*)
- Frame 7: **Do the red team do it well?** (*Yes.*)
- Frame 8: **Why do they win?** (*Teamwork.*)

- Organise the class into groups (one for each character) and play the CD. Each group joins in when their character speaks.
- Repeat, with groups swapping roles.

After you read: Pupil's Book Activity 3

Ask and answer.

- Ask a pupil to read out the first question and answer. Then repeat with the other questions.
- In pairs, the pupils practise asking and answering. The pupils can do this orally or in their notebooks.

Answers: **1** It's called 'Teamwork'. **2** They carry water. **3** They carry a flag. **4** They jump over a moving pole. **5** The red team are the winners.

Pupil's Book Activity 4: Values

Read and discuss.

- Read out the questions and discuss them as a class.
- Encourage the class to think about why it is sometimes good to work in a team. (*To listen to each other, help each other, be kind, be patient.*)

After you read: Activity Book

Activity 1

Read and match.

- The pupils read the sentences and match them to the correct games.

Answers: **1** Game 3 **2** Game 1 **3** Game 2 **4** Game 1 **5** Game 2 **6** Game 3

Activity 2

Listen and circle the eight mistakes. Listen again. Write the correct words.

▶ *CD4 Track 01 p277*

- Play the CD. The pupils circle the eight mistakes.
- Play the CD again. The pupils write the correct words.

Answers: **1** ~~radio~~ TV **2** ~~green~~ red **3** ~~jumpers~~ T-shirts **4** ~~food~~ water **5** ~~hill~~ slide **6** ~~five~~ ten **7** ~~climb~~ jump **8** ~~drinks~~ prizes

Activity 3

Read and complete. What do you think?

- Invite pupils to read out and complete the sentences.
- The pupils complete the task in their Activity Books and then share opinions with a Talk Partner.

Code activity

- The pupils complete the code activity.

Answer: sink

Ending the lesson

Review the lesson and reflect on learning.

- Say **Today we've listened to a story about a TV programme.** Elicit the story from the pupils.
- Ask **Which was your favourite activity today? Which activity was easy / difficult?**

Extra activity

Reinforcement

- Retell the story as a class. Say **Let's tell the story together.** Prompt the pupils by saying **The children are in a programme called …** (*Teamwork*). Use mime, gesture and drawings to support the class.

Key Competences and Key Learning Outcomes

- Identify and say regular verbs
- Follow and correct the grammar tables
- Make positive and negative statements in the past simple using regular verbs

- Sing a song

Key language

- Regular verbs *climb a tree, paint a picture, phone a friend, plant seeds, play cards, skip*
- *I (painted a picture) yesterday. He didn't (watch TV) last night. Yesterday was (cool)!*
- Extension: *bake-baked, skate-skated, study-studied, travel-travelled*
- Recycled: *last night, last week, yesterday; played football, watched TV; Did she (watch TV) yesterday?*

Materials

- Pupil's Book p86; Activity Book p83; Class CD4; Teacher's App on Navio
- Teacher's Resource Bank: Talk cards

Optional materials

- Teacher's Resource Bank: Trinity Exams Practice cards (selected from the Starter Unit and Units 1, 2, 3, 4, 5, 6 and 7)

At a Glance Lesson Plan

Pupil's Book

Starting the lesson

- Use the Trinity Exams Practice cards (optional).
- Review the story.
- Set learning outcomes and use the talk cards.

Activity 1

- Listen, point and say.
- ▶ *CD4 Track 02 p277*

Activity 2

- Listen and sing *Did you watch TV?*
- ▶ *CD4 Track 03 p277*

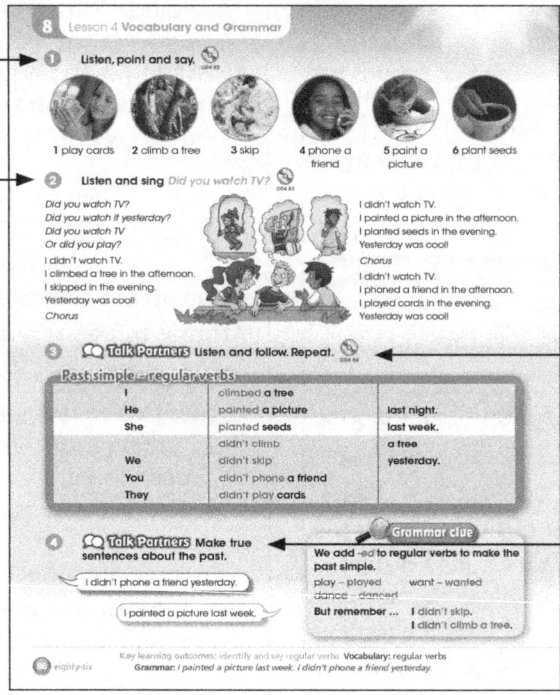

Activity 3

- Listen and follow.
- ▶ *CD4 Track 04 p278*
- Repeat.
- **Grammar clue:** Read about making the past simple with regular verbs.

Activity 4

- Make true sentences about the past.
- Go to the Activity Book.

Ending the lesson

- Review the lesson and reflect on learning.

Extra activities

Reinforcement

- Review other regular verbs and make true sentences about the past.

Vocabulary extension

- Present four additional vocabulary items.

Activity Book

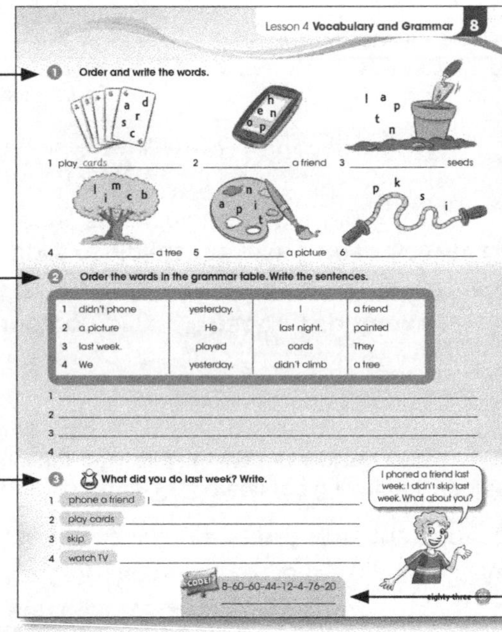

Activity Book

Activity 1

- Order and write the words.

Activity 2

- Order the words in the grammar table.
- Write the sentences.

Activity 3

- What did you do last week?
- Write.

Code activity

- Complete the code activity.

Digital resources

Teacher's Digital: You can also teach this lesson using the Teacher's App on Navio.

Pupil's Digital: Encourage your pupils to use the Pupil's App on Navio to practise the activities from this lesson.

Powered By NAVIO

Starting the lesson

Use the Trinity Exams Practice cards (optional).

- The pupils practise asking and answering questions.

Review the story.

- Ask the pupils if they remember the story that they read in the previous lesson.
- Organise the class into small groups. Ask each group a question about the story. The pupils should collaborate before they give the answer.

Set learning outcomes and use the talk cards.

- Say **Today we're going to learn the names of some free-time activities and we're going to learn how to talk about these activities in the past.**
- Point to the talk cards to show the pupils the different ways they will be working in the lesson.

Pupil's Book Activity 1

Listen, point and say.

▶ *CD4 Track 02 p277*

- Point to the first photo and say **What's she doing?** (*Playing cards.*) Ask **Do you like playing cards? How often do you play cards? What's your favourite card game?**
- Repeat the procedure with the other photos, encouraging the class to talk about the free-time activities.
- Play the CD. The pupils listen, point to the photos and repeat.

Pupil's Book Activity 2

Listen and sing *Did you watch TV?*

▶ *CD4 Track 03 p277*

- Focus the pupils' attention on the pictures and ask **What did Lily do yesterday?** Repeat the question for Josh and Ravi.
- Play the CD. The pupils listen and read.
- Play the CD again. The pupils join in singing the song and miming the free-time activities in each verse.

Pupil's Book Activity 3

Listen and follow. Repeat.

▶ *CD4 Track 04 p278*

- Focus the class on the grammar table.
- Play the CD. The pupils listen to the first sentence and point to the corresponding parts in the table. They then repeat the complete sentence. Repeat the procedure with the other sentences.
- Use the grammar table to make a sentence that is true for you, e.g. **I planted seeds last night. / I didn't skip yesterday.** Prompt the class to use the table to make other true sentences.

Grammar clue

- Read the grammar clue as a class. Ask the pupils to repeat the examples of the past simple with you. Highlight the different pronunciation of the endings.

Pupil's Book Activity 4

Make true sentences about the past.

- Organise the class into Talk Partners. The pupils make true sentences. They can do this orally or in their notebooks.

Activity Book

Activity 1

Order and write the words.

- Invite a pupil to say and spell the first missing word.
- The pupils work on their own to order and write the remaining words.

Answers: **1** cards **2** phone **3** plant **4** climb **5** paint **6** skip

Activity 2

Order the words in the grammar table. Write the sentences.

- Explain that the grammar table is mixed up and that the pupils need to reorder the words. Invite a pupil to read out the first sentence.
- The pupils order and write the remaining sentences. If they need more support, remind them that a sentence begins with a capital letter and ends with a full stop.

Answers: **1** I didn't phone a friend yesterday. **2** He painted a picture last night. **3** They played cards last week. **4** We didn't climb a tree yesterday.

Activity 3

What did you do last week? Write.

- Invite a pupil to read out Josh's speech bubble. Then ask different pupils to say if they phoned or didn't phone a friend last week. If necessary, repeat the procedure with the prompts.
- The pupils work on their own to write their sentences.

Code activity

- The pupils complete the code activity.

Answer: bookcase

Ending the lesson

Review the lesson and reflect on learning.

- Say **Today we've learnt the names of some new free-time activities and we've practised talking about them in the past.** Elicit example sentences.
- Ask **Which was your favourite activity today? Which activity was easy / difficult?**

Extra activities

Reinforcement

- Write a list of regular verbs that the class knows on the board (*walk, kick, smile, wash, skate, dance*).
- Prompt the pupils to use these verbs to make true sentences about what they did and didn't do yesterday, last week and last year.

Vocabulary extension

- Use the Vocabulary Booster on Navio and present and practise four additional regular verbs: *bake-baked, skate-skated, study-studied, travel-travelled.*

Key Competences and Key Learning Outcomes

- Say a tongue twister with the 'f' sound
- Practise spelling and learn an alternative spelling for the 'f' sound
- Listen for specific information
- Play a communication game using questions with *did*

Key language

- *climbed a tree, danced, listened to music, painted a picture, phoned a friend, planted seeds, played basketball, played cards, played tennis, played the drums, played the violin, skipped, washed the car, watched TV*
- *What did (Daisy) do (yesterday morning)? She (played cards). Thank you. You're welcome.*
- Recycled: *alphabet, dolphin, elephant, farm, film, fish, friend, frog, fur, photo; yesterday afternoon / evening / morning, last night*

Materials

- Pupil's Book p87; Activity Book p84; Class CD4; Teacher's App on Navio
- Teacher's Resource Bank: Talk Cards
- TV programmes flashcards
- Teacher's Resource Bank: Unit 8 Lesson 5 Communication Activity

Optional materials

- Teacher's Resource Bank: Trinity Exams Practice cards (selected from the Starter Unit and Units 1, 2, 3, 4, 5, 6 and 7)

At a Glance Lesson Plan

Pupil's Book

Starting the lesson

- Use the Trinity Exams Practice cards (optional).
- Review the past simple of regular verbs.
- Review the *Did you watch TV?* song.
- ▶ ***CD4 Track 03 p277***
- Set learning outcomes and use the talk cards.

Activity 1: Speak and spell

- Listen, read and say.
- ▶ ***CD4 Track 05 p278***
- Go to the Activity Book.

Activity 2

- Look at the chart.
- Listen and identify four differences.
- ▶ ***CD4 Track 06 p278***

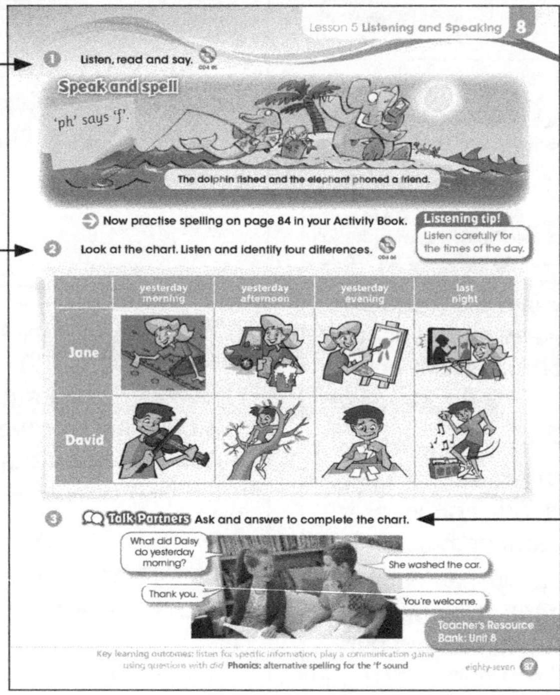

Activity 3

- Ask and answer to complete the chart (Teacher's Resource Bank: Unit 8).

Ending the lesson

- Review the lesson and reflect on learning.

Extra activities

Reinforcement

- Play *Disappearing flashcards*.

Extension

- Make your own tongue twister to practise the 'f' sound.

Activity Book

Activity Book

Activity 1: Speak and spell

- Complete and say.

Activity 2

- Find and circle the words.
- Classify and write.

Activity 3

- Test your friend.
- Ask and answer.

Code activity

- Complete the code activity.

Digital resources

Teacher's Digital: You can also teach this lesson using the Teacher's App on Navio.

Pupil's Digital: Encourage your pupils to use the Pupil's App on Navio to practise the activities from this lesson.

Powered By NAVIO

Starting the lesson

Use the Trinity Exams Practice cards (optional).

- The pupils practise asking and answering questions.

Review the past simple of regular verbs.

- Invite a pupil to the front of the class and show him / her one of the pictures of the free-time activities in Lesson 4. Ask the pupil to mime the activity and ask the class **What did (Carmen) do yesterday?** When a pupil answers correctly, ask the whole class to repeat the verb in the past simple. Repeat the procedure with the remaining five free-time activities.

Review the *Did you watch TV?* song.

▶ *CD4 Track 03 p277*

- Play the CD. The pupils join in singing the song and doing the actions.

Set learning outcomes and use the talk cards.

- Say **Today we're going to say a tongue twister, practise spelling and complete a chart together.**
- Point to the talk cards to show the pupils the different ways they will be working in the lesson.

Pupil's Book Activity 1: Speak and spell

Listen, read and say.

▶ *CD4 Track 05 p278*

- (Books closed.) Write the letter 'f' on the board and ask **What sound does this letter make?** (*'f'*) List the words the pupils know that begin with this letter. Say **Today you're going to learn another way of writing the 'f' sound.**
- (Books open.) Focus on the picture and ask **Which animals can you see?** (*A dolphin and an elephant.*) **What are they doing?** (*Fishing and phoning.*)
- Say **Let's listen to the tongue twister.** Play the CD. The pupils follow the text in their books.
- Play the CD again. The pupils join in with the tongue twister.
- Finally, ask the class to identify the alternative way of writing the 'f' sound (*'ph'*).

Activity Book

Activity 1: Speak and spell

Complete and say.

- The pupils write the letters and say the tongue twister.

Answer: The dolphin fished and the elephant phoned a friend.

Activity 2

Find and circle the words. Classify and write.

- The pupils find and circle the words in the border which contain the 'f' sound.
- The pupils classify and write the words according to whether they are spelt with 'f' or 'ph'.

Answers: ph: elephant, dolphin, phone, alphabet, photo
f: fish, film, farm, frog, fur

Activity 3

Talk Partners. Test your friend. Ask and answer.

- Invite two pupils to read out the speech bubbles.
- Organise the pupils into Talk Partners. The pupils take turns to identify the words in Activity 2. Stress the importance of encouraging and helping each other.

Code activity

- The pupils complete the code activity.

Answer: mat

Pupil's Book Activity 2

Look at the chart. Listen and identify four differences.

▶ *CD4 Track 06 p278*

- Ask the class to name the activities. Explain that all the verbs are regular, so they finish in '–ed' in the past simple. Prompt the class to say the activities in the past simple.
- Tell the pupils they need to listen out for four differences between the activities in the chart and those mentioned on the audio.
- Play the CD, pausing after the first exchange to elicit the difference. Repeat the procedure with the other exchanges.

Answers: Jane climbed a tree yesterday afternoon. David played the guitar yesterday morning. Jane listened to music last night. David played video games yesterday evening.

Pupil's Book Activity 3

Ask and answer to complete the chart (Teacher's Resource Bank: Unit 8).

- Invite two pupils to read out the speech bubbles. Explain that the pupils are going to do the same activity with a Talk Partner.
- Organise the class into Talk Partners. Check that the pupils know all the activities that appear on the chart and highlight that they all end in '–ed'. If necessary, review language for clarification: *Can you repeat that, please? How do you spell that, please?*
- The pupils take turns to ask and answer the questions to complete the chart.

Ending the lesson

Review the lesson and reflect on learning.

- Say **Today we've practised a tongue twister.** Elicit the tongue twister.
- Ask **Which was your favourite activity today? Which activity was easy / difficult?**

Extra activities

Reinforcement

- Play *Disappearing flashcards* (see p27) with the TV programmes flashcards.

Extension

- Ask the pupils to open their Activity Books at page 84 and read out the list of words in Activity 2. Explain that you want them to use these words to make a new tongue twister. They do this in pairs and then read their new tongue twister to the rest of the class.

Key Competences and Key Learning Outcomes

- Predict content from a title
- Scan the text for specific information
- Read and understand a review
- Give a personal response to the information

Key language

- *ending, strange*
- *This programme is about (sea animals). It's on Channel (2) on (Wednesday evening). It begins at (eight o'clock). I (love) this programme because (it's funny).*
- Recycled: *adventure, comedy programme, dangerous, documentary, exciting, famous, funny, information, interesting, judges, music programme, newspaper, scary, scientists, sea animals, singers, submarine, surprise*

Materials

- Pupil's Book p88; Activity Book p85; Class CD4; Teacher's App on Navio
- Teacher's Resource Bank: Talk cards

Optional materials

- Teacher's Resource Bank: Trinity Exams Practice cards (selected from the Starter Unit and Units 1, 2, 3, 4, 5, 6 and 7)

At a Glance Lesson Plan

Pupil's Book

Starting the lesson

- Use the Trinity Exams Practice cards (optional).
- Review the tongue twister.
- ▶ *CD4 Track 05 p278*
- Set learning outcomes and use the talk cards.

Before you read: Activity 1

- What type of TV programmes do you think these are?

Activity 2

- Read and listen to find out.
- ▶ *CD4 Track 07 p278*
- Go to the Activity Book.

Ending the lesson

- Review the lesson and reflect on learning.

Extra activity

Reinforcement

- Complete sentences about the TV programmes you watch.

Activity Book

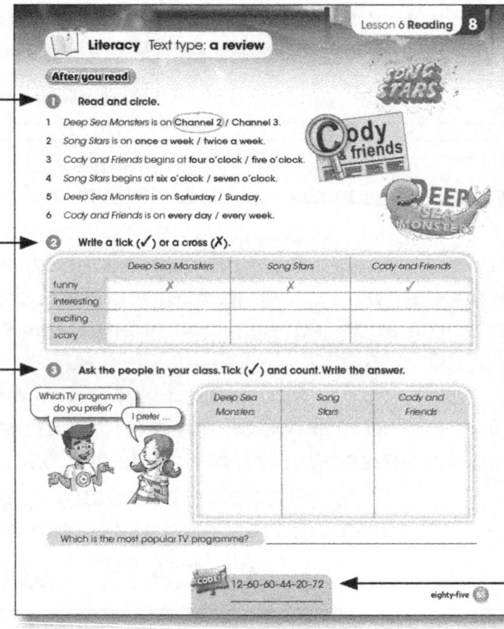

After you read: Activity Book

Activity 1

- Read and circle.

Activity 2

- Write a tick (✓) or a cross (✗).

Activity 3

- Ask the people in your class.
- Tick (✓) and count.
- Write the answer.

Code activity

- Complete the code activity.

Digital resources

Teacher's Digital: You can also teach this lesson using the Teacher's App on Navio.

Pupil's Digital: Encourage your pupils to use the Pupil's App on Navio to practise the activities from this lesson.

Powered By NAVIO

Starting the lesson

Use the Trinity Exams Practice cards (optional).

- The pupils practise asking and answering questions.

Review the tongue twister.

▶ *CD4 Track 05 p278*

- Ask **What sound did you practise in the tongue twister?** (*'f'*)
- Play the CD. Practise the tongue twister as a class.
- Remind the pupils that they know two spellings for this sound ('f' and 'ph'). The pupils list the words they know which contain these letters.

Set learning outcomes and use the talk cards.

- Say **Today we're going to read some reviews of TV programmes.** Explain that a review gives information about a book, a film or a TV programme.
- Point to the talk cards to show the pupils the different ways they will be working in the lesson.

Before you read: Pupil's Book Activity 1

What type of TV programmes do you think these are?

- Invite a pupil to read the first name and encourage the class to predict what kind of TV programme it is.
- Repeat with the other two names.

Pupil's Book Activity 2

Read and listen to find out.

▶ *CD4 Track 07 p278*

- Explain to the pupils that the first time they read they should try to understand the most important information. If you want the pupils to read the text without the support of the CD, set a time limit for this task. Otherwise, play the CD, pausing at the end of each section of the text.
- The pupils report back on the types of TV programmes they are.
- Ask **Which of these programmes do you want to watch?**

Answers: Song Stars: music programme; Deep Sea Monsters: documentary; Cody and Friends: comedy programme

After you read: Activity Book

Activity 1

Read and circle.

- Invite a pupil to read out the first statement. The class scans the review of *Deep Sea Monsters* in the Pupil's Book to find the information.
- The pupils work on their own or in pairs to read the sentences, scan the text and circle the correct information.

Answers: **1** Channel 2 **2** once a week **3** four o'clock **4** seven o'clock **5** Sunday **6** every day

Activity 2

Write a tick (✓) or a cross (✗).

- Read out the list of adjectives in the chart. Check understanding by asking the class to mime watching a funny programme, an interesting programme, an exciting programme and a scary programme. Then say each adjective and ask the class to repeat.
- Point to the first row and ask **Is *Deep Sea Monsters* funny?** (*No.*) **Is *Cody and Friends* funny?** (*Yes.*) If necessary, repeat the procedure with the second adjective.
- The pupils work on their own or in pairs to scan the texts and write a tick or a cross in the different columns of the chart.

	Deep Sea Monsters	*Song Stars*	*Cody and Friends*
funny	✗	✗	✓
interesting	✓	✗	✗
exciting	✗	✓	✗
scary	✓	✗	✗

Activity 3

Ask the people in your class. Tick (✓) and count. Write the answer.

- Explain to the pupils that they are going to find out which TV programme is the most popular. Say **I prefer (*Deep Sea Monsters*).** Then ask a pupil **Which TV programme do you prefer?** Ask several more pupils.
- The pupils ask and answer the question in pairs.
- Explain that the pupils will need to ask ten other pupils in the class the question. They will then write ticks in the chart to show the programmes their friends prefer.
- Ask half the class to stand up. Prompt them to ask the question to ten pupils who are sitting down. When they've finished, the pupils swap roles.
- Finally, the pupils add up the number of ticks to find out which is the most popular TV programme and write the answer under the chart.

Code activity

- The pupils complete the code activity.

Answer: cooker

Ending the lesson

Review the lesson and reflect on learning.

- Say **Today we've read some reviews.** Then ask **What were the names of the TV programmes? What type of programmes were they?**
- Ask **Which was your favourite activity today? Which activity was easy / difficult?**

Extra activity

Reinforcement

- Write the following sentence endings on the board: *… is a scary programme. … is an interesting programme. … is an exciting programme. … is a funny programme.*
- The pupils should think about the TV programmes that they watch and then copy and complete the sentences in their notebooks.

Key Competences and Key Learning Outcomes

- Use *because* to give a reason
- Identify the text features of a review
- Read and listen for specific information
- Use criteria to check your writing
- Share your writing with a partner
- Prepare and write a review

Key language

- *last minute, saves the world*
- *My favourite (character) is (Tina) because (she's very funny).*
- Recycled: *adventures, cartoon, detective, dog, exciting, funny, pet, programme; This (cartoon) is about (a clever dog). It's on Channel (3) (every afternoon) at (half past five). I (love) the programme because (it's exciting).*

Materials

- Pupil's Book p89; Activity Book p86; Class CD4; Teacher's App on Navio
- Teacher's Resource Bank: Talk cards

Optional materials

- Teacher's Resource Bank: Trinity Exams Practice cards (selected from the Starter Unit and Units 1, 2, 3, 4, 5, 6 and 7)
- Paper, card, crayons or coloured pencils

At a Glance Lesson Plan

Pupil's Book

Starting the lesson

- Use the Trinity Exams Practice cards (optional).
- Review the past simple.
- Set learning outcomes and use the talk cards.

Investigate a text: Activity 1

- Look at the picture.
- Think of questions to ask about this TV programme.

Investigate a text: Activity 2

- Read and listen.
- ▶ *CD4 Track 08 p278*
- Does the review answer your questions?

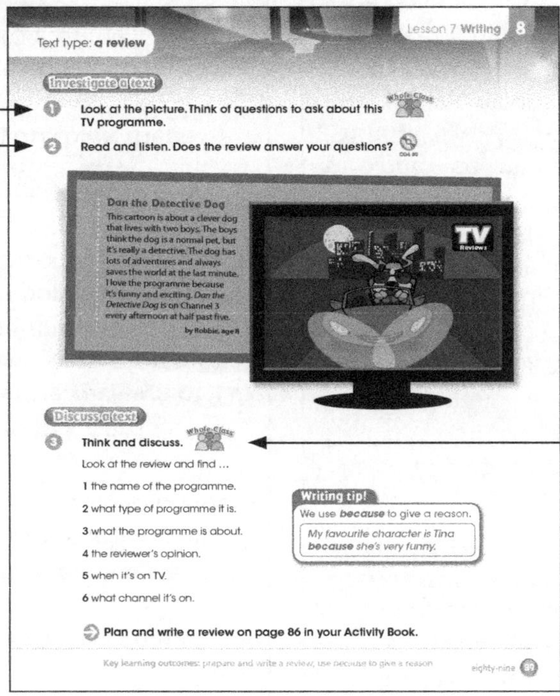

Lesson 7 Writing 8

Text type: a review

Investigate a text

1 Look at the picture. Think of questions to ask about this TV programme.

2 Read and listen. Does the review answer your questions?

Dan the Detective Dog

This cartoon is about a clever dog that lives with two boys. The boys think the dog is a normal pet, but it's really a detective. The dog has lots of adventures and always saves the world at the last minute. I love the programme because it's funny and exciting. Dan the Detective Dog is on Channel 3 every afternoon at half past five.

by Robbie, age 8

Discuss a text

3 Think and discuss.

Look at the review and find ...

1 the name of the programme.
2 what type of programme it is.
3 what the programme is about.
4 the reviewer's opinion.
5 when it's on TV.
6 what channel it's on.

Writing tip!
We use *because* to give a reason.
My favourite character is Tina because she's very funny.

Plan and write a review on page 86 in your Activity Book.

Discuss a text: Activity 3

- Think and discuss.
- **Writing tip:** Read about using 'because' to give a reason.
- Go to the Activity Book.

Ending the lesson

- Review the lesson and reflect on learning.

Extra activity

Reinforcement

- Rewrite and decorate your review for a class display.

Activity Book

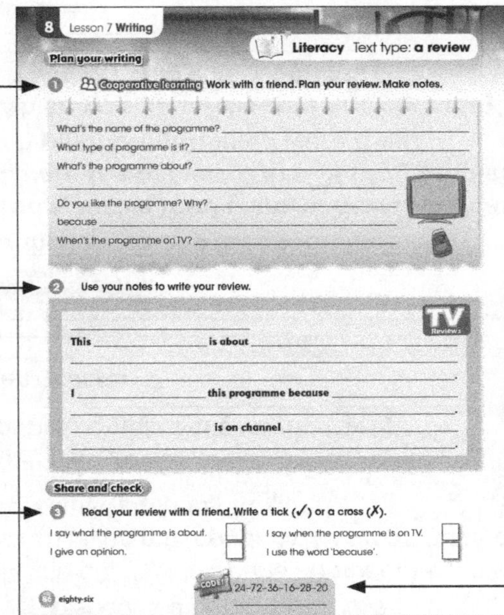

8 Lesson 7 Writing

Literacy Text type: a review

Plan your writing

1 Cooperative learning Work with a friend. Plan your review. Make notes.

What's the name of the programme?
What type of programme is it?
What's the programme about?
Do you like the programme? Why?
because
When's the programme on TV?

2 Use your notes to write your review.

This ___ is about ___
I ___ this programme because ___
___ is on channel ___

Share and check

3 Read your review with a friend. Write a tick (✓) or a cross (✗).

I say what the programme is about. ☐ I say when the programme is on TV. ☐
I give an opinion. ☐ I use the word 'because'. ☐

CODE 24-72-36-16-28-20

eighty-six

Activity Book

Plan your writing: Activity 1

- Work with a friend.
- Plan your review.
- Make notes.

Activity 2

- Use your notes to write your review.

Share and check: Activity 3

- Read your review with a friend.
- Write a tick (✓) or a cross (✗).

Code activity

- Complete the code activity.

Digital resources

Teacher's Digital: You can also teach this lesson using the Teacher's App on Navio.

Pupil's Digital: Encourage your pupils to use the Pupil's App on Navio to practise the activities from this lesson.

Powered By NAVIO

Starting the lesson

Use the Trinity Exams Practice cards (optional).

- The pupils practise asking and answering questions.

Review the past simple.

- Explain that you are going to say some sentences about yesterday, e.g. **I played football yesterday.** The pupils should listen to each sentence and stand up if it's true for them. Those who are standing up repeat the sentence and then sit down. Repeat the procedure with other sentences, using regular verbs, e.g. **I painted a picture. I played a video game. I watched TV. I climbed a tree. I walked to school.**

Set learning outcomes and use the talk cards.

- Ask **How many reviews did we read in the last lesson?** (*Three.*) **What kind of programmes did they review?** (*A comedy programme, a documentary, a music programme.*) Say **Today we're going to read another review. Then we're going to plan and write a review.**
- Point to the talk cards to show the pupils the different ways they will be working in the lesson.

Investigate a text: Pupil's Book Activity 1

Look at the picture. Think of questions to ask about this TV programme.

- Focus on the picture and ask the class to describe the cartoon character in as much detail as possible. Then say **This review is about a cartoon. What questions can we ask about this cartoon?** Elicit questions and write them on the board, e.g. *What's the dog's name? What does the dog do? When can I watch the cartoon? Is the cartoon funny?*

Investigate a text: Pupil's Book Activity 2

Read and listen. Does the review answer your questions?

▶ *CD4 Track 08 p278*

- The pupils read the text to find out if their questions are answered. If you want the pupils to read the text without the support of the CD, set a time limit. Otherwise, play the CD.

Discuss a text: Pupil's Book Activity 3

Think and discuss.

- Read the instructions and find the text features as a class. Highlight that reviews give the name and type of programme, information about what the programme is about and a personal opinion. They also give information about the channel and the time the programme begins.

Answers: **1** *Dan the Detective Dog* **2** It's a cartoon. **3** It's about a dog who's a detective. **4** The reviewer loves it. **5** It's on TV at half past five every afternoon. **6** It's on Channel 3.

Writing tip

- Read the information about using 'because'.
- Prompt the pupils to find other examples of 'because' in the text.
- Write on the board the prompt *I like … because …* Give an example of a sentence, e.g. *I like the (news) because it's interesting.* Then prompt the class to make similar sentences.

Activity Book

Plan your writing: Activity 1

Writing Partners. Work with a friend. Plan your review. Make notes.

- Organise the class into Talk Partners and explain that they are going to write a review of a TV programme they like.
- The pupils work with their partner to decide on a programme and then write their notes.

Activity 2

Use your notes to write your review.

- Focus the class on the activity. If necessary, model how to write a review. Choose a programme that the whole class is familiar with and prompt the pupils to give you the information. Correct or fine-tune their suggestions and write the text on the board.
- The pupils work with their partners to write their own TV review in their Activity Books. This text may be as short or as long as the pupils like.

Share and check: Activity 3

Writing Partners. Read your review with a friend. Write a tick (✓) or a cross (✗).

- Focus on the statements and read through them as a class.
- Organise the class into new pairs. One pupil in each pair should read their text aloud to their partner. The other pupil listens. The pupils work together to decide if the text fulfils all the criteria and tick or cross the corresponding boxes. The pupils can add to, improve, or correct the text at this stage.
- The pupils swap roles.

Code activity

- The pupils complete the code activity.

Answer: fridge

Ending the lesson

Review the lesson and reflect on learning.

- Say **Today we've written a review. Are you happy with your review?** Elicit the pupils' opinions.
- Ask **Which was your favourite activity today? Which activity was easy / difficult?**

Extra activity

Reinforcement

- Ask the class to copy their reviews onto a piece of paper and to decorate their writing with drawings or pictures.
- Stick the pupils' work onto card and write the title *What's on TV?*
- Put up the display in the classroom or in another area of the school.

Key Competences and Key Learning Outcomes

- Use the Internet to investigate the USA
- Read and listen for specific information
- Read about Hollywood
- Think about your own culture and identity

Key language

- *actor, actress, car chase, coast, explosion, handprints, Oscars, red carpet, script, sign, special effects, star, studio*
- *Do you want to (feel like a star)?*
- Recycled: *city, exciting, famous, film, floor, hills, music, prizes, surprises; There are (more than 2,000 stars). You can (visit a real studio). It's (incredible).*

Materials

- Pupil's Book p90; Activity Book p87; Class CD4; Teacher's App on Navio
- Teacher's Resource Bank: Talk cards
- An online world map
- Coloured pencils (red, white and blue)

Optional materials

- Teacher's Resource Bank: Trinity Exams Practice cards (selected from the Starter Unit and Units 1, 2, 3, 4, 5, 6 and 7)

At a Glance Lesson Plan

Pupil's Book

Starting the lesson

- Use the Trinity Exams Practice cards (optional).
- Review film vocabulary and the past tense.
- Set learning outcomes and use the talk cards.

Activity 1

- Read Luke's questions.
- What do you think?

Activity 2

- Read and listen.
- ▶ *CD4 Track 09 p278*
- Answer Luke's questions.
- **Think about your culture** Do you watch American films in your country? Which are your favourite films?

Go to the Activity Book.

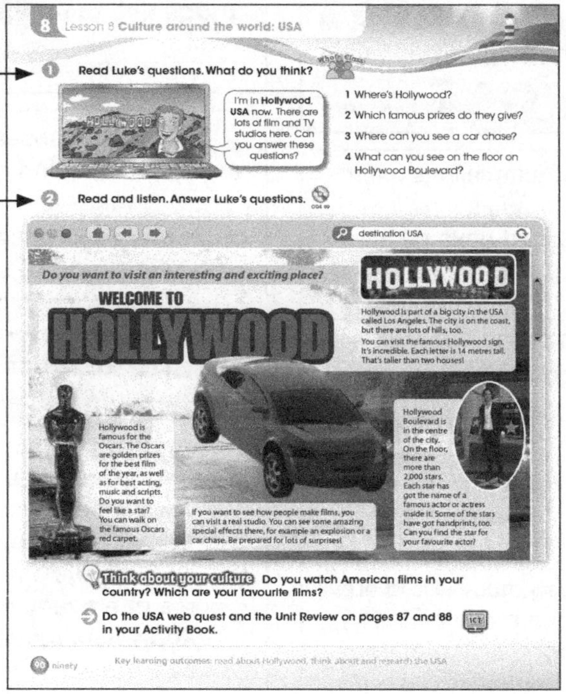

8 Lesson 8 Culture around the world: USA

1 Read Luke's questions. What do you think?

I'm in **Hollywood, USA** now. There are lots of film and TV studios here. Can you answer these questions?

1 Where's Hollywood?
2 Which famous prizes do they give?
3 Where can you see a car chase?
4 What can you see on the floor on Hollywood Boulevard?

2 Read and listen. Answer Luke's questions.

Do you want to visit an interesting and exciting place?

WELCOME TO HOLLYWOOD

Hollywood is part of a big city in the USA called Los Angeles. The city is on the coast, but there are lots of hills, too. You can visit the famous Hollywood sign. It's incredible. Each letter is 14 metres tall. That's taller than two houses!

Hollywood is famous for the Oscars. The Oscars are golden prizes for the best film of the year, as well as for best acting, music and scripts. Do you want to feel like a star? You can walk on the famous Oscars red carpet.

If you want to see how people make films, you can visit a real studio. You can see some amazing special effects there, for example an explosion or a car chase. Be prepared for lots of surprises!

Hollywood Boulevard is in the centre of the city. On the floor, there are more than 2,000 stars. Each star has got the name of a famous actor or actress inside it. Some of the stars have got handprints, too. Can you find the star for your favourite actor?

Think about your culture Do you watch American films in your country? Which are your favourite films?

Do the USA web quest and the Unit Review on pages 87 and 88 in your Activity Book.

90 ninety

Ending the lesson

- Review the lesson and reflect on learning.

Extra activity

Extension

- Use the Internet to plan an imaginary visit to a Hollywood film studio.

Activity Book

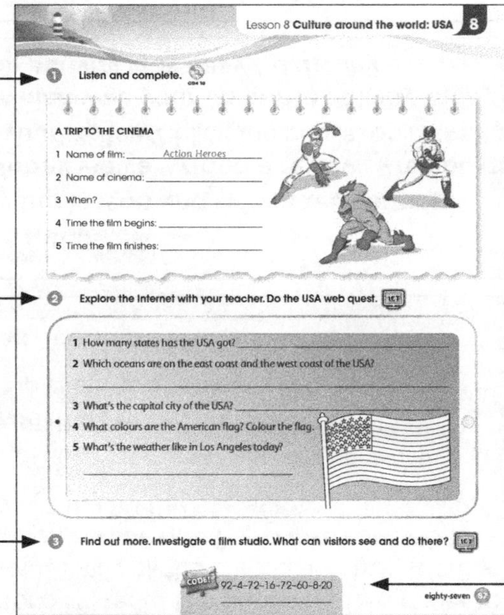

Lesson 8 Culture around the world: USA 8

1 Listen and complete.

A TRIP TO THE CINEMA
1 Name of film: Action Heroes
2 Name of cinema:
3 When?
4 Time the film begins:
5 Time the film finishes:

2 Explore the Internet with your teacher. Do the USA web quest.

1 How many states has the USA got?
2 Which oceans are on the east coast and the west coast of the USA?
3 What's the capital city of the USA?
4 What colours are the American flag? Colour the flag.
5 What's the weather like in Los Angeles today?

3 Find out more. Investigate a film studio. What can visitors see and do there?

CODE 92-4-72-16-72-60-8-20

eighty-seven 87

Activity Book

Activity 1

- Listen and complete.
- ▶ *CD4 Track 10 p278*

Activity 2

- Explore the Internet with your teacher.
- Do the USA web quest.

Activity 3

- Find out more.
- Investigate a film studio.
- What can visitors see and do there?

Code activity

- Complete the code activity.

Digital resources

Teacher's Digital: You can also teach this lesson using the Teacher's App on Navio.

Powered By NAVIO

Starting the lesson

Use the Trinity Exams Practice cards (optional).

- The pupils practise asking and answering questions.

Review film vocabulary and the past tense.

- Ask **Did you go to the cinema last week / month? Which film did you watch? Was it good? Did you like it?** Encourage different pupils to respond.

Set learning outcomes and use the talk cards.

- Say **Today we're going to investigate the United States of America.**
- Point to the talk cards to show the pupils the different ways they will be working in the lesson.

Pupil's Book Activity 1

Read Luke's questions. What do you think?

- Read the speech bubble as a class. Encourage the pupils to tell you what they know about Hollywood. Show the pupils where the USA is on an online world map. Then show them where Hollywood is.
- Read Luke's questions as a class. Encourage the pupils to predict the answers.

Pupil's Book Activity 2

Read and listen. Answer Luke's questions.

▸ *CD4 Track 09 p278*

- Focus the class on the photos. Ask **What can you see?**
- Ask the pupils to read the text. If you want them to read the text without the support of the CD, set a time limit for this task. Otherwise, play the CD, pausing after each section to check understanding.
- The pupils answer Luke's questions.

Answers: **1** It's in Los Angeles in the USA. **2** They give the Oscars. **3** You can see a car chase in a real studio. **4** You can see stars with the names of famous actors and actresses.

Think about your culture

- Read out the questions and prompt the pupils to tell you about their favourite American film. Ask **What's the film about? Who are the characters? Why do you like it?**
- Organise the class into pairs. The pupils take turns to ask and answer the questions.

Activity Book

Activity 1

Listen and complete.

▸ *CD4 Track 10 p278*

- Invite a pupil to read out the information in the notebook. Then play the CD, pausing after each piece of information. Prompt the class to give you the answer each time and to complete the notes.
- When the pupils have completed the notes, play the CD again without pausing. The pupils should listen and follow the notes in their Activity Books.

Answers: **1** Action Heroes **2** Zoom **3** Saturday **4** five o'clock **5** half past six

Activity 2

Explore the Internet with your teacher. Do the USA web quest.

- Read out the instructions for the activity.
- Connect to a children's website (see suggested websites opposite) that provides geographical information about the USA. Read out questions 1–4. The pupils work as a class to find and write the answers. They should also colour the flag.
- Read out question 5. Connect to a website that shows the weather around the world. The pupils complete the information.

Answers: **1** 50 **2** the Atlantic Ocean (east coast) and the Pacific Ocean (west coast) **3** Washington, D.C. **4** red, white and blue

Activity 3

Find out more. Investigate a film studio. What can visitors see and do there?

- If you are doing the investigation as a class, go to a suitable website. The pupils scan the information to find out what you can see and do there.
- If you are working in a computer room, organise the class into small groups to do the activity.

Suggested websites

http://maps.google.es/
http://kids.nationalgeographic.com/
http://www.bbc.co.uk/weather
http://www.universalstudioshollywood.com

Code activity

- The pupils complete the code activity.

Answer: wardrobe

Ending the lesson

Review the lesson and reflect on learning.

- Say **Today we've learnt about Hollywood in the USA. Is it an interesting place? What can you see and do there?** Elicit the information from the pupils.
- Ask **Which was your favourite activity today? Which activity was easy / difficult?**

Extra activity

Extension

- Explain that you want the pupils to plan an imaginary trip to a film studio. Write the following prompts on the board: *The studio opens at … and closes at … We can have lunch at … We can ride on … We can see … We can't miss the … We can buy …*
- The pupils can either use the Universal Studio webpage to find the information, or invent their own details to complete the sentences.

Go to the AB Unit Review on page 257.

Key Competences and Key Learning Outcomes

- Watch and understand a video about television
- Work collaboratively to plan a video
- Learn about professions in the TV industry

Key language

- *actor, camera, camera operator, camerawoman, director, drone, edit, editor, headphones, presenter, studio, upload*
- *The presenter reads the news. You need (a lot of light). Let's make a documentary.*

Materials

- Pupil's Book p91; Activity Book p89; Class CD4; Teacher's App on Navio
- TV programmes flashcards
- Teacher's Resource Bank: Talk cards

Optional materials

- Teacher's Resource Bank: Trinity Exams Practice cards (selected from the Starter Unit and Units 1, 2, 3, 4, 5, 6 and 7)

At a Glance Lesson Plan

Pupil's Book

Starting the lesson

- Use the Trinity Exams Practice cards (optional).
- **Think-Pair-Share.** Review TV programmes.
- Set learning outcomes and use the talk cards.

Activity 1

- Before you watch
- Watch the video.
  Unit 8 video p286
- What do people do with this equipment?

Activity 2

- Watch the video again.
  Unit 8 video
- Read and say *true* or *false*.
- Correct the false sentences.

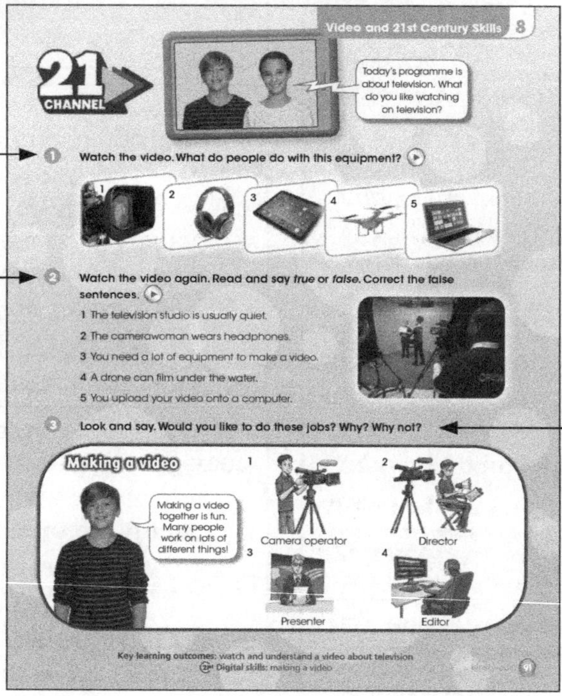

Activity 3

- Look and say.
- Would you like to do these jobs?
- Why? Why not?
  Go to the Activity Book.

Ending the lesson

- Review the lesson and reflect on learning.

Extra activity

Reinforcement

- Make a video.

Activity Book

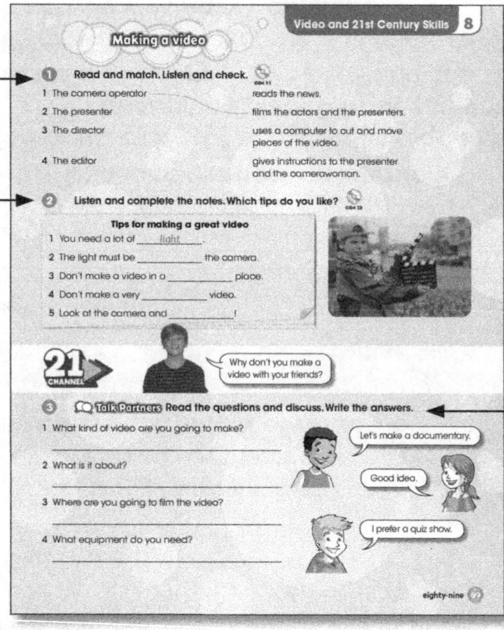

Activity Book

Activity 1

- Read and match.
- Listen and check.

▶ *CD4 Track 11 p279*

Activity 2

- Listen and complete the notes.

▶ *CD4 Track 12 p279*

- Which tips do you like?

Activity 3

- Read the questions and discuss.
- Write the answers.

Digital resources

Teacher's Digital: You can also teach this lesson using the Teacher's App on Navio.

Pupil's Digital: Encourage your pupils to use the Pupil's App on Navio to practise the activities from this lesson.

Powered By NAVIO

Starting the lesson

Use the Trinity Exams Practice cards (optional).

- The pupils practise asking and answering questions.

Think-Pair-Share. Review TV programmes.

- Ask **Can you remember the vocabulary for TV programmes?** The class thinks silently for a minute.
- Then the pupils work with a Talk Partner to name TV programmes.
- Invite different Talk Partners to say a different item. Hold up the corresponding flashcard and prompt the class to repeat the word.
- Finally, repeat the procedure, asking different pairs of Talk Partners each time, until all the TV programmes have been named.

Set learning outcomes and use the talk cards.

- Say **Today we're going to watch a video and then ask and answer questions about television**.
- Point to the talk cards to show the pupils the different ways they will be working in the lesson.

Pupil's Book Activity 1

Before you watch

- Read the speech bubble to the pupils. Ask **What do you like watching on television?** Elicit responses from a number of pupils. You could use the flashcards to prompt a variety of different answers.

Watch the video. What do people do with this equipment? *p286*

- Watch Part 1. Ask pupils **What are you going to see next?** Check that they understand that they will see a video about how to make television programmes.
- Play Part 2. Ask general questions to check understanding. Focus the pupils' attention on the photos in Activity 1. Check vocabulary. Say **What do people do with this equipment?** Elicit ideas.
- Play Part 2 again for the pupils to answer the questions. Check answers as a class.

Answers: **1** film the actors and presenters **2** listen to instructions **3** film your TV programme **4** film from the sky **5** edit the video

Pupil's Book Activity 2

Watch the video again. Read and say *true* or *false*. Correct the false sentences.

- Explain that you are going to do a true or false activity.
- Ask a pupil to read out sentence 1. Ask the class whether they think the sentence is true or false. Repeat with sentences 2–5.
- Play Part 2. Students work in pairs to decide whether the sentences are true or false. They correct the false sentences.

Answers: **1** F The television studio is usually noisy. **2** T **3** F You don't need a lot of equipment to make a video. **4** F A drone can film from the sky. **5** T

Pupil's Book Activity 3

Look and say. Would you like to do these jobs? Why? Why not?

- Tell pupils that in the last part of the video Chloe and Mark suggest making your own TV programme. Look at the pictures and elicit the roles of each person.
- Ask pupils to work on their own to think about which jobs they would like to do. Encourage them to think of reasons.
- Ask pupils **Would you like to be a (camera operator)?**

Activity Book

Activity 1

Read and match. Listen and check.

▸ *CD4 Track 11 p279*

- Pupils work on their own to match the people with their roles.
- Play the CD and check answers.

Answers: **1** The camera operator films the actors and the presenters. **2** The presenter reads the news. **3** The director gives instructions to the presenter and the camerawoman. **4** The editor uses a computer to cut and move pieces of the video.

Activity 2

Listen and complete the notes. Which tips do you like?

▸ *CD4 Track 12 p279*

- Explain to the pupils that they are going to listen to a boy and a girl talking about tips for making a great video. Ask pupils for their ideas. Read out the information. Then play the CD, pausing to allow the pupils to write the missing information.
- Play the CD again without pausing.

Answers: **1** light **2** behind **3** noisy **4** long **5** smile

- Ask pupils which tips they like best.

Activity 3

Read the questions and discuss. Write the answers.

- Read out the speech bubble. Explain that pupils will work in groups of four to plan the video that they are going to make. Remind them that they need to each have a job.
- Organise the pupils into groups and ask each pupil to choose one of the four roles. Ensure that there is one camera operator, director, presenter and editor in each group.
- The pupils ask and answer the questions to plan their video.

Ending the lesson

Review the lesson and reflect on learning.

- Say **Today we've watched a video about television and learnt how to make a video.**
- Ask **Which was your favourite activity today? Which activity was easy / difficult?**

Extra activity

Reinforcement

- Pupils work in their groups to make a short video.

Date: ______________ Unit: ______________

1 What did my pupils learn in this unit?

2 How did my pupils work? (✓)

individually ☐ in pairs ☐ in small groups ☐

in large groups ☐ as a class ☐

3 Which key competences did my pupils develop?

- Competence in linguistic communication ☐
- Competence in mathematics, science and technology ☐
- Digital competence ☐
- Learning to learn ☐
- Social and civic competences ☐
- Sense of initiative and entrepreneurship ☐
- Cultural awareness and expression ☐

4 Which lessons / activities were the most successful and why?

5 Which lessons / activities did my pupils find the most difficult and why?

6 What did I try in the classroom for the first time? How did it go?

7 Which resources did I find most useful? (including webpages)

8 What could I do differently next time I teach this unit?

Unit overview

Key Competences and Key Learning Outcomes

- Identify and name attractions at festivals (Lesson 1)
- Say the vocabulary chant (Lesson 1)
- Understand and act out a conversation (Lesson 2)
- Talk about festivals in the past tense (Lesson 2)
- Follow, complete and correct the grammar tables (Lessons 2 and 4)
- Tell the time (Lesson 4)
- Understand how to use 'but' (Lesson 7)
- Watch and understand a video (Video and 21st Century Skills)

- Use a code to read a message (Lesson 3)

- Use the Pupil's App on Navio
- Investigate Canada (Lesson 8)

- Say a tongue twister, learn another spelling for the 's' sound and practise spelling (Lesson 5)
- Practise activity types found in the Cambridge Exams: A1 Movers
- Review your own learning (Review)

- Understand the importance of doing nice things for others (Lesson 3)
- Work collaboratively to plan a fete (Video and 21st Century Skills)

- Work with a Talk Partner to practise and reinforce learning (all lessons)
- Play a communication game (Lesson 5)

- Sing two songs (Lessons 1 and 4)
- Understand, act out and give an opinion on a story (Lesson 3)
- Read an email (Lesson 6)
- Plan and write an email (Lesson 7)
- Learn about Canada (Lesson 8)
- Think about your own culture (Lesson 8)

Vocabulary

Core vocabulary
band, big wheel, bumper cars, candyfloss, clown, costume, fireworks, ghost train, merry-go-round, parade, roller coaster, toffee apple; ten past (three), twenty past (one), twenty-five past (eleven), twenty-five to (four), ten to (eight), five to (twelve)

Extension vocabulary (optional)
barbecue, bonfire, bouncy castle, display, helter-skelter, stall; five past two, ten past seven, twenty to three, ten to nine

Other vocabulary
concert, email, face painting, haggis, log rolling, lumberjack, maypole, Morris dancers, Mounties, photo, poet, ribbon, school fete, show, snacks, sweets

Recycled vocabulary
months of the year; ordinal numbers (1st–31st); *beach, bike, birthday, burger, cake, chocolate, festival, fish, half past, ice cream, last week / night, played, quarter past / to, sunglasses, surprise party, TV programmes, watched TV, water, yesterday (evening)*

Structures

Core structures
What did (you) wear / eat / drink / do / see (yesterday)? I wore / ate / drank / did / saw; I had / went / rode; What time did (you) (go to bed) yesterday? (I) (went to bed) at (twenty past nine).

Other structures
In the (evening), I had (a big dinner). Then I (sang songs), but I didn't (dance). When's (Canada Day)?

Recycled structures
Let's (watch the parade). Do you (eat candyfloss)? Yes, I do. No, I don't. What (a mess)! What did (Peter) watch / ride on / see? What was (Joey's) favourite activity? What about candyfloss?

Phonics

The 's' sound (***C**ecil **s**nake **s**ang dan**c**ed **c**ity **c**elebration*)

Literacy

Text type: an email (email form; writing preparation)
Reading skills: guessing meaning from context (inferring)
Writing skills: using 'but' to give opposite information

Culture ... around the world

Canada Day celebrations

21st Century Skills

Working in a group: accepting ideas and suggestions

Thinking skills

Thinking about your culture (Lesson 1); Applying rules (Lessons 2 and 4); Predicting (Lessons 3 and 8); Discussing values (Lesson 3); Expressing opinions (Lesson 3); Making connections (Review)

Cooperative learning

Team building (Lesson 2); Collaborating (Lesson 3); Checking learning (Lesson 5); Sharing information (Lesson 5); Peer evaluation and feedback (Lesson 7); Working together (Review)

Values

Understanding the importance of doing nice things for others

Cross-curricular links

Link to Science
Work: Reviewing the three job sectors (primary, secondary, tertiary)
Suggested Arts and Crafts concepts
Identifying the use of lines to show movement in illustrations and drawing a comic strip

Key Competences and Key Learning Outcomes

- Identify and say attractions at festivals
- Say the vocabulary chant
- Review festivals
- Ask and answer questions using a recycled structure
- Sing a song about a festival

Key language

- Attractions at festivals: *band, big wheel, bumper cars, candyfloss, clown, costume, fireworks, ghost train, merry-go-round, parade, roller coaster, toffee apple; scream*
- *Turn (round and round).*
- Extension: *barbecue, bonfire, bouncy castle, display, helter-skelter, stall*
- Recycled: *eat, ride, watch, wear; festivals; Let's watch (the parade). Do you (eat candyfloss)? Yes, I do. No, I don't.*

Materials

- Pupil's Book p92; Activity Book p90; Class CD4; Teacher's App on Navio
- Teacher's Resource Bank: Attractions at festivals word cards
- Attractions at festivals flashcards
- Teacher's Resource Bank: Talk cards

Optional materials

- Teacher's Resource Bank: Trinity Exams Practice cards (selected from the Starter Unit and Units 1, 2, 3, 4, 5, 6, 7 and 8)

At a Glance Lesson Plan

Pupil's Book

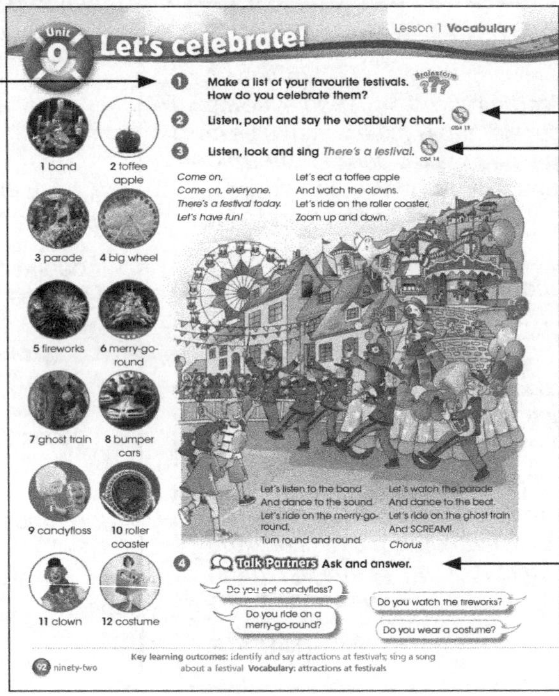
Unit 9 Let's celebrate! Lesson 1 Vocabulary

1 Make a list of your favourite festivals. How do you celebrate them?

2 Listen, point and say the vocabulary chant.

3 Listen, look and sing *There's a festival.*

1 band 2 toffee apple 3 parade 4 big wheel 5 fireworks 6 merry-go-round 7 ghost train 8 bumper cars 9 candyfloss 10 roller coaster 11 clown 12 costume

Come on,
Come on, everyone.
There's a festival today.
Let's have fun!
Let's eat a toffee apple
And watch the clowns.
Let's ride on the roller coaster.
Zoom up and down.

Let's listen to the band
And dance to the sound.
Let's ride on the merry-go-round.
Turn round and round.

Let's watch the parade
And dance to the beat.
Let's ride on the ghost train
And SCREAM!
Chorus

4 Talk Partners Ask and answer.

Do you eat candyfloss?
Do you ride on a merry-go-round?
Do you watch the fireworks?
Do you wear a costume?

92 ninety-two

Key learning outcomes: identify and say attractions at festivals; sing a song about a festival Vocabulary: attractions at festivals

Starting the lesson

- Use the Trinity Exams Practice cards (optional).
- Review talking about activities in the past.
- Set learning outcomes and use the talk cards.

Activity 1

- Make a list of your favourite festivals.
- How do you celebrate them?

Vocabulary presentation

- Present the new vocabulary using the attractions at festivals flashcards.

Word cards

- Introduce the spellings of the vocabulary using the attractions at festivals word cards.

Activity 2

- Listen, point and say the vocabulary chant.

▶ ***CD4 Track 13 p279***

Activity 3

- Listen, look and sing *There's a festival.*

▶ ***CD4 Track 14 p279***

Activity 4

- Ask and answer.

Go to the Activity Book.

Ending the lesson

- Review the lesson and reflect on learning.

Extra activities

Reinforcement

- Order the new vocabulary alphabetically.

Vocabulary extension

- Present six additional vocabulary items.

Activity Book

Unit 9 Let's celebrate! Lesson 1 Vocabulary

1 Read and complete the puzzle.

1 ... explode in the sky.
2 A ... goes round and up and down very quickly.
3 A ... is clothes you wear on special days.
4 ... is a pink food that you eat at the funfair.
5 This exciting attraction is called ... cars.
6 A ... wears colourful clothes, a red nose and is funny.
7 This round attraction is called a big ... .
8 This scary attraction is called a ... train.

2 Think about a festival you celebrate. Look and write. Thinking skills

I eat a toffee apple. I don't watch a parade. What about you?

CODE 12-4-72-80-60-60-56

90 ninety

Activity Book

Activity 1

- Read and complete the puzzle.

Activity 2

- Think about a festival you celebrate.
- Look and write.

Code activity

- Complete the code activity.

Digital resources

Teacher's Digital: You can also teach this lesson using the Teacher's App on Navio.

Pupil's Digital: Encourage your pupils to use the Pupil's App on Navio to practise the activities from this lesson.

Powered By NAVIO

Starting the lesson

Use the Trinity Exams Practice cards (optional).

- The pupils practise asking and answering questions.

Review talking about activities in the past.

- Briefly tell the class what you did yesterday / at the weekend. Then ask **What did you do?** Encourage the pupils to say what they did, providing the past tense forms when necessary. Respond to what the pupils say and ask for more information, e.g. **Was it interesting? Did you like it?**

Set learning outcomes and use the talk cards.

- Say **Today we're going to learn the names of attractions at festivals.** Explain that a festival day is a holiday for everyone and we have festival days to celebrate different things. Some festivals are for the whole country and other festivals are for a town or village.
- Point to the talk cards to show the pupils the different ways they will be working in the lesson.

Pupil's Book Activity 1

Make a list of your favourite festivals. How do you celebrate them?

- (Books closed.) Ask **Which festivals do we celebrate?** Prompt the class to name the festivals they know. Make a list on the board. They may mention Christmas, Easter and Halloween. With each suggestion, ask **What do you eat / wear / do on this festival day?**

Vocabulary presentation

- (Books closed.) Say **Some festivals have fireworks.** Show the class the *fireworks* flashcard and ask **Do you like fireworks?** Say the keyword again. The pupils repeat the word once or twice. Stick the flashcard on the board. Then repeat the procedure with the other attractions at festivals flashcards.

Word cards

- (Books closed.) Organise the class into pairs and hand out an attractions at festivals word card to each pair.
- The pairs of pupils take turns to come to the board, read out their attraction and stick their word card next to the corresponding flashcard.

Pupil's Book Activity 2

Listen, point and say the vocabulary chant.

▶ ***CD4 Track 13 p279***

- Focus the pupils' attention on the 12 photos. Say **Let's listen and say the words.** Play the CD. The pupils listen, point and repeat.

Pupil's Book Activity 3

Listen, look and sing *There's a festival.*

▶ ***CD4 Track 14 p279***

- Focus the pupils' attention on the scene. Ask **What are Lily and Josh looking at?** (*A parade, a band, clowns.*) **What's Lily eating?** (*Candyfloss.*)
- Say **Let's listen to the song.** Play the CD. The pupils listen and read.
- Ask **Which attractions that you can ride on do the children sing about?** (*The roller coaster, the merry-go-round and the ghost train.*) **What do you do on the merry-go-round?** (*Turn round and round.*)
- Play the song again. The pupils join in singing the song.

Pupil's Book Activity 4

Ask and answer.

- Choose a local festival that the pupils all know and ask a pupil **Do you eat candyfloss at (the festival)?** Ask other questions, inviting a different pupil to answer each time.
- Organise the class into Talk Partners to ask and answer the questions in the speech bubbles.

Activity Book

Activity 1

Read and complete the puzzle.

- Ask different pupils to read out the clues and say the missing words.
- The pupils write the words in the puzzle.

Answers: **1** fireworks **2** roller coaster **3** costume **4** candyfloss **5** bumper **6** clown **7** wheel **8** ghost

Activity 2

Think about a festival you celebrate. Look and write.

- Invite a pupil to read out the speech bubble and complete the first sentence so that it's true for him / her.
- Ask the pupils to identify the pictures (*toffee apple, parade, merry-go-round, band, roller coaster*). The pupils then work on their own to write their sentences.

Code activity

- The pupils complete the code activity.

Answer: cartoon

Ending the lesson

Review the lesson and reflect on learning.

- Say **Today we've learnt the names of attractions at festivals. What do you remember?** Elicit the attractions from the pupils.
- Ask **Which was your favourite activity today? Which activity was easy / difficult?**

Extra activities

Reinforcement

- Organise the class into pairs and ask them to copy the new vocabulary into their notebooks in alphabetical order. Challenge them to complete the task in a certain time period, e.g. five minutes.

Vocabulary extension

- Present six additional festival attractions: *barbecue, bonfire, bouncy castle, display, helter-skelter, stall*.
- Use the Vocabulary Booster on Navio to practise these new words.

Key Competences and Key Learning Outcomes

- Listen, repeat and act out a conversation
- Listen, follow the grammar table and identify the parts of a question
- Use irregular verbs in the past simple

Key language

- *ate, did, drank, had, rode, saw, went, wore*
- *What did (you) wear / eat / drink / do / see (yesterday)? I wore / ate / drank / did / saw … I had … I went … I rode …*
- Recycled: *band, big wheel, bumper cars, candyfloss, clown, costume, fireworks, ghost train, merry-go-round, parade, roller coaster, toffee apple; last night, last week, yesterday, yesterday evening; beach, bike, clown, fish, ice cream, sunglasses, water*

Materials

- Pupil's Book p93; Activity Book p91; Class CD4; Teacher's App on Navio
- Attractions at festivals flashcards
- Teacher's Resource Bank: Talk cards

Optional materials

- Teacher's Resource Bank: Trinity Exams Practice cards (selected from the Starter Unit and Units 1, 2, 3, 4, 5, 6, 7 and 8)

At a Glance Lesson Plan

Pupil's Book

Starting the lesson

- Use the Trinity Exams Practice cards (optional).
- **Think-Pair-Share.** Review vocabulary for attractions at festivals.
- Review the *There's a festival* song.
- ▶ *CD4 Track 14 p279*
- ▶ *CD4 Track 15 p279*
- Set learning outcomes and use the talk cards.

Activity 1

- Listen and read.
- Listen and repeat.
- ▶ *CD4 Track 16 p279*
- Act out.

Activity 2

- Read again.
- Did Lily do activities with these objects?

Activity 3

- Listen and follow.
- ▶ *CD4 Track 17 p279*
- Repeat.
- **Grammar clue:** Read about regular and irregular verbs in the past simple.

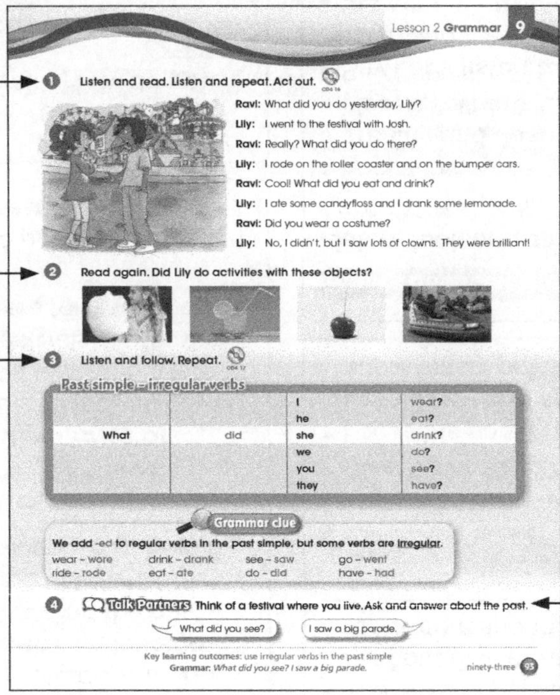
Lesson 2 Grammar 9

1 Listen and read. Listen and repeat. Act out.

Ravi: What did you do yesterday, Lily?
Lily: I went to the festival with Josh.
Ravi: Really? What did you do there?
Lily: I rode on the roller coaster and on the bumper cars.
Ravi: Cool! What did you eat and drink?
Lily: I ate some candyfloss and I drank some lemonade.
Ravi: Did you wear a costume?
Lily: No, I didn't, but I saw lots of clowns. They were brilliant!

2 Read again. Did Lily do activities with these objects?

3 Listen and follow. Repeat.

Past simple – irregular verbs

		I	wear?
		he	eat?
What	did	she	drink?
		we	do?
		you	see?
		they	have?

Grammar clue
We add -ed to regular verbs in the past simple, but some verbs are irregular.
wear – wore, drink – drank, see – saw, go – went
ride – rode, eat – ate, do – did, have – had

4 Talk Partners Think of a festival where you live. Ask and answer about the past.
What did you see? I saw a big parade.

Key learning outcomes: use irregular verbs in the past simple
Grammar: What did you see? I saw a big parade.
ninety-three 93

Activity 4

- Think of a festival where you live.
- Ask and answer about the past.
- Go to the Activity Book.

Ending the lesson

- Review the lesson and reflect on learning.

Extra activity

Reinforcement

- Play a matching game to practise irregular verbs in the past simple.

Digital resources

Teacher's Digital: You can also teach this lesson using the Teacher's App on Navio.

Pupil's Digital: Encourage your pupils to use the Pupil's App on Navio to practise the activities from this lesson.

Powered By NAVIO

Activity Book

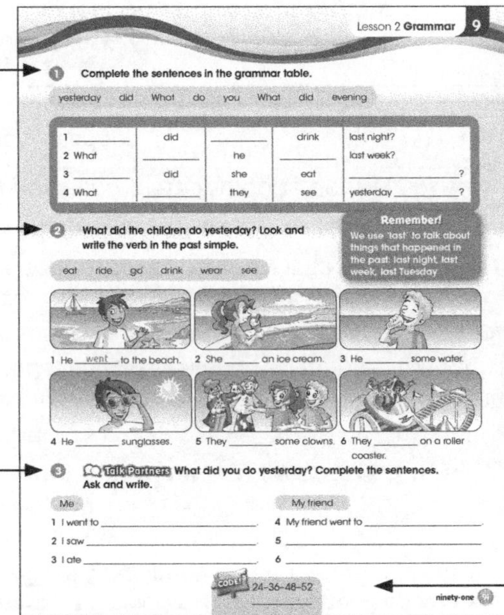
Lesson 2 Grammar 9

1 Complete the sentences in the grammar table.
yesterday did What do you What did evening

1 ____	did	____	drink	last night?
2 What	____	he	____	last week?
3 ____	did	she	eat	____?
4 What	____	they	see	yesterday ____?

2 What did the children do yesterday? Look and write the verb in the past simple.
eat ride go drink wear see

Remember! We use 'last' to talk about things that happened in the past: last night, last week, last Tuesday

1 He went to the beach. 2 She ____ an ice cream. 3 He ____ some water.
4 He ____ sunglasses. 5 They ____ some clowns. 6 They ____ on a roller coaster.

3 Talk Partners What did you do yesterday? Complete the sentences. Ask and write.

Me: 1 I went to ____ 2 I saw ____ 3 I ate ____
My friend: 4 My friend went to ____ 5 ____ 6 ____

Code! 24-36-48-52
ninety-one 91

Activity Book

Activity 1

- Complete the sentences in the grammar table.

Activity 2

- What did the children do yesterday?
- Look and write the verb in the past simple.

Activity 3

- What did you do yesterday?
- Complete the sentences.
- Ask and write.

Code activity

- Complete the code activity.

Starting the lesson

Use the Trinity Exams Practice cards (optional).

- The pupils practise asking and answering questions.

Think-Pair-Share. Review vocabulary for attractions at festivals.

- Ask **Can you remember the vocabulary for attractions at festivals?** The class thinks silently for a minute.
- Then the pupils work with a Talk Partner to name the attractions at festivals.
- Invite Talk Partners to say a different attraction at a festival. Hold up the corresponding flashcard and prompt the class to repeat the word.

Review the *There's a festival* song.

▶ *CD4 Track 14 p279*

▶ *CD4 Track 15 p279 (optional karaoke version)*

- Play the CD (or use the karaoke version). The pupils sing along.

Set learning outcomes and use the talk cards.

- Say **Today we're going to talk about festivals in the past simple.**
- Point to the talk cards to show the pupils the different ways they will be working in the lesson.

Pupil's Book Activity 1

Listen and read. Listen and repeat. Act out.

▶ *CD4 Track 16 p279*

- The pupils look at the picture. Ask **Where are Ravi and Lily? What do you think they are talking about?**
- Play the CD. The pupils listen and read the conversation.
- Ask **Which attractions did Lily ride on?** (*The roller coaster and the bumper cars.*)
- Play the CD again, pausing after each sentence for the pupils to repeat.
- The pupils act out the conversation in pairs.

Pupil's Book Activity 2

Read again. Did Lily do activities with these objects?

- The pupils read the conversation again and say whether Lily did activities with the objects.

Answers: 1, 2 and 4

Pupil's Book Activity 3

Listen and follow. Repeat.

▶ *CD4 Track 17 p279*

- Play the CD. The pupils listen to the first question and point to the words they hear. They then repeat the complete question. Repeat the procedure with the other questions.

Grammar clue

- Read the grammar clue as a class. Ask the class to find the irregular verbs in the conversation in Activity 1.
- Say the past simple of the irregular verbs and ask the pupils to repeat each one with you two or three times.

Pupil's Book Activity 4

Think of a festival where you live. Ask and answer about the past.

- Name a local festival that all the pupils know. Prompt a confident pupil to use the grammar table to ask you a question, e.g. *What did you see?* Give your answer, highlighting the irregular verb. Repeat several times with different pupils.
- Organise the class into Talk Partners. They take turns to ask and answer questions about the festival.

Activity Book

Activity 1

Complete the sentences in the grammar table.

- Invite a pupil to read out the words in the word box. Then read the *Remember!* tip.
- The pupils work on their own or with a partner to write the words in the grammar table.

Answers: **1** What, you **2** did, do **3** What, yesterday **4** did, evening

Activity 2

What did the children do yesterday? Look and write the verb in the past simple.

- Read out the verbs in the word box as a class. Invite a pupil to read out the first sentence.
- The pupils work on their own to complete the other sentences, writing the correct verb in the past simple.

Answers: **1** went **2** ate **3** drank **4** wore **5** saw **6** rode

Activity 3

What did you do yesterday? Complete the sentences. Ask and write.

- Invite different pupils to read out and complete the first sentence about them. If necessary, repeat the procedure with the next two sentences.
- The pupils work on their own to write their sentences.
- Organise the pupils into Talk Partners. The pupils take turns to read their sentences to each other and they record their partner's answers.

Code activity

- The pupils complete the code activity.

Answer: film

Ending the lesson

Review the lesson and reflect on learning.

- Say **Today we've learnt how to use some irregular verbs in the past simple. Which verbs do you remember?** Elicit the verbs.
- Ask **Which was your favourite activity today? Which activity was easy / difficult?**

Extra activity

Reinforcement

- Write a row of numbers (1–8) on the board and below it a row of letters (A–H). Explain that each number is a verb in the present and each letter is a verb in the past. The pupils must find and match a present and past verb.
- Organise the class into two teams. The teams take turns to say a number and a letter. Read out the corresponding verbs (see below). If the verbs match, write them on the board and award the team a point. Then continue the game.

1	2	3	4	5	6	7	8
go	see	eat	drink	wear	have	ride	do
A	B	C	D	E	F	G	H
drank	had	went	wore	did	saw	rode	ate

Key Competences and Key Learning Outcomes

- Read the story with some fluency
- Use a code to read a message
- Do a pre-reading task
- Understand the importance of doing nice things for others
- Read, listen and understand a story about a surprise birthday party
- Give an opinion on the story

Key language

- *cook, decorate, fancy dress, painter, sandwiches, surprise birthday party*
- *Yesterday was Lily's birthday. Josh painted a message for Lily. Dad made some sandwiches. It's (ten to four). Are you ready for (Lily's surprise birthday party)? That's in (one hour)! Mind (the step).*
- Recycled: *birthday, cake, chocolate; message, What a mess!*

Materials

- Pupil's Book pp94–95; Activity Book p92; Class CD4; Teacher's App on Navio
- Teacher's Resource Bank: Talk cards

Optional materials

- Teacher's Resource Bank: Trinity Exams Practice cards (selected from the Starter Unit and Units 1, 2, 3, 4, 5, 6, 7 and 8)

At a Glance Lesson Plan

Pupil's Book

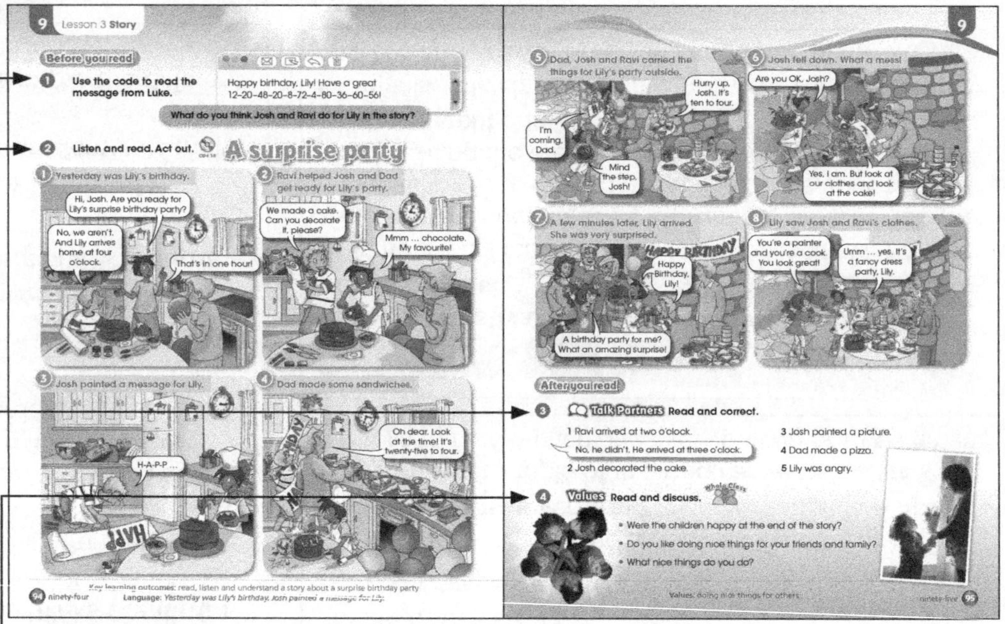

Activity Book

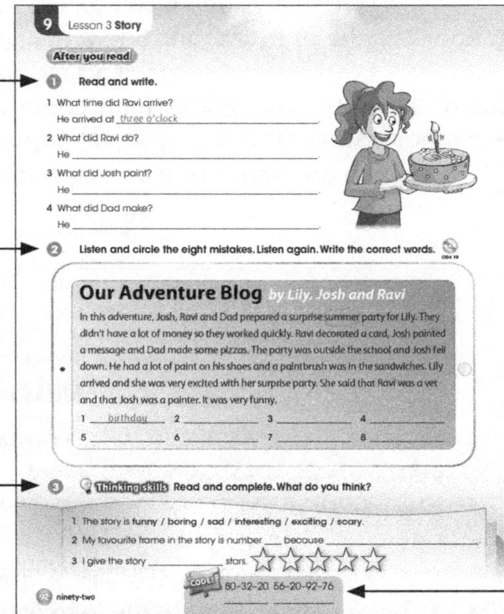

Starting the lesson

- Use the Trinity Exams Practice cards (optional).
- Review regular and irregular verbs in the past simple.
- Set learning outcomes and use the talk cards.

Before you read: Activity 1

- Use the code to read the message from Luke.

Activity 2

- Listen and read.
- ▶ *CD4 Track 18 p279*
- Act out.

After you read: Activity 3

- Read and correct.

Activity 4: Values

- Read and discuss.
- Go to the Activity Book.

Ending the lesson

- Review the lesson and reflect on learning.

Extra activity

Reinforcement

- Retell the story as a class.
- Congratulate each other on good and kind behaviour.

After you read: Activity Book

Activity 1

- Read and write.

Activity 2

- Listen and circle the eight mistakes.
- ▶ *CD4 Track 19 p279*
- Listen again.
- Write the correct words.

Activity 3

- Read and complete.
- What do you think?

Code activity

- Complete the code activity.

Digital resources

Teacher's Digital: You can also teach this lesson using the Teacher's App on Navio.

Pupil's Digital: Encourage your pupils to use the Pupil's App on Navio to practise the activities from this lesson.

Powered By NAVIO

Starting the lesson

Use the Trinity Exams Practice cards (optional).

- The pupils practise asking and answering questions.

Review regular and irregular verbs in the past simple.

- Draw a 4 x 4 grid on the board with the numbers 1–16 in the squares. Organise the class into two teams: noughts (0) and crosses (X). One team says a number. Say the corresponding present tense verb from this list: 1 wear 2 drink 3 is 4 eat 5 see 6 paint 7 watch TV, 8 do 9 have 10 climb 11 phone 12 go 13 ride 14 play 15 skip 16 plant.
- If the team gives you the correct verb in the past simple, draw a nought or cross in the square. The teams win a point when they have three noughts or crosses in a row.

Set learning outcomes and use the talk cards.

- Say **Today we're going to read and listen to a story.**
- Point to the talk cards to show the pupils the different ways they will be working in the lesson.

Before you read: Pupil's Book Activity 1

Use the code to read the message from Luke.

- Say **Josh and Lily have received another message from Luke.** Ask the pupils to use the code (Pupil's Book page 7) to discover the mystery word (*celebration*).
- Read the story title and ask **What do you think Josh and Ravi do for Lily in the story?** The pupils make their predictions.

Pupil's Book Activity 2

Listen and read. Act out.

▶ *CD4 Track 18 p279*

- Play the CD. The pupils follow in their books.
- Confirm that Josh and Ravi prepare a party for Lily.
- Ask questions to check comprehension.

Suggested comprehension questions

- Frame 1: **What are Josh and Dad doing?** (*Getting ready for Lily's party.*) **Why is Josh worried?** (*Lily arrives home in one hour.*)
- Frame 2: **What does Ravi do?** (*Decorate the cake.*)
- Frame 3: **What does Josh paint?** (*A message.*)
- Frame 4: **What does Dad make?** (*Sandwiches.*) **Why are they in a hurry?** (*They've only got 25 minutes.*)
- Frame 6: **Where does Josh fall?** (*On the step.*) **What have the boys got on their clothes?** (*Paint and cake.*)
- Frame 7: **Is Lily happy?** (*Yes.*)
- Frame 8: **What does Ravi look like?** (*A cook.*) **What does Josh look like?** (*A painter.*)

- Organise the class into four groups (Lily, Ravi, Josh and Dad) and play the CD. Each group joins in when their character speaks.
- Repeat, with groups swapping roles.

After you read: Pupil's Book Activity 3

Read and correct.

- Ask a pupil to read out the first sentence and its correction. Ask the class to identify the story frame which has this information. (*Frame 1.*)
- Repeat, highlighting the past simple verb each time.
- Working with a Talk Partner, the pupils correct the sentences. They can do this orally or in their notebooks.

Answers: **1** No, he didn't. He arrived at three o'clock. **2** No, he didn't. Ravi decorated the cake. **3** No, he didn't. He painted a message. **4** No, he didn't. He made some sandwiches. **5** No, she wasn't. She was very happy.

Pupil's Book Activity 4: Values

Read and discuss.

- Read out the questions and discuss them as a class.
- Encourage the pupils to describe the nice things they do for their friends and family and praise them for their behaviour.

After you read: Activity Book

Activity 1

Read and write.

- Ask pupils to read out the questions and to say the answers. If necessary, write the past simple verbs on the board.
- The pupils write their answers.

Answers: **1** three o'clock **2** decorated the cake **3** painted a message **4** made some sandwiches

Activity 2

Listen and circle the eight mistakes. Listen again. Write the correct words.

▶ *CD4 Track 19 p279*

- Play the CD. The pupils listen and circle the mistakes.
- Play the CD again. The pupils write the correct words.

Answers: **1** ~~summer~~ birthday **2** ~~money~~ time **3** ~~card~~ cake **4** ~~pizzas~~ sandwiches **5** ~~school~~ lighthouse **6** ~~shoes~~ clothes **7** ~~sandwiches~~ cake **8** ~~vet~~ cook

Activity 3

Read and complete. What do you think?

- Invite pupils to read out and complete the sentences.
- The pupils complete the task in their Activity Books and then share opinions with a Talk Partner.

Code activity

- The pupils complete the code activity.

Answer: the news

Ending the lesson

Review the lesson and reflect on learning.

- Say **Today we've listened to a story about a surprise party.** Elicit the story.
- Ask **Which was your favourite activity today? Which activity was easy / difficult?**

Extra activity

Reinforcement

- Retell the story as a class, using prompts, mime, gesture and drawings to support the pupils.
- Organise the pupils into a circle and ask them to close their eyes and think of a nice or kind thing that a friend did. The pupils share their experiences.

Key Competences and Key Learning Outcomes

- Identify and tell the time
- Use the past simple to ask and answer about the timing of events
- Follow and correct the grammar tables
- Use the past simple with regular and irregular verbs
- Sing a song

Key language

- Telling the time: *ten past (three), twenty past (one), twenty-five past (eleven), twenty-five to (four), ten to (eight), five to (twelve); did (my) homework, had lunch, played, started school, watched TV, went to bed*
- *We didn't (stop). We raced the clock. What time did you (go to bed) yesterday? I (went to bed) at (twenty past nine).*
- Extension: *five past two, ten past seven, twenty to three, ten to nine*
- Recycled: *do, go, have, play, start, watch*

Materials

- Pupil's Book p96; Activity Book p93; Class CD4; Teacher's App on Navio
- Teacher's Resource Bank: Talk cards

Optional materials

- Teacher's Resource Bank: Trinity Exams Practice cards (selected from the Starter Unit and Units 1, 2, 3, 4, 5, 6, 7 and 8)

At a Glance Lesson Plan

Pupil's Book

Starting the lesson

- Use the Trinity Exams Practice cards (optional).
- Review telling the time.
- Set learning outcomes and use the talk cards.

Activity 1

- Listen, point and say.

▶ ***CD4 Track 20 p280***

Activity 2

- Listen and sing *Tick-tock.*

▶ ***CD4 Track 21 p280***

Activity 3

- Listen and follow.

▶ ***CD4 Track 22 p280***

- Repeat.
- **Grammar clue:** Read about using the past simple to answer 'What time did …?' questions.

Activity 4

- Ask and answer about yesterday.

Go to the Activity Book.

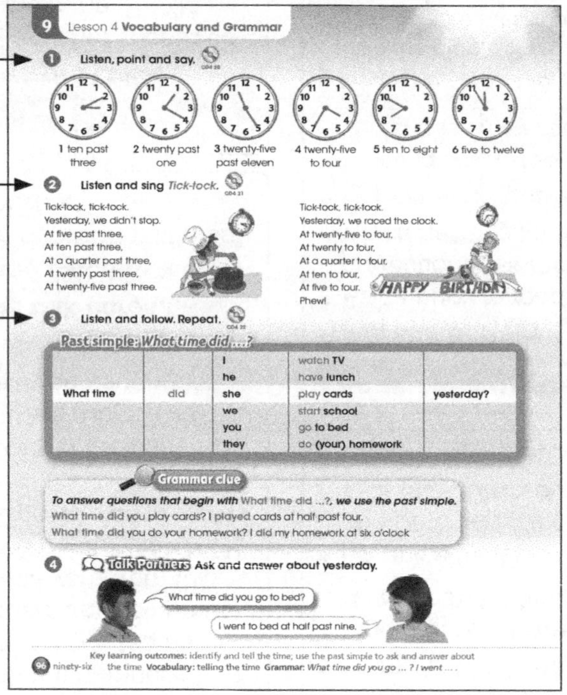

Ending the lesson

- Review the lesson and reflect on learning.

Extra activity

Reinforcement

- Play *Human clocks* in pairs.

Vocabulary extension

- Present four additional vocabulary items.

Digital resources

Teacher's Digital: You can also teach this lesson using the Teacher's App on Navio.

Pupil's Digital: Encourage your pupils to use the Pupil's App on Navio to practise the activities from this lesson.

Powered By NAVIO

Activity Book

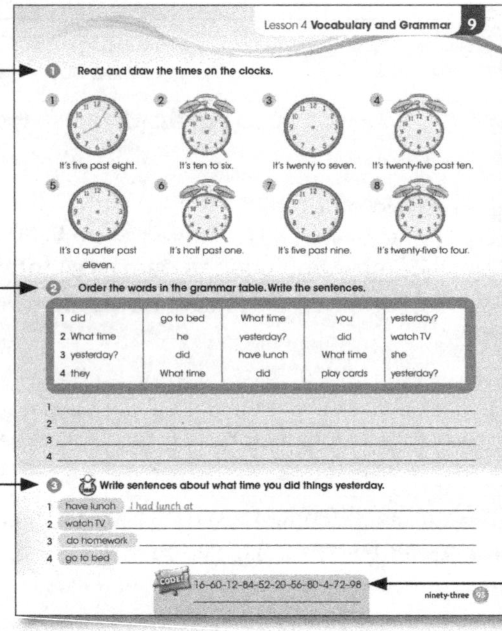

Activity Book

Activity 1

- Read and draw the times on the clocks.

Activity 2

- Order the words in the grammar table.
- Write the sentences.

Activity 3

- Write sentences about what time you did things yesterday.

Code activity

- Complete the code activity.

Starting the lesson

Use the Trinity Exams Practice cards (optional).

- The pupils practise asking and answering questions.

Review telling the time.

- Draw two large analogue clock faces without hands on the board. Divide the class into two teams and give a pupil from each team a board pen. Say a time that the class knows, e.g. **half past seven**. One pupil from each team draws the missing hands on the clocks. Repeat with other times (*o'clock, half past, a quarter past / to*) and different pairs of pupils.

Set learning outcomes and use the talk cards.

- Say **Today we're going to learn how to say what time it is and we're also going to talk about what time we did things yesterday.**
- Point to the talk cards to show the pupils the different ways they will be working in the lesson.

Pupil's Book Activity 1

Listen, point and say.

▸ *CD4 Track 20 p280*

- Point to the first clock and ask **What time is it?** If necessary, draw a clock on the board and count the minutes to ten past the hour, then draw the clock hands. Elicit the time. (*Ten past three.*)
- Repeat with the other times, counting the minutes past / to the hour each time, if necessary.
- Play the CD. The pupils listen, repeat the time and point to the clocks.

Pupil's Book Activity 2

Listen and sing *Tick-tock*.

▸ *CD4 Track 21 p280*

- Focus on the pictures and ask **Do you remember the story? What did Ravi do? What did Josh do? Did they have lots of time to do these jobs?** Say **They worked quickly. They didn't stop. They raced the clock.** Mime running a race.
- Play the CD. The pupils listen and read.
- Play the CD again. The pupils join in singing the song.

Pupil's Book Activity 3

Listen and follow. Repeat.

▸ *CD4 Track 22 p280*

- Focus the class on the grammar table. Play the CD. The pupils listen to the first question and point to the table. They then repeat the question. Repeat the procedure with the other questions.

Grammar clue

- Read the grammar clue.
- Ask a pupil **What time did you go to bed yesterday?** Prompt the pupil to answer using the past simple, supporting him / her if necessary by pointing to the grammar clue.
- Repeat several times, then invite pupils to ask you the questions.

Pupil's Book Activity 4

Ask and answer about yesterday.

- Organise the class into Talk Partners. The pupils ask and answer the questions with a Talk Partner.

Activity Book

Activity 1

Read and draw the times on the clocks.

- Invite a pupil to read out the first time. Then draw a clock face on the board and ask a pupil to read out the second time. Draw the hands on the clock.
- The pupils draw the times on the clocks and then check their answers in pairs.

Activity 2

Order the words in the grammar table. Write the sentences.

- Explain that the grammar table is mixed up and that the pupils need to reorder the words. Invite a pupil to read out the first sentence.
- The pupils order and write the remaining sentences. If they need more support, remind them that a sentence begins with a capital letter and ends with a full stop.

Answers: **1** What time did you go to bed yesterday? **2** What time did he watch TV yesterday? **3** What time did she have lunch yesterday? **4** What time did they play cards yesterday?

Activity 3

Write sentences about what time you did things yesterday.

- Complete the first sentence: **I had lunch at (one o'clock).** Then ask **What time did you have lunch yesterday?** Prompt different pupils to answer.
- Repeat with the remaining three prompts and, if necessary, write the past simple on the board.
- The pupils write their answers.
- The pupils ask and answer in pairs about things they did yesterday.

Code activity

- The pupils complete the code activity.

Answer: documentary

Ending the lesson

Review the lesson and reflect on learning.

- Say **Today we've learnt how to tell the time and we've talked about what time we did things yesterday.** Elicit examples.
- Ask **Which was your favourite activity today? Which activity was easy / difficult?**

Extra activity

Reinforcement

- Play *Human clocks.* Organise the class into pairs. Pupil A in each pair is a clock. Say **It's twelve o'clock.** Pupil B places Pupil A's arms in the correct position (both arms raised vertically).
- Repeat with other times.

Vocabulary extension

- Use the Vocabulary Booster on Navio and present and practise four additional times: *five past two, ten past seven, twenty to three, ten to nine*.

Key Competences and Key Learning Outcomes

- Say a tongue twister with the 's' sound
- Practise spelling and learn an alternative spelling for the 's' sound
- Listen for specific information
- Play a communication game using *What time did …?*

Key language

- *celebration, city, cycle, face, sang, summer, sun; arrived at the festival, ate some candyfloss, rode on the ghost train, rode on the roller coaster, watched the fireworks, went home*
- *What time did (Freddy) (arrive at the festival)? He (arrived) at (ten past six). At (ten past six)? Yes, that's right.*
- Recycled: *circle, danced, festival, ghost train, sing, snake, sweet*

Materials

- Pupil's Book p97; Activity Book p94; Class CD4; Teacher's App on Navio
- Teacher's Resource Bank: Talk cards
- Teacher's Resource Bank: Unit 9 Lesson 5 Communication Activity

Optional materials

- Teacher's Resource Bank: Trinity Exams Practice cards (selected from the Starter Unit and Units 1, 2, 3, 4, 5, 6, 7 and 8)
- Attractions at festivals flashcards

At a Glance Lesson Plan

Pupil's Book

Starting the lesson

- Use the Trinity Exams Practice cards (optional).
- Review telling the time.
- Review the *Tick-tock* song.
- ▶ ***CD4 Track 21 p280***
- Set learning outcomes and use the talk cards.

Activity 1: Speak and spell

- Listen, read and say.
- ▶ ***CD4 Track 23 p280***
- Go to the Activity Book.

Activity 2

- Look at the clocks.
- Listen and identify four differences.
- ▶ ***CD4 Track 24 p280***

Activity 3

- Ask and answer.
- Draw the times (Teacher's Resource Bank: Unit 9).

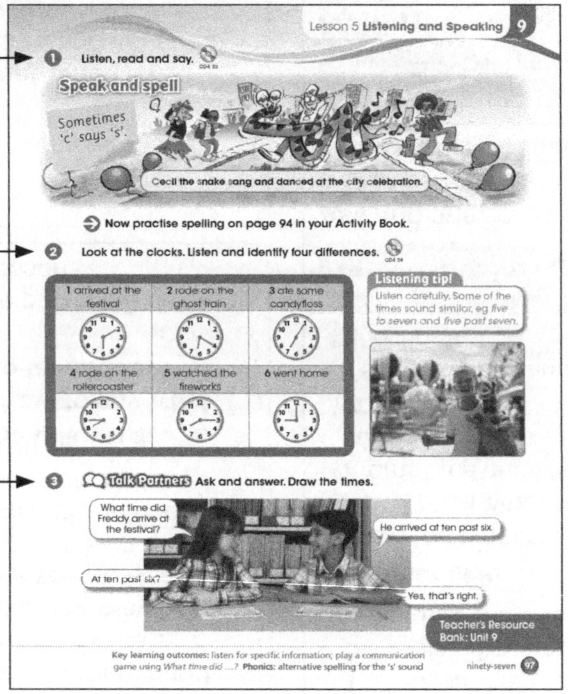

Ending the lesson

- Review the lesson and reflect on learning.

Extra activities

Reinforcement

- Play *Flashcard elimination*.

Extension

- Make your own tongue twister to practise the 's' sound.

Activity Book

Activity Book

Activity 1: Speak and spell

- Complete and say.

Activity 2

- Find and circle the words.
- Classify and write.

Activity 3

- Test your friend.
- Ask and answer.

Code activity

- Complete the code activity.

Digital resources

Teacher's Digital: You can also teach this lesson using the Teacher's App on Navio.

Pupil's Digital: Encourage your pupils to use the Pupil's App on Navio to practise the activities from this lesson.

Powered By NAVIO

Starting the lesson

Use the Trinity Exams Practice cards (optional).

- The pupils practise asking and answering questions.

Review telling the time.

- Instruct the class to stand up. Ask **What time did you go to bed last night? Did you go to bed at (nine o'clock)?** The pupils who went to bed at this time sit down. Ask **Did you go to bed at (ten past nine)?** The pupils who went to bed at this time sit down. Continue asking questions, getting later and later, until all the pupils are sitting in their chairs.

Review the *Tick-tock* song.

▶ *CD4 Track 21 p280*

- Play the CD. The pupils join in singing the song.

Set learning outcomes and use the talk cards.

- Say **Today we're going to say a tongue twister, practise spelling and draw the times in a chart.**
- Point to the talk cards to show the pupils the different ways they will be working in the lesson.

Pupil's Book Activity 1: Speak and spell

Listen, read and say.

▶ *CD4 Track 23 p280*

- (Books closed.) Write the letter 's' on the board and ask **What sound does this letter make?** ('s') List the words the pupils know that begin with this letter. Say **Today you're going to learn another way of writing the 's' sound.**
- (Books open.) Ask **Which animal can you see?** (*A snake.*) **Where is it?** (*In the city.*) **What's the snake doing?** (*Dancing.*)
- Say **Let's listen to the tongue twister.** Play the CD. The pupils follow the text in their books. Highlight that the past simple of the verb 'sing' is 'sang'.
- Play the CD again. The pupils say the tongue twister.
- Finally, ask the class to identify the alternative way of writing the 's' sound ('*c*').
- If you wish, teach the class that when the letter 'c' is followed by the letter 'e', 'i' or 'y', it is pronounced as an 's' sound. When it is followed by any other letter, it is pronounced as a 'k' sound.

Activity Book

Activity 1: Speak and spell

Complete and say.

- The pupils write the letters and say the tongue twister.

Answer: Cecil the snake sang and danced at the city celebration.

Activity 2

Find and circle the words. Classify and write.

- The pupils find and circle the words in the border which contain the 's' sound.
- The pupils classify and write the words according to whether they are spelt with 's' or 'c'.

Answers: s: sun, sweet, snake, sing, summer
c: city, cycle, danced, face, circle

Activity 3

Talk Partners. Test your friend. Ask and answer.

- Invite two pupils to read out the speech bubbles.
- Organise the pupils into Talk Partners. The pupils test their partners on the spelling of the words in Activity 2. Stress the importance of prompting, encouraging and helping each other.

Code activity

- The pupils complete the code activity.

Answer: game show

Pupil's Book Activity 2

Look at the clocks. Listen and identify four differences.

▶ *CD4 Track 24 p280*

- Elicit the time on each clock. Tell the pupils that they need to listen and identify four differences.
- Play the CD. The pupils raise their hand when they hear a difference. Elicit what the difference is.
- Play the CD again, pausing after each exchange to confirm the correct time and the activity.

Answers: **1** ✓ **2** quarter past six **3** five to seven **4** ten to eight **5** ✓ **6** ten o'clock

Pupil's Book Activity 3

Ask and answer. Draw the times (Teacher's Resource Bank: Unit 9).

- Invite two pupils to read out the speech bubbles.
- Explain to the pupils that they are going to do the same activity in pairs.
- Organise the class into Talk Partners and give each pupil a chart.
- Ask a pair to demonstrate. Then the rest of the class does the activity.
- At the end of the activity, the Talk Partners should show each other their chart and check / correct their answers.

Ending the lesson

Review the lesson and reflect on learning.

- Say **Today we've practised a tongue twister.** Elicit the tongue twister.
- Ask **Which was your favourite activity today? Which activity was easy / difficult?**

Extra activities

Reinforcement

- Play *Flashcard elimination* (see p27) with the attractions at festivals flashcards.

Extension

- Ask the pupils to open their Activity Books at page 94 and read out the list of words in Activity 2. Explain that you want them to use these words to make a new tongue twister. The pupils do this in pairs and then read their new tongue twister to the rest of the class.

Key Competences and Key Learning Outcomes

- Predict content from photos
- Scan the text for specific information
- Guess the meaning of words from context (inferring)
- Read and understand an email

Key language

- *concert, email, May Day, maypole, Morris dancers*
- *I wore / watched / did / painted / danced / had / went / rode; They were (fantastic)!*
- Recycled: *afternoon, evening, morning; big wheel, celebrate, festival, fireworks, ghost train, park, roller coaster*

Materials

- Pupil's Book p98; Activity Book p95; Class CD4; Teacher's App on Navio
- Teacher's Resource Bank: Talk cards

Optional materials

- Teacher's Resource Bank: Trinity Exams Practice cards (selected from the Starter Unit and Units 1, 2, 3, 4, 5, 6, 7 and 8)

At a Glance Lesson Plan

Pupil's Book

Starting the lesson

- Use the Trinity Exams Practice cards (optional).
- Review the tongue twister.

▶ *CD4 Track 23 p280*

- Set learning outcomes and use the talk cards.

Before you read: Activity 1

- Do you send emails?
- Who do you send emails to?

Before you read: Activity 2

- Look at the photos in the email.
- What do you think the email is about?

Activity 3

- Read and listen to find out.

▶ *CD4 Track 25 p280*

Go to the Activity Book.

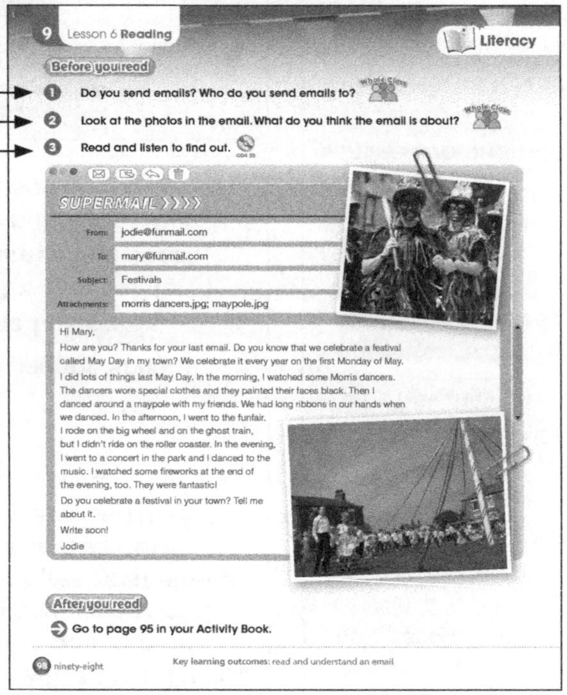

Ending the lesson

- Review the lesson and reflect on learning.

Extra activity

Extension

- Describe / comment on Morris dancing and maypole dancing video clips.

Activity Book

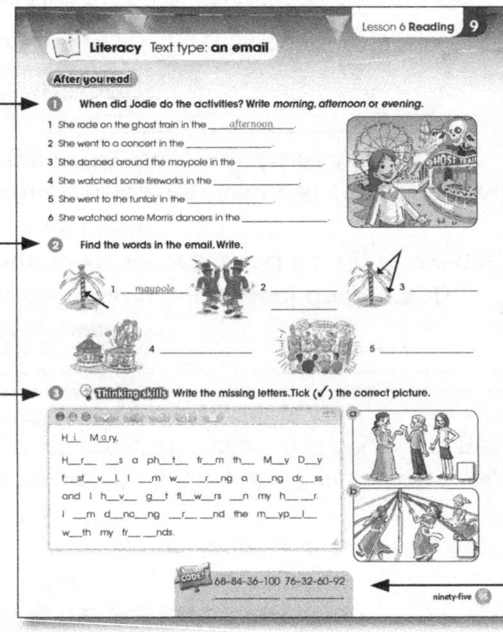

After you read: Activity Book

Activity 1

- When did Jodie do the activities?
- Write *morning, afternoon* or *evening*.

Activity 2

- Find the words in the email.
- Write.

Activity 3

- Write the missing letters.
- Tick (✓) the correct picture.

Code activity

- Complete the code activity.

Digital resources

Teacher's Digital: You can also teach this lesson using the Teacher's App on Navio.

Pupil's Digital: Encourage your pupils to use the Pupil's App on Navio to practise the activities from this lesson.

Powered By NAVIO

Starting the lesson

Use the Trinity Exams Practice cards (optional).

- The pupils practise asking and answering questions.

Review the tongue twister.

▶ *CD4 Track 23 p280*

- Ask **What sound did you practise in the tongue twister?** ('s')
- Play the CD. Practise the tongue twister as a class.
- Remind the pupils that they know two spellings for this sound ('s' and 'c').The pupils list the words they know which contain these letters.

Set learning outcomes and use the talk cards.

- Say **Today we're going to read an email.**
- Point to the talk cards to show the pupils the different ways they will be working in the lesson.

Before you read: Pupil's Book Activity 1

Do you send emails? Who do you send emails to?

- Invite a pupil to read out the questions and encourage the rest of the pupils to say whether they send or receive emails.
- Ask **Who do you send emails to? Who do you receive emails from? What do you write about?**

Before you read: Pupil's Book Activity 2

Look at the photos in the email. What do you think the email is about?

- Focus the class on the photos and ask **What do you think the email is about?** Encourage the pupils to make their predictions.

Pupil's Book Activity 3

Read and listen to find out.

▶ *CD4 Track 25 p280*

- Explain that the first time the pupils read they should try to understand the most important information. If you want the pupils to read the text without the support of the CD, set a time limit for this task. Otherwise, play the CD, pausing at the end of each section of the text.
- The pupils report back on what the email is about (*the May Day festival*) and what is happening in the attached photos (*maypole dancing and Morris dancing*).
- Ask the pupils to read the text again on their own and choose two activities they like.
- After reading the text, the pupils report back as a class.

After you read: Activity Book

Activity 1

When did Jodie do the activities? Write *morning, afternoon* or *evening.*

- Read out the first statement. Then invite a pupil to read out the second statement. The class should quickly scan the email to find the information. Confirm that Jodie went to a concert in the evening.
- The pupils work on their own or in pairs to complete the code activity.

Answers: **1** afternoon **2** evening **3** morning **4** evening **5** afternoon **6** morning

Activity 2

Find the words in the email. Write.

- Focus the class on the first picture and ask **What is it?** (*A maypole.*) Then encourage the class to scan the email to identify what's in the next picture. Confirm that they are Morris dancers and ask the pupils to label the picture.
- The pupils work on their own or in pairs to find the other words and label the pictures.

Answers: **1** maypole **2** Morris dancers **3** ribbon **4** funfair **5** concert

Activity 3

Write the missing letters. Tick (✓) the correct picture.

- Explain to the class that Jodie sent another email with a photo. The pupils need to complete the email by writing the missing letters. The letters are *a, e, i, o* or *u*. Read out the beginning of the email as a class.
- The pupils work on their own or in pairs to complete the email and then tick the correct photo.

Answers: Hi Mary, Here is a photo from the May Day festival. I am wearing a long dress and I have got flowers in my hair. I am dancing around the maypole with my friends. (Picture b)

Code activity

- The pupils complete the code activity.

Answer: quiz show

Ending the lesson

Review the lesson and reflect on learning.

- Say **Today we've read an email.** Then ask **Who wrote the email? What did she write about?** Elicit the content of Jodie's email.
- Ask **Which was your favourite activity today? Which activity was easy / difficult?**

Extra activity

Extension

- Play a video clip of maypole dancing and Morris dancers and ask the pupils to describe and comment on what they can see.
- The pupils find similar clips on the Internet (keywords: school maypole dancing / Morris dancing).

Key Competences and Key Learning Outcomes

- Use 'but' to give opposite information
- Identify the informational content of an email
- Identify the text features of an email
- Use criteria to check your writing
- Share your writing with a partner
- Prepare and write an email

Key language

- *Burns Night, haggis, meat, poet, Scotland, sheep's stomach, traditional dish*
- *I enjoyed / had / ate / listened to / went / saw; I (sang songs), but I didn't (dance).*
- Recycled: months of the year; ordinal numbers (1st to 31st); *evening; It's (delicious).*

Materials

- Pupil's Book p99; Activity Book p96; Class CD4; Teacher's App on Navio
- Teacher's Resource Bank: Talk cards

Optional materials

- Teacher's Resource Bank: Trinity Exams Practice cards (selected from the Starter Unit and Units 1, 2, 3, 4, 5, 6, 7 and 8)

At a Glance Lesson Plan

Pupil's Book

Starting the lesson

- Use the Trinity Exams Practice cards (optional).
- Review how to say dates.
- Set learning outcomes and use the talk cards.

Investigate a text: Activity 1

- In what order does this information appear in the email?

Investigate a text: Activity 2

- Read and listen to find out.

▶ *CD4 Track 26 p280*

Discuss a text: Activity 3

- Think and discuss.
- **Writing tip:** Read about using 'but' to give opposite information.

Go to the Activity Book.

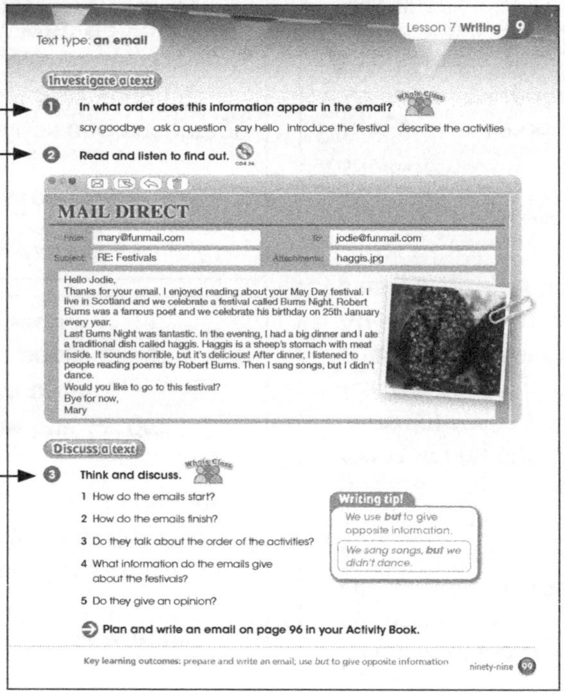
Lesson 7 Writing 9

Text type: an email

Investigate a text

1 In what order does this information appear in the email?

say goodbye ask a question say hello introduce the festival describe the activities

2 Read and listen to find out.

MAIL DIRECT

From: mary@funmail.com To: jodie@funmail.com

Subject: RE: Festivals Attachments: haggis.jpg

Hello Jodie,
Thanks for your email. I enjoyed reading about your May Day festival. I live in Scotland and we celebrate a festival called Burns Night. Robert Burns was a famous poet and we celebrate his birthday on 25th January every year.
Last Burns Night was fantastic. In the evening, I had a big dinner and I ate a traditional dish called haggis. Haggis is a sheep's stomach with meat inside. It sounds horrible, but it's delicious! After dinner, I listened to people reading poems by Robert Burns. Then I sang songs, but I didn't dance.
Would you like to go to this festival?
Bye for now,
Mary

Discuss a text

3 Think and discuss.

1 How do the emails start?
2 How do the emails finish?
3 Do they talk about the order of the activities?
4 What information do the emails give about the festivals?
5 Do they give an opinion?

Writing tip! We use *but* to give opposite information. *We sang songs, but we didn't dance.*

Plan and write an email on page 96 in your Activity Book.

Key learning outcomes: prepare and write an email; use *but* to give opposite information ninety-nine 99

Ending the lesson

- Review the lesson and reflect on learning.

Extra activity

Reinforcement

- Send an email to your teacher or a friend in English.

Digital resources

Teacher's Digital: You can also teach this lesson using the Teacher's App on Navio.

Pupil's Digital: Encourage your pupils to use the Pupil's App on Navio to practise the activities from this lesson.

Powered By NAVIO

Activity Book

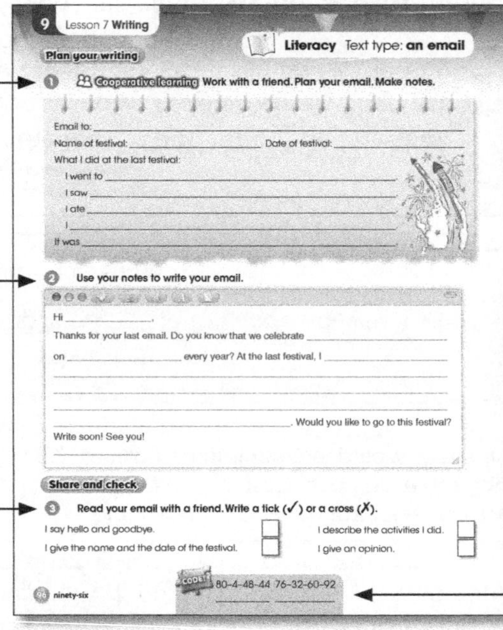
9 Lesson 7 Writing

Literacy Text type: an email

Plan your writing

1 Cooperative learning Work with a friend. Plan your email. Make notes.

Email to:
Name of festival: Date of festival:
What I did at the last festival:
I went to
I saw
I ate
I
It was

2 Use your notes to write your email.

Hi ______,
Thanks for your last email. Do you know that we celebrate ______ on ______ every year? At the last festival, I ______
______ Would you like to go to this festival?
Write soon! See you!

Share and check

3 Read your email with a friend. Write a tick (✓) or a cross (✗).

I say hello and goodbye. ☐ I describe the activities I did. ☐
I give the name and the date of the festival. ☐ I give an opinion. ☐

CODE 80-4-48-44 76-32-60-92

96 ninety-six

Activity Book

Plan your writing: Activity 1

- Work with a friend.
- Plan your email.
- Make notes.

Activity 2

- Use your notes to write your email.

Share and check: Activity 3

- Read your email with a friend.
- Write a tick (✓) or a cross (✗).

Code activity

- Complete the code activity.

Starting the lesson

Use the Trinity Exams Practice cards (optional).

- The pupils practise asking and answering questions.

Review how to say dates.

- Quickly review the months of the year with the class.
- Write *1/6* on the board and elicit the date (*1st June*). Remind the pupils that the first number is the day and the second number is the month. Repeat with other dates and review the ordinal numbers (1st–31st).
- Write between ten and twenty more dates on the board at random.
- Give the board pen to a pupil and say one of the dates. The pupil finds and circles the date and passes the pen to the next pupil. Repeat several times.

Set learning outcomes and use the talk cards.

- Ask **What did we read in the last lesson?** (*An email.*) **Who sent the email?** (*Jodie.*) **What was the email about?** (*The May Day festival.*) Say **Today we're going to read Mary's answer. Then we're going to plan and write an email.**
- Point to the talk cards to show the pupils the different ways they will be working in the lesson.

Investigate a text: Pupil's Book Activity 1

In what order does this information appear in the email?

- Read the task as a class and ask different pupils to read out the information.
- The pupils predict the order of the information in the email.

Investigate a text: Pupil's Book Activity 2

Read and listen to find out.

▶ *CD4 Track 26 p280*

- Ask the pupils to read the text quickly to see if their predictions were correct. If you want the pupils to read the text without the support of the CD, set a time limit for this task. Otherwise, play the CD.
- The pupils report the order of the information. Then ask the class general comprehension questions: **What's the name of the festival? Where and when do people celebrate it? What do they do?** Point to the photo and ask **What's this? What's it made of?**

Answers: say hello, introduce the festival, describe the activities, ask a question, say goodbye

Discuss a text: Pupil's Book Activity 3

Think and discuss.

- Read the first question and confirm that both emails (in Lessons 6 and 7) begin with a greeting.
- Discuss the other questions. Confirm that the emails give the name and date of the festivals and information about the activities you can do. They also order the activities, give an opinion and end with the writer's name.

Writing tip

- Read the information. Then prompt the pupils to find another example of 'but' in the email.
- Write on the board the prompt *I ate a … but I didn't eat …* Give an example, e.g. **I ate (a burger), but I didn't eat (an ice cream).** Then prompt the class to make similar sentences. Repeat the procedure with different verbs.

Activity Book

Plan your writing: Activity 1

Writing Partners. Work with a friend. Plan your email. Make notes.

- Brainstorm the festivals that the pupils celebrate. Write the names and dates on the board.
- The pupils work in pairs to decide on the content of their email and write their notes.

Activity 2

Use your notes to write your email.

- If necessary, model how to write an email. Choose a festival that the whole class is familiar with and prompt the class to give you the information. Correct or fine-tune the pupils' suggestions and write the text on the board.
- The pupils work with their partners to write their own text in their Activity Books. This text may be as short or as long as the pupils like.

Share and check: Activity 3

Writing Partners. Read your email with a friend. Write a tick (✓) or a cross (✗).

- Focus on the statements and read through them as a class.
- Organise the class into new pairs. One pupil in each pair should read their text aloud to their partner. The other pupil listens. The pupils work together to decide if the text fulfils all the criteria and tick or cross the corresponding boxes. The pupils can add to, improve, or correct the text at this stage.
- The pupils swap roles.

Code activity CODE!

- The pupils complete the code activity.

Answer: talk show

Ending the lesson

Review the lesson and reflect on learning.

- Say **Today we've written an email. Are you happy with your email?** Elicit the pupils' opinions.
- Ask **Which was your favourite activity today? Which activity was easy / difficult?**

Extra activity

Reinforcement

- If you are happy to do so, give the pupils your school email address and ask them to send you a message in English describing what they did at the weekend. Alternatively, they can send an email to a friend including this information.

Key Competences and Key Learning Outcomes

- Use the Internet to investigate Canada
- Review the primary, secondary and tertiary job sectors (optional)
- Read and listen for specific information
- Read about Canada Day
- Think about your own culture and identity

Key language

- *helicopters, hop, log rolling, lumberjack, marching band, motorbikes, police, pony, winner*
- Recycled: *cars, dancers, forest, horses, prize, race, trees, wood; What did (Peter) watch / ride on / see? What was (Joey's) favourite activity?*

Materials

- Pupil's Book p100; Activity Book p97; Class CD4; Teacher's App on Navio
- Teacher's Resource Bank: Talk cards
- An online world map
- Coloured pencils (red and white)

Optional materials

- Teacher's Resource Bank: Trinity Exams Practice cards (selected from the Starter Unit and Units 1, 2, 3, 4, 5, 6, 7 and 8)

At a Glance Lesson Plan

Pupil's Book

Starting the lesson

- Use the Trinity Exams Practice cards (optional).
- Review the names of countries.
- Set learning outcomes and use the talk cards.

Activity 1

- Read Luke's questions.
- What do you think?

Activity 2

- Read and listen.

▶ *CD4 Track 27 p280*

- Answer Luke's questions.
- **Think about your culture** Do you celebrate your town, region or country? Which day is it? What do you do?

Go to the Activity Book.

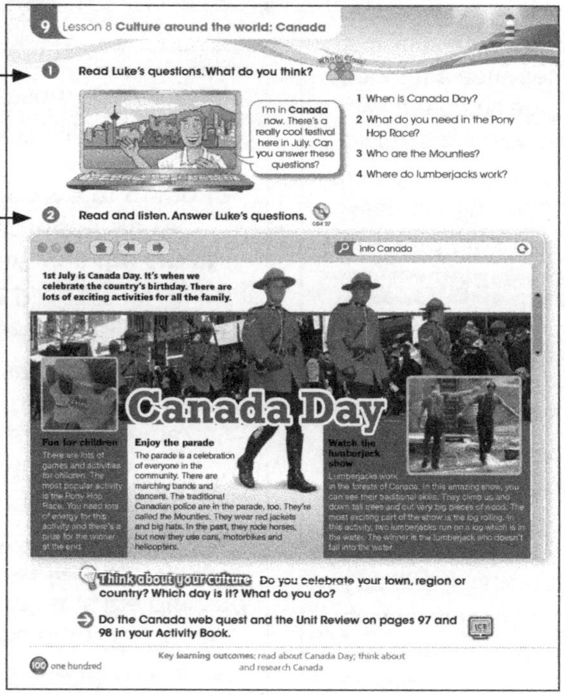

Ending the lesson

- Review the lesson and reflect on learning.

Link to Science

- **Work:** Review the primary, secondary and tertiary sectors.

Activity Book

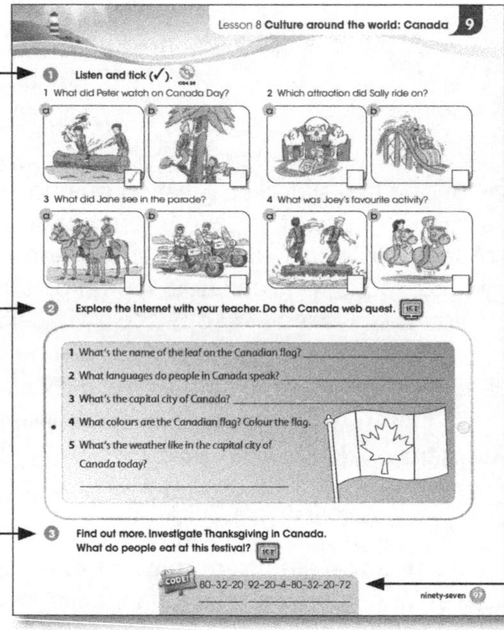

Activity Book

Activity 1

- Listen and tick (✓).

▶ *CD4 Track 28 p280*

Activity 2

- Explore the Internet with your teacher. Do the Canada web quest.

Activity 3

- Find out more. Investigate Thanksgiving in Canada. What do people eat at this festival?

Code activity

- Complete the code activity.

Digital resources

Teacher's Digital: You can also teach this lesson using the Teacher's App on Navio.

Powered By NAVIO

Starting the lesson

Use the Trinity Exams Practice cards (optional).

- The pupils practise asking and answering questions.

Review the names of countries.

- Ask **What's Lily and Josh's brother's name?** (*Luke.*) **What's his job?** (*He's a scientist.*) **Which places did he visit in Units 1–8?** Prompt the class to remember as many places as possible and write the countries on the board. The pupils should then look back through the Pupil's Book to identify the other places Luke visited. (*1 Ireland, 2 Scotland, 3 Malta, 4 India, 5 Hawaii, 6 New Zealand, 7 Australia, 8 the USA.*)

Set learning outcomes and use the talk cards.

- Say **Today we're going to investigate Canada.**
- Point to the talk cards to show the pupils the different ways they will be working in the lesson.

Pupil's Book Activity 1

Read Luke's questions. What do you think?

- Read the speech bubble as a class.
- Encourage the pupils to tell you what they know about Canada. Show the pupils where Canada is on an online world map.
- Read the questions as a class. Encourage the pupils to predict the answers.

Pupil's Book Activity 2

Read and listen. Answer Luke's questions.

▶ *CD4 Track 27 p280*

- Focus on the photos. Ask **What can you see?**
- Ask the pupils to read the text. If you want them to read the text without the support of the CD, set a time limit for this task. Otherwise, play the CD, pausing after each section to check understanding.
- The pupils answer Luke's questions.

Answers: **1** Canada Day is on 1st July. **2** You need lots of energy for the race. **3** The Mounties are the traditional Canadian police. **4** Lumberjacks work in the forests.

Think about your culture

- Read out the questions and prompt the pupils to tell you about a local, regional or national festival.

Activity Book

Activity 1

Listen and tick (✓).

▶ *CD4 Track 28 p280*

- Ask the pupils to read out the first question and to describe what they can see in the two pictures.
- Play the CD, pausing to allow the pupils to tick the activity they hear in the exchange.
- Repeat the procedure with the other questions.

Answers: **1** a **2** b **3** a **4** a

Activity 2

Explore the Internet with your teacher. Do the Canada web quest. ICT

- Read out the instructions for the activity.
- Connect to a children's website (see suggested websites opposite) that provides geographical information about Canada. Read out questions 1–4. The pupils work as a class to find and write the answers. They should also colour the flag.
- Read out question 5. Connect to a website that shows the weather around the world. The pupils complete the information about the day's weather in Ottawa.

Answers: **1** maple leaf **2** English and French **3** Ottawa **4** red and white

Activity 3

Find out more. Investigate Thanksgiving in Canada. What do people eat at this festival? ICT

- Read the question as a class and encourage the pupils to predict what people eat at Thanksgiving.
- If you are doing the investigation as a class, go to a suitable website, and ask the pupils to scan the information to find the answer.
- If you are working in a computer room, organise the class into small groups. The groups should go to the website and do the activity.

Answer: People eat turkey, mashed potato and pumpkin pie on Thanksgiving.

Suggested websites

http://maps.google.es/
http://www.bbc.co.uk/weather
https://www.natgeokids.com/uk/easyscienceforkids.com/all-about-canada/

Code activity CODE!

- The pupils complete the code activity.

Answer: the weather

Ending the lesson

Review the lesson and reflect on learning.

- Say **Today we've learnt about Canada. Is it an interesting country? When is there a national holiday? What can you see and do on that day?** Elicit the information from the pupils.
- Ask **Which was your favourite activity today? Which activity was easy / difficult?**

Link to Science

- If you are studying the Science topic of **Work** in English, review the different job sectors by asking **Which sector does a lumberjack work in?** (*Primary.*) **Which sector does a Mountie work in?** (*Tertiary.*) Quickly brainstorm other jobs that pupils know in the primary, secondary and tertiary sectors.

Go to the AB Unit Review on page 259.

Video and 21st Century Skills

Key Competences and Key Learning Outcomes

- Watch and understand a video about a school fete
- Work collaboratively to plan a fete
- Learn about school fete activities

Key language

- *bouncy castle, candyfloss, coconut, duck, fete, fireworks, ice cream, instruments, parade, school band, snack, sponge, sticky*
- *What did (the children) do (in the morning)? What did (Mark) (eat)? What about (ice cream)?*

Materials

- Pupil's Book p101; Activity Book p99; Class CD4; Teacher's App on Navio
- Attractions at festivals flashcards
- Teacher's Resource Bank: Talk cards

Optional materials

- Teacher's Resource Bank: Trinity Exams Practice cards (selected from the Starter Unit and Units 1, 2, 3, 4, 5, 6, 7 and 8)

At a Glance Lesson Plan

Pupil's Book

Starting the lesson

- Use the Trinity Exams Practice cards (optional).
- **Think-Pair-Share.** Review vocabulary for attractions at festivals.
- Set learning outcomes and use the talk cards.

Activity 1

- Before you watch
- Watch the video.
- *Unit 9 video p286*
- Which things were at the children's school fete last year?

Activity 2

- Watch the video again.
- *Unit 9 video*
- Read and answer the questions.

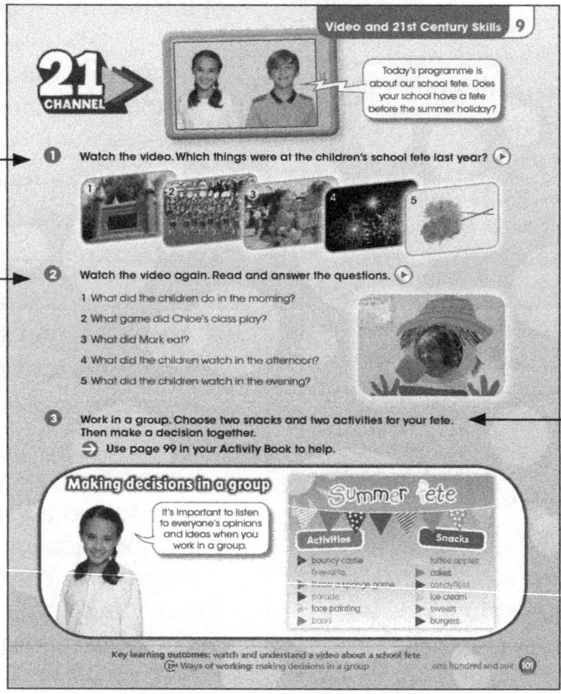
Video and 21st Century Skills 9

21 CHANNEL

Today's programme is about our school fete. Does your school have a fete before the summer holiday?

1 Watch the video. Which things were at the children's school fete last year?

2 Watch the video again. Read and answer the questions.

1 What did the children do in the morning?
2 What game did Chloe's class play?
3 What did Mark eat?
4 What did the children watch in the afternoon?
5 What did the children watch in the evening?

3 Work in a group. Choose two snacks and two activities for your fete. Then make a decision together.
Use page 99 in your Activity Book to help.

Making decisions in a group

It's important to listen to everyone's opinions and ideas when you work in a group.

Summer fete — Activities: bouncy castle ... face painting — Snacks: toffee apples, cakes, candyfloss, ice cream, sweets, burgers

Key learning outcomes: watch and understand a video about a school fete
Ways of working: making decisions in a group

one hundred and one 101

Activity 3

- Work in a group. Choose two snacks and two activities for your fete.
- Then make a decision together.
- Use page 99 in your Activity Book to help.
- Go to the Activity Book.

Ending the lesson

- Review the lesson and reflect on learning.

Extra activity

Reinforcement

- Make decisions in a group.

Activity Book

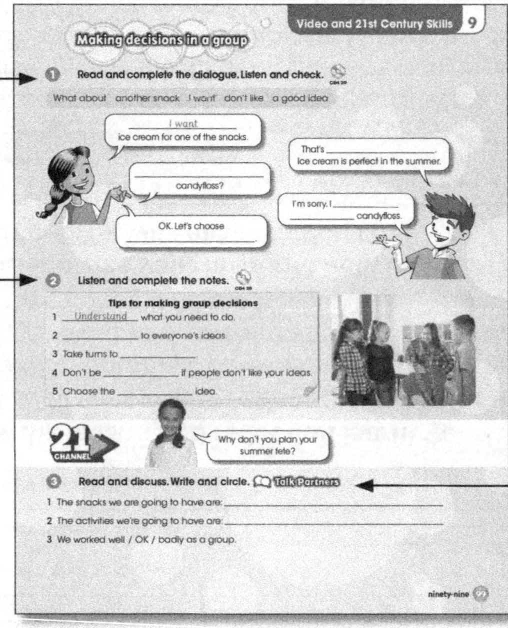
Video and 21st Century Skills 9

Making decisions in a group

1 Read and complete the dialogue. Listen and check.

What about · another snack · I want · don't like · a good idea

I want ice cream for one of the snacks.
That's ___ Ice cream is perfect in the summer.
___ candyfloss?
I'm sorry. I ___ candyfloss.
OK. Let's choose ___

2 Listen and complete the notes.

Tips for making group decisions
1 Understand what you need to do.
2 ___ to everyone's ideas
3 Take turns to ___
4 Don't be ___ if people don't like your ideas.
5 Choose the ___ idea.

Why don't you plan your summer fete?

3 Read and discuss. Write and circle. Talk Partners

1 The snacks we are going to have are: ___
2 The activities we're going to have are: ___
3 We worked well / OK / badly as a group.

ninety-nine 99

Activity Book

Activity 1

- Read and complete the dialogue.
- Listen and check.
- ▶ *CD4 Track 29 p281*

Activity 2

- Listen and complete the notes.
- ▶ *CD4 Track 30 p281*

Activity 3

- Read and discuss.
- Write and circle.

Digital resources

Teacher's Digital: You can also teach this lesson using the Teacher's App on Navio.

Pupil's Digital: Encourage your pupils to use the Pupil's App on Navio to practise the activities from this lesson.

Powered By NAVIO

Starting the lesson

Use the Trinity Exams Practice cards (optional).

- The pupils practise asking and answering questions.

Think-Pair-Share. Review vocabulary for attractions at festivals.

- Ask **Can you remember the vocabulary for attractions at festivals?** The class thinks silently for a minute.
- Then the pupils work with a Talk Partner to name the attractions at festivals.
- Invite different Talk Partners to say a different attraction at a festival. Hold up the corresponding flashcard and prompt the class to repeat the word.
- Finally, repeat the procedure, asking different pairs of Talk Partners each time, until all the attractions at festivals have been named.

Set learning outcomes and use the talk cards.

- Say **Today we're going to watch a video and then ask and answer questions about a school fete**.
- Point to the talk cards to show the pupils the different ways they will be working in the lesson.

Pupil's Book Activity 1

Before you watch

- Read the speech bubble to the pupils. Ask **Does your school have a fete before the summer holiday? What attractions does it normally have?** Elicit responses from a number of pupils. You could use the flashcards to prompt a variety of different answers.

Watch the video. Which things were at the children's school fete last year? *p286*

- Watch Part 1. Ask pupils **What are you going to see next?** Check they understand that they will see a video about Mark and Chloe's school fete last year.
- Play Part 2. Ask general questions to check understanding. Focus the pupils' attention on the photos in Activity 1. Say **Which things were at the children's school fete last year?** Elicit ideas.
- Play Part 2 again for the pupils to answer the questions. Check answers as a class.

Answers: 1, 2, 3, 4, 5

Pupil's Book Activity 2

Watch the video again. Read and answer the questions.

- Ask a pupil to read out sentence 1. Ask the class what they think the answer is. Repeat with sentences 2–5.
- Play Part 2. Students work in pairs to answer the questions.

Answers: **1** In the morning, they went on the bouncy castle. **2** Chloe's class played the throw a sponge game. **3** Mark ate candyfloss. **4** In the afternoon, everybody watched a parade. **5** In the evening, everybody watched the fireworks.

Pupil's Book Activity 3

Work in a group. Choose two snacks and two activities for your fete. Then make a decision together. Use page 99 in your Activity Book to help.

- Ask **What does Mark suggest at the end of the video?** (*Planning a fete at your school.*) **What does Chloe say is important?** (*All the children work together and we listen to everyone's ideas.*)
- Explain that this activity is all about working in a group to make suggestions and decisions for their own school fete. Look at the summer fete poster with the class and check vocabulary.
- Pupils work in groups to choose two snacks and two activities for their school fete.
- Invite groups to tell their decisions to the class.

Activity Book

Activity 1

Read and complete the dialogue. Listen and check.

▶ *CD4 Track 29 p281*

- Look at the words in the box and check vocabulary.
- Pupils work on their own to complete the conversation.
- Play the CD and check answers.

Answers: **1** I want ice cream for one of the snacks. **2** That's a good idea. Ice cream is perfect in the summer. **3** What about candyfloss? **4** I'm sorry. I don't like candyfloss. **5** OK. Let's choose another snack.

Activity 2

Listen and complete the notes.

▶ *CD4 Track 30 p281*

- Explain to the pupils that they are going to listen to some tips for making group decisions. Ask pupils for their own ideas. Read out the information. Then play the CD, pausing to allow the pupils to write the missing information.
- Play the CD again without pausing.

Answers: **1** Understand **2** Listen **3** speak **4** angry **5** best

Activity 3

Read and discuss. Write and circle.

- Pupils write down their decisions.
- Invite groups to tell their decisions to the class.
- At the end of the activity ask **How well did you work as a group and accept ideas and suggestions from others?** Reflect on whether working as a group and making decisions was easier after taking into account the sentences in Activity 1 and the tips for making group decisions.

Ending the lesson

Review the lesson and reflect on learning.

- Say **Today we've watched a video about a school fete and we've tested how well we make decisions in a group.**
- Ask **Which was your favourite activity today? Which activity was easy / difficult?**

Extra activity

Reinforcement

- Ask pupils to work in groups to make other decisions, for example the food for a picnic, the lessons in a timetable or the sports offered in a summer camp.
- Review the language of making and accepting suggestions and ask pupils to reflect on whether working in a group gets easier.

My project 3: A London adventure

Key Competences and Key Learning Outcomes

- Review and learn the names of places and attractions in London
- Discuss the advantages and disadvantages of city life (optional)
- Use the Internet to investigate two London attractions
- Share information about London

Key language

- Places in the city; transport; city attractions: *bike, boat, bus, taxi, Underground; aquarium, attraction, building, cathedral, museum, park, Queen, river cruise, tower, trip, zoo*
- *What's your (first / second) attraction? What can you (do) there? You can (visit some rooms).*

Materials

- Pupil's Book p102; Activity Book p100; Class CD4
- Teacher's Resource Bank: Talk cards

Optional materials

- Teacher's Resource Bank: Trinity Exams Practice cards (selected from the Starter Unit and Units 1, 2, 3, 4, 5, 6, 7, 8 and 9)

At a Glance Lesson Plan

Starting the lesson

- Use the Trinity Exams Practice cards (optional).
- Set learning outcomes and use the talk cards.

Investigate: Activity 1

- What do you know about London?
- What can you see and do there?

Investigate: Activity 2

- Work in groups.
- Look at the map of London and make lists.

Activity 3:

- Listen and check your lists.
- ▶ *CD4 Track 31 p281*
- Listen again and repeat the words.

Link to Science

- **Where we live:** Discuss the advantages and disadvantages of city life.

Pupil's Book

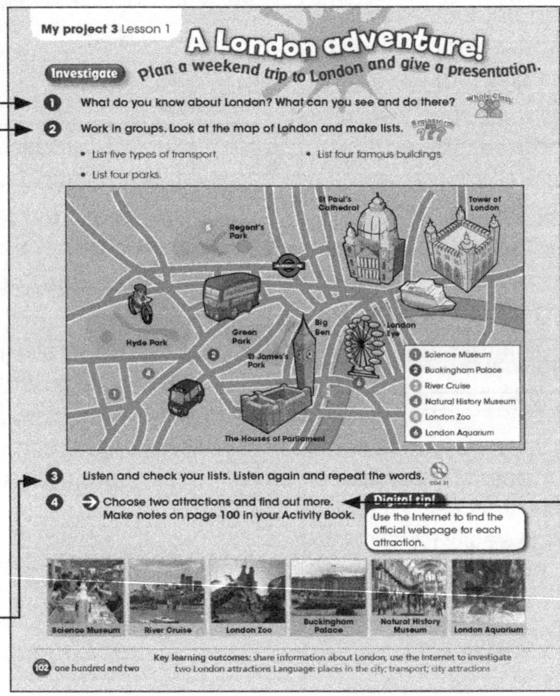

Activity 4: Share information

- Choose two attractions and find out more.
- Make notes on page 100 in your Activity Book.

Go to the Activity Book.

Ending the lesson

- Review the lesson and reflect on learning.

Extra activity

Reinforcement

- Use the map to practise giving directions.

Activity Book

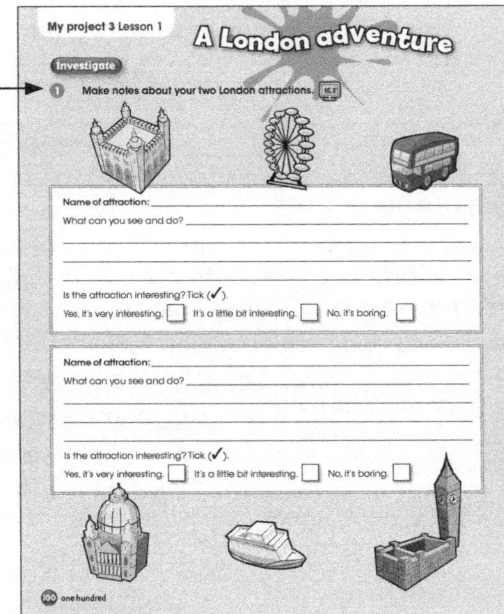

Activity Book

Activity 1

- Make notes about your two London attractions.

Digital resources

Teacher's Digital: You can also teach this lesson using the Teacher's App on Navio.

Pupil's Digital: Encourage your pupils to use the Pupil's App on Navio to practise the activities from this lesson.

Powered By NAVIO

Starting the lesson

Use the Trinity Exams Practice cards (optional).

- The pupils practise asking and answering questions.

Set learning outcomes and use the talk cards.

- Say **Today we're going to begin a project.**
- Point to the talk cards to show the pupils the different ways they will be working in the lesson.
- Focus the pupils' attention on the task at the top of Pupil's Book page 102. Read the challenge.

Investigate: Pupil's Book Activity 1

What do you know about London? What can you see and do there?

- Read out the questions to be discussed as a class. Encourage the pupils to report what they know about London. Prompt the class to give more information. Ask **Have you visited London? What did you do / see / eat there? How did you travel? Did you speak English?**

Investigate: Pupil's Book Activity 2

Work in groups. Look at the map of London and make lists.

- Focus the pupils on the map of London and ask **What can you see?** Read out the three tasks, check understanding and prompt the class to find examples on the map.
- Organise the class into groups of four and ask each group to choose a scribe who will write the lists in his / her notebook. Set a time limit. The pupils identify and list items that appear on the map. Remind them of the importance of good teamwork.
- At the end of the time limit, the groups read out their lists. Write the words on the board and elicit / give the pupils the names of any unknown items.

Answers: Transport: bus, bike, taxi, Underground, river boat
Parks: Regent's Park, Hyde Park, Green Park, St James's Park
Famous buildings: London Eye, Tower of London, St Paul's Cathedral, The Houses of Parliament, Big Ben

Pupil's Book Activity 3

Listen and check your lists. Listen again and repeat the words.

▶ *CD4 Track 31 p281*

- Pupils listen and check their lists. Then they listen again and repeat the words.

Pupil's Book Activity 4

Choose two attractions and find out more. Make notes on page 100 in your Activity Book.

- The pupils can do this as a whole-class activity or in groups.
- Ask the pupils to describe what they can see in the photos. Explain that the photos show famous attractions in London.

Activity Book

Activity 1

Make notes about your two London attractions.

- Focus the pupils on the activity and check understanding of the task.
- If you do the investigation as a whole-class activity, connect to the official website of each attraction in turn. Talk about what you can see and do at each attraction, but only the pupils who have been allocated this attraction should take notes.
- If you have access to several computers, the pupils who are investigating the same two attractions should work together. Give each group the links to the official website of their attractions and ask them to make notes.
- Alternatively, the pupils can do the investigation for homework.
- Use trusted websites such as:
  Science Museum: http://www.sciencemuseum.org.uk
  River Cruises: www.citycruises.com
  London Zoo: http://www.zsl.org/zsl-london-zoo/
  Buckingham Palace: http://www.royal.gov.uk/theroyalresidences/buckinghampalace/buckinghampalace.aspx
  Natural History Museum: http://www.nhm.ac.uk/
  London Aquarium: http://www.visitsealife.com/London/

Ending the lesson

Review the lesson and reflect on learning.

- Say **Today we've learnt about London. Would you like to visit the city?** The pupils respond.
- Ask **Which was your favourite activity? Which activity was easy / difficult?**

Extra activity

Reinforcement

- The pupils use the map on Pupil's Book page 102 to practise giving directions. Ask **Where's (the Tower of London)? How do you get from (Hyde Park) to (Buckingham Palace)?** The pupils respond accordingly.

Link to Science

- If you are studying the Science topic of **Where we live** in English, you could discuss the advantages and disadvantages of living in a city. Encourage the class to use the comparative form: *A city is (noisier) than a small town.*

My project 3: A London adventure

Key Competences and Key Learning Outcomes

- Present your trip to the class
- Reflect on what you've learnt and how you've worked together
- Work in a group to design a digital presentation of your trip

Key language

- *bike, boat, bus, taxi, Underground; aquarium, attraction, cathedral, museum, park, Queen, river cruise, tower, trip, zoo; Saturday, Sunday; do experiments, ride a bike, take a photo*
- *You can (do experiments) there. Why don't we (go on the London Eye)? Shall we (go to Regent's Park)? On Saturday we're going to (take the Underground). We're going to visit (Buckingham Palace). Let's (visit Regent's Park).*

Materials

- Pupil's Book p103; Activity Book p101
- Teacher's Resource Bank: Talk cards

Optional materials

- Teacher's Resource Bank: Trinity Exams Practice cards (selected from the Starter Unit and Units 1, 2, 3, 4, 5, 6, 7, 8 and 9)

At a Glance Lesson Plan

Pupil's Book

Starting the lesson

- Use the Trinity Exams Practice cards (optional).
- Set learning outcomes and use the talk cards.

Plan and create your project: Activity 1

- Discuss the questions.
- Write the information on page 101 in your Activity Book.

Go to the Activity Book.

Cooperative learning

- Try to stay calm when you don't agree with your group.

Activity 2

- Create a digital presentation of your trip.

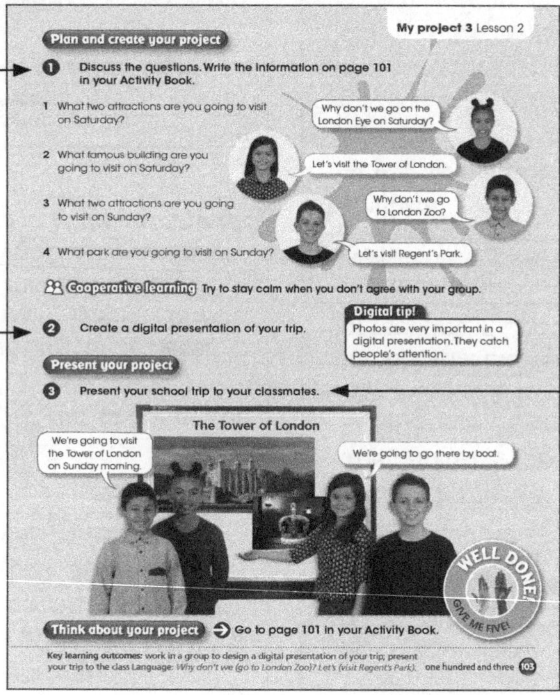

Present your project: Activity 3

- Present your school trip to your classmates.
- Think about your project

Go to the Activity Book.

Ending the lesson

- Review the lesson and reflect on learning.

Extra activity

Extension

- Plan what items you will take on your trip.

Activity Book

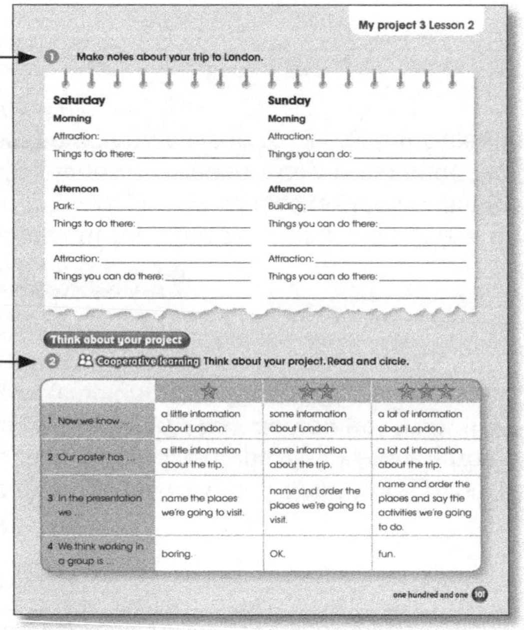

Activity Book

Activity 1

- Make notes about your trip to London.

Think about your project: Activity 2

- Think about your project.
- Read and circle.

Digital resources

Teacher's Digital: You can also teach this lesson using the Teacher's App on Navio.

Pupil's Digital: Encourage your pupils to use the Pupil's App on Navio to practise the activities from this lesson.

Powered By NAVIO

Starting the lesson

Use the Trinity Exams Practice cards (optional).

- The pupils practise asking and answering questions.

Set learning outcomes and use the talk cards.

- Say **Today we're going to continue the project.** Prompt the pupils to tell you what they did in the last lesson.
- Prompt the class to tell you what they must do when they work in groups: *listen, take turns, respect different opinions,* etc.
- Point to the talk cards to show the pupils the different ways they will be working in the lesson.

Plan and create your project: Pupil's Book Activity 1

Discuss the questions. Write the information on page 101 in your Activity Book.

- Explain that the pupils should work in their groups of four to plan a weekend trip to London. This information is to be recorded in their Activity Books.
- Focus the class on the activity and invite a pupil to read out the information. Highlight the two structures for making suggestions: *Why don't we …? Let's …*

Cooperative learning

Try to stay calm when you don't agree with your group.

- Read out the rubric. Discuss with the class ways in which we can show respect for each others' opinions and stay calm if we don't agree.
- Emphasise the importance of listening to others.

Activity Book

Activity 1

Make notes about your trip to London.

- The pupils record their decisions about their two-day trip to London.

Plan and create your project: Pupil's Book Activity 2

Create a digital presentation of your trip.

- Once the pupils have worked together to complete their plan, they create a digital presentation.
- Refer the pupils to the Digital tip to highlight the importance of using photos in a digital presentation to catch people's attention.

Present your project: Pupil's Book Activity 3

Present your school trip to your classmates.

- Focus the pupils on the photo and encourage them to talk about what they can see. Ask **What are the children talking about? What can you see in their presentation?** Then ask a pupil to read out the speech bubbles.
- Invite different groups in turn to present their London trip to the rest of the class. Ensure that each pupil in the group participates in the presentation, but accept that some pupils may contribute more than others. At the end of each presentation, ask the group a question and encourage the rest of the class to think of questions they'd like to ask. The group giving the presentation should answer the questions.
- If you wish, at the end of the activity, tell the class that they are going to vote on which trip is the best. Give each group a number and explain that the pupils can only vote for one trip and they can't vote for their own group. Say the number of each group in turn and ask the pupils to raise their hands if they think that trip is the best. Alternatively, hand out a slip of paper to each pupil and ask them to write the number of the trip they think is best. Collect in and count the papers.

Think about your project

- Tell the pupils that they are now going to think about what they have achieved and evaluate how their project went. Ask the pupils to turn to page 101 in their Activity Book.

Activity Book

Activity 2: Think about your project.

Read and circle.

- Explain to the pupils that they are now going to think about their project and how they've worked as a group. Read out each statement and ask the pupils to circle the appropriate number of stars depending on their project.

Ending the lesson

Review the lesson and reflect on learning.

- Say **We've completed our project about London.** Ask **Did you enjoy planning your two-day trip?** Elicit the pupils' opinions.
- Ask **Which was your favourite activity? Which activity was easy / difficult?**

Extra activity

Extension

- Explain to the pupils that they need to pack an imaginary suitcase for their trip. Ask **What items will you need to pack for a trip to London?**
- The pupils make a list of the clothes and objects that they need to take, taking into the account the weather in London.

Chinese New Year

Key Competences and Key Learning Outcomes

- Learn about Chinese New Year
- Do research on the Internet
- Write a riddle for a mystery word
- Read and solve some riddles
- Make a Chinese lantern

Key language

- *chopsticks, dragons, envelopes, festival, fish, lanterns, lions, lucky, money, noodles, riddles, soup, tradition*
- *(People) eat / use / decorate ..., (Children) have / receive / read ..., The (envelopes) have got (money inside them). They often have (drawings of lucky animals). What letter is it?*

Materials

- Pupil's Book p104; Class CD4
- Teacher's Resource Bank: Talk cards; Chinese lantern

Optional materials

- Teacher's Resource Bank: Trinity Exams Practice cards (selected from the Starter Unit and Units 1, 2, 3, 4, 5, 6, 7, 8 and 9)
- Paper, coloured pens and pencils for each pair

At a Glance Lesson Plan

Starting the lesson

- Use the Trinity Exams Practice cards (optional).
- Set learning outcomes and use the talk cards.

Activity 1

- Read and answer.

Activity 2

- Read and listen. Which tradition do you like the most? Why?

▶ *CD4 Track 32 p281*

Pupil's Book

Festivals

Chinese New Year

1 Read and answer.

Millions of people around the world celebrate Chinese New Year. The exact date of this festival changes every year, but it's always in January or February. The festival has got lots of amazing traditions. Look at the pictures. What do you think people do?

2 Read and listen. Which tradition do you like the most? Why? CD4 32

1 At Chinese New Year, families have a special meal together. There are always lots of traditional dishes. People eat soup, fish, green vegetables and long noodles. Do you know that it's bad luck to cut the noodles with a knife? People use chopsticks to eat them.

2 Children receive special envelopes from their family at Chinese New Year. The envelopes have got money inside them. The envelopes are red because it's a lucky colour. They often have drawings of lucky animals like lions and dragons, too.

3 People decorate their houses with beautiful lanterns at Chinese New Year. The lanterns are made of paper and there are riddles at the bottom. Riddles are clever questions. Children read the riddles when they visit a house. If they know the answer, they get a present.

3 Read again and find the names of these things.

1 2 3 4 5 6

4 Solve the riddles with a partner. Order the six letters to find the mystery word.

1 It's in one, but not in toe. What letter is it?
2 There are two in spoon and one in fork. What letter is it?
3 This letter is in word, but not in window. What letter is it?
4 This letter is in golf, but not in flower. What letter is it?
5 There are two in address and one in dress. What letter is it?
6 This letter is in read, but not in drive. What letter is it?

Now write your riddle and make a Chinese lantern.

ICT Each year has got the name of an animal in the Chinese calendar. Use the internet to find out the animals.

104 one hundred and four

Activity 3

- Read again and find the names of these things.

Activity 4

- Solve the riddles with a partner. Order the six letters to find the mystery word.
- Each year has got the name of an animal in the Chinese calendar. Use the Internet to find out the animals.

Ending the lesson

- Review the lesson and reflect on learning.

Extra activity

Extension

- Now write your riddle and make a Chinese lantern.

Digital resources

Teacher's Digital: You can also teach this lesson using the Teacher's App on Navio.

Pupil's Digital: Encourage your pupils to use the Pupil's App on Navio to practise the activities from this lesson.

Powered By NAVIO

Detailed Lesson Plan

Starting the lesson

Use the Trinity Exams Practice cards (optional).

- The pupils practise asking and answering questions.

Set learning outcomes and use the talk cards.

- Say **Today we're going to learn about Chinese New Year and some of its traditions, solve some riddles and write our own riddles**.
- Point to the talk cards to show the pupils the different ways they will be working in the lesson.

At a Glance Lesson Plan

Pupil's Book Activity 1

Read and answer.

- (Books closed.) Work as a class to find out what pupils know about Chinese New Year. Write the information that the pupils give you on the board. To elicit the information, ask **When is Chinese New Year? How do people celebrate it?**
- (Books open.) Ask pupils to read the text and look at the photos. Ask pupils again **When is Chinese New Year?** Ask pupils how they think Chinese New Year is celebrated and add ideas to the board.

Pupil's Book Activity 2

Read and listen. Which tradition do you like the most? Why?

▶ *CD4 Track 32 p281*

- Explain that you are going to read and listen to descriptions of three Chinese New Year traditions. Play the CD. The pupils listen and read.
- Check understanding. Ask **What do people eat at Chinese New Year?** (*Soup, fish, green vegetables, noodles.*) **What's in the envelopes?** (*Money.*) **What's on the bottom of the lanterns?** (*Riddles.*)
- Ask pupils **Which tradition do you like the most?** Ask them to justify their answer.

Pupil's Book Activity 3

Read again and find the names of these things.

- Point to the first picture and ask **What's this?** The pupils find the word in the texts.
- Organise the class into pairs. They find the words in the text and write them in their notebooks.
- Check the answers and spelling as a class.

Answers: **1** envelopes **2** lantern **3** chopsticks **4** riddles **5** noodles **6** dragon

Pupil's Book Activity 4

Solve the riddles with a partner. Order the six letters to find the mystery word.

- Look again at the third photo in Activity 2 and remind pupils that at the bottom of each lantern is a riddle. Say **A riddle is a clever question.**
- Read the first riddle to the class and ask pupils **What letter is it?** Ensure that all pupils understand why the answer is *N*.
- Organise the class into pairs. They continue to solve the riddles and write the letters in their notebooks.
- When they have solved all of the riddles, tell the pupils to rearrange the letters to find the mystery word. Ask **What is the mystery word?** (*Dragon.*)

Each year has got the name of an animal in the Chinese calendar. Use the Internet to find out the animals. ICT

- Read the instructions at the bottom of the page. Challenge the pupils to find out the information on the Internet, in groups or as a homework activity.

Answers: rat, ox, tiger, rabbit, dragon, snake, horse, sheep / goat, monkey, rooster, dog, pig

Ending the lesson

Review the lesson and reflect on learning.

- Say **Today we've learnt lots of things about Chinese New Year. What do you remember?** Elicit the information from the pupils.
- Ask **Which was your favourite activity today? Which activity was easy / difficult?**

Extra activity

Extension

Now write your riddle and make a Chinese lantern.

- Tell the pupils they are going to work in pairs to write their own riddle for another pair to solve.
- Give each pair some paper and coloured pens or pencils. The pupils decide on a mystery word and write their own riddle to reveal it. They can colour and decorate their riddle if they wish.
- Pairs swap riddles with another pair to try and find the mystery word. You could give a small prize to the first pair to solve their riddle.
- The pupils now make a Chinese lantern.

World Book Day

Key Competences and Key Learning Outcomes

- Ask and answer questions about books and reading
- Do research on the Internet
- Make a poster about a favourite book
- Learn about World Book Day
- Read and enjoy a poem

Key language

- *adventure, black hole, books, buy, chest, desert, detective, dragon, faraway land, follow, gold, grow, ice, land, magic beans, magic carpet, pirate, poems, read, sand, snow, stories, treasure, tree, white rabbit, witch, write*
- *Do you like (writing stories and poems)? How often do (you read a book)? I (read a book) three times a week. What's your (favourite book)? My favourite book is (Geronimo Stilton). What's it (about)? It's (about a mouse).*

Materials

- Pupil's Book p105; Class CD4
- Teacher's Resource Bank: Talk cards

Optional materials

- Paper, coloured pens and pencils for each pupil
- Teacher's Resource Bank: Trinity Exams Practice cards (sselected from the Starter Unit and Units 1, 2, 3, 4, 5, 6, 7, 8 and 9)

At a Glance Lesson Plan

Starting the lesson

- Use the Trinity Exams Practice cards (optional).
- Set learning outcomes and use the talk cards.

Activity 1

- Read and answer.

Activity 2

- Listen, read and match.
- ▶ *CD4 Track 33 p281*
- Read the poem aloud.

Activity 3

- Ask and answer.
- Find out when children in the UK celebrate World Book Day.

Pupil's Book

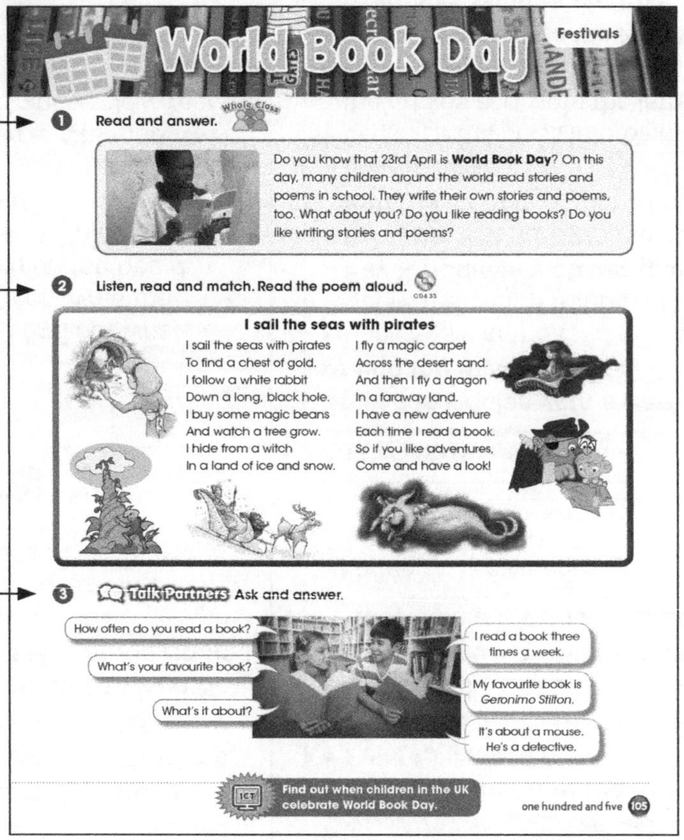

Ending the lesson

- Review the lesson and reflect on learning.

Extra activity

Extension

- Make a poster for World Book Day.

Digital resources

Teacher's Digital: You can also teach this lesson using the Teacher's App on Navio.

Pupil's Digital: Encourage your pupils to use the Pupil's App on Navio to practise the activities from this lesson.

Powered By NAVIO

Starting the lesson

Use the Trinity Exams Practice cards (optional).

- The pupils practise asking and answering questions.

Set learning outcomes and use the talk cards.

- Say **It's (almost) World Book Day. Today we're going to read a poem about books. We're also going to ask and answer about books, and make a poster.**
- Point to the talk cards to show the pupils the different ways they will be working in the lesson.

Pupil's Book Activity 1

Read and answer.

- Read the introduction as a class. Check understanding.
- Prompt different individual pupils to say whether they like reading and writing stories and poems.

Pupil's Book Activity 2

Listen, read and match. Read the poem aloud.

▶ *CD4 Track 33 p281*

- Point to the first picture and ask **What can you see?** Repeat the procedure with the other illustrations.
- If you wish to do so, ask **Do you know a story about a girl and a white rabbit?** Elicit / explain that it is the story *Alice in Wonderland*. The other stories that are illustrated are: *Treasure Island, Jack and the Beanstalk, The Lion, the Witch and the Wardrobe, Aladdin* and *The Never Ending Story.*
- Say **Let's listen to a poem about books.** Play the CD. The pupils listen and read.
- Read out the first two lines of the poem and ask the class to point to the matching picture. Repeat the procedure with the following lines.
- Play the CD a second time, pausing after each line of the poem. The pupils should repeat each line in turn.
- Finally, play the CD again. The pupils join in, saying the poem. If you wish, encourage the class to mime the different actions.

Pupil's Book Activity 3

Ask and answer.

- Focus the class on the activity and ask a pair of pupils to read out the conversation. Prompt another pair of pupils to ask and answer the same questions.
- Organise the class into Talk Partners. The pupils ask and answer the questions in pairs.

Find out when children in the UK celebrate World Book Day. ICT

- Read the instructions at the bottom of the page. Challenge the pupils to find out the information on the Internet, in groups or as a homework activity.

Answer: World Book Day is celebrated in the UK on the first Thursday in March.

Ending the lesson

Review the lesson and reflect on learning.

- Say **Today we've learnt a poem. Did you like it?** Elicit the pupils' opinions. Then say **We've talked about our favourite books, too.** Ask a few pupils around the class what their favourite book is.
- Ask **Which was your favourite activity today? Which activity was easy / difficult?**

Extra activity

Extension

- Tell the pupils they are going to make a poster for World Book Day. Give each pupil some paper and coloured pens or pencils. The pupils draw a picture of their favourite book and write the title of the book.
- They can also write what it is about and why they like it. Refer them back to the conversation in Activity 3 if they need ideas of what to write.
- Collect the posters and make a World Book Day class display.

Key Competences and Key Learning Outcomes

- Read and understand sentences
- Talk about which picture is different

- Review learning and reflect on progress
- Practise for A1 Movers Reading and Writing Parts 2&6, Speaking Part 3 and Listening Part 4

Key language

- *Which subjects are you good at? I'm (very) good at (Maths). What do you like doing at school? I like (English). What activities do you do after school? Which subjects do you have on (Tuesday)?*
- Recycled: classroom objects; days of the week; places in a school; school and after-school activities; school subjects; *capital letter*

Materials

- Pupil's Book p115; Activity Book p14, 102 and p111; Class CD4; Teacher's App on Navio
- Teacher's Resource Bank: Talk cards

Optional materials

- Teacher's Resource Bank: Trinity Exams Practice cards (selected from Unit 1)

At a Glance Lesson Plan

Pupil's Book

Starting the lesson

- Use the Trinity Exams Practice cards (optional).
- Review a song from the unit.
- Set learning outcomes and use the talk cards.

Go to the Activity Book.

Activity 1

- Read the text and choose the best answer.

Activity 2

- Listen and follow.

▶ *CD4 Track 34 p281*

- Which picture is different in number 1?
- Why?

External Exams Video

- Additional Cambridge Exams Practice Video: A1 Movers.

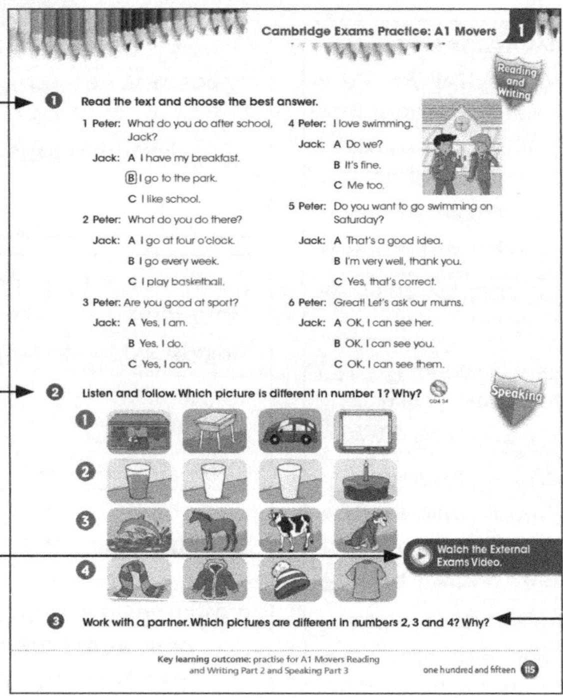
Cambridge Exams Practice: A1 Movers 1

1 Read the text and choose the best answer.

1 Peter: What do you do after school, Jack?
Jack: A I have my breakfast. B I go to the park. C I like school.

2 Peter: What do you do there?
Jack: A I go at four o'clock. B I go every week. C I play basketball.

3 Peter: Are you good at sport?
Jack: A Yes, I am. B Yes, I do. C Yes, I can.

4 Peter: I love swimming.
Jack: A Do we? B It's fine. C Me too.

5 Peter: Do you want to go swimming on Saturday?
Jack: A That's a good idea. B I'm very well, thank you. C Yes, that's correct.

6 Peter: Great! Let's ask our mums.
Jack: A OK. I can see her. B OK. I can see you. C OK. I can see them.

2 Listen and follow. Which picture is different in number 1? Why?

Watch the External Exams Video.

3 Work with a partner. Which pictures are different in numbers 2, 3 and 4? Why?

Key learning outcome: practise for A1 Movers Reading and Writing Part 2 and Speaking Part 3

one hundred and fifteen 115

Activity 3

- Work with a partner.
- Which pictures are different in numbers 2, 3 and 4?
- Why?

Go to the Activity Book.

Ending the lesson

- Review the lesson and reflect on learning.

Extra activity

Reinforcement

- Find illustrations of places in a school.

Activity Book

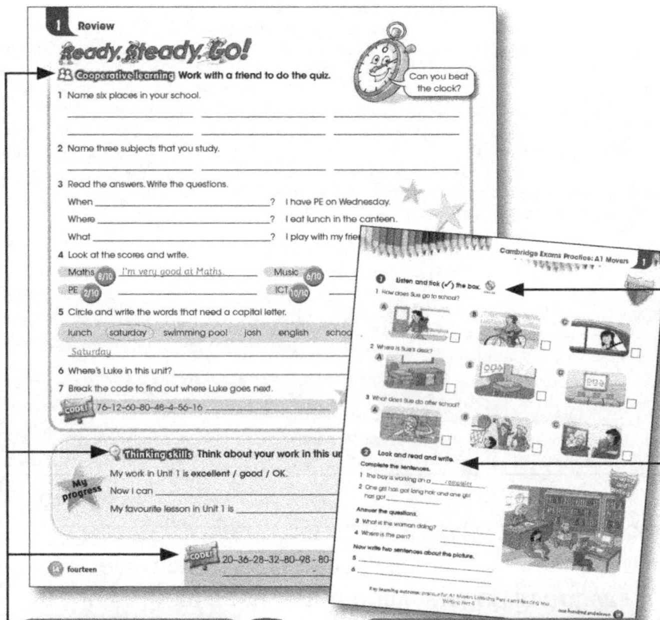
1 Review

Ready, Steady, Go!

Cooperative learning Work with a friend to do the quiz.

Can you beat the clock?

1 Name six places in your school.

2 Name three subjects that you study.

3 Read the answers. Write the questions.

4 Look at the scores and write.

5 Circle and write the words that need a capital letter.

6 Where's Luke in this unit?

7 Break the code to find out where Luke goes next.

Thinking skills Think about your work in this unit.

My work in Unit 1 is excellent / good / OK.

Now I can

My favourite lesson in Unit 1 is

fourteen

Cambridge Exams Practice: A1 Movers 1

1 Listen and tick (✓) the box.

2 Look and read and write.

Activity Book page 14: Review

- Work with a friend to do the quiz.

My progress

- Think about your work in this unit.
- Read, circle and write.

Code activity

- Complete the code activity.

Activity Book page 111: Cambridge Exams Practice

Activity 1

- Listen and tick (✓) the box.

▶ *CD4 Track 43 p282*

Activity 2

- Look and read and write.

Digital resources

Teacher's Digital: You can also teach this lesson using the Teacher's App on Navio.

Pupil's Digital: Encourage your pupils to use the Pupil's App on Navio to practise the activities from this lesson.

Powered By NAVIO

Starting the lesson

Use the Trinity Exams Practice cards (optional).

- The pupils practise asking and answering questions with the Unit 1 cards.

Review a song from the unit.

- Invite the class to choose one of the songs from the unit. The pupils sing and do the corresponding actions.

Set learning outcomes and use the talk cards.

- Say **Today we're going to practise activities for an exam and remember what we've learnt in Unit 1.**
- Point to the talk cards to show the pupils the different ways they will be working in the lesson.

Activity Book page 14: Review

Work with a friend to do the quiz.

- Organise the class into pairs. Set a time limit (10–15 minutes). Stress that the pupils are racing against the clock, not each other.
- Read out the seven tasks and check understanding. Then say **Ready, steady, go!**
- Check and correct the answers as a class.

Answers: **1** Six of the following: gym, corridor, computer room, football pitch, school hall, playground, library, bike stand, music room, basketball court, canteen, vegetable garden **2** Three of the following: ICT, Geography, History, Arts and Crafts, PE, Drama, Science **3** When do you have PE? Where do you eat lunch? What do you do in the playground? **4** I'm very good at Maths. I'm not very good at PE. I'm good at Music. I'm brilliant at ICT. **5** Saturday, Josh, English, Ravi, Monday **6** Ireland **7** Scotland

My progress

Think about your work in this unit. Read, circle and write.

- Say **Now you're going to think about your work.**
- Prompt the pupils to say what they can do after studying Unit 1. Ask **What can you say?** (*Places in a school, school subjects, after-school activities.*) **What can you write?** (*A poster.*) The pupils circle 'excellent', 'good' or 'OK' and complete the two sentences.

Code activity

- The pupils complete the code activity.

Answer: eighty-two

Pupil's Book Activity 1

Read the text and choose the best answer.

- The pupils read the line from a conversation. They choose the best response.

Answers: **1** B **2** C **3** A **4** C **5** A **6** C

Pupil's Book Activity 2

Listen and follow. Which picture is different in number 1? Why?

▶ *CD4 Track 34 p281*

- Ask the pupils to look at the four pictures in number 1. Ask which picture they think is different.
- Play the CD. The pupils listen and identify which picture is different and why.

Answers: **1** car (the others are classroom objects)

Pupil's Book Activity 3

Work with a partner. Which pictures are different in numbers 2, 3 and 4? Why?

- Ask the pupils to look at the four pictures in numbers 2–4. Pupils work together to decide which picture is different in each set.

Answers: **2** cake (the others are drinks) **3** dolphin (the others are land animals) **4** T-shirt (the others are clothes for cold weather)

External Exams Video

Additional Cambridge Exams Practice Video: A1 Movers.

- Additional external exams preparation material, including videos, worksheets and practice tests, can be found in the Teacher's Resource Bank on Navio.

Activity Book page 111: Cambridge Exams Practice: A1 Movers 1

Activity 1

Listen and tick (✓) the box.

▶ *CD4 Track 43 p282*

- Ask the pupils to describe what they can see in the first set of pictures.
- Play the CD, pausing after the first exchange. The pupils listen and tick the correct picture. Repeat the procedure with the other exchanges.

Answers: **1** B **2** C **3** B

Activity 2

Look and read and write.

- Ask the pupils to describe the picture.
- The pupils work on their own or in pairs to read each sentence and answer the questions.

Answers: **1** computer **2** short hair **3** writing **4** on the desk **5 & 6** Pupils' own answers

Ending the lesson

Review the lesson and reflect on learning.

- Say **Today we've practised activities for an exam and remembered what we've learnt in Unit 1.**
- Ask **Which was your favourite activity today? Which activity was easy / difficult?**

Extra activity

Reinforcement

- Ask **Can you find a (bike stand)?** The pupils look through Unit 1 in the Pupil's Book to find and point to the correct place in a school. Repeat with other places and objects that are illustrated in the unit.
- Organise the class into pairs to play the game.

Activity Book page 102: Vocabulary and Grammar Practice

Answers: **1.1** football pitch **1.2** bike stand **1.3** school hall **1.4** vegetable garden
2.1 ICT **2.2** History **2.3** Geography **2.4** PE **2.5** Drama
3.1 do you eat lunch? **3.2** When do you have PE? **3.3** What do you do in the library? **3.4** Where do you play football? **3.5** What do you do in the school hall?
4.1 very good/brilliant **4.2** not very good at pottery **4.3** She's very good at/brilliant at Maths.

Key Competences and Key Learning Outcomes

- Read and complete a text
- Tell a story

- Review learning and reflect on progress
- Practise for A1 Movers Reading and Writing Parts 1&3, Speaking Part 2 and Listening Part 3

Key language

- *I sometimes (use a dictionary). I (listen to songs) in (English).*
- Recycled: free-time activities; frequency words; household chores; household objects; rooms in a house; *How often do you (play football)? When / Where do you (have lunch)? Do you like (swimming)?*

Materials

- Pupil's Book p116; Activity Book p24, 103 and p112; Class CD4; Teacher's App on Navio
- Teacher's Resource Bank: Talk cards

Optional materials

- Teacher's Resource Bank: Trinity Exams Practice cards (selected from Unit 2)

At a Glance Lesson Plan

Pupil's Book

Starting the lesson

- Use the Trinity Exams Practice cards (optional).
- Review a song from the unit.
- Set learning outcomes and use the talk cards.

Go to the Activity Book.

Activity 1

- Read the story.
- Choose a word from the box.
- Write the correct words in your notebook.

Activity 2

- Now choose the best name for the story.

External Exams Video

- Additional Cambridge Exams Practice Video: A1 Movers.

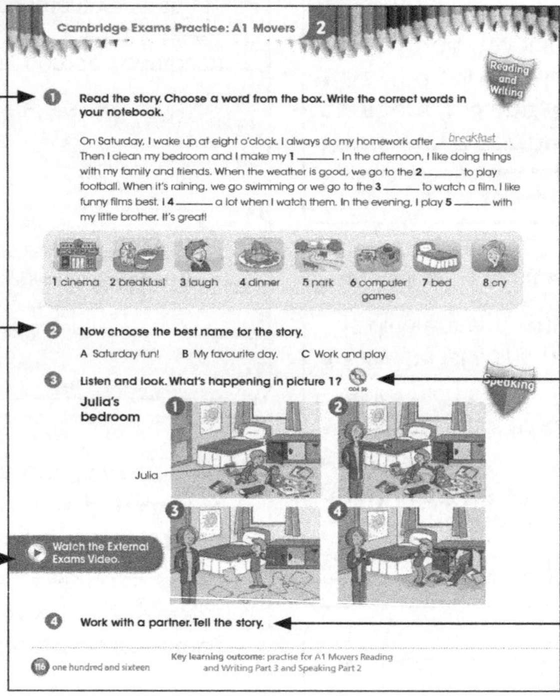

Activity 3

- Listen and look.

▶ *CD4 Track 35 p281*

- What's happening in picture 1?

Activity 4

- Work with a partner.
- Tell the story.

Go to the Activity Book.

Ending the lesson

- Review the lesson and reflect on learning.

Extra activity

Reinforcement

- Prepare three questions about the unit.

Activity Book

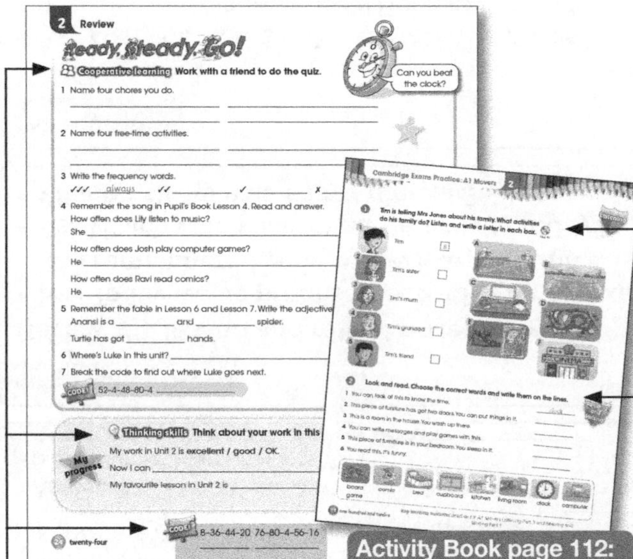

Activity Book page 24: Review

- Work with a friend to do the quiz.

My progress

- Think about your work in this unit. Read, circle and write.

Code activity

- Complete the code activity.

Activity Book page 112: Cambridge Exams Practice

Activity 1

- Tim is telling Mrs Jones about his family.
- What activities do his family do?
- Listen and write a letter in each box.

▶ *CD4 Track 44 p282*

Activity 2

- Look and read.
- Choose the correct words and write them on the lines.

Digital resources

Teacher's Digital: You can also teach this lesson using the Teacher's App on Navio.

Pupil's Digital: Encourage your pupils to use the Pupil's App on Navio to practise the activities from this lesson.

Powered By NAVIO

Starting the lesson

Use the Trinity Exams Practice cards (optional).

- The pupils practise asking and answering questions using the Unit 2 cards.

Review a song from the unit.

- Invite the class to choose one of the songs from the unit. The pupils sing and do the corresponding actions.

Set learning outcomes and use the talk cards.

- Say **Today we're going to practise activities for an exam and remember what we've learnt in Unit 2.**
- Point to the talk cards to show the pupils the different ways they will be working in the lesson.

Activity Book page 24: Review

Work with a friend to do the quiz.

- Organise the class into pairs. Set a time limit (10–15 minutes). Stress that the pupils are racing against the clock, not each other.
- Read out the seven tasks and check understanding. Then say **Ready, steady, go!** Check and correct the answers as a class.

Answers: **1** Four of the following: make my bed, tidy up, feed my pet, wash up, cook dinner, hoover the floor, lay the table, clear the table, walk the dog, wash the car, water the plants, dust **2** Four of the following: watch DVDs, do puzzles, read comics, draw pictures, play computer games, play board games **3** always, often, sometimes, never **4** She listens to music once a week. He plays computer games twice a week. He reads comics three times a week. **5** lazy / greedy, dirty **6** Scotland **7** Malta

My progress

Think about your work in this unit. Read, circle and write.

- Say **Now you're going to think about your work.**
- Prompt the pupils to say what they can do after studying Unit 2. Ask **What can you say?** (*Household chores, free-time activities*.) **What can you write?** (*A fable ending*.)
- The pupils circle 'excellent', 'good' or 'OK' and complete the two sentences.

Code activity

- The pupils complete the code activity.

Answer: bike stand

Pupil's Book Activity 1

Read the story. Choose a word from the box. Write the correct words in your notebook.

- The pupils read the story. They choose the best words to complete the text. There are two extra words.

Answers: **1** bed **2** park **3** cinema **4** laugh **5** computer games

Pupil's Book Activity 2

Now choose the best name for the story.

- The pupils decide which name is best.

Answer: **A** Saturday fun!

Pupil's Book Activity 3

Listen and look. What's happening in picture 1?

▶ *CD4 Track 35 p281*

- Play the CD while the pupils look at the picture. Elicit what is happening in picture 1.

Pupil's Book Activity 4

Work with a partner. Tell the story.

- Organise the class into Talk Partners. The pupils describe what is happening in the story.

External Exams Video

Additional Cambridge Exams Practice Video: A1 Movers.

- Additional external exams preparation material, including videos, worksheets and practice tests, can be found in the Teacher's Resource Bank on Navio.

Activity Book page 112: Cambridge Exams Practice: A1 Movers 2

Activity 1

Tim is telling Mrs Jones about his family. What activities do his family do? Listen and write a letter in each box.

▶ *CD4 Track 44 p282*

- The pupils describe the pictures. Play the CD, pausing after each exchange. The pupils listen and write a letter in each box.

Answers: **1** B **2** E **3** F **4** D **5** B

Activity 2

Look and read. Choose the correct words and write them on the lines.

- Ask, e.g. **Where can you find a (bed)? What do we use a (clock) for?**
- The pupils work in pairs to read the sentences and write the words. Check the answers and spellings.

Answers: **1** clock **2** cupboard **3** kitchen **4** computer **5** bed **6** comic

Ending the lesson

Review the lesson and reflect on learning.

- Say **Today we've practised activities for an exam and remembered what we've learnt in Unit 2.**
- Ask **Which was your favourite activity today? Which activity was easy / difficult?**

Extra activity

Reinforcement

- In pairs, the pupils write three questions about the unit. Reorganise the class into new pairs. The pupils take it in turns to ask and answer the questions.

Activity Book page 103: Vocabulary and Grammar Practice

Answers: **1.1** wash up **1.2** hoover the floor **1.3** make the bed **1.4** water the plants **1.5** cook lunch / dinner
2.1 do **2.2** read **2.3** draw **2.4** watch **2.5** play **2.6** play
3.1 Peter always feeds his pet. **3.2** Lily sometimes makes her bed. **3.3** My sister often hoovers the floor.
3.4 My brother never cooks dinner.
4.1 How often does your friend watch TV? **4.2** How often does your friend play computer games? **4.3** How often does your friend cook dinner?

Key Competences and Key Learning Outcomes

- Read and complete a text
- Talk about the differences between two pictures

- Practise for A1 Movers Reading and Writing Parts 2&4, Speaking Part 1 and Listening Part 2

Key language

- *apple, blond hair, burger, cloudy, grass, jacket, jumper, ride a bike, T-shirt*
- *The boy is eating (an apple). The girl is wearing (a jacket). The boy's got (blond hair). It's (cloudy). How do you spell (jacket)? What does (jumper) mean? How do you say (this word) in English? Shall I (tell a teacher)? That's a (good idea).*
- Recycled: health problems; *I've got (earache). You must (wear a hat and scarf). You mustn't (swim). How often do you (eat fruit)? I (eat fruit) (every day). How are you today? I'm (not very well).*

Materials

- Pupil's Book p117; Activity Book p34, 104 and p113; Class CD4; Teacher's App on Navio
- Teacher's Resource Bank: Talk cards

Optional materials

- Teacher's Resource Bank: Trinity Exams Practice cards (selected from Unit 3)

At a Glance Lesson Plan

Pupil's Book

Starting the lesson

- Use the Trinity Exams Practice cards (optional).
- Review a song from the unit.
- Set learning outcomes and use the talk cards.

Go to the Activity Book.

Activity 1

- Read the text.
- Choose the right words and write them in your notebook.

Activity 2

- Listen and look. What's the difference?

▶ *CD4 Track 36 p281*

Activity 3

- Work with a partner.
- Look and find more differences.

Go to the Activity Book.

Ending the lesson

- Review the lesson and reflect on learning.

Extra activity

Reinforcement

- Prepare three questions about the unit.

External Exams Video

- Additional Cambridge Exams Practice Video: A1 Movers.

Activity Book

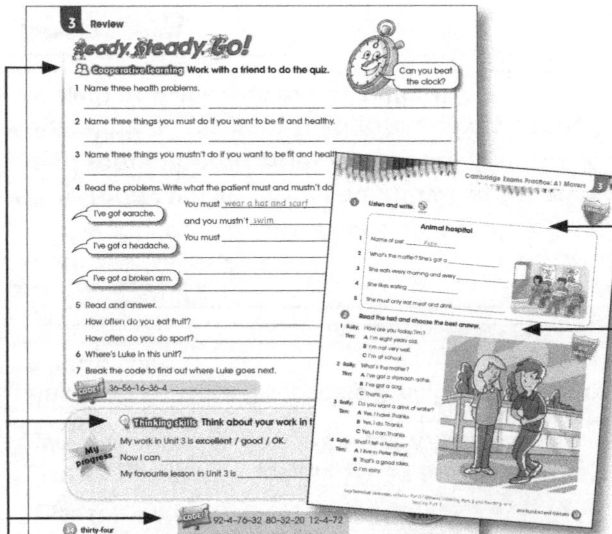

Activity Book page 34: Review

- Work with a friend to do the quiz.

My progress

- Think about your work in this unit.
- Read, circle and write.

Code activity

- Complete the code activity.

Activity Book page 113: Cambridge Exams Practice

Activity 1

- Listen and write.

▶ *CD4 Track 45 p282*

Activity 2

- Read the text and choose the best answer.

Digital resources

Teacher's Digital: You can also teach this lesson using the Teacher's App on Navio.

Pupil's Digital: Encourage your pupils to use the Pupil's App on Navio to practise the activities from this lesson.

Powered By NAVIO

Starting the lesson

Use the Trinity Exams Practice cards (optional).

- The pupils practise asking and answering questions using the Unit 3 cards.

Review a song from the unit.

- Invite the class to choose one of the songs from the unit. The pupils sing and do the corresponding actions.

Set learning outcomes and use the talk cards.

- Say **Today we're going to practise activities for an exam and remember what we've learnt in Unit 3.**
- Point to the talk cards to show the pupils the different ways they will be working in the lesson.

Activity Book page 34: Review

Work with a friend to do the quiz.

- Organise the class into pairs. Set a time limit (10–15 minutes). Stress that the pupils are racing against the clock, not each other.
- Read out the tasks and check understanding. Then say **Ready, steady, go!**
- Check and correct the answers as a class.

Answers: **1** Three of the following: headache, stomach ache, earache, cold, cough, sore throat, flu, temperature, cut, broken leg, feel dizzy, feel sick **2** go to bed early, eat healthy snacks, be active **3** go to bed late, eat lots of sweets, be lazy **4** You must wear a hat and scarf and you mustn't swim. You must be quiet and you mustn't shout. You must go to hospital and you mustn't run. **6** Malta **7** India

My progress

Think about your work in this unit. Read, circle and write.

- Say **Now you're going to think about your work.**
- Prompt the pupils by asking **What can you say?** (*Health problems, healthy / unhealthy habits.*) **What can you write?** (*A quiz.*) The pupils circle 'excellent', 'good' or 'OK' and complete the two sentences.

Code activity

- The pupils complete the code activity.

Answer: wash the car

Pupil's Book Activity 1

Read the text. Choose the right words and write them in your notebook.

- The pupils read the text. They choose the best words to complete the text.

Answers: **1** help **2** at **3** mustn't **4** well **5** asks **6** because

Pupil's Book Activity 2

Listen and look. What's the difference?

▶ *CD4 Track 36 p281*

- Explain to pupils that they are going to listen to a description of one difference.
- Play the CD while the pupils look at the pictures. Say **What's the difference?** (*The boy is eating a burger in picture A but an apple in picture B.*)

Pupil's Book Activity 3

Work with a partner. Look and find more differences.

- The pupils work in pairs to identify three more differences between the pictures.

Answers: In picture A the girl is playing football. In picture B she is riding a bike. In picture A the dog is with the boy. In picture B the dog is with the girl. In picture A it's sunny. In picture B it's cloudy.

External Exams Video

Additional Cambridge Exams Practice Video: A1 Movers.

- Additional external exams preparation material, including videos, worksheets and practice tests, can be found in the Teacher's Resource Bank on Navio.

Activity Book page 113: Cambridge Exams Practice: A1 Movers 3

Activity 1

Listen and write.

▶ *CD4 Track 45 p282*

- Play the CD, pausing after the first exchange. Check the answer with the class.
- Repeat the procedure with the other exchanges.

Answers: **1** Katie **2** stomach ache **3** evening **4** cake **5** water

Activity 2

Read the text and choose the best answer.

- Focus the class on the picture and ask **What's the matter with the boy?**
- Read out the first question and invite a pupil to read out the three possible answers. Ask the class to tell you whether the correct response is A, B or C.
- The pupils choose the best answer to each question.

Answers: **1** B **2** A **3** B **4** B

Ending the lesson

Review the lesson and reflect on learning.

- Say **Today we've practised activities for an exam and remembered what we've learnt in Unit 3.**
- Ask **Which was your favourite activity today? Which activity was easy / difficult?**

Extra activity

Reinforcement

- In pairs, the pupils prepare three questions about the unit. Reorganise the class into new pairs. The pupils take turns to ask and answer the questions.

Activity Book page 104: Vocabulary and Grammar Practice

Answers: **1.1** cut **1.2** headache **1.3** cough **1.4** sore throat **1.5** stomach ache
2.1 early **2.2** late **2.3** healthy **2.4** sweets **2.5** active **2.6** lazy
3.1 Has the boy got a cut? **3.2** Do the children feel dizzy? **3.3** Have they got stomach ache? **3.4** Does she have a sore throat?
4.1 You mustn't eat lots of sweets. **4.2** You must brush your teeth. **4.3** You must eat healthy food. **4.4** You must go to bed early.

Key Competences and Key Learning Outcomes

- Complete and write sentences about a picture
- Ask and answer questions

- Review learning and reflect on progress
- Practise for A1 Movers Reading and Writing Parts 5&6, Speaking Part 4 and Listening Part 1

Key language

- *cereals, fruit, toast, watermelon*
- *How do you (like to work)? I like to work with the whole class / with a Talk Partner / in small groups / on my own.*
- Recycled: pizza toppings; *crunchy, plain, savoury, soft, spicy, sweet; chocolate, curry, ice cream, milk, sweets; every day, about (three) times a (month), (twice) a (week); cake, pizza, presents, restaurant; What do you have for (breakfast)? I have (cereal). Do you prefer eating (at home) or (in a restaurant)? I prefer eating (in a restaurant). Which food do you (love eating)? I love eating (cheese). How often do you eat (cheese)? I eat (cheese) (about) (once a week).*

Materials

- Pupil's Book p118; Activity Book p46, 105 and p114; Class CD4; Teacher's App on Navio
- Teacher's Resource Bank: Talk cards

Optional materials

- Teacher's Resource Bank: Trinity Exams Practice cards (selected from Unit 4)

At a Glance Lesson Plan

Pupil's Book

Starting the lesson

- Use the Trinity Exams Practice cards (optional).
- Review a song from the unit.
- Set learning outcomes and use the talk cards.

Go to the Activity Book.

Activity 1

- Look, read and write.

Activity 2

- Listen and follow.

▶ *CD4 Track 37 p282*

- What's the missing information?

Activity 3

- Work with a partner.
- Ask and answer.

Go to the Activity Book.

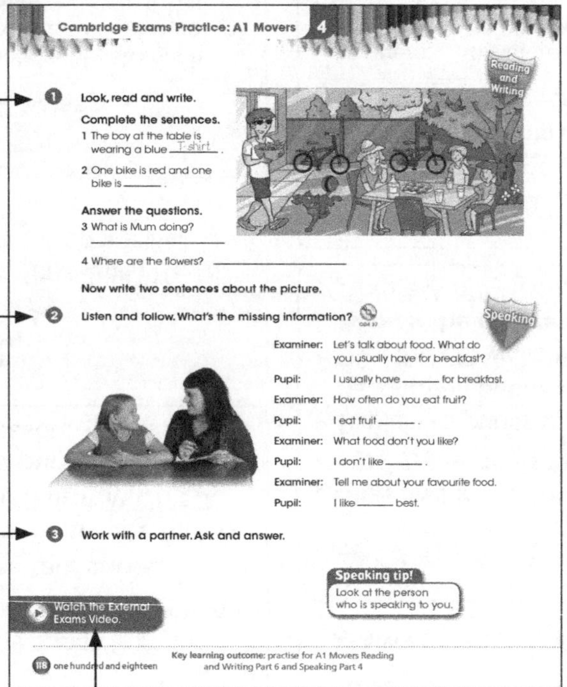

Ending the lesson

- Review the lesson and reflect on learning.

Extra activity

Reinforcement

- Prepare three questions about the unit.

External Exams Video

- Additional Cambridge Exams Practice Video: A1 Movers.

Digital resources

Teacher's Digital: You can also teach this lesson using the Teacher's App on Navio.

Pupil's Digital: Encourage your pupils to use the Pupil's App on Navio to practise the activities from this lesson.

Powered By NAVIO

Activity Book

Activity Book page 46: Review

- Work with a friend to do the quiz.

My progress

- Think about your work in this unit.
- Read, circle and write.

Code activity

- Complete the code activity.

Activity Book page 114: Cambridge Exams Practice

Activity 1

- Listen and draw lines.

▶ *CD4 Track 46 p283*

Activity 2

- Read the story.
- Choose a word from the box.
- Write the correct word next to the numbers.

Starting the lesson

Use the Trinity Exams Practice cards (optional).

- The pupils practise asking and answering questions using the Unit 4 cards.

Review a song from the unit.

- Invite the class to choose one of the songs from the unit. The pupils sing and do the actions.

Set learning outcomes and use the talk cards.

- Say **Today we're going to practise activities for an exam and remember what we've learnt in Unit 4.**
- Point to the talk cards to show the pupils the different ways they will be working in the lesson.

Activity Book page 46: Review

Activity 1

Work with a friend to do the quiz.

- Organise the class into pairs. Set a time limit (10–15 minutes). Stress that pupils are racing against the clock, not each other.
- Read out the tasks and check understanding. Then say **Ready, steady, go!**
- Check and correct the answers as a class.

Answers: **1** Nine of the following: cheese, chillies, onions, olives, tomato sauce, peppers, prawns, tuna, mushrooms, spinach, sweetcorn, pineapple **3** Ice cream is soft and sweet. Apples are sweet and crunchy. Curry is hot and spicy. **4** Pupils' own answers **5** India **6** Hawaii

My progress

Think about your work in this unit. Read, circle and write.

- Say **Now you're going to think about your work.**
- Prompt the pupils to say what they can do after studying Unit 4 by asking **What can you say?** (*Food and adjectives to describe food.*) **What can you write?** (*A shape poem.*) The pupils circle 'excellent', 'good' or 'OK' and complete the two sentences.

Code activity

- The pupils complete the code activity.

Answer: sore throat

Pupil's Book Activity 1

Look, read and write.

- The pupils look at the picture, then complete the sentences and answer the questions. They then write two sentences about the picture.

Answers: **1** T-shirt **2** purple **3** drinking water **4** next to the tree

Pupil's Book Activity 2

Listen and follow. What's the missing information?

▶ *CD4 Track 37 p282*

- Ask pupils to read the conversation and look at the information that is missing.
- Play the rest of the CD, pausing after the first question and answer. Say **What's the missing information?**
- Play the CD. The pupils listen and identify the missing information.

Answers: bread and cheese, every day, onions, ice cream

Pupil's Book Activity 3

Work with a partner. Ask and answer.

- The pupils work in pairs to ask and answer questions about food preferences.

External Exams Video

Additional Cambridge Exams Practice Video: A1 Movers.

- Additional external exams preparation material, including videos, worksheets and practice tests, can be found in the Teacher's Resource Bank on Navio.

Activity Book page 114: Cambridge Exams Practice: A1 Movers 4

Activity 1

Listen and draw lines.

▶ *CD4 Track 46 p283*

- Point to the different people in the picture and ask **What's this boy / girl doing / wearing?** Explain that pupils must match six names to six children.
- Play the CD, pausing after each exchange. The pupils listen and draw matching lines.

Answers: Peter – eating an ice cream. Jim – eating cake. Anna – eating pizza. John – riding a blue bike. Jane – flying the kite. Tom – walking the dog and eating a banana.

Activity 2

Read the story. Choose a word from the box. Write the correct word next to the numbers.

- Read the words in the box. Then read out the complete text, pausing slightly at each missing word. In pairs, the pupils read the text again and write the missing words.
- The pupils choose the best name for the story.

Answers: **1** cooks **2** bowl **3** salad **4** cake **5** presents **6** computer game **7** Tim's birthday

Ending the lesson

Review the lesson and reflect on learning.

- Say **Today we've practised activities for an exam and remembered what we've learnt in Unit 4.**
- Ask **Which was your favourite activity today? Which activity was easy / difficult?**

Extra activity

Reinforcement

- In pairs, the pupils write three questions about the unit. Reorganise the class into new pairs. The pupils take it in turns to ask and answer the questions.

Activity Book page 105: Vocabulary and Grammar Practice

Answers: **1.1** cheese, tomato sauce and onion **1.2** cheese, mushrooms and olives **1.3** peppers, pineapple and sweetcorn
2.1 No, it isn't. It's soft and sweet. **2.2** No, it isn't. It's crunchy and sweet. **2.3** No, it isn't. It's soft and sweet. **2.4** No, it isn't. It's savoury and plain.

Key Competences and Key Learning Outcomes

- Read and understand a story
- Talk about differences between pictures

- Review learning and reflect on progress
- Practise for A1 Movers Reading and Writing Parts 1&5, Speaking Part 1 and Listening Part 4

Key language

- *dictionary*
- *Which (sea animal) do you prefer? How often do you (go to the beach)? Which activities do you do (at the beach)? Which (sea activities) would you like to try?*
- Recycled: animals; sea animals; *big, colourful, dangerous, heavy, intelligent, pretty, ugly; blowhole, sea, shell*

Materials

- Pupil's Book p119; Activity Book p56, 106 and p115; Class CD4; Teacher's App on Navio
- Teacher's Resource Bank: Talk cards

Optional materials

- Teacher's Resource Bank: Trinity Exams Practice cards (selected from Unit 5)

At a Glance Lesson Plan

Pupil's Book

Starting the lesson

- Use the Trinity Exams Practice cards (optional).
- Review a song from the unit.
- Set learning outcomes and use the talk cards.

Go to the Activity Book.

Activity 1

- Look at the pictures and read the story.
- Write some words in your notebook to complete the sentences about the story.
- You can use 1, 2 or 3 words.

Activity 2

- Listen and look.

▶ *CD4 Track 38 p282*

- What's the difference?

Activity 3

- Work with a partner.
- Look and find more differences.

Go to the Activity Book.

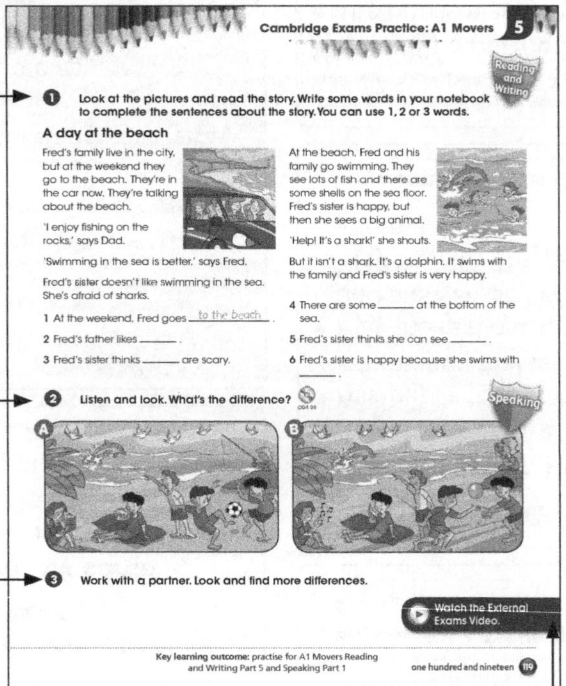
Cambridge Exams Practice: A1 Movers 5

1 Look at the pictures and read the story. Write some words in your notebook to complete the sentences about the story. You can use 1, 2 or 3 words.

A day at the beach

Fred's family live in the city, but at the weekend they go to the beach. They're in the car now. They're talking about the beach.

'I enjoy fishing on the rocks,' says Dad.

'Swimming in the sea is better,' says Fred.

Fred's sister doesn't like swimming in the sea. She's afraid of sharks.

At the beach, Fred and his family go swimming. They see lots of fish and there are some shells on the sea floor. Fred's sister is happy, but then she sees a big animal.

'Help! It's a shark!' she shouts.

But it isn't a shark. It's a dolphin. It swims with the family and Fred's sister is very happy.

1 At the weekend, Fred goes to the beach.
2 Fred's father likes ______.
3 Fred's sister thinks ______ are scary.
4 There are some ______ at the bottom of the sea.
5 Fred's sister thinks she can see ______.
6 Fred's sister is happy because she swims with ______.

2 Listen and look. What's the difference?

3 Work with a partner. Look and find more differences.

Watch the External Exams Video.

Key learning outcome: practise for A1 Movers Reading and Writing Part 5 and Speaking Part 1

one hundred and nineteen 119

Ending the lesson

- Review the lesson and reflect on learning.

Extra activity

Reinforcement

- Prepare three questions about the unit.

External Exams Video

- Additional Cambridge Exams Practice Video: A1 Movers.

Digital resources

Teacher's Digital: You can also teach this lesson using the Teacher's App on Navio.

Pupil's Digital: Encourage your pupils to use the Pupil's App on Navio to practise the activities from this lesson.

Powered By NAVIO

Activity Book

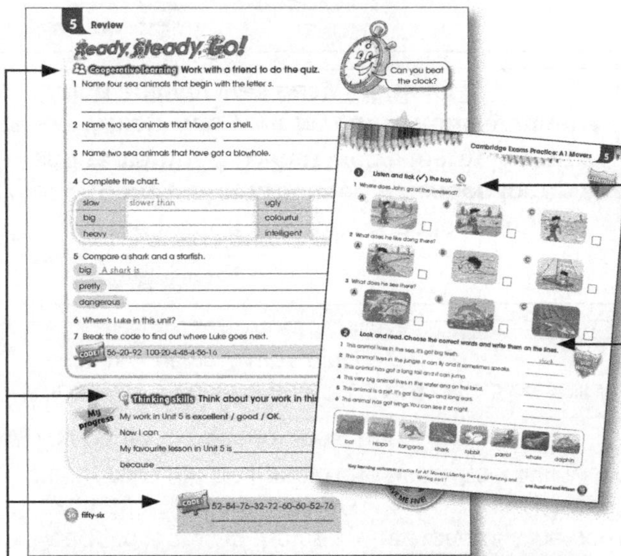

Activity Book page 56: Review

- Work with a friend to do the quiz.

My progress

- Think about your work in this unit.
- Read, circle and write.

Code activity

- Complete the code activity.

Activity Book page 115: Cambridge Exams Practice

Activity 1

- Listen and tick (✓) the box.

▶ *CD4 Track 47 p283*

Activity 2

- Look and read.
- Choose the correct words and write them on the lines.

Starting the lesson

Use the Trinity Exams Practice cards (optional).

- The pupils practise asking and answering questions using the Unit 5 cards.

Review a song from the unit.

- Invite the class to choose one of the songs from the unit. The pupils sing and do the actions.

Set learning outcomes and use the talk cards.

- Say **Today we're going to practise activities for an exam and we're going to remember what we've learnt in Unit 5.**
- Point to the talk cards to show the pupils the different ways they will be working in the lesson.

Activity Book page 56: Review

Work with a friend to do the quiz.

- Organise the class into pairs. Set a time limit (10–15 minutes). Stress that the pupils are racing against the clock, not each other.
- Read out the tasks and check understanding. Then say **Ready, steady, go!**
- Check and correct the answers as a class.

Answers: **1** Four of the following: shark, seal, squid, seahorse, starfish **2** crab, turtle **3** whale, dolphin **4** slower than, bigger than, heavier than, uglier than, more colourful than, more intelligent than **5** A shark is bigger than a starfish. A starfish is prettier than a shark. A shark is more dangerous than a starfish. **6** Hawaii **7** New Zealand

My progress

Think about your work in this unit. Read, circle and write.

- Say **Now you're going to think about your work.**
- Prompt the pupils to say what they can do after studying Unit 5 by asking **What can you say?** (*Names of sea animals.*) **What can you write?** (*A magazine article.*) **What can you compare?** (*Animals.*) The pupils circle 'excellent', 'good' or 'OK' and complete the two sentences.

Code activity

- The pupils complete the code activity.

Answer: mushrooms

Pupil's Book Activity 1

Look at the pictures and read the story. Write some words in your notebook to complete the sentences about the story. You can use 1, 2 or 3 words.

- Read the story and look at the pictures with the class.
- Pupils complete the sentences about the story using between one and three words.

Answers: **1** to the beach **2** fishing **3** sharks **4** shells **5** a shark **6** a dolphin

Pupil's Book Activity 2

Listen and look. What's the difference?

▶ *CD4 Track 38 p282*

- Play the CD. Say **What's the difference?** (*The boys in picture A are playing football, but the boys in picture B are playing volleyball.*)

Pupil's Book Activity 3

Work with a partner. Look and find more differences.

Answers: The girl on the left in picture A is reading, but in picture B she's listening to music. The boy on the rock is fishing in picture A, but he's taking a photo in picture B. The boy is eating a sandwich in picture A, but he's eating a slice of melon in picture B. There are five seagulls in picture A, but only four in picture B.

External Exams Video

Additional Cambridge Exams Practice Video: A1 Movers.

- Additional external exams preparation material, including videos, worksheets and practice tests, can be found in the Teacher's Resource Bank on Navio.

Activity Book page 115: Cambridge Exams Practice: A1 Movers 5

Activity 1

Listen and tick (✓) the box.

▶ *CD4 Track 47 p283*

- The pupils describe the first set of pictures.
- Play the CD. The pupils listen and tick the correct picture.

Answers: **1** C **2** C **3** A

Activity 2

Look and read. Choose the correct words and write them on the lines.

- The pupils read each sentence and write the corresponding animal. (There are two extra animals.)

Answers: **1** shark **2** parrot **3** kangaroo **4** hippo **5** rabbit **6** bat

Ending the lesson

Review the lesson and reflect on learning.

- Say **Today we've practised activities for an exam and remembered what we've learnt in Unit 5.**
- Ask **Which was your favourite activity today? Which activity was easy / difficult?**

Extra activity

Reinforcement

- In pairs, the pupils write three questions about the unit. Reorganise the class into new pairs. The pairs take it in turns to ask and answer the questions.

Activity Book page 106: Vocabulary and Grammar Practice

Answers: **1.1** squid **1.2** whale **1.3** dolphin **1.4** starfish **1.5** jellyfish **1.6** turtle

2.1 heavy **2.2** intelligent **2.3** colourful **2.4** dangerous **2.5** ugly **2.6** pretty

3.1 A shark is bigger than a seal. **3.2** A shark is slower than a seal. **3.3** A shark is heavier than a seal. **3.4** A shark is uglier than a seal. **3.5** A shark is more dangerous than a seal.

4.1 An apple is healthier than a sweet. **4.2** Science is more interesting than Maths. **4.3** A motorbike is faster than a skateboard. **4.4** A train is heavier than a bus. **4.5** A dog is more intelligent than a cat.

Cambridge Exams Practice, Review and Vocabulary and Grammar Practice answers

Key Competences and Key Learning Outcomes

- Read and understand a conversation
- Listen and understand colours
- Complete a text with the correct words

- Review learning and reflect on progress
- Practise for A1 Movers Reading and Writing Parts 2&4 and Listening Part 5

Key language

- *Where's (the boy)? (The boy) is (on the beach). What's (he doing)? He's (playing football). How does he (feel)? He's (very happy).*
- Recycled: sports equipment; *rollerblade, sing, swim; What (are you) going to do (tomorrow)? (I'm) going to (go swimming).*

Materials

- Pupil's Book p120; Activity Book p66, 107 and p116; Class CD4; Teacher's App on Navio
- Teacher's Resource Bank: Talk cards
- Coloured pencils (red, brown, purple)

Optional materials

- Teacher's Resource Bank: Trinity Exams Practice cards (selected from Unit 6)

At a Glance Lesson Plan

Pupil's Book

Starting the lesson

- Use the Trinity Exams Practice cards (optional).
- Review a song from the unit.
- Set learning outcomes and use the talk cards.

Go to the Activity Book.

Activity 1

- Read the text and choose the best answer.

Go to the Activity Book.

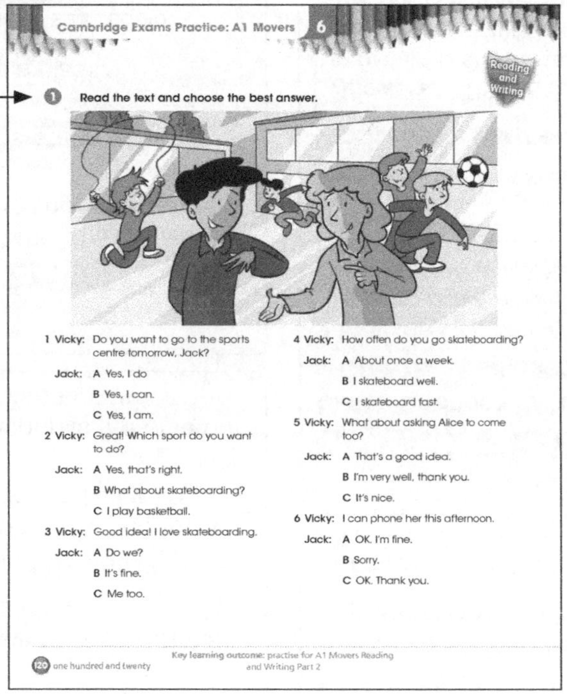
Cambridge Exams Practice: A1 Movers 6

1 Read the text and choose the best answer.

1 Vicky: Do you want to go to the sports centre tomorrow, Jack?
Jack: A Yes, I do B Yes, I can. C Yes, I am.
2 Vicky: Great! Which sport do you want to do?
Jack: A Yes, that's right. B What about skateboarding? C I play basketball.
3 Vicky: Good idea! I love skateboarding.
Jack: A Do we? B It's fine. C Me too.
4 Vicky: How often do you go skateboarding?
Jack: A About once a week. B I skateboard well. C I skateboard fast.
5 Vicky: What about asking Alice to come too?
Jack: A That's a good idea. B I'm very well, thank you. C It's nice.
6 Vicky: I can phone her this afternoon.
Jack: A OK. I'm fine. B Sorry. C OK. Thank you.

120 one hundred and twenty — Key learning outcome: practise for A1 Movers Reading and Writing Part 2

Ending the lesson

- Review the lesson and reflect on learning.

Extra activity

Reinforcement

- Prepare three questions about the unit.

External Exams Video

- Additional Cambridge Exams Practice Video: A1 Movers.

Activity Book

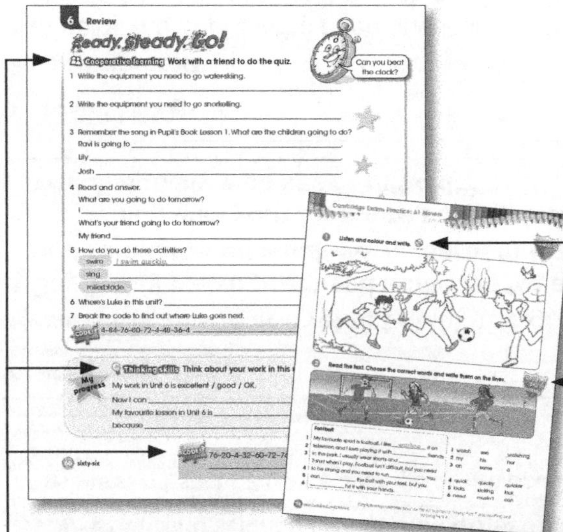

Activity Book page 66: Review

- Work with a friend to do the quiz.

My progress

- Think about your work in this unit.
- Read, circle and write.

Code activity

- Complete the code activity.

Activity Book page 116: Cambridge Exams Practice

Activity 1

- Listen and colour and write.

▶ *CD4 Track 48 p283*

Activity 2

- Read the text.
- Choose the correct words and write them on the lines.

Digital resources

Teacher's Digital: You can also teach this lesson using the Teacher's App on Navio.

Pupil's Digital: Encourage your pupils to use the Pupil's App on Navio to practise the activities from this lesson.

Powered By NAVIO

Starting the lesson

Use the Trinity Exams Practice cards (optional).

- The pupils practise asking and answering questions using the Unit 6 cards.

Review a song from the unit.

- Invite the class to choose one of the songs from the unit. The pupils sing and do the actions.

Set learning outcomes and use the talk cards.

- Say **Today we're going to practise activities for an exam and remember what we've learnt in Unit 6.**
- Point to the talk cards to show the pupils the different ways they will be working in the lesson.

Activity Book page 66: Review

Work with a friend to do the quiz.

- Organise the class into pairs. Set a time limit (10–15 minutes). Stress that the pupils are racing the clock, not each other.
- Read out the tasks and check understanding. Then say **Ready, steady, go!**
- Check and correct the answers as a class.

Answers: **1** wetsuit, life jacket, water-skis, gloves **2** mask, flippers, snorkel **3** Ravi is going to go snorkelling. Lily is going to go kayaking. Josh is going to go water-skiing. **4** Pupils' own answers. **5** (Possible answers) I swim quickly. I sing quietly. I rollerblade well. **6** New Zealand **7** Australia

My progress

Think about your work in this unit. Read, circle and write.

- Say **Now you're going to think about your work.**
- Prompt the pupils to say what they can do after studying Unit 6 by asking **What can you say?** (*Names of sports equipment.*) **What can you write?** (*A letter.*) The pupils circle 'excellent', 'good' or 'OK' and complete the two sentences.

Code activity

- The pupils complete the code activity.

Answer: seahorse

Pupil's Book Activity 1

Read the text and choose the best answer.

- Look at the picture and read the text with pupils.
- Read the answer options.
- Pupils choose the best answer to complete the conversation.

Answers: **1** A **2** B **3** C **4** A **5** A **6** C

External Exams Video

Additional Cambridge Exams Practice Video: A1 Movers.

- Additional external exams preparation material, including videos, worksheets and practice tests, can be found in the Teacher's Resource Bank on Navio.

Activity Book page 116: Cambridge Exams Practice: A1 Movers 6

Activity 1

Listen and colour and write.

▸ *CD4 Track 48 p283*

- Focus on the picture and ask **What can you see?**
- Explain that the pupils must listen carefully to find out how to colour the picture and where to write a number.
- Play the CD, pausing after each exchange. The pupils listen, colour and write the number.
- The pupils compare their work with their partner.

Answers: Pupils colour the boy's curly hair brown, the girl's T-shirt red, the bird in the tree brown and the kite purple. Pupils write the number 7 on the tall boy's T-shirt.

Activity 2

Read the text. Choose the correct words and write them on the lines.

- Ask **How do you play football?** Read out the text, pausing slightly before each missing word.
- The pupils work in pairs to read the text again and write the correct words. Check the answers as a class.

Answers: **1** watching **2** my **3** a **4** quickly **5** kick **6** mustn't

Ending the lesson

Review the lesson and reflect on learning.

- Say **Today we've practised activities for an exam and remembered what we've learnt in Unit 6.**
- Ask **Which was your favourite activity today? Which activity was easy / difficult?**

Extra activity

Reinforcement

- In pairs, the pupils write three questions about the unit. Reorganise the class into new pairs. The pairs take it in turns to ask and answer the questions.

Activity Book page 107: Vocabulary and Grammar Practice

Answers: **1.1** gloves **1.2** mask **1.3** helmet **1.4** paddle **1.5** flippers **1.6** wetsuit
2.1 badly **2.2** loudly **2.3** well **2.4** slowly **2.5** quietly
3.1 Peter isn't going to play football after school. **3.2** Peter is going to watch TV tonight. **3.3** Peter is going to speak English tomorrow. **3.4** Peter isn't going to swim next week.
4.1 A horse runs quickly. **4.2** A seal swims well. **4.3** A bird runs badly. **4.4** A tortoise moves slowly.

Key Competences and Key Learning Outcomes

- Read and understand descriptions
- Listen and understand descriptions
- Ask and answer questions

- Review learning and reflect on progress
- Practise for A1 Movers Reading and Writing Parts 1&6, Speaking Part 4 and Listening Part 1

Key language

- Recycled: adverbs of frequency; free-time activities; household objects; *What do you like doing (at the weekend)? I like (swimming). Do you usually (play football)? Where were you last (Saturday)? I was (at the supermarket). What are you going to do this (Saturday)? I'm going to (play tennis). Were the (earrings) under the (sofa)?*

Materials

- Pupil's Book p121; Activity Book p78, 108 and p117; Class CD4; Teacher's App on Navio
- Teacher's Resource Bank: Talk cards

Optional materials

- Teacher's Resource Bank: Trinity Exams Practice cards (selected from Unit 7)

At a Glance Lesson Plan

Pupil's Book

Starting the lesson

- Use the Trinity Exams Practice cards (optional).
- Review a song from the unit.
- Set learning outcomes and use the talk cards.

Go to the Activity Book.

Activity 1

- Look and read.
- Choose the correct words and write them in your notebook.

Activity 2

- Listen and follow.

▶ *CD4 Track 39 p282*

- What's the missing information?

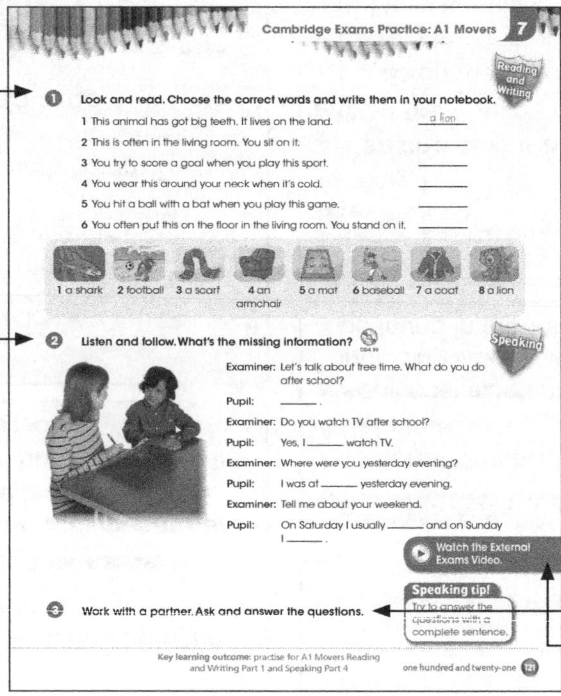

Activity 3

- Work with a partner.
- Ask and answer the questions.

Go to the Activity Book.

Ending the lesson

- Review the lesson and reflect on learning.

Extra activity

Reinforcement

- Prepare three questions about the unit.

External Exams Video

- Additional Cambridge Exams Practice Video: A1 Movers.

Activity Book

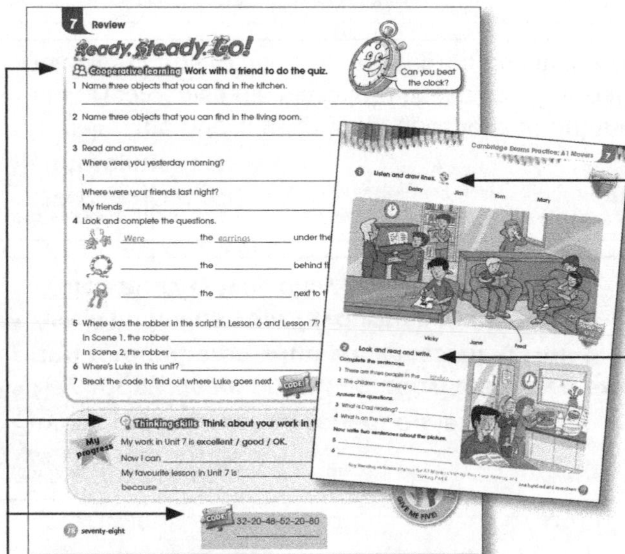

Activity Book page 78: Review

- Work with a friend to do the quiz.

My progress

- Think about your work in this unit.
- Read, circle and write.

Code activity

- Complete the code activity.

Activity Book page 117: Cambridge Exams Practice

Activity 1

- Listen and draw lines.

▶ *CD4 Track 49 p283*

Activity 2

- Look and read and write.

Digital resources

Teacher's Digital: You can also teach this lesson using the Teacher's App on Navio.

Pupil's Digital: Encourage your pupils to use the Pupil's App on Navio to practise the activities from this lesson.

Powered By NAVIO

Starting the lesson

Use the Trinity Exams Practice cards (optional).

- The pupils practise asking and answering questions using the Unit 7 cards.

Review a song from the unit.

- Invite the class to choose a song from the unit. The pupils sing and do the actions.

Set learning outcomes and use the talk cards.

- Say **Today we're going to practise activities for an exam and remember what we've learnt in Unit 7.**
- Point to the talk cards to show the pupils the different ways they will be working in the lesson.

Activity Book page 78: Review

Work with a friend to do the quiz.

- Organise the class into pairs. Set a time limit (10–15 minutes). Stress that the pupils are racing against the clock, not each other.
- Read out the tasks and check understanding. Then say **Ready, steady, go!**
- Check and correct the answers as a class.

Answers: **1** Three of the following: sink, cooker, fridge, cupboard **2** Three of the following: armchair, mirror, bookcase, painting, sofa, mat **4** Were, earrings, Was, bracelet, Were, keys **5** was in the living room; was in the bush **6** Australia **7** USA

My progress

Think about your work in this unit. Read, circle and write.

- Say **Now you're going to think about your work.**
- Prompt the pupils to say what they can do after studying Unit 7 by asking **What can you say?** (*Household objects, personal belongings*) **What can you write?** (*A script.*) The pupils circle 'excellent,' 'good' or 'OK' then complete the two sentences.

Code activity

- The pupils complete the code activity.

Answer: helmet

Pupil's Book Activity 1

Look and read. Choose the correct words and write them in your notebook.

- Read the descriptions and look at the pictures with the class. The pupils choose the correct words and write them in their notebooks.

Answers: **1** a lion **2** an armchair **3** football **4** a scarf **5** baseball **6** a mat

Pupil's Book Activity 2

Listen and follow. What's the missing information?

▶ *CD4 Track 39 p282*

- Play the CD, pausing after the first question and answer. Say **What's the missing information?**
- Play the rest of the CD while the pupils complete the missing information.

Answers: I do my homework, usually, home, go swimming, visit my grandparents

Pupil's Book Activity 3

Work with a partner. Ask and answer the questions.

- The pupils work in pairs to ask and answer questions about free-time activities.

External Exams Video

Additional Cambridge Exams Practice Video: A1 Movers.

- Additional external exams preparation material, including videos, worksheets and practice tests, can be found in the Teacher's Resource Bank on Navio.

Activity Book page 117: Cambridge Exams Practice: A1 Movers 7

Activity 1

Listen and draw lines.

▶ *CD4 Track 49 p283*

- Focus the class on the picture and ask **What can you see? What is this boy / girl doing? What is this boy / girl wearing?** Read out the children's names.
- Play the CD, pausing after each exchange. The pupils draw matching lines from the names to the children.

Answers: Fred – drawing. Mary – listening to music. Tom – reading in front of the bookcase. Daisy – playing the piano. Jane – standing next to the piano. Jim – behind the sofa.

Activity 2

Look and read and write.

- Ask the pupils to describe the picture.
- The pupils work on their own or in pairs to read each sentence and answer the questions.

Answers: **1** kitchen **2** cake **3** a book **4** a clock **5 & 6** Pupils' own answers

Ending the lesson

Review the lesson and reflect on learning.

- Say **Today we've practised activities for an exam and remembered what we've learnt in Unit 7.**
- Ask **Which was your favourite activity today? Which activity was easy / difficult?**

Extra activity

Reinforcement

- In pairs, the pupils write three questions about the unit. Reorganise the class into new pairs. The pairs take it in turns to ask and answer the questions.

Activity Book page 108: Vocabulary and Grammar Practice

Answers: **1** Kitchen: fridge, cooker, sink Living room: lamp, armchair, sofa
2.1 earrings **2.2** sunglasses **2.3** umbrella **2.4** keys
3.1 Peter wasn't at home yesterday. **3.2** Zoe and Julia were at the supermarket yesterday. **3.3** Peter was at the cinema yesterday. **3.4** Julia wasn't at school yesterday. **3.5** Zoe and Julia weren't at the beach yesterday.
4.1 Were you at the beach yesterday? **4.2** Were you at school yesterday? **4.3** Were you at the cinema yesterday?

Key Competences and Key Learning Outcomes

- Complete a text using the correct words
- Tell a story
- Read and understand a story

- Review learning and reflect on progress
- Practise for A1 Movers Reading and Writing Part 4, Speaking Part 2 and Listening Part 3

Key language

- *What's the programme about? Who appears in the programme? When's the programme on TV? Why do you like it?*
- Recycled: TV programmes; *Did you watch (a cartoon) yesterday? Yes, I did. No, I didn't. I (painted a picture) yesterday. My favourite (TV programme) is (the news).*

Materials

- Pupil's Book p122; Activity Book p88, 109 and p118; Class CD4; Teacher's App on Navio
- Teacher's Resource Bank: Talk cards

Optional materials

- Teacher's Resource Bank: Trinity Exams Practice cards (selected from Unit 8)

At a Glance Lesson Plan

Pupil's Book

Starting the lesson

- Use the Trinity Exams Practice cards (optional).
- Review a song from the unit.
- Set learning outcomes and use the talk cards.

Go to the Activity Book.

Activity 1

- Read the text.
- Choose the correct words and write them in your notebook.

Activity 2

- Listen and look.

▶ *CD4 Track 40 p282*

- What's happening in picture 1?

Activity 3

- Work with a partner.
- Tell the story.

Activity 4

- Now listen to the story.

▶ *CD4 Track 41 p282*

Go to the Activity Book.

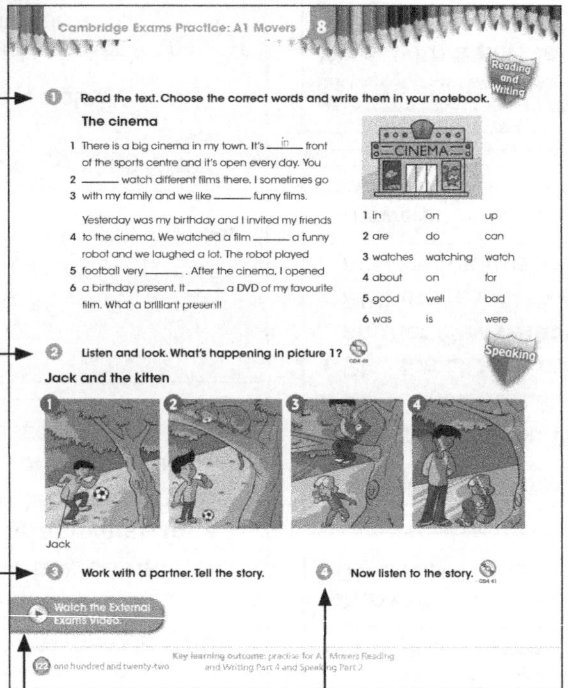

Ending the lesson

- Review the lesson and reflect on learning.

Extra activity

Reinforcement

- Prepare three questions about the unit.

External Exams Video

- Additional Cambridge Exams Practice Video: A1 Movers.

Digital resources

Teacher's Digital: You can also teach this lesson using the Teacher's App on Navio.

Pupil's Digital: Encourage your pupils to use the Pupil's App on Navio to practise the activities from this lesson.

Powered By NAVIO

Activity Book

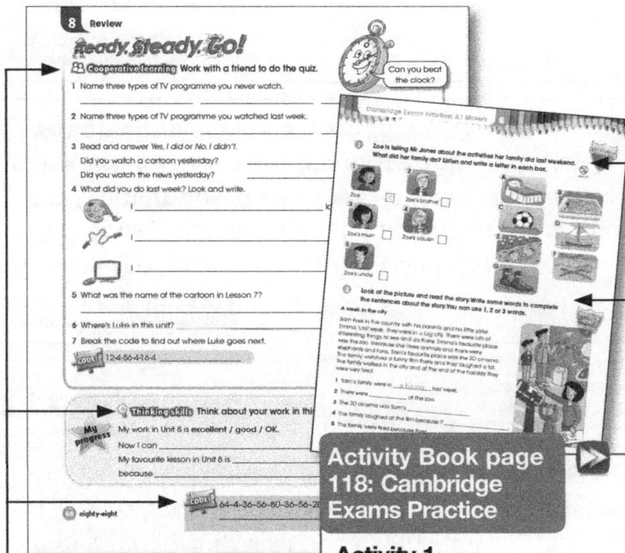

Activity Book page 88: Review

- Work with a friend to do the quiz.

My progress

- Think about your work in this unit.
- Read, circle and write.

Code activity

- Complete the code activity.

Activity Book page 118: Cambridge Exams Practice

Activity 1

- Zoe is telling Mr Jones about the activities her family did last weekend.
- What did her family do?
- Listen and write a letter in each box.

▶ *CD4 Track 50 p284*

Activity 2

- Look at the picture and read the story.
- Write some words to complete the sentences about the story.
- You can use 1, 2 or 3 words.

Starting the lesson

Use the Trinity Exams Practice cards (optional).

- The pupils practise asking and answering questions using the Unit 8 cards.

Review a song from the unit.

- Invite the class to choose one of the songs from the unit. The pupils sing and do the corresponding actions.

Set learning outcomes and use the talk cards.

- Say **Today we're going to practise activities for an exam and remember what we've learnt in Unit 8.**
- Point to the talk cards to show the pupils the different ways they will be working in the lesson.

Activity Book page 88: Review

Work with a friend to do the quiz.

- Organise the class into pairs. Set a time limit (10–15 minutes). Stress that pupils are racing against the clock, not each other.
- Read out the tasks and check understanding. Then say **Ready, steady, go!**
- Check and correct the answers as a class.

Answers: **1–4** Pupils' own answers **5** Dan the Detective Dog **6** the USA **7** Canada

My progress

Think about your work in this unit. Read, circle and write.

- Say **Now you're going to think about your work.**
- Prompt the pupils to say what they can do after studying Unit 8 by asking **What can you say?** (*Types of TV programme.*) **What can you write?** (*A review.*) **What can you talk about?** (*A TV programme, activities in the past.*) The pupils circle 'excellent', 'good' or 'OK' and complete the two sentences.

Code activity

- The pupils complete the code activity.

Answer: painting

Pupil's Book Activity 1

Read the text. Choose the correct words and write them in your notebook.

- Read the text with the class.
- Pupils choose the correct words and write them in their notebooks.

Answers: **1** in **2** can **3** watching **4** about **5** well **6** was

Pupil's Book Activity 2

Listen and look. What's happening in picture 1?

▶ *CD4 Track 40 p282*

- Play the CD. The pupils listen to the description. Elicit what is happening in picture 1.

Pupil's Book Activity 3

Work with a partner. Tell the story.

- The pupils work in pairs to tell the story.

Pupil's Book Activity 4

Now listen to the story.

▶ *CD4 Track 41 p282*

- Pupils listen to the story.

External Exams Video

Additional Cambridge Exams Practice Video: A1 Movers.

- Additional external exams preparation material, including videos, worksheets and practice tests, can be found in the Teacher's Resource Bank on Navio.

Activity Book page 118: Cambridge Exams Practice: A1 Movers 8

Activity 1

Zoe is telling Mr Jones about the activities her family did last weekend. What did her family do? Listen and write a letter in each box.

▶ *CD4 Track 50 p284*

- The pupils describe the pictures.
- Play the CD, pausing after each exchange. The pupils listen and write the correct letters.

Answers: **1** C **2** A **3** E **4** D **5** F

Activity 2

Look at the picture and read the story. Write some words to complete the sentences about the story. You can use 1, 2 or 3 words.

- Focus the pupils on the picture. Ask **What can you see? Where are Sam and his family?** (*At the planetarium.*)
- Ask **Can you name the planets?** Discuss the solar system, including the moon, with the pupils.
- Read out the text as a class. Check comprehension.
- Complete the first two sentences as a class. Remind the pupils to only write one, two or three words in each space.
- The pupils complete the remaining sentences.
- Check the answers as a class.

Answers: **1** a big city **2** elephants and lions **3** favourite place **4** was funny **5** walked

Ending the lesson

Review the lesson and reflect on learning.

- Say **Today we've practised activities for an exam and remembered what we've learnt in Unit 8.**
- Ask **Which was your favourite activity today? Which activity was easy / difficult?**

Extra activity

Reinforcement

- In pairs, the pupils write three questions about the unit. Reorganise the class into new pairs. The pairs take it in turns to ask and answer the questions.

Activity Book page 109: Vocabulary and Grammar Practice

Answers: **1.1** cartoon **1.2** documentary **1.3** advert **1.4** quiz show **1.5** the news **1.6** game show **2.1** play **2.2** skip **2.3** phone **2.4** paint **2.5** climb **2.6** plant

Key Competences and Key Learning Outcomes

- Read and understand a story
- Talk about which picture is different
- Listen and understand details about a party
- Read and complete a story

- Review learning and reflect on progress
- Practise Movers Reading and Writing Parts 3&5, Speaking Part 3 and Listening Part 2

Key language

- *(The tiger) is different. It isn't (a sea animal).*
- Recycled: rooms in a house; places in a school; sea animals; healthy habits; attractions at a festival; *I wore / ate / saw … yesterday.*

Materials

- Pupil's Book p123; Activity Book p98, 110 and p119; Class CD4; Teacher's App on Navio
- Teacher's Resource Bank: Talk cards

Optional materials

- Teacher's Resource Bank: Trinity Exams Practice cards (selected from Unit 9)

At a Glance Lesson Plan

Pupil's Book

Starting the lesson

- Use the Trinity Exams Practice cards (optional).
- Review a song from the unit.
- Set learning outcomes and use the talk cards.

Go to the Activity Book.

Activity 1

- Look at the pictures and read the story.
- Write some words in your notebook to complete the sentences about the story.
- You can use 1, 2 or 3 words.

Activity 2

- Listen and follow
- ▶ *CD4 Track 42 p282*
- Which picture is different in number 1?
- Why?

Activity 3

- Work with a partner.
- Which pictures are different in numbers 2, 3 and 4?
- Why?

Go to the Activity Book.

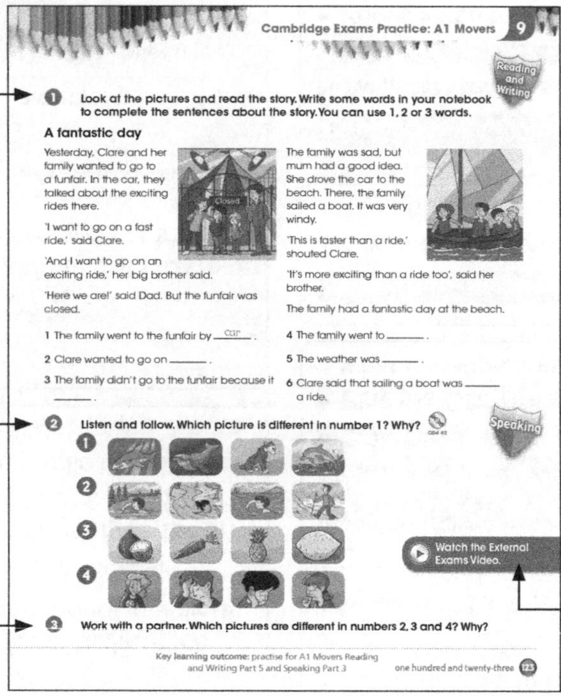

Ending the lesson

- Review the lesson and reflect on learning.

Extra activity

Reinforcement

- Prepare three questions about the unit.

External Exams Video

- Additional Cambridge Exams Practice Video A1: Movers.

Digital resources

Teacher's Digital: You can also teach this lesson using the Teacher's App on Navio.

Pupil's Digital: Encourage your pupils to use the Pupil's App on Navio to practise the activities from this lesson.

Powered By NAVIO

Activity Book

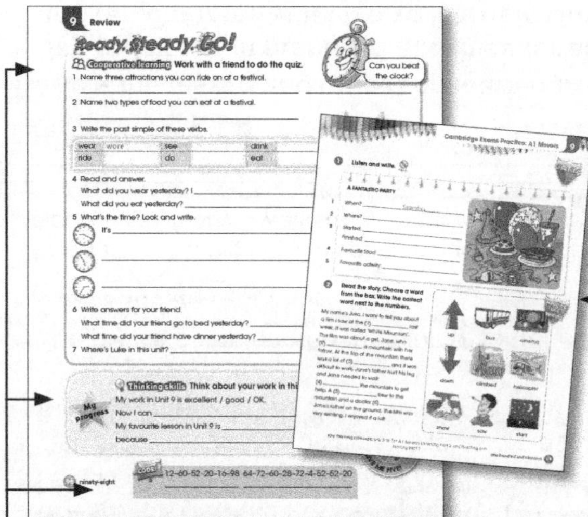

Activity Book page 98: Review

- Work with a friend to do the quiz.

My progress

- Think about your work in this unit.
- Read, circle and write.

Code activity

- Complete the code activity.

Activity Book page 119: Cambridge Exams Practice

Activity 1

- Listen and write.
- ▶ *CD4 Track 51 p284*

Activity 2

- Read the story.
- Choose a word from the box.
- Write the correct word next to the numbers.

Starting the lesson

Use the Trinity Exams Practice cards (optional).

- The pupils practise asking and answering questions using the Unit 9 cards.

Review a song from the unit.

- Invite the class to choose one of the songs from the unit. The pupils sing and do the actions.

Set learning outcomes and use the talk cards.

- Say **Today we're going to practise activities for an exam and remember what we've learnt in Units 1–9.**
- Point to the talk cards to show the pupils the different ways they will be working in the lesson.

Activity Book page 98: Review

Work with a friend to do the quiz.

- Organise the class into pairs. Set a time limit (10–15 minutes). Stress that the pupils are racing against the clock, not each other.
- Read out the tasks and check understanding. Then say **Ready, steady, go!**
- Check and correct the answers as a class.

Answers: **1** Three of the following: ghost train, big wheel, merry-go-round, bumper cars, roller coaster **2** toffee apple, candyfloss **3** wear-wore, ride-rode, see-saw, do-did, drink-drank, eat-ate, go-went, have-had **4** Pupils' own answers **5** It's twenty past nine. It's five to six. It's twenty-five to three. **6** Pupils' own answers. **7** Canada

My progress

Think about your work in this unit. Read, circle and write.

- Say **Now you're going to think about your work.**
- Prompt the pupils to say what they can do after studying Unit 9 by asking **What can you write?** (*An email.*) **What can you talk about?** (*Festivals.*) The pupils then complete the two sentences.

Code activity

- The pupils complete the code activity.

Answer: comedy programme

Pupil's Book Activity 1

Look at the pictures and read the story. Write some words in your notebook to complete the sentences about the story. You can use 1, 2 or 3 words.

- Pupils write between one and three words to complete the sentences about the story.

Answers: **1** car **2** a fast ride **3** was closed **4** the beach **5** very windy **6** faster than

Pupil's Book Activity 2

Listen and follow. Which picture is different in number 1? Why?

▶ *CD4 Track 42 p282*

- Ask the pupils which picture they think is different.
- Play the CD. The pupils listen to the description.

Answer: **1** tiger (the others live in the sea)

Pupil's Book Activity 3

Work with a partner. Which pictures are different in numbers 2, 3 and 4? Why?

Answer: **2** man walking (the others are swimming) **3** carrot (the others are fruit) **4** smiling girl (the others are unwell)

External Exams Video

Additional Cambridge Exams Practice Video: A1 Movers.

- Additional external exams preparation material, including videos, worksheets and practice tests, can be found in the Teacher's Resource Bank on Navio.

Activity Book page 119: Cambridge Exams Practice: A1 Movers 9

Activity 1

Listen and write.

▶ *CD4 Track 51 p284*

- Play the CD, pausing after the first exchange. Check the answer with the class. Repeat the procedure.

Answers: **1** Saturday **2** On the beach **3** Four o'clock / Eight o'clock **4** Cake **5** Singing

Activity 2

Read the story. Choose a word from the box. Write the correct word next to the numbers.

- Read out the whole text as a class. Prompt the pupils to predict what the missing words are. The pupils confirm their guesses by choosing words from the box. Finally, the pupils write the words in the activity.

Answers: **1** cinema **2** climbed **3** snow **4** down **5** helicopter **6** saw

Ending the lesson

Review the lesson and reflect on learning.

- Say **Today we've practised activities for an exam and remembered what we've learnt in Units 1–9.** Elicit the pupils' opinions on the unit content.
- Ask **Which was your favourite activity today? Which activity was easy / difficult?**

Extra activity

Reinforcement

- In pairs, the pupils write three questions about the unit. Reorganise the class into new pairs. The pupils take it in turns to ask and answer the questions.

Activity Book page 110: Vocabulary and Grammar Practice

Answers: **1** Things I watch: band, parade, fireworks
Things I ride: big wheel, bumper cars, roller coaster
2.2 It's twenty to twelve. **2.4** It's five to three.
3.1 wore **3.2** drank **3.3** saw **3.4** went **3.5** rode **3.6** ate **3.7** did **3.8** had
4.1 What did you eat yesterday? **4.2** What did you wear yesterday? **4.3** What did you drink yesterday?
4.4 What time did you go to bed yesterday?

Audioscript

Starter Unit Lesson 1

Pupil's Book

CD1 TRACK 01

PB page 4 Activity 2

Josh: Hello. My name's Josh and I'm nine. What's your name?
Ravi: I'm Ravi and I'm nine years old, too.
Lily: Hi. I'm Lily and I'm eight. Josh is my brother.
Ravi: Is the lighthouse your new home?
Lily: Yes, it is. Where do you live?
Ravi: I live in the town. I live in a flat with my mum, dad and little sister.
Lily: Our grandparents live in the town, too.

Starter Unit Lesson 1

Pupil's Book

CD1 TRACK 02

PB page 4 Activity 4

***Welcome to the lighthouse!* song**

Welcome to the lighthouse!
It's next to the sea.
Welcome to the lighthouse!
It's a great place to be.

Let's explore the lighthouse
From the bottom to the top.
Let's explore the lighthouse
With Ravi, Lily and Josh.

Starter Unit Lesson 1

Pupil's Book

CD1 TRACK 03

PB page 4 Activity 4

Karaoke version: *Welcome to the lighthouse!* song

Starter Unit Lesson 2

Pupil's Book

CD1 TRACK 04

PB page 5 Activity 1

Ravi: What activities do you like, Josh?
Josh: I like swimming. I like swimming in the sea and in the swimming pool.
Ravi: What about you, Lily?
Lily: I love singing. It's my favourite activity. Do you like singing, Ravi?
Ravi: No, I don't.
Lily: What do you like doing?
Ravi: I like making models.

Starter Unit Lesson 2

Pupil's Book

CD1 TRACK 05

PB page 5 Activity 2

dancing, singing, cycling, reading, skateboarding, playing tennis, making models, swimming

Starter Unit Lesson 3

Pupil's Book

CD1 TRACK 06

PB page 6 Activity 1

The secret message

Frame 1
Narrator: Dad is moving boxes into the lighthouse.
Lily: Hi, Dad. Can we help you?
Dad: Yes, please. Take these boxes to the blue room. Be careful!

Frame 2
Narrator: The children go up the steps to the blue room.
Ravi: Who's this?
Josh: He's our big brother, Luke. He's a scientist and he travels around the world.

Frame 3
Narrator: Suddenly, the children hear a noise.
Ravi: What's that noise?
Josh: It's the computer. There's a message.
From: Luke
To: Josh and Lily
Subject: Top Secret
Do you like secret messages?
Break the code and write the password.
4–16–88–20–56–80–84–72–20

Frame 4
Narrator: The children work together.
Ravi: It's an alphabet code. Number four is the letter A.
Lily: And number sixteen is the letter D.
Josh: OK. So, A-D-V-E-N-T-U-R-E. The password is 'adventure'.

Frame 5
Narrator: The password is correct. Luke appears on the screen.
Luke: Well done! You can use the code to read my secret messages and my travel blog.
Lily: Great! We can write a blog about our adventures, too.

Starter Unit Lesson 3

Activity Book

CD1 TRACK 07

AB page 4 Activity 3

Our Adventure Blog by Lily, Josh and Ravi

In this adventure, we take some boxes to the blue room. In this room, there are more boxes on the floor and a photo of Luke on the wall. Luke is our brother. There's a computer on a table, too. We hear a noise. There's a secret message on the computer screen. We work together to break a code. Luke appears on the screen and we talk to him. Now we can read and write an adventure blog together.

Starter Unit Lesson 4

Pupil's Book

CD1 TRACK 08

PB page 7 Activity 1

The secret code rap

A B C D E F G, write a secret message with me.
H I J K L M N, we can send it to a friend.
O P Q R S and T, use this code to write and read.
U V W X Y Z, shh, keep this code in your head.

Starter Unit Lesson 4

Pupil's Book

CD1 TRACK 09

PB page 7 Activity 3

How do you spell message?
How do you spell password?
How do you spell school?

Starter Unit Lesson 4

Activity Book

CD1 TRACK 10

AB page 5 Activity 1

1 A, C, F, H, I, J, K, L, W
2 B, C, D, E, G, S, P, T, V
3 F, C, L, M, N, O, S, X, Z

Unit 1 Lesson 1

Pupil's Book

CD1 TRACK 11

PB page 8 Activity 2

gym, corridor, computer room, football pitch, school hall, playground, library, bike stand, music room, basketball court, canteen, vegetable garden

Unit 1 Lesson 1

Pupil's Book

CD1 TRACK 12

PB page 8 Activity 3

***My school is cool* song**

From Monday to Friday
I go to school.
This is my school.
My school is cool.

Where do you play the drums?
Where do you go online?
I play the drums in the music room.
And I go online
In the computer room.

From Monday to Friday
I go to school.
This is my school.
My school is cool.

Where do you hang your coat?
Where do you throw a ball?
I hang my coat in the corridor.
And I throw a ball
On the basketball court.

From Monday to Friday
I go to school.
This is my school.
My school is cool.

Unit 1 Lesson 1

Pupil's Book

CD1 TRACK 13

PB page 8 Activity 3

Karaoke version: *My school is cool* song

Unit 1 Lesson 2

Pupil's Book

CD1 TRACK 14

PB page 9 Activity 1

Ravi: This is the school gym.
Josh: Wow! It's really big. What do you do in here?
Ravi: I do gymnastics in my PE lesson.
Josh: When do you have PE?
Ravi: I have PE on Monday and Friday.
Josh: And where do you play football?
Ravi: I play football on the football pitch. It's behind the school. Come and see.

Unit 1 Lesson 2

Pupil's Book

CD1 TRACK 15

PB page 9 Activity 3

When do you play with your friends?
Where do you study Maths?
What do you do in the music room?

Unit 1 Lesson 3

Pupil's Book

CD1 TRACK 16

PB page 10 Activity 2

The new school

Frame 1
Narrator: It's nine o'clock. The children are in their classroom.
Teacher: Welcome to your new school, Lily and Josh.
Lily and Josh: Thank you.

Frame 2
Narrator: The first lesson is Arts and Crafts. The children are making bracelets.
Lily: What's the matter, Josh?
Josh: I'm not very good at Arts and Crafts.
Lily: Don't worry. I can help you.

Frame 3
Narrator: The next lesson is Music.
Josh: And I'm not very good at Music. I can't play the drums.
Ravi: Come on, Josh. You can do it.

Frame 4
Narrator: It's break time. The children are in the playground.
Ravi: Let's play basketball.
Josh: Great! I love sport. When do we have PE?
Ravi: We have PE after the break. We have a swimming lesson today.

Frame 5
Narrator: The swimming pool is next to the school.
Josh: Wow! This swimming pool is amazing.
Lily: You can see the lighthouse. Look!

Frame 6
Narrator: Ravi and Lily jump into the water.
PE teacher: Kick your legs, everyone.
Ravi: Phew! This is difficult.

Frame 7
Narrator: Five minutes later …
Lily: Oh no! Where's my new bracelet?
Ravi: It's at the bottom of the pool.
Josh: Don't worry. I can get it.

Frame 8
Narrator: Josh finds the bracelet.
Josh: Here's your bracelet.
Lily: Thanks, Josh. You're good at PE.
Ravi: Josh isn't good at PE. He's brilliant at it!

Unit 1 Lesson 3

Activity Book

CD1 TRACK 17

AB page 8 Activity 2

Our Adventure Blog by Lily, Josh and Ravi
Today is the first day in our new school. We have Arts and Crafts in the morning and we make a bracelet. Then we have Music and we play the drums. At break time, we play basketball in the playground. After the break, we have a PE lesson. The swimming pool is next to the school. Lily loses her bracelet and she is sad. The bracelet is at the bottom of the swimming pool. Josh finds the bracelet.

Unit 1 Lesson 4

Pupil's Book

CD1 TRACK 18

PB page 12 Activity 1

1 ICT
2 Geography
3 History
4 Arts and Crafts
5 PE
6 Drama

Unit 1 Lesson 4

Pupil's Book

CD1 TRACK 19

PB page 12 Activity 2

***I'm brilliant at PE* song**

I'm very good at Maths
And I'm good at Arts and Crafts.
I'm good at ICT
And I'm brilliant at PE.
Yes, I'm brilliant.
I'm brilliant at PE!
Brilliant!

Are you good at Maths?
Are you good at Arts and Crafts?
Are you good at ICT?
Are you brilliant at PE?
Are you brilliant?
Are you brilliant at PE?
Brilliant!

Unit 1 Lesson 4

Pupil's Book

CD1 TRACK 20

PB page 12 Activity 3

I'm very good at History.
I'm brilliant at Drama.
I'm not very good at Arts and Crafts.

Audioscript

Unit 1 Lesson 5

Pupil's Book

CD1 TRACK 21

PB page 13 Activity 1

giraffes – jumping – judo – gym
The giraffes are jumping and doing judo in the gym.
The giraffes are jumping and doing judo in the gym.
The giraffes are jumping and doing judo in the gym.

Unit 1 Lesson 5

Pupil's Book

CD1 TRACK 22

PB page 13 Activity 2

Boy: Hi Tanya. I haven't got my timetable. Can you help me?
Girl: Yes, of course. No problem.
Boy: When do we have Music?
Girl: We have Music on Monday at nine o'clock.
Boy: Great. It's my favourite subject. Where do we have Music?
Girl: We have it in the classroom.
Boy: Are you sure?
Girl: Yes, I am. What other subjects do you like?
Boy: I love Science. When do we have Science?
Girl: We have Science on Thursday at eleven o'clock.
Boy: Thursday at eleven o'clock. OK. Thanks. What about Maths? I like Maths, too.
Girl: We have Maths on Tuesday at nine o'clock and Friday at eleven o'clock.
Boy: Cool!
Girl: Do you like Drama?
Boy: No. I'm not very good at Drama. When do we have Drama?
Girl: We have it on Wednesday at eleven o'clock.
Boy: Where do we have it?
Girl: I'm not sure. I think we have it in the gym.
Boy: It's time for class. Thanks for your help, Tanya.
Girl: You're welcome.

Unit 1 Lesson 6

Pupil's Book

CD1 TRACK 23

PB page 14 Activity 3

Are you bored after school? Do you want to learn a fast and exciting sport?
Join the Roller Hockey Heroes
We meet on Tuesday and Thursday in the school playground. The classes begin at five o'clock and finish at six.
We have hockey sticks and balls for everyone. We also have gloves for your hands, pads for your legs and a helmet for your head. The classes cost £2 and you need to wear comfortable clothes and bring your rollerblades.
For more information, email emma@fun.uk
Come and have fun with the Roller Hockey Heroes!

Unit 1 Lesson 7

Pupil's Book

CD1 TRACK 24

PB page 15 Activity 1

Do you love computers?
Do you want to play cool games and draw amazing pictures? Join the school computer club. We meet on Wednesday in the computer room. The classes begin at four o'clock and finish at six. The classes are free, but you need to bring a memory stick for your work.
For more information, contact Mr Smith.
Come and have fun!

Unit 1 Lesson 8

Pupil's Book

CD1 TRACK 25

PB page 16 Activity 2

Springhill School
Welcome to Springhill School. On this webpage, you can learn about the amazing activities we do after school.
Sheona: Hi. My name's Sheona and my favourite activity is Gaelic football. It's a traditional sport in Ireland. Do you know that you can carry the ball in your hands? You can hit and kick the ball, too. I play Gaelic football with my friends every Friday afternoon.
Teresa: My name's Teresa and my favourite activity is Irish dancing. I go to a dance class every Monday and Wednesday after school. It's good fun because we skip and jump a lot. We wear traditional dresses, too. They're beautiful.
Liam: Hi, I'm Liam. Hurling is a traditional sport in Ireland and I play it in my free time. I practise on Tuesday evenings and I play in competitions. I'm very good at running and passing the ball. I always wear a helmet.
Pat: Hello, I'm Pat. I love music and I play a tin whistle in my free time. This traditional instrument is small, but it makes a lot of noise. I practise with my friends every Thursday afternoon and we have a concert in the summer. It's good fun!

Unit 1 Lesson 8

Activity Book

CD1 TRACK 26

AB page 13 Activity 1

1
Girl: Hi, Peter. Do you do an activity after school?
Boy: Yes, I do. I play hurling. It's really exciting.
Girl: When do you play?
Boy: I play on Friday.

2
Boy: Hello, Sue. Do you do an activity after school?
Girl: Yes, I do. I do Irish dancing.
Boy: When do you go to dance classes?
Girl: I go to a dance class every Wednesday. It's great fun!

3
Boy: Hi, Mary. What activity do you do after school?
Girl: I play the tin whistle.
Boy: Really? That's very interesting. When do you practise?
Girl: I practise on Monday, after school.

4
Girl: What activity do you do after school, Daniel?
Boy: I play Gaelic football.
Girl: When do you play?
Boy: I play on Thursday at six o'clock.

Unit 1 Video and 21st Century Skills

Activity Book

CD1 TRACK 27

AB page 15 Activity 1

1
Boy: Do you want to play the guitar?
Girl: Yes, I do. Music is fun.
2
Girl: Do you want to do street dance?
Boy: Yes, I do. I'm good at dancing.
3
Boy: Do you want to play rugby?
Girl: Yes, I do. It's a great sport.
4
Girl: Do you want to build a robot?
Boy: Yes, I do. I love technology.

Unit 1 Video and 21st Century Skills

Activity Book

CD1 TRACK 28

AB page 15 Activity 2

Adult: Do you want to play tennis, Sarah?
Girl: No, I don't. I can't play tennis!
Adult: It's important to try new activities.
Girl: I know, but I don't like it.
Adult: Let's look for some tips to help you.
Girl: OK … Here's a good webpage. Look!
Adult: Tip number 1: don't be afraid. Everybody needs to learn.
Girl: That's true.
Adult: And tip number 2 is: listen to the instructions. Then you know what to do.
Girl: That's a good idea.
Adult: Tip number 3 is: watch what other people do. Then you can copy them.
Girl: I like that tip. What's number 4.
Adult: Tip number 4 is: ask people to help you. It's important to ask for help.
Girl: Yes, it is. These are great tips. What's the last one?
Adult: Tip number five is … have fun! Are you ready to play tennis now?
Girl: Yes, I am.
Adult: Fantastic!

Unit 2 Lesson 1

Pupil's Book

CD1 TRACK 29

PB page 18 Activity 2

make my bed, lay the table, tidy up, clear the table, feed my pet, walk the dog, wash up, wash the car, cook dinner, water the plants, hoover the floor, dust

Unit 2 Lesson 1

Pupil's Book

CD1 TRACK 30

PB page 18 Activity 3

***What a busy day!* song**

Saturday, Saturday.
What a busy day!
We do chores in the morning
And then we play.

I clear the kitchen table,
Then I make my bed.
I hoover the living room floor
And then I feed my pet.

Saturday, Saturday.
What a busy day!
We do chores in the morning
And then we play.

I wash the car outside,
Then I tidy up.
I water the plants in the living room
And then I wash up.

Saturday, Saturday.
What a busy day!
We do chores in the morning
And then we play.
Yes, we do chores in the morning
And then we play.

Unit 2 Lesson 1

Pupil's Book

CD1 TRACK 31

PB page 18 Activity 3

Karaoke version: *What a busy day!* song

Unit 2 Lesson 2

Pupil's Book

CD1 TRACK 32

PB page 19 Activity 1

Ravi: What's the matter, Josh?
Josh: It isn't fair. I always wash up.
Ravi: What about Lily?
Josh: She never washes up.
Ravi: Oh dear. Does she do other chores?
Josh: Yes, she does. She often clears the table and she sometimes hoovers the floor.
Ravi: So Lily helps at home, too.
Josh: Yes, I suppose you're right.

Unit 2 Lesson 2

Pupil's Book

CD1 TRACK 33

PB page 19 Activity 3

My brother often lays the table.
My sister never cooks dinner.
My dad sometimes hoovers the floor.

Unit 2 Lesson 3

Pupil's Book

CD1 TRACK 34

PB page 20 Activity 2

The secret tunnel

Frame 1
Narrator: It's Saturday morning. Lily and Josh are doing chores.
Ravi: Are you ready to play now?
Josh: Yes, Ravi. I'm ready. What about you, Lily?
Lily: Not yet. I need to hoover the floor first.

Frame 2
Narrator: Josh shows Ravi an old book in the living room.
Josh: Look at this book. It's about the ghost of a drummer boy who lives in the lighthouse.
Ravi: Is it scary?
Josh: Yes, it is. It's great!

Frame 3
Narrator: Lily moves a curtain and has a surprise.
Lily: What's this?
Josh: Wow! It's a secret tunnel. Let's explore.
Ravi: I can hear drums.

Frame 4
Narrator: The children go down the steps and into the tunnel.
Lily: Oh dear. It's very dark in here.
Ravi: Be careful. The floor is wet.
Josh: I think we're under the sea.

Frame 5
Narrator: The drums are loud now.
Lily: I don't like that noise.
Ravi: Maybe it's the ghost of the drummer boy.

Frame 6
Narrator: There's a light at the end of the tunnel.
Lily: Look at that shadow on the wall.
Ravi: It's very big. What is it?
Josh: It *is* the ghost!

Frame 7
Narrator: They hear a voice.
Grandma: Come in here, children.

Frame 8
Narrator: The children walk slowly into the cave.
Lily: Grandma! Why are you in this cave?
Grandma: Grandad always tidies up on Saturday morning, so I practise the drums here once a week.
Ravi: Phew! I'm glad you aren't a ghost.

Unit 2 Lesson 3

Activity Book

CD1 TRACK 35

AB page 18 Activity 2

Our Adventure Blog by Lily, Josh and Ravi

In this adventure, we discover a secret tunnel behind a curtain. We go down some steps. The tunnel is very dark and wet. It goes under the sea. In the tunnel, we hear some drums and we see a very big shadow on the wall. Finally, we go into a cave and we see Grandma. She's practising the drums.

Audioscript

Unit 2 Lesson 4

Pupil's Book

CD1 TRACK 36

PB page 22 Activity 1

1 watch DVDs
2 do puzzles
3 read comics
4 draw pictures
5 play computer games
6 play board games

Unit 2 Lesson 4

Pupil's Book

CD1 TRACK 37

PB page 22 Activity 2

***Free time* song**

Free time at the weekend.
Free time after school.
Free time is great.
What do you do?

Lily plays board games.
She watches DVDs.
And she listens to music
Once a week.

Free time at the weekend.
Free time after school.
Free time is great.
What do you do?

Josh draws pictures.
He watches DVDs.
And he plays computer games
Twice a week.

Free time at the weekend.
Free time after school.
Free time is great.
What do you do?

Ravi does puzzles.
He watches DVDs.
And he reads comics
Three times a week.

Free time at the weekend.
Free time after school.
Free time is great.
What do you do?

Unit 2 Lesson 4

Pupil's Book

CD1 TRACK 38

PB page 22 Activity 3

How often does your dad read comics?
How often does your mum play board games?
How often does your brother play computer games?

Unit 2 Lesson 5

Pupil's Book

CD1 TRACK 39

PB page 23 Activity 1

witch – chops – chicken – kitchen
The witch chops chicken in the kitchen.
The witch chops chicken in the kitchen.
The witch chops chicken in the kitchen.

Unit 2 Lesson 5

Pupil's Book

CD1 TRACK 40

PB page 23 Activity 2

Girl: Excuse me, can I ask you some questions, please?
Boy: Yes, of course.
Girl: Great. Thanks. What's your name?
Boy: It's Marc.
Girl: How do you spell that?
Boy: M-A-R-C.
Girl: And how old are you?
Boy: I'm twelve.
Girl: My first question is – How often do you clear the table?
Boy: Hmmm … I don't do it every day. I clear the table about twice a week.
Girl: OK. Next question – Have you got a pet?
Boy: Yes, I've got a fish.
Girl: How often do you feed your pet?
Boy: Oh. I feed it every day before I go to school.
Girl: And have you got a dog?
Boy: No, I haven't.
Girl: So … you never walk the dog.
Boy: That's right.
Girl: The next question is – How often do you wash up?
Boy: That's easy. I wash up every day. I wash my plate at breakfast time.
Girl: That's good. How often do you cook dinner?
Boy: I sometimes help my mum to cook dinner. So … about once a week.
Girl: That's fantastic. Thanks for your help, Mark.
Boy: You're welcome.

Unit 2 Lesson 6

Pupil's Book

CD1 TRACK 41

PB page 24 Activity 3

Why Anansi has got eight long, thin legs

One day, Anansi goes for a walk and visits his friend, Rabbit. It's lunchtime and Rabbit is cooking vegetables. Rabbit invites his friend to lunch. Anansi is hungry and the vegetables smell good, but he doesn't want to help with the cooking. He has a clever idea. He makes a web, gives it to Rabbit and says, 'Pull this web when lunch is ready.'
Next, Anansi visits Monkey. Monkey is cooking beans and honey. They smell delicious. Monkey also invites his friend to lunch, but Anansi is lazy and doesn't want to help. He makes another web, gives it to Monkey and says, 'Pull this web when lunch is ready.'
Anansi is greedy and he looks for more food. He gives a web to six more friends. Now he's got a web for each leg. When he's next to the river, all eight friends pull the webs at the same time and Anansi falls into the river. When Anansi climbs out of the river, he's very surprised.
Anansi: Look at my legs! They're long and thin now.
And that's why Anansi has got eight long, thin legs.

Unit 2 Lesson 7

Pupil's Book

CD1 TRACK 42

PB page 25 Activity 2

One lunchtime, Turtle visits Anansi. He's very hungry. Anansi has got a lot of food, but he doesn't want to share it with Turtle. Anansi has a clever idea. He says, 'You can't eat lunch with dirty hands. Go to the river and wash.'
Turtle can't walk fast. When he returns, the food is finished.
One week later, Turtle invites Anansi to his house at the bottom of the river. Anansi puts on a heavy coat so he can swim to Turtle's house. There's a lot of delicious food on the table. Turtle has a clever idea. He says, 'You can't wear a coat when you eat lunch … .'

Unit 2 Lesson 8

Pupil's Book

CD1 TRACK 43

PB page 26 Activity 2

Life on a Scottish island

Sarah: I'm Sarah and I live on a small island in the north of Scotland. There isn't a school here, so I go to school on another island. I travel to school by ferry five days a week and I have to get up very early. I love travelling by ferry in the winter because there are lots of big waves. But when the weather is very bad, I study on the computer at home.
Olivia: My name's Olivia and I live on a small island in the west of Scotland. The island is famous for its sheep and my parents have got a farm. I help my parents look after the animals every day and I often feed the sheep before I go to school. I love playing with the baby animals, too.

James: I'm James and this is my sister, Fiona. We're from an island in the west of Scotland. Life here is very quiet. I often ride my bike in my free time. It's very safe because there aren't any cars. I go to the beach with my sister, too. You can sometimes see seals and dolphins in the sea. They're beautiful.

Unit 2 Lesson 8

Activity Book

CD1 TRACK 44

AB page 23 Activity 1

Girl: Hello. Can I ask you some questions?
Boy: Yes, of course.
Girl: What's your name?
Boy: It's Neil.
Girl: How do you spell that?
Boy: It's N-E-I-L.
Girl: OK. Thanks. And how old are you, Neil?
Boy: I'm nine.
Girl: Do you go to school on the island?
Boy: Yes, I do.
Girl: And how do you go to school?
Boy: I ride my bike to school.
Girl: How many children are in your class?
Boy: There are six children.
Girl: Six!
Boy: Yes, it's a very small school.
Girl: And what do you do in your free time?
Boy: I like playing basketball, but my favourite activity is sailing. I go sailing with my dad every weekend.
Girl: That's great. Thank you for answering the questions.
Boy: You're welcome.

Unit 2 Video and 21st Century Skills

Activity Book

CD1 TRACK 45

AB page 25 Activity 1

1
I tidy up the classroom.
2
I wash up my plates.
3
I share my snack.
4
I take out the rubbish.
5
I explain an exercise.
6
I clean the board.

Unit 2 Video and 21st Century Skills

Activity Book

CD1 TRACK 46

AB page 25 Activity 2

Boy: Hello, Emma. What are you doing?
Girl: I'm reading a webpage.
Boy: What's it about?
Girl: It's about how children can help at home.
Boy: Really? What things can children do?
Girl: Well, they can pick up their clothes from the floor.
Boy: That's easy. What else?
Girl: They can tidy up their toys and games when they play.
Boy: Oh! I always tidy up my toys and games.
Girl: Children can look after their pets, too.
Boy: That's true. Children can feed and clean their pets.
Girl: And it says that children can take out the rubbish.
Boy: Oh no! I never take out the rubbish.
Girl: The last thing it says is that children can lay the table.
Boy: I sometimes lay the table at home.
Girl: Me too. It's dinner time now. Let's go and help.
Boy: Good idea.

Unit 3 Lesson 1

Pupil's Book

CD1 TRACK 47

PB page 28 Activity 2

headache, flu, stomach ache, temperature, earache, cut, cold, broken leg, cough, feel dizzy, sore throat, feel sick

Unit 3 Lesson 1

Pupil's Book

CD1 TRACK 48

PB page 28 Activity 3

***I'm not very well* song**

Oh dear.
I'm not very well.
I've got a cough
And stomach ache, too.
I feel sick.
Have I got flu?

Oh dear.
I'm not very well.
I've got a headache
And a sore throat, too.
I feel dizzy.
Have I got flu?

Oh dear.
You aren't very well.
Go to bed.
There's no school for you.

Unit 3 Lesson 1

Pupil's Book

CD2 TRACK 01

PB page 28 Activity 3

Karaoke version: *I'm not very well* song

Unit 3 Lesson 2

Pupil's Book

CD2 TRACK 02

PB page 29 Activity 1

Ravi: Hi, Lily. Where's Josh?
Lily: He's at home.
Ravi: What's the matter?
Lily: He isn't very well today.
Ravi: Oh dear. Has he got a headache?
Lily: Yes, he has. And he's got a cough.
Ravi: Does he feel sick, too?
Lily: Yes, he does.
Ravi: Poor Josh!

Unit 3 Lesson 2

Pupil's Book

CD2 TRACK 03

PB page 29 Activity 3

Has she got a sore throat?
Do you feel sick?
Does he feel dizzy?

Unit 3 Lesson 3

Pupil's Book

CD2 TRACK 04

PB page 30 Activity 2

The dolphin rescue

Frame 1
Narrator: It's four o'clock. Lily and Ravi arrive home from school.
Ravi: Hi, Josh. Are you better now?
Josh: Yes, I am. Thanks.

Frame 2
Narrator: Josh wants to play.
Josh: Can we play outside, Mum?
Mum: Yes, you can. But put your coat on. It's cold and windy today.

Frame 3
Narrator: The children go to the beach.
Josh: Look at that dog! Why is it barking?
Ravi: I don't know. Let's find out.

Audioscript

Frame 4
Narrator: The children follow the dog.
Lily: Oh no! There's a dolphin on the beach.
Ravi: I think it's hurt.
Josh: Quick! Let's tell Mum.

Frame 5
Narrator: The children run to the lighthouse.
Mum: What's the matter?
Josh: There's a dolphin on the beach and it isn't very well.
Mum: Oh no! I'll phone the vet.

Frame 6
Narrator: The vets arrive. They know what to do.
Vet 1: We must protect the dolphin's skin.
Vet 2: And dolphins don't like loud noises. We mustn't shout.

Frame 7
Narrator: The vets put the dolphin into the water.
Lily: Excuse me. How's the dolphin, please?
Vet 3: It's tired and it's got some cuts, but it's OK.

Frame 8
Narrator: A TV station hears about the rescue.
Reporter: Well done for finding the dolphin.
Ravi: Thank you, but we must also say thank you to a very clever dog!
Dog: Woof!

Unit 3 Lesson 3

Activity Book

CD2 TRACK 05

AB page 28 Activity 2

Our Adventure Blog by Lily, Josh and Ravi
In this adventure, we play outside. We put our coats on because it is cold and windy. We walk to the beach and we hear a dog barking. Then we see a dolphin on the sand. It's hurt. We run to the lighthouse and Mum phones the vet. The vets protect the dolphin's skin. Then they put the dolphin into the water. The dolphin has got some cuts, but it's OK. Later, we are on the TV. It's exciting!

Unit 3 Lesson 4

Pupil's Book

CD2 TRACK 06

PB page 32 Activity 1

1 go to bed early
2 go to bed late
3 eat healthy snacks
4 eat lots of sweets
5 be active
6 be lazy

Unit 3 Lesson 4

Pupil's Book

CD2 TRACK 07

PB page 32 Activity 2

***Fit and healthy* song**

If you want to be fit
And healthy, too.
This is what you must do.
You must be active.
Run and play.
And eat healthy snacks
Every day.

If you want to be fit
And healthy, too.
This is what you mustn't do.
You mustn't be lazy.
Get up on your feet!
And you mustn't eat lots of sweets.
They're bad for your teeth.

Unit 3 Lesson 4

Pupil's Book

CD2 TRACK 08

PB page 32 Activity 3

You must be active.
You mustn't eat lots of sweets.
You mustn't be lazy.

Unit 3 Lesson 5

Pupil's Book

CD2 TRACK 09

PB page 33 Activity 1

pink – chameleon – headache – king – stomach ache
The pink chameleon's got a headache and the king's got stomach ache.
The pink chameleon's got a headache and the king's got stomach ache.
The pink chameleon's got a headache and the king's got stomach ache.

Unit 3 Lesson 5

Pupil's Book

CD2 TRACK 10

PB page 33 Activity 2

1
Boy: Hello.
Girl: Hello, Doctor.
Boy: What's your name?
Girl: It's Sally.
Boy: And how old are you?
Girl: I'm nine.
Boy: What's the matter?
Girl: I don't feel very well. I've got earache.
Boy: Oh dear. Does it hurt?
Girl: Yes, it does.
Boy: Hmm. You must wear a hat and a scarf. And you mustn't go swimming.
Girl: Thank you, Doctor.
Boy: You're welcome.
2
Girl: Hello.
Boy: Hello, Doctor.
Girl: What's your name?
Boy: It's Joe.
Girl: How old are you, Joe?
Boy: I'm eleven.
Girl: What's the matter with you?
Boy: I've got a sore throat.
Girl: Let me see. Say aaah!
Boy: Aaah!
Girl: Oh dear. You must take some medicine and you mustn't shout.
Boy: OK. Thank you, Doctor.
Girl: You're welcome.

Unit 3 Lesson 6

Pupil's Book

CD2 TRACK 11

PB page 34 Activity 2

Are you fit and healthy?

1 Do you walk to school?
a) always
b) sometimes
c) never

2 How often do you eat fruit?
a) every day
b) five times a week
c) once or twice a week

3 What time do you go to bed?
a) about nine o'clock
b) about ten o'clock
c) about eleven o'clock

4 How much TV do you watch every day?
a) less than one hour
b) one to two hours
c) more than two hours

5 How often do you do sport?
a) every day
b) five times a week
c) once or twice a week

Unit 3 Lesson 7

Pupil's Book

CD2 TRACK 12

PB page 35 Activity 2

Do you have a healthy diet?
Do the quiz to find out.

1 How often do you eat vegetables?
a) every day
b) five times a week
c) once or twice a week

2 Do you eat breakfast?
a) always
b) sometimes
c) never

3 Do you drink fizzy drinks with your dinner?
a) never
b) sometimes
c) always

Unit 3 Lesson 8

Pupil's Book

CD2 TRACK 13

PB page 36 Activity 2

Animal Rescue

Marine animals sometimes need our help. In Malta, there are many people who work to help animals that are hurt or ill. Divers swim under the water to rescue the animals. Scientists investigate why the animals are ill and vets help make the animals better.

Turtles sometimes need help because they eat plastic bags that are in the water. Boats can hit turtles and hurt them, too. A rescue team takes these animals to the vets at a rescue centre.

The vets inspect the animals. Some turtles have got cuts and some have got broken bones. The vets wash them and give them some medicine. Then the vets put the turtles in a warm pool.

When the turtles are better, the vets put them back into the sea. They do this in the summer because the water is warm. Everyone feels very happy and proud when the turtles are in the wild again.

Unit 3 Lesson 8

Activity Book

CD2 TRACK 14

AB page 33 Activity 1

1 Where does Jane go every summer?
Boy: Hi, Jane.
Girl: Hi, Paul. Do you want to see my holiday photos?
Boy: Yes, please.
Girl: Look! This is a photo of a beach in Malta. We go there every summer.
Boy: Oh. It's very nice.
2 What does she often do there?
Boy: What do you do at the beach, Jane?
Girl: Hmm … we do lots of things. We sometimes swim and we sometimes play volleyball.
Boy: What's your favourite beach activity?
Girl: It's sailing. I often go sailing with my dad.
3 Which animals does she sometimes see?
Boy: Do you see wild animals when you go sailing?
Girl: Yes, I do.
Boy: Which animals do you see?
Girl: I see lots of fish, of course. And I sometimes see dolphins, too.
Boy: Dolphins! That's amazing.
4 What does she eat?
Boy: What do you eat when you go to the beach, Jane?
Girl: I always eat watermelon.
Boy: Why?
Girl: It's good for you and it's delicious, too!

Unit 3 Video and 21st Century Skills

Activity Book

CD2 TRACK 15

AB page 35 Activity 1

The healthy activities are:
do exercise
eat breakfast
go to bed early.

The not very healthy activities are:
drink fizzy drinks
eat burgers
watch TV.

Unit 3 Video and 21st Century Skills

Activity Book

CD2 TRACK 16

AB page 35 Activity 2

Dad: Tim, please, switch off the computer. You need to be more active.
Boy: But, what can I do?
Dad: Look! I've got some tips here. The first tip is: walk to school. Don't go to school by car.
Boy: OK. I can walk to school with my friend Sam. What's tip number 2?
Dad: At school, play in the playground. Don't just sit and chat with your friends.
Boy: That's a good idea!
Dad: Tip number three is: join a sports club.
Boy: A sports club? My friend David goes to the swimming club. I love swimming.
Dad: Tip number four is: walk the dog.
Boy: I *sometimes* walk the dog …
Dad: You can walk the dog every day …
Boy: What's the last tip?
Dad: Tip number 5 is: go to the park at the weekend.
Boy: I like that tip. It's my favourite one!
Dad: Me too. Let's go to the park now. We can play basketball.
Boy: Fantastic!

My project 1 Lesson 1

Pupil's Book

CD2 TRACK 17

PB page 38 Activity 3

The animals in the zoo are:
an elephant, an ostrich, monkeys, a crocodile, a giraffe, penguins, a tortoise, parrots, lizards, a tiger, an eagle, snakes.

Five services for visitors are:
a gift shop, a restaurant, a first aid post, a playground, a picnic area.

Five things you can see in the animals' living areas are:
trees, bushes, rocks, a pool, grass.

Unit 4 Lesson 1

Pupil's Book

CD2 TRACK 18

PB page 40 Activity 2

cheese, tuna, chillies, prawns, onions, mushrooms, olives, spinach, tomato sauce, sweetcorn, peppers, pineapple

Unit 4 Lesson 1

Pupil's Book

CD2 TRACK 19

PB page 40 Activity 3

***Let's make a pizza* song**

Mix it, push it,
Roll it out.
Throw the pizza
Up and down.

You can add tuna
And mushrooms, too.
There are lots of toppings
For you to choose.

Mix it, push it,
Roll it out.
Throw the pizza
Up and down.

You can add olives
And spinach, too.
There are lots of toppings
For you to choose.

Mix it, push it,
Roll it out.
Throw the pizza
Up and down.

You can add pineapple
And peppers, too.
There are lots of toppings
For you to choose.

Audioscript

Mix it, push it,
Roll it out.
Throw the pizza
Up and down.

Unit 4 Lesson 1

Pupil's Book

CD2 TRACK 20

PB page 40 Activity 3

Karaoke version: ***Let's make a pizza*** **song**

Unit 4 Lesson 2

Pupil's Book

CD2 TRACK 21

PB page 41 Activity 1

Josh: Good evening. What would you like, Madam?
Grandma: I'd like a salad, please.
Josh: What would you like in your salad?
Grandma: I'd like some spinach and some tuna, please.
Josh: Would you like anything else in your salad?
Grandma: Yes, please. I'd like some olives.
Narrator: A few minutes later …
Josh: Sorry, Madam. There isn't any spinach and there isn't any tuna, but there are lots of olives. Here you are.

Unit 4 Lesson 2

Pupil's Book

CD2 TRACK 22

PB page 41 Activity 3

She would like a lot of tuna.
I would like lots of spinach.
We would like some cheese.

Unit 4 Lesson 3

Pupil's Book

CD2 TRACK 23

PB page 42 Activity 2

The amazing pizza

Frame 1
Narrator: Lily and Josh go to Ravi's flat. He's in the kitchen with his sister.
Lily: Hi, Ravi and Aarti. What are you doing?
Ravi: We're making a pizza. There's a competition at Mario's restaurant today.

Frame 2
Narrator: Lily and Josh help make the pizza.
Ravi: First we need to mix these ingredients.
Now we need to wait for half an hour.
Aarti: Let's play computer games.

Frame 3
Narrator: The children forget about the mixture. It grows and grows and grows.
Lily: Oh no! Look at the mixture now.
Josh: It's too big for the oven!
Ravi: It's OK. We can bake it at the restaurant.

Frame 4
Narrator: They roll out the mixture. The pizza is enormous.
Ravi: What toppings would you like on your slice of pizza?
Lily: I'd like mushrooms and chilli, please.
Josh: And I'd like tuna and olives, please.

Frame 5
Narrator: The children put the toppings on the pizza.
Ravi: What about you, Aarti?
Aarti: I prefer sweet food. I'd like some pineapple and banana, please.

Frame 6
Narrator: It's time to bake the pizza.
Mario: Wow! That's a big pizza.
Ravi: Can we bake it in your oven, please?
Mario: Yes, of course.

Frame 7
Narrator: The judges taste the pizza.
Mario: Mmm. This part of the pizza is spicy.
Judge 1: This part of the pizza is savoury.
Judge 2: And this part is sweet. It's delicious!

Frame 8
Narrator: The judges are ready to give the prizes.
Mario: The first prize is for the big, spicy, savoury and sweet pizza.
Judge 2: Well done, children.
Ravi, Josh and Aarti: Thank you very much.

Unit 4 Lesson 3

Activity Book

CD2 TRACK 24

AB page 40 Activity 2

Our Adventure Blog by Lily, Josh and Ravi
In this adventure, we make a pizza for a competition. First we mix the ingredients. Then we play computer games in the living room. We forget about the mixture and it grows a lot. We roll out the mixture and the pizza is very big. Lily puts some mushrooms and chilli on it. Josh puts some tuna and olives on it. Aarti puts some pineapple and banana on it. We take the pizza to the restaurant. The judges taste the pizza. They think that it's delicious and we win first prize.

Unit 4 Lesson 4

Pupil's Book

CD2 TRACK 25

PB page 44 Activity 1

1 sweet
2 savoury
3 plain
4 spicy
5 soft
6 crunchy

Unit 4 Lesson 4

Pupil's Book

CD2 TRACK 26

PB page 44 Activity 2

The delicious food rap

Food, food,
Delicious food.
Which do you prefer?
Sweet or savoury?
Plain or spicy?
Soft or crunchy?
Food, food,
Delicious food.
Which do you prefer?

Unit 4 Lesson 4

Pupil's Book

CD2 TRACK 27

PB page 44 Activity 3

I prefer spicy food.
We prefer crunchy food.
She prefers soft food.

Unit 4 Lesson 5

Pupil's Book

CD2 TRACK 28

PB page 45 Activity 1

zebra – sneezes – cheese – cherries
The zebra sneezes when it eats cheese and cherries.
The zebra sneezes when it eats cheese and cherries.
The zebra sneezes when it eats cheese and cherries.

Unit 4 Lesson 5

Pupil's Book

CD2 TRACK 29

PB page 45 Activity 2

1
Girl: Let's play a game.
Boy: Good idea!
Girl: First, you need to choose a favourite food.
Boy: OK.
Girl: Now I ask questions to find the food … Ready?
Boy: Yes.
Girl: Do you prefer sweet food or savoury food?
Boy: I prefer savoury food.
Girl: Do you prefer hot food or cold food?
Boy: I prefer hot food.
Girl: Do you prefer plain food or spicy food?
Boy: I prefer spicy food.
Girl: I know! Your favourite food is … CURRY!
2
Boy: Now it's my turn. Choose a favourite food.
Girl: OK. I'm ready.
Boy: Do you prefer sweet food or savoury food?
Girl: I prefer sweet food.
Boy: Do you prefer crunchy food or soft food?
Girl: I prefer soft food.
Boy: Do you prefer hot food or cold food?
Girl: I prefer cold food.
Boy: Your favourite food is … ICE CREAM!
3
Girl: It's my turn again. Are you ready?
Boy: Yes, I am.
Girl: Do you prefer sweet food or savoury food?
Boy: I prefer savoury food.
Girl: Do you prefer hot food or cold food?
Boy: I prefer cold food.
Girl: Do you prefer plain food or spicy food?
Boy: I prefer spicy food.
Girl: I know! Your favourite food is … SPICY CRISPS!
4
Boy: Now it's my turn. Choose a favourite food.
Girl: OK.
Boy: Good. Do you prefer sweet food or savoury food?
Girl: I prefer sweet food.
Boy: Do you prefer crunchy food or soft food?
Girl: I prefer soft food.
Boy: Do you prefer hot food or cold food?
Girl: I prefer hot food.
Boy: Your favourite food is … PANCAKES!

Unit 4 Lesson 6

Pupil's Book

CD2 TRACK 30

PB page 46 Activity 3

Boy: It's long and thin. It's yellow on the outside. It's white on the inside. It's soft and sticky and sweet. I peel it. I eat it. Yum, yum, yum. It's delicious!
Girl: It's thin and square. It's brown on the outside. It's white on the inside. It's soft and savoury. I eat it with cheese. I eat it with meat. I sometimes toast it and I eat it with jam. Yum, yum, yum. It's delicious!
Boy: It's small and round. It's got a stone in the middle. It's red and shiny. It's sweet and juicy. I eat it in the summer. Yum, yum, yum. It's delicious!

Unit 4 Lesson 7

Pupil's Book

CD2 TRACK 31

PB page 47 Activity 2

It's big and round. It's sweet and sticky. It's red and yellow and green. I hold the stick. Then I lick it and I lick it. My favourite flavour is strawberry.

Unit 4 Lesson 8

Pupil's Book

CD2 TRACK 32

PB page 48 Activity 2

Food around the world: India
Breakfast is an important meal in India. There are lots of different breakfasts, but many people eat curry with rice and vegetables in the morning. Do you know that people put spicy sauces on their breakfast food, too?
India is famous for its spicy food, but there's a lot of sweet food, too. People use milk, sugar, cheese and nuts to make traditional cakes. These small cakes are sticky and very sweet. People eat these cakes on birthdays or on festival days.
People in India often eat their meals with their fingers. They use bread to pick up the rice and vegetables, and some people also use bread to eat soup. Do you know that you can only eat with your right hand in India?
You can buy many different snacks in the street in India. These snacks can be sweet, savoury or spicy.

Unit 4 Lesson 8

Activity Book

CD2 TRACK 33

AB page 45 Activity 1

Boy 1: What's your favourite sweet food from India?
Boy 2: My favourite sweet food is Kaju burfi.
Boy 1: How do you make it?
Boy 2: It's very easy. You need three cups of cashew nuts and you need half a cup of water. You need two cups of sugar, too.
Boy 1: What do you do with the ingredients?
Boy 2: First, you chop the cashew nuts into small pieces.
Boy 1: What do you do next?
Boy 2: Then you mix the cashew nuts with hot water and sugar.
Boy 1: Wow. Is it very sticky?
Boy 2: Yes, it is.
Boy 1: What do you do next?
Boy 2: You put the mixture on a plate and wait for two hours.
Boy 1: Can you eat it then?
Boy 2: Yes, you can. It's delicious.

Unit 4 Video and 21st Century Skills

Activity Book

CD2 TRACK 34

AB page 47 Activity 1

1
Boy: Which shape do you prefer?
Girl: I prefer a circle. What about you?
2
Girl: Which colour do you prefer?
Boy: I prefer purple. Do you?
3
Boy: Which decorations do you prefer?
Girl: I prefer flowers.
4
Girl: What else can we do?
Boy: Let's write our names.

Unit 4 Video and 21st Century Skills

Activity Book

CD2 TRACK 35

AB page 47 Activity 2

Mum: What are you doing Ellie?
Girl: I'm writing a story, but it isn't very good. I haven't got any imagination.
Mum: Don't worry. Look at this website. There are some tips for you.
Girl: OK. What's the first tip?
Mum: Tip number 1 is: read lots of books. You get lots of ideas when you read books.
Girl: That's true.
Mum: And tip number 2 is: ask lots of questions.
Girl: That's a good tip. You find out about a lot of new things when you ask questions.

Audioscript

Mum: Tip number 3 is: try new activities. You can try new food, new hobbies …
Girl: I like trying new food! What else?
Mum: Tip number 4 is: switch off the TV and play.
Girl: What's the last tip?
Mum: Number 5 is: talk about your ideas.
Girl: OK! Can I talk about my story with you?
Mum: Yes, of course.

Unit 5 Lesson 1

Pupil's Book

CD2 TRACK 36

PB page 50 Activity 2

fish, turtle, crab, squid, shark, seahorse, whale, starfish, seal, jellyfish, dolphin, octopus

Unit 5 Lesson 1

Pupil's Book

CD2 TRACK 37

PB page 50 Activity 3

***Under the sea* song**
There's a wonderful world.
There's a wonderful world to see.
Under the sea.
Yes, under the sea.

There are fish.
There are turtles.
They're in the seaweed.
There's a very big shark
And it's got sharp teeth.

There's a wonderful world.
There's a wonderful world to see.
Under the sea.
Yes, under the sea.

There are squids.
There are starfish.
They're on the sea floor.
There's a very big crab
And it's got sharp claws.

There's a wonderful world.
There's a wonderful world to see.
Under the sea.
Yes, under the sea.

Unit 5 Lesson 1

Pupil's Book

CD2 TRACK 38

PB page 50 Activity 3

Karaoke version: *Under the sea* song

Unit 5 Lesson 2

Pupil's Book

CD2 TRACK 39

PB page 51 Activity 1

Josh: Excuse me. Can I ask a question?
Biologist: Yes, of course.
Josh: It says here that a squid is faster than an octopus. Is it true?
Biologist: Yes, it is.
Josh: And it says that there are giant squids.
Biologist: That's right. A giant squid is bigger than a car.
Josh: Wow! That's amazing!

Unit 5 Lesson 2

Pupil's Book

CD2 TRACK 40

PB page 51 Activity 3

A dolphin is faster than a fish.
A seahorse is smaller than a seal.
A whale is longer than a turtle.

Unit 5 Lesson 3

Pupil's Book

CD2 TRACK 41

PB page 52 Activity 2

An underwater adventure

Frame 1
Narrator: It's the end of the visit to the aquarium.
Lily: The aquarium is very interesting.
Josh: But it's more interesting to see animals in the wild.
Grandad: Mmm … I've got an idea.

Frame 2
Narrator: Later that day …
Grandad: Would you like to go on the mini submarine, children?
Josh: Wow! Thanks, Grandad.
Captain: All aboard! Let's see some sea animals in the wild.

Frame 3
Narrator: The children go inside the mini submarine.
Captain: Hold tight. We're going to the bottom of the sea.
Josh: Hurray!

Frame 4
Narrator: The children look through the windows.
Ravi: There are lots of fish down here.
Lily: Is that a shark?
Josh: Don't be silly. It's only a big fish.

Frame 5
Narrator: The sea animal comes closer and closer …
Ravi: It's bigger than a fish.
Lily: And it's heavier than a shark.
Josh: It's a whale. Amazing!

Frame 6
Narrator: Now the captain takes the children to an old pirate ship.
Ravi: I can see some shiny objects on the sand. Look!

Frame 7
Narrator: The captain uses robot arms to pick up the objects.
Lily: I think they're gold coins.
Josh: Hurray! We're rich!

Frame 8
Narrator: The children are back on land.
Ravi: Oh no! These aren't gold coins.
Josh: And we aren't rich.
Lily: Yuck! Let's put these cans in the bin.

Unit 5 Lesson 3

Activity Book

CD2 TRACK 42

AB page 50 Activity 2

Our Adventure Blog by Lily, Josh and Ravi
In this adventure, we go on a mini submarine. We go to the bottom of the sea and we see lots of fish. We also see a very big whale. Next, we visit an old pirate ship. It's very exciting because Ravi sees some shiny objects on the sand. We think the objects are gold coins. The captain uses the robot arms to pick them up. Later, we find out that the objects are cans and we put them in the bin.

Unit 5 Lesson 4

Pupil's Book

CD2 TRACK 43

PB page 54 Activity 1

1 heavy
2 ugly
3 pretty
4 colourful
5 intelligent
6 dangerous

Unit 5 Lesson 4

Pupil's Book

CD2 TRACK 44

PB page 54 Activity 2

The sea animal rap

Ugly, pretty,
Heavy, light.
Which sea animal
Do you like?

He likes jellyfish.
I like dolphins.
A dolphin is prettier
And more intelligent.

Ugly, pretty,
Heavy, light.
Which sea animal
Do you like?

She likes dolphins.
I like jellyfish.
A jellyfish is uglier
And more dangerous.

Ugly, pretty,
Heavy, light.
Which sea animal
Do you like?

Unit 5 Lesson 4

Pupil's Book

CD2 TRACK 45

PB page 54 Activity 3

A dolphin is heavier than a seahorse.
An octopus is uglier than a whale.
A jellyfish is more dangerous than a crab.

Unit 5 Lesson 5

Pupil's Book

CD2 TRACK 46

PB page 55 Activity 1

Why – white – whale – wearing – watch
Why is the white whale wearing a watch?
Why is the white whale wearing a watch?
Why is the white whale wearing a watch?

Unit 5 Lesson 5

Pupil's Book

CD2 TRACK 47

PB page 55 Activity 2

Boy: What are you doing, Lucy?
Girl: I'm doing an animal quiz. Look!
Boy: Do you want me to look at the answers for you?
Girl: Yes, please.
Boy: What's the first question?
Girl: The first question is: Is an elephant taller than a giraffe? I say 'no' for that one. I think a giraffe is taller than an elephant.
Boy: You're right! The answer is 'no'.
Girl: Great! Let's look at number two. The question is: Is a snail slower than a turtle?
Boy: What's your answer?
Girl: My answer is 'yes'. I think a snail IS slower than a turtle.
Boy: You're right again. The answer is 'yes'.
Girl: Excellent! Question number 3 is: Is a hippo heavier than a whale?
Boy: That's a difficult question.
Girl: I know. My answer is 'yes'. I think a hippo IS heavier than a whale.
Boy: Oh! That's the wrong answer. The answer is 'no'. A whale is heavier than a hippo.
Girl: It doesn't matter. The last question is: Is a dog more intelligent than a mouse?
Boy: What's your answer?
Girl: It's 'yes', of course. Dogs are very intelligent.
Boy: You're right. The answer is 'yes'. Your score is three out of four. Well done!
Girl: Thanks.

Unit 5 Lesson 6

Pupil's Book

CD2 TRACK 48

PB page 56 Activity 3

Amazing Animals
Blue whale
Blue whales are about 30 metres long. That's the same as three buses! They've got soft skin and a long, round body. On their head, there are two blowholes for breathing. They've got a very big mouth, but they haven't got any teeth. They eat tiny sea animals called krill. Do you know that 50 humans can stand on a blue whale's tongue?
Seahorse
Seahorses are between one and 30 centimetres long. They've got a long, curled tail and a long, thin head. They've got very hard skin and they can change colour, too. Seahorses eat tiny fish and plants. Do you know that seahorses haven't got any teeth or a stomach?
Spider crab
There are many types of crabs. They're different sizes and different colours. Crabs have got a hard shell, ten legs and sharp claws. Crabs use their claws to eat plants and smaller sea animals. Do you know that a crab's teeth are in its stomach?

Unit 5 Lesson 7

Pupil's Book

CD3 TRACK 01

PB page 57 Activity 1

Super starfish
Starfish are between 12 and 24 centimetres long. They've got very hard skin. Most starfish have got five arms, but some starfish have got more. They've got an eye at the end of each arm, too. Starfish eat smaller sea animals. Do you know that starfish haven't got a brain? That's amazing!

Unit 5 Lesson 8

Pupil's Book

CD3 TRACK 02

PB page 58 Activity 2

Welcome to the islands of Hawaii
There are lots of exciting activities for all the family.
Learn to surf
Do you like water sports? In Hawaii, there are lots of beaches where you can learn to surf. It isn't easy, but it's exciting and fun. Give it a try!
Watch the whales
More than 6,000 humpback whales visit Hawaii every year. They arrive in December and stay until May. Take a boat trip and get close to these amazing animals. If you're lucky, you can see them jump out of the water. It's amazing!
Snorkel
There are beautiful coral reefs around the islands of Hawaii. You can swim with colourful, tropical fish and see enormous manta rays. Manta rays look quite scary, but they aren't dangerous.
Make a sandcastle
Hawaii is famous for its beautiful beaches, but the sand isn't always yellow. You can find red, black, green and white sand here. It's the perfect place to make a fantastic sandcastle!

Unit 5 Lesson 8

Activity Book

CD3 TRACK 03

AB page 55 Activity 1

Man: Look, Sue! There's a trip to watch the whales.
Girl: Wow! That sounds fantastic.
Man: It begins at eleven o'clock.
Girl: What time is it now, Dad?
Man: It's half past ten.
Girl: And what time does the trip finish?
Man: The trip is for one hour so it finishes at twelve o'clock.

Audioscript

Girl: And what can you see on the trip?
Man: You can see whales and you can see dolphins, too.
Girl: Fantastic. How much is it?
Man: Let me see … it's ten dollars for adults and it's five dollars for children.
Girl: Can we go, Dad? Please!
Man: OK. Let's go and buy the tickets.
Girl: Hurray!

Unit 5 Video and 21st Century Skills

Activity Book

CD3 TRACK 04

AB page 57 Activity 1

1
search engine
2
keywords
3
website
4
webpage

Unit 5 Video and 21st Century Skills

Activity Book

CD3 TRACK 05

AB page 57 Activity 2

Dad: What's the matter, Emma?
Girl: I need to find some information for my homework. Can you help me?
Dad: Yes, of course. We can look online.
Girl: What do we need to do?
Dad: First, we need to use a search engine for children. Search engines for children are safer than search engines for adults.
Girl: Do I write a question in the search engine?
Dad: No, not really. Don't write a question. Use keywords.
Girl: OK … Look! There are lots of websites.
Dad: Now read the name of the websites and choose the best one.
Girl: This one looks good.
Dad: Remember to check the information on another webpage.
Girl: Why?
Dad: Because sometimes the information you find online is wrong. You need to check the information is correct.
Girl: OK. Thanks, Dad.

Unit 6 Lesson 1

Pupil's Book

CD3 TRACK 06

PB page 60 Activity 2

flippers, wetsuit, mask, kayak, snorkel, helmet, life jacket, swimsuit, paddle, water-skis, surfboard, gloves

Unit 6 Lesson 1

Pupil's Book

CD3 TRACK 07

PB page 60 Activity 3

***Fun in the sea* song**

Under the water
And on the waves.
Let's have fun
In the sea today.

I'm wearing a mask
And flippers, too.
I'm ready to snorkel.
What about you?

Under the water
And on the waves.
Let's have fun
In the sea today.

I'm wearing a helmet
And a life jacket, too.
I'm ready to kayak.
What about you?

Under the water
And on the waves.
Let's have fun
In the sea today.

I'm wearing gloves
And a wetsuit, too.
I'm ready to water-ski.
What about you?

Under the water
And on the waves.
Let's have fun
In the sea today.

Unit 6 Lesson 1

Pupil's Book

CD3 TRACK 08

PB page 60 Activity 3

Karaoke version: *Fun in the sea* song

Unit 6 Lesson 2

Pupil's Book

CD3 TRACK 09

PB page 61 Activity 1

Lily: Look, Dad. I'm ready to do some water sports.
Dad: Great! Are you going to go water-skiing?
Lily: No, I'm not. I'm going to go kayaking. Look, here's my paddle.
Dad: What are you going to do after that?
Lily: I'm going to go surfing. There are lots of surfboards over there.
Dad: Have fun, Lily! See you later.

Unit 6 Lesson 2

Pupil's Book

CD3 TRACK 10

PB page 61 Activity 3

He is going to watch TV after school.
I am not going to play football tomorrow.
We are going to go surfing at the weekend.

Unit 6 Lesson 3

Pupil's Book

CD3 TRACK 11

PB page 62 Activity 2

The raft race

Frame 1
Narrator: There are lots of things to do at the Water Sports Day.
Dad: Look. There's a raft race. Are you going to enter it?
Lily, Josh and Ravi: Definitely!

Frame 2
Narrator: It's three o'clock.
Lily: What are you doing here, Dad?
Dad: I'm going to enter the race, too.

Frame 3
Narrator: The teams listen to the rules of the race.
Man: You must build your raft with these things.
Woman: And you must paddle your raft around that flag.

Frame 4
Narrator: The children begin to build their raft.
Lily: Let's use these plastic bottles.
Ravi: OK. We can tie them to the wood with this rope.
Josh: Good idea, Ravi!

Frame 5
Narrator: Dad begins to build his raft, too.
Josh: Why don't you use this rope, Dad?
Dad: No. My raft is faster like this.
Josh: OK.

Frame 6
Narrator: The rafts are ready. It's time for the race.
Woman: Ready, steady, … Go!
Lily: Come on, everyone! Paddle quickly!

Frame 7
Narrator: Dad is having problems.
Dad: Oh no! My raft is sinking.
Ravi: We can help you. Hold this!

Frame 8
Narrator: The children help Dad get back to the beach.
Dad: Next time, I'm going to listen to your ideas, Josh.
Josh: Thanks, Dad!

Unit 6 Lesson 3

Activity Book

CD3 TRACK 12

AB page 60 Activity 2

Our Adventure Blog by Lily, Josh and Ravi
In this adventure, we enter a raft race. Dad enters the race, too. We build a raft with some plastic bottles and some wood. We tie the bottles to the wood with rope, but Dad doesn't use rope. We paddle quickly. Dad has problems because his raft is sinking. We help Dad get back to the beach. At the end of the race, Dad is wet and tired and he wants to go home.

Unit 6 Lesson 4

Pupil's Book

CD3 TRACK 13

PB page 64 Activity 1

1 swim quickly
2 swim slowly
3 ride well
4 ride badly
5 play quietly
6 play loudly

Unit 6 Lesson 4

Pupil's Book

CD3 TRACK 14

PB page 64 Activity 2

***Warm up!* song**

Warm up.
Warm up your body.
Warm up.
Are you ready?
Warm up.
Warm up your body.
One, two. One, two, three.

Let's move slowly.
Stretch your arms.
Slowly, slowly, slowly.
Let's move slowly.
Bend your knees.
Slowly, slowly, slowly.

Warm up.
Warm up your body.
Warm up.
Are you ready?
Warm up.
Warm up your body.
One, two. One, two, three.

Let's move quickly.
Wiggle your fingers.
Quickly, quickly, quickly.
Let's move quickly.
Shake your body.
Quickly, quickly, quickly.

Warm up.
Warm up your body.
Warm up.
Are you ready?
Warm up.
Warm up your body.
One, two. One, two, three.

Unit 6 Lesson 4

Pupil's Book

CD3 TRACK 15

PB page 64 Activity 3

I rollerblade slowly.
You swim quickly.
He plays chess well.

Unit 6 Lesson 5

Pupil's Book

CD3 TRACK 16

PB page 65 Activity 1

black – monkey – kayaks – quickly – lake
The black monkey kayaks quickly on the lake.
The black monkey kayaks quickly on the lake.
The black monkey kayaks quickly on the lake.

Unit 6 Lesson 5

Pupil's Book

CD3 TRACK 17

PB page 65 Activity 2

Boy: Hello. I'm doing a sports questionnaire. Can I ask you some questions, please?
Girl: Yes, of course.
Boy: Thanks. What's your name?
Girl: It's Anna Jones.
Boy: How do you spell Jones?
Girl: J-O-N-E-S.
Boy: And how old are you?
Girl: I'm nine.
Boy: What's your favourite sport, Anna?
Girl: It's volleyball. I love it!
Boy: Me too! How often do you do sport?
Girl: Well, I play volleyball on Monday and Wednesday. And I go swimming every Saturday. So … three times a week.
Boy: That's great. How do you ride a bike? Do you ride it well or badly?
Girl: I ride a bike well.
Boy: And how do you swim? Do you swim fast or slowly?
Girl: I swim fast because I go swimming every week.
Boy: Oh yes, of course. What about tennis? Do you play tennis well or badly?
Girl: I play it well.
Boy: And how do you skate. Do you skate quickly or slowly?
Girl: I skate quickly.
Boy: Wow! You are sporty!
Girl: Yes, I am.

Unit 6 Lesson 6

Pupil's Book

CD3 TRACK 18

PB page 66 Activity 2

95 Sun Road
Newtown
NT1 8BN
The 15th March
Dear Grandma and Grandad,
How are you? I'm very happy because I'm going to go to a sports camp with my friends tomorrow. The camp is in the middle of a beautiful forest and I can do sport all day. There are lots of exciting sports to try. First, I'm going to play volleyball because that's my favourite sport. Next, I'm going to go kayaking. The lessons are on a lake and I need to wear a life jacket and a helmet. Finally, I'm going to go mountain biking in the forest with my friends. I can't wait!
See you after the camp.
Love, Robert xxx

Unit 6 Lesson 7

Pupil's Book

CD3 TRACK 19

PB page 67 Activity 2

37 Silver Street
London
NW1 8AP
The 18th March
Dear Grandma,
How are you? I'm very excited because I'm going to go to an adventure camp on Friday. It's in the mountains and there are lots of great activities for me to try.
First, I'm going to go horse riding because I love horses and I can ride very well. Next, I'm going to do archery. It looks fun! Finally, I'm going to go windsurfing on the lake. I need to wear a wetsuit because the water is cold. I'm not going to go rock climbing because it's very scary.
See you soon,
Love, Laura xxx

Audioscript

Unit 6 Lesson 8

Pupil's Book

CD3 TRACK 20

PB page 68 Activity 2

Extreme sports

New Zealand has got some very exciting sports, but you must be very brave!

Bungee Jumping
In this sport, you put an elastic rope around your ankles. Then you jump from a very high bridge. You fall very quickly through the air and you bounce up and down. It's amazing!

Rafting
Do you like adventure? In this sport, you ride down a fast river on a raft. You need lots of energy and you get very wet, but it's good fun!

Zorbing
This is the newest extreme sport in New Zealand. In this sport, you get inside a big, plastic ball and you roll down a hill or on water. Some balls move at 50 km an hour. That's the same as a car!

Sand surfing
If you like travelling fast, sand surfing is the sport for you. You can sit, stand or lie down on a surfboard. It's fantastic!

Unit 6 Lesson 8

Activity Book

CD3 TRACK 21

AB page 65 Activity 1

1
Boy: What's your favourite extreme sport, Anne?
Girl: It's bungee jumping.
Boy: And what equipment do you need?
Girl: You need a helmet, a harness and a special rope.

2
Girl: What about you, Tony? What's your favourite extreme sport?
Boy: It's zorbing.
Girl: Do you need any special equipment?
Boy: Oh yes, you do. You need to wear a helmet and a harness when you do this sport.

3
Boy: Do you like rafting, Anne?
Girl: Yes, I do.
Boy: Do you need any special equipment?
Girl: Yes, you do. You need a wetsuit and a helmet. You need a paddle and a life jacket, too.

4
Girl: Do you like sand surfing?
Boy: Yes, I do. I think it's exciting.
Girl: What equipment do you need?
Boy: You need a surfboard and a helmet. You need lots of energy, too.

Unit 6 Video and 21st Century Skills

Activity Book

CD3 TRACK 22

AB page 67 Activity 1

1
You need to wear sun cream.
2
You need to warm up.
3
You need to drink plenty of water.
4
You need to follow the rules.
5
You need to wear knee pads.
6
You need to wear goggles.

Unit 6 Video and 21st Century Skills

Activity Book

CD3 TRACK 23

AB page 67 Activity 2

Monitor: Hello. Welcome to the skateboarding class.
Girl and boy: Thank you.
Monitor: Before we begin, let's remember the safety rules.
Girl: OK
Monitor: First, you must always wear a helmet. It protects your head if you fall down. Have you got helmets?
Boy: Yes.
Girl: Here's my helmet.
Monitor: Great! It's also a good idea to wear gloves. Gloves protect your hands. And pads protect your elbows and your knees.
Boy: Oh dear! I've got some gloves, but I haven't got any pads.
Monitor: Don't worry. I've got some extra pads. Here you are.
Boy: Thank you. Can we skate on the road?
Monitor: No, you can't skate on the road. It's dangerous. There are lots of cars and bikes.
Boy: OK.
Monitor: And never ride your skateboard behind a bike. It looks fun, but it's easy to have an accident.
Girl: You're right.
Monitor: Great. Now, let's begin the class.

My project 2 Lesson 1

Pupil's Book

CD3 TRACK 24

PB page 70 Activity 3

Five man-made things on the island are:
a lighthouse, a pyramid, a port, a village and a bridge.
Five natural things in the middle of the island are:
a volcano, a waterfall, a lake, a river and a jungle.
Five natural things on the coast are:
a cave, cliffs, a bay, a beach and rocks.

Unit 7 Lesson 1

Pupil's Book

CD3 TRACK 25

PB page 72 Activity 2

armchair, fridge, mirror, wardrobe, sink, painting, bookcase, sofa, mat, bath, cooker, cupboard

Unit 7 Lesson 1

Pupil's Book

CD3 TRACK 26

PB page 72 Activity 3

***There's a mystery* song**

There's a mystery,
A mystery to solve.
Whose are these tracks?
And where do they go?

They're on the fridge
And in front of the cooker.
They're near the cupboard
And near the mirror.

There's a mystery,
A mystery to solve.
Whose are these tracks?
And where do they go?

They're on the sofa
And behind the armchair.
They're on the bookcase
And on the stairs.

There's a mystery,
A mystery to solve.
Whose are these tracks?
And where do they go?

Unit 7 Lesson 1

Pupil's Book

CD3 TRACK 27

PB page 72 Activity 3

Karaoke version: *There's a mystery* song

Unit 7 Lesson 2

Pupil's Book

CD3 TRACK 28

PB page 73 Activity 1

Ravi: Whose are these tracks, Lily?
Lily: They aren't mine. I wasn't here this morning.
Ravi: What about Josh?
Lily: He was at the swimming pool with me.
Ravi: And what about your parents?
Lily: They weren't here. They were at the library.
Ravi: Mmm … it's a mystery.
Lily: No, it isn't. Look!
Ravi: Oh no! It's my dog chasing a bird. What a mess!

Unit 7 Lesson 2

Pupil's Book

CD3 TRACK 29

PB page 73 Activity 3

I was at home yesterday afternoon.
We weren't at school last night.
They were at the swimming pool yesterday morning.

Unit 7 Lesson 3

Pupil's Book

CD3 TRACK 30

PB page 74 Activity 2

The missing watch

Frame 1
Narrator: Mum is worried. Her watch is missing.
Mum: I can't find my watch. It was in the living room, but it isn't there now.
Lily: Don't worry, Mum. We can help you.

Frame 2
Narrator: The children look for Mum's watch.
Lily: It's no good. It isn't here.
Ravi: We've got a real mystery now.
Josh: Let's look for clues.

Frame 3
Narrator: Josh finds a clue in Lily's bedroom.
Josh: There's a black feather under the wardrobe.
Ravi: That magpie has got black feathers.
Lily: And it's got my bracelet. Look!

Frame 4
Narrator: The children follow the magpie.
Josh: The magpie is flying to the island.
Lily: Can you take us to the island, Dad?
Dad: Yes, of course. Jump in!

Frame 5
Narrator: Dad takes the children to the island in his boat.
Josh: Can you see the magpie now, Lily?
Lily: Yes, I can. It's flying into the castle.
Ravi: Let's go! We must find its nest.

Frame 6
Narrator: The children find the magpie's nest.
Ravi: Wow! Look at all the shiny things in the nest.
Lily: Here's my bracelet and Mum's watch!

Frame 7
Narrator: The children have an idea.
Ravi: Let's put this sweet wrapper in the nest.
Josh: And these shiny marbles.
Lily: Now we can take our things.

Frame 8
Narrator: Lily gives Mum her watch.
Mum: My watch! Where was it?
Lily: It was in a magpie's nest in the castle.
Mum: That's incredible! Good work, detectives.

Unit 7 Lesson 3

Activity Book

CD3 TRACK 31

AB page 72 Activity 2

Our Adventure Blog by Lily, Josh and Ravi
In this adventure, Mum can't find her watch. We look for clues and Josh finds a feather under the wardrobe. Then Ravi sees a magpie and it's got Lily's bracelet. The magpie flies to the island and Dad takes us there in his boat. We find the magpie's nest in the castle. Mum's watch and Lily's bracelet are in the nest. We put a sweet wrapper and some shiny marbles in the nest. Then we take the watch and the bracelet home. Mum is very surprised and happy.

Unit 7 Lesson 4

Pupil's Book

CD3 TRACK 32

PB page 76 Activity 1

1 earrings
2 bracelet
3 sunglasses
4 watch
5 keys
6 umbrella

Unit 7 Lesson 4

Pupil's Book

CD3 TRACK 33

PB page 76 Activity 2

The memory chant

M-E-M-O-R-Y. Memory.
What do you remember?

Was the watch in the box?
Yes, it was.

Was the bracelet in the box?
No, it wasn't.

Were the keys on the floor?
Yes, they were.

Were the earrings on the floor?
No, they weren't.

M-E-M-O-R-Y. Memory.
What do you remember?

Unit 7 Lesson 4

Pupil's Book

CD3 TRACK 34

PB page 76 Activity 3

Was the bracelet under the armchair?
Was the watch in the cupboard?
Were the earrings on the table?

Unit 7 Lesson 5

Pupil's Book

CD3 TRACK 35

PB page 77 Activity 1

Ron – robber – writes – red – wrapper
Ron the robber writes on the red wrapper.
Ron the robber writes on the red wrapper.
Ron the robber writes on the red wrapper.

Unit 7 Lesson 5

Pupil's Book

CD3 TRACK 36

PB page 77 Activity 2

Girl: Have you got a good memory, Charlie?
Boy: Yes. I've got an excellent memory.
Girl: Really? Let's play a memory game to see if that's true.
Boy: OK.
Girl: Look at this picture from yesterday for thirty seconds. … Ready?
Boy: Yes.
Girl: OK. Give me the picture … Thank you … I've got five questions. Here's question 1: Where were the sunglasses yesterday?
Boy: They were on the table.
Girl: Here's question number two: Where was the mobile phone yesterday?
Boy: It was behind the sofa.

Audioscript

Girl: Question number three: Where was the magazine yesterday?
Boy: Err … It was under the cupboard.
Girl: Question number four: Where was the book yesterday?
Boy: It was under the mat?
Girl: And the last question: Where were the earrings yesterday?
Boy: Ah ha! I know this. They were in front of the TV.
Girl: Oh dear, Charlie. You haven't got an excellent memory. Only [beep] answers are correct!

Unit 7 Lesson 6

Pupil's Book

CD3 TRACK 37

PB page 78 Activity 3

The missing necklace: Scene 1
Narrator: Lady Muck's necklace is missing. A police officer arrives to investigate.
Police officer: Good afternoon, Madam. What's the problem?
Lady Muck: My necklace isn't here.
Police officer: What kind of necklace is it?
Lady Muck: It's a diamond necklace.
Police officer: … a diamond necklace. And where was it?
Lady Muck: It was on that table.
Narrator: Suddenly, Lady Muck sees something behind the sofa.
Lady Muck: There's someone behind the sofa.
Police officer: You're right. Hands up!
Robber: It's time for me to go.
Police officer: Come back!
Robber: Ha, ha, ha! You can't catch me.

Unit 7 Lesson 7

Pupil's Book

CD3 TRACK 38

PB page 79 Activity 1

The missing necklace: Scene 2
Narrator: Two police officers are looking for the robber. They're in Lady Muck's garden.

Unit 7 Lesson 7

Pupil's Book

CD3 TRACK 39

PB page 79 Activity 2

Police officer 1: Can you see the robber?
Police officer 2: No, I can't.
Police officer 1: Shh! What's that noise?
Police officer 2: I don't know. Is it a fox?
Police officer 1: Don't be silly.
Police officer 2: I can hear the noise again. Is it a wolf?
Police officer 1: No, it isn't.
Police officer 2: Look! The bush over there is moving.
Police officer 1: Shh! Got you!
Police officer 2: It isn't a fox or a wolf. It's the robber!
Police officer 1: And she's got the diamond necklace.

Unit 7 Lesson 8

Pupil's Book

CD3 TRACK 40

PB page 80 Activity 2

Living in an underground town
Hi, everyone. My name's Joey and I live in a small town called Coober Pedy in Australia. It's in the middle of a desert, so there isn't a lot of rain and it's very hot in the summer. Do you know that many people build their houses under the ground in my town? Living underground is cooler than living above ground. My house is underground. It's got three bedrooms, a living room, a kitchen and a bathroom.
I love my bedroom. It hasn't got a window, but it's got beautiful stone walls and a colourful blanket on the bed. There are pictures of my favourite sports stars on the walls, too.
There's lots to do in my town. You can visit an underground museum or go shopping at the underground shops. One of my favourite activities is golf. I play above ground on the sand. I can't play in the day because it's too hot, so I play at night. The balls are yellow so that you can see them in the dark. It's fantastic!

Unit 7 Lesson 8

Activity Book

CD3 TRACK 41

AB page 77 Activity 1

1 Who does Joey live with?
Girl: Hi, Joey. Who do you live with in your underground house?
Boy: I live with my mum, my dad and my sister.
Girl: Is your sister older or younger than you?
Boy: She's older than me. She's fifteen.
2 Which sport does Joey do at the weekend?
Girl: Do you like doing sport, Joey?
Boy: Yes, I do. My favourite sport is swimming.
Girl: Do you go swimming at the weekend?
Boy: No, I don't. I usually play golf at the weekend.
3 Which picture is on Joey's bedroom wall?
Girl: Have you got any pictures on your bedroom wall?
Boy: Yes, I have.
Girl: Which is your favourite picture?
Boy: It's a picture of a rugby player. He's running and throwing the ball.
4 What has Joey got in his bedroom?
Girl: Have you got a computer, Joey?
Boy: Yes, I have.
Girl: Is it in your bedroom?
Boy: No, it isn't. But I've got a CD player in my bedroom. It's fantastic.

Unit 7 Video and 21st Century Skills

Activity Book

CD3 TRACK 42

AB page 79 Activity 1

1
Where were the flowers?
2
What colour was the mat?
3
Where was the dog?
4
What colour were the sunglasses?
5
Was the painting next to the door?
6
Were the flowers on the table?

Unit 7 Video and 21st Century Skills

Activity Book

CD3 TRACK 43

AB page 79 Activity 2

Dad: What's the matter, Lucy?
Girl: I can't remember my homework.
Dad: You need to pay attention in class, Lucy. Look at this webpage. Here are five tips to help you.
Girl: Oh, OK. What's number 1?
Dad: Tip number one is: listen carefully to instructions.
Girl: That's important. What's number two?
Dad: Tip number two is: repeat the important information you hear. You can repeat it in your head.
Girl: What else?
Dad: Tip number three is: look at the person speaking. Look at their face. It helps you understand and remember.
Girl: Ah, OK. What's number four?
Dad: Tip number four is: ask questions. It's important to ask questions if you don't understand.

Girl: I always ask questions! What's the last tip?
Dad: Play memory games and do puzzles. They help you pay attention and remember.
Girl: They're great tips. And now I remember my homework, too. Thanks, dad.

Unit 8 Lesson 1

Pupil's Book

CD3 TRACK 44

PB page 82 Activity 2

cartoon, quiz show, film, music programme, the news, talk show, documentary, the weather, game show, comedy programme, sports programme, advert

Unit 8 Lesson 1

Pupil's Book

CD3 TRACK 45

PB page 82 Activity 3

The TV song

I like watching game shows.
I love watching cartoons.
I don't like watching talk shows.
What about you?
What do you like watching
In the afternoon?
What about you?

I like watching the news.
I love watching cartoons.
I don't like watching quiz shows.
What about you?
What do you like watching
In the afternoon?
What about you?

Unit 8 Lesson 1

Pupil's Book

CD3 TRACK 46

PB page 82 Activity 3

Karaoke version: *The TV song*

Unit 8 Lesson 2

Pupil's Book

CD3 TRACK 47

PB page 83 Activity 1

Ravi: Did you watch TV yesterday, Josh?
Josh: Yes, I did.
Ravi: What did you watch?
Josh: Can you guess?
Ravi: Hmm … did you watch a sports programme?
Josh: No, I didn't.
Ravi: Did you watch a cartoon?
Josh: Yes, I did.
Ravi: I know! Did you watch *Super snake*?
Josh: Yes, I did. It's my favourite programme.

Unit 8 Lesson 2

Pupil's Book

CD3 TRACK 48

PB page 83 Activity 3

Did she watch a comedy programme last week?
Did you watch the news yesterday?
Did we watch a game show last week?

Unit 8 Lesson 3

Pupil's Book

CD3 TRACK 49

PB page 84 Activity 2

Great teamwork!

Frame 1
Narrator: Ravi, Josh and Lily are going to be on a TV game show.
Lily: This is so exciting! *Teamwork* is my favourite TV programme.
Josh: What's the first game?
Ravi: The teams work together to carry water through some rings.

Frame 2
Narrator: The first game starts and Josh wants to win.
Lily: Slow down, Josh!
Josh: But the other team are faster.
Ravi: It doesn't matter. We need to work together.

Frame 3
Narrator: The blue team were faster, but the red team have got more water.
Man: The red team are the winners! You get ten points.
Josh, Lily and Ravi: Hooray!

Frame 4
Narrator: Next, the teams must carry a flag up the slide.
Ravi: Wait for us, Josh. We need to climb together.
Josh: Oh no! The slide is slippery. I'm falling!

Frame 5
Narrator: The blue team win. Now they've got ten points, too.
Josh: I'm sorry.
Lily: It doesn't matter, Josh. There's one more game.

Frame 6
Narrator: In the final game, each team must jump over a moving pole.
Ravi: Remember. We must jump together.
Josh and Lily: OK!

Frame 7
Narrator: The children hold hands.
Lily: Here comes the pole.
Ravi: One, two, three, jump!
Josh: We're the winners!

Frame 8
Narrator: One hour later …
Mum: What great prizes! How did you win?
Josh: Teamwork! First, we carried some water through rings.
Ravi: Then we all jumped together. It was fantastic!

Unit 8 Lesson 3

Activity Book

CD4 TRACK 01

AB page 82 Activity 2

Our Adventure Blog by Lily, Josh and Ravi
In this adventure, we appear on a TV programme called *Teamwork*. We're the red team and we wear red T-shirts and caps. In the first game, we carry some water through some rings and we win ten points. In the second game, we must carry a flag up a slide, but Josh falls. The blue team wins ten points. In the last game, we must jump over a pole together. We work together and we win the competition. We get lots of prizes. It's a fantastic adventure!

Unit 8 Lesson 4

Pupil's Book

CD4 TRACK 02

PB page 86 Activity 1

1 play cards
2 climb a tree
3 skip
4 phone a friend
5 paint a picture
6 plant seeds

Unit 8 Lesson 4

Pupil's Book

CD4 TRACK 03

PB page 86 Activity 2

***Did you watch TV?* song**

Did you watch TV?
Did you watch it yesterday?
Did you watch TV
Or did you play?

I didn't watch TV.
I climbed a tree in the afternoon.
I skipped in the evening.
Yesterday was cool!

Audioscript

Did you watch TV?
Did you watch it yesterday?
Did you watch TV
Or did you play?

I didn't watch TV.
I painted a picture in the afternoon.
I planted seeds in the evening.
Yesterday was cool!

Did you watch TV?
Did you watch it yesterday?
Did you watch TV
Or did you play?

I didn't watch TV.
I phoned a friend in the afternoon.
I played cards in the evening.
Yesterday was cool!

Unit 8 Lesson 4

Pupil's Book

CD4 TRACK 04

PB page 86 Activity 3

She planted seeds last week.
We didn't play cards yesterday.
They painted a picture last night.

Unit 8 Lesson 5

Pupil's Book

CD4 TRACK 05

PB page 87 Activity 1

Dolphin – fished – elephant – phoned – friend
The dolphin fished and the elephant phoned a friend.
The dolphin fished and the elephant phoned a friend.
The dolphin fished and the elephant phoned a friend.

Unit 8 Lesson 5

Pupil's Book

CD4 TRACK 06

PB page 87 Activity 2

Boy: Hi, Emma. Did you see Jane yesterday?
Girl: No, I didn't. She was very busy.
Boy: What did she do in the morning?
Girl: She worked in the garden in the morning. She planted seeds. Then in the afternoon she climbed a tree.
Boy: That was active! What did she do in the evening?
Girl: She painted a picture in the evening.
Boy: Really? What did she do last night?
Girl: She listened to music.
Boy: What a cool day! What about David? Did you see him yesterday?
Girl: Yes, in the evening. We played video games together. Then last night, we listened to music and we danced. It was fun!
Boy: What did David do in the morning?
Girl: He played the guitar in the morning. Then, in the afternoon, he played in the garden and he climbed a tree.

Unit 8 Lesson 6

Pupil's Book

CD4 TRACK 07

PB page 88 Activity 2

TV Reviews
What's on TV this week? Read these children's reviews to find out.
Girl: Song Stars
This music programme is about some singers who want to be famous. They must learn a new song every week and sing it in front of lots of people. I love this programme because the singers are really good. It's also exciting when the judges choose the best singer. *Song Stars* is on Channel 1 on Thursday evening and it begins at seven o'clock.
Boy: Deep Sea Monsters
This documentary is about strange and dangerous sea animals. There are two scientists and they travel to the bottom of the sea in a submarine. I love the programme because you learn lots of interesting information. It's also scary because the scientists get very close to the animals. *Deep Sea Monsters* is on Channel 2 on Sunday afternoon and it begins at five o'clock.
Girl: Cody and Friends
This comedy programme is about a group of friends who write a school newspaper. The friends investigate things that happen in their school and always get into trouble. I don't think it's a very good programme. It's sometimes funny, but the ending is never a surprise. *Cody and Friends* is on Channel 3 every afternoon at four o'clock.

Unit 8 Lesson 7

Pupil's Book

CD4 TRACK 08

PB page 89 Activity 2

Dan the Detective Dog
This cartoon is about a clever dog that lives with two boys. The boys think the dog is a normal pet, but it's really a detective. The dog has lots of adventures and always saves the world at the last minute. I love the programme because it's funny and exciting. *Dan the Detective Dog* is on Channel 3 every afternoon at half past five.

Unit 8 Lesson 8

Pupil's Book

CD4 TRACK 09

PB page 90 Activity 2

Do you want to visit an interesting and exciting place?
Welcome to Hollywood
Hollywood is part of a big city in the USA called Los Angeles. The city is on the coast, but there are lots of hills, too. You can visit the famous Hollywood sign. It's incredible. Each letter is 14 metres tall. That's taller than two houses!
Hollywood is famous for the Oscars. The Oscars are golden prizes for the best film of the year, as well as for best acting, music and scripts. Do you want to feel like a star? You can walk on the famous Oscars red carpet.
If you want to see how people make films, you can visit a real studio. You can see some amazing special effects there, for example an explosion or a car chase. Be prepared for lots of surprises!
Hollywood Boulevard is in the centre of the city. On the floor, there are more than 2,000 stars. Each star has got the name of a famous actor or actress inside it. Some of the stars have got handprints, too. Can you find the star for your favourite actor?

Unit 8 Lesson 8

Activity Book

CD4 TRACK 10

AB page 87 Activity 1

Girl: Do you want to go to the cinema, Peter?
Boy: Yes, please. Which film is on?
Girl: Action Heroes.
Boy: Brilliant! I love action films.
Girl: It's on at the Zoom cinema.
Boy: Zoom. How do you spell that?
Girl: Z-O-O-M.
Boy: And when do you want to go?
Girl: What about Saturday?
Boy: Saturday. That's a good idea. What time does the film begin?
Girl: It begins at five o'clock.
Boy: And what time does it finish?
Girl: It finishes at half past six.
Boy: Great! Thanks, Emma. See you on Saturday.
Girl: Bye.
Boy: Bye.

Unit 8 Video and 21st Century Skills

Activity Book

CD4 TRACK 11

AB page 89 Activity 1

1
The camera operator films the actors and the presenters.
2
The presenter reads the news.
3
The director gives instructions to the presenter and the camerawoman.
4
The editor uses a computer to cut and move pieces of the video.

Unit 8 Video and 21st Century Skills

Activity Book

CD4 TRACK 12

AB page 89 Activity 2

Girl: Do you want to make a video, Sam? My mum says we can use this video camera.
Boy: OK. That's fun!
Girl: I've got some tips here. Let's read them first.
Boy: Good idea. What's tip number one?
Girl: Tip number 1 is: you need a lot of light. It's not a good idea to film at night.
Boy: That's true. What's number 2?
Girl: Tip number 2 is: the light must be behind the camera.
Boy: OK …
Girl: And tip number 3 is: don't make a video in a noisy place. You need to hear the actors or the presenters talk.
Boy: What's tip number 4?
Girl: Tip number 4 is: don't make a very long video.
Boy: Yes … Long videos are boring.
Girl: And tip number 5 is: look at the camera and smile!
Boy: Ha ha … That's easy. Let's plan the video now.

Unit 9 Lesson 1

Pupil's Book

CD4 TRACK 13

PB page 92 Activity 2

band, toffee apple, parade, big wheel, fireworks, merry-go-round, ghost train, bumper cars, candyfloss, roller coaster, clown, costume

Unit 9 Lesson 1

Pupil's Book

CD4 TRACK 14

PB page 92 Activity 3

***There's a festival* song**

Come on,
Come on, everyone.
There's a festival today.
Let's have fun!

Let's eat a toffee apple
And watch the clowns.
Let's ride on the roller coaster,
Zoom up and down.

Let's listen to the band
And dance to the sound.
Let's ride on the merry-go-round,
Turn round and round.

Let's watch the parade
And dance to the beat.
Let's ride on the ghost train
And scream!

Come on,
Come on, everyone.
There's a festival today.
Let's have fun!

Unit 9 Lesson 1

Pupil's Book

CD4 TRACK 15

PB page 92 Activity 3

Karaoke version: *There's a festival* song

Unit 9 Lesson 2

Pupil's Book

CD4 TRACK 16

PB page 93 Activity 1

Ravi: What did you do yesterday, Lily?
Lily: I went to the festival with Josh.
Ravi: Really? What did you do there?
Lily: I rode on the roller coaster and on the bumper cars.
Ravi: Cool! What did you eat and drink?
Lily: I ate some candyfloss and I drank some lemonade.
Ravi: Did you wear a costume?
Lily: No, I didn't, but I saw lots of clowns. They were brilliant!

Unit 9 Lesson 2

Pupil's Book

CD4 TRACK 17

PB page 93 Activity 3

What did she drink?
What did we eat?
What did they see?

Unit 9 Lesson 3

Pupil's Book

CD4 TRACK 18

PB page 94 Activity 2

A surprise party

Frame 1
Narrator: Yesterday was Lily's birthday.
Ravi: Hi, Josh. Are you ready for Lily's surprise birthday party?
Josh: No, we aren't. And Lily arrives home at four o'clock.
Ravi: That's in one hour!

Frame 2
Narrator: Ravi helped Josh and Dad get ready for Lily's party.
Josh: We made a cake. Can you decorate it, please?
Ravi: Mmm … chocolate. My favourite!

Frame 3
Narrator: Josh painted a message for Lily.
Josh: H-A-P-P …

Frame 4
Narrator: Dad made some sandwiches.
Dad: Oh dear. Look at the time! It's twenty-five to four.

Frame 5
Narrator: Dad, Josh and Ravi carried the things for Lily's party outside.
Dad: Hurry up, Josh. It's ten to four.
Josh: I'm coming, Dad.
Ravi: Mind the step, Josh!

Frame 6
Narrator: Josh fell down. What a mess!
Ravi: Are you OK, Josh?
Josh: Yes, I am. But look at our clothes and look at the cake!

Frame 7
Narrator: A few minutes later, Lily arrived. She was very surprised.
Josh and Ravi: Happy Birthday, Lily!
Lily: A birthday party for me? What an amazing surprise!

Frame 8
Narrator: Lily saw Josh and Ravi's clothes.
Lily: You're a painter and you're a cook. You look great!
Josh: Umm … yes. It's a fancy dress party, Lily.

Unit 9 Lesson 3

Pupil's Book

CD4 TRACK 19

AB page 92 Activity 2

Our Adventure Blog by Lily, Josh and Ravi
In this adventure, Josh, Ravi and Dad prepared a surprise birthday party for Lily. They didn't have a lot of time so they worked quickly. Ravi decorated a cake, Josh painted a message and Dad made some sandwiches. The party was outside the lighthouse and Josh fell down. He had a lot of paint on his clothes and a paintbrush was in the cake. Lily arrived and she was very excited with her surprise party. She said that Ravi was a cook and that Josh was a painter. It was very funny.

Audioscript

Unit 9 Lesson 4

Pupil's Book

CD4 TRACK 20

PB page 96 Activity 1

1 ten past three
2 twenty past one
3 twenty-five past eleven
4 twenty-five to four
5 ten to eight
6 five to twelve

Unit 9 Lesson 4

Pupil's Book

CD4 TRACK 21

PB page 96 Activity 2

***Tick-tock* song**

Tick-tock, tick-tock.
Yesterday, we didn't stop.

At five past three,
At ten past three,
At a quarter past three,
At twenty past three,
At twenty-five past three.

Tick-tock, tick-tock.
Yesterday, we raced the clock.

At twenty-five to four,
At twenty to four,
At a quarter to four,
At ten to four,
At five to four.
Phew!

Unit 9 Lesson 4

Pupil's Book

CD4 TRACK 22

PB page 96 Activity 3

What time did she play cards yesterday?
What time did we have lunch yesterday?
What time did you go to bed yesterday?

Unit 9 Lesson 5

Pupil's Book

CD4 TRACK 23

PB page 97 Activity 1

Cecil – snake – sang – danced – city – celebration
Cecil the snake sang and danced at the city celebration.
Cecil the snake sang and danced at the city celebration.
Cecil the snake sang and danced at the city celebration.

Unit 9 Lesson 5

Pupil's Book

CD4 TRACK 24

PB page 97 Activity 2

Girl: Hey, Paul. Did you go to the festival yesterday?
Boy: Yes, I did. It was fantastic.
Girl: What time did you arrive at the festival?
Boy: I arrived at ten past six.
Girl: Did you ride on the ghost train?
Boy: Yes, I did. It was brilliant!
Girl: What time did you ride on the ghost train?
Boy: I rode on the ghost train at quarter past six.
Girl: Did you eat any candyfloss?
Boy: Yes, I did. I ate some candyfloss at five to seven.
Girl: What did you do after that?
Boy: I rode on the roller coaster.
Girl: What time did you ride on the roller coaster?
Boy: I rode on it at ten to eight.
Girl: Was it high?
Boy: Yes, it was. It was very high and very fast!
Girl: What did you do next?
Boy: I watched the fireworks. I watched them at quarter past eight. They were great.
Girl: What time did you go home?
Boy: I went home at ten o'clock. It was a great festival!

Unit 9 Lesson 6

Pupil's Book

CD4 TRACK 25

PB page 98 Activity 3

Hi Mary,
How are you? Thanks for your last email. Do you know that we celebrate a festival called May Day in my town? We celebrate it every year on the first Monday of May.
I did lots of things last May Day. In the morning, I watched some Morris dancers. The dancers wore special clothes and they painted their faces black. Then I danced around a maypole with my friends. We had long ribbons in our hands when we danced.
In the afternoon, I went to the funfair. I rode on the big wheel and on the ghost train, but I didn't ride on the roller coaster. In the evening, I went to a concert in the park and I danced to the music. I watched some fireworks at the end of the evening, too. They were fantastic!
Do you celebrate a festival in your town? Tell me about it.
Write soon!
Jodie

Unit 9 Lesson 7

Pupil's Book

CD4 TRACK 26

PB page 99 Activity 2

Hello Jodie,
Thanks for your email. I enjoyed reading about your May Day festival.
I live in Scotland and we celebrate a festival called Burns Night. Robert Burns was a famous poet and we celebrate his birthday on 25th January every year.
Last Burns Night was fantastic. In the evening, I had a big dinner and I ate a traditional dish called haggis. Haggis is a sheep's stomach with meat inside. It sounds horrible, but it's delicious! After dinner, I listened to people reading poems by Robert Burns. Then I sang songs, but I didn't dance.
Would you like to go to this festival?
Bye for now,
Mary

Unit 9 Lesson 8

Pupil's Book

CD4 TRACK 27

PB page 100 Activity 2

Canada Day
The first of July is Canada Day. It's when we celebrate the country's birthday. There are lots of exciting activities for all the family.
Fun for children
There are lots of games and activities for children. The most popular activity is the Pony Hop Race. You need lots of energy for this activity and there's a prize for the winner at the end.
Enjoy the parade
The parade is a celebration of everyone in the community. There are marching bands and dancers. The traditional Canadian police are in the parade, too. They're called the Mounties. They wear red jackets and big hats. In the past, they rode horses, but now they use cars, motorbikes and helicopters.
Watch the lumberjack show
Lumberjacks work in the forests of Canada. In this amazing show, you can see their traditional skills. They climb up and down tall trees and cut very big pieces of wood. The most exciting part of the show is the log rolling. In this activity, two lumberjacks run on a log which is in the water. The winner is the lumberjack who doesn't fall into the water.

Unit 9 Lesson 8

Activity Book

CD4 TRACK 28

AB page 97 Activity 1

1 What did Peter watch on Canada Day?
Girl: Hi, Peter. Did you enjoy the Canada Day festival?

Boy: Yes, I did.
Girl: What did you do?
Boy: I watched the lumberjack show.
Girl: Was it good?
Boy: Yes, it was. A lumberjack cut a big piece of wood in only fifteen seconds.
Girl: That's amazing.
2 Which attraction did Sally ride on?
Boy: Did you go to the funfair, Sally?
Girl: Yes, I did.
Boy: Did you ride on the ghost train?
Girl: No, I didn't. I rode on the roller coaster.
Boy: Was it exciting?
Girl: Yes, of course.
3 What did Jane see in the parade?
Boy: Did you watch the Canada Day parade yesterday, Jane?
Girl: Yes, I did. It was great.
Boy: What did you see?
Girl: I saw some traditional Canadian police.
Boy: Did they ride motorbikes?
Girl: No, they didn't. They rode horses. It was fantastic.
4 What was Joey's favourite activity?
Girl: What was your favourite activity at the Canada Day festival, Joey?
Boy: Hmm … that's difficult. I liked the log rolling and the Pony Hop Race. But, I think the log rolling was my favourite.
Girl: Are you sure?
Boy: Yes, it was great.

Unit 9 Video and 21st Century Skills

Activity Book

CD4 TRACK 29

AB page 99 Activity 1

Girl: I want ice cream for one of the snacks.
Boy: That's a good idea. Ice cream is perfect in the summer.
Girl: What about candyfloss?
Boy: I'm sorry. I don't like candyfloss.
Girl: OK. Let's choose another snack.

Unit 9 Video and 21st Century Skills

Activity Book

CD4 TRACK 30

AB page 99 Activity 2

Teacher: Good morning class. It's the school summer fete soon and we need to make some decisions. Here are some tips to help you. Can you read them, Peter?
Boy: OK. Tip number one is: understand what you need to do.
Teacher: If you don't understand what you need to do, ask a question.
Boy: Tip number 2 is: listen to everyone's ideas.
Teacher: Listening to everyone's ideas is very important!
Boy: And tip number 3 is take turns to speak.
Teacher: Yes, don't speak at the same time.
Boy: Now tip number 4: don't be angry if people don't like your ideas.
Teacher: No shouting in this classroom, please.
Boy: And the last tip is: Choose the best idea.
Teacher: That's right. Thank you, Peter. OK, everyone: get into your groups …

My project 3 Lesson 1

Pupil's Book

CD4 TRACK 31

PB page 102 Activity 3

Five types of transport are: a bus, a bike, a boat, a taxi, the Underground.
Four parks are: Regent's Park, Hyde Park, Green Park, Saint James's Park
Four famous buildings are: The Houses of Parliament, Big Ben, Saint Paul's Cathedral, the Tower of London.

Festivals: Chinese New Year

Pupil's Book

CD4 TRACK 32

PB page 104 Activity 2

1
At Chinese New Year, families have a special meal together. There are always lots of traditional dishes. People eat soup, fish, green vegetables and long noodles. Do you know that it's bad luck to cut the noodles with a knife? People use chopsticks to eat them.
2
Children receive special envelopes from their family at Chinese New Year. The envelopes have got money inside them. The envelopes are red because it's a lucky colour. They often have drawings of lucky animals like lions and dragons, too.
3
People decorate their houses with beautiful lanterns at Chinese New Year. The lanterns are made of paper and there are riddles at the bottom. Riddles are clever questions. Children read the riddles when they visit a house. If they know the answer, they get a present.

Festivals: World Book Day

Pupil's Book

CD4 TRACK 33

PB page 105 Activity 2

I sail the seas with pirates

I sail the seas with pirates
To find a chest of gold.
I follow a white rabbit
Down a long, black hole.
I buy some magic beans
And watch a tree grow.
I hide from a witch
In a land of ice and snow.
I fly a magic carpet
Across the desert sand.
And then I fly a dragon
In a faraway land.
I have a new adventure
Each time I read a book.
So if you like adventures,
Come and have a look!

Unit 1 Cambridge Exams Practice

Pupil's Book

CD4 TRACK 34

PB page 115 Activity 2

Look at these four pictures. One is different. The car is different. A cupboard, a desk and a board are in the classroom. A car isn't in the classroom. It's in the street.

Unit 2 Cambridge Exams Practice

Pupil's Book

CD4 TRACK 35

PB page 116 Activity 3

These pictures show a story. It's called Julia's bedroom. Look at the pictures. Julia is in her bedroom. She's playing with a robot. There are lots of toys on the floor.

Unit 3 Cambridge Exams Practice

Pupil's Book

CD4 TRACK 36

PB page 117 Activity 2

Look at these pictures. They look the same, but some things are different. This boy is eating a burger. But this boy is eating an apple.

Audioscript

Unit 4 Cambridge Exams Practice

Pupil's Book

CD4 TRACK 37

PB page 118 Activity 2

Adult: Let's talk about food. What do you usually have for breakfast?
Pupil: I usually have bread and cheese for breakfast.
Adult: How often do you eat fruit?
Pupil: I eat fruit every day.
Adult: What food don't you like?
Pupil: I don't like onions.
Adult: Tell me about your favourite food.
Pupil: I like ice cream best. I often eat it at the weekend. It's great!

Unit 5 Cambridge Exams Practice

Pupil's Book

CD4 TRACK 38

PB page 119 Activity 2

Look at these pictures. They look the same but some things are different. These boys are playing football, but these boys are playing volleyball.

Unit 7 Cambridge Exams Practice

Pupil's Book

CD4 TRACK 39

PB page 121 Activity 2

Adult: Let's talk about free time. What do you do after school?
Pupil: I do my homework.
Adult: Do you watch TV after school?
Pupil: Yes, I usually watch TV.
Adult: Where were you yesterday evening?
Pupil: I was at home yesterday evening.
Adult: Tell me about your weekend.
Pupil: On Saturday I usually go swimming and on Sunday I visit my grandparents.

Unit 8 Cambridge Exams Practice

Pupil's Book

CD4 TRACK 40

PB page 122 Activity 2

These pictures show a story. It's called Jack and the kitten. Look at the pictures. It's a sunny day. Jack's in the garden and he's playing football.

Unit 8 Cambridge Exams Practice

Pupil's Book

CD4 TRACK 41

PB page 122 Activity 4

It's a sunny day. Jack's in the garden and he's playing football. There's a tree in the garden. Jack sees a kitten in the tree. It can't come down. Jack climbs the tree. He can see his sister in the garden. She's looking for the kitten. Jack gives the kitten to his sister. She's very happy. The kitten is happy, too.

Unit 9 Cambridge Exams Practice

Pupil's Book

CD4 TRACK 42

PB page 123 Activity 2

Look at these four pictures. One is different. The tiger is different. A shark, a whale and a dolphin live in the sea. A tiger doesn't live in the sea. It lives in the jungle.

Unit 1 Cambridge Exams Practice

Activity Book

CD4 TRACK 43

AB page 111 Activity 1

1 How does Sue go to school?
Boy: Do you walk to school, Sue?
Girl: No, I don't. I don't live near the school.
Boy: Oh. Do you go to school by car, then?
Girl: No, I ride my bike. It's good fun.
2 Where is Sue's desk?
Boy: Is your desk next to the window, Sue?
Girl: No, it isn't.
Boy: Where is it?
Girl: It's in front of the board, between Peter's desk and Zoe's desk.
Boy: That's nice.
3 What does Sue do after school?
Boy: Do you do any sport, Sue?
Girl: Yes, I do. I go swimming and I play basketball.
Boy: When do you go swimming?
Girl: I go swimming at the weekend. And I play basketball on Tuesday and Thursday after school.
Boy: That's cool!

Unit 2 Cambridge Exams Practice

Activity Book

CD4 TRACK 44

AB page 112 Activity 1

1
Adult: What do you do at the weekend, Tim?
Boy: I usually go to the park with my friends.
Adult: That's nice. Do you play basketball there?
Boy: No, we play football on the grass.
2
Adult: What about your big sister? What does she do at the weekend?
Boy: Lucy? She likes being outside, too.
Adult: Does she do sport in the park?
Boy: No, she usually goes to the mountains. She walks with her friends there.
3
Adult: Does your mum like doing sport?
Boy: Yes, sometimes. But at the weekend she usually watches a film.
Adult: Does she watch the film on television?
Boy: No, she usually goes to the cinema with my dad.
4
Adult: And what about your grandad?
Boy: He comes to our house on Sunday.
Adult: What do you do together?
Boy: We have lunch and then we play a board game. It's great!
5
Adult: Do you see your friend, Sam, at the weekend?
Boy: No, I don't.
Adult: Why not? Does he do a lot of homework?
Boy: No, he plays football on Saturday and on Sunday. He's brilliant at football!

Unit 3 Cambridge Exams Practice

Activity Book

CD4 TRACK 45

AB page 113 Activity 1

1
Adult: What a lovely kitten!
Boy: Thank you.
Adult: What's her name?
Boy: She's called Katie.
Adult: Katie? How do you spell that?
Boy: K-A-T-I-E.
2
Adult: And what's the matter with Katie.
Boy: She isn't very well.
Adult: Oh dear.
Boy: She isn't eating her food. I think she's got a stomach ache.
3
Adult: Hmm. What does she usually eat?
Boy: She usually eats meat.
Adult: And how often does she eat meat?
Boy: I give her some food every morning and every evening.
Adult: I see …
4
Adult: Does she eat any different food?
Boy: Well … I sometimes give her some milk.
Adult: Yes …
Boy: And I sometimes give her some cake. It's her favourite food. She likes eating cake.
5
Adult: How often do you give her cake?
Boy: Two or three times a week. Is that wrong?
Adult: Yes, it is. You mustn't give her cake or biscuits. Cats must only eat meat and drink water. But don't worry. She's going to be fine.
Boy: Good!

Unit 4 Cambridge Exams Practice

Activity Book

CD4 TRACK 46

AB page 114 Activity 1

1
Girl: Lots of my school friends are in the park today.
Adult: Really?
Girl: Yes. There's Peter. He's having a snack.
Adult: Is he eating an apple?
Girl: No, he isn't, He's eating a big ice cream.
Adult: Oh yes. I can see him now.
2
Adult: Who's the boy eating a cake?
Girl: Is he sitting next to Peter at the table?
Adult: Yes, he is.
Girl: Oh. He's called Jim. He loves eating cake!
3
Girl: I can see Anna.
Adult: Is she eating an ice cream, too?
Girl: No, she isn't. She's eating some pizza.
Adult: Oh yes. That looks delicious.
4
Adult: Who's the boy riding a bike?
Girl: Which one?
Adult: The one with shorts and a T-shirt.
Girl: Oh. He's called John. He's my friend, too.
5
Adult: And who's the girl flying a kite?
Girl: The girl with long hair?
Adult: Yes.
Girl: She's my best friend. Her name's Jane.
Adult: I love her kite.
6
Adult: Can you see any more friends?
Girl: Yes. I can see Tom.
Adult: What's Tom doing?
Girl: He's walking the dog.
Adult: Is he eating an apple or a banana?
Girl: He's eating a banana.

Unit 5 Cambridge Exams Practice

Activity Book

CD4 TRACK 47

AB page 115 Activity 1

1 Where does John go at the weekend?
Girl: Do you want to come to the lake on Saturday, John?
Boy: I'm sorry, I can't. I go to my grandparents' house at the weekend.
Girl: That's nice. Where do they live?
Boy: They live next to the sea. It's fantastic.
2 What does John like doing there?
Girl: What do you do at your grandparents' house?
Boy: I usually go to the beach with my cousins. They like fishing.
Girl: Do you like fishing, too?
Boy: Not really. My favourite activity is sailing. I love it!
3 What does John see there?
Girl: Do you see any animals in the sea?
Boy: Oh yes. There are lots of animals.
Girl: Do you see any fish?
Boy: Yes, I do. But I never see any sharks or dolphins

Unit 6 Cambridge Exams Practice

Activity Book

CD4 TRACK 48

AB page 116 Activity 1

1
Adult: Do you want to colour something in the picture?
Girl: Yes, please.
Adult: Can you see the boy with curly hair?
Girl: Yes, I can.
Adult: His hair is brown.
Girl: OK. I'm colouring his hair brown.
2
Girl: Can I colour the girl's T-shirt now?
Adult: OK. What colour?
Girl: Red is my favourite colour.
Adult: OK. Colour the girl's T-shirt red.
3
Adult: Now I want you to write a number.
Girl: OK. Where?
Adult: Write the number 7 on the boy's T-shirt.
Girl: Which boy?
Adult: The tall boy. Write the number 7 on his T-shirt.
4
Adult: Look at the bird.
Girl: Which one?
Adult: The bird in the tree.
Girl: Oh yes. What colour is it?
Adult: It's brown.
Girl: OK. I'm colouring the bird brown.
5
Adult: What do you want to colour now?
Girl: Can I colour the kite?
Adult: That's a good idea. Colour it purple.
Girl: Great. I'm colouring the kite purple.

Unit 7 Cambridge Exams Practice

Activity Book

CD4 TRACK 49

AB page 117 Activity 1

1
Girl: Look. This is a photo of me and my cousins.
Boy: That's nice. Who's the boy that's sitting at the table?
Girl: That's Fred. He loves drawing.
Boy: Does he draw well?
Girl: Yes, Fred draws very well.
2
Girl: Can you see my cousin Mary?
Boy: What's she doing?
Girl: She's listening to music.
Boy: Oh yes. She's sitting on the sofa.
Girl: That's right.
3
Boy: Who's the boy that's reading?
Girl: Which one?
Boy: The one that's standing in front of the bookcase.
Girl: Oh. That's my cousin Tom.
4
Girl: Look at Daisy.

Boy: Is she the girl with long hair?
Girl: No, she's got short hair.
Boy: Oh yes. She's playing the piano.
5
Boy: Who's that girl with long hair?
Girl: Which one?
Boy: She's standing next to the piano.
Girl: Oh yes. That's Jane.
6
Girl: Where's Jim? I can't see him.
Boy: He's behind the sofa.
Girl: Oh yes. What's he doing?
Boy: He's looking for his watch.

Unit 8 Cambridge Exams Practice

Activity Book

CD4 TRACK 50

AB page 118 Activity 1

1
Adult: Did you go to the park last Saturday, Zoe?
Girl: Yes, I did. I was there in the afternoon.
Adult: Did you go skating?
Girl: No, I didn't. The skate park was closed. I played football with my dad.
2
Adult: What about your brother? Did he go to the park, too?
Girl: No. He wasn't very well at the weekend. He needed to go to bed.
Adult: Oh! Is he better now?
Girl: Yes, he's fine now, thanks.
3
Adult: Did your mum have a good weekend, Zoe?
Girl: Yes, she did. She usually works in the hospital on Saturday, but last Saturday she was at home. She planted some flowers in the garden.
Adult: That's nice!
4
Adult: What about your cousin? Did you see her?
Girl: No, I didn't. She was at the beach with her mum and dad.
Adult: Did she swim in the sea?
Girl: No! The water was very cold. She went sailing.
5
Adult: Did your uncle swim?
Girl: No. He likes fishing. He fished on the beach with my aunt.
Adult: Did he catch a fish?
Girl: Yes, he did. But he put it in the sea again.
Adult: Oh good!

Unit 9 Cambridge Exams Practice

Activity Book

CD4 TRACK 51

AB page 119 Activity 1

1
Girl: What did you do last weekend, Tom?
Boy: I went to a party.
Girl: Really? Which day did you go?
Boy: I went on Saturday. It was great fun.
2
Girl: Was the party in a house?
Boy: No, it wasn't.
Girl: Oh! Where was it?
Boy: It was on the beach.
Girl: How exciting!
3
Girl: What time did the party start?
Boy: It started at four o'clock.
Girl: At five o'clock?
Boy: No, it started at four o'clock and it finished at eight o'clock.
4
Girl: Did you eat a lot?
Boy: Yes, I did. The food was delicious.
Girl: What was your favourite food?
Boy: It was the cake. I ate three pieces.
Girl: I don't believe it!
5
Girl: Did you play any games?
Boy: Yes, we did. We danced and sang songs, too.
Girl: What was your favourite activity?
Boy: My favourite activity was singing.
Girl: Of course. You're very good at singing.

Videoscript

Unit 1 21st Century Video

PB page 17 Activities 1 and 2

Chloe: Hello everyone, welcome to Channel 21!
Mark: My name's Mark.
Chloe: And I'm Chloe.
Mark: We work together to find fun and interesting videos.
Chloe: Because it's a new school year, we've got some videos about after-school activities. Let's look at the cool things children do after school!

Narrator: These children go to a robotics club. They build robots there. Look at the children's robots. They can move, but they can't talk.
Narrator: This girl goes to a pottery class. She's making a bowl today. She's got very dirty hands. Pottery is creative. It's fun, too!
Narrator: Lots of children go to a sports club after school. This boy goes to a roller hockey club. Roller hockey is a fast and exciting game. This boy is the goalkeeper. He's wearing gloves and a helmet. He's wearing pads on his legs, too.
These children go to a rugby club. You need a lot of energy to play rugby. Boys and girls can play rugby. This girl is fast!
Narrator: Lots of children go to a dance class after school. This type of dancing is slow and beautiful. Do you like dancing?
Narrator: This boy goes to a drum class after school. He's practising now. Wow! He's brilliant at the drums!

Mark: My favourite activity is playing the drums.
Chloe: Really? Why don't you go to the drum class after school?
Mark: Because I'm not very good at music …
Chloe: Look! Here are some African drums. We can play together.
Mark: See … I can't play!
Chloe: You need to keep going. Look at me.
Mark: Drumming is great. I love it!
Chloe: It's important to try new activities.
Mark: Yes! It's fun to learn new things!
Chloe: See you next time.
Mark: Bye!

Unit 2 21st Century Video

PB page 27 Activities 1 and 2

Mark and Chloe: Hello!
Chloe: Welcome back to Channel 21. Today's programme is about helping people. Do you help people, Mark?
Mark: Yes, I do. I help my mum and dad.
Chloe: What do you do?
Mark: I tidy up my bedroom. My mum says my bedroom's a cave!
Chloe: That's funny! Now, let's see how other children help at home.

Narrator: This girl walks the dog every day after school. Look! They're in the park today. What a happy dog!
Narrator: This boy often helps his dad in the garden. He's watering the new plants now. Whoops! Not too much water!
Narrator: At bedtime, this girl reads a story to her brother. This story is his favourite!
Narrator: These two brothers sometimes cook dinner together. There's pizza for dinner today. Delicious!
Narrator: It's dinner time in this house, too. These sisters are laying the table. They lay the table every evening. Good work, girls!
Narrator: These brothers usually wash the car with their dad. It's hard work today because it's hot and sunny.

Chloe: What a fantastic video! There are lots of ways to help at home.
Mark: And working together is fun!
Chloe: I think we need to tidy up. Look at the studio. What a mess!
Mark: Let's tidy up together!
Chloe: That's better …
Mark: See you next time everyone.
Chloe: Bye!

Unit 3 21st Century Video

PB page 37 Activities 1 and 2

Chloe: Hello everyone!
Mark: Welcome back to Channel 21. Today's programme is about being healthy.
Chloe: Are you fit and healthy, Mark?
Mark: Yes, I am. I've got **LOTS** of energy.
Chloe: Great! Let's watch the video.

Narrator: To stay healthy you need to eat lots of fruit and vegetables. A salad is very healthy, and it's fun to make, too! Fruit is a fantastic snack. Why don't you eat an orange … or an apple?
Narrator: Don't drink fizzy drinks when you're thirsty. Drink water. It hasn't got any sugar.
Narrator: It's important to do exercise. Playing outside is a good way to stay fit and healthy. It's fun to play with your friends!
Narrator: You need to do sports two or three times a week. There are lots of sports to choose. Why don't you try basketball, football or baseball?

Chloe: What a fun video!
Mark: How often do you do exercise, Chloe?
Chloe: Mmm … About once a week.
Mark: Only once a week? I think it's time to do some exercise …
Chloe: What … now?
Mark: Yes! It's important to warm up first. Stretch your arms … good! Stretch your legs … excellent! And bend your body. Now let's go for a run in the park …
Chloe: OK … Bye everyone.
Mark: See you next time!

Unit 4 21st Century Video

PB page 49 Activities 1 and 2

Chloe: Hello everyone!
Mark: Welcome back to Channel 21. Today's programme is about fruit.
Mark: Do you like eating fruit, Chloe?
Chloe: Hmm … Not really.
Mark: Fruit is very healthy. It's important to eat it every day.
Chloe: I know. But fruit is so boring …
Mark: Fruit isn't boring. Eating fruit can be fun! Let's watch a video about being creative with fruit.

Narrator: Fruits are different colours, different shapes and different sizes. Take a look at these desserts.
Narrator: There are strawberries in this dessert. Look! They're on a pancake. It's a happy sun!
Narrator: Look at this juicy orange. There's melon in this dessert, too. They're flowers. How pretty!
Narrator: This dessert has got kiwi in it. It's got banana, too. Wow! Two palm trees. That's amazing!
Narrator: This dessert has got bananas in it, too. What picture does it make? Two dolphins. How creative!
Narrator: This dessert has got lots of apple in it. Can you see what it is? It's a crab. Amazing!
Narrator: Some people cut fruit to make beautiful shapes. Look at the flowers on this watermelon!
Narrator: What's this person making? Can you guess? It's a bird. What a fantastic imagination.

Chloe: That was a great video! I'd like to be creative with fruit … and eat those desserts, too!
Mark: Well, I've got a surprise for you. Close your eyes. Ta-da!
Chloe: That's amazing! You're very creative, Mark. Mmmm … it's sweet and crunchy! Delicious! Thank you!
Mark: You're welcome.
Chloe and Mark: Bye!

Unit 5 21st Century Video

PB page 59 Activities 1 and 2

Chloe: Hi everyone!
Mark: Welcome back to Channel 21.
Chloe: Today's programme is about our favourite sea animals.
Mark: That's right. Get ready for a trip under the sea …

Narrator: Look at this sea turtle. It's slow, but it can swim for hundreds of kilometres. Sea turtles love eating jellyfish. They think jellyfish are delicious!
Narrator: Octopuses usually live on the sea floor. Do you know that octopus blood is blue? Octopuses have got three hearts, too!
Narrator: Look at this beautiful jellyfish. It's more than four metres long. That's longer than a car! A jellyfish is 95% water, but it eats small fish and crabs.
Narrator: Great white sharks are big and very heavy. They are faster than a small boat, too. These sharks have got 300 teeth. The teeth are triangular and very sharp.
Narrator: Japanese spider crabs have got eight long, thin legs. But they are very slow. Do you know that they can live 100 years? That's amazing!

Mark: What a great video!
Chloe: I love learning facts about animals. You can look for more facts on the Internet.
Mark: It's a good idea to use keywords when you look for information. You find information faster!
Chloe: Keywords are the important words. I want to know what seahorses eat. So, I write *seahorse food*.
Mark: Have fun looking for animal facts.
Mark and Chloe: Bye!

Unit 6 21st Century Video

PB page 69 Activities 1 and 2

Chloe: Hi everyone!
Mark: Welcome back to Channel 21.
Chloe: Today's programme is very exciting. It's about extreme sports in New Zealand.
Mark: Are extreme sports dangerous, Chloe?
Chloe: I'm not sure … Let's watch the video and see.

Narrator: This sport is called zorbing. There's a person inside this plastic ball. Hold tight!
Narrator: This family is going to go rafting. Look! They're putting on helmets. They're wearing life jackets, too.
Narrator: These men are rafting. They're getting very wet, but it's fun!
Narrator: Rock climbing is a popular sport. These climbers are wearing a harness and a helmet. They've got ropes, too.
Narrator: These people are caving. It's very dark so they need a torch. And they need to wear a helmet.
Narrator: Lots of people go mountain biking in New Zealand. It's fantastic to cycle down the mountain!
Narrator: This man is getting ready to do a bungee jump. It's almost time … 3, 2, 1 Jump!

Chloe: So … extreme sports **are** dangerous.
Mark: But not if you're careful. It's very important to be safe. You need to have the correct equipment.
Chloe: I always have the correct equipment when I do sport. Look! I've got gloves, I've got knee pads and I've got a helmet.
Mark: What are you going to do?
Chloe: Guess!
Mark: Are you going to go climbing?
Chloe: No, I'm not. I'm going to go skateboarding!
Mark: See you next time, everyone.
Chloe and Mark: Bye.

Videoscript

Unit 7 21st Century Video

PB page 81 Activities 1 and 2

Chloe: Hi everyone!
Mark: Welcome back to Channel 21.
Chloe: Today's programme is about houses.
Mark: Houses? That isn't very interesting.
Chloe: These houses are interesting.
Chloe: Let's watch the video. Which house would you like to live in?

Narrator: This house is in Germany. People don't live in this house. It's an attraction. Can you see the car in the garage? Amazing!
Narrator: People live in this house. The shape of the house is a turtle. Look! The roof of the house is a shell!
Narrator: This tall building is a lighthouse. It's on a beach in England. The lighthouse has got nine long legs.
Narrator: This traditional house is in Iceland. It's got grass on the roof and on the walls. This keeps the house warm in the winter.
Narrator: This house was a train before, but now it hasn't got any wheels. Can you see the tall chimney?
Narrator: This very tall house is in England. There are five bedrooms and a big living room at the top.
Narrator: This house is in Portugal. It's a stone house under a big rock. Look at the small window!
Narrator: Here's another attraction. It's the dining room. Can you see the upside-down food on that table?

Mark: I think my favourite house was the lighthouse.
Chloe: That was my favourite, too! I'd like to live there.
Mark: What colour was it? I don't remember …
Chloe: Was it blue and white? Or was it green and white?
Mark: Let's look at the lighthouse again. It was **red** and white!
Chloe: It's important to pay attention to what we see. It helps us remember.
Mark: You're right.
Chloe: See you next time everyone!
Mark: Bye!

Unit 8 21st Century Video

PB page 91 Activities 1 and 2

Chloe: Hi everyone!
Mark: Welcome back to Channel 21.
Chloe: Today's programme is about television.
Mark: I LOVE watching television.
Chloe: Me too. It's also fun to make television programmes.
Mark: This video shows you how people do it.

Narrator: This is a television studio. It's quiet here now, but it's usually noisy. Can you see the big camera?
Narrator: This is a camerawoman. She films the actors and the presenters. Look! She's got headphones on her ears. She uses them to listen to instructions.
Narrator: This man is the director. He gives instructions to the actors and the camera woman.
Narrator: You can make a video, too. It's easy! This boy has got a small camera. He's filming his friends.
Narrator: These children are making a television programme.
Narrator: You don't need a lot of equipment to make a video. You can use a video camera, a tablet or a phone to film.
Narrator: A drone can film from the sky, too.
Narrator: Then you upload your video onto a computer. You use a computer programme to edit the video. You can cut and move pieces of the video.
Narrator: Finally, you show your video to your family and your friends!

Mark: That was great! I loved the drone!
Chloe: Why don't you make a television programme with your friends?
Mark: You can make a documentary or a quiz show!
Chloe: Or a sports programme!
Mark: Have fun!
Chloe and Mark: Bye!

Unit 9 21st Century Video

PB page 101 Activities 1 and 2

Mark: Hi everyone!
Chloe: Welcome back to Channel 21.
Mark: It's the last programme today.
Chloe: And it's the end of the school year, too.
Mark: Our school always has a fete at the end of the year. Last year's fete was fun!
Chloe: Let's watch a video about our school fete.

Narrator: A lot of people went to the fete. It was a hot and sunny day.
Narrator: There were lots of things for the children to do. In the morning, the children went on the bouncy castle. It was fun!
Narrator: Look at these children. They won a duck. It was great!
Narrator: In this game people threw balls at a coconut. It was **very** difficult!
Narrator: Chloe's class played the throw a sponge game. How funny!
Narrator: A teacher painted children's faces, too. She was brilliant at painting. Look at this girl's face!
Narrator: There were lots of delicious things at the fete. Mark ate candyfloss. It was pink and sticky.
Narrator: There were lots of cakes, too!
Narrator: In the afternoon, everybody watched a parade. There was a school band. The children played the instruments very well.
Narrator: Finally, in the evening everybody watched the fireworks. They were amazing!

Mark: It was a great day! At school, we always work hard to prepare the fete.
Chloe: All the children work together and we listen to everyone's ideas.
Mark: Why don't you plan a fete at your school?
Mark and Chloe: Have a great time! Bye!

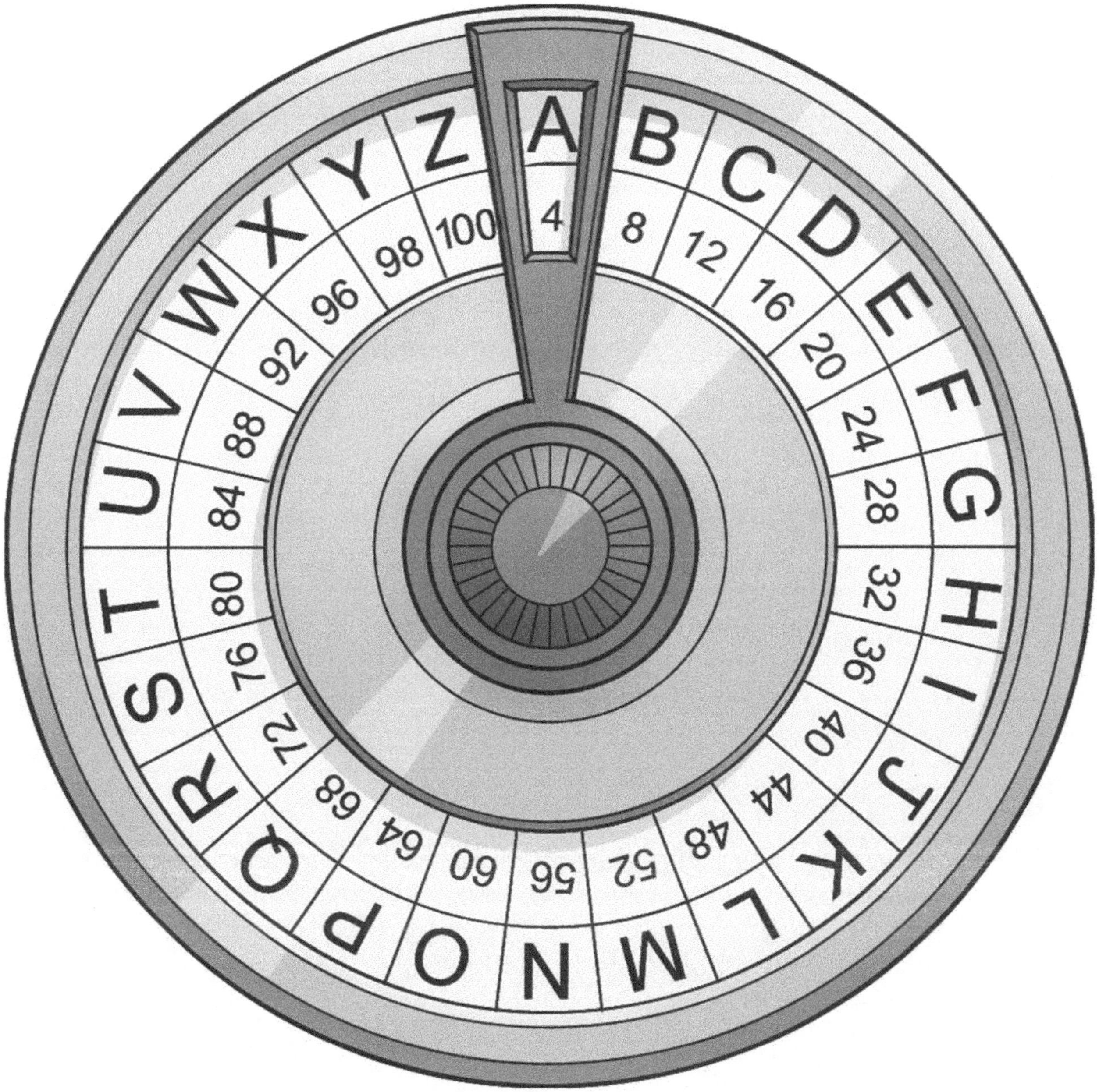
A
4
B
8
C
12
D
16
E
20
F
24
G
28
H
32
I
36
J
40
K
44
L
48
M
52
N
56
O
60
P
64
Q
68
R
72
S
76
T
80
U
84
V
88
W
92
X
96
Y
98
Z
100